●START !

THE BIBLE FOR NEW BELIEVERS
NEW TESTAMENT

GREG LAURIE
GENERAL EDITOR

THOMAS NELSON
Since 1798

NASHVILLE   DALLAS   MEXICO CITY   RIO DE JANEIRO

Printed in the United States of America
3 4 5 6 7 8 9 – 15 14 13 12

TABLE OF CONTENTS//

THE PLAN OF SALVATION//

Have you ever wished you could have a second chance in life? Maybe you did something so shameful that you wish you could turn back the clock and avoid making the same stupid mistake. But now you feel as though it's too late.

I have good news for you! God specializes in second chances. No matter how radically you have sinned, or what horrible things you have done, God has made it possible for you to be totally and completely forgiven.

Many doubt this. Maybe you have doubted it. Perhaps you've wondered, *can a person really change?* Can someone *really* be delivered from addiction? Can a person *really* make a clean break from an immoral lifestyle? Can you *really* go from being cynical and hard to having faith and love?

The answer is YES! It's called salvation.

Although all of us were created in God's image and therefore are wired for meaning and purpose, a huge barrier stands in our way: sin. We are not sinners because we sin, but we sin because we are sinners. And because God sees and hears *everything*, He knows every sin we have committed. Jesus said, "There is nothing covered that will not be revealed, and hidden that will not be known" (Matt. 10:26). And the Bible plainly declares, "The wages of sin is death" (Rom. 6:23), and "The soul who sins shall die" (Ezek. 18:4).

This is where Jesus comes in.

Some 2,000 years ago, Jesus Christ, the Son of God, died on the Cross for *your* sins. He did this so you could know God, so you could discover the purpose for which He created you and have fulfillment in this life—and most importantly, the hope of eternal life when you die.

So let me ask: Do you know God? Not just, "Do you know *about* Him," but do you *personally* know Him? This is a crucial question, because if you don't know Him *now*, He won't know you *then*. If you say no to Him now, He will say, "Depart from Me" then. But if you say yes to Him now, He will say, "Enter into the joy of the Lord" then.

The moment you confess your sins and ask Jesus to become your Savior and Lord, through faith, some incredible things happen. First, *all* of your sins are forgiven instantaneously (Mic. 7:18, 19; Acts 13:38, 39). God tramples your sins under His feet and throws them into the depths of the ocean. According to God's Word, they are *gone!* God will toss your guilt into the sea of His forgetfulness and then post a sign: "No fishing allowed!"

But there is even more. God will also put to your credit the infinite righteousness of Christ (Phil. 3:9). This is not a gradual process, either. It is immediate! The amazing things that happen to you when you place your faith in Jesus are something like what happened to a guy we'll call Joe.

Back in 1989, Joe was puttering around a flea market in Adamstown, Pennsylvania, when he spotted a fraying old print tucked inside a picture frame he thought he could use. He bought the artwork for four bucks and tucked it in his car.

When he got home and tried to remove the print, however, the rickety frame disintegrated. What can you expect for four dollars, right? But something caught his eye among the debris—a crisply folded document that had been hiding, apparently for decades, between the print and its wooden backing. When Joe unfolded the document, he discovered what looked to be a vintage copy of the Declaration of Independence, still in excellent shape. A few days later, when he had it appraised, he discovered his old document was in fact one of only 500 copies of an official printing by John Dunlap in 1776. Until that

point in time, only twenty-four copies of the original 500 were known still to exist, and only three of them were in private hands. Joe's copy turned out to be one of three finest documents of their kind.

Two years later, on June 4, 1991, Joe put his rare find up for auction with Sotheby's. Estimators predicted Joe's pristine copy of the Declaration of Independence would likely sell for between $800,000 to $1.2 million. The estimates proved seriously wrong. When bidding finally ended, Joe wound up with a check for *$2.42 million*. His four dollar investment earned him a sixty million, five hundred thousand percent return.

The value of Joe's document was not in its quality of paper or in the frame that had hidden it for so long. Its worth had nothing to do with its smell or how it felt to the touch. Its value was completely tied to the fact that in 1776 it was one of an official group of prints that carried the earth-shattering news of America's independence to the waiting, anxious colonies.

In a similar way, the moment you place your faith in Jesus, God puts to your account all the riches of Christ. It has nothing to do with your worthiness or performance. It has everything to do with Jesus Christ, the rarest Treasure of all, who wants to take up residence in your heart *right now!* The Bible says, "As many as received Him, to them He gave the right to become children of God, to those who believe in His name" (John 1:12).

Have you received Him yet? That's what it means to be saved.

When a Roman jailer asked the apostle Paul what it took to be saved, Paul replied, "Believe on the Lord Jesus Christ" (Acts 16:31). To believe doesn't mean only to acknowledge the existence of God—the demons believe that and tremble (James 2:19). To believe means to trust in, cling to, rely on.

Are you saved right now?

If not, the same Jesus who forgave and changed the hardened Philippian jailer can forgive and change *you!* Your life really *can* change, and right now. You must simply do what the jailer did: put your whole trust in Jesus Christ. There is no more serious issue than this.

If you are not sure whether you personally know God, then why not settle that issue right now? Jesus says, "Behold, I stand at the door and knock. If anyone hears My voice and opens the door, I will come in" (Rev. 3:20). Jesus wants to come into your life right now and forgive you of every sin you have ever committed. Would you like Him to come in? If so, why not pray this suggested prayer:

Lord Jesus, I know that I am a sinner. Thank you for dying for me on the Cross and paying the price for every sin I have ever committed. I turn from that sin now and ask you to come into my life as my Savior, Lord, and friend. Thank you for hearing this prayer. In Jesus' name I pray, Amen.

If you just prayed that prayer (and meant it!), then you are now a brand new Christian! The Bible says, "These things I have written to you who believe in the name of the Son of God, that you may know that you have eternal life" (1 John 5:13). God gave you eternal life the moment you put your trust in Him.

Congratulations, and welcome to the family of God!

SECRETS TO SPIRITUAL SUCCESS//

I assume that either you are a new believer in Jesus Christ or someone who wants to know more about what it means to be a Christian. Then again, you may be a growing believer who just wants to learn more about your life of faith.

So, let me say first of all, I'm glad you have this *Start!* Bible. The title says it all: *Start!*

Just as in a race all runners get on their line and take off when the starter pistol fires, so we must begin the most important race we will ever run—the spiritual race. Our objective is also to win.

But not every person who runs this spiritual race does well.

While some cross the finish line with flying colors, other crash and burn. What makes the difference? Why does it seem as though Christianity works for some people and not for others?

"I've tried Christianity," I've heard some individuals say, "but it didn't work for me." Please know this: Christianity is *not* a product that works for some, but not for others. Plain and simple,

Christianity is Christ. And He can and will work in any life that is truly dedicated to Him.

So again: why do some succeed while others fail? It comes down to personal choice. If you want to succeed in the Christian life—if you go for it—then you can and you will succeed. Not without some failure or shortcoming! But if you choose to win, you can indeed become a spiritual success. On the other hand, if you don't really go for it, then you will most certainly fail.

I am not suggesting that the Christian life depends on human effort, because Scripture teaches, "It is God who works in you both to will and to do for His good pleasure" (Phil. 2:13). But at the same time, the Bible makes it clear that there are some things only *God* can do and some things only *you and I* can do. Only God can save a person, for example. Only God can forgive and forget our sins. Only God can change the human heart. But only *you and I* can believe. Only *you and I* can repent. Only *you and I* can follow. God will not do those things for us, because He has given us a free will. We have to choose.

The verse that precedes the one just quoted says, "Work out your own salvation with fear and trembling; for it is God who works in you both to will and to do for His good pleasure" (Phil. 2:12, 13). That phrase "work out" means "carry it to the goal and fully complete." In other words, we must work out what God has worked in. We are not working for our salvation, for that is a gift to us from God (Eph. 2:8). We are implementing and applying it.

Most of us are well aware of the things we *should not* do as Christians. So let's focus on what we *should do.* After all, the best defense is a good offense, as the saying goes, so let's take a look at some critical starting places to build a successful Christian life.

THE PLACE TO START

To spiritually succeed as a follower of Jesus Christ, several things must become a part of your life on a regular, even daily, basis. These are nonnegotiable. They are not for some believers but not for others. *They are for every follower of Jesus Christ.* They are the disciplines of the Christian life, and they go hand-in-hand with success.

Now, *discipline,* of course, is not a word we particularly like. In the twenty-first century we live in an instant society, so we are always looking for ways to do things faster and easier. The same is true when it comes to our spiritual lives. We expect instant spirituality. We want it *all,* and we want it *now.* Yet the Bible speaks about slowing down, taking root spiritually, studying carefully, denying oneself, and as one author once

put it, "a long obedience in the same direction." In other words, Scripture talks about discipline.

The very word *disciple* comes from the same root word for *discipline.* Do you want to be a disciple of Jesus? Do you want to grow and succeed as a Christian? If so, then you must learn discipline.

The First Secret

The best place to begin in this *Start!* Bible is with the Word of God itself. And why is the Bible so important for spiritual growth and success?

The Bible is for people who feel some sense of desperation about where they are in life. It is for people who lack purpose in their lives. It is for people who don't want to be controlled any longer by their passions, who don't want to be constant victims of circumstance, and who want to improve their relationships. It is for people who want solid direction in life, who want to know how to live well, and who want to go to heaven. It is for people who want to know God. The Bible is for people who don't have all the answers but who want something better.

The Bible is God's very Word to us. And if you want spiritual success, it must be integrated into your life. The Lord once told a strong leader named Joshua,

This Book of the Law shall not depart from your mouth, but you shall meditate in it day and night, that you may observe to do according to all that is written in it. For then you will

make your way prosperous, and then you will have good success. (Joshua 1:8)

Secret number one: If you want to be a successful Christian, then you must read, study, and love God's Word.

Many years ago, when a young man named Billy Sunday became a Christian, an older believer gave him some advice that he never forgot. The man told him, "William, there are three simple rules I wish you'd practice. If you do, no one will ever write 'backslider' after your name. Take fifteen minutes each day to let God talk to you; allow fifteen minutes to talk to Him; and then spend fifteen minutes telling others about the Savior." Billy Sunday faithfully followed that advice, and ultimately became a powerful evangelist whom God used to bring thousands of people into His kingdom.

That is good advice and a good place to begin. So let's look at the first principle: letting God talk to us. How does God speak to us today? First and foremost, He speaks to us through His Word, the Bible.

A successful Christian will *always* be a Bible-studying Christian. The psalmist wrote, "Consider how I love Your precepts; revive me, O LORD, according to Your lovingkindness. The entirety of Your word is truth, and every one of Your righteous judgments endures forever" (Ps. 119:159, 160).

A fruitful believer always will love God's Word. There is no getting around this. It's Spiritual Success 101!

Just Read the Directions

The Bible is God's Word to us. It is the user's manual written by the Manufacturer, showing us who God is and how to know Him and His will. The Bible gives us directions and warnings to guide us and protect us. The apostle Paul, who wrote more than half of the New Testament, reminded us,

All Scripture is given by inspiration of God, and is profitable for doctrine, for reproof, for correction, for instruction in righteousness, that the man of God may be complete, thoroughly equipped for every good work. (2 Tim. 3:16, 17)

The Word of God is also alive. Hebrews 4:12 says, "For the word of God is living and powerful, and sharper than any two-edged sword, piercing even to the division of soul and spirit, and of joints and marrow, and is a discerner of the thoughts and intents of the heart." The Bible reveals who we really are, deep inside—and that may be one reason why some people don't like to read it. They don't like what it says about *them*. They don't like its revealing light shining into their lives. The Bible tells the truth. As the sixteenth century reformer Martin Luther said, "The Bible is alive. It speaks to me. It has feet. It runs after me."

Success or failure in the Christian life depends on how much of the Bible we get into our hearts and minds every day—and how completely we obey it. If we neglect the study of Scripture, our spiritual life will ultimately unravel, because everything we need to know about God we learn in the Bible. Show me a Christian who is failing, someone who is drifting and not growing spiritually, and I will show you someone who is not spending time in God's Word. We neglect the Bible at our own peril.

You Need to Eat

A hungry person is a healthy person. One way a physician knows whether a patient is healthy is by the person's appetite. A lack of appetite usually means something is wrong. In the same way, some Christians have no appetite for the Word of God. And when that happens, something has gone wrong spiritually. The Bible urges us, "As newborn babes, desire the pure milk of the word, that you may grow thereby, if indeed you have tasted that the Lord is gracious" (1 Pet. 2:2, 3).

You know the feeling when you haven't eaten for a while. Your mood turns sour, you feel tired, listless, and you may even get a headache. You might even think you're getting sick. But what a difference a good meal can make! It can revive you.

The same is true of the study of God's Word. The prophet Jeremiah wrote, "Your words were found, and I ate them, and Your word was to me the joy and rejoicing of my heart; for I am called by Your name, O LORD God of hosts" (Jer. 15:16).

The Bible tells us that God has given us His Word, along with gifted people to teach it to us, so "that we should no longer be children, tossed to and fro and carried about with every wind of doctrine, by the trickery of men, in the cunning craftiness of deceitful plotting, but, speaking the truth in love, may

grow up in all things into Him who is the head—Christ" (Eph. 4:14, 15).

The best way to spot a counterfeit is to know the genuine. I once spoke with a law enforcement officer about a counterfeit ring that had just been exposed. When I asked him how authentic the money looked, he told me that he could not tell the difference. Bank tellers could, however, because they constantly handle money. The same principle applies to living successfully as a Christian: we must be familiar with the genuine Word of God. Jesus said, "If you abide in My word, you are My disciples indeed" (John 8:31).

All of us need to learn how to think biblically. And in so doing, we will develop a Christian worldview. This means that we look at our culture, our questions, and our challenges through the lens of Scripture. The Bible is our foundation for life, and it is our final authority.

It's Perfect

Now let's see what the Word of God has to say about itself and its benefits. The phrase "the law of the Lord" was term used in the Old Testament to define Scripture:

The law of the LORD is perfect, converting the soul; the testimony of the LORD is sure, making wise the simple; the statutes of the LORD are right, rejoicing the heart; the commandment of the LORD is pure, enlightening the eyes; the fear of the LORD is clean, enduring forever; the judgments of the LORD are true and righteous altogether. More to be desired are they than gold, yea, than much fine gold; sweeter also than honey and the honeycomb. Moreover by them Your servant is warned, and in keeping them there is great reward. (Ps. 19:7–11)

First, we discover "the law of the LORD is perfect" (v. 7), in direct contrast to the flawed, imperfect reasoning of humanity. As society changes, we don't need to flow with the winds of change. We can stand on the firm foundation of God's Word.

Things go in and out of style, after all. Consider how dated an old yearbook is. We look at our hair back then and ask, "What was I thinking?" And with access to instant news on the Internet and twenty-four hour news channels, even the morning newspaper can be dated. But God's Word is always current; it's as fresh as the morning dew. This is why the British writer C.S. Lewis once said, "everything that is not eternal is eternally out of date." Scripture tells us that His mercies "are new every morning" (Lam. 3:23). God's Word is perfect, whole, complete, and sufficient. We need to add nothing to it and take away nothing from it. When 2 Timothy 3:16 tells us that "all Scripture is given by inspiration of God," it literally means, "all Scripture is *breathed* by God."

This means that the Bible is God's infallible Word. The original writings, the "autographs," were without errors. They made no mistakes and committed no contradictions. A few decades ago with the discovery of the Dead Sea Scrolls—ancient Bible texts that predated by centuries most of the manuscripts we had before then—we found the copies we had were accurate. God's Word is perfect.

God's Word is also sufficient. Everything you need to know about God is found in the Bible. God's Word is sufficient for your life.

It Transforms Us

We also see from Psalm 19 that the Word of God transforms us: "The law of the LORD is perfect, *converting the soul*" (v. 7, emphasis mine). The word "converting" can be translated, "to revive, to restore, to transform." So when you read God's Word, you are revived, restored, and transformed.

It Gives Wisdom

It is not enough to simply read and study God's Word. We must do what it says. James reminds us:

But be doers of the word, and not hearers only, deceiving yourselves. For if anyone is a hearer of the word and not a doer, he is like a man observing his natural face in a mirror; for he observes himself, goes away, and immediately forgets what kind of man he was. But he who looks into the perfect law of liberty and continues in it, and is not a forgetful hearer but a doer of the work, this one will be blessed in what he does. (James 1:22–25)

The study of God's Word, with a commitment to obeying it, brings us untold benefits, another of which is described in Psalm 19:7: "The testimony of the LORD is sure, making wise the simple." God's Word gives us incredible wisdom. The word "simple" in this verse is translated from a root word in the original Hebrew (the language of the Old Testament) that speaks of an open door. It suggests the idea of a person who has a mind like an open door—everything comes in and goes out. It is the idea of a person who is completely naïve, open to everything, and closed to nothing. This verse tells us that the Bible is able to make such a person wise.

We need a Christian and biblical worldview and that comes from careful study of Scripture.

It Tells the Truth about Life

If you believe that human beings are intrinsically good and that no one is really evil, then you will have a hard time reconciling human behavior with your ideals. If you believe people are merely the product of their environment, and you can change them simply by altering their environment, then you will wind up with a lot of questions.

But if you accept what the Bible says, that all people have a sinful bent and are *not* basically good, then life will make much more sense. If you believe that only God can change the human heart, then you will be able to make sense of this world. If you believe that one day Christ will return and true justice will prevail, then you will have hope. That's what happens when you believe the Bible rather than relying on your own opinions, emotions, or what is currently popular or politically correct. We can't let such changeable things dictate how we feel or how we act. We need to think and act biblically and look at the world through a scriptural lens.

It's Right

We also see from Psalm 19 that God's Word is right: "The statutes of the LORD are right, rejoicing the heart" (v. 8).

God has presented to us, in the pages of Scripture, the right way to live. Do you want peace, joy, meaning, and purpose in life? The Bible says, "Blessed are those who hear the word of God and keep it!" (Luke 11:28).

Sometimes people wrongly feel that God is out to make their life miserable and restrictive. "He has too many rules," they'll say. And I admit the Bible *does* tell us not to do certain things, as well as urging us to do certain other things. But whatever God commands, He commands for our own good spiritually, and often physically. Moses wrote, "what does the LORD your God require of you, but to fear the LORD your God, to walk in all His ways and to love Him, to serve the LORD your God with all your heart and with all your soul, and to keep the commandments of the LORD and His statutes which I command you today *for your good*?" (Deut. 10:12, 13, emphasis mine). If the Bible tells you to steer clear of a certain activity, relationship, or situation, it is for your spiritual protection and well-being. Psalm 84:11 reminds us, "No good thing will He withhold from those who walk uprightly." If it's a good thing, God will not keep you from it. But often what we think of as good is spiritually destructive.

The Second Secret

Now let's take a look at the second secret to spiritual success: *To be a successful Christian, you must have an active prayer life.*

Simply put, prayer is communicating with and listening to God, and there are many ways to pray and various forms of prayer. The apostle Paul wrote in Ephesians, "Praying always with all prayer and supplication in the Spirit, being watchful to this end with all perseverance and supplication for all the saints" (6:18). Growing Christians "pray always" and "with all prayer." We can pray publicly, privately, verbally, or silently. We can pray kneeling, sitting, lying down, or even while we are driving. We can pray with our eyes open or closed. (If you pray while you're driving, I strongly recommend the first option.) You can pray in any position, at any time, anywhere.

Sometimes we think the Lord will perhaps hear our prayers better if they are spoken in a church building, but that is not necessarily true. Daniel prayed from a lion's den. David prayed in a field. Peter prayed both in and on the water. And Jonah prayed from the belly of a very large fish. Surely God will hear your prayer, wherever you are!

The main thing is that you pray—and that you are praying always. The word "all" from Ephesians 6:18 speaks of the frequency of prayer: morning, afternoon, and evening. When the Bible speaks of "all prayer," it means that everywhere you go, you remain conscious of the fact that God is present and is listening to what you have to say.

A Good Reason to Pray

So *why* pray?

First and foremost, we pray because Jesus told us to. He left us a model to follow. Throughout the Gospels, we read that Jesus was constantly praying. If you

want to read the real "Lord's Prayer," then look at John 17, where Jesus offered a lengthy and beautiful prayer to His Father. We see Him in prayer before He raised Lazarus from the dead, as He spoke first to His Father: " 'Father, I thank You that You have heard Me. And I know that You always hear Me, but because of the people who are standing by I said this, that they may believe that You sent Me.' Now when He had said these things, He cried with a loud voice, 'Lazarus, come forth!' " (John 11:41–43).

When Jesus fed five thousand men (not counting the women and children) with just a few small loaves of bread and a few fish, He asked God's blessing on the food (see John 6:11). And mothers brought their children to Him "that He might put His hands on them and pray" (Matt. 19:13).

During the hardest phase of His ministry, Jesus remained in constant prayer. In the Garden of Gethsemane, He prayed, calling on His Father and saying, "O My Father, if it is possible, let this cup pass from Me; nevertheless, not as I will, but as You will' " (Matt. 26:39). Even on the cross, He prayed, "Father, forgive them, for they do not know what they do" (Luke 23:34), and "My God, My God, why have You forsaken Me?" (Matt. 27:46).

So if prayer was such an important part of Jesus' life, then shouldn't it be all the more so in ours? In Luke, we read that Jesus told His disciples a parable about a persistent widow to show them that they "always ought to pray and not lose heart" (Luke 18:1). Is there really any better reason to pray? His words alone should be enough to cause us to pray. Of course, even beyond that, we have the promise that God answers our prayers. We have the joy of being able to see the hand of God move at our request! Still, the first reason to pray is simply because Jesus told us to. Even if prayer was an extremely difficult task (which it is not), or very unpleasant (which it is not), or even if we never received answers (which we do), we should pray simply because we are commanded to pray.

Just Ask

Second, we should pray because prayer is God's appointed way for us to obtain things. As James 4:2 tells us, "You do not have because you do not ask." That may sound rather mercenary and selfish, but the fact is that God wants to hear and answer your prayers.

You may wonder, *Why it is that I never seem to know the will of God for my life?* "You do not have because you do not ask." *Why am I always just scraping by, never having enough?*" "You do not have because you do not ask."

Do you have a need right now? If so, just stop and pray about it.

I am *not* saying that God will answer every one of our prayers in the affirmative, simply because we have taken the time to ask Him. But I *am* saying there are some wonderful things God wants to do in your life, and He is simply waiting for you to ask so that He can show you His love and power.

Don't Worry About It

Third, prayer is the way through which God helps us overcome our anxiety and worry. Life certainly fills up with troubles and worry. Among other things, we worry about our future. We worry about who we will marry (or if we will get married.) After we get married and have children, we worry about them. We worry about our aging parents. We worry about our grandchildren. We worry about our spouse's health. We worry about our own health. We worry about our income.

Yet the Book of Philippians says, "Be anxious for nothing, but in everything by prayer and supplication, with thanksgiving, let your requests be made known to God; and the peace of God, which surpasses all understanding, will guard your hearts and minds through Christ Jesus" (Phil. 4:6, 7).

There is much to worry about—but prayer is the primary way we overcome our anxiety and worry. As it has been said, "If your knees are shaking, kneel on them."

Get Ready

Fourth, prayer is one of the ways in which we make ourselves ready for Christ's return. Jesus said,

But take heed to yourselves, lest your hearts be weighed down with carousing, drunkenness, and cares of this life, and that Day come on you unexpectedly. For it will come as a snare on all those who dwell on the face of the whole earth. Watch therefore, and pray always that you may be counted worthy to escape all these things that will come to pass, and to stand before the Son of Man. (Luke 21:34–36, emphasis mine)

In speaking of His coming, Jesus said, "But of that day and hour no one knows, not even the angels in heaven, nor the Son, but only the Father. Take heed, watch and pray; for you do not know when the time is" (Mark 13:32, 33).

All of this should make it clear that prayer is not an option for a believer. If you want God to speak to you, provide for you, help you not to worry, and be ready for Christ's return, then you must pray. To succeed spiritually, along with having a love for God's Word and a desire to study and obey it, we must learn and practice this essential discipline of the Christian life.

A Simple Guideline

Even when we pray according to Jesus' command, yet all of us have had prayers go unanswered—at least, in the affirmative. Consider a simple guideline to keep in mind when you are waiting for your prayers to be answered:

If the request is wrong, God says, "No."

If the timing is wrong, God says, "Slow."

If you are wrong, God says, "Grow."

But if the request is right, the timing is right, and you are right, God says, "Go!"

So how can we hear God's "Yes" and "Go!" more often? Are there secrets to answered prayer? Well, yes and no. On one hand, these are not really secrets, because the Bible clearly tells us how

to approach God and have meaningful communion with Him through prayer. On the other hand, if you don't know these principles, then they indeed could be secrets that will give you the key to unlock a more effective prayer life.

A Pattern for Prayer

These keys to answered prayer can be found in what we usually call "The Lord's Prayer." Technically, it was not so much the Lord's Prayer as much as it is the disciples' prayer. Or to be more specific, it is a form to follow, a pattern to keep in mind as we approach God:

Now it came to pass, as He was praying in a certain place, when He ceased, that one of His disciples said to Him, "Lord, teach us to pray, as John also taught his disciples." So He said to them, "When you pray, say: Our Father in heaven, hallowed be Your name. Your kingdom come. Your will be done on earth as it is in heaven. Give us day by day our daily bread. And forgive us our sins, for we also forgive everyone who is indebted to us. And do not lead us into temptation, but deliver us from the evil one." (Luke 11:1–4)

Before we utter a word of personal petition, we must first consider to whom we are speaking. He is the Almighty God, and yet also our Heavenly Father. So we begin our prayer with worship, adoration, and acceptance of His will.

Pray According to God's Will

This brings us to the first key to answered prayer: If you want your prayer answered in the affirmative, then you must pray according to the will of God. "Your kingdom come. Your will be done" (Luke 11:2). Jesus modeled this again in the Garden of Gethsemane, just before His arrest and crucifixion, as He prayed, "Nevertheless, not as I will, but as You will" (Matt. 26:39).

The primary objective of prayer is to align our will with the will of God. It is only when we do this that we will see more of our prayers answered in the affirmative. True praying is not overcoming God's reluctance, but laying hold of His willingness. Prayer is not getting our will in heaven, but it is getting God's will on earth.

The apostle John wrote, "Now this is the confidence that we have in Him, that if we ask anything according to His will, He hears us. And if we know that He hears us, whatever we ask, we know that we have the petitions that we have asked of Him" (1 John 5:14, 15). Nothing lies outside the reach of prayer except that which lies outside the will of God. God answers only the requests that He inspires.

Prayer is surrender—surrender to the will of God and cooperation with His will. It's like being on a boat and throwing the boathook to the shore and pulling. Do you pull the shore to you, or do you pull yourself to the shore? Prayer is not pulling God to our will; it is you being pulled toward His.

Next we come to the place in prayer to mention our personal needs: "Give us day by day our daily bread" (Luke 11:3). It is an amazing thing to consider that this all-knowing, all-powerful, omnipresent, Creator of the universe would take *any* interest in us personally. As

Job observed, "What is man, that You should exalt him, that You should set Your heart on him?" (Job 7:17). Why would God be concerned about what concerns us? Why would He care about your needs—much less your wants? Why would He commit Himself personally to providing your daily bread? Many reasons could be cited, but the most notable is simply that He loves you. Just as earthly parents love to give gifts to their children, so our Heavenly Father loves to give gifts to His sons and daughters.

Confess Your Sins

Now we come to the second key to answered prayer: *If you want your prayer answered in the affirmative, then you must confess your personal sin.* "Forgive us our sins" (Luke 11:4). Or literally, "Forgive us our trespasses, shortcomings, resentments, what we owe to You, and the wrong we have done."

Some think they don't need forgiveness, but according to Jesus, it is something we should be asking for regularly. According to 1 John 1:8, "If we say that we have no sin, we deceive ourselves, and the truth is not in us." Those who do not see a constant need for regular cleansing do not spend much time in God's presence, because when we have truly prayed, "Our Father in heaven, hallowed be Your name," then we will also pray, "Forgive us our sins."

The more we contemplate the holiness of God, the more we will see our own sinfulness. It has been said, "The greater the saint, the greater is the sense of sin and the awareness of sin within." I find it interesting in the apostle Paul's writings that he went from being "the least of all the saints" (Eph. 3:8) to the chief of sinners (see 1 Tim. 1:15).

Now, *that* is spiritual growth!

If you have unconfessed sin in your life, then your prayers will go nowhere. The psalmist said, "If I regard iniquity in my heart, the Lord will not hear" (Ps. 66:18). The fact is, we don't necessarily even know what sins we may have committed. The Bible speaks both of sins of commission and omission. The sin of commission is to do what God prohibits. By contrast, a sin of omission is failing to do what God commands. Generally, if our hearts are tender toward the Lord, we know when we fall into a sin of commission and have crossed the line or done something that displeases Him. But the sin of omission is a bit trickier. James tells us, "Therefore, to him who knows to do good and does not do it, to him it is sin" (James 4:17). Maybe the Lord directs you to pray more or perhaps share the gospel with someone (more on that later), and you find yourself refusing.

All of this helps to explain why Jesus tells us in the model prayer to ask regularly for the forgiveness of our sins. Why is this important? Because unconfessed sin is like a wall between God and us. When we have unconfessed sin in our lives, God is far less likely to answer our prayers. The prophet Isaiah said, "Your iniquities have separated you from your God; and your sins have hidden His face from you, so that He will not hear" (Is. 59:2). There may be some sin in your past that has remained unjudged and unconfessed. But God cannot forgive the sin you will not confess. So, to the best of your ability, ask the Lord to forgive the sin in your life.

Forgive Others

The third key to answered prayer is that *we must forgive others*. "And forgive us our sins, for we also forgive everyone who is indebted to us" (Luke 11:4). This is a very important principle, and often missed. This verse isn't saying that God's forgiveness hinges on our forgiveness of others. Rather, our forgiveness of others should hinge on our understanding of God's gracious and generous forgiveness of us. The proof that you and I are forgiven and have accepted God's forgiveness is that we forgive. The person who has known God's forgiveness must forgive others.

In many ways, forgiveness is the key to all healthy, strong, and lasting relationships, because as fatally flawed people, we all sin. We hurt one another, whether intentionally or unintentionally. Husbands offend wives, and wives offend husbands. Parents hurt their children, and children hurt their parents. Family members offend one another. This is why we must learn to forgive.

Ephesians 4:32 instructs us to "be kind to one another, tenderhearted, forgiving one another, even as God in Christ forgave you." And Jesus said, "Therefore if you bring your gift to the altar, and there remember that your brother has something against you, leave your gift there before the altar, and go your way. First be reconciled to your brother, and then come and offer your gift" (Matt. 5:23, 24).

Is there someone you need to forgive? If you want your prayers answered, then you need to forgive that individual.

Failing to forgive is like drinking rat poison and then waiting for the rat to die. You are the one who is being hurt spiritually. When you forgive someone, you set a prisoner free . . . yourself!

Stay Out of Temptation's Way

Now let's look at the fourth key to answered prayer: *As much as possible, stay out of the way of temptation.* "And do not lead us into temptation, but deliver us from the evil one" (Luke 11:4). I recognize that we cannot completely remove ourselves from temptation. Otherwise, we would have to leave the planet. But this prayer says, "Lord, don't let me be tempted above my capacity to resist."

The problem with temptation is that we often rationalize it. We tell ourselves that whatever it is we're tempted to do, is not a sin. But if we could see our own temptations as well as we see the temptations of others, they wouldn't be so hard to identify. We see others give in to temptation and we ask, "How could they do that?" Their sin looks so ugly and foolish. Yet we manage to rationalize our own sin. It somehow seems different, even acceptable. It's the classic plank-in-the-eye syndrome:

For with what judgment you judge, you will be judged; and with the measure you use, it will be measured back to you. And why do you look at the speck in your brother's eye, but do not consider the plank in your own eye?

Or how can you say to your brother, "Let me remove the speck from your eye"; and look, a plank is in your own eye? (Matt. 7:2–4)

One day, our little house of cards will collapse and we will see our sin for what it is. Here's a little test to apply when you are not sure whether something is enticing you to do evil:

1. *Pray about it and bring it into the clear light of the presence of God.* Ask yourself, "Should I allow myself to be in this potentially vulnerable situation?" Jesus said, "Watch and pray, lest you enter into temptation" (Matt. 26:41). Often we refuse to pray about it because we already know the answer.

2. *Consider how you would react if you saw another Christian doing the same thing.* How would it look to you? A good prayer to lift up to your Heavenly Father at a time like this would be, "Lord, I know my own sinful vulnerabilities, and I ask You to keep me from the power of sin. Help me to make the right choices and avoid anything that would pull me away from you."

Don't Give Up

Now we arrive at the fifth and final key to answered prayer: *Don't give up.* Jesus followed up His lesson on how to pray with a parable that illustrates the importance of persistent prayer:

And He said to them, "Which of you shall have a friend, and go to him at midnight and say to him, 'Friend, lend me three loaves; for a friend of mine has come to me on his journey, and I have nothing to set before him'; and he will answer from within and say, 'Do not trouble me; the door is now shut, and my children are with me in bed; I cannot rise and give to you'? I say to you, though he will not rise and give to him because he is his friend, yet because of his persistence he will rise and give him as many as he needs." (Luke 11:5–8)

Jesus used an example familiar to the people of His culture. In that day, family members generally did not have their own rooms. The entire family had a common sleeping area. So, one person getting up in the middle of the night would wake everyone. Yet here comes this neighbor who refused to take "no" for an answer. Jesus concluded, "So I say to you, ask, and it will be given to you; seek, and you will find; knock, and it will be opened to you. For everyone who asks receives, and he who seeks finds, and to him who knocks it will be opened" (Luke 11:9, 10).

Jesus' language is unusually compelling in these verses, as the verbs "ask," "seek," and "knock" indicate an ascending intensity. The word "ask" implies a request for assistance. We realize our need and ask for help. It implies a certain humble, low-key approach, like gently trying to get the attention of your server in a restaurant. "Seek" denotes asking, but adds action to it. It is the idea of not just expressing our need, but actually looking around for help. It involves effort. "Knock" includes asking, in addition to acting and persevering. It is like someone pounding on a closed door. The sequence of the words in these verses is extremely forceful. A literal translation of the text would read, "*Keep on asking, and it will be given to you. Keep*

on seeking, and you will find it. Keep on knocking, and the door will be opened."

Jesus calls us to passionate, persistent prayer. Much of our prayer has no power because it has no heart. If we put so little heart into our prayers, then we cannot expect God to put much heart into answering them. God promises that His people will find Him when they search for Him with all of their heart (see Jer. 29:13).

So don't give up! Don't stop praying! As J. Sidlow Baxter said, "Men may spurn our appeals, reject our message, oppose our arguments, despise our persons—but they are helpless against our prayers."

The Third Secret

Because you are reading this section of the *Start!* Bible, I'm assuming you want to know the secrets of spiritual success. So let me give you the third secret to spiritual success: *To be a successful Christian, you must be actively involved in a local church.*

You need to find a good, Bible-teaching church and become an active part of it. Don't try to be a solo-Christian. You need to develop close relationships with other believers who share your faith.

When you miss church, you miss out on a lot, because something wonderful and even supernatural happens when God's people gather in His name. Certainly you can and will benefit from personal Bible study. You can also have a great time worshiping the Lord by yourself. But when you get together with other believers to study His Word and to worship and pray, the Lord manifests His presence in a special way.

We miss out on so much when we ignore fellowship with other believers at church! Some people claim that the Bible doesn't command them to go to church, and that others invented the idea. But the Bible does indeed command us to be an active part of His church. For example, Hebrews 10:24, 25 says plainly, "And let us consider one another in order to stir up love and good works, *not forsaking the assembling of ourselves together*, as is the manner of some, *but exhorting one another*, and so much the more as you see the Day approaching" (emphasis mine).

The fact is that neglect of fellowship with other believers is a sure sign of backsliding. Backsliding takes place when we start falling back in the direction of our old life, before we committed ourselves to follow Jesus Christ. Studies have shown that if you don't go to church for one month, the odds are almost two to one that you won't go for more than a year.

Being in fellowship with other believers is a proof that you are indeed a child of God. We are told in 1 John 3:14, "We know that we have passed from death to life, because we love the brethren. He who does not love his brother abides in death." And we read in Psalm 133:1, "Behold, how good and how pleasant it is for brethren to dwell together in unity!"

A person's failure to get involved with a local church is proof there is something

wrong with them spiritually. As 1 John 2:19 says, "They went out from us, but they were not of us; for if they had been of us, they would have continued with us; but they went out that they might be made manifest, that none of them were of us."

I hope that you have discovered the joy and the blessing of being an active part of a body of believers! We receive many spiritual benefits from gathering to hear God's Word, worship, and serve together. Jesus himself established the church and said, "The gates of Hades shall not prevail against it" (Matt. 16:18). It is a place where we refocus, learn, and grow, a place where we can come to God and help others to do the same. It is a place to both receive from God and give back to others. And it is something we all need to be a part of if we want to succeed spiritually.

When we isolate ourselves from other believers, we quickly lose perspective. We can get fearful, confused, angry, and even bitter. This was true of the skeptical Thomas, who was not present with the other disciples when the resurrected Jesus appeared among them. When they told him about it, he said, "Unless I see in His hands the print of the nails, and put my finger into the print of the nails, and put my hand into His side, I will not believe" (John 20:25). But the next time they met, Thomas had joined them. And his faithfulness was rewarded as he saw the risen Lord for himself.

An Old Testament man named Asaph grappled with the age-old question of why the ungodly prosper. And then it dawned on him: "When I thought how to understand this, it was too painful for me—until I went into the sanctuary of God; then I understood their end" (Ps. 73:16, 17). In other words, "I didn't understand why things were the way they were until I came into God's presence to study His Word with His people. Then my questions came into their proper perspective." Worship affects every aspect of our lives, and when we neglect it, it affects everything about us.

The Fourth Secret

To succeed spiritually, you must understand and apply a fourth secret: *You must learn the joy of giving to and serving others.*

All of us must grow past that early phase in our spiritual lives in which we come to church only to receive. We must learn the joy and blessing of giving to God and to others. We may think that happiness and joy come from being served, but the ultimate fulfillment and joy come from serving others.

We were blessed to be a blessing.

Serving others is also a sign of spiritual maturity. Jesus said, "And whoever of you desires to be first shall be slave of all. For even the Son of Man did not come to be served, but to serve, and to give His life a ransom for many" (Mark 10:44, 45). Jesus came not only to save us from our sin, but also to make us like himself. Philippians 2:5–7 tells us, "Let this mind be in you which was also in Christ Jesus, who, being in the form of God, did not consider it robbery to be equal with God, but made Himself

of no reputation, taking the form of a bondservant, and coming in the likeness of men."

Ironically, young believers often want to serve, while older and more mature believers sometimes don't want to. We must make the choice to serve. Joshua made that choice. He told the people of Israel, "And if it seems evil to you to serve the LORD, choose for yourselves this day whom you will serve, whether the gods which your fathers served that were on the other side of the River, or the gods of the Amorites, in whose land you dwell. But as for me and my house, we will serve the LORD" (Josh. 24:15). The fact is that serving the Lord is a true test of who is right with God and who is not. As Malachi 3:18 says, "Then you shall again discern between the righteous and the wicked, between one who serves God and one who does not serve Him."

We All Have a Part to Play

So, *how* do we serve the Lord? First, *we serve Him by finding and using our spiritual gifts.* In the Book of Ephesians, Paul compares the church to a body in which everyone does his or her part:

That we should no longer be children, tossed to and fro and carried about with every wind of doctrine, by the trickery of men, in the cunning craftiness of deceitful plotting, but, speaking the truth in love, may grow up in all things into Him who is the head—Christ—from whom the whole body, joined and knit together by what every joint supplies, according to the effective working by which every part does its share, causes growth of the body for the edifying of itself in love. (Eph. 4:14–16)

Each part of the body is important. And our service, our involvement in the church, grows out of our worship.

Second, *we serve Him by learning how to give.* Many believers haven't yet learned how to do this. Or at least, they may have heard about the importance of giving, but they just don't want to do it. It reminds me of the man who went to church with his family. As they drove home afterward, he began complaining about everything. "The music was too loud, the sermon was too long, the announcements were unclear, the building was hot, and the people were unfriendly," he said. He went on and on. Finally, his son, a very observant boy, said, "Dad, you've got to admit that it wasn't a bad show just for a dollar."

The Blessing of Giving

Many of us don't like to think about giving to God. For some, the very mention of money and giving makes us uncomfortable, especially when it comes to the prospect of parting with any of it. But the Bible tells us there can be great joy in giving.

Have you discovered that joy?

Jesus said, "It is more blessed to give than to receive" (Acts 20:35). The word "blessed" means "happy." So if you want to be a happy person, then be a generous person.

Money is such an important topic in the Bible that it is the main subject of nearly half of the parables Jesus told. In addition, one of every seven verses in the New Testament deals with finances. To give you an idea of how this compares with other subjects, Scripture offers about five hundred verses on prayer, fewer than five hundred on faith, and more than two thousand on the subject of money. Maybe that is because, as Jesus said, "Where your treasure is, there your heart will be also" (Matt. 6:21).

To be a successful Christian means that God will have control in every area of your life. No one follows Jesus completely without learning how to give.

The Final Secret

Now we come to our fifth and final secret of spiritual growth and success. In many ways, this is the natural outgrowth of having the other principles in play: *We need to tell others about Jesus Christ.*

Many people have not yet discovered this relationship that you have found with Christ, so you need to tell them. I believe that God wants to use all of us to bring others to Himself. The Bible says, "The fruit of the righteous is a tree of life, and he who wins souls is wise" (Prov. 11:30). Daniel 12:3 says, "Those who are wise shall shine like the brightness of the firmament, and those who turn many to righteousness like the stars forever and ever." After His crucifixion and resurrection from the dead, Jesus gathered His disciples and gave to them what is often referred to as "The Great Commission." Jesus said,

Go therefore and make disciples of all the nations, baptizing them in the name of the Father and of the Son and of the Holy Spirit, teaching them to observe all things that I have commanded you; and lo, I am with you always, even to the end of the age. (Matt. 28:19, 20)

In the original language, Jesus addressed these words to everyone—not merely to pastors, evangelists, and missionaries, but to everyone. He is speaking to businessmen, to housewives, to students . . . to everyone. No one is exempt.

That, of course, includes you.

Consider, too, that these words of Jesus in the original language are in the form of a command. Jesus is not saying, "If you can find time in your busy schedule, as a personal favor to Me, would you mind going and sharing the gospel?" No, as our Savior, Lord, and Commander-in-Chief, He says, "Go!"

This is called *evangelism*, which means to share your faith in Jesus Christ with others. You might protest "But I'm not gifted as an evangelist!" That may be true. For indeed some are given that actual gift from God (Eph 4:1). Nevertheless, every believer is called to evangelize.

I know the idea of evangelism seems daunting, even overwhelming. So how can we do it?

One Bite at a Time

The answer to the question, "How can we do evangelism?" is the same as the answer to the question, "How do you eat an elephant?" The answer: "One bite at a time."

So, how do we fulfill the Great Commission? One bite at a time.

The Gospel of Mark gives us a slight variation on the Great Commission: "And He said to them, 'Go into all the world and preach the gospel to every creature' " (16:15).

Maybe it would help if we localized it: "Go into all of YOUR world and preach the gospel." Go into your family, your workplace, your campus, your sphere of influence.

And what does it mean to "make disciples?" Jesus defines that for us: "Teaching them to observe all things that I have commanded you" (Matt. 28:20). Simply put, to disciple someone means to teach him or her to observe what God has commanded. It is to live out our faith in this world and also to share it with others—to teach it by word and model it by example. The full concept of "going into all the world and making disciples" is to share our faith, to seek to lead people to Christ, and then, to the best of your ability, to help them to mature spiritually. Colossians 1:28 says, "Him we preach, warning every man and teaching every man in all wisdom, that we may present every man perfect in Christ Jesus."

Why Do This?

But why are we to share the gospel and disciple young believers? Why doesn't God just poke His face out of the heavens and say, "Believe in me now!"? Why does He want to use flawed people like us?

I don't really know; I just know He does.

The primary way God has chosen to reach people is through people. People like you and me. The apostle Paul, in his letter to the church in Rome, wrote,

"How then shall they call on Him in whom they have not believed? And how shall they believe in Him of whom they have not heard? And how shall they hear without a preacher? And how shall they preach unless they are sent? As it is written: 'How beautiful are the feet of those who preach the gospel of peace, who bring glad tidings of good things!' " (Rom. 10:14, 15). And the primary way we are to share this message is verbally.

This is not to say that you should not live out the gospel first, for indeed you should. But we need to look for opportunities to verbalize our faith to others. The apostle Paul reminds us, "For since, in the wisdom of God, the world through wisdom did not know God, it pleased God through the foolishness of the message preached to save those who believe" (1 Cor. 1:21).

So what is the essential gospel message we are to share with others? Paul gives a simple summation of the gospel in 1 Corinthians 15:1–4:

Moreover, brethren, I declare to you the gospel which I preached to you, which also you received and in which you stand, by which also you are saved, if you hold fast that word which I preached to you—unless you believed in vain. For I delivered to you first of all that which I also received: that Christ died for our sins according to the Scriptures, and that He was buried, and that He rose again the third day according to the Scriptures.

Imbed that last thought deeply into your mind. The gospel in a nutshell is this: Christ died for our sins, was buried, and raised on the third day. There are other important elements to the message, but the cornerstone is the death and resurrection of Jesus Christ.

Back in the nineteenth century, someone once asked the great British preacher C.H. Spurgeon if he could put into a few words his Christian faith. "It is all in four words," replied Spurgeon, "Jesus died for me."

In the Book of Romans, Paul refers to the power of the gospel: "I am not ashamed of the gospel of Christ, for it is the power of God unto salvation to everyone who believes." He is reminding us that there is a distinct power in the simple message of the life, words, death, and resurrection of Jesus Christ from the dead.

Don't underestimate its appeal.

Don't be ashamed of its simplicity.

Don't add to it or take away from it.

Just proclaim it, stand back, and watch what God will do.

That's a great place for you to start! So then—let's start running this race of life to *win!*

A Few More Helps

To give you a little more assistance in running your race of faith, I've included in this *Start!* Bible several features designed to help ground you in some basics of spiritual growth. You'll find these features scattered throughout the Bible, and each one of them should give you further insight into how to run your race to win. Let me briefly describe each of them for you.

1. Bible Book Introductions

The Bible is made up of sixty-six individual books, thirty-nine in the Old Testament and twenty-seven in the New Testament. For each of these sixty-six books I've provided a short introduction that should give you a good overview of the book, as well as some highlights that could have special importance for your growth in God's grace.

2. Live.

These short articles focus on various aspects of what it means to be a Christian. According to the Bible, when you place your faith in Jesus Christ, you are justified, sanctified, redeemed, sealed with the Holy Spirit, and much more. Now you are probably wondering what that all means. I'll explain it to you in the "Live" entries.

3. Grow.

These tips give you helpful guidance on some of the key principles for living the Christian life, including prayer, Bible study, telling others about your faith, resisting temptation, and more. Your spiritual growth will blossom as you put these truths into daily practice.

4. Know.

These short articles highlight some of the core beliefs of the Christian faith. It's like Faith 101. Here you'll discover some crucial ideas about God the Father, Jesus Christ, the Holy Spirit, angels and demons, what the Bible says about end times events, and more. These teachings will help to give you a firm foundation for further growth.

5. Learn.

These mini-commentaries on key Bible passages for spiritual growth will help you to better understand some crucial portions of God's Word and will encourage you and help motivate you to draw closer to God.

In an effort to make these features even more helpful to you, we have created an index that lists every entry, found at the back of the Bible. This index should help you to easily locate articles that may be of special interest to you. In addition, you will find all of these features linked to other features in various parts of the Bible, in order to make it easier for you to more effectively build a solid understanding of your new faith, bit by bit.

One last thing. At the back of the Bible you will find a longer article I've called "Essentials." This resource gives you a simple but important overview of some of the most important things every growing believer needs to know about God and Jesus Christ, His Son. Don't miss this! It should encourage you as it clearly puts together some of the key pieces of the puzzle in understanding our God and His loving relationship with us.

Again, I want to welcome you to the family of God. You're in for quite an adventure! As I've put this *Start!* Bible together I've been praying for you that as the apostle Peter wrote, you may "grow in the grace and knowledge of our Lord and Savior Jesus Christ. To Him be the glory both now and forever. Amen" (2 Pet. 3:18).

PREFACE//
TO THE NEW KING JAMES VERSION®

The purpose of this most recent revision of the King James Version is in harmony with the purpose of the original King James scholars: "Not to make a new translation . . . but to make a good one better." The New King James Version is a continuation of the labors of the King James translators, unlocking for today's readers the spiritual treasures found especially in the Authorized Version of the Holy Bible.

While seeking to maintain the excellent *form* of the traditional English Bible, special care has also been taken to preserve the work of *precision* which is the legacy of the King James translators.

Where new translation has been necessary, the most complete representation of the original has been rendered by considering the definition and usage of the Hebrew, Aramaic, and Greek words in their contexts. This translation principle, known as *complete equivalence,* seeks to preserve accurately all of the information in the text while presenting it in good literary form.

In addition to accuracy, the translators have also sought to maintain those lyrical and devotional qualities that are so highly regarded in the King James Version. The thought flow and selection of phrases from the King James Version have been preserved wherever possible without sacrificing clarity.

The format of the New King James Version is designed to enhance the vividness, devotional quality, and usefulness of the Bible. Words or phrases in italics indicate expressions in the original language that require clarification by additional English words, as was done in the King James Version. Oblique type in the New Testament indicates a quotation from the Old Testament. Poetry is structured as verse to reflect the form and beauty of the passage in the original language. The covenant name of God was usually translated from the Hebrew as LORD or GOD, using capital letters as shown, as in the King James Version. This convention is also maintained in the New King James Version when the Old Testament is quoted in the New.

The Hebrew text used for the Old Testament is the 1967/1977 Stuttgart edition of the *Biblia Hebraica,* with frequent comparisons to the Bomberg edition of

1524-25. Ancient versions and the Dead Sea Scrolls were consulted, but the Hebrew is followed wherever possible. Significant variations, explanations, and alternate renderings are mentioned in footnotes.

The Greek text used for the New Testament is the one that was followed by the King James translators: the traditional text of the Greek-speaking churches, called the Received Text or Textus Receptus, first published in 1516. Footnotes indicate significant variants from the Textus Receptus as found in two other editions of the Greek New Testament:

(1) NU-Text: These variations generally represent the Alexandrian or Egyptian text type as found in the critical text published in the twenty-sixth edition of the Nestle-Aland Greek New Testament (N) and in the United Bible Societies' third edition (U).

(2) M-Text: These variations represent readings found in the text of the first edition of *The Greek New Testament According to the Majority Text,* which follows the consensus of the majority of surviving New Testament manuscripts.

The textual notes in the New King James Version make no evaluation, but objectively present the facts about variant readings.

MATTHEW ↙

INTRODUCTION//

Matthew wrote his Gospel approximately thirty years after the death and resurrection of Jesus (A.D. 60–65), in order to prove to the Jewish people that this Nazarene born in Bethlehem was indeed the Messiah for whom they had been waiting many centuries. Matthew therefore frequently quotes the Hebrew Scriptures to show how Jesus fulfilled ancient prophecies about the Messiah (at least 129 quotations or allusions from the Old Testament).

Only Matthew tells us about Joseph's dream (1:20–24), the visit of the Magi (2:1–12), and the escape to Egypt (2:13–15). His account of Jesus' genealogy (1:1–17) traces the Savior's lineage through Joseph, rather than Mary, and has an interesting focus on grace (compare Luke 3:23–38). Matthew mentions four women in Jesus' line, all of them outcasts whom God had redeemed through His grace (Tamar, Gen. 38; Rahab, Josh. 2; 6:17–23; Ruth; and Bathsheba, 2 Sam. 11). Matthew is the only synoptic Gospel (Mark and Luke are the others) written as an eyewitness account by one of the twelve apostles.

Matthew also records many specific teachings and sermons given by Jesus. It is the only Gospel in which we find the Sermon on the Mount (5–7), a clear blueprint for how to live as an effective disciple of Christ. In this famous sermon we encounter the Beatitudes (5:3–10) and the Lord's Prayer (6:9–13), where Jesus teaches us about anger, lust, divorce, love, money, charity, and worry. And in what is often called the Olivet Discourse (24), we hear what Jesus has to say about the future and His Second Coming. Matthew closes his Gospel with a compelling description of Christ's arrest, trial, crucifixion and resurrection, and a final challenge by the risen Jesus to His church to "make disciples of all the nations"—what we often call "The Great Commission."

The Genealogy of Jesus Christ

1 The book of the genealogy of Jesus Christ, the Son of David, the Son of Abraham:

²Abraham begot Isaac, Isaac begot Jacob, and Jacob begot Judah and his brothers. ³Judah begot Perez and Zerah by Tamar, Perez begot Hezron, and Hezron begot Ram. ⁴Ram begot Amminadab, Amminadab begot Nahshon, and Nahshon begot Salmon. ⁵Salmon begot Boaz by Rahab, Boaz begot Obed by Ruth, Obed begot Jesse, ⁶and Jesse begot David the king.

David the king begot Solomon by her *who had been the wife*ᵃ of Uriah. ⁷Solomon begot Rehoboam, Rehoboam begot Abijah, and Abijah begot Asa.ᵃ ⁸Asa begot Jehoshaphat, Jehoshaphat begot Joram, and Joram begot Uzziah. ⁹Uzziah begot Jotham, Jotham begot Ahaz, and Ahaz begot Hezekiah. ¹⁰Hezekiah begot Manasseh, Manasseh begot Amon,ᵃ and Amon begot Josiah. ¹¹Josiah begot Jeconiah and his brothers about the time they were carried away to Babylon.

¹²And after they were brought to Babylon, Jeconiah begot Shealtiel, and Shealtiel begot Zerubbabel. ¹³Zerubbabel begot Abiud, Abiud begot Eliakim, and Eliakim begot Azor. ¹⁴Azor begot Zadok, Zadok begot Achim, and Achim begot Eliud. ¹⁵Eliud begot Eleazar, Eleazar begot Matthan, and Matthan begot Jacob. ¹⁶And Jacob begot Joseph the husband of Mary, of whom was born Jesus who is called Christ.

¹⁷So all the generations from Abraham to David *are* fourteen generations, from David until the captivity in Babylon *are* fourteen generations, and from the captivity in Babylon until the Christ *are* fourteen generations.

Christ Born of Mary

¹⁸Now the birth of Jesus Christ was as follows: After His mother Mary was betrothed to Joseph, before they came together, she was found with child of the Holy Spirit. ¹⁹Then Joseph her husband, being a just *man,* and not wanting to make her a public example, was minded to put her away secretly. ²⁰But while he thought about these things, behold, an angel of the Lord appeared to him in a dream, saying, "Joseph, son of David, do not be afraid to take to you Mary your wife, for that which is conceived in her is of the Holy Spirit. ²¹And she will bring forth a Son, and you shall call His name JESUS, for He will save His people from their sins."

> → *And she will bring forth a Son, and you shall call His name JESUS, for He will save His people from their sins.* Matt. 1:21

²²So all this was done that it might be fulfilled which was spoken by the Lord through the prophet, saying: ²³*"Behold, the virgin shall be with child, and bear a Son, and they shall call His name Immanuel,"*ᵃ which is translated, "God with us."

²⁴Then Joseph, being aroused from sleep, did as the angel of the Lord commanded him and took to him his wife, ²⁵and did not know her till she had brought forth her firstborn Son.ᵃ And he called His name JESUS.

Wise Men from the East

2 Now after Jesus was born in Bethlehem of Judea in the days of Herod the king, behold, wise men from the East came to Jerusalem, ²saying, "Where is He who has been born King of the Jews? For we have seen His star in the East and have come to worship Him."

³When Herod the king heard *this,* he was troubled, and all Jerusalem with him. ⁴And when he had gathered all the chief priests and scribes of the people together, he inquired of them where the Christ was to be born.

⁵So they said to him, "In Bethlehem of Judea, for thus it is written by the prophet:

⁶'*But you, Bethlehem, in the land of Judah,
Are not the least among the rulers of
Judah;
For out of you shall come a Ruler
Who will shepherd My people Israel.'* "ᵃ

⁷Then Herod, when he had secretly called the wise men, determined from them what time the star appeared. ⁸And he sent them to Bethlehem and said, "Go and search carefully for the young Child, and when you have found *Him,* bring back word to me, that I may come and worship Him also."

⁹When they heard the king, they departed; and behold, the star which they had seen in the East went before them, till it came and stood over where the young Child was. ¹⁰When they saw the star, they rejoiced with exceedingly great joy. ¹¹And when they had come into the house, they saw the young Child with Mary His mother, and fell down and worshiped Him. And when they had opened their treasures, they presented gifts to Him: gold, frankincense, and myrrh.

¹²Then, being divinely warned in a dream that they should not return to Herod, they departed for their own country another way.

The Flight into Egypt

¹³Now when they had departed, behold, an angel of the Lord appeared to Joseph in a dream, saying, "Arise, take the young Child and His mother, flee to Egypt, and stay there until I bring you word; for Herod will seek the young Child to destroy Him."

¹⁴When he arose, he took the young Child and His mother by night and departed for Egypt, ¹⁵and was there until the death of Herod, that it might be fulfilled which was spoken by the Lord through the prophet, saying, *"Out of Egypt I called My Son."*ᵃ

Massacre of the Innocents

¹⁶Then Herod, when he saw that he was deceived by the wise men, was exceedingly angry; and he sent forth and put to death all the male children who were in Bethlehem and in all its districts, from two years old and under, according to the time which he had determined from the wise men. ¹⁷Then was fulfilled what was spoken by Jeremiah the prophet, saying:

18 *"A voice was heard in Ramah,*
   Lamentation, weeping, and great
      mourning,
   Rachel weeping for her children,
   Refusing to be comforted,
   *Because they are no more."*ᵃ

The Home in Nazareth

¹⁹Now when Herod was dead, behold, an angel of the Lord appeared in a dream to Joseph in Egypt, ²⁰saying, "Arise, take the young Child and His mother, and go to the land of Israel, for those who sought the young Child's life are dead." ²¹Then he arose, took the young Child and His mother, and came into the land of Israel.

²²But when he heard that Archelaus was reigning over Judea instead of his father Herod, he was afraid to go there. And being warned by God in a dream, he turned aside into the region of Galilee. ²³And he came and dwelt in a city called Nazareth, that it might be fulfilled which was spoken by the prophets, "He shall be called a Nazarene."

2:15 ᵃHosea 11:1 2:18 ᵃJeremiah 31:15

↓ KNOW (MATT. 1:23)

We often romanticize the very first Christmas. We see the babe swathed in blue night, sitting serenely in the stable with Mary and Joseph, with the shepherds looking on adoringly. In fact, Jesus was born in unsanitary conditions, surrounded by a stable full of filthy animals. His birth is not only the story of an arrival on earth; it is also the story of a departure from heaven. From earth's perspective, unto us a Child was born. But from heaven's perspective, a Son was given (see Is. 9:6). Jesus, who was fully God, became a human born of a woman, who grew up in Israel, lived for about thirty years among His countrymen—every moment without committing a single sin or displeasing His heavenly Father to the slightest degree—and willingly died on a Roman cross in order to make a way for us to live with Him in eternity. *For more about* Jesus' Life, *see Matt. 4:2.*

John the Baptist Prepares the Way

3 In those days John the Baptist came preaching in the wilderness of Judea, [2]and saying, "Repent, for the kingdom of heaven is at hand!" [3]For this is he who was spoken of by the prophet Isaiah, saying:

"The voice of one crying in the wilderness:
'Prepare the way of the LORD;
Make His paths straight.' "[a]

[4]Now John himself was clothed in camel's hair, with a leather belt around his waist; and his food was locusts and wild honey. [5]Then Jerusalem, all Judea, and all the region around the Jordan went out to him [6]and were baptized by him in the Jordan, confessing their sins.

[7]But when he saw many of the Pharisees and Sadducees coming to his baptism, he said to them, "Brood of vipers! Who warned you to flee from the wrath to come? [8]Therefore bear fruits worthy of repentance, [9]and do not think to say to yourselves, 'We have Abraham as *our* father.' For I say to you that God is able to raise up children to Abraham from these stones. [10]And even now the ax is laid to the root of the trees. Therefore every tree which does not bear good fruit is cut down and thrown into the fire. [11]I indeed baptize you with water unto repentance, but He who is coming after me is mightier than I, whose sandals I am not worthy to carry. He will baptize you with the Holy Spirit and fire.[a] [12]His winnowing fan *is* in His hand, and He will thoroughly clean out His threshing floor, and gather His wheat into the barn; but He will burn up the chaff with unquenchable fire."

John Baptizes Jesus

[13]Then Jesus came from Galilee to John at the Jordan to be baptized by him. [14]And John *tried to* prevent Him, saying, "I need to be baptized by You, and are You coming to me?"

[15]But Jesus answered and said to him, "Permit *it to be so* now, for thus it is fitting for us to fulfill all righteousness." Then he allowed Him.

[16]When He had been baptized, Jesus came up immediately from the water; and behold, the heavens were opened to Him, and He[a] saw the Spirit of God descending like a dove and alighting upon Him. [17]And suddenly a voice *came* from heaven, saying, "This is My beloved Son, in whom I am well pleased."

Satan Tempts Jesus

4 Then Jesus was led up by the Spirit into the wilderness to be tempted by the devil. [2]And when He had fasted forty days and forty nights, afterward He was hungry. [3]Now when the tempter came to Him, he said, "If You are the Son of God, command that these stones become bread."

[4]But He answered and said, "It is written, *'Man shall not live by bread alone, but by every word that proceeds from the mouth of God.' "*[a]

[5]Then the devil took Him up into the holy city, set Him on the pinnacle of the temple,

---

3:3 [a]Isaiah 40:3   3:11 [a]M-Text omits *and fire.*   3:16 [a]Or *he*   4:4 [a]Deuteronomy 8:3

↓ KNOW (MATT. 4:2)
· ·

As a man, Jesus became tired, just as we do. When He needed to get from point A to point B, He walked, just like everybody else. Jesus felt physical hunger. We know that after He fasted for forty days and nights, He got hungry. He got thirsty. When He hung on the Cross, He said, "I thirst" (John 19:28). I think we can safely say that Jesus was a man's man, but even so, He could grow weary and weak. He died like a man when His battered body ceased to function. And although He never flew off the handle or lost His temper, Jesus sometimes got angry—a genuine righteous indignation. When Jesus came to the tomb of one of His closest friends who had just died, He also felt deep, deep sorrow. The Scripture says simply, "Jesus wept" (John 11:35). *For more about Jesus' Life, see Mark 1:35.*

[6]and said to Him, "If You are the Son of God, throw Yourself down. For it is written:

'He shall give His angels charge over you,'

and,

'In their hands they shall bear you up,
Lest you dash your foot against a stone.' "[a]

[7]Jesus said to him, "It is written again, *'You shall not tempt the LORD your God.' "*[a] [8]Again, the devil took Him up on an exceedingly high mountain, and showed Him all the kingdoms of the world and their glory. [9]And he said to Him, "All these things I will give You if You will fall down and worship me." [10]Then Jesus said to him, "Away with you,[a] Satan! For it is written, *'You shall worship the LORD your God, and Him only you shall serve.' "*[b] [11]Then the devil left Him, and behold, angels came and ministered to Him.

Jesus Begins His Galilean Ministry

[12]Now when Jesus heard that John had been put in prison, He departed to Galilee. [13]And leaving Nazareth, He came and dwelt in Capernaum, which is by the sea, in the regions of Zebulun and Naphtali, [14]that it might be fulfilled which was spoken by Isaiah the prophet, saying:

[15] *"The land of Zebulun and the land of*
Naphtali,
By the way of the sea, beyond the Jordan,
Galilee of the Gentiles:
[16] *The people who sat in darkness have seen*
a great light,
And upon those who sat in the region and
shadow of death
Light has dawned."[a]

[17]From that time Jesus began to preach and to say, "Repent, for the kingdom of heaven is at hand."

Four Fishermen Called as Disciples

[18]And Jesus, walking by the Sea of Galilee, saw two brothers, Simon called Peter, and Andrew his brother, casting a net into the sea; for they were fishermen. [19]Then He said to them, "Follow Me, and I will make you fishers of men." [20]They immediately left *their* nets and followed Him.

> ➤ **Then He said to them, "Follow Me, and I will make you fishers of men."** Matt. 4:19

[21]Going on from there, He saw two other brothers, James *the son* of Zebedee, and John his brother, in the boat with Zebedee their father, mending their nets. He called them, [22]and immediately they left the boat and their father, and followed Him.

Jesus Heals a Great Multitude

[23]And Jesus went about all Galilee, teaching in their synagogues, preaching the gospel of the kingdom, and healing all kinds of sickness and all kinds of disease among the people. [24]Then His fame went throughout all Syria; and they brought to Him all sick people who were afflicted with various diseases and torments, and those who were demon-possessed, epileptics, and paralytics; and He healed them. [25]Great multitudes followed Him—from Galilee, and *from* Decapolis, Jerusalem, Judea, and beyond the Jordan.

The Beatitudes

5 And seeing the multitudes, He went up on a mountain, and when He was seated His disciples came to Him. [2]Then He opened His mouth and taught them, saying:

[3]"Blessed *are* the poor in spirit,
For theirs is the kingdom of heaven.
[4]Blessed *are* those who mourn,
For they shall be comforted.
[5]Blessed *are* the meek,
For they shall inherit the earth.
[6]Blessed *are* those who hunger and thirst
for righteousness,
For they shall be filled.
[7]Blessed *are* the merciful,
For they shall obtain mercy.

4:6 [a]Psalm 91:11, 12   **4:7** [a]Deuteronomy 6:16   **4:10** [a]M-Text reads *Get behind Me.*   [b]Deuteronomy 6:13   **4:16** [a]Isaiah 9:1, 2

[8]Blessed *are* the pure in heart,
For they shall see God.
[9]Blessed *are* the peacemakers,
For they shall be called sons of God.
[10]Blessed *are* those who are persecuted for
righteousness' sake,
For theirs is the kingdom of heaven.

[11]"Blessed are you when they revile and persecute you, and say all kinds of evil against you falsely for My sake. [12]Rejoice and be exceedingly glad, for great *is* your reward in heaven, for so they persecuted the prophets who were before you.

Believers Are Salt and Light

[13]"You are the salt of the earth; but if the salt loses its flavor, how shall it be seasoned? It is then good for nothing but to be thrown out and trampled underfoot by men.
[14]"You are the light of the world. A city that is set on a hill cannot be hidden. [15]Nor do they light a lamp and put it under a basket,

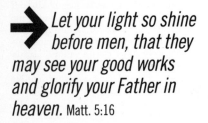

Let your light so shine before men, that they may see your good works and glorify your Father in heaven. Matt. 5:16

but on a lampstand, and it gives light to all *who are* in the house. [16]Let your light so shine before men, that they may see your good works and glorify your Father in heaven.

Christ Fulfills the Law

[17]"Do not think that I came to destroy the Law or the Prophets. I did not come to destroy but to fulfill. [18]For assuredly, I say to you, till heaven and earth pass away, one jot or one tittle will by no means pass from the law till all is fulfilled. [19]Whoever therefore breaks one of the least of these commandments, and teaches men so, shall be called least in the kingdom of heaven; but whoever does and teaches *them*, he shall be called great in the kingdom of heaven. [20]For I say to you, that unless your righteousness exceeds

→LIVE

5:20 • I remember when I first read that our righteousness must exceed that of the Pharisees. I knew these men were devoutly religious and I thought, *How could my righteousness surpass theirs?* But this is not a righteousness I can produce personally. Even on my best day, my righteousness is pretty much throw-away. To the proud, self-confident individual who thinks he doesn't need Jesus, the Holy Spirit comes with convicting power and sets him straight. When we believe in Jesus, we are justified. This means that God deposits the righteousness of Christ into our spiritual bank account (Phil. 3:9). *For more about* New Life in Christ, *see Luke 18:14; the* Holy Spirit, *Mark 5:30.*

the righteousness of the scribes and Pharisees, you will by no means enter the kingdom of heaven.

Murder Begins in the Heart

[21]"You have heard that it was said to those of old, *'You shall not murder,*[a] and whoever murders will be in danger of the judgment.' [22]But I say to you that whoever is angry with his brother without a cause[a] shall be in danger of the judgment. And whoever says to his brother, 'Raca!' shall be in danger of the council. But whoever says, 'You fool!' shall be in danger of hell fire. [23]Therefore if you bring your gift to the altar, and there remember that your brother has something against you, [24]leave your gift there before the altar, and go your way. First be reconciled to your brother,

↘LEARN

5:21–24 • If you want to grow spiritually, be careful to develop and maintain good relationships, especially within the church. God has designed us to need one another, which means that *nobody* can get far in his or her life of faith by going it alone. There is no place for a solo Christian. Jesus felt so strongly about this that He insisted His followers put reconciliation above any religious duty—so if you have a conflict with a fellow believer, get it settled. How we treat one another greatly impacts how we grow spiritually. So bury the hatchet—and not in the other person's back. *For more about* Fellowship, *see Matt. 18:19, 20;* Growing in Christ, *Matt. 14:28–31;* Loving Others, *Matt. 22:37–40;* Forgiveness, *Mark 1:14.*

5:21 [a]Exodus 20:13; Deuteronomy 5:17   5:22 [a]NU-Text omits *without a cause.*

and then come and offer your gift. ²⁵Agree with your adversary quickly, while you are on the way with him, lest your adversary deliver you to the judge, the judge hand you over to the officer, and you be thrown into prison. ²⁶Assuredly, I say to you, you will by no means get out of there till you have paid the last penny.

Adultery in the Heart

²⁷"You have heard that it was said to those of old,ᵃ *'You shall not commit adultery.'*ᵇ ²⁸But I say to you that whoever looks at a woman to lust for her has already committed adultery with her in his heart. ²⁹If your right eye causes you to sin, pluck it out and cast *it* from you; for it is more profitable for you that one of your members perish, than for your whole body to be cast into hell. ³⁰And if your right hand causes you to sin, cut it off and cast *it* from you; for it is more profitable for you that one of your members perish, than for your whole body to be cast into hell.

Marriage Is Sacred and Binding

³¹"Furthermore it has been said, 'Whoever divorces his wife, let him give her a certificate of divorce.' ³²But I say to you that whoever divorces his wife for any reason except sexual immorsalityᵃ causes her to commit adultery; and whoever marries a woman who is divorced commits adultery.

Jesus Forbids Oaths

³³"Again you have heard that it was said to those of old, 'You shall not swear falsely, but shall perform your oaths to the Lord.' ³⁴But I say to you, do not swear at all: neither by heaven, for it is God's throne; ³⁵nor by the earth, for it is His footstool; nor by Jerusalem, for it is the city of the great King. ³⁶Nor shall you swear by your head, because you cannot make one hair white or black. ³⁷But let your 'Yes' be 'Yes,' and your 'No,' 'No.' For whatever is more than these is from the evil one.

Go the Second Mile

³⁸"You have heard that it was said, *'An eye for an eye and a tooth for a tooth.'*ᵃ ³⁹But I tell you not to resist an evil person.

But whoever slaps you on your right cheek, turn the other to him also. ⁴⁰If anyone wants to sue you and take away your tunic, let him have *your* cloak also. ⁴¹And whoever compels you to go one mile, go with him two. ⁴²Give to him who asks you, and from him who wants to borrow from you do not turn away.

Love Your Enemies

⁴³"You have heard that it was said, *'You shall love your neighbor*ᵃ and hate your enemy.' ⁴⁴But I say to you, love your enemies, bless those who curse you, do good to those who hate you, and pray for those who spitefully use you and persecute you,ᵃ ⁴⁵that you may be sons of your Father in heaven; for He makes His sun rise on the evil and on the good, and sends rain on the just and on the unjust. ⁴⁶For if you love those who love you, what reward have you? Do not even the tax collectors do the same? ⁴⁷And if you greet your brethrenᵃ only, what do you do more *than others?* Do not even the tax collectorsᵇ do so? ⁴⁸Therefore you shall be perfect, just as your Father in heaven is perfect.

Do Good to Please God

6 "Take heed that you do not do your charitable deeds before men, to be seen by them. Otherwise you have no reward from your Father in heaven. ²Therefore, when you do a charitable deed, do not sound a trumpet before you as the hypocrites do in the synagogues and in the streets, that they may have glory from men. Assuredly, I say to you, they have their reward. ³But when you do a charitable deed, do not let your left hand know what your right hand is doing, ⁴that your charitable deed may be in secret; and your Father who sees in secret will Himself reward you openly.ᵃ

The Model Prayer

⁵"And when you pray, you shall not be like the hypocrites. For they love to pray standing in the synagogues and on the corners of the streets, that they may be seen by men. Assuredly, I say to you, they have their reward. ⁶But you, when you pray, go into your room, and when you have shut your door, pray to

---

5:27 ᵃNU-Text and M-Text omit *to those of old.* ᵇExodus 20:14; Deuteronomy 5:18   **5:32** ᵃOr *fornication*   **5:38** ᵃExodus 21:24; Leviticus 24:20; Deuteronomy 19:21   **5:43** ᵃCompare Leviticus 19:18   **5:44** ᵃNU-Text omits three clauses from this verse, leaving, *"But I say to you, love your enemies and pray for those who persecute you."*   **5:47** ᵃM-Text reads *friends.* ᵇNU-Text reads *Gentiles.*   **6:4** ᵃNU-Text omits *openly.*

your Father who *is* in the secret *place;* and your Father who sees in secret will reward you openly.[a] [7]And when you pray, do not use vain repetitions as the heathen *do.* For they think that they will be heard for their many words.

[8]"Therefore do not be like them. For your Father knows the things you have need of before you ask Him. [9]In this manner, therefore, pray:

> Our Father in heaven,
> Hallowed be Your name.
> [10]Your kingdom come.
> Your will be done
> On earth as *it is* in heaven.
> [11]Give us this day our daily bread.
> [12]And forgive us our debts,
> As we forgive our debtors.
> [13]And do not lead us into temptation,
> But deliver us from the evil one.
> For Yours is the kingdom and the power
> and the glory forever. Amen.[a]

[14]"For if you forgive men their trespasses, your heavenly Father will also forgive you. [15]But if you do not forgive men their trespasses, neither will your Father forgive your trespasses.

Fasting to Be Seen Only by God

[16]"Moreover, when you fast, do not be like the hypocrites, with a sad countenance. For they disfigure their faces that they may appear to men to be fasting. Assuredly, I say to you, they have their reward. [17]But you, when you fast, anoint your head and wash your face, [18]so that you do not appear to men to be fasting, but to your Father who *is* in the secret *place;* and your Father who sees in secret will reward you openly.[a]

Lay Up Treasures in Heaven

[19]"Do not lay up for yourselves treasures on earth, where moth and rust destroy and where thieves break in and steal; [20]but lay up for yourselves treasures in heaven, where neither moth nor rust destroys and where thieves do not break in and steal. [21]For where your treasure is, there your heart will be also.

The Lamp of the Body

[22]"The lamp of the body is the eye. If therefore your eye is good, your whole body will be full of light. [23]But if your eye is bad, your whole body will be full of darkness. If therefore the light that is in you is darkness, how great *is* that darkness!

You Cannot Serve God and Riches

[24]"No one can serve two masters; for either he will hate the one and love the other, or else he will be loyal to the one and despise the other. You cannot serve God and mammon.

Do Not Worry

[25]"Therefore I say to you, do not worry about your life, what you will eat or what you will drink; nor about your body, what you will put on. Is not life more than food and

---

6:6 [a]NU-Text omits *openly.*   **6:13** [a]NU-Text omits *For Yours* through *Amen.*   **6:18** [a]NU-Text and M-Text omit *openly.*

↑ GROW (MATT. 6:10)

. . . .

In the Lord's Prayer, a template for all prayer, Jesus shows us prayer's true objective. *In Prayer we line up our will with the will of God.* True praying is not overcoming God's reluctance, but rather laying hold of His willingness. Prayer is not getting our will done in heaven, but getting God's will done on earth. So we ought to pray, "Lord, what do you want done here? I am about to ask for what I think is right, but if I'm wrong, I want to agree with Jesus and say, 'Nevertheless, not my will but Yours be done.'" When you have lived a little and walked a few years with Jesus, you begin to realize that God knows much more than you do! And so it gets easier and easier to pray, "Your will be done." Never be afraid to commit an unknown future to a known God. *For more about* Prayer, *see Matt. 7:7;* God's Will, *John 12:24, 25.*

the body more than clothing? ²⁶Look at the birds of the air, for they neither sow nor reap nor gather into barns; yet your heavenly Father feeds them. Are you not of more value than they? ²⁷Which of you by worrying can add one cubit to his stature?

²⁸"So why do you worry about clothing? Consider the lilies of the field, how they grow: they neither toil nor spin; ²⁹and yet I say to you that even Solomon in all his glory was not arrayed like one of these. ³⁰Now if God so clothes the grass of the field, which today is, and tomorrow is thrown into the oven, *will He* not much more *clothe* you, O you of little faith?

³¹"Therefore do not worry, saying, 'What shall we eat?' or 'What shall we drink?' or 'What shall we wear?' ³²For after all these things the Gentiles seek. For your heavenly Father knows that you need all these things. ³³But seek first the kingdom of God and His righteousness, and all these things shall be added to you. ³⁴Therefore do not worry about tomorrow, for tomorrow will worry about its own things. Sufficient for the day *is* its own trouble.

Do Not Judge

7 "Judge not, that you be not judged. ²For with what judgment you judge, you will be judged; and with the measure you use, it will be measured back to you. ³And why do you look at the speck in your brother's eye, but do not consider the plank in your own eye? ⁴Or how can you say to your brother, 'Let me remove the speck from your eye'; and look, a plank *is* in your own eye? ⁵Hypocrite! First remove the plank from your

> **But seek first the kingdom of God and His righteousness, and all these things shall be added to you.** Matt. 6:33

own eye, and then you will see clearly to remove the speck from your brother's eye.

⁶"Do not give what is holy to the dogs; nor cast your pearls before swine, lest they trample them under their feet, and turn and tear you in pieces.

Keep Asking, Seeking, Knocking

⁷"Ask, and it will be given to you; seek, and you will find; knock, and it will be opened to you. ⁸For everyone who asks receives, and he who seeks finds, and to him who knocks it will be opened. ⁹Or what man is there among you who, if his son asks for bread, will give him a stone? ¹⁰Or if he asks for a fish, will he give him a serpent? ¹¹If you then, being evil, know how to give good gifts to your children, how much more will your Father who is in heaven give good things to those who ask Him! ¹²Therefore, whatever you want men to do to you, do also to them, for this is the Law and the Prophets.

The Narrow Way

¹³"Enter by the narrow gate; for wide *is* the gate and broad *is* the way that leads to destruction, and there are many who go in by

↑ GROW (MATT. 7:7)

When you are praying for someone's salvation, or when you are petitioning God for a prodigal son or daughter, don't give up. You don't know what is happening behind the scenes! And don't think, *My prayer isn't getting answered as quickly as I would like it to be. God must be saying no.* In fact, He might be saying no today, but maybe He will say yes tomorrow or the day after. Just as God has His perfect will, so also He has His perfect timing. Your job is to keep on praying. When Jesus told us to knock and seek and find, in the original language the clear implication is, "Keep on asking, keep on knocking, keep on seeking." God's delays are not necessarily His denials. There may be a reason for the delay. So Jesus instructs us to keep praying until we sense Him telling us to stop. *For more about* Prayer *and* God at Work, *see Matt. 18:19, 20.*

it. [14]Because[a] narrow *is* the gate and difficult *is* the way which leads to life, and there are few who find it.

You Will Know Them by Their Fruits

[15]"Beware of false prophets, who come to you in sheep's clothing, but inwardly they are ravenous wolves. [16]You will know them by their fruits. Do men gather grapes from thornbushes or figs from thistles? [17]Even so, every good tree bears good fruit, but a bad tree bears bad fruit. [18]A good tree cannot bear bad fruit, nor *can* a bad tree bear good fruit. [19]Every tree that does not bear good fruit is cut down and thrown into the fire. [20]Therefore by their fruits you will know them.

I Never Knew You

[21]"Not everyone who says to Me, 'Lord, Lord,' shall enter the kingdom of heaven, but he who does the will of My Father in heaven. [22]Many will say to Me in that day, 'Lord, Lord, have we not prophesied in Your name, cast out demons in Your name, and done many wonders in Your name?' [23]And then I will declare to them, 'I never knew you; depart from Me, you who practice lawlessness!'

Build on the Rock

[24]"Therefore whoever hears these sayings of Mine, and does them, I will liken him to a wise man who built his house on the rock: [25]and the rain descended, the floods came, and the winds blew and beat on that house; and it did not fall, for it was founded on the rock.

> ↘ **LEARN**
> • • • • • • • • • • • • • •
> 7:21–23 • It's not enough to know about Jesus or even perform miracles. We must *know* Him, which we demonstrate by our obedience to Him. Just as Jesus came to earth to do His Father's will, not to do His own will (see John 6:38), so He equips us through the power of the Holy Spirit to obey God. Prophesying in Jesus' name, casting out demons, and performing miracles is no proof of salvation. What delights the heart of God is wholehearted, joyful obedience—and He promises to richly reward everyone who honors Him in this way. *For more about* How to Live Out Your Faith, *see* Matt. 16:13–17.

[26]"But everyone who hears these sayings of Mine, and does not do them, will be like a foolish man who built his house on the sand: [27]and the rain descended, the floods came, and the winds blew and beat on that house; and it fell. And great was its fall."

[28]And so it was, when Jesus had ended these sayings, that the people were astonished at His teaching, [29]for He taught them as one having authority, and not as the scribes.

Jesus Cleanses a Leper

8 When He had come down from the mountain, great multitudes followed Him. [2]And behold, a leper came and worshiped Him, saying, "Lord, if You are willing, You can make me clean."

[3]Then Jesus put out *His* hand and touched him, saying, "I am willing; be cleansed." Immediately his leprosy was cleansed.

[4]And Jesus said to him, "See that you tell no one; but go your way, show yourself to the priest, and offer the gift that Moses commanded, as a testimony to them."

Jesus Heals a Centurion's Servant

[5]Now when Jesus had entered Capernaum, a centurion came to Him, pleading with Him, [6]saying, "Lord, my servant is lying at home paralyzed, dreadfully tormented."

[7]And Jesus said to him, "I will come and heal him."

[8]The centurion answered and said, "Lord, I am not worthy that You should come under my roof. But only speak a word, and my servant will be healed. [9]For I also am a man under authority, having soldiers under me. And I say to this *one*, 'Go,' and he goes; and to another, 'Come,' and he comes; and to my servant, 'Do this,' and he does *it*."

[10]When Jesus heard *it*, He marveled, and said to those who followed, "Assuredly, I say to you, I have not found such great faith, not even in Israel! [11]And I say to you that many will come from east and west, and sit down with Abraham, Isaac, and Jacob in the kingdom of heaven. [12]But the sons of the kingdom will be cast out into outer darkness. There will be weeping and gnashing of teeth." [13]Then Jesus said to the centurion, "Go your way; and as you have believed, *so* let it be

7:14 [a]NU-Text and M-Text read *How . . . !*

done for you." And his servant was healed that same hour.

Peter's Mother-in-Law Healed

[14]Now when Jesus had come into Peter's house, He saw his wife's mother lying sick with a fever. [15]So He touched her hand, and the fever left her. And she arose and served them.[a]

Many Healed in the Evening

[16]When evening had come, they brought to Him many who were demon-possessed. And He cast out the spirits with a word, and healed all who were sick, [17]that it might be fulfilled which was spoken by Isaiah the prophet, saying:

"He Himself took our infirmities
And bore our sicknesses."[a]

The Cost of Discipleship

[18]And when Jesus saw great multitudes about Him, He gave a command to depart to the other side. [19]Then a certain scribe came and said to Him, "Teacher, I will follow You wherever You go."

[20]And Jesus said to him, "Foxes have holes and birds of the air *have* nests, but the Son of Man has nowhere to lay *His* head."

[21]Then another of His disciples said to Him, "Lord, let me first go and bury my father."

[22]But Jesus said to him, "Follow Me, and let the dead bury their own dead."

Wind and Wave Obey Jesus

[23]Now when He got into a boat, His disciples followed Him. [24]And suddenly a great tempest arose on the sea, so that the boat was covered with the waves. But He was asleep. [25]Then His disciples came to *Him* and awoke Him, saying, "Lord, save us! We are perishing!"

[26]But He said to them, "Why are you fearful, O you of little faith?" Then He arose and rebuked the winds and the sea, and there was a great calm. [27]So the men marveled, saying, "Who can this be, that even the winds and the sea obey Him?"

Two Demon-Possessed Men Healed

[28]When He had come to the other side, to the country of the Gergesenes,[a] there met Him two demon-possessed *men,* coming out of the tombs, exceedingly fierce, so that no one could pass that way. [29]And suddenly they cried out, saying, "What have we to do with You, Jesus, You Son of God? Have You come here to torment us before the time?"

[30]Now a good way off from them there was a herd of many swine feeding. [31]So the demons begged Him, saying, "If You cast us out, permit us to go away[a] into the herd of swine."

[32]And He said to them, "Go." So when they had come out, they went into the herd of swine. And suddenly the whole herd of swine ran violently down the steep place into the sea, and perished in the water.

[33]Then those who kept *them* fled; and they went away into the city and told everything, including what *had happened* to the demon-possessed *men.* [34]And behold, the whole city came out to meet Jesus. And when they saw Him, they begged *Him* to depart from their region.

Jesus Forgives and Heals a Paralytic

9 So He got into a boat, crossed over, and came to His own city. [2]Then behold, they brought to Him a paralytic lying on a bed. When Jesus saw their faith, He said to the paralytic, "Son, be of good cheer; your sins are forgiven you."

[3]And at once some of the scribes said within themselves, "This Man blasphemes!"

[4]But Jesus, knowing their thoughts, said, "Why do you think evil in your hearts? [5]For which is easier, to say, 'Your sins are forgiven you,' or to say, 'Arise and walk'? [6]But that you may know that the Son of Man has power on earth to forgive sins"—then He said to the paralytic, "Arise, take up your bed, and go to your house." [7]And he arose and departed to his house.

[8]Now when the multitudes saw *it,* they marveled[a] and glorified God, who had given such power to men.

Matthew the Tax Collector

[9]As Jesus passed on from there, He saw a man named Matthew sitting at the tax office.

8:15 [a]NU-Text and M-Text read *Him.*   8:17 [a]Isaiah 53:4   8:28 [a]NU-Text reads *Gadarenes.*   8:31 [a]NU-Text reads *send us.*   9:8 [a]NU-Text reads *were afraid.*

And He said to him, "Follow Me." So he arose and followed Him.

[10]Now it happened, as Jesus sat at the table in the house, *that* behold, many tax collectors and sinners came and sat down with Him and His disciples. [11]And when the Pharisees saw *it,* they said to His disciples, "Why does your Teacher eat with tax collectors and sinners?"

[12]When Jesus heard *that,* He said to them, "Those who are well have no need of a physician, but those who are sick. [13]But go and learn what *this* means: '*I desire mercy and not sacrifice.*'ᵃ For I did not come to call the righteous, but sinners, to repentance."ᵇ

Jesus Is Questioned About Fasting

[14]Then the disciples of John came to Him, saying, "Why do we and the Pharisees fast often,ᵃ but Your disciples do not fast?"

[15]And Jesus said to them, "Can the friends of the bridegroom mourn as long as the bridegroom is with them? But the days will come when the bridegroom will be taken away from them, and then they will fast. [16]No one puts a piece of unshrunk cloth on an old garment; for the patch pulls away from the garment, and the tear is made worse. [17]Nor do they put new wine into old wineskins, or else the wineskins break, the wine is spilled, and the wineskins are ruined. But they put new wine into new wineskins, and both are preserved."

A Girl Restored to Life and a Woman Healed

[18]While He spoke these things to them, behold, a ruler came and worshiped Him, saying, "My daughter has just died, but come and lay Your hand on her and she will live." [19]So Jesus arose and followed him, and so *did* His disciples.

[20]And suddenly, a woman who had a flow of blood for twelve years came from behind and touched the hem of His garment. [21]For she said to herself, "If only I may touch His garment, I shall be made well." [22]But Jesus turned around, and when He saw her He said, "Be of good cheer, daughter; your faith has made you well." And the woman was made well from that hour.

[23]When Jesus came into the ruler's house, and saw the flute players and the noisy crowd wailing, [24]He said to them, "Make room, for the girl is not dead, but sleeping." And they ridiculed Him. [25]But when the crowd was put outside, He went in and took her by the hand, and the girl arose. [26]And the report of this went out into all that land.

Two Blind Men Healed

[27]When Jesus departed from there, two blind men followed Him, crying out and saying, "Son of David, have mercy on us!"

[28]And when He had come into the house, the blind men came to Him. And Jesus said to them, "Do you believe that I am able to do this?"

They said to Him, "Yes, Lord."

[29]Then He touched their eyes, saying, "According to your faith let it be to you." [30]And their eyes were opened. And Jesus sternly warned them, saying, "See *that* no one knows *it.*" [31]But when they had departed, they spread the news about Him in all that country.

A Mute Man Speaks

[32]As they went out, behold, they brought to Him a man, mute and demon-possessed. [33]And when the demon was cast out, the mute spoke. And the multitudes marveled, saying, "It was never seen like this in Israel!"

[34]But the Pharisees said, "He casts out demons by the ruler of the demons."

The Compassion of Jesus

[35]Then Jesus went about all the cities and villages, teaching in their synagogues, preaching the gospel of the kingdom, and healing every sickness and every disease among the people.ᵃ [36]But when He saw the multitudes, He was moved with compassion for them, because they were wearyᵃ and scattered, like sheep having no shepherd. [37]Then He said to His disciples, "The harvest truly *is* plentiful, but the laborers *are* few. [38]Therefore pray the Lord of the harvest to send out laborers into His harvest."

9:13 ᵃHosea 6:6 ᵇNU-Text omits *to repentance.*   9:14 ᵃNU-Text brackets *often* as disputed.   9:35 ᵃNU-Text omits *among the people.*
9:36 ᵃNU-Text and M-Text read *harassed.*

The Twelve Apostles

10 And when He had called His twelve disciples to *Him,* He gave them power *over* unclean spirits, to cast them out, and to heal all kinds of sickness and all kinds of disease. [2]Now the names of the twelve apostles are these: first, Simon, who is called Peter, and Andrew his brother; James the *son* of Zebedee, and John his brother; [3]Philip and Bartholomew; Thomas and Matthew the tax collector; James the *son* of Alphaeus, and Lebbaeus, whose surname was[a] Thaddaeus; [4]Simon the Cananite,[a] and Judas Iscariot, who also betrayed Him.

Sending Out the Twelve

[5]These twelve Jesus sent out and commanded them, saying: "Do not go into the way of the Gentiles, and do not enter a city of the Samaritans. [6]But go rather to the lost sheep of the house of Israel. [7]And as you go, preach, saying, 'The kingdom of heaven is at hand.' [8]Heal the sick, cleanse the lepers, raise the dead,[a] cast out demons. Freely you have received, freely give. [9]Provide neither gold nor silver nor copper in your money belts, [10]nor bag for *your* journey, nor two tunics, nor sandals, nor staffs; for a worker is worthy of his food.

[11]"Now whatever city or town you enter, inquire who in it is worthy, and stay there till you go out. [12]And when you go into a household, greet it. [13]If the household is worthy, let your peace come upon it. But if it is not worthy, let your peace return to you. [14]And whoever will not receive you nor hear your words, when you depart from that house or city, shake off the dust from your feet. [15]Assuredly, I say to you, it will be more tolerable for the land of Sodom and Gomorrah in the day of judgment than for that city!

Persecutions Are Coming

[16]"Behold, I send you out as sheep in the midst of wolves. Therefore be wise as serpents and harmless as doves. [17]But beware of men, for they will deliver you up to councils and scourge you in their synagogues. [18]You will be brought before governors and kings for My sake, as a testimony to them and to the Gentiles. [19]But when they deliver you up, do not worry about how or what you should speak. For it will be given to you in that hour what you should speak; [20]for it is not you who speak, but the Spirit of your Father who speaks in you.

[21]"Now brother will deliver up brother to death, and a father *his* child; and children will rise up against parents and cause them to be put to death. [22]And you will be hated by all for My name's sake. But he who endures to the end will be saved. [23]When they persecute you in this city, flee to another. For assuredly, I say to you, you will not have gone through the cities of Israel before the Son of Man comes.

[24]"A disciple is not above *his* teacher, nor a servant above his master. [25]It is enough for a disciple that he be like his teacher, and a servant like his master. If they have called the master of the house Beelzebub,[a] how much more *will they call* those of his household! [26]Therefore do not fear them. For there is nothing covered that will not be revealed, and hidden that will not be known.

Jesus Teaches the Fear of God

[27]"Whatever I tell you in the dark, speak in the light; and what you hear in the ear, preach on the housetops. [28]And do not fear those who kill the body but cannot kill the soul. But rather fear Him who is able to destroy both soul and body in hell. [29]Are not two sparrows sold for a copper coin? And not one of them falls to the ground apart from your Father's will. [30]But the very hairs of your head are all numbered. [31]Do not fear therefore; you are of more value than many sparrows.

Confess Christ Before Men

[32]"Therefore whoever confesses Me before men, him I will also confess before My Father who is in heaven. [33]But whoever denies Me before men, him I will also deny before My Father who is in heaven.

Christ Brings Division

[34]"Do not think that I came to bring peace on earth. I did not come to bring peace but a sword. [35]For I have come to 'set a man against

---

10:3 [a]NU-Text omits *Lebbaeus, whose surname was.*   **10:4** [a]NU-Text reads *Canaanean.*   **10:8** [a]NU-Text reads *raise the dead, cleanse the lepers;* M-Text omits *raise the dead.*   **10:25** [a]NU-Text and M-Text read *Beelzebul.*

→LIVE
• • • • • • • • • • • • • • • •

10:32 • Have you confessed Jesus as Lord? You say, "People know I am a Christian. I try to be moral. I try to be caring." Those things are nice, but a moment must come when you say, "I believe in Jesus Christ and confess Him as my Savior and Lord." That is why we call people forward in many of our evangelistic meetings. Walking down an aisle doesn't make anyone a Christian. But if they will confess Christ before men, He will confess them before the Father. Look for an opportunity to confess Jesus Christ before this day is over. *For more about* Becoming a Christian, Mark 10:27.

his father, a daughter against her mother, and a daughter-in-law against her mother-in-law'; ³⁶and 'a man's enemies will be those of his own household.'ᵃ ³⁷He who loves father or mother more than Me is not worthy of Me. And he who loves son or daughter more than Me is not worthy of Me. ³⁸And he who does not take his cross and follow after Me is not worthy of Me. ³⁹He who finds his life will lose it, and he who loses his life for My sake will find it.

A Cup of Cold Water

⁴⁰"He who receives you receives Me, and he who receives Me receives Him who sent Me. ⁴¹He who receives a prophet in the name of a prophet shall receive a prophet's reward. And he who receives a righteous man in the name of a righteous man shall receive a righteous man's reward. ⁴²And whoever gives one of these little ones only a cup of cold *water* in the name of a disciple, assuredly, I say to you, he shall by no means lose his reward."

John the Baptist Sends Messengers to Jesus

11 Now it came to pass, when Jesus finished commanding His twelve disciples, that He departed from there to teach and to preach in their cities.

²And when John had heard in prison about the works of Christ, he sent two ofᵃ his disciples ³and said to Him, "Are You the Coming One, or do we look for another?"

⁴Jesus answered and said to them, "Go and tell John the things which you hear and see: ⁵*The* blind see and *the* lame walk; *the*

lepers are cleansed and *the* deaf hear; *the* dead are raised up and *the* poor have the gospel preached to them. ⁶And blessed is he who is not offended because of Me."

⁷As they departed, Jesus began to say to the multitudes concerning John: "What did you go out into the wilderness to see? A reed shaken by the wind? ⁸But what did you go out to see? A man clothed in soft garments? Indeed, those who wear soft *clothing* are in kings' houses. ⁹But what did you go out to see? A prophet? Yes, I say to you, and more than a prophet. ¹⁰For this is *he* of whom it is written:

'Behold, I send My messenger before
   Your face,
Who will prepare Your way before
   You.'ᵃ

¹¹"Assuredly, I say to you, among those born of women there has not risen one greater than John the Baptist; but he who is least in the kingdom of heaven is greater than he. ¹²And from the days of John the Baptist until now the kingdom of heaven suffers violence, and the violent take it by force. ¹³For all the prophets and the law prophesied until John. ¹⁴And if you are willing to receive *it*, he is Elijah who is to come. ¹⁵He who has ears to hear, let him hear!

¹⁶"But to what shall I liken this generation? It is like children sitting in the marketplaces and calling to their companions, ¹⁷and saying:

'We played the flute for you,
   And you did not dance;
We mourned to you,
   And you did not lament.'

¹⁸For John came neither eating nor drinking, and they say, 'He has a demon.' ¹⁹The Son of Man came eating and drinking, and they say, 'Look, a glutton and a winebibber, a friend of tax collectors and sinners!' But wisdom is justified by her children."ᵃ

Woe to the Impenitent Cities

²⁰Then He began to rebuke the cities in which most of His mighty works had been done, because they did not repent: ²¹"Woe to

10:36 ᵃMicah 7:6   11:2 ᵃNU-Text reads *by* for *two of*.   11:10 ᵃMalachi 3:1   11:19 ᵃNU-Text reads *works*.

you, Chorazin! Woe to you, Bethsaida! For if the mighty works which were done in you had been done in Tyre and Sidon, they would have repented long ago in sackcloth and ashes. ²²But I say to you, it will be more tolerable for Tyre and Sidon in the day of judgment than for you. ²³And you, Capernaum, who are exalted to heaven, will beª brought down to Hades; for if the mighty works which were done in you had been done in Sodom, it would have remained until this day. ²⁴But I say to you that it shall be more tolerable for the land of Sodom in the day of judgment than for you."

Jesus Gives True Rest

²⁵At that time Jesus answered and said, "I thank You, Father, Lord of heaven and earth, that You have hidden these things from *the* wise and prudent and have revealed them to babes. ²⁶Even so, Father, for so it seemed good in Your sight. ²⁷All things have been delivered to Me by My Father, and no one knows the Son except the Father. Nor does anyone know the Father except the Son, and *the one* to whom the Son wills to reveal *Him.* ²⁸Come to Me, all *you* who labor and are heavy laden, and I will give you rest. ²⁹Take My yoke upon you and learn from Me, for I am gentle and lowly in heart, and you will find rest for your souls. ³⁰For My yoke *is* easy and My burden is light."

Jesus Is Lord of the Sabbath

12 At that time Jesus went through the grainfields on the Sabbath. And His disciples were hungry, and began to pluck heads of grain and to eat. ²And when the Pharisees saw *it,* they said to Him, "Look, Your disciples are doing what is not lawful to do on the Sabbath!"

³But He said to them, "Have you not read what David did when he was hungry, he and those who were with him: ⁴how he entered the house of God and ate the showbread which was not lawful for him to eat, nor for those who were with him, but only for the priests? ⁵Or have you not read in the law that on the Sabbath the priests in the temple profane the Sabbath, and are blameless? ⁶Yet I say to you that in this place there is *One* greater

than the temple. ⁷But if you had known what *this* means, '*I desire mercy and not sacrifice,*'ª you would not have condemned the guiltless. ⁸For the Son of Man is Lord evenª of the Sabbath."

Healing on the Sabbath

⁹Now when He had departed from there, He went into their synagogue. ¹⁰And behold, there was a man who had a withered hand. And they asked Him, saying, "Is it lawful to heal on the Sabbath?"—that they might accuse Him.

¹¹Then He said to them, "What man is there among you who has one sheep, and if it falls into a pit on the Sabbath, will not lay hold of it and lift *it* out? ¹²Of how much more value then is a man than a sheep? Therefore it is lawful to do good on the Sabbath." ¹³Then He said to the man, "Stretch out your hand." And he stretched *it* out, and it was restored as whole as the other. ¹⁴Then the Pharisees went out and plotted against Him, how they might destroy Him.

Behold, My Servant

¹⁵But when Jesus knew *it,* He withdrew from there. And great multitudesª followed Him, and He healed them all. ¹⁶Yet He warned them not to make Him known, ¹⁷that it might be fulfilled which was spoken by Isaiah the prophet, saying:

¹⁸ *"Behold! My Servant whom I have chosen,*
  My Beloved in whom My soul is well
    pleased!
  I will put My Spirit upon Him,
  And He will declare justice to the
    Gentiles.
¹⁹ *He will not quarrel nor cry out,*
  Nor will anyone hear His voice in the
    streets.
²⁰ *A bruised reed He will not break,*
  And smoking flax He will not quench,
  Till He sends forth justice to victory;
²¹ *And in His name Gentiles will trust.* "ª

A House Divided Cannot Stand

²²Then one was brought to Him who was demon-possessed, blind and mute; and He

---

11:23 ªNU-Text reads *will you be exalted to heaven? No, you will be.*   12:7 ªHosea 6:6   12:8 ªNU-Text and M-Text omit *even.*
12:15 ªNU-Text brackets *multitudes* as disputed.   12:21 ªIsaiah 42:1–4

healed him, so that the blind and[a] mute man both spoke and saw. [23]And all the multitudes were amazed and said, "Could this be the Son of David?"

[24]Now when the Pharisees heard *it* they said, "This *fellow* does not cast out demons except by Beelzebub,[a] the ruler of the demons."

[25]But Jesus knew their thoughts, and said to them: "Every kingdom divided against itself is brought to desolation, and every city or house divided against itself will not stand. [26]If Satan casts out Satan, he is divided against himself. How then will his kingdom stand? [27]And if I cast out demons by Beelzebub, by whom do your sons cast *them* out? Therefore they shall be your judges. [28]But if I cast out demons by the Spirit of God, surely the kingdom of God has come upon you. [29]Or how can one enter a strong man's house and plunder his goods, unless he first binds the strong man? And then he will plunder his house. [30]He who is not with Me is against Me, and he who does not gather with Me scatters abroad.

The Unpardonable Sin

[31]"Therefore I say to you, every sin and blasphemy will be forgiven men, but the blasphemy *against* the Spirit will not be forgiven men. [32]Anyone who speaks a word against the Son of Man, it will be forgiven him; but whoever speaks against the Holy Spirit, it will not be forgiven him, either in this age or in the *age* to come.

A Tree Known by Its Fruit

[33]"Either make the tree good and its fruit good, or else make the tree bad and its fruit bad; for a tree is known by *its* fruit. [34]Brood of vipers! How can you, being evil, speak good things? For out of the abundance of the heart the mouth speaks. [35]A good man out of the good treasure of his heart[a] brings forth good things, and an evil man out of the evil treasure brings forth evil things. [36]But I say to you that for every idle word men may speak, they will give account of it in the day of judgment. [37]For by your words you will be justified, and by your words you will be condemned."

The Scribes and Pharisees Ask for a Sign

[38]Then some of the scribes and Pharisees answered, saying, "Teacher, we want to see a sign from You."

[39]But He answered and said to them, "An evil and adulterous generation seeks after a sign, and no sign will be given to it except the sign of the prophet Jonah. [40]For as Jonah was three days and three nights in the belly of the great fish, so will the Son of Man be three days and three nights in the heart of the earth. [41]The men of Nineveh will rise up in the judgment with this generation and condemn it, because they repented at the preaching of Jonah; and indeed a greater than Jonah *is* here. [42]The queen of the South will rise up in the judgment with this generation and condemn it, for she came from the ends of the earth to hear the wisdom of Solomon; and indeed a greater than Solomon *is* here.

An Unclean Spirit Returns

[43]"When an unclean spirit goes out of a man, he goes through dry places, seeking rest, and finds none. [44]Then he says, 'I will return to my house from which I came.' And when he comes, he finds *it* empty, swept, and put in order. [45]Then he goes and takes with him seven other spirits more wicked than himself, and they enter and dwell there; and the last *state* of that man is worse than the first. So shall it also be with this wicked generation."

Jesus' Mother and Brothers Send for Him

[46]While He was still talking to the multitudes, behold, His mother and brothers stood outside, seeking to speak with Him. [47]Then one said to Him, "Look, Your mother and Your brothers are standing outside, seeking to speak with You."

[48]But He answered and said to the one who told Him, "Who is My mother and who are My brothers?" [49]And He stretched out His hand toward His disciples and said, "Here are My mother and My brothers! [50]For whoever does the will of My Father in heaven is My brother and sister and mother."

12:22 [a]NU-Text omits *blind and.*   **12:24** [a]NU-Text and M-Text read *Beelzebul.*   **12:35** [a]NU-Text and M-Text omit *of his heart.*

The Parable of the Sower

13 On the same day Jesus went out of the house and sat by the sea. [2]And great multitudes were gathered together to Him, so that He got into a boat and sat; and the whole multitude stood on the shore.

[3]Then He spoke many things to them in parables, saying: "Behold, a sower went out to sow. [4]And as he sowed, some *seed* fell by the wayside; and the birds came and devoured them. [5]Some fell on stony places, where they did not have much earth; and they immediately sprang up because they had no depth of earth. [6]But when the sun was up they were scorched, and because they had no root they withered away. [7]And some fell among thorns, and the thorns sprang up and choked them. [8]But others fell on good ground and yielded a crop: some a hundredfold, some sixty, some thirty. [9]He who has ears to hear, let him hear!"

The Purpose of Parables

[10]And the disciples came and said to Him, "Why do You speak to them in parables?"

[11]He answered and said to them, "Because it has been given to you to know the mysteries of the kingdom of heaven, but to them it has not been given. [12]For whoever has, to him more will be given, and he will have abundance; but whoever does not have, even what he has will be taken away from him. [13]Therefore I speak to them in parables, because seeing they do not see, and hearing they do not hear, nor do they understand. [14]And in them the prophecy of Isaiah is fulfilled, which says:

'Hearing you will hear and shall not
       understand,
   And seeing you will see and not perceive;
[15] For the hearts of this people have grown
       dull.
   Their ears are hard of hearing,
   And their eyes they have closed,
   Lest they should see with their eyes and
       hear with their ears,
   Lest they should understand with their
       hearts and turn,
   So that I should[a] heal them.'[b]

[16]But blessed *are* your eyes for they see, and your ears for they hear; [17]for assuredly, I say to you that many prophets and righteous *men* desired to see what you see, and did not see *it*, and to hear what you hear, and did not hear *it*.

The Parable of the Sower Explained

[18]"Therefore hear the parable of the sower: [19]When anyone hears the word of the kingdom, and does not understand *it*, then the wicked *one* comes and snatches away what was sown in his heart. This is he who received seed by the wayside. [20]But he who received the seed on stony places, this is he who hears the word and immediately receives it with joy; [21]yet he has no root in himself, but endures only for a while. For when tribulation or persecution arises because of the word, immediately he stumbles. [22]Now he who received seed among the thorns is he who hears the word, and the cares of this world and the deceitfulness of riches choke the word, and he becomes unfruitful. [23]But he who received seed on the good ground is he who hears the word and understands *it*, who indeed bears fruit and produces: some a hundredfold, some sixty, some thirty."

The Parable of the Wheat and the Tares

[24]Another parable He put forth to them, saying: "The kingdom of heaven is like a man who sowed good seed in his field; [25]but while men slept, his enemy came and sowed tares among the wheat and went his way. [26]But when the grain had sprouted and produced a crop, then the tares also appeared. [27]So the servants of the owner came and said to him, 'Sir, did you not sow good seed in your field? How then does it have tares?' [28]He said to them, 'An enemy has done this.' The servants said to him, 'Do you want us then to go and gather them up?' [29]But he said, 'No, lest while you gather up the tares you also uproot the wheat with them. [30]Let both grow together until the harvest, and at the time of harvest I will say to the reapers, "First gather together the tares and bind them in bundles to burn them, but gather the wheat into my barn." ' "

The Parable of the Mustard Seed

[31]Another parable He put forth to them, saying: "The kingdom of heaven is like a

13:15 [a]NU-Text and M-Text read *would.* [b]Isaiah 6:9, 10

mustard seed, which a man took and sowed in his field, ³²which indeed is the least of all the seeds; but when it is grown it is greater than the herbs and becomes a tree, so that the birds of the air come and nest in its branches."

The Parable of the Leaven

³³Another parable He spoke to them: "The kingdom of heaven is like leaven, which a woman took and hid in three measures[a] of meal till it was all leavened."

Prophecy and the Parables

³⁴All these things Jesus spoke to the multitude in parables; and without a parable He did not speak to them, ³⁵that it might be fulfilled which was spoken by the prophet, saying:

"I will open My mouth in parables;
I will utter things kept secret from the
foundation of the world."[a]

The Parable of the Tares Explained

³⁶Then Jesus sent the multitude away and went into the house. And His disciples came to Him, saying, "Explain to us the parable of the tares of the field."
³⁷He answered and said to them: "He who sows the good seed is the Son of Man. ³⁸The field is the world, the good seeds are the sons of the kingdom, but the tares are the sons of the wicked *one.* ³⁹The enemy who sowed them is the devil, the harvest is the end of the age, and the reapers are the angels. ⁴⁰Therefore as the tares are gathered and burned in the fire, so it will be at the end of this age. ⁴¹The Son of Man will send out His angels, and they will gather out of His kingdom all things that offend, and those who practice lawlessness, ⁴²and will cast them into the furnace of fire. There will be wailing and gnashing of teeth. ⁴³Then the righteous will shine forth as the sun in the kingdom of their Father. He who has ears to hear, let him hear!

The Parable of the Hidden Treasure

⁴⁴"Again, the kingdom of heaven is like treasure hidden in a field, which a man found and hid; and for joy over it he goes and sells all that he has and buys that field.

The Parable of the Pearl of Great Price

⁴⁵"Again, the kingdom of heaven is like a merchant seeking beautiful pearls, ⁴⁶who, when he had found one pearl of great price, went and sold all that he had and bought it.

The Parable of the Dragnet

⁴⁷"Again, the kingdom of heaven is like a dragnet that was cast into the sea and gathered some of every kind, ⁴⁸which, when it was full, they drew to shore; and they sat down and gathered the good into vessels, but threw the bad away. ⁴⁹So it will be at the end of the age. The angels will come forth, separate the wicked from among the just, ⁵⁰and cast them into the furnace of fire. There will be wailing and gnashing of teeth."
⁵¹Jesus said to them,[a] "Have you understood all these things?"
They said to Him, "Yes, Lord."[b]
⁵²Then He said to them, "Therefore every scribe instructed concerning[a] the kingdom of heaven is like a householder who brings out of his treasure *things* new and old."

Jesus Rejected at Nazareth

⁵³Now it came to pass, when Jesus had finished these parables, that He departed from there. ⁵⁴When He had come to His own country, He taught them in their synagogue, so that they were astonished and said, "Where did this *Man* get this wisdom and *these* mighty works? ⁵⁵Is this not the carpenter's son? Is not His mother called Mary? And His brothers James, Joses,[a] Simon, and Judas? ⁵⁶And His sisters, are they not all with us? Where then did this *Man* get all these things?" ⁵⁷So they were offended at Him.

But Jesus said to them, "A prophet is not without honor except in his own country and in his own house." ⁵⁸Now He did not do many mighty works there because of their unbelief.

John the Baptist Beheaded

14 At that time Herod the tetrarch heard the report about Jesus ²and said to his servants, "This is John the Baptist; he is risen from the dead, and therefore these powers are at work in him."

13:33 [a]Greek *sata,* approximately two pecks in all   **13:35** [a]Psalm 78:2   **13:51** [a]NU-Text omits *Jesus said to them.*
[b]NU-Text omits *Lord.*   **13:52** [a]Or *for*   **13:55** [a]NU-Text reads *Joseph.*

[3]For Herod had laid hold of John and bound him, and put *him* in prison for the sake of Herodias, his brother Philip's wife. [4]Because John had said to him, "It is not lawful for you to have her." [5]And although he wanted to put him to death, he feared the multitude, because they counted him as a prophet.

[6]But when Herod's birthday was celebrated, the daughter of Herodias danced before them and pleased Herod. [7]Therefore he promised with an oath to give her whatever she might ask.

[8]So she, having been prompted by her mother, said, "Give me John the Baptist's head here on a platter."

[9]And the king was sorry; nevertheless, because of the oaths and because of those who sat with him, he commanded *it* to be given to *her*. [10]So he sent and had John beheaded in prison. [11]And his head was brought on a platter and given to the girl, and she brought *it* to her mother. [12]Then his disciples came and took away the body and buried it, and went and told Jesus.

Feeding the Five Thousand

[13]When Jesus heard *it,* He departed from there by boat to a deserted place by Himself. But when the multitudes heard it, they followed Him on foot from the cities. [14]And when Jesus went out He saw a great multitude; and He was moved with compassion for them, and healed their sick. [15]When it was evening, His disciples came to Him, saying, "This is a deserted place, and the hour is already late. Send the multitudes away, that they may go into the villages and buy themselves food."

[16]But Jesus said to them, "They do not need to go away. You give them something to eat."

[17]And they said to Him, "We have here only five loaves and two fish."

[18]He said, "Bring them here to Me." [19]Then He commanded the multitudes to sit down on the grass. And He took the five loaves and the two fish, and looking up to heaven, He blessed and broke and gave the loaves to the disciples; and the disciples gave to the multitudes. [20]So they all ate and were filled, and they took up twelve baskets full of the fragments that remained. [21]Now those

who had eaten were about five thousand men, besides women and children.

Jesus Walks on the Sea

[22]Immediately Jesus made His disciples get into the boat and go before Him to the other side, while He sent the multitudes away. [23]And when He had sent the multitudes away, He went up on the mountain by Himself to pray. Now when evening came, He was alone there. [24]But the boat was now in the middle of the sea,[a] tossed by the waves, for the wind was contrary.

[25]Now in the fourth watch of the night Jesus went to them, walking on the sea. [26]And when the disciples saw Him walking on the sea, they were troubled, saying, "It is a ghost!" And they cried out for fear.

[27]But immediately Jesus spoke to them, saying, "Be of good cheer! It is I; do not be afraid."

[28]And Peter answered Him and said, "Lord, if it is You, command me to come to You on the water."

[29]So He said, "Come." And when Peter had come down out of the boat, he walked on the water to go to Jesus. [30]But when he saw that the wind *was* boisterous,[a] he was afraid; and beginning to sink he cried out, saying, "Lord, save me!"

[31]And immediately Jesus stretched out *His* hand and caught him, and said to him, "O you of little faith, why did you doubt?" [32]And when they got into the boat, the wind ceased.

[33]Then those who were in the boat came

↘ LEARN
• • • • • • • • • • • • • • • •

14:28–31 • Peter started out well. He did not impetuously leap out of the boat, but asked the Lord to bid him walk on the water. And Jesus said, "Come!" (4:29). That's always a wise way to operate! Soon, however, Peter let circumstances get the better of him. By focusing on the danger of his call, he forgot the Lord's word. That's when he sank. Do you want to grow in faith? Then lock your eyes on Jesus (Heb. 12:2). Corrie Ten Boom once said, "Look without and be distressed. Look within and be depressed. Look at Jesus and be at rest." *For more about* Faith, *see Matt. 14:30;* Growing in Christ, *Matt. 18:8;* Adversity, Mark 14:36.

14:24 [a]NU-Text reads *many furlongs away from the land.*   **14:30** [a]NU-Text brackets *that* and *boisterous* as disputed.

and[a] worshiped Him, saying, "Truly You are the Son of God."

Many Touch Him and Are Made Well

[34]When they had crossed over, they came to the land of[a] Gennesaret. [35]And when the men of that place recognized Him, they sent out into all that surrounding region, brought to Him all who were sick, [36]and begged Him that they might only touch the hem of His garment. And as many as touched *it* were made perfectly well.

Defilement Comes from Within

15 Then the scribes and Pharisees who were from Jerusalem came to Jesus, saying, [2]"Why do Your disciples transgress the tradition of the elders? For they do not wash their hands when they eat bread."

[3]He answered and said to them, "Why do you also transgress the commandment of God because of your tradition? [4]For God commanded, saying, *'Honor your father and your mother';*[a] and, *'He who curses father or mother, let him be put to death.'*[b] [5]But you say, 'Whoever says to his father or mother, "Whatever profit you might have received from me *is* a gift *to God*"— [6]then he need not honor his father or mother.'[a] Thus you have made the commandment[b] of God of no effect by your tradition. [7]Hypocrites! Well did Isaiah prophesy about you, saying:

[8]*'These people draw near to Me with their mouth,*

And[a] *honor Me with their lips,*
But their heart is far from Me.
[9]*And in vain they worship Me,*
Teaching as doctrines the
commandments of men.' "[a]

[10]When He had called the multitude to *Himself*, He said to them, "Hear and understand: [11]Not what goes into the mouth defiles a man; but what comes out of the mouth, this defiles a man."

[12]Then His disciples came and said to Him, "Do You know that the Pharisees were offended when they heard this saying?"

[13]But He answered and said, "Every plant which My heavenly Father has not planted will be uprooted. [14]Let them alone. They are blind leaders of the blind. And if the blind leads the blind, both will fall into a ditch."

[15]Then Peter answered and said to Him, "Explain this parable to us."

[16]So Jesus said, "Are you also still without understanding? [17]Do you not yet understand that whatever enters the mouth goes into the stomach and is eliminated? [18]But those things which proceed out of the mouth come from the heart, and they defile a man. [19]For out of the heart proceed evil thoughts, murders, adulteries, fornications, thefts, false witness, blasphemies. [20]These are *the things* which defile a man, but to eat with unwashed hands does not defile a man."

A Gentile Shows Her Faith

[21]Then Jesus went out from there and departed to the region of Tyre and Sidon. [22]And

---

14:33 [a]NU-Text omits *came and*.   14:34 [a]NU-Text reads *came to land at*.   15:4 [a]Exodus 20:12; Deuteronomy 5:16   [b]Exodus 21:17
15:6 [a]NU-Text omits *or mother*.   [b]NU-Text reads *word*.   15:8 [a]NU-Text omits *draw near to Me with their mouth, And*.   15:9 [a]Isaiah 29:13

↑ GROW (MATT. 14:30)
. . . .

We all have lapses of faith. Maybe we start something in faith and then bail. Unfortunately, the situation is not at all unusual. So what should you do when you have a lapse of faith? Call out to Jesus. Too many of us doubt our beliefs and believe our doubts. Don't doubt in the dark what you have believed in the light! Some have criticized Peter's failure, but note that Jesus indeed told him to come (v. 29). And Peter is the only apostle ever to walk on water! Have you ever tried to do something for God and failed? If so, I want to say to you, "Thank you for trying!" I would rather try and fail than never try at all. Sometimes we learn crucial lessons through so-called "failure" that set us up for success later on. The doorway to success often comes through the hallway of failure. *For more about* Faith, *see Matt. 17:20.*

behold, a woman of Canaan came from that region and cried out to Him, saying, "Have mercy on me, O Lord, Son of David! My daughter is severely demon-possessed."

[23]But He answered her not a word.

And His disciples came and urged Him, saying, "Send her away, for she cries out after us."

[24]But He answered and said, "I was not sent except to the lost sheep of the house of Israel."

[25]Then she came and worshiped Him, saying, "Lord, help me!"

[26]But He answered and said, "It is not good to take the children's bread and throw *it* to the little dogs."

[27]And she said, "Yes, Lord, yet even the little dogs eat the crumbs which fall from their masters' table."

[28]Then Jesus answered and said to her, "O woman, great *is* your faith! Let it be to you as you desire." And her daughter was healed from that very hour.

Jesus Heals Great Multitudes

[29]Jesus departed from there, skirted the Sea of Galilee, and went up on the mountain and sat down there. [30]Then great multitudes came to Him, having with them *the* lame, blind, mute, maimed, and many others; and they laid them down at Jesus' feet, and He healed them. [31]So the multitude marveled when they saw *the* mute speaking, *the* maimed made whole, *the* lame walking, and *the* blind seeing; and they glorified the God of Israel.

Feeding the Four Thousand

[32]Now Jesus called His disciples to *Himself* and said, "I have compassion on the multitude, because they have now continued with Me three days and have nothing to eat. And I do not want to send them away hungry, lest they faint on the way."

[33]Then His disciples said to Him, "Where could we get enough bread in the wilderness to fill such a great multitude?"

[34]Jesus said to them, "How many loaves do you have?"

And they said, "Seven, and a few little fish."

[35]So He commanded the multitude to sit down on the ground. [36]And He took the seven loaves and the fish and gave thanks, broke *them* and gave *them* to His disciples; and the disciples *gave* to the multitude. [37]So they all ate and were filled, and they took up seven large baskets full of the fragments that were left. [38]Now those who ate were four thousand men, besides women and children. [39]And He sent away the multitude, got into the boat, and came to the region of Magdala.[a]

The Pharisees and Sadducees Seek a Sign

16 Then the Pharisees and Sadducees came, and testing Him asked that He would show them a sign from heaven. [2]He answered and said to them, "When it is evening you say, '*It will be* fair weather, for the sky is red'; [3]and in the morning, '*It will be* foul weather today, for the sky is red and threatening.' Hypocrites![a] You know how to discern the face of the sky, but you cannot *discern* the signs of the times. [4]A wicked and adulterous generation seeks after a sign, and no sign shall be given to it except the sign of the prophet[a] Jonah." And He left them and departed.

The Leaven of the Pharisees and Sadducees

[5]Now when His disciples had come to the other side, they had forgotten to take bread. [6]Then Jesus said to them, "Take heed and beware of the leaven of the Pharisees and the Sadducees."

[7]And they reasoned among themselves, saying, "*It is* because we have taken no bread."

[8]But Jesus, being aware of *it,* said to them, "O you of little faith, why do you reason among yourselves because you have brought no bread?[a] [9]Do you not yet understand, or remember the five loaves of the five thousand and how many baskets you took up? [10]Nor the seven loaves of the four thousand and how many large baskets you took up? [11]How is it you do not understand that I did not speak to you concerning bread?—*but* to beware of the leaven of the Pharisees and Sadducees." [12]Then they understood that He did not tell *them* to beware of the leaven of bread, but of the doctrine of the Pharisees and Sadducees.

15:39 [a]NU-Text reads *Magadan.*   **16:3** [a]NU-Text omits *Hypocrites.*   **16:4** [a]NU-Text omits *the prophet.*
16:8 [a]NU-Text reads *you have no bread.*

Peter Confesses Jesus as the Christ

¹³When Jesus came into the region of Caesarea Philippi, He asked His disciples, saying, "Who do men say that I, the Son of Man, am?" ¹⁴So they said, "Some *say* John the Baptist, some Elijah, and others Jeremiah or one of the prophets." ¹⁵He said to them, "But who do you say that I am?" ¹⁶Simon Peter answered and said, "You are the Christ, the Son of the living God." ¹⁷Jesus answered and said to him, "Blessed are you, Simon Bar-Jonah, for flesh and blood has not revealed *this* to you, but My Father who is in heaven. ¹⁸And I also say to you that you are Peter, and on this rock I

> ↘ **LEARN**
> • • • • • • • • • • • • • • • • •
> 16:13–17 • Ask a dozen people today who Jesus is, and you're likely to get a dozen answers. "He was a great teacher." "He was a miracle worker." "He was a prophet." But the key question is, *Who do* you *say that He is?* What is your relationship to Him? Can you say, along with Peter, that He is the Messiah, God's Son? Have you given your allegiance to Him? Is He your Savior and your Lord? And if He is, are you living like it? Do others know that Jesus is your Master by the way you live? That's the question. *For more about* How to Live Out Your Faith, *see Matt. 19:21–24.*

will build My church, and the gates of Hades shall not prevail against it. ¹⁹And I will give you the keys of the kingdom of heaven, and whatever you bind on earth will be bound in heaven, and whatever you loose on earth will be loosed[a] in heaven." ²⁰Then He commanded His disciples that they should tell no one that He was Jesus the Christ.

Jesus Predicts His Death and Resurrection

²¹From that time Jesus began to show to His disciples that He must go to Jerusalem, and suffer many things from the elders and chief priests and scribes, and be killed, and be raised the third day. ²²Then Peter took Him aside and began to rebuke Him, saying, "Far be it from You, Lord; this shall not happen to You!" ²³But He turned and said to Peter, "Get behind Me, Satan! You are an offense to Me, for you are not mindful of the things of God, but the things of men."

Take Up the Cross and Follow Him

²⁴Then Jesus said to His disciples, "If anyone desires to come after Me, let him deny himself, and take up his cross, and follow Me. ²⁵For whoever desires to save his life will lose it, but whoever loses his life for My sake will find it. ²⁶For what profit is it to a man if he

> ➜ *For whoever desires to save his life will lose it, but whoever loses his life for My sake will find it.* Matt. 16:25

gains the whole world, and loses his own soul? Or what will a man give in exchange for his soul? ²⁷For the Son of Man will come in the glory of His Father with His angels, and then He will reward each according to his works.

Jesus Transfigured on the Mount

²⁸Assuredly, I say to you, there are some standing here who shall not taste death till they see the Son of Man coming in His kingdom."

17 Now after six days Jesus took Peter, James, and John his brother, led them up on a high mountain by themselves; ²and He was transfigured before them. His face shone like the sun, and His clothes became as white as the light. ³And behold, Moses and Elijah appeared to them, talking with Him. ⁴Then Peter answered and said to Jesus, "Lord, it is good for us to be here; if You wish, let us[a] make here three tabernacles: one for You, one for Moses, and one for Elijah."

⁵While he was still speaking, behold, a bright cloud overshadowed them; and suddenly a voice came out of the cloud, saying, "This is My beloved Son, in whom I am well pleased. Hear Him!" ⁶And when the disciples heard *it,* they fell on their faces and were greatly afraid. ⁷But Jesus came and touched them and said, "Arise, and do not be afraid."

16:19 [a]Or *will have been bound . . . will have been loosed*   **17:4** [a]NU-Text reads *I will.*

⁸When they had lifted up their eyes, they saw no one but Jesus only.

⁹Now as they came down from the mountain, Jesus commanded them, saying, "Tell the vision to no one until the Son of Man is risen from the dead."

¹⁰And His disciples asked Him, saying, "Why then do the scribes say that Elijah must come first?"

¹¹Jesus answered and said to them, "Indeed, Elijah is coming firstᵃ and will restore all things. ¹²But I say to you that Elijah has come already, and they did not know him but did to him whatever they wished. Likewise the Son of Man is also about to suffer at their hands." ¹³Then the disciples understood that He spoke to them of John the Baptist.

A Boy Is Healed

¹⁴And when they had come to the multitude, a man came to Him, kneeling down to Him and saying, ¹⁵"Lord, have mercy on my son, for he is an epilepticᵃ and suffers severely; for he often falls into the fire and often into the water. ¹⁶So I brought him to Your disciples, but they could not cure him."

¹⁷Then Jesus answered and said, "O faithless and perverse generation, how long shall I be with you? How long shall I bear with you? Bring him here to Me." ¹⁸And Jesus rebuked the demon, and it came out of him; and the child was cured from that very hour.

¹⁹Then the disciples came to Jesus privately and said, "Why could we not cast it out?"

²⁰So Jesus said to them, "Because of your unbelief;ᵃ for assuredly, I say to you, if you have faith as a mustard seed, you will say to this mountain, 'Move from here to there,' and it will move; and nothing will be impossible for you. ²¹However, this kind does not go out except by prayer and fasting."ᵃ

Jesus Again Predicts His Death and Resurrection

²²Now while they were stayingᵃ in Galilee, Jesus said to them, "The Son of Man is about to be betrayed into the hands of men, ²³and they will kill Him, and the third day He will be raised up." And they were exceedingly sorrowful.

↘ LEARN
• • • • • • • • • • • • • • • • • •

17:20 • Is mountain-moving faith reserved for the elite? Not according to Jesus. He requires genuine faith, not necessarily gargantuan faith. A mustard seed is tiny, but a living seed can produce an enormous plant. When we place our whole trust in Jesus, even when we're shaking in our boots, God goes to work. The size of the difficulty does not matter, so long as we come to God humbly and with full confidence that He is able. If we have a small god, then we'll have big problems. But if we have a big God, then we'll have small problems. *For more about* Faith, *see Matt. 18:1–4.*

Peter and His Master Pay Their Taxes

²⁴When they had come to Capernaum,ᵃ those who received the *temple* tax came to Peter and said, "Does your Teacher not pay the *temple* tax?"

²⁵He said, "Yes."

And when he had come into the house, Jesus anticipated him, saying, "What do you think, Simon? From whom do the kings of the earth take customs or taxes, from their sons or from strangers?"

²⁶Peter said to Him, "From strangers."

Jesus said to him, "Then the sons are free. ²⁷Nevertheless, lest we offend them, go to the sea, cast in a hook, and take the fish that comes up first. And when you have opened its mouth, you will find a piece of money;ᵃ take that and give it to them for Me and you."

Who Is the Greatest?

18 At that time the disciples came to Jesus, saying, "Who then is greatest in the kingdom of heaven?"

²Then Jesus called a little child to Him, set him in the midst of them, ³and said, "Assuredly, I say to you, unless you are converted and become as little children, you will by no means enter the kingdom of heaven. ⁴Therefore whoever humbles himself as this little child is the greatest in the kingdom of heaven. ⁵Whoever receives one little child like this in My name receives Me.

Jesus Warns of Offenses

⁶"Whoever causes one of these little ones who believe in Me to sin, it would be better

---

17:11 ᵃNU-Text omits *first.*   **17:15** ᵃLiterally *moonstruck*   **17:20** ᵃNU-Text reads *little faith.*   **17:21** ᵃNU-Text omits this verse.
17:22 ᵃNU-Text reads *gathering together.*   **17:24** ᵃNU-Text reads *Capharnaum* (here and elsewhere).   **17:27** ᵃGreek *stater*, the exact amount to pay the temple tax (didrachma) for two

⌁ LEARN

18:1–4 • What does it mean to come to Jesus "as a little child"? It doesn't mean to approach Him innocently—all of us are guilty. It doesn't mean to have childish thoughts of Him—the Bible tells us to think like adults (1 Cor. 14:20). It means instead to give up big-shot notions of ourselves and to approach Him humbly, with nothing in our hands except our need. It is to come to Jesus with a childlike sense of wonder and expectation, along with total dependence on Him. We are not to be child*ish*, but child-*like* in our faith. *For more about* Faith, *see Matt. 18:8.*

for him if a millstone were hung around his neck, and he were drowned in the depth of the sea. [7]Woe to the world because of offenses! For offenses must come, but woe to that man by whom the offense comes!

[8]"If your hand or foot causes you to sin, cut it off and cast *it* from you. It is better for you to enter into life lame or maimed, rather than having two hands or two feet, to be cast into the everlasting fire. [9]And if your

→ LIVE

18:8 • Anybody can fall away from the Lord. One sign of the end times is that some will fall away from the faith (1 Tim. 4:1). Anybody can depart from the faith. I don't care how much of the Bible she has memorized. I don't care if God has spoken through him and used him. You could fall away. I could fall away. Anyone can fall away. This is why we need to take practical precautions against drifting. If you're not where you once were, take action immediately. The best way to not go backward spiritually is to go forward. *For more about* Growing in Christ, *see Mark 1:16–20;* Faith, *Luke 7:19.*

eye causes you to sin, pluck it out and cast *it* from you. It is better for you to enter into life with one eye, rather than having two eyes, to be cast into hell fire.

The Parable of the Lost Sheep

[10]"Take heed that you do not despise one of these little ones, for I say to you that in heaven their angels always see the face of My Father who is in heaven. [11]For the Son of Man has come to save that which was lost.[a]

[12]"What do you think? If a man has a hundred sheep, and one of them goes astray, does he not leave the ninety-nine and go to the mountains to seek the one that is straying? [13]And if he should find it, assuredly, I say to you, he rejoices more over that *sheep* than over the ninety-nine that did not go astray. [14]Even so it is not the will of your Father who is in heaven that one of these little ones should perish.

Dealing with a Sinning Brother

[15]"Moreover if your brother sins against you, go and tell him his fault between you and him alone. If he hears you, you have gained your brother. [16]But if he will not hear, take with you one or two more, that *'by the mouth of two or three witnesses every word may be established.'*[a] [17]And if he refuses to hear them, tell *it* to the church. But if he refuses even to hear the church, let him be to you like a heathen and a tax collector.

[18]"Assuredly, I say to you, whatever you bind on earth will be bound in heaven, and whatever you loose on earth will be loosed in heaven.

[19]"Again I say[a] to you that if two of you agree on earth concerning anything that they ask, it will be done for them by My Father in heaven. [20]For where two or three are gathered together in My name, I am there in the midst of them."

⌁ LEARN

18:19, 20 • God goes to work in amazing ways when His people agree with one another in prayer. Group prayer invites God to take things to a higher level. When the church prays as a unit, sometimes the ground shakes (Acts 4:31) and prison doors get flung open (Acts 12:5–10). In prayer, we strive to align our will with the will of God. Prayer is not pulling God our way, but us His way. Nevertheless, when two or more believers receive a burden from the Lord Himself and it aligns with His will—and we pray together—amazing things can happen! *For more about* Prayer, *see Mark 1:35;* God at Work, *John 11:5, 6;* Fellowship, *Mark 6:7.*

The Parable of the Unforgiving Servant

[21]Then Peter came to Him and said, "Lord, how often shall my brother sin against me, and I forgive him? Up to seven times?"

18:11 [a]NU-Text omits this verse.   **18:16** [a]Deuteronomy 19:15   **18:19** [a]NU-Text and M-Text read *Again, assuredly, I say.*

> **➤ *For where two or three are gathered together in My name, I am there in the midst of them.*** Matt 18:20

²²Jesus said to him, "I do not say to you, up to seven times, but up to seventy times seven. ²³Therefore the kingdom of heaven is like a certain king who wanted to settle accounts with his servants. ²⁴And when he had begun to settle accounts, one was brought to him who owed him ten thousand talents. ²⁵But as he was not able to pay, his master commanded that he be sold, with his wife and children and all that he had, and that payment be made. ²⁶The servant therefore fell down before him, saying, 'Master, have patience with me, and I will pay you all.' ²⁷Then the master of that servant was moved with compassion, released him, and forgave him the debt.

²⁸"But that servant went out and found one of his fellow servants who owed him a hundred denarii; and he laid hands on him and took *him* by the throat, saying, 'Pay me what you owe!' ²⁹So his fellow servant fell down at his feet[a] and begged him, saying, 'Have patience with me, and I will pay you all.'[b] ³⁰And he would not, but went and threw him into prison till he should pay the debt. ³¹So when his fellow servants saw what had been done, they were very grieved, and came and told their master all that had been done. ³²Then his master, after he had called him, said to him, 'You wicked servant! I forgave you all that debt because you begged me. ³³Should you not also have had compassion on your fellow servant, just as I had pity on you?' ³⁴And his master was angry, and delivered him to the torturers until he should pay all that was due to him.

³⁵"So My heavenly Father also will do to you if each of you, from his heart, does not forgive his brother his trespasses."[a]

Marriage and Divorce

19 Now it came to pass, when Jesus had finished these sayings, *that* He departed from Galilee and came to the region of Judea beyond the Jordan. ²And great multitudes followed Him, and He healed them there.

³The Pharisees also came to Him, testing Him, and saying to Him, "Is it lawful for a man to divorce his wife for *just* any reason?"

⁴And He answered and said to them, "Have you not read that He who made[a] *them* at the beginning *'made them male and female,'*[b] ⁵and said, *'For this reason a man shall leave his father and mother and be joined to his wife, and the two shall become one flesh'?*[a] ⁶So then, they are no longer two but one flesh. Therefore what God has joined together, let not man separate."

⁷They said to Him, "Why then did Moses command to give a certificate of divorce, and to put her away?"

⁸He said to them, "Moses, because of the hardness of your hearts, permitted you to divorce your wives, but from the beginning it was not so. ⁹And I say to you, whoever divorces his wife, except for sexual immorality,[a] and marries another, commits adultery; and whoever marries her who is divorced commits adultery."

¹⁰His disciples said to Him, "If such is the case of the man with *his* wife, it is better not to marry."

Jesus Teaches on Celibacy

¹¹But He said to them, "All cannot accept this saying, but only *those* to whom it has been given: ¹²For there are eunuchs who were born thus from *their* mother's womb, and there are eunuchs who were made eunuchs by men, and there are eunuchs who have made themselves eunuchs for the kingdom of heaven's sake. He who is able to accept *it,* let him accept *it.*"

Jesus Blesses Little Children

¹³Then little children were brought to Him that He might put *His* hands on them and pray, but the disciples rebuked them. ¹⁴But Jesus said, "Let the little children come to Me, and do not forbid them; for of such is the kingdom of heaven." ¹⁵And He laid *His* hands on them and departed from there.

Jesus Counsels the Rich Young Ruler

¹⁶Now behold, one came and said to Him, "Good[a] Teacher, what good thing shall I do that I may have eternal life?"

18:29 [a]NU-Text omits *at his feet.* [b]NU-Text and M-Text omit *all.*   **18:35** [a]NU-Text omits *his trespasses.*   **19:4** [a]NU-Text reads *created.*
[b]Genesis 1:27; 5:2   **19:5** [a]Genesis 2:24   **19:9** [a]Or *fornication*   **19:16** [a]NU-Text omits *Good.*

[17]So He said to him, "Why do you call Me good?[a] No one *is* good but One, *that is,* God.[b] But if you want to enter into life, keep the commandments."

[18]He said to Him, "Which ones?"

Jesus said, "*'You shall not murder,' 'You shall not commit adultery,' 'You shall not steal,' 'You shall not bear false witness,'* [19]*'Honor your father and your mother,'*[a] and, *'You shall love your neighbor as yourself.'* "[b]

[20]The young man said to Him, "All these things I have kept from my youth.[a] What do I still lack?"

[21]Jesus said to him, "If you want to be perfect, go, sell what you have and give to the poor, and you will have treasure in heaven; and come, follow Me."

↘ LEARN

19:21–24 • Jesus does not call us all to give away everything we own, as He did the man we often name "the rich young ruler." But He does call each of us to make Him first in our lives, to give Him total priority, to eject anything that hinders us from following Him wholeheartedly. Jesus put a test before this young man, and he failed it. Clearly his idol was his wealth—what is it for you? What keeps you from giving Jesus the top spot in your life? What would it take for you to give Jesus preeminence in *everything*? *For more about* How to Live Out Your Faith, *see Matt. 22:37–40;* Submitting to God, *Mark 9:33–37.*

[22]But when the young man heard that saying, he went away sorrowful, for he had great possessions.

With God All Things Are Possible

[23]Then Jesus said to His disciples, "Assuredly, I say to you that it is hard for a rich man to enter the kingdom of heaven. [24]And again I say to you, it is easier for a camel to go through the eye of a needle than for a rich man to enter the kingdom of God."

[25]When His disciples heard *it,* they were greatly astonished, saying, "Who then can be saved?"

[26]But Jesus looked at *them* and said to them, "With men this is impossible, but with God all things are possible."

[27]Then Peter answered and said to Him,

"See, we have left all and followed You. Therefore what shall we have?"

[28]So Jesus said to them, "Assuredly I say to you, that in the regeneration, when the Son of Man sits on the throne of His glory, you who have followed Me will also sit on twelve thrones, judging the twelve tribes of Israel. [29]And everyone who has left houses or brothers or sisters or father or mother or wife[a] or children or lands, for My name's sake, shall receive a hundredfold, and inherit eternal life. [30]But many *who are* first will be last, and the last first.

The Parable of the Workers in the Vineyard

20 "For the kingdom of heaven is like a landowner who went out early in the morning to hire laborers for his vineyard. [2]Now when he had agreed with the laborers for a denarius a day, he sent them into his vineyard. [3]And he went out about the third hour and saw others standing idle in the marketplace, [4]and said to them, 'You also go into the vineyard, and whatever is right I will give you.' So they went. [5]Again he went out about the sixth and the ninth hour, and did likewise. [6]And about the eleventh hour he went out and found others standing idle,[a] and said to them, 'Why have you been standing here idle all day?' [7]They said to him, 'Because no one hired us.' He said to them, 'You also go into the vineyard, and whatever is right you will receive.'[a]

[8]"So when evening had come, the owner of the vineyard said to his steward, 'Call the laborers and give them *their* wages, beginning with the last to the first.' [9]And when those came who *were hired* about the eleventh hour, they each received a denarius. [10]But when the first came, they supposed that they would receive more; and they likewise received each a denarius. [11]And when they had received *it,* they complained against the landowner, [12]saying, 'These last *men* have worked *only* one hour, and you made them equal to us who have borne the burden and the heat of the day.' [13]But he answered one of them and said, 'Friend, I am doing you no wrong. Did you not agree with me for a denarius? [14]Take *what is* yours and go your way. I wish to give to this last man *the same* as to you. [15]Is it

19:17 [a]NU-Text reads *Why do you ask Me about what is good?* [b]NU-Text reads *There is One who is good.* **19:19** [a]Exodus 20:12–16; Deuteronomy 5:16–20 [b]Leviticus 19:18 **19:20** [a]NU-Text omits *from my youth.* **19:29** [a]NU-Text omits *or wife.* **20:6** [a]NU-Text omits *idle.* **20:7** [a]NU-Text omits the last clause of this verse.

not lawful for me to do what I wish with my own things? Or is your eye evil because I am good?' [16]So the last will be first, and the first last. For many are called, but few chosen."[a]

Jesus a Third Time Predicts His Death and Resurrection

[17]Now Jesus, going up to Jerusalem, took the twelve disciples aside on the road and said to them, [18]"Behold, we are going up to Jerusalem, and the Son of Man will be betrayed to the chief priests and to the scribes; and they will condemn Him to death, [19]and deliver Him to the Gentiles to mock and to scourge and to crucify. And the third day He will rise again."

> **→ LIVE**
> • • • • • • • • • • • • • • • •
> **20:19 •** Jesus Christ is the only way to the Father. On the Cross, all the sin of the world was poured upon Jesus as He became the sin sacrifice for us. *In the Cross is the only way of salvation.* If there had been any other way to save you, God would have found it. If living a good, moral life could save you, then Jesus never would have died. But He *did* die. Because there was—and is—no other way. Nails did not hold Him to that Cross 2,000 years ago; love did. Love for you, and love for me. *For more about* The Cross, *see Matt. 27:46;* God's Love, *Mark 15:15.*

Greatness Is Serving

[20]Then the mother of Zebedee's sons came to Him with her sons, kneeling down and asking something from Him.

[21]And He said to her, "What do you wish?"

She said to Him, "Grant that these two sons of mine may sit, one on Your right hand and the other on the left, in Your kingdom."

[22]But Jesus answered and said, "You do not know what you ask. Are you able to drink the cup that I am about to drink, and be baptized with the baptism that I am baptized with?"[a]

They said to Him, "We are able."

[23]So He said to them, "You will indeed drink My cup, and be baptized with the baptism that I am baptized with;[a] but to sit on

My right hand and on My left is not Mine to give, but *it is for those* for whom it is prepared by My Father."

[24]And when the ten heard *it,* they were greatly displeased with the two brothers. [25]But Jesus called them to *Himself* and said, "You know that the rulers of the Gentiles lord it over them, and those who are great exercise authority over them. [26]Yet it shall not be so among you; but whoever desires to become great among you, let him be your servant. [27]And whoever desires to be first among you, let him be your slave— [28]just as the Son of Man did not come to be served, but to serve, and to give His life a ransom for many."

Two Blind Men Receive Their Sight

[29]Now as they went out of Jericho, a great multitude followed Him. [30]And behold, two blind men sitting by the road, when they heard that Jesus was passing by, cried out, saying, "Have mercy on us, O Lord, Son of David!"

[31]Then the multitude warned them that they should be quiet; but they cried out all the more, saying, "Have mercy on us, O Lord, Son of David!"

[32]So Jesus stood still and called them, and said, "What do you want Me to do for you?"

[33]They said to Him, "Lord, that our eyes may be opened." [34]So Jesus had compassion and touched their eyes. And immediately their eyes received sight, and they followed Him.

The Triumphal Entry

21 Now when they drew near Jerusalem, and came to Bethphage,[a] at the Mount of Olives, then Jesus sent two disciples, [2]saying to them, "Go into the village opposite you, and immediately you will find a donkey tied, and a colt with her. Loose *them* and bring *them* to Me. [3]And if anyone says anything to you, you shall say, 'The Lord has need of them,' and immediately he will send them."

[4]All[a] this was done that it might be fulfilled which was spoken by the prophet, saying:

[5] *"Tell the daughter of Zion,*
   'Behold, your King is coming to you,
   Lowly, and sitting on a donkey,
   A colt, the foal of a donkey.' "[a]

[6]So the disciples went and did as Jesus commanded them. [7]They brought the donkey and the colt, laid their clothes on them, and set *Him*[a] on them. [8]And a very great multitude spread their clothes on the road; others cut down branches from the trees and spread *them* on the road. [9]Then the multitudes who went before and those who followed cried out, saying:

   "Hosanna to the Son of David!
   'Blessed is He who comes in the name of
      the LORD!'[a]
   Hosanna in the highest!"

[10]And when He had come into Jerusalem, all the city was moved, saying, "Who is this?" [11]So the multitudes said, "This is Jesus, the prophet from Nazareth of Galilee."

Jesus Cleanses the Temple

[12]Then Jesus went into the temple of God[a] and drove out all those who bought and sold in the temple, and overturned the tables of the money changers and the seats of those who sold doves. [13]And He said to them, "It is written, *'My house shall be called a house of prayer,'*[a] but you have made it a *'den of thieves.' "*[b]

[14]Then *the* blind and *the* lame came to Him in the temple, and He healed them. [15]But when the chief priests and scribes saw the wonderful things that He did, and the children crying out in the temple and saying, "Hosanna to the Son of David!" they were indignant [16]and said to Him, "Do You hear what these are saying?"

And Jesus said to them, "Yes. Have you never read,

   'Out of the mouth of babes and nursing
      infants
   You have perfected praise'?"[a]

[17]Then He left them and went out of the city to Bethany, and He lodged there.

The Fig Tree Withered

[18]Now in the morning, as He returned to the city, He was hungry. [19]And seeing a fig tree by the road, He came to it and found nothing on it but leaves, and said to it, "Let no fruit grow on you ever again." Immediately the fig tree withered away.

The Lesson of the Withered Fig Tree

[20]And when the disciples saw *it,* they marveled, saying, "How did the fig tree wither away so soon?" [21]So Jesus answered and said to them, "Assuredly, I say to you, if you have faith and do not doubt, you will not only do what was done to the fig tree, but also if you say to this mountain, 'Be removed and be cast into the sea,' it will be done. [22]And whatever things you ask in prayer, believing, you will receive."

Jesus' Authority Questioned

[23]Now when He came into the temple, the chief priests and the elders of the people confronted Him as He was teaching, and said, "By what authority are You doing these things? And who gave You this authority?" [24]But Jesus answered and said to them, "I also will ask you one thing, which if you tell Me, I likewise will tell you by what authority I do these things: [25]The baptism of John— where was it from? From heaven or from men?"

And they reasoned among themselves, saying, "If we say, 'From heaven,' He will say to us, 'Why then did you not believe him?' [26]But if we say, 'From men,' we fear the multitude, for all count John as a prophet." [27]So they answered Jesus and said, "We do not know."

And He said to them, "Neither will I tell you by what authority I do these things.

The Parable of the Two Sons

[28]"But what do you think? A man had two sons, and he came to the first and said, 'Son, go, work today in my vineyard.' [29]He answered and said, 'I will not,' but afterward he regretted it and went. [30]Then he came to the second and said likewise. And he answered

---

21:5 [a]Zechariah 9:9   21:7 [a]NU-Text reads *and He sat.*   21:9 [a]Psalm 118:26   21:12 [a]NU-Text omits *of God.*
21:13 [a]Isaiah 56:7   [b]Jeremiah 7:11   21:16 [a]Psalm 8:2

and said, 'I *go*, sir,' but he did not go. [31]Which of the two did the will of *his* father?"

They said to Him, "The first."

Jesus said to them, "Assuredly, I say to you that tax collectors and harlots enter the kingdom of God before you. [32]For John came to you in the way of righteousness, and you did not believe him; but tax collectors and harlots believed him; and when you saw *it*, you did not afterward relent and believe him.

The Parable of the Wicked Vinedressers

[33]"Hear another parable: There was a certain landowner who planted a vineyard and set a hedge around it, dug a winepress in it and built a tower. And he leased it to vinedressers and went into a far country. [34]Now when vintage-time drew near, he sent his servants to the vinedressers, that they might receive its fruit. [35]And the vinedressers took his servants, beat one, killed one, and stoned another. [36]Again he sent other servants, more than the first, and they did likewise to them. [37]Then last of all he sent his son to them, saying, 'They will respect my son.' [38]But when the vinedressers saw the son, they said among themselves, 'This is the heir. Come, let us kill him and seize his inheritance.' [39]So they took him and cast *him* out of the vineyard and killed *him*.

[40]"Therefore, when the owner of the vineyard comes, what will he do to those vinedressers?"

[41]They said to Him, "He will destroy those wicked men miserably, and lease *his* vineyard to other vinedressers who will render to him the fruits in their seasons."

[42]Jesus said to them, "Have you never read in the Scriptures:

'The stone which the builders rejected
Has become the chief cornerstone.
This was the LORD's doing,
And it is marvelous in our eyes'?[a]

[43]"Therefore I say to you, the kingdom of God will be taken from you and given to a nation bearing the fruits of it. [44]And whoever falls on this stone will be broken; but on whomever it falls, it will grind him to powder."

[45]Now when the chief priests and Pharisees heard His parables, they perceived that He was speaking of them. [46]But when they sought to lay hands on Him, they feared the multitudes, because they took Him for a prophet.

The Parable of the Wedding Feast

22 And Jesus answered and spoke to them again by parables and said: [2]"The kingdom of heaven is like a certain king who arranged a marriage for his son, [3]and sent out his servants to call those who were invited to the wedding; and they were not willing to come. [4]Again, he sent out other servants, saying, 'Tell those who are invited, "See, I have prepared my dinner; my oxen and fatted cattle *are* killed, and all things *are* ready. Come to the wedding." ' [5]But they made light of it and went their ways, one to his own farm, another to his business. [6]And the rest seized his servants, treated *them* spitefully, and killed *them*. [7]But when the king heard *about it*, he was furious. And he sent out his armies, destroyed those murderers, and burned up their city. [8]Then he said to his servants, 'The wedding is ready, but those who were invited were not worthy. [9]Therefore go into the highways, and as many as you find, invite to the wedding.' [10]So those servants went out into the highways and gathered together all whom they found, both bad and good. And the wedding *hall* was filled with guests.

[11]"But when the king came in to see the guests, he saw a man there who did not have on a wedding garment. [12]So he said to him, 'Friend, how did you come in here without a wedding garment?' And he was speechless. [13]Then the king said to the servants, 'Bind him hand and foot, take him away, and[a] cast *him* into outer darkness; there will be weeping and gnashing of teeth.'

[14]"For many are called, but few *are* chosen."

The Pharisees: Is It Lawful to Pay Taxes to Caesar?

[15]Then the Pharisees went and plotted how they might entangle Him in *His* talk. [16]And they sent to Him their disciples with the Herodians, saying, "Teacher, we know that You are true, and teach the way of God in truth; nor do You care about anyone, for

21:42 [a]Psalm 118:22, 23   22:13 [a]NU-Text omits *take him away, and*.

You do not regard the person of men. [17]Tell us, therefore, what do You think? Is it lawful to pay taxes to Caesar, or not?"

[18]But Jesus perceived their wickedness, and said, "Why do you test Me, *you* hypocrites? [19]Show Me the tax money."

So they brought Him a denarius.

[20]And He said to them, "Whose image and inscription *is* this?"

[21]They said to Him, "Caesar's."

And He said to them, "Render therefore to Caesar the things that are Caesar's, and to God the things that are God's." [22]When they had heard *these words,* they marveled, and left Him and went their way.

The Sadducees: What About the Resurrection?

[23]The same day the Sadducees, who say there is no resurrection, came to Him and asked Him, [24]saying: "Teacher, Moses said that if a man dies, having no children, his brother shall marry his wife and raise up offspring for his brother. [25]Now there were with us seven brothers. The first died after he had married, and having no offspring, left his wife to his brother. [26]Likewise the second also, and the third, even to the seventh. [27]Last of all the woman died also. [28]Therefore, in the resurrection, whose wife of the seven will she be? For they all had her."

[29]Jesus answered and said to them, "You are mistaken, not knowing the Scriptures nor the power of God. [30]For in the resurrection they neither marry nor are given in marriage, but are like angels of God[a] in heaven. [31]But concerning the resurrection of the dead, have you not read what was spoken to you by God, saying, [32]*'I am the God of Abraham, the God of Isaac, and the God of Jacob'?*[a] God is not the God of the dead, but of the living." [33]And when the multitudes heard *this,* they were astonished at His teaching.

The Scribes: Which Is the First Commandment of All?

[34]But when the Pharisees heard that He had silenced the Sadducees, they gathered together. [35]Then one of them, a lawyer, asked *Him a question,* testing Him, and saying, [36]"Teacher, which *is* the great commandment in the law?"

↘ LEARN

22:37–40 • With this statement Jesus neatly sums up the Ten Commandments (Ex. 20:1–17). The first four commandments relate to my relationship with God; the next six relate to my relationships with others. If I truly love God, then I will have no other gods before Him, worship idols, or take His name in vain. If I truly love my neighbor as myself, I will not steal from him, lie to him, covet his possessions, or kill him. Jesus is not teaching self-love here, but rather, since we already love ourselves (Eph. 5:29), we are to extend that same love to others. *For more about* Loving Others *and* How to Live Out Your Faith, *see* Matt. 25:34–40.

[37]Jesus said to him, " '*You shall love the* LORD *your God with all your heart, with all your soul, and with all your mind.* '[a] [38]This is *the* first and great commandment. [39]And *the* second *is* like it: *'You shall love your neighbor as yourself.* '[a] [40]On these two commandments hang all the Law and the Prophets."

Jesus: How Can David Call His Descendant Lord?

[41]While the Pharisees were gathered together, Jesus asked them, [42]saying, "What do you think about the Christ? Whose Son is He?"

They said to Him, "*The Son* of David."

[43]He said to them, "How then does David in the Spirit call Him *'Lord,'* saying:

[44]*'The* LORD *said to my Lord,*
  "*Sit at My right hand,*
  Till I make Your enemies Your
     footstool " '?[a]

[45]If David then calls Him *'Lord,'* how is He his Son?" [46]And no one was able to answer Him a word, nor from that day on did anyone dare question Him anymore.

Woe to the Scribes and Pharisees

23 Then Jesus spoke to the multitudes and to His disciples, [2]saying: "The scribes and the Pharisees sit in Moses' seat. [3]Therefore whatever they tell you to observe,[a] *that* observe and do, but do not do according to their works; for they say, and do

---

22:30 [a]NU-Text omits *of God.*   22:32 [a]Exodus 3:6, 15   22:37 [a]Deuteronomy 6:5   22:39 [a]Leviticus 19:18   22:44 [a]Psalm 110:1
23:3 [a]NU-Text omits *to observe.*

not do. [4]For they bind heavy burdens, hard to bear, and lay *them* on men's shoulders; but they *themselves* will not move them with one of their fingers. [5]But all their works they do to be seen by men. They make their phylacteries broad and enlarge the borders of their garments. [6]They love the best places at feasts, the best seats in the synagogues, [7]greetings in the marketplaces, and to be called by men, 'Rabbi, Rabbi.' [8]But you, do not be called 'Rabbi'; for One is your Teacher, the Christ,[a] and you are all brethren. [9]Do not call anyone on earth your father; for One is your Father, He who is in heaven. [10]And do not be called teachers; for One is your Teacher, the Christ. [11]But he who is greatest among you shall be your servant. [12]And whoever exalts himself will be humbled, and he who humbles himself will be exalted.

[13]"But woe to you, scribes and Pharisees, hypocrites! For you shut up the kingdom of heaven against men; for you neither go in *yourselves,* nor do you allow those who are entering to go in. [14]Woe to you, scribes and Pharisees, hypocrites! For you devour widows' houses, and for a pretense make long prayers. Therefore you will receive greater condemnation.[a]

[15]"Woe to you, scribes and Pharisees, hypocrites! For you travel land and sea to win one proselyte, and when he is won, you make him twice as much a son of hell as yourselves.

[16]"Woe to you, blind guides, who say, 'Whoever swears by the temple, it is nothing; but whoever swears by the gold of the temple, he is obliged *to perform it.'* [17]Fools and blind! For which is greater, the gold or the temple that sanctifies[a] the gold? [18]And, 'Whoever swears by the altar, it is nothing; but whoever swears by the gift that is on it, he is obliged *to perform it.'* [19]Fools and blind! For which is greater, the gift or the altar that sanctifies the gift? [20]Therefore he who swears by the altar, swears by it and by all things on it. [21]He who swears by the temple, swears by it and by Him who dwells[a] in it. [22]And he who swears by heaven, swears by the throne of God and by Him who sits on it.

[23]"Woe to you, scribes and Pharisees, hypocrites! For you pay tithe of mint and anise and cummin, and have neglected the weightier *matters* of the law: justice and mercy and faith. These you ought to have done, without leaving the others undone. [24]Blind guides, who strain out a gnat and swallow a camel!

[25]"Woe to you, scribes and Pharisees, hypocrites! For you cleanse the outside of the cup and dish, but inside they are full of extortion and self-indulgence.[a] [26]Blind Pharisee, first cleanse the inside of the cup and dish, that the outside of them may be clean also.

[27]"Woe to you, scribes and Pharisees, hypocrites! For you are like whitewashed tombs which indeed appear beautiful outwardly, but inside are full of dead *men's* bones and all uncleanness. [28]Even so you also outwardly appear righteous to men, but inside you are full of hypocrisy and lawlessness.

[29]"Woe to you, scribes and Pharisees, hypocrites! Because you build the tombs of the prophets and adorn the monuments of the righteous, [30]and say, 'If we had lived in the days of our fathers, we would not have been partakers with them in the blood of the prophets.'

[31]"Therefore you are witnesses against yourselves that you are sons of those who murdered the prophets. [32]Fill up, then, the measure of your fathers' *guilt.* [33]Serpents, brood of vipers! How can you escape the condemnation of hell? [34]Therefore, indeed, I send you prophets, wise men, and scribes: *some* of them you will kill and crucify, and *some* of them you will scourge in your synagogues and persecute from city to city, [35]that on you may come all the righteous blood shed on the earth, from the blood of righteous Abel to the blood of Zechariah, son of Berechiah, whom you murdered between the temple and the altar. [36]Assuredly, I say to you, all these things will come upon this generation.

Jesus Laments over Jerusalem

[37]"O Jerusalem, Jerusalem, the one who kills the prophets and stones those who are sent to her! How often I wanted to gather your children together, as a hen gathers her chicks under *her* wings, but you were not willing! [38]See! Your house is left to you desolate; [39]for I say to you, you shall see Me no more till you say, *'Blessed is He who comes in the name of the Lord!'* "[a]

Jesus Predicts the Destruction of the Temple

24 Then Jesus went out and departed from the temple, and His disciples came up to show Him the buildings of the temple. [2]And Jesus said to them, "Do you not see all these things? Assuredly, I say to you, not *one* stone shall be left here upon another, that shall not be thrown down."

The Signs of the Times and the End of the Age

[3]Now as He sat on the Mount of Olives, the disciples came to Him privately, saying, "Tell us, when will these things be? And what *will be* the sign of Your coming, and of the end of the age?"

[4]And Jesus answered and said to them: "Take heed that no one deceives you. [5]For many will come in My name, saying, 'I am the Christ,' and will deceive many. [6]And you will hear of wars and rumors of wars. See that you are not troubled; for all[a] *these things* must come to pass, but the end is not yet. [7]For nation will rise against nation, and kingdom against kingdom. And there will be famines, pestilences,[a] and earthquakes in various places. [8]All these *are* the beginning of sorrows.

[9]"Then they will deliver you up to tribulation and kill you, and you will be hated by all nations for My name's sake. [10]And then many will be offended, will betray one another, and will hate one another. [11]Then many false prophets will rise up and deceive many. [12]And because lawlessness will abound, the love of many will grow cold. [13]But he who endures to the end shall be saved. [14]And this gospel of the kingdom will be preached in all the world as a witness to all the nations, and then the end will come.

The Great Tribulation

[15]"Therefore when you see the *'abomination of desolation,'*[a] spoken of by Daniel the prophet, standing in the holy place" (whoever reads, let him understand), [16]"then let those who are in Judea flee to the mountains. [17]Let him who is on the housetop not go down to take anything out of his house. [18]And let him who is in the field not go back to get his clothes. [19]But woe to those who are pregnant and to those who are nursing babies in those days! [20]And pray that your flight may not be in winter or on the Sabbath. [21]For then there will be great tribulation, such as has not been since the beginning of the world until this time, no, nor ever shall be. [22]And unless those days were shortened, no flesh would be saved; but for the elect's sake those days will be shortened.

[23]"Then if anyone says to you, 'Look, here *is* the Christ!' or 'There!' do not believe *it.* [24]For false christs and false prophets will rise and show great signs and wonders to deceive, if possible, even the elect. [25]See, I have told you beforehand.

[26]"Therefore if they say to you, 'Look, He is in the desert!' do not go out; *or* 'Look, *He is* in the inner rooms!' do not believe *it.* [27]For as the lightning comes from the east and flashes to the west, so also will the coming of the Son of Man be. [28]For wherever the carcass is, there the eagles will be gathered together.

The Coming of the Son of Man

[29]"Immediately after the tribulation of those days the sun will be darkened, and the moon will not give its light; the stars will fall from heaven, and the powers of the heavens will be shaken. [30]Then the sign of the Son of Man will appear in heaven, and then all the tribes of the earth will mourn, and they will see the Son of Man coming on the clouds of heaven with power and great glory. [31]And He will send His angels with a great sound of a trumpet, and they will gather together His elect from the four winds, from one end of heaven to the other.

The Parable of the Fig Tree

[32]"Now learn this parable from the fig tree: When its branch has already become tender and puts forth leaves, you know that summer *is* near. [33]So you also, when you see all these things, know that it[a] is near—at the doors! [34]Assuredly, I say to you, this generation will by no means pass away till all these things take place. [35]Heaven and earth will pass away, but My words will by no means pass away.

No One Knows the Day or Hour

[36]"But of that day and hour no one knows, not even the angels of heaven,[a] but My Father only. [37]But as the days of Noah *were,* so also

---

24:6 [a]NU-Text omits *all.*   **24:7** [a]NU-Text omits *pestilences.*   **24:15** [a]Daniel 11:31; 12:11   **24:33** [a]Or *He*
24:36 [a]NU-Text adds *nor the Son.*

will the coming of the Son of Man be. [38]For as in the days before the flood, they were eating and drinking, marrying and giving in marriage, until the day that Noah entered the ark, [39]and did not know until the flood came and took them all away, so also will the coming of the Son of Man be. [40]Then two *men* will be in the field: one will be taken and the other left. [41]Two *women will be* grinding at the mill: one will be taken and the other left. [42]Watch therefore, for you do not know what hour[a] your Lord is coming. [43]But know this, that if the master of the house had known what hour the thief would come, he would have watched and not allowed his house to be broken into. [44]Therefore you also be ready, for the Son of Man is coming at an hour you do not expect.

↘ LEARN

• • • • • • • • • • • • • • • • •

24:42–44 • When does the UPS or Federal Express man arrive at your door? Probably, he has no set schedule. He comes whenever he has a package to deliver, and that means he might arrive at 10 A.M. Monday or 3:37 P.M. Friday—there's no way for you to know. In a similar way, Jesus will return to earth whenever His Father's divine timetable calls for it, and He will not come back one second before or one second after. Since none of us knows when that moment will arrive, we are to remain constantly ready for His return. Eyes open, everybody! *For more about* Jesus' Return, *see John 20:29.*

The Faithful Servant and the Evil Servant

[45]"Who then is a faithful and wise servant, whom his master made ruler over his household, to give them food in due season? [46]Blessed *is* that servant whom his master, when he comes, will find so doing. [47]Assuredly, I say to you that he will make him ruler over all his goods. [48]But if that evil servant says in his heart, 'My master is delaying his coming,'[a] [49]and begins to beat *his* fellow servants, and to eat and drink with the drunkards, [50]the master of that servant will come on a day when he is not looking for *him* and at an hour that he is not aware of, [51]and will cut him in two and appoint *him* his portion with the hypocrites. There shall be weeping and gnashing of teeth.

The Parable of the Wise and Foolish Virgins

25 "Then the kingdom of heaven shall be likened to ten virgins who took their lamps and went out to meet the bridegroom. [2]Now five of them were wise, and five *were* foolish. [3]Those who *were* foolish took their lamps and took no oil with them, [4]but the wise took oil in their vessels with their lamps. [5]But while the bridegroom was delayed, they all slumbered and slept.

[6]"And at midnight a cry was *heard:* 'Behold, the bridegroom is coming;[a] go out to meet him!' [7]Then all those virgins arose and trimmed their lamps. [8]And the foolish said to the wise, 'Give us *some* of your oil, for our lamps are going out.' [9]But the wise answered, saying, '*No,* lest there should not be enough for us and you; but go rather to those who sell, and buy for yourselves.' [10]And while they went to buy, the bridegroom came, and those who were ready went in with him to the wedding; and the door was shut.

[11]"Afterward the other virgins came also, saying, 'Lord, Lord, open to us!' [12]But he answered and said, 'Assuredly, I say to you, I do not know you.'

[13]"Watch therefore, for you know neither the day nor the hour[a] in which the Son of Man is coming.

The Parable of the Talents

[14]"For *the kingdom of heaven is* like a man traveling to a far country, *who* called his own servants and delivered his goods to them. [15]And to one he gave five talents, to another two, and to another one, to each according to his own ability; and immediately he went on a journey. [16]Then he who had received the five talents went and traded with them, and made another five talents. [17]And likewise he who *had received* two gained two more also. [18]But he who had received one went and dug in the ground, and hid his lord's money. [19]After a long time the lord of those servants came and settled accounts with them.

[20]"So he who had received five talents came and brought five other talents, saying, 'Lord, you delivered to me five talents; look, I have gained five more talents besides them.' [21]His lord said to him, 'Well *done,* good and faithful servant; you were faithful over a few things,

---

24:42 [a]NU-Text reads *day.*   **24:48** [a]NU-Text omits *his coming.*   **25:6** [a]NU-Text omits *is coming.*
25:13 [a]NU-Text omits the rest of this verse.

I will make you ruler over many things. Enter into the joy of your lord.' ²²He also who had received two talents came and said, 'Lord, you delivered to me two talents; look, I have gained two more talents besides them.' ²³His lord said to him, 'Well *done,* good and faithful servant; you have been faithful over a few things, I will make you ruler over many things. Enter into the joy of your lord.'

²⁴"Then he who had received the one talent came and said, 'Lord, I knew you to be a hard man, reaping where you have not sown, and gathering where you have not scattered seed. ²⁵And I was afraid, and went and hid your talent in the ground. Look, *there* you have *what is* yours.'

²⁶"But his lord answered and said to him, 'You wicked and lazy servant, you knew that I reap where I have not sown, and gather where I have not scattered seed. ²⁷So you ought to have deposited my money with the bankers, and at my coming I would have received back my own with interest. ²⁸So take the talent from him, and give *it* to him who has ten talents.

²⁹'For to everyone who has, more will be given, and he will have abundance; but from him who does not have, even what he has will be taken away. ³⁰And cast the unprofitable servant into the outer darkness. There will be weeping and gnashing of teeth.'

The Son of Man Will Judge the Nations

³¹"When the Son of Man comes in His glory, and all the holyᵃ angels with Him, then He will sit on the throne of His glory. ³²All the nations will be gathered before Him, and He will separate them one from another, as a shepherd divides *his* sheep from the goats. ³³And He will set the sheep on His right hand, but the goats on the left. ³⁴Then the King will say to those on His right hand, 'Come, you blessed of My Father, inherit the kingdom prepared for you from the foundation of the world: ³⁵for I was hungry and you gave Me food; I was thirsty and you gave Me drink; I was a stranger and you took Me in; ³⁶I *was* naked and you clothed Me; I was sick and you visited Me; I was in prison and you came to Me.'

³⁷"Then the righteous will answer Him, saying, 'Lord, when did we see You hungry

> ## ↘ LEARN
>
> . . . .
>
> **25:34–40** • When did you last feed a hungry person or visit someone in a jail? When did you last minister to someone in a hospital or convalescent home? When did you last give a thirsty person something to drink, or a poor person some clothes, or a weary traveler a comfortable place to get some rest? Jesus is saying that when we show acts of mercy like these to others, we are doing it for Him. And it's such a big deal to Him that He promises to reward our simple acts of mercy with heavenly gifts beyond our imagination. *For more about* Loving Others, *see John 13:9–14;* How to Live Out Your Faith, *Mark 28:18–20.*

and feed *You,* or thirsty and give *You* drink? ³⁸When did we see You a stranger and take *You* in, or naked and clothe *You?* ³⁹Or when did we see You sick, or in prison, and come to You?' ⁴⁰And the King will answer and say to them, 'Assuredly, I say to you, inasmuch as you did *it* to one of the least of these My brethren, you did *it* to Me.'

⁴¹"Then He will also say to those on the left hand, 'Depart from Me, you cursed, into the everlasting fire prepared for the devil and his angels: ⁴²for I was hungry and you gave Me no food; I was thirsty and you gave Me no drink; ⁴³I was a stranger and you did not take Me in, naked and you did not clothe Me, sick and in prison and you did not visit Me.'

⁴⁴"Then they also will answer Him,ᵃ saying, 'Lord, when did we see You hungry or thirsty or a stranger or naked or sick or in prison, and did not minister to You?' ⁴⁵Then He will answer them, saying, 'Assuredly, I say to you, inasmuch as you did not do *it* to one of the least of these, you did not do *it* to Me.' ⁴⁶And these will go away into everlasting punishment, but the righteous into eternal life."

The Plot to Kill Jesus

26 Now it came to pass, when Jesus had finished all these sayings, *that* He said to His disciples, ²"You know that after two days is the Passover, and the Son of Man will be delivered up to be crucified."

³Then the chief priests, the scribes,ᵃ and the elders of the people assembled at the palace of the high priest, who was called Caiaphas, ⁴and plotted to take Jesus by trickery and kill *Him.*

⁵But they said, "Not during the feast, lest there be an uproar among the people."

The Anointing at Bethany

⁶And when Jesus was in Bethany at the house of Simon the leper, ⁷a woman came to Him having an alabaster flask of very costly fragrant oil, and she poured *it* on His head as He sat *at the table.* ⁸But when His disciples saw *it,* they were indignant, saying, "Why this waste? ⁹For this fragrant oil might have been sold for much and given to *the* poor."

¹⁰But when Jesus was aware of *it,* He said to them, "Why do you trouble the woman? For she has done a good work for Me. ¹¹For you have the poor with you always, but Me you do not have always. ¹²For in pouring this fragrant oil on My body, she did *it* for My burial. ¹³Assuredly, I say to you, wherever this gospel is preached in the whole world, what this woman has done will also be told as a memorial to her."

Judas Agrees to Betray Jesus

¹⁴Then one of the twelve, called Judas Iscariot, went to the chief priests ¹⁵and said, "What are you willing to give me if I deliver Him to you?" And they counted out to him thirty pieces of silver. ¹⁶So from that time he sought opportunity to betray Him.

Jesus Celebrates Passover with His Disciples

¹⁷Now on the first *day of the Feast* of the Unleavened Bread the disciples came to Jesus, saying to Him, "Where do You want us to prepare for You to eat the Passover?"

¹⁸And He said, "Go into the city to a certain man, and say to him, 'The Teacher says, "My time is at hand; I will keep the Passover at your house with My disciples." ' "

¹⁹So the disciples did as Jesus had directed them; and they prepared the Passover.

²⁰When evening had come, He sat down with the twelve. ²¹Now as they were eating, He said, "Assuredly, I say to you, one of you will betray Me."

²²And they were exceedingly sorrowful, and each of them began to say to Him, "Lord, is it I?"

²³He answered and said, "He who dipped

his hand with Me in the dish will betray Me. ²⁴The Son of Man indeed goes just as it is written of Him, but woe to that man by whom the Son of Man is betrayed! It would have been good for that man if he had not been born."

²⁵Then Judas, who was betraying Him, answered and said, "Rabbi, is it I?"

He said to him, "You have said it."

Jesus Institutes the Lord's Supper

²⁶And as they were eating, Jesus took bread, blessed[a] and broke *it,* and gave *it* to the disciples and said, "Take, eat; this is My body."

²⁷Then He took the cup, and gave thanks, and gave *it* to them, saying, "Drink from it, all of you. ²⁸For this is My blood of the new[a] covenant, which is shed for many for the remission of sins. ²⁹But I say to you, I will not drink of this fruit of the vine from now on until that day when I drink it new with you in My Father's kingdom."

³⁰And when they had sung a hymn, they went out to the Mount of Olives.

Jesus Predicts Peter's Denial

³¹Then Jesus said to them, "All of you will be made to stumble because of Me this night, for it is written:

> '*I will strike the Shepherd,*
> *And the sheep of the flock will be*
>   *scattered.*'[a]

³²But after I have been raised, I will go before you to Galilee."

³³Peter answered and said to Him, "Even if all are made to stumble because of You, I will never be made to stumble."

³⁴Jesus said to him, "Assuredly, I say to you that this night, before the rooster crows, you will deny Me three times."

³⁵Peter said to Him, "Even if I have to die with You, I will not deny You!"

And so said all the disciples.

The Prayer in the Garden

³⁶Then Jesus came with them to a place called Gethsemane, and said to the disciples,

26:26 ªM-Text reads *gave thanks for.*   26:28 ªNU-Text omits *new.*   26:31 ªZechariah 13:7

"Sit here while I go and pray over there." [37]And He took with Him Peter and the two sons of Zebedee, and He began to be sorrowful and deeply distressed. [38]Then He said to them, "My soul is exceedingly sorrowful, even to death. Stay here and watch with Me."

[39]He went a little farther and fell on His face, and prayed, saying, "O My Father, if it is possible, let this cup pass from Me; nevertheless, not as I will, but as You *will*."

[40]Then He came to the disciples and found them sleeping, and said to Peter, "What! Could you not watch with Me one hour? [41]Watch and pray, lest you enter into temptation. The spirit indeed *is* willing, but the flesh *is* weak."

[42]Again, a second time, He went away and prayed, saying, "O My Father, if this cup cannot pass away from Me unless[a] I drink it, Your will be done." [43]And He came and found them asleep again, for their eyes were heavy.

[44]So He left them, went away again, and prayed the third time, saying the same words. [45]Then He came to His disciples and said to them, "Are *you* still sleeping and resting? Behold, the hour is at hand, and the Son of Man is being betrayed into the hands of sinners. [46]Rise, let us be going. See, My betrayer is at hand."

Betrayal and Arrest in Gethsemane

[47]And while He was still speaking, behold, Judas, one of the twelve, with a great multitude with swords and clubs, came from the chief priests and elders of the people. [48]Now His betrayer had given them a sign, saying, "Whomever I kiss, He is the One; seize Him." [49]Immediately he went up to Jesus and said, "Greetings, Rabbi!" and kissed Him.

[50]But Jesus said to him, "Friend, why have you come?"

Then they came and laid hands on Jesus and took Him. [51]And suddenly, one of those *who were* with Jesus stretched out *his* hand and drew his sword, struck the servant of the high priest, and cut off his ear.

[52]But Jesus said to him, "Put your sword in its place, for all who take the sword will perish[a] by the sword. [53]Or do you think that

I cannot now pray to My Father, and He will provide Me with more than twelve legions of angels? [54]How then could the Scriptures be fulfilled, that it must happen thus?"

[55]In that hour Jesus said to the multitudes, "Have you come out, as against a robber, with swords and clubs to take Me? I sat daily with you, teaching in the temple, and you did not seize Me. [56]But all this was done that the Scriptures of the prophets might be fulfilled."

Then all the disciples forsook Him and fled.

Jesus Faces the Sanhedrin

[57]And those who had laid hold of Jesus led *Him* away to Caiaphas the high priest, where the scribes and the elders were assembled. [58]But Peter followed Him at a distance to the high priest's courtyard. And he went in and sat with the servants to see the end.

[59]Now the chief priests, the elders,[a] and all the council sought false testimony against Jesus to put Him to death, [60]but found none. Even though many false witnesses came forward, they found none.[a] But at last two false witnesses[b] came forward [61]and said, "This *fellow* said, 'I am able to destroy the temple of God and to build it in three days.'"

[62]And the high priest arose and said to Him, "Do You answer nothing? What *is it* these men testify against You?" [63]But Jesus kept silent. And the high priest answered and said to Him, "I put You under oath by the living God: Tell us if You are the Christ, the Son of God!"

[64]Jesus said to him, "*It is as* you said. Nevertheless, I say to you, hereafter you will see the Son of Man sitting at the right hand of the Power, and coming on the clouds of heaven."

[65]Then the high priest tore his clothes, saying, "He has spoken blasphemy! What further need do we have of witnesses? Look, now you have heard His blasphemy! [66]What do you think?"

They answered and said, "He is deserving of death."

[67]Then they spat in His face and beat Him; and others struck *Him* with the palms of their hands, [68]saying, "Prophesy to us, Christ! Who is the one who struck You?"

26:42 [a]NU-Text reads *if this may not pass away unless.*   26:52 [a]M-Text reads *die.*   26:59 [a]NU-Text omits *the elders.*
26:60 [a]NU-Text puts a comma after *but found none,* does not capitalize *Even,* and omits *they found none.* [b]NU-Text omits *false witnesses.*

Peter Denies Jesus, and Weeps Bitterly

[69]Now Peter sat outside in the courtyard. And a servant girl came to him, saying, "You also were with Jesus of Galilee."

[70]But he denied it before *them* all, saying, "I do not know what you are saying."

[71]And when he had gone out to the gateway, another *girl* saw him and said to those *who were* there, "This *fellow* also was with Jesus of Nazareth."

[72]But again he denied with an oath, "I do not know the Man!"

[73]And a little later those who stood by came up and said to Peter, "Surely you also are *one* of them, for your speech betrays you."

[74]Then he began to curse and swear, *saying,* "I do not know the Man!"

Immediately a rooster crowed. [75]And Peter remembered the word of Jesus who had said to him, "Before the rooster crows, you will deny Me three times." So he went out and wept bitterly.

Jesus Handed Over to Pontius Pilate

27 When morning came, all the chief priests and elders of the people plotted against Jesus to put Him to death. [2]And when they had bound Him, they led Him away and delivered Him to Pontius[a] Pilate the governor.

Judas Hangs Himself

[3]Then Judas, His betrayer, seeing that He had been condemned, was remorseful and brought back the thirty pieces of silver to the chief priests and elders, [4]saying, "I have sinned by betraying innocent blood."

And they said, "What *is that* to us? You see *to it!*"

[5]Then he threw down the pieces of silver in the temple and departed, and went and hanged himself.

[6]But the chief priests took the silver pieces and said, "It is not lawful to put them into the treasury, because they are the price of blood." [7]And they consulted together and bought with them the potter's field, to bury strangers in. [8]Therefore that field has been called the Field of Blood to this day.

[9]Then was fulfilled what was spoken by Jeremiah the prophet, saying, *"And they took the thirty pieces of silver, the value of Him who was priced,* whom they of the children of Israel priced, [10]*and gave them for the potter's field, as the LORD directed me."*[a]

Jesus Faces Pilate

[11]Now Jesus stood before the governor. And the governor asked Him, saying, "Are You the King of the Jews?"

Jesus said to him, "*It is as* you say." [12]And while He was being accused by the chief priests and elders, He answered nothing.

[13]Then Pilate said to Him, "Do You not hear how many things they testify against You?" [14]But He answered him not one word, so that the governor marveled greatly.

Taking the Place of Barabbas

[15]Now at the feast the governor was accustomed to releasing to the multitude one prisoner whom they wished. [16]And at that time they had a notorious prisoner called Barabbas.[a] [17]Therefore, when they had gathered together, Pilate said to them, "Whom do you want me to release to you? Barabbas, or Jesus who is called Christ?" [18]For he knew that they had handed Him over because of envy.

[19]While he was sitting on the judgment seat, his wife sent to him, saying, "Have nothing to do with that just Man, for I have suffered many things today in a dream because of Him."

[20]But the chief priests and elders persuaded the multitudes that they should ask for Barabbas and destroy Jesus. [21]The governor answered and said to them, "Which of the two do you want me to release to you?"

They said, "Barabbas!"

[22]Pilate said to them, "What then shall I do with Jesus who is called Christ?"

They all said to him, "Let Him be crucified!"

[23]Then the governor said, "Why, what evil has He done?"

But they cried out all the more, saying, "Let Him be crucified!"

[24]When Pilate saw that he could not prevail at all, but rather *that* a tumult was rising, he took water and washed *his* hands before

27:2 [a]NU-Text omits *Pontius.*   27:10 [a]Jeremiah 32:6–9   27:16 [a]NU-Text reads *Jesus Barabbas.*

the multitude, saying, "I am innocent of the blood of this just Person.[a] You see *to it*."

²⁵And all the people answered and said, "His blood *be* on us and on our children."

²⁶Then he released Barabbas to them; and when he had scourged Jesus, he delivered *Him* to be crucified.

The Soldiers Mock Jesus

²⁷Then the soldiers of the governor took Jesus into the Praetorium and gathered the whole garrison around Him. ²⁸And they stripped Him and put a scarlet robe on Him. ²⁹When they had twisted a crown of thorns, they put *it* on His head, and a reed in His right hand. And they bowed the knee before Him and mocked Him, saying, "Hail, King of the Jews!" ³⁰Then they spat on Him, and took the reed and struck Him on the head. ³¹And when they had mocked Him, they took the robe off Him, put His *own* clothes on Him, and led Him away to be crucified.

The King on a Cross

³²Now as they came out, they found a man of Cyrene, Simon by name. Him they compelled to bear His cross. ³³And when they had come to a place called Golgotha, that is to say, Place of a Skull, ³⁴they gave Him sour[a] wine mingled with gall to drink. But when He had tasted *it*, He would not drink.

³⁵Then they crucified Him, and divided His garments, casting lots,[a] that it might be fulfilled which was spoken by the prophet:

> "They divided My garments among them,
> And for My clothing they cast lots."[b]

³⁶Sitting down, they kept watch over Him there. ³⁷And they put up over His head the accusation written against Him:

THIS IS JESUS
THE KING OF THE JEWS.

³⁸Then two robbers were crucified with Him, one on the right and another on the left.

³⁹And those who passed by blasphemed Him, wagging their heads ⁴⁰and saying, "You who destroy the temple and build *it* in three days, save Yourself! If You are the Son of God, come down from the cross."

⁴¹Likewise the chief priests also, mocking with the scribes and elders,[a] said, ⁴²"He saved others; Himself He cannot save. If He is the King of Israel,[a] let Him now come down from the cross, and we will believe Him.[b] ⁴³He trusted in God; let Him deliver Him now if He will have Him; for He said, 'I am the Son of God.' "

⁴⁴Even the robbers who were crucified with Him reviled Him with the same thing.

Jesus Dies on the Cross

⁴⁵Now from the sixth hour until the ninth hour there was darkness over all the land. ⁴⁶And about the ninth hour Jesus cried out with a loud voice, saying, "Eli, Eli, lama sabachthani?" that is, *"My God, My God, why have You forsaken Me?"*[a]

⁴⁷Some of those who stood there, when

27:24 [a]NU-Text omits *just*.   27:34 [a]NU-Text omits *sour*.   27:35 [a]NU-Text and M-Text omit the rest of this verse. [b]Psalm 22:18
27:41 [a]M-Text reads *with the scribes, the Pharisees, and the elders*.   27:42 [a]NU-Text reads *He is the King of Israel!*
[b]NU-Text and M-Text read *we will believe in Him*.   27:46 [a]Psalm 22:1

↓ KNOW (MATT. 27:46)

Jesus died to absorb the wrath of God. He took the punishment we deserve because we broke God's commandments and fell short of God's standards. All of us have offended a holy God by our sins. As a result, judgment had to be meted out—and that is exactly what happened at the Cross. If God were not just, there would have been no need for Jesus to suffer and die. If God were not loving, there would have been no willingness for His Son to suffer and die in our place. But God is both just and willing, and at the Cross His love willingly met the demands of His justice. Jesus took the full brunt of God's judgment, in our place. Jesus died on the Cross to cancel the legal demands against us and to disarm the devil. Jesus suffered and died to provide our forgiveness and justification. *For more about* The Cross, *see* Mark 8:34, 35.

they heard *that,* said, "This Man is calling for Elijah!" [48]Immediately one of them ran and took a sponge, filled *it* with sour wine and put *it* on a reed, and offered it to Him to drink.

[49]The rest said, "Let Him alone; let us see if Elijah will come to save Him."

[50]And Jesus cried out again with a loud voice, and yielded up His spirit.

[51]Then, behold, the veil of the temple was torn in two from top to bottom; and the earth quaked, and the rocks were split, [52]and the graves were opened; and many bodies of the saints who had fallen asleep were raised; [53]and coming out of the graves after His resurrection, they went into the holy city and appeared to many.

[54]So when the centurion and those with him, who were guarding Jesus, saw the earthquake and the things that had happened, they feared greatly, saying, "Truly this was the Son of God!"

[55]And many women who followed Jesus from Galilee, ministering to Him, were there looking on from afar, [56]among whom were Mary Magdalene, Mary the mother of James and Joses,[a] and the mother of Zebedee's sons.

Jesus Buried in Joseph's Tomb

[57]Now when evening had come, there came a rich man from Arimathea, named Joseph, who himself had also become a disciple of Jesus. [58]This man went to Pilate and asked for the body of Jesus. Then Pilate commanded the body to be given to him. [59]When Joseph had taken the body, he wrapped it in a clean linen cloth, [60]and laid it in his new tomb which he had hewn out of the rock; and he rolled a large stone against the door of the tomb, and departed. [61]And Mary Magdalene was there, and the other Mary, sitting opposite the tomb.

Pilate Sets a Guard

[62]On the next day, which followed the Day of Preparation, the chief priests and Pharisees gathered together to Pilate, [63]saying, "Sir, we remember, while He was still alive, how that deceiver said, 'After three days I will rise.' [64]Therefore command that the tomb be made secure until the third day, lest His disciples come by night[a] and steal Him *away,* and say

to the people, 'He has risen from the dead.' So the last deception will be worse than the first."

[65]Pilate said to them, "You have a guard; go your way, make *it* as secure as you know how." [66]So they went and made the tomb secure, sealing the stone and setting the guard.

He Is Risen

28 Now after the Sabbath, as the first *day* of the week began to dawn, Mary Magdalene and the other Mary came to see the tomb. [2]And behold, there was a great earthquake; for an angel of the Lord descended from heaven, and came and rolled back the stone from the door,[a] and sat on it. [3]His countenance was like lightning, and his clothing as white as snow. [4]And the guards shook for fear of him, and became like dead *men.*

[5]But the angel answered and said to the women, "Do not be afraid, for I know that you seek Jesus who was crucified. [6]He is not here; for He is risen, as He said. Come, see the place where the Lord lay. [7]And go quickly and tell His disciples that He is risen from the dead, and indeed He is going before you into Galilee; there you will see Him. Behold, I have told you."

[8]So they went out quickly from the tomb with fear and great joy, and ran to bring His disciples word.

The Women Worship the Risen Lord

[9]And as they went to tell His disciples,[a] behold, Jesus met them, saying, "Rejoice!" So they came and held Him by the feet and worshiped Him. [10]Then Jesus said to them, "Do not be afraid. Go *and* tell My brethren to go to Galilee, and there they will see Me."

The Soldiers Are Bribed

[11]Now while they were going, behold, some of the guard came into the city and reported to the chief priests all the things that had happened. [12]When they had assembled with the elders and consulted together, they gave a large sum of money to the soldiers, [13]saying, "Tell them, 'His disciples came at night and stole Him *away* while we slept.'

27:56 [a]NU-Text reads *Joseph.*   27:64 [a]NU-Text omits *by night.*   28:2 [a]NU-Text omits *from the door.*
28:9 [a]NU-Text omits the first clause of this verse.

[14]And if this comes to the governor's ears, we will appease him and make you secure." [15]So they took the money and did as they were instructed; and this saying is commonly reported among the Jews until this day.

The Great Commission

[16]Then the eleven disciples went away into Galilee, to the mountain which Jesus had appointed for them. [17]When they saw Him, they worshiped Him; but some doubted.

> ## ↘ LEARN
> . . . .
> 28:18–20 • These well-known words of Jesus, often referred to as the "Great Commission," have unfortunately for many become the great omission! We must realize that Jesus *commands* us to go and proclaim the gospel and then to help new believers grow spiritually. These are His marching orders for all believers throughout history, including us. To make it all possible, Jesus promises to be with us, empowering us each step of the way (v. 20). The Great Commission is not the great suggestion, so let's look for opportunities! As Jesus said, "The harvest truly is great, but the laborers are few" (Luke 10:2). *For more about* Sharing Your Faith, *see Mark 2:21, 22;* How to Live Out Your Faith, *Mark 1:16–20.*

28:19 [a]M-Text omits *therefore.*   28:20 [a]NU-Text omits *Amen.*

> ➤ *Go therefore and make disciples of all the nations, baptizing them in the name of the Father and of the Son and of the Holy Spirit, teaching them to observe all things that I have commanded you; and lo, I am with you always, even to the end of the age.* Matt. 28:19, 20

[18]And Jesus came and spoke to them, saying, "All authority has been given to Me in heaven and on earth. [19]Go therefore[a] and make disciples of all the nations, baptizing them in the name of the Father and of the Son and of the Holy Spirit, [20]teaching them to observe all things that I have commanded you; and lo, I am with you always, *even* to the end of the age." Amen.[a]

MARK

INTRODUCTION//

The Gospel of Mark was likely the first of the four New Testament Gospels to be written; certainly it was composed before the destruction of Jerusalem in A.D. 70. It is not a first-hand account, but rather comes to us through the lens of the other apostles, especially Peter. Some scholars think Mark might have been the unidentified "young man" who ran away at Jesus' arrest in 14:51. Mark does not record many of Jesus' sermons, but instead emphasizes what Jesus *did* more than what He *said*. His Gospel does not dwell on Jesus' family, history or ministry, but records His achievements, action packed from beginning to end.

Mark is much like a reporter, with an almost breathless quality about his writing, as though you are there, seeing and hearing everything as it happens. You could call it, "The Gospel for Busy People." One of Mark's favorite words is *immediately;* he uses it forty-two times. He also uses the historical present tense 150 times—Jesus *comes,* Jesus *says,* Jesus *heals.* He portrays Christ's life as extremely busy, even having trouble finding time to eat (3:20; 6:31)!

Mark emphasizes the servanthood of Christ, showing Christ healing the sick, raising the dead, and feeding the hungry. His works provide a compelling argument for salvation, because they show powerfully the incredible love of God for us. Because of God's love and grace, Mark invites us to run into the arms of our Father—and then He points us to Jesus as the perfect example of how we should live. Mark's version of Jesus' ministry is a simple, direct, and easy-to-understand manual for our salvation and spiritual transformation. With its beautiful collection of miracles, parables, and teachings, Mark is foundational to understanding the words of Christ that we find in the other Gospels.

John the Baptist Prepares the Way

1 The beginning of the gospel of Jesus Christ, the Son of God. [2]As it is written in the Prophets:[a]

"*Behold, I send My messenger before Your face,*
Who will prepare Your way before You."[b]
[3]"*The voice of one crying in the wilderness:*
'*Prepare the way of the* LORD;
Make His paths straight.' "[a]

[4]John came baptizing in the wilderness and preaching a baptism of repentance for the remission of sins. [5]Then all the land of Judea, and those from Jerusalem, went out to him and were all baptized by him in the Jordan River, confessing their sins.

[6]Now John was clothed with camel's hair and with a leather belt around his waist, and he ate locusts and wild honey. [7]And he preached, saying, "There comes One after me who is mightier than I, whose sandal strap I am not worthy to stoop down and loose. [8]I indeed baptized you with water, but He will baptize you with the Holy Spirit."

John Baptizes Jesus

[9]It came to pass in those days *that* Jesus came from Nazareth of Galilee, and was baptized by John in the Jordan. [10]And immediately, coming up from[a] the water, He saw the heavens parting and the Spirit descending upon Him like a dove. [11]Then a voice came from heaven, "You are My beloved Son, in whom I am well pleased."

Satan Tempts Jesus

[12]Immediately the Spirit drove Him into the wilderness. [13]And He was there in the wilderness forty days, tempted by Satan, and was with the wild beasts; and the angels ministered to Him.

Jesus Begins His Galilean Ministry

[14]Now after John was put in prison, Jesus came to Galilee, preaching the gospel of the kingdom[a] of God, [15]and saying, "The time is fulfilled, and the kingdom of God is at hand. Repent, and believe in the gospel."

→ LIVE

1:14 • Men feel guilty for one simple reason: they are (Rom. 3:19). The guilt feeling is only the symptom of the real problem, sin. All the psychological counseling in the world cannot relieve a person of guilt. You can pretend it's not there or find someone to blame, but the only effective way to remove guilt is to get to the root of the problem. The word *gospel* means "Good News," which offers the way of salvation from sin. And until a person admits his sin and turns to Jesus for forgiveness, he cannot find the solution to remove his guilt. *For more about* Sin, *see Mark 7:18–23;* Forgiveness, *Luke 18:14.*

Four Fishermen Called as Disciples

[16]And as He walked by the Sea of Galilee, He saw Simon and Andrew his brother casting a net into the sea; for they were fishermen. [17]Then Jesus said to them, "Follow Me, and I will make you become fishers of men." [18]They immediately left their nets and followed Him.

[19]When He had gone a little farther from there, He saw James the *son* of Zebedee, and John his brother, who also *were* in the boat mending their nets. [20]And immediately He called them, and they left their father Zebedee in the boat with the hired servants, and went after Him.

Jesus Casts Out an Unclean Spirit

[21]Then they went into Capernaum, and immediately on the Sabbath He entered the synagogue and taught. [22]And they were

↘ LEARN

1:16–20 • The men who became Jesus' disciples were all *doing something* when Jesus called them. Throughout Scripture, we find the same pattern. God is not looking for ability as much as He is looking for availability. If you want to grow spiritually, don't sit around waiting for something to happen. Get busy! Mend those nets, tend those sheep, plow those fields, teach that Sunday school class, tell someone about Christ, give that tithe. Do what you can, where you can. If God wants to call you to do even more, He will. But be faithful with what is before you *now. For more about* How to Live Out Your Faith, *see Mark 8:34, 35;* Growing in Christ, *Mark 9:43.*

1:2 [a]NU-Text reads *Isaiah the prophet.* [b]Malachi 3:1   **1:3** [a]Isaiah 40:3   **1:10** [a]NU-Text reads *out of.* **1:14** [a]NU-Text omits *of the kingdom.*

astonished at His teaching, for He taught them as one having authority, and not as the scribes.

²³Now there was a man in their synagogue with an unclean spirit. And he cried out, ²⁴saying, "Let *us* alone! What have we to do with You, Jesus of Nazareth? Did You come to destroy us? I know who You are—the Holy One of God!"

²⁵But Jesus rebuked him, saying, "Be quiet, and come out of him!" ²⁶And when the unclean spirit had convulsed him and cried out with a loud voice, he came out of him. ²⁷Then they were all amazed, so that they questioned among themselves, saying, "What is this? What new doctrine *is* this? For with authority[a] He commands even the unclean spirits, and they obey Him." ²⁸And immediately His fame spread throughout all the region around Galilee.

Peter's Mother-in-Law Healed

²⁹Now as soon as they had come out of the synagogue, they entered the house of Simon and Andrew, with James and John. ³⁰But Simon's wife's mother lay sick with a fever, and they told Him about her at once. ³¹So He came and took her by the hand and lifted her up, and immediately the fever left her. And she served them.

Many Healed After Sabbath Sunset

³²At evening, when the sun had set, they brought to Him all who were sick and those who were demon-possessed. ³³And the whole city was gathered together at the door. ³⁴Then He healed many who were sick with various diseases, and cast out many demons; and He did not allow the demons to speak, because they knew Him.

Preaching in Galilee

³⁵Now in the morning, having risen a long while before daylight, He went out and departed to a solitary place; and there He prayed. ³⁶And Simon and those *who were* with Him searched for Him. ³⁷When they found Him, they said to Him, "Everyone is looking for You."

³⁸But He said to them, "Let us go into the next towns, that I may preach there also, because for this purpose I have come forth." ³⁹And He was preaching in their synagogues throughout all Galilee, and casting out demons.

Jesus Cleanses a Leper

⁴⁰Now a leper came to Him, imploring Him, kneeling down to Him and saying to Him, "If You are willing, You can make me clean." ⁴¹Then Jesus, moved with compassion, stretched out *His* hand and touched him, and said to him, "I am willing; be cleansed." ⁴²As soon as He had spoken, immediately the leprosy left him, and he was cleansed. ⁴³And He strictly warned him and sent him away at once, ⁴⁴and said to him, "See that you say nothing to anyone; but go your way, show yourself to the priest, and offer for your cleansing those things which Moses commanded, as a testimony to them."

1:27 [a]NU-Text reads *What is this? A new doctrine with authority.*

↑ GROW (MARK 1:35)

Why should you pray? Here's the short answer: because Jesus told you to. And He not only told you to pray, but He personally left us an amazing example of prayer. Frequently in the Gospels we see Jesus praying, sometimes by Himself and sometimes with others. Here was God in human form, walking our planet, breathing our air, and yet feeling the need to remain in constant communion with His Father. So if Jesus felt the necessity to pray constantly, then how much more should we feel the need to stay in communion with our God? Pray all the time—when you get up, when you eat, when you're in the shower, when you get in your car. Pray about all things—your neighbor's salvation, your son's study habits, your job, your commute. Pray about whatever concerns or troubles you (Phil. 4:6). Jesus has given us a tremendous example to follow. *For more about* Prayer, *see Mark 6:31;* Jesus' Life, *Mark 5:30.*

[45]However, he went out and began to proclaim *it* freely, and to spread the matter, so that Jesus could no longer openly enter the city, but was outside in deserted places; and they came to Him from every direction.

Jesus Forgives and Heals a Paralytic

2 And again He entered Capernaum after *some* days, and it was heard that He was in the house. [2]Immediately[a] many gathered together, so that there was no longer room to receive *them,* not even near the door. And He preached the word to them. [3]Then they came to Him, bringing a paralytic who was carried by four *men.* [4]And when they could not come near Him because of the crowd, they uncovered the roof where He was. So when they had broken through, they let down the bed on which the paralytic was lying.

[5]When Jesus saw their faith, He said to the paralytic, "Son, your sins are forgiven you."

[6]And some of the scribes were sitting there and reasoning in their hearts, [7]"Why does this *Man* speak blasphemies like this? Who can forgive sins but God alone?"

[8]But immediately, when Jesus perceived in His spirit that they reasoned thus within themselves, He said to them, "Why do you reason about these things in your hearts? [9]Which is easier, to say to the paralytic, 'Your sins are forgiven you,' or to say, 'Arise, take up your bed and walk'? [10]But that you may know that the Son of Man has power on earth to forgive sins"—He said to the paralytic, [11]"I say to you, arise, take up your bed, and go to your house." [12]Immediately he arose, took up the bed, and went out in the presence of them all, so that all were amazed and glorified God, saying, "We never saw *anything* like this!"

Matthew the Tax Collector

[13]Then He went out again by the sea; and all the multitude came to Him, and He taught them. [14]As He passed by, He saw Levi the *son* of Alphaeus sitting at the tax office. And He said to him, "Follow Me." So he arose and followed Him.

[15]Now it happened, as He was dining in *Levi's* house, that many tax collectors and sinners also sat together with Jesus and His disciples; for there were many, and they followed Him. [16]And when the scribes and[a]

Pharisees saw Him eating with the tax collectors and sinners, they said to His disciples, "How *is it* that He eats and drinks with tax collectors and sinners?"

[17]When Jesus heard *it,* He said to them, "Those who are well have no need of a physician, but those who are sick. I did not come to call *the* righteous, but sinners, to repentance."[a]

Jesus Is Questioned About Fasting

[18]The disciples of John and of the Pharisees were fasting. Then they came and said to Him, "Why do the disciples of John and of the Pharisees fast, but Your disciples do not fast?"

[19]And Jesus said to them, "Can the friends of the bridegroom fast while the bridegroom is with them? As long as they have the bridegroom with them they cannot fast. [20]But the days will come when the bridegroom will be taken away from them, and then they will fast in those days. [21]No one sews a piece of unshrunk cloth on an old garment; or else the new piece pulls away from the old, and the tear is made worse. [22]And no one puts new wine into old wineskins; or else the new wine bursts the wineskins, the wine is spilled, and the wineskins are ruined. But new wine must be put into new wineskins."

Jesus Is Lord of the Sabbath

[23]Now it happened that He went through the grainfields on the Sabbath; and as they went His disciples began to pluck the heads of grain. [24]And the Pharisees said to Him,

↘ LEARN

2:21, 22 • The dead religion of the Pharisees, full of unbiblical rules and regulations—old garments and old wineskins—drove people away from God. Unfortunately, we see this happening still today. We start majoring on minors, get caught up in cultural tradition, and miss divine opportunity. We must always look for fresh ways to bring the Good News to this generation. Infiltrate, don't isolate! Instead of cutting off contact with non-believers, engage them and seek to bring them to Christ. Some churches turn into old wineskins by living in the past. God wants to do a fresh and powerful work in every generation. *For more about* Sharing Your Faith, *see Mark 5:30.*

2:2 [a]NU-Text omits *Immediately.*   2:16 [a]NU-Text reads *of the.*   2:17 [a]NU-Text omits *to repentance.*

"Look, why do they do what is not lawful on the Sabbath?"

²⁵But He said to them, "Have you never read what David did when he was in need and hungry, he and those with him: ²⁶how he went into the house of God *in the days* of Abiathar the high priest, and ate the show-bread, which is not lawful to eat except for the priests, and also gave some to those who were with him?"

²⁷And He said to them, "The Sabbath was made for man, and not man for the Sabbath. ²⁸Therefore the Son of Man is also Lord of the Sabbath."

Healing on the Sabbath

3 And He entered the synagogue again, and a man was there who had a withered hand. ²So they watched Him closely, whether He would heal him on the Sabbath, so that they might accuse Him. ³And He said to the man who had the withered hand, "Step forward." ⁴Then He said to them, "Is it lawful on the Sabbath to do good or to do evil, to save life or to kill?" But they kept silent. ⁵And when He had looked around at them with anger, being grieved by the hardness of their hearts, He said to the man, "Stretch out your hand." And he stretched *it* out, and his hand was restored as whole as the other.ᵃ ⁶Then the Pharisees went out and immediately plotted with the Herodians against Him, how they might destroy Him.

A Great Multitude Follows Jesus

⁷But Jesus withdrew with His disciples to the sea. And a great multitude from Galilee followed Him, and from Judea ⁸and Jerusalem and Idumea and beyond the Jordan; and those from Tyre and Sidon, a great multitude, when they heard how many things He was doing, came to Him. ⁹So He told His disciples that a small boat should be kept ready for Him because of the multitude, lest they should crush Him. ¹⁰For He healed many, so that as many as had afflictions pressed about Him to touch Him. ¹¹And the unclean spirits, whenever they saw Him, fell down before Him and cried out, saying, "You are the Son of God." ¹²But He sternly warned them that they should not make Him known.

The Twelve Apostles

¹³And He went up on the mountain and called to *Him* those He Himself wanted. And they came to Him. ¹⁴Then He appointed twelve,ᵃ that they might be with Him and that He might send them out to preach, ¹⁵and to have power to heal sicknesses andᵃ to cast out demons: ¹⁶Simon,ᵃ to whom He gave the name Peter; ¹⁷James the *son* of Zebedee and John the brother of James, to whom He gave the name Boanerges, that is, "Sons of Thunder"; ¹⁸Andrew, Philip, Bartholomew, Matthew, Thomas, James the *son* of Alphaeus, Thaddaeus, Simon the Cananite; ¹⁹and Judas Iscariot, who also betrayed Him. And they went into a house.

A House Divided Cannot Stand

²⁰Then the multitude came together again, so that they could not so much as eat bread. ²¹But when His own people heard *about this,* they went out to lay hold of Him, for they said, "He is out of His mind."

²²And the scribes who came down from Jerusalem said, "He has Beelzebub," and, "By the ruler of the demons He casts out demons."

²³So He called them to *Himself* and said to them in parables: "How can Satan cast out Satan? ²⁴If a kingdom is divided against itself, that kingdom cannot stand. ²⁵And if a house is divided against itself, that house cannot stand. ²⁶And if Satan has risen up against himself, and is divided, he cannot stand, but has an end. ²⁷No one can enter a strong man's house and plunder his goods, unless he first binds the strong man. And then he will plunder his house.

The Unpardonable Sin

²⁸"Assuredly, I say to you, all sins will be forgiven the sons of men, and whatever blasphemies they may utter; ²⁹but he who blasphemes against the Holy Spirit never has forgiveness, but is subject to eternal condemnation"— ³⁰because they said, "He has an unclean spirit."

Jesus' Mother and Brothers Send for Him

³¹Then His brothers and His mother came, and standing outside they sent to Him,

---

3:5 ᵃNU-Text omits *as whole as the other.*   **3:14** ᵃNU-Text adds *whom He also named apostles.*   **3:15** ᵃNU-Text omits *to heal sicknesses and.*   **3:16** ᵃNU-Text reads *and He appointed the twelve: Simon. . . .*

calling Him. [32]And a multitude was sitting around Him; and they said to Him, "Look, Your mother and Your brothers[a] are outside seeking You."

[33]But He answered them, saying, "Who is My mother, or My brothers?" [34]And He looked around in a circle at those who sat about Him, and said, "Here are My mother and My brothers! [35]For whoever does the will of God is My brother and My sister and mother."

The Parable of the Sower

4 And again He began to teach by the sea. And a great multitude was gathered to Him, so that He got into a boat and sat *in it* on the sea; and the whole multitude was on the land facing the sea. [2]Then He taught them many things by parables, and said to them in His teaching:

[3]"Listen! Behold, a sower went out to sow. [4]And it happened, as he sowed, *that* some *seed* fell by the wayside; and the birds of the air[a] came and devoured it. [5]Some fell on stony ground, where it did not have much earth; and immediately it sprang up because it had no depth of earth. [6]But when the sun was up it was scorched, and because it had no root it withered away. [7]And some *seed* fell among thorns; and the thorns grew up and choked it, and it yielded no crop. [8]But other *seed* fell on good ground and yielded a crop that sprang up, increased and produced: some thirtyfold, some sixty, and some a hundred."

[9]And He said to them,[a] "He who has ears to hear, let him hear!"

↘ LEARN

• • • • • • • • • • • • • • • • •

4:9 • While I believe we need anointed preaching today, I also believe we need anointed *listening*—not only with our heads, but also our hearts. To grow spiritually, we must remain open to God's Word. To hear His words and not do them is to damage our spiritual lives. *How* we listen is vitally important. We must give attention with intention. Whenever we come into contact with holy things, we will be either converted or hardened. If the light of Jesus Christ does not convert us, it will plunge us into deeper darkness. "The same sun that softens the wax, hardens the clay." *For more about* Growing in Christ, *see* Mark 8:23–25; Spiritual Disciplines, Mark 6:31.

The Purpose of Parables

[10]But when He was alone, those around Him with the twelve asked Him about the parable. [11]And He said to them, "To you it has been given to know the mystery of the kingdom of God; but to those who are outside, all things come in parables, [12]so that

'Seeing they may see and not perceive,
And hearing they may hear and not
understand;
Lest they should turn,
And their sins be forgiven them.' "[a]

The Parable of the Sower Explained

[13]And He said to them, "Do you not understand this parable? How then will you understand all the parables? [14]The sower sows the word. [15]And these are the ones by the wayside where the word is sown. When they hear, Satan comes immediately and takes away the word that was sown in their hearts. [16]These likewise are the ones sown on stony ground who, when they hear the word, immediately receive it with gladness; [17]and they have no root in themselves, and so endure only for a time. Afterward, when tribulation or persecution arises for the word's sake, immediately they stumble. [18]Now these are the ones sown among thorns; *they are* the ones who hear the word, [19]and the cares of this world, the deceitfulness of riches, and the desires for other things entering in choke the word, and it becomes unfruitful. [20]But these are the ones sown on good ground, those who hear the word, accept *it,* and bear fruit: some thirtyfold, some sixty, and some a hundred."

Light Under a Basket

[21]Also He said to them, "Is a lamp brought to be put under a basket or under a bed? Is it not to be set on a lampstand? [22]For there is nothing hidden which will not be revealed, nor has anything been kept secret but that it should come to light. [23]If anyone has ears to hear, let him hear."

[24]Then He said to them, "Take heed what you hear. With the same measure you use, it will be measured to you; and to you who hear, more will be given. [25]For whoever has,

---

3:32 [a]NU-Text and M-Text add *and Your sisters.* 4:4 [a]NU-Text and M-Text omit *of the air.* 4:9 [a]NU-Text and M-Text omit *to them.* 4:12 [a]Isaiah 6:9, 10

to him more will be given; but whoever does not have, even what he has will be taken away from him."

The Parable of the Growing Seed

26And He said, "The kingdom of God is as if a man should scatter seed on the ground, 27and should sleep by night and rise by day, and the seed should sprout and grow, he himself does not know how. 28For the earth yields crops by itself: first the blade, then the head, after that the full grain in the head. 29But when the grain ripens, immediately he puts in the sickle, because the harvest has come."

The Parable of the Mustard Seed

30Then He said, "To what shall we liken the kingdom of God? Or with what parable shall we picture it? 31*It is* like a mustard seed which, when it is sown on the ground, is smaller than all the seeds on earth; 32but when it is sown, it grows up and becomes greater than all herbs, and shoots out large branches, so that the birds of the air may nest under its shade."

Jesus' Use of Parables

33And with many such parables He spoke the word to them as they were able to hear *it.* 34But without a parable He did not speak to them. And when they were alone, He explained all things to His disciples.

Wind and Wave Obey Jesus

35On the same day, when evening had come, He said to them, "Let us cross over to the other side." 36Now when they had left the multitude, they took Him along in the boat as He was. And other little boats were also with Him. 37And a great windstorm arose, and the waves beat into the boat, so that it was already filling. 38But He was in the stern, asleep on a pillow. And they awoke Him and said to Him, "Teacher, do You not care that we are perishing?"

39Then He arose and rebuked the wind, and said to the sea, "Peace, be still!" And the wind ceased and there was a great calm. 40But He said to them, "Why are you so fearful? How *is it* that you have no faith?"a 41And they feared exceedingly, and said to one another, "Who can this be, that even the wind and the sea obey Him!"

A Demon-Possessed Man Healed

5 Then they came to the other side of the sea, to the country of the Gadarenes.a 2And when He had come out of the boat, immediately there met Him out of the tombs a man with an unclean spirit, 3who had *his* dwelling among the tombs; and no one could bind him,a not even with chains, 4because he had often been bound with shackles and chains. And the chains had been pulled apart by him, and the shackles broken in pieces; neither could anyone tame him. 5And always, night and day, he was in the mountains and in the tombs, crying out and cutting himself with stones.

6When he saw Jesus from afar, he ran and worshiped Him. 7And he cried out with a loud voice and said, "What have I to do with You, Jesus, Son of the Most High God? I implore You by God that You do not torment me."

8For He said to him, "Come out of the man, unclean spirit!" 9Then He asked him, "What *is* your name?"

And he answered, saying, "My name *is* Legion; for we are many." 10Also he begged Him earnestly that He would not send them out of the country. 11Now a large herd of swine was feeding there near the mountains. 12So all the demons begged Him, saying, "Send us to the swine, that we may enter them." 13And at once Jesusa gave them permission. Then the unclean spirits went out and entered the swine (there were about two thousand); and the herd ran violently down the steep place into the sea, and drowned in the sea.

14So those who fed the swine fled, and they told *it* in the city and in the country. And they went out to see what it was that had happened. 15Then they came to Jesus, and saw the one *who had been* demon-possessed and had the legion, sitting and clothed and in his right mind. And they were afraid. 16And those who saw it told them how it happened to him *who had been* demon-possessed, and

---

4:40 aNU-Text reads *Have you still no faith?*   **5:1** aNU-Text reads *Gerasenes.*   **5:3** aNU-Text adds *anymore.*
5:13 aNU-Text reads *And He gave.*

about the swine. [17]Then they began to plead with Him to depart from their region.

[18]And when He got into the boat, he who had been demon-possessed begged Him that he might be with Him. [19]However, Jesus did not permit him, but said to him, "Go home to your friends, and tell them what great things the Lord has done for you, and how He has had compassion on you." [20]And he departed and began to proclaim in Decapolis all that Jesus had done for him; and all marveled.

A Girl Restored to Life and a Woman Healed

[21]Now when Jesus had crossed over again by boat to the other side, a great multitude gathered to Him; and He was by the sea. [22]And behold, one of the rulers of the synagogue came, Jairus by name. And when he saw Him, he fell at His feet [23]and begged Him earnestly, saying, "My little daughter lies at the point of death. Come and lay Your hands on her, that she may be healed, and she will live." [24]So *Jesus* went with him, and a great multitude followed Him and thronged Him.

[25]Now a certain woman had a flow of blood for twelve years, [26]and had suffered many things from many physicians. She had spent all that she had and was no better, but rather grew worse. [27]When she heard about Jesus, she came behind *Him* in the crowd and touched His garment. [28]For she said, "If only I may touch His clothes, I shall be made well."

[29]Immediately the fountain of her blood was dried up, and she felt in *her* body that she was healed of the affliction. [30]And Jesus, immediately knowing in Himself that power had gone out of Him, turned around in the crowd and said, "Who touched My clothes?"

[31]But His disciples said to Him, "You see the multitude thronging You, and You say, 'Who touched Me?' "

[32]And He looked around to see her who had done this thing. [33]But the woman, fearing and trembling, knowing what had happened to her, came and fell down before Him and told Him the whole truth. [34]And He said to her, "Daughter, your faith has made you well. Go in peace, and be healed of your affliction."

[35]While He was still speaking, *some* came from the ruler of the synagogue's *house* who said, "Your daughter is dead. Why trouble the Teacher any further?"

[36]As soon as Jesus heard the word that was spoken, He said to the ruler of the synagogue, "Do not be afraid; only believe." [37]And He permitted no one to follow Him except Peter, James, and John the brother of James. [38]Then He came to the house of the ruler of the synagogue, and saw a tumult and those who wept and wailed loudly. [39]When He came in, He said to them, "Why make this commotion and weep? The child is not dead, but sleeping."

[40]And they ridiculed Him. But when He had put them all outside, He took the father and the mother of the child, and those *who were* with Him, and entered where the child was lying. [41]Then He took the child by the hand, and said to her, "Talitha, cumi," which is translated, "Little girl, I say to you, arise." [42]Immediately the girl arose and walked, for she was twelve years *of age*. And they were overcome with great amazement. [43]But He commanded them strictly that no one should

↑ GROW (MARK 5:30)

Just as the Spirit came upon Jesus in power in order to bless a needy woman, so God wants His Spirit and His power to come upon *you* so that He may bless others through you. You will receive power to speak up and be counted. You will receive power to turn your world upside down. The same power poured out at Pentecost is available to you today. God wants to give *you* the power to find the courage to approach someone you don't know and tell him or her about Jesus Christ. He wants *you* to have the power to lovingly confront someone about his or her sin. God makes His power available to you so that you may tell others what great things Jesus has done—and is doing—for you. The key, as with this woman, is to reach out and touch Jesus and receive that power. *For more about the* Holy Spirit, *see Mark 10:27;* Jesus' Life, *see Mark 6:31;* Sharing Your Faith, *Luke 24:47.*

know it, and said that *something* should be given her to eat.

Jesus Rejected at Nazareth

6 Then He went out from there and came to His own country, and His disciples followed Him. ²And when the Sabbath had come, He began to teach in the synagogue. And many hearing *Him* were astonished, saying, "Where *did* this Man *get* these things? And what wisdom *is* this which is given to Him, that such mighty works are performed by His hands! ³Is this not the carpenter, the Son of Mary, and brother of James, Joses, Judas, and Simon? And are not His sisters here with us?" So they were offended at Him.

⁴But Jesus said to them, "A prophet is not without honor except in his own country, among his own relatives, and in his own house." ⁵Now He could do no mighty work there, except that He laid His hands on a few sick people and healed *them.* ⁶And He marveled because of their unbelief. Then He went about the villages in a circuit, teaching.

Sending Out the Twelve

⁷And He called the twelve to *Himself,* and began to send them out two *by* two, and gave them power over unclean spirits. ⁸He commanded them to take nothing for the journey except a staff—no bag, no bread, no copper in *their* money belts— ⁹but to wear sandals, and not to put on two tunics.

↘ LEARN
. . . .

6:7 • Have you noticed that the Gospels usually describe the apostles in pairs? Peter and Andrew, James and John, Philip and Bartholomew. Jesus tended to send His men out in pairs since it is easier and safer for people serving the Lord to travel and work together. While one spoke, the other could pray. Two are better than one (Eccl. 4:9). They also kept each other accountable. This is one reason why the devil wants to isolate us. When we're alone, we're like the stray wildebeest that always seems to get picked off by the hungry predator. To whom are *you* accountable? *For more about* Fellowship, *see Acts 2:42.*

---

¹⁰Also He said to them, "In whatever place you enter a house, stay there till you depart from that place. ¹¹And whoeverᵃ will not receive you nor hear you, when you depart from there, shake off the dust under your feet as a testimony against them.ᵇ Assuredly, I say to you, it will be more tolerable for Sodom and Gomorrah in the day of judgment than for that city!"

¹²So they went out and preached that *people* should repent. ¹³And they cast out many demons, and anointed with oil many who were sick, and healed *them.*

John the Baptist Beheaded

¹⁴Now King Herod heard *of Him,* for His name had become well known. And he said, "John the Baptist is risen from the dead, and therefore these powers are at work in him."

¹⁵Others said, "It is Elijah."

And others said, "It is the Prophet, orᵃ like one of the prophets."

¹⁶But when Herod heard, he said, "This is John, whom I beheaded; he has been raised from the dead!" ¹⁷For Herod himself had sent and laid hold of John, and bound him in prison for the sake of Herodias, his brother Philip's wife; for he had married her. ¹⁸Because John had said to Herod, "It is not lawful for you to have your brother's wife." ¹⁹Therefore Herodias held it against him and wanted to kill him, but she could not; ²⁰for Herod feared John, knowing that he *was* a just and holy man, and he protected him. And when he heard him, he did many things, and heard him gladly.

²¹Then an opportune day came when Herod on his birthday gave a feast for his nobles, the high officers, and the chief *men* of Galilee. ²²And when Herodias' daughter herself came in and danced, and pleased Herod and those who sat with him, the king said to the girl, "Ask me whatever you want, and I will give *it* to you." ²³He also swore to her, "Whatever you ask me, I will give you, up to half my kingdom."

²⁴So she went out and said to her mother, "What shall I ask?"

And she said, "The head of John the Baptist!"

²⁵Immediately she came in with haste to the king and asked, saying, "I want you to

6:11 ᵃNU-Text reads *whatever place.* ᵇNU-Text omits the rest of this verse.   6:15 ᵃNU-Text and M-Text omit *or.*

give me at once the head of John the Baptist on a platter."

[26]And the king was exceedingly sorry; *yet,* because of the oaths and because of those who sat with him, he did not want to refuse her. [27]Immediately the king sent an executioner and commanded his head to be brought. And he went and beheaded him in prison, [28]brought his head on a platter, and gave it to the girl; and the girl gave it to her mother. [29]When his disciples heard *of it,* they came and took away his corpse and laid it in a tomb.

Feeding the Five Thousand

[30]Then the apostles gathered to Jesus and told Him all things, both what they had done and what they had taught. [31]And He said to them, "Come aside by yourselves to a deserted place and rest a while." For there were many coming and going, and they did not even have time to eat. [32]So they departed to a deserted place in the boat by themselves.

> ### ↘ LEARN
> . . . .
> 6:31 • We often forget that our Lord lived in a very human body. Like anyone else, He grew tired. And so He took time to rest and instructed His men to do the same. Likewise, we need to remember to take care of our bodies as well as our spirits. We need times to rest. It has been said that if we do not "come apart," we will come apart! We also need time to recharge spiritually. If you make time for God's Word and prayer, it will help you throughout the day—and God will surely honor it (Matt. 6:33). *For more about* Jesus' Life, *see Mark* 14:36; Spiritual Disciplines, *Mark* 14:22–25; Prayer, *Mark* 14:36.

[33]But the multitudes[a] saw them departing, and many knew Him and ran there on foot from all the cities. They arrived before them and came together to Him. [34]And Jesus, when He came out, saw a great multitude and was moved with compassion for them, because they were like sheep not having a shepherd. So He began to teach them many things. [35]When the day was now far spent, His disciples came to Him and said, "This is a deserted place, and already the hour *is* late. [36]Send them away, that they may go into the surrounding country and villages and buy themselves bread;[a] for they have nothing to eat."

[37]But He answered and said to them, "You give them something to eat."

And they said to Him, "Shall we go and buy two hundred denarii worth of bread and give them *something* to eat?"

[38]But He said to them, "How many loaves do you have? Go and see."

And when they found out they said, "Five, and two fish."

[39]Then He commanded them to make them all sit down in groups on the green grass. [40]So they sat down in ranks, in hundreds and in fifties. [41]And when He had taken the five loaves and the two fish, He looked up to heaven, blessed and broke the loaves, and gave *them* to His disciples to set before them; and the two fish He divided among *them* all. [42]So they all ate and were filled. [43]And they took up twelve baskets full of fragments and of the fish. [44]Now those who had eaten the loaves were about[a] five thousand men.

Jesus Walks on the Sea

[45]Immediately He made His disciples get into the boat and go before Him to the other side, to Bethsaida, while He sent the multitude away. [46]And when He had sent them away, He departed to the mountain to pray. [47]Now when evening came, the boat was in the middle of the sea; and He *was* alone on the land. [48]Then He saw them straining at rowing, for the wind was against them. Now about the fourth watch of the night He came to them, walking on the sea, and would have passed them by. [49]And when they saw Him walking on the sea, they supposed it was a ghost, and cried out; [50]for they all saw Him and were troubled. But immediately He talked with them and said to them, "Be of good cheer! It is I; do not be afraid." [51]Then He went up into the boat to them, and the wind ceased. And they were greatly amazed in themselves beyond measure, and marveled. [52]For they had not understood about the loaves, because their heart was hardened.

Many Touch Him and Are Made Well

[53]When they had crossed over, they came to the land of Gennesaret and anchored there.

6:33 [a]NU-Text and M-Text read *they.*   6:36 [a]NU-Text reads *something to eat* and omits the rest of this verse.
6:44 [a]NU-Text and M-Text omit *about.*

[54]And when they came out of the boat, immediately the people recognized Him, [55]ran through that whole surrounding region, and began to carry about on beds those who were sick to wherever they heard He was. [56]Wherever He entered, into villages, cities, or the country, they laid the sick in the marketplaces, and begged Him that they might just touch the hem of His garment. And as many as touched Him were made well.

Defilement Comes from Within

7 Then the Pharisees and some of the scribes came together to Him, having come from Jerusalem. [2]Now when[a] they saw some of His disciples eat bread with defiled, that is, with unwashed hands, they found fault. [3]For the Pharisees and all the Jews do not eat unless they wash *their* hands in a special way, holding the tradition of the elders. [4]*When they come* from the marketplace, they do not eat unless they wash. And there are many other things which they have received and hold, *like* the washing of cups, pitchers, copper vessels, and couches.

[5]Then the Pharisees and scribes asked Him, "Why do Your disciples not walk according to the tradition of the elders, but eat bread with unwashed hands?"

[6]He answered and said to them, "Well did Isaiah prophesy of you hypocrites, as it is written:

'This people honors Me with their lips,
    But their heart is far from Me.
[7]And in vain they worship Me,
    Teaching as doctrines the commandments
        of men.'[a]

[8]For laying aside the commandment of God, you hold the tradition of men[a]—the washing of pitchers and cups, and many other such things you do."

[9]He said to them, "*All too* well you reject the commandment of God, that you may keep your tradition. [10]For Moses said, 'Honor your father and your mother';[a] and, 'He who curses father or mother, let him be put to death.'[b] [11]But you say, 'If a man says to his father or mother, "Whatever profit you might have received from me *is* Corban"—' (that is,

a gift *to God*), [12]then you no longer let him do anything for his father or his mother, [13]making the word of God of no effect through your tradition which you have handed down. And many such things you do."

[14]When He had called all the multitude to *Himself,* He said to them, "Hear Me, everyone, and understand: [15]There is nothing that enters a man from outside which can defile him; but the things which come out of him, those are the things that defile a man. [16]If anyone has ears to hear, let him hear!"[a]

[17]When He had entered a house away from the crowd, His disciples asked Him concerning the parable. [18]So He said to them, "Are you thus without understanding also? Do you not perceive that whatever enters a man from outside cannot defile him, [19]because it does not enter his heart but his stomach, and is eliminated, *thus* purifying all foods?"[a] [20]And He said, "What comes out of a man, that defiles a man. [21]For from within, out of the heart of men, proceed evil thoughts, adulteries, fornications, murders, [22]thefts, covetousness, wickedness, deceit, lewdness, an evil eye, blasphemy, pride, foolishness. [23]All these evil things come from within and defile a man."

↘ LEARN

• • • • • • • • • • • • • • • • •

7:18–23 • Sometimes it is said, "The truth is within." The Bible teaches that the *problem* is within—and that problem is sin. Man's opinion of sin and God's opinion of sin are quite different. Man says sin is a chance; God says it's a choice. Man says it's an error; God says it's enmity. Man says it's a failure; God says it's a fatality. Man says it's a weakness; God says it's wickedness. The Pharisees regarded sin primarily as an outward thing, while Jesus insisted it's an inward thing. What defiles us comes not from the outside, but from the inside. *For more about* Sin, *see Mark 15:34.*

A Gentile Shows Her Faith

[24]From there He arose and went to the region of Tyre and Sidon.[a] And He entered a house and wanted no one to know *it,* but He could not be hidden. [25]For a woman whose young daughter had an unclean spirit heard about Him, and she came and fell at His feet.

7:2 [a]NU-Text omits *when* and *they found fault.*   **7:7** [a]Isaiah 29:13   **7:8** [a]NU-Text omits the rest of this verse.   **7:10** [a]Exodus 20:12; Deuteronomy 5:16 [b]Exodus 21:17   **7:16** [a]NU-Text omits this verse.   **7:19** [a]NU-Text ends quotation with *eliminated,* setting off the final clause as Mark's comment that Jesus has declared all foods clean.   **7:24** [a]NU-Text omits *and Sidon.*

²⁶The woman was a Greek, a Syro-Phoenician by birth, and she kept asking Him to cast the demon out of her daughter. ²⁷But Jesus said to her, "Let the children be filled first, for it is not good to take the children's bread and throw *it* to the little dogs."

²⁸And she answered and said to Him, "Yes, Lord, yet even the little dogs under the table eat from the children's crumbs."

²⁹Then He said to her, "For this saying go your way; the demon has gone out of your daughter."

³⁰And when she had come to her house, she found the demon gone out, and her daughter lying on the bed.

Jesus Heals a Deaf-Mute

³¹Again, departing from the region of Tyre and Sidon, He came through the midst of the region of Decapolis to the Sea of Galilee. ³²Then they brought to Him one who was deaf and had an impediment in his speech, and they begged Him to put His hand on him. ³³And He took him aside from the multitude, and put His fingers in his ears, and He spat and touched his tongue. ³⁴Then, looking up to heaven, He sighed, and said to him, "Ephphatha," that is, "Be opened."

³⁵Immediately his ears were opened, and the impediment of his tongue was loosed, and he spoke plainly. ³⁶Then He commanded them that they should tell no one; but the more He commanded them, the more widely they proclaimed *it*. ³⁷And they were astonished beyond measure, saying, "He has done all things well. He makes both the deaf to hear and the mute to speak."

Feeding the Four Thousand

8 In those days, the multitude being very great and having nothing to eat, Jesus called His disciples *to Him* and said to them, ²"I have compassion on the multitude, because they have now continued with Me three days and have nothing to eat. ³And if I send them away hungry to their own houses, they will faint on the way; for some of them have come from afar."

⁴Then His disciples answered Him, "How can one satisfy these people with bread here in the wilderness?"

⁵He asked them, "How many loaves do you have?"

And they said, "Seven."

⁶So He commanded the multitude to sit down on the ground. And He took the seven loaves and gave thanks, broke *them* and gave *them* to His disciples to set before *them;* and they set *them* before the multitude. ⁷They also had a few small fish; and having blessed them, He said to set them also before *them.* ⁸So they ate and were filled, and they took up seven large baskets of leftover fragments. ⁹Now those who had eaten were about four thousand. And He sent them away, ¹⁰immediately got into the boat with His disciples, and came to the region of Dalmanutha.

The Pharisees Seek a Sign

¹¹Then the Pharisees came out and began to dispute with Him, seeking from Him a sign from heaven, testing Him. ¹²But He sighed deeply in His spirit, and said, "Why does this generation seek a sign? Assuredly, I say to you, no sign shall be given to this generation."

Beware of the Leaven of the Pharisees and Herod

¹³And He left them, and getting into the boat again, departed to the other side. ¹⁴Now the disciples[a] had forgotten to take bread, and they did not have more than one loaf with them in the boat. ¹⁵Then He charged them, saying, "Take heed, beware of the leaven of the Pharisees and the leaven of Herod."

¹⁶And they reasoned among themselves, saying, "*It is* because we have no bread."

¹⁷But Jesus, being aware of *it*, said to them, "Why do you reason because you have no bread? Do you not yet perceive nor understand? Is your heart still[a] hardened? ¹⁸Having eyes, do you not see? And having ears, do you not hear? And do you not remember? ¹⁹When I broke the five loaves for the five thousand, how many baskets full of fragments did you take up?"

They said to Him, "Twelve."

²⁰"Also, when I broke the seven for the four thousand, how many large baskets full of fragments did you take up?"

And they said, "Seven."

²¹So He said to them, "How *is it* you do not understand?"

8:14 [a]NU-Text and M-Text read *they*.   **8:17** [a]NU-Text omits *still.*

A Blind Man Healed at Bethsaida

[22]Then He came to Bethsaida; and they brought a blind man to Him, and begged Him to touch him. [23]So He took the blind man by the hand and led him out of the town. And when He had spit on his eyes and put His hands on him, He asked him if he saw anything.

[24]And he looked up and said, "I see men like trees, walking."

[25]Then He put *His* hands on his eyes again and made him look up. And he was restored and saw everyone clearly. [26]Then He sent him away to his house, saying, "Neither go into the town, nor tell anyone in the town."[a]

↘ LEARN

8:23–25 • This is the only instance in Scripture where Jesus healed a man gradually, and it illustrates that the Christian life is one of gradual change. Sure, many immediate changes take place when we place our faith in Christ: Jesus forgives our sins and gives us an eternal address. But our character, who we are, takes time to change. That's why it is called the "fruit of the Spirit" (Gal. 5:22). Fruit does not grow overnight. Alan Redpath wrote, "The salvation of the soul is the miracle of the moment; the manufacturing of a saint is the task of a lifetime." *For more about* Growing in Christ, *see Mark 9:43.*

Peter Confesses Jesus as the Christ

[27]Now Jesus and His disciples went out to the towns of Caesarea Philippi; and on the road He asked His disciples, saying to them, "Who do men say that I am?"

[28]So they answered, "John the Baptist; but some *say,* Elijah; and others, one of the prophets."

[29]He said to them, "But who do you say that I am?"

Peter answered and said to Him, "You are the Christ."

[30]Then He strictly warned them that they should tell no one about Him.

Jesus Predicts His Death and Resurrection

[31]And He began to teach them that the Son of Man must suffer many things, and be rejected by the elders and chief priests and scribes, and be killed, and after three days rise again. [32]He spoke this word openly. Then Peter took Him aside and began to rebuke Him. [33]But when He had turned around and looked at His disciples, He rebuked Peter, saying, "Get behind Me, Satan! For you are not mindful of the things of God, but the things of men."

Take Up the Cross and Follow Him

[34]When He had called the people to *Himself,* with His disciples also, He said to them, "Whoever desires to come after Me, let him deny himself, and take up his cross, and follow Me. [35]For whoever desires to save his life will lose it, but whoever loses his life for My sake and the gospel's will save it. [36]For

↘ LEARN

8:34, 35 • What does it mean to take up our cross and follow Jesus? It means we must die to self. Jesus used this phrase to tell Peter, "As I take up My cross, so must you, along with anyone else who wants the life I offer." It's not misery to do this; it's life as it was meant to be lived. Samuel Rutherford confessed, "The cross of Christ is the sweetest burden that I ever bore. It is a burden to me such as wings are to a bird or sails are to a ship to carry me forward to my harbor." *For more about* How to Live Out Your Faith, *see Mark 9:33–37;* The Cross, *Mark 15:15.*

what will it profit a man if he gains the whole world, and loses his own soul? [37]Or what will a man give in exchange for his soul? [38]For whoever is ashamed of Me and My words in this adulterous and sinful generation, of him the Son of Man also will be ashamed when He comes in the glory of His Father with the holy angels."

➔ *For whoever desires to save his life will lose it, but whoever loses his life for My sake and the gospel's will save it.* Mark 8:35

8:26 [a]NU-Text reads *"Do not even go into the town."*

Jesus Transfigured on the Mount

9 And He said to them, "Assuredly, I say to you that there are some standing here who will not taste death till they see the kingdom of God present with power."

[2]Now after six days Jesus took Peter, James, and John, and led them up on a high mountain apart by themselves; and He was transfigured before them. [3]His clothes became shining, exceedingly white, like snow, such as no launderer on earth can whiten them. [4]And Elijah appeared to them with Moses, and they were talking with Jesus. [5]Then Peter answered and said to Jesus, "Rabbi, it is good for us to be here; and let us make three tabernacles: one for You, one for Moses, and one for Elijah"— [6]because he did not know what to say, for they were greatly afraid.

[7]And a cloud came and overshadowed them; and a voice came out of the cloud, saying, "This is My beloved Son. Hear Him!" [8]Suddenly, when they had looked around, they saw no one anymore, but only Jesus with themselves.

[9]Now as they came down from the mountain, He commanded them that they should tell no one the things they had seen, till the Son of Man had risen from the dead. [10]So they kept this word to themselves, questioning what the rising from the dead meant. [11]And they asked Him, saying, "Why do the scribes say that Elijah must come first?"

[12]Then He answered and told them, "Indeed, Elijah is coming first and restores all things. And how is it written concerning the Son of Man, that He must suffer many things and be treated with contempt? [13]But I say to you that Elijah has also come, and they did to him whatever they wished, as it is written of him."

A Boy Is Healed

[14]And when He came to the disciples, He saw a great multitude around them, and scribes disputing with them. [15]Immediately, when they saw Him, all the people were greatly amazed, and running to *Him,* greeted Him. [16]And He asked the scribes, "What are you discussing with them?"

[17]Then one of the crowd answered and said, "Teacher, I brought You my son, who has a mute spirit. [18]And wherever it seizes him, it throws him down; he foams at the mouth, gnashes his teeth, and becomes rigid. So I spoke to Your disciples, that they should cast it out, but they could not."

[19]He answered him and said, "O faithless generation, how long shall I be with you? How long shall I bear with you? Bring him to Me." [20]Then they brought him to Him. And when he saw Him, immediately the spirit convulsed him, and he fell on the ground and wallowed, foaming at the mouth.

[21]So He asked his father, "How long has this been happening to him?"

And he said, "From childhood. [22]And often he has thrown him both into the fire and into the water to destroy him. But if You can do anything, have compassion on us and help us."

[23]Jesus said to him, "If you can believe,[a] all things *are* possible to him who believes."

[24]Immediately the father of the child cried out and said with tears, "Lord, I believe; help my unbelief!"

[25]When Jesus saw that the people came running together, He rebuked the unclean spirit, saying to it, "Deaf and dumb spirit, I command you, come out of him and enter him no more!" [26]Then *the spirit* cried out, convulsed him greatly, and came out of him. And he became as one dead, so that many said, "He is dead." [27]But Jesus took him by the hand and lifted him up, and he arose.

[28]And when He had come into the house, His disciples asked Him privately, "Why could we not cast it out?"

[29]So He said to them, "This kind can come out by nothing but prayer and fasting."[a]

Jesus Again Predicts His Death and Resurrection

[30]Then they departed from there and passed through Galilee, and He did not want anyone to know *it.* [31]For He taught His disciples and said to them, "The Son of Man is being betrayed into the hands of men, and they will kill Him. And after He is killed, He will rise the third day." [32]But they did not understand this saying, and were afraid to ask Him.

Who Is the Greatest?

[33]Then He came to Capernaum. And when He was in the house He asked them,

---

9:23 [a]NU-Text reads *"If You can!' All things. . . ."*   **9:29** [a]NU-Text omits *and fasting.*

"What was it you disputed among yourselves on the road?" ³⁴But they kept silent, for on the road they had disputed among themselves who *would be the* greatest. ³⁵And He sat down, called the twelve, and said to them, "If anyone desires to be first, he shall be last of all and servant of all." ³⁶Then He took a little child and set him in the midst of them. And when He had taken him in His arms, He said to them, ³⁷"Whoever receives one of these little children in My name receives Me; and whoever receives Me, receives not Me but Him who sent Me."

> ↘ **LEARN**
> • • • • • • • • • • • • • • • •
>
> 9:33–37 • The disciples were so much like us, each wanting to be greater than the other. Jesus helped them get perspective when He told them if they really wanted to be first, they needed to become the servant of all. In the Bible, the way up is down. If you want to find your life, you must lose it by putting God first. Jesus illustrates His point by setting a child in their midst and telling them to accept God's truth with a childlike sense of wonder. Children trust and believe, and we must do the same when God tells us these things. *For more about* How to Live Out Your Faith, *see Mark 14:36;* Submitting to God, *Mark 9:43.*

Jesus Forbids Sectarianism

³⁸Now John answered Him, saying, "Teacher, we saw someone who does not follow us casting out demons in Your name, and we forbade him because he does not follow us."

³⁹But Jesus said, "Do not forbid him, for no one who works a miracle in My name can soon afterward speak evil of Me. ⁴⁰For he who is not against us is on our[a] side. ⁴¹For whoever gives you a cup of water to drink in My name, because you belong to Christ, assuredly, I say to you, he will by no means lose his reward.

Jesus Warns of Offenses

⁴²"But whoever causes one of these little ones who believe in Me to stumble, it would be better for him if a millstone were hung around his neck, and he were thrown into the sea. ⁴³If your hand causes you to sin, cut it off.

> → **LIVE**
> • • • • • • • • • • • • • • • •
>
> 9:43 • God wants Christians to lead a sanctified life (1 Thess. 4:3), one of holiness, consecration, and dedication to God. Sanctification means being made holy and set apart, but it also includes gaining the power of Christ in order to live a life both set apart and holy. We cannot hope to live how Christ has asked us to without the strength He offers. All the power necessary to carry forth the work is available whenever we want it. We gain that strength by knowing Him; we must seek Him so that we may find the power to walk with Him. *For more about* Submitting to God, *see Mark 14:36;* Growing in Christ, *Luke 2:19.*

It is better for you to enter into life maimed, rather than having two hands, to go to hell, into the fire that shall never be quenched— ⁴⁴where

> 'Their worm does not die
> And the fire is not quenched.'[a]

⁴⁵And if your foot causes you to sin, cut it off. It is better for you to enter life lame, rather than having two feet, to be cast into hell, into the fire that shall never be quenched— ⁴⁶where

> 'Their worm does not die
> And the fire is not quenched.'[a]

⁴⁷And if your eye causes you to sin, pluck it out. It is better for you to enter the kingdom of God with one eye, rather than having two eyes, to be cast into hell fire— ⁴⁸where

> 'Their worm does not die
> And the fire is not quenched.'[a]

Tasteless Salt Is Worthless

⁴⁹"For everyone will be seasoned with fire,[a] and every sacrifice will be seasoned with salt. ⁵⁰Salt *is* good, but if the salt loses its flavor, how will you season it? Have salt in yourselves, and have peace with one another."

Marriage and Divorce

10 Then He arose from there and came to the region of Judea by the other side of the Jordan. And multitudes

---

9:40 [a]M-Text reads *against you is on your side.*   **9:44** [a]NU-Text omits this verse.   **9:46** [a]NU-Text omits the last clause of verse 45 and all of verse 46.   **9:48** [a]Isaiah 66:24   **9:49** [a]NU-Text omits the rest of this verse.

gathered to Him again, and as He was accustomed, He taught them again.

²The Pharisees came and asked Him, "Is it lawful for a man to divorce *his* wife?" testing Him.

³And He answered and said to them, "What did Moses command you?"

⁴They said, "Moses permitted *a man* to write a certificate of divorce, and to dismiss *her*."

⁵And Jesus answered and said to them, "Because of the hardness of your heart he wrote you this precept. ⁶But from the beginning of the creation, God *'made them male and female.'*ᵃ ⁷*'For this reason a man shall leave his father and mother and be joined to his wife,* ⁸*and the two shall become one flesh';*ᵃ so then they are no longer two, but one flesh. ⁹Therefore what God has joined together, let not man separate."

¹⁰In the house His disciples also asked Him again about the same *matter.* ¹¹So He said to them, "Whoever divorces his wife and marries another commits adultery against her. ¹²And if a woman divorces her husband and marries another, she commits adultery."

Jesus Blesses Little Children

¹³Then they brought little children to Him, that He might touch them; but the disciples rebuked those who brought *them.* ¹⁴But when Jesus saw *it,* He was greatly displeased and said to them, "Let the little children come to Me, and do not forbid them; for of such is the kingdom of God. ¹⁵Assuredly, I say to you, whoever does not receive the kingdom

of God as a little child will by no means enter it." ¹⁶And He took them up in His arms, laid *His* hands on them, and blessed them.

Jesus Counsels the Rich Young Ruler

¹⁷Now as He was going out on the road, one came running, knelt before Him, and asked Him, "Good Teacher, what shall I do that I may inherit eternal life?"

¹⁸So Jesus said to him, "Why do you call Me good? No one *is* good but One, *that is,* God. ¹⁹You know the commandments: *'Do not commit adultery,' 'Do not murder,' 'Do not steal,' 'Do not bear false witness,'* 'Do not defraud,' *'Honor your father and your mother.'* "ᵃ

²⁰And he answered and said to Him, "Teacher, all these things I have kept from my youth."

²¹Then Jesus, looking at him, loved him, and said to him, "One thing you lack: Go your way, sell whatever you have and give to the poor, and you will have treasure in heaven; and come, take up the cross, and follow Me."

²²But he was sad at this word, and went away sorrowful, for he had great possessions.

With God All Things Are Possible

²³Then Jesus looked around and said to His disciples, "How hard it is for those who have riches to enter the kingdom of God!" ²⁴And the disciples were astonished at His words. But Jesus answered again and said to them, "Children, how hard it is for those who trust in richesᵃ to enter the kingdom of God!

10:6 ᵃGenesis 1:27; 5:2   **10:8** ᵃGenesis 2:24   **10:19** ᵃExodus 20:12–16; Deuteronomy 5:16–20
10:24 ᵃNU-Text omits *for those who trust in riches.*

↓ KNOW (MARK 10:18)

What does it mean to be good? I may say, "God is good," until something bad happens . . . and then I wonder. Maybe my definition of good differs from God's idea of good? Some people define "good" as blue skies, robust health, paid bills, and no problems to speak of. They would never regard an illness or a major crisis as good. For them, good means smooth sailing and the absence of conflict and pain. And no doubt, if most of us could have our way, that is exactly the kind of life we would choose. God, however, who alone is good, has a very different idea. He considers good anything that brings us into closer conformity with the image of His Son, Jesus. He wants the absolute best for us, and often securing that absolute best involves big doses of difficulty, challenge, hardship, and pain. *For more about the* Attributes of God, *see Luke 11:5–9.*

²⁵It is easier for a camel to go through the eye of a needle than for a rich man to enter the kingdom of God."

²⁶And they were greatly astonished, saying among themselves, "Who then can be saved?"

²⁷But Jesus looked at them and said, "With men *it is* impossible, but not with God; for with God all things are possible."

> **→LIVE**
> • • • • • • • • • • • • • • •
> 10:27 • Sometimes we think we initiate our salvation, that our actions bring us to God. The fact is, God begins salvation. Throughout the Bible we see God taking the first step. It is He who gave His Son, who offers us grace and grants us forgiveness. Only by His will do we have a Bible to tell us of His gifts. The Holy Spirit convicts us of sin and convinces us of our need of Jesus (John 16:8). We need to respond to the Spirit's work, turn from our sins, and put our faith in Jesus Christ as Savior and Lord. *For more about* Becoming a Christian, *see* Luke 23:42; *the* Holy Spirit, *Luke 4:1.*

²⁸Then Peter began to say to Him, "See, we have left all and followed You."

²⁹So Jesus answered and said, "Assuredly, I say to you, there is no one who has left house or brothers or sisters or father or mother or wifeᵃ or children or lands, for My sake and the gospel's, ³⁰who shall not receive a hundredfold now in this time—houses and brothers and sisters and mothers and children and lands, with persecutions—and in the age to come, eternal life. ³¹But many *who are* first will be last, and the last first."

Jesus a Third Time Predicts His Death and Resurrection

³²Now they were on the road, going up to Jerusalem, and Jesus was going before them; and they were amazed. And as they followed they were afraid. Then He took the twelve aside again and began to tell them the things that would happen to Him: ³³"Behold, we are going up to Jerusalem, and the Son of Man will be betrayed to the chief priests and to the scribes; and they will condemn Him to death and deliver Him to the Gentiles; ³⁴and they will mock Him, and scourge Him, and spit on Him, and kill Him. And the third day He will rise again."

Greatness Is Serving

³⁵Then James and John, the sons of Zebedee, came to Him, saying, "Teacher, we want You to do for us whatever we ask."

³⁶And He said to them, "What do you want Me to do for you?"

³⁷They said to Him, "Grant us that we may sit, one on Your right hand and the other on Your left, in Your glory."

³⁸But Jesus said to them, "You do not know what you ask. Are you able to drink the cup that I drink, and be baptized with the baptism that I am baptized with?"

³⁹They said to Him, "We are able."

So Jesus said to them, "You will indeed drink the cup that I drink, and with the baptism I am baptized with you will be baptized; ⁴⁰but to sit on My right hand and on My left is not Mine to give, but *it is for those* for whom it is prepared."

⁴¹And when the ten heard *it,* they began to be greatly displeased with James and John. ⁴²But Jesus called them to *Himself* and said to them, "You know that those who are considered rulers over the Gentiles lord it over them, and their great ones exercise authority over them. ⁴³Yet it shall not be so among you; but whoever desires to become great among you shall be your servant. ⁴⁴And whoever of you desires to be first shall be slave of all. ⁴⁵For even the Son of Man did not come to be served, but to serve, and to give His life a ransom for many."

> **→** *For even the Son of Man did not come to be served, but to serve, and to give His life a ransom for many.* Mark 10:45

Jesus Heals Blind Bartimaeus

⁴⁶Now they came to Jericho. As He went out of Jericho with His disciples and a great multitude, blind Bartimaeus, the son of Timaeus, sat by the road begging. ⁴⁷And when he heard that it was Jesus of Nazareth, he began to cry out and say, "Jesus, Son of David, have mercy on me!"

10:29 ᵃNU-Text omits *or wife.*

[48]Then many warned him to be quiet; but he cried out all the more, "Son of David, have mercy on me!"

[49]So Jesus stood still and commanded him to be called.

Then they called the blind man, saying to him, "Be of good cheer. Rise, He is calling you."

[50]And throwing aside his garment, he rose and came to Jesus.

[51]So Jesus answered and said to him, "What do you want Me to do for you?"

The blind man said to Him, "Rabboni, that I may receive my sight."

[52]Then Jesus said to him, "Go your way; your faith has made you well." And immediately he received his sight and followed Jesus on the road.

The Triumphal Entry

11 Now when they drew near Jerusalem, to Bethphage[a] and Bethany, at the Mount of Olives, He sent two of His disciples; [2]and He said to them, "Go into the village opposite you; and as soon as you have entered it you will find a colt tied, on which no one has sat. Loose it and bring *it*. [3]And if anyone says to you, 'Why are you doing this?' say, 'The Lord has need of it,' and immediately he will send it here."

[4]So they went their way, and found the[a] colt tied by the door outside on the street, and they loosed it. [5]But some of those who stood there said to them, "What are you doing, loosing the colt?"

[6]And they spoke to them just as Jesus had commanded. So they let them go. [7]Then they brought the colt to Jesus and threw their clothes on it, and He sat on it. [8]And many spread their clothes on the road, and others cut down leafy branches from the trees and spread *them* on the road. [9]Then those who went before and those who followed cried out, saying:

"Hosanna!
'Blessed is He who comes in the name of the LORD!'[a]
[10]Blessed *is* the kingdom of our father David
That comes in the name of the Lord![a]
Hosanna in the highest!"

[11]And Jesus went into Jerusalem and into the temple. So when He had looked around at all things, as the hour was already late, He went out to Bethany with the twelve.

The Fig Tree Withered

[12]Now the next day, when they had come out from Bethany, He was hungry. [13]And seeing from afar a fig tree having leaves, He went to see if perhaps He would find something on it. When He came to it, He found nothing but leaves, for it was not the season for figs. [14]In response Jesus said to it, "Let no one eat fruit from you ever again."

And His disciples heard *it.*

Jesus Cleanses the Temple

[15]So they came to Jerusalem. Then Jesus went into the temple and began to drive out those who bought and sold in the temple, and overturned the tables of the money changers and the seats of those who sold doves. [16]And He would not allow anyone to carry wares through the temple. [17]Then He taught, saying to them, "Is it not written, 'My house shall be called a house of prayer for all nations'?[a] But you have made it a 'den of thieves.' "[b]

[18]And the scribes and chief priests heard it and sought how they might destroy Him; for they feared Him, because all the people were astonished at His teaching. [19]When evening had come, He went out of the city.

The Lesson of the Withered Fig Tree

[20]Now in the morning, as they passed by, they saw the fig tree dried up from the roots. [21]And Peter, remembering, said to Him, "Rabbi, look! The fig tree which You cursed has withered away."

[22]So Jesus answered and said to them, "Have faith in God. [23]For assuredly, I say to you, whoever says to this mountain, 'Be removed and be cast into the sea,' and does not doubt in his heart, but believes that those things he says will be done, he will have whatever he says. [24]Therefore I say to you, whatever things you ask when you pray, believe that you receive *them,* and you will have *them.*

11:1 [a]M-Text reads *Bethsphage.*   11:4 [a]NU-Text and M-Text read *a.*   11:9 [a]Psalm 118:26   11:10 [a]NU-Text omits *in the name of the Lord.*   11:17 [a]Isaiah 56:7   [b]Jeremiah 7:11

Forgiveness and Prayer

25"And whenever you stand praying, if you have anything against anyone, forgive him, that your Father in heaven may also forgive you your trespasses. 26But if you do not forgive, neither will your Father in heaven forgive your trespasses."a

Jesus' Authority Questioned

27Then they came again to Jerusalem. And as He was walking in the temple, the chief priests, the scribes, and the elders came to Him. 28And they said to Him, "By what authority are You doing these things? And who gave You this authority to do these things?"

29But Jesus answered and said to them, "I also will ask you one question; then answer Me, and I will tell you by what authority I do these things: 30The baptism of John—was it from heaven or from men? Answer Me."

31And they reasoned among themselves, saying, "If we say, 'From heaven,' He will say, 'Why then did you not believe him?' 32But if we say, 'From men' "—they feared the people, for all counted John to have been a prophet indeed. 33So they answered and said to Jesus, "We do not know."

And Jesus answered and said to them, "Neither will I tell you by what authority I do these things."

The Parable of the Wicked Vinedressers

12 Then He began to speak to them in parables: "A man planted a vineyard and set a hedge around it, dug a place for the wine vat and built a tower. And he leased it to vinedressers and went into a far country. 2Now at vintage-time he sent a servant to the vinedressers, that he might receive some of the fruit of the vineyard from the vinedressers. 3And they took him and beat him and sent him away empty-handed. 4Again he sent them another servant, and at him they threw stones,a wounded him in the head, and sent him away shamefully treated. 5And again he sent another, and him they killed; and many others, beating some and killing some. 6Therefore still having one son, his beloved, he also sent him to them last, saying, 'They will respect my son.' 7But those vinedressers said among themselves, 'This is

the heir. Come, let us kill him, and the inheritance will be ours.' 8So they took him and killed him and cast him out of the vineyard.

9"Therefore what will the owner of the vineyard do? He will come and destroy the vinedressers, and give the vineyard to others. 10Have you not even read this Scripture:

'The stone which the builders rejected
Has become the chief cornerstone.
11*This was the LORD's doing,*
And it is marvelous in our eyes'?"a

12And they sought to lay hands on Him, but feared the multitude, for they knew He had spoken the parable against them. So they left Him and went away.

The Pharisees: Is It Lawful to Pay Taxes to Caesar?

13Then they sent to Him some of the Pharisees and the Herodians, to catch Him in His words. 14When they had come, they said to Him, "Teacher, we know that You are true, and care about no one; for You do not regard the person of men, but teach the way of God in truth. Is it lawful to pay taxes to Caesar, or not? 15Shall we pay, or shall we not pay?"

But He, knowing their hypocrisy, said to them, "Why do you test Me? Bring Me a denarius that I may see it." 16So they brought it.

And He said to them, "Whose image and inscription is this?" They said to Him, "Caesar's."

17And Jesus answered and said to them, "Render to Caesar the things that are Caesar's, and to God the things that are God's."

And they marveled at Him.

The Sadducees: What About the Resurrection?

18Then some Sadducees, who say there is no resurrection, came to Him; and they asked Him, saying: 19"Teacher, Moses wrote to us that if a man's brother dies, and leaves his wife behind, and leaves no children, his brother should take his wife and raise up offspring for his brother. 20Now there were seven brothers. The first took a wife; and dying, he left no offspring. 21And the second took her, and he died; nor did he leave any offspring. And the third likewise. 22So the seven had her and left no offspring. Last of all

---

11:26 aNU-Text omits this verse.   **12:4** aNU-Text omits *and at him they threw stones.*   **12:11** aPsalm 118:22, 23

the woman died also. [23]Therefore, in the resurrection, when they rise, whose wife will she be? For all seven had her as wife."

[24]Jesus answered and said to them, "Are you not therefore mistaken, because you do not know the Scriptures nor the power of God? [25]For when they rise from the dead, they neither marry nor are given in marriage, but are like angels in heaven. [26]But concerning the dead, that they rise, have you not read in the book of Moses, in the *burning* bush *passage,* how God spoke to him, saying, *'I am the God of Abraham, the God of Isaac, and the God of Jacob'*?[a] [27]He is not the God of the dead, but the God of the living. You are therefore greatly mistaken."

The Scribes: Which Is the First Commandment of All?

[28]Then one of the scribes came, and having heard them reasoning together, perceiving[a] that He had answered them well, asked Him, "Which is the first commandment of all?"

[29]Jesus answered him, "The first of all the commandments *is: 'Hear, O Israel, the* Lord *our God, the* Lord *is one.* [30]*And you shall love the* Lord *your God with all your heart, with all your soul, with all your mind, and with all your strength.'*[a] This *is* the first commandment.[b] [31]And the second, like it, *is* this: *'You shall love your neighbor as yourself.'*[a] There is no other commandment greater than these."

[32]So the scribe said to Him, "Well *said,* Teacher. You have spoken the truth, for there is one God, and there is no other but He. [33]And to love Him with all the heart, with all the understanding, with all the soul,[a] and with all the strength, and to love one's neighbor as oneself, is more than all the whole burnt offerings and sacrifices."

[34]Now when Jesus saw that he answered wisely, He said to him, "You are not far from the kingdom of God."

But after that no one dared question Him.

Jesus: How Can David Call His Descendant Lord?

[35]Then Jesus answered and said, while He taught in the temple, "How *is it* that the scribes say that the Christ is the Son of David? [36]For David himself said by the Holy Spirit:

'The Lord *said to my Lord,*
"Sit at My right hand,
*   Till I make Your enemies Your*
*   footstool." '*[a]

[37]Therefore David himself calls Him *'Lord';* how is He *then* his Son?"

And the common people heard Him gladly.

Beware of the Scribes

[38]Then He said to them in His teaching, "Beware of the scribes, who desire to go around in long robes, *love* greetings in the marketplaces, [39]the best seats in the synagogues, and the best places at feasts, [40]who devour widows' houses, and for a pretense make long prayers. These will receive greater condemnation."

The Widow's Two Mites

[41]Now Jesus sat opposite the treasury and saw how the people put money into the treasury. And many *who were* rich put in much. [42]Then one poor widow came and threw in two mites,[a] which make a quadrans. [43]So He called His disciples to *Himself* and said to them, "Assuredly, I say to you that this poor widow has put in more than all those who have given to the treasury; [44]for they all put in out of their abundance, but she out of her poverty put in all that she had, her whole livelihood."

Jesus Predicts the Destruction of the Temple

13 Then as He went out of the temple, one of His disciples said to Him, "Teacher, see what manner of stones and what buildings *are here!*"

[2]And Jesus answered and said to him, "Do you see these great buildings? Not *one* stone shall be left upon another, that shall not be thrown down."

The Signs of the Times and the End of the Age

[3]Now as He sat on the Mount of Olives opposite the temple, Peter, James, John, and Andrew asked Him privately, [4]"Tell us, when will these things be? And what *will be* the sign when all these things will be fulfilled?"

12:26 [a]Exodus 3:6, 15   12:28 [a]NU-Text reads *seeing.*   12:30 [a]Deuteronomy 6:4, 5   [b]NU-Text omits this sentence.
12:31 [a]Leviticus 19:18   12:33 [a]NU-Text omits *with all the soul.*   12:36 [a]Psalm 110:1
12:42 [a]Greek *lepta,* very small copper coins worth a fraction of a penny

[5]And Jesus, answering them, began to say: "Take heed that no one deceives you. [6]For many will come in My name, saying, 'I am *He*,' and will deceive many. [7]But when you hear of wars and rumors of wars, do not be troubled; for *such things* must happen, but the end *is* not yet. [8]For nation will rise against nation, and kingdom against kingdom. And there will be earthquakes in various places, and there will be famines and troubles.[a] These *are* the beginnings of sorrows.

[9]"But watch out for yourselves, for they will deliver you up to councils, and you will be beaten in the synagogues. You will be brought[a] before rulers and kings for My sake, for a testimony to them. [10]And the gospel must first be preached to all the nations. [11]But when they arrest *you* and deliver you up, do not worry beforehand, or premeditate[a] what you will speak. But whatever is given you in that hour, speak that; for it is not you who speak, but the Holy Spirit. [12]Now brother will betray brother to death, and a father *his* child; and children will rise up against parents and cause them to be put to death. [13]And you will be hated by all for My name's sake. But he who endures to the end shall be saved.

The Great Tribulation

[14]"So when you see the *'abomination of desolation,'*[a] spoken of by Daniel the prophet,[b] standing where it ought not" (let the reader understand), "then let those who are in Judea flee to the mountains. [15]Let him who is on the housetop not go down into the house, nor enter to take anything out of his house. [16]And let him who is in the field not go back to get his clothes. [17]But woe to those who are pregnant and to those who are nursing babies in those days! [18]And pray that your flight may not be in winter. [19]For *in* those days there will be tribulation, such as has not been since the beginning of the creation which God created until this time, nor ever shall be. [20]And unless the Lord had shortened those days, no flesh would be saved; but for the elect's sake, whom He chose, He shortened the days. [21]"Then if anyone says to you, 'Look, here *is* the Christ!' or, 'Look, *He is* there!' do not believe it. [22]For false christs and false prophets will rise and show signs and wonders to deceive, if possible, even the elect. [23]But take

heed; see, I have told you all things beforehand.

The Coming of the Son of Man

[24]"But in those days, after that tribulation, the sun will be darkened, and the moon will not give its light; [25]the stars of heaven will fall, and the powers in the heavens will be shaken. [26]Then they will see the Son of Man coming in the clouds with great power and glory. [27]And then He will send His angels, and gather together His elect from the four winds, from the farthest part of earth to the farthest part of heaven.

The Parable of the Fig Tree

[28]"Now learn this parable from the fig tree: When its branch has already become tender, and puts forth leaves, you know that summer is near. [29]So you also, when you see these things happening, know that it[a] is near—at the doors! [30]Assuredly, I say to you, this generation will by no means pass away till all these things take place. [31]Heaven and earth will pass away, but My words will by no means pass away.

No One Knows the Day or Hour

[32]"But of that day and hour no one knows, not even the angels in heaven, nor the Son, but only the Father. [33]Take heed, watch and pray; for you do not know when the time is. [34]*It is* like a man going to a far country, who left his house and gave authority to his servants, and to each his work, and commanded the doorkeeper to watch. [35]Watch therefore, for you do not know when the master of the house is coming—in the evening, at midnight, at the crowing of the rooster, or in the morning— [36]lest, coming suddenly, he find you sleeping. [37]And what I say to you, I say to all: Watch!"

The Plot to Kill Jesus

14 After two days it was the Passover and *the Feast* of Unleavened Bread. And the chief priests and the scribes sought how they might take Him by trickery and put *Him* to death. [2]But they said, "Not during the feast, lest there be an uproar of the people."

13:8 [a]NU-Text omits *and troubles.*   **13:9** [a]NU-Text and M-Text read *will stand.*   **13:11** [a]NU-Text omits *or premeditate.*   **13:14** [a]Daniel 11:31; 12:11   [b]NU-Text omits *spoken of by Daniel the prophet.*   **13:29** [a]Or He

The Anointing at Bethany

³And being in Bethany at the house of Simon the leper, as He sat at the table, a woman came having an alabaster flask of very costly oil of spikenard. Then she broke the flask and poured *it* on His head. ⁴But there were some who were indignant among themselves, and said, "Why was this fragrant oil wasted? ⁵For it might have been sold for more than three hundred denarii and given to the poor." And they criticized her sharply.

⁶But Jesus said, "Let her alone. Why do you trouble her? She has done a good work for Me. ⁷For you have the poor with you always, and whenever you wish you may do them good; but Me you do not have always. ⁸She has done what she could. She has come beforehand to anoint My body for burial. ⁹Assuredly, I say to you, wherever this gospel is preached in the whole world, what this woman has done will also be told as a memorial to her."

Judas Agrees to Betray Jesus

¹⁰Then Judas Iscariot, one of the twelve, went to the chief priests to betray Him to them. ¹¹And when they heard *it,* they were glad, and promised to give him money. So he sought how he might conveniently betray Him.

Jesus Celebrates the Passover with His Disciples

¹²Now on the first day of Unleavened Bread, when they killed the Passover *lamb,* His disciples said to Him, "Where do You want us to go and prepare, that You may eat the Passover?"

¹³And He sent out two of His disciples and said to them, "Go into the city, and a man will meet you carrying a pitcher of water; follow him. ¹⁴Wherever he goes in, say to the master of the house, 'The Teacher says, "Where is the guest room in which I may eat the Passover with My disciples?" ' ¹⁵Then he will show you a large upper room, furnished *and* prepared; there make ready for us."

¹⁶So His disciples went out, and came into the city, and found it just as He had said to them; and they prepared the Passover.

¹⁷In the evening He came with the twelve. ¹⁸Now as they sat and ate, Jesus said, "Assuredly, I say to you, one of you who eats with Me will betray Me."

¹⁹And they began to be sorrowful, and to say to Him one by one, "*Is it* I?" And another *said,* "*Is* it I?"ᵃ

²⁰He answered and said to them, "*It is* one of the twelve, who dips with Me in the dish. ²¹The Son of Man indeed goes just as it is written of Him, but woe to that man by whom the Son of Man is betrayed! It would have been good for that man if he had never been born."

Jesus Institutes the Lord's Supper

²²And as they were eating, Jesus took bread, blessed and broke *it,* and gave *it* to them and said, "Take, eat;ᵃ this is My body."

²³Then He took the cup, and when He had given thanks He gave *it* to them, and they all drank from it. ²⁴And He said to them, "This is My blood of the newᵃ covenant, which is

14:19 ᵃNU-Text omits this sentence.   14:22 ᵃNU-Text omits *eat.*   14:24 ᵃNU-Text omits *new.*

↑ GROW (MARK 14:22–25)
. . . .

Every time we come to the communion table, we are to examine ourselves (1 Cor. 11:28). Why? After we have been Christians for a while, unfortunately, we tend to forget our roots. It slips our minds that at one time we were all miserable sinners who had offended God, but that God graciously extended His forgiveness to us through Jesus, who voluntarily went to the Cross, died, and shed His blood for us. So Jesus gave us a reminder of His work. The bread and the fruit of the vine represent His broken body and His shed blood. He told us to "do this" in remembrance of Him so that we would periodically recall how we came into this relationship with Him in the first place. Communion is no mere ritual; we are to examine ourselves before we partake of the elements, lest we eat and drink judgment upon ourselves. *For more about* Spiritual Disciplines, *see Luke 4:2.*

shed for many. ²⁵Assuredly, I say to you, I will no longer drink of the fruit of the vine until that day when I drink it new in the kingdom of God."

²⁶And when they had sung a hymn, they went out to the Mount of Olives.

Jesus Predicts Peter's Denial

²⁷Then Jesus said to them, "All of you will be made to stumble because of Me this night,ᵃ for it is written:

*'I will strike the Shepherd,
And the sheep will be scattered.'*ᵇ

²⁸"But after I have been raised, I will go before you to Galilee."

²⁹Peter said to Him, "Even if all are made to stumble, yet I *will* not *be.*"

³⁰Jesus said to him, "Assuredly, I say to you that today, *even* this night, before the rooster crows twice, you will deny Me three times."

³¹But he spoke more vehemently, "If I have to die with You, I will not deny You!"

And they all said likewise.

The Prayer in the Garden

³²Then they came to a place which was named Gethsemane; and He said to His disciples, "Sit here while I pray." ³³And He took Peter, James, and John with Him, and He began to be troubled and deeply distressed. ³⁴Then He said to them, "My soul is exceedingly sorrowful, *even* to death. Stay here and watch."

14:27 ᵃNU-Text omits *because of Me this night.* ᵇZechariah 13:7

³⁵He went a little farther, and fell on the ground, and prayed that if it were possible, the hour might pass from Him. ³⁶And He said, "Abba, Father, all things *are* possible for You. Take this cup away from Me; nevertheless, not what I will, but what You *will.*"

↘ LEARN

• • • • • • • • • • •

14:36 • Each of us must come to the point where we say along with Jesus, "Not my will, but Thine be done." For every believer there comes a Gethsemane, a place where obedience overrules personal desire and where Spirit becomes more important than flesh. A place where the glory of God becomes more important than my glory. Jesus promised, "He who loses his life for My sake will find it" (Matt. 10:39). So don't be afraid to pray, "Abba, Father"—a term of endearment and tenderness, like a child calling her father "Daddy"—and then surrender yourself to His perfect will for your life. *For more about* Submitting to God *and* How to Live Out Your Faith, *see Luke 9:59;* Prayer, *Luke 11:5–9.*

³⁷Then He came and found them sleeping, and said to Peter, "Simon, are you sleeping? Could you not watch one hour? ³⁸Watch and pray, lest you enter into temptation. The spirit indeed *is* willing, but the flesh *is* weak."

³⁹Again He went away and prayed, and spoke the same words. ⁴⁰And when He returned, He found them asleep again, for their eyes were heavy; and they did not know what to answer Him.

⁴¹Then He came the third time and said to them, "Are you still sleeping and resting? It is enough! The hour has come; behold, the Son of Man is being betrayed into the hands

↓ KNOW (MARK 14:36)

• •

Even before His arrest, Jesus knew that Judas Iscariot was coming with the temple guard. He knew He would appear before Annas, and then Caiaphas, and then Pilate, and then Herod, and finally back again to Pilate. He knew the soldiers would rip the beard off of His face. He knew they would punch Him in the mouth. He knew they would take the cat-o'-nine-tails and tear open His back. He knew they would nail Him to a cross. But worst of all, He knew He would have to bear the sin of the entire world. And that is why He prayed, "Take this cup away from Me; nevertheless, not what I will, but what You will." But He addressed His prayer to "Abba, Father." Jewish children called their father, "Abba," implying trust and affection. You can say the same to God as you face your own trials. *For more about* Prayer, *see Luke 11:5–9;* Adversity, *Mark 15:15;* Jesus' Life, *Luke 1:1–4.*

of sinners. [42]Rise, let us be going. See, My betrayer is at hand."

Betrayal and Arrest in Gethsemane

[43]And immediately, while He was still speaking, Judas, one of the twelve, with a great multitude with swords and clubs, came from the chief priests and the scribes and the elders. [44]Now His betrayer had given them a signal, saying, "Whomever I kiss, He is the One; seize Him and lead *Him* away safely."

[45]As soon as he had come, immediately he went up to Him and said to Him, "Rabbi, Rabbi!" and kissed Him.

[46]Then they laid their hands on Him and took Him. [47]And one of those who stood by drew his sword and struck the servant of the high priest, and cut off his ear.

[48]Then Jesus answered and said to them, "Have you come out, as against a robber, with swords and clubs to take Me? [49]I was daily with you in the temple teaching, and you did not seize Me. But the Scriptures must be fulfilled."

[50]Then they all forsook Him and fled.

A Young Man Flees Naked

[51]Now a certain young man followed Him, having a linen cloth thrown around *his* naked *body*. And the young men laid hold of him, [52]and he left the linen cloth and fled from them naked.

Jesus Faces the Sanhedrin

[53]And they led Jesus away to the high priest; and with him were assembled all the chief priests, the elders, and the scribes. [54]But Peter followed Him at a distance, right into the courtyard of the high priest. And he sat with the servants and warmed himself at the fire.

[55]Now the chief priests and all the council sought testimony against Jesus to put Him to death, but found none. [56]For many bore false witness against Him, but their testimonies did not agree.

[57]Then some rose up and bore false witness against Him, saying, [58]"We heard Him say, 'I will destroy this temple made with hands, and within three days I will build another made without hands.' " [59]But not even then did their testimony agree.

[60]And the high priest stood up in the midst and asked Jesus, saying, "Do You answer nothing? What *is it* these men testify against You?" [61]But He kept silent and answered nothing.

Again the high priest asked Him, saying to Him, "Are You the Christ, the Son of the Blessed?"

[62]Jesus said, "I am. And you will see the Son of Man sitting at the right hand of the Power, and coming with the clouds of heaven."

[63]Then the high priest tore his clothes and said, "What further need do we have of witnesses? [64]You have heard the blasphemy! What do you think?"

And they all condemned Him to be deserving of death.

[65]Then some began to spit on Him, and to blindfold Him, and to beat Him, and to say to Him, "Prophesy!" And the officers struck Him with the palms of their hands.[a]

Peter Denies Jesus, and Weeps

[66]Now as Peter was below in the courtyard, one of the servant girls of the high priest came. [67]And when she saw Peter warming himself, she looked at him and said, "You also were with Jesus of Nazareth."

[68]But he denied it, saying, "I neither know nor understand what you are saying." And he went out on the porch, and a rooster crowed.

[69]And the servant girl saw him again, and began to say to those who stood by, "This is *one* of them." [70]But he denied it again.

And a little later those who stood by said to Peter again, "Surely you are *one* of them; for you are a Galilean, and your speech shows *it*."[a]

[71]Then he began to curse and swear, "I do not know this Man of whom you speak!"

[72]A second time *the* rooster crowed. Then Peter called to mind the word that Jesus had said to him, "Before the rooster crows twice, you will deny Me three times." And when he thought about it, he wept.

Jesus Faces Pilate

15 Immediately, in the morning, the chief priests held a consultation with the elders and scribes and the whole council; and they bound Jesus, led *Him* away, and delivered *Him* to Pilate. [2]Then

---

14:65 [a]NU-Text reads *received Him with slaps.*   **14:70** [a]NU-Text omits *and your speech shows it.*

Pilate asked Him, "Are You the King of the Jews?"

He answered and said to him, "*It is as* you say."

³And the chief priests accused Him of many things, but He answered nothing. ⁴Then Pilate asked Him again, saying, "Do You answer nothing? See how many things they testify against You!"ᵃ ⁵But Jesus still answered nothing, so that Pilate marveled.

Taking the Place of Barabbas

⁶Now at the feast he was accustomed to releasing one prisoner to them, whomever they requested. ⁷And there was one named Barabbas, *who was* chained with his fellow rebels; they had committed murder in the rebellion. ⁸Then the multitude, crying aloud,ᵃ began to ask *him to do* just as he had always done for them. ⁹But Pilate answered them, saying, "Do you want me to release to you the King of the Jews?" ¹⁰For he knew that the chief priests had handed Him over because of envy.

¹¹But the chief priests stirred up the crowd, so that he should rather release Barabbas to them. ¹²Pilate answered and said to them again, "What then do you want me to do *with Him* whom you call the King of the Jews?"

¹³So they cried out again, "Crucify Him!"

¹⁴Then Pilate said to them, "Why, what evil has He done?"

But they cried out all the more, "Crucify Him!"

¹⁵So Pilate, wanting to gratify the crowd, released Barabbas to them; and he delivered Jesus, after he had scourged *Him,* to be crucified.

The Soldiers Mock Jesus

¹⁶Then the soldiers led Him away into the hall called Praetorium, and they called together the whole garrison. ¹⁷And they clothed Him with purple; and they twisted a crown of thorns, put it on His *head,* ¹⁸and began to salute Him, "Hail, King of the Jews!" ¹⁹Then they struck Him on the head with a reed and spat on Him; and bowing the knee, they worshiped Him. ²⁰And when they had mocked Him, they took the purple off Him, put His own clothes on Him, and led Him out to crucify Him.

The King on a Cross

²¹Then they compelled a certain man, Simon a Cyrenian, the father of Alexander and Rufus, as he was coming out of the country and passing by, to bear His cross. ²²And they brought Him to the place Golgotha, which is translated, Place of a Skull. ²³Then they gave Him wine mingled with myrrh to drink, but He did not take *it.* ²⁴And when they crucified Him, they divided His garments, casting lots for them *to determine* what every man should take.

²⁵Now it was the third hour, and they crucified Him. ²⁶And the inscription of His accusation was written above:

THE KING OF THE JEWS.

²⁷With Him they also crucified two robbers, one on His right and the other on His left. ²⁸So the Scripture was fulfilledᵃ which says, *"And He was numbered with the transgressors."*ᵇ

15:4 ᵃNU-Text reads *of which they accuse You.*   15:8 ᵃNU-Text reads *going up.*   15:28 ᵃIsaiah 53:12 ᵇNU-Text omits this verse.

↓ KNOW (MARK 15:15)

• •

Maybe we can understand, at least partly, why Jesus had to die on the Cross. But why did He have to *suffer?* And indeed He did suffer, far beyond our limited comprehension. God can, of course, do whatever He wants to, so long as it's consistent with His character. So if you were God, would *you* suffer if you didn't have to? Why would you *choose* to suffer? One answer seems to be, "So that we will recognize we serve a God who knows what we're going through." Are you suffering? Maybe you feel as though you are the only person going through this painful circumstance. You need to know you're not alone in your pain. For good reason Jesus was called the Man of Sorrows. No matter how great your difficulty or need, know that He understands. Jesus suffered and died to show you how much God loves you. *For more about* Adversity, *see Luke 7:19;* God's Love, *Luke 15:19;* The Cross, *Mark 15:34.*

[29]And those who passed by blasphemed Him, wagging their heads and saying, "Aha! *You* who destroy the temple and build *it* in three days, [30]save Yourself, and come down from the cross!"

[31]Likewise the chief priests also, mocking among themselves with the scribes, said, "He saved others; Himself He cannot save. [32]Let the Christ, the King of Israel, descend now from the cross, that we may see and believe."[a]

Even those who were crucified with Him reviled Him.

Jesus Dies on the Cross

[33]Now when the sixth hour had come, there was darkness over the whole land until the ninth hour. [34]And at the ninth hour Jesus cried out with a loud voice, saying, "Eloi, Eloi, lama sabachthani?" which is translated, *"My God, My God, why have You forsaken Me?"*[a]

→LIVE
. . . .

15:34 • On the Cross Jesus bore the sins of the world and died as a substitute for others. To Him was imputed the guilt of our sins, and He suffered the just punishment for those sins. In some mysterious way, during those awful hours as Jesus hung on the Cross, the Father poured out the full measure of His wrath against sin upon His own beloved Son. God was punishing Jesus as if He had personally committed every wicked deed committed by every wicked sinner. Jesus was forsaken by the Father for a time so that I could enjoy His presence forever. *For more about* The Cross, *see Acts 4:27, 28;* Sin, *Luke 7:39.*

[35]Some of those who stood by, when they heard *that*, said, "Look, He is calling for Elijah!" [36]Then someone ran and filled a sponge full of sour wine, put *it* on a reed, and offered *it* to Him to drink, saying, "Let Him alone; let us see if Elijah will come to take Him down."

[37]And Jesus cried out with a loud voice, and breathed His last.

[38]Then the veil of the temple was torn in two from top to bottom. [39]So when the centurion, who stood opposite Him, saw that He cried out like this and breathed His last,[a] he said, "Truly this Man was the Son of God!"

[40]There were also women looking on from afar, among whom were Mary Magdalene, Mary the mother of James the Less and of Joses, and Salome, [41]who also followed Him and ministered to Him when He was in Galilee, and many other women who came up with Him to Jerusalem.

Jesus Buried in Joseph's Tomb

[42]Now when evening had come, because it was the Preparation Day, that is, the day before the Sabbath, [43]Joseph of Arimathea, a prominent council member, who was himself waiting for the kingdom of God, coming and taking courage, went in to Pilate and asked for the body of Jesus. [44]Pilate marveled that He was already dead; and summoning the centurion, he asked him if He had been dead for some time. [45]So when he found out from the centurion, he granted the body to Joseph. [46]Then he bought fine linen, took Him down, and wrapped Him in the linen. And he laid Him in a tomb which had been hewn out of the rock, and rolled a stone against the door of the tomb. [47]And Mary Magdalene and Mary *the mother* of Joses observed where He was laid.

He Is Risen

16 Now when the Sabbath was past, Mary Magdalene, Mary *the mother* of James, and Salome bought spices, that they might come and anoint Him. [2]Very early in the morning, on the first *day* of the week, they came to the tomb when the sun had risen. [3]And they said among themselves, "Who will roll away the stone from the door of the tomb for us?" [4]But when they looked up, they saw that the stone had been rolled away—for it was very large. [5]And entering the tomb, they saw a young man clothed in a long white robe sitting on the right side; and they were alarmed.

[6]But he said to them, "Do not be alarmed. You seek Jesus of Nazareth, who was crucified. He is risen! He is not here. See the place where they laid Him. [7]But go, tell His disciples—and Peter—that He is going before you into Galilee; there you will see Him, as He said to you."

[8]So they went out quickly[a] and fled from the tomb, for they trembled and were

---

15:32 [a]M-Text reads *believe Him.*   **15:34** [a]Psalm 22:1   **15:39** [a]NU-Text reads *that He thus breathed His last.*
16:8 [a]NU-Text and M-Text omit *quickly.*

amazed. And they said nothing to anyone, for they were afraid.

Mary Magdalene Sees the Risen Lord

[9]Now when *He* rose early on the first *day* of the week, He appeared first to Mary Magdalene, out of whom He had cast seven demons. [10]She went and told those who had been with Him, as they mourned and wept. [11]And when they heard that He was alive and had been seen by her, they did not believe.

Jesus Appears to Two Disciples

[12]After that, He appeared in another form to two of them as they walked and went into the country. [13]And they went and told *it* to the rest, *but* they did not believe them either.

The Great Commission

[14]Later He appeared to the eleven as they sat at the table; and He rebuked their unbelief

and hardness of heart, because they did not believe those who had seen Him after He had risen. [15]And He said to them, "Go into all the world and preach the gospel to every creature. [16]He who believes and is baptized will be saved; but he who does not believe will be condemned. [17]And these signs will follow those who believe: In My name they will cast out demons; they will speak with new tongues; [18]they[a] will take up serpents; and if they drink anything deadly, it will by no means hurt them; they will lay hands on the sick, and they will recover."

Christ Ascends to God's Right Hand

[19]So then, after the Lord had spoken to them, He was received up into heaven, and sat down at the right hand of God. [20]And they went out and preached everywhere, the Lord working with *them* and confirming the word through the accompanying signs. Amen.[a]

16:18 [a]NU-Text reads *and in their hands they will.* **16:20** [a]Verses 9–20 are bracketed in NU-Text as not original. They are lacking in Codex Sinaiticus and Codex Vaticanus, although nearly all other manuscripts of Mark contain them.

LUKE

INTRODUCTION//

Luke, a Gentile Christian who became a close friend of the apostle Paul, wrote his own account of Jesus Christ's life to make the message of salvation understandable to those outside the Jewish world. As a doctor, his scientific training prompted him to do a great amount of research. He read many accounts of Jesus' ministry and likely interviewed those who knew Him best—including Mary, Jesus' mother—in order to get the most detail possible. Yet, at times Luke writes in an almost poetic way, giving to us the most beloved version of the Christmas story. His account therefore gives us an in-depth perspective on Jesus' life and ministry, giving us facts about His birth, childhood, and ministry found nowhere else. The birth of John the Baptist (1:5–25, 57–80), the birth of Jesus in Bethlehem (2:1–40), and a solitary glimpse of Jesus' childhood (2:41–52) are found only here. He also gives us three of Jesus' most famous parables: the parables of the lost sheep (15:1–7), the lost coin (15:8–10), and the prodigal son (15:11–32). He also highlights the role of the Holy Spirit and the contributions of women.

While Matthew focuses on Jesus as the Messiah who fulfilled Old Testament prophecy, and Mark writes of Jesus' actions and how He served those who came to Him, Luke focuses on the humanity of Christ. In no way does he deny the divinity of Christ—in fact, he records many miracles pointing to His deity—but by focusing on the physical aspects of His birth and death, Luke shows us that Jesus was God *incarnate*, God walking on earth as a man. Luke demonstrates that Jesus lived a perfect life as a man, just as dependent as we are on the Holy Spirit; therefore, Jesus gives us a perfect example to follow.

Dedication to Theophilus

1 Inasmuch as many have taken in hand to set in order a narrative of those things which have been fulfilled[a] among us, [2]just as those who from the beginning were eyewitnesses and ministers of the word delivered them to us, [3]it seemed good to me also, having had perfect understanding of all things from the very first, to write to you an orderly account, most excellent Theophilus, [4]that you may know the certainty of those things in which you were instructed.

> ↘ **LEARN**
> • • • • • • • • • • • • • • • • •
>
> 1:1–4 • Luke, a Christian physician from a Gentile background, desired to create a record of Jesus' life designed for individuals outside of a Jewish culture. With the education of a doctor and the flair of a poet, Luke produced an orderly, systematic record of the life of Christ. Many accounts about Jesus were floating around at the time, some of them badly distorted. Because the tabloids of Luke's day made up outright lies about Jesus, Luke wanted his readers to know the "certainty" of Christ's story. Then as now, the proper telling of the Christian story produces belief in its truth. *For more about* Jesus' Life, *see Luke 1:34;* God's Word, *Luke 4:2.*

John's Birth Announced to Zacharias

[5]There was in the days of Herod, the king of Judea, a certain priest named Zacharias, of the division of Abijah. His wife *was* of the daughters of Aaron, and her name *was* Elizabeth. [6]And they were both righteous before God, walking in all the commandments and ordinances of the Lord blameless. [7]But they had no child, because Elizabeth was barren, and they were both well advanced in years.

[8]So it was, that while he was serving as priest before God in the order of his division, [9]according to the custom of the priesthood, his lot fell to burn incense when he went into the temple of the Lord. [10]And the whole multitude of the people was praying outside at the hour of incense. [11]Then an angel of the Lord appeared to him, standing on the right side of the altar of incense. [12]And when Zacharias saw *him,* he was troubled, and fear fell upon him.

[13]But the angel said to him, "Do not be afraid, Zacharias, for your prayer is heard; and your wife Elizabeth will bear you a son, and you shall call his name John. [14]And you will have joy and gladness, and many will rejoice at his birth. [15]For he will be great in the sight of the Lord, and shall drink neither wine nor strong drink. He will also be filled with the Holy Spirit, even from his mother's womb. [16]And he will turn many of the children of Israel to the Lord their God. [17]He will also go before Him in the spirit and power of Elijah, *'to turn the hearts of the fathers to the children,'*[a] and the disobedient to the wisdom of the just, to make ready a people prepared for the Lord."

[18]And Zacharias said to the angel, "How shall I know this? For I am an old man, and my wife is well advanced in years."

[19]And the angel answered and said to him, "I am Gabriel, who stands in the presence of God, and was sent to speak to you and bring you these glad tidings. [20]But behold, you will be mute and not able to speak until the day these things take place, because you did not believe my words which will be fulfilled in their own time."

[21]And the people waited for Zacharias, and marveled that he lingered so long in the temple. [22]But when he came out, he could not speak to them; and they perceived that he had seen a vision in the temple, for he beckoned to them and remained speechless.

[23]So it was, as soon as the days of his service were completed, that he departed to his own house. [24]Now after those days his wife Elizabeth conceived; and she hid herself five months, saying, [25]"Thus the Lord has dealt with me, in the days when He looked on *me,* to take away my reproach among people."

Christ's Birth Announced to Mary

[26]Now in the sixth month the angel Gabriel was sent by God to a city of Galilee named Nazareth, [27]to a virgin betrothed to a man whose name was Joseph, of the house of David. The virgin's name *was* Mary. [28]And having come in, the angel said to her, "Rejoice, highly favored *one,* the Lord *is* with you; blessed *are* you among women!"[a]

[29]But when she saw *him,*[a] she was troubled at his saying, and considered what manner of greeting this was. [30]Then the angel said to

---

1:1 [a]*Or are most surely believed*   1:17 [a]Malachi 4:5, 6   1:28 [a]NU-Text omits *blessed are you among women.*
1:29 [a]NU-Text omits *when she saw him.*

her, "Do not be afraid, Mary, for you have found favor with God. ³¹And behold, you will conceive in your womb and bring forth a Son, and shall call His name JESUS. ³²He will be great, and will be called the Son of the Highest; and the Lord God will give Him the throne of His father David. ³³And He will reign over the house of Jacob forever, and of His kingdom there will be no end."

³⁴Then Mary said to the angel, "How can this be, since I do not know a man?"

³⁵And the angel answered and said to her, "*The* Holy Spirit will come upon you, and the power of the Highest will overshadow you; therefore, also, that Holy One who is to be born will be called the Son of God. ³⁶Now indeed, Elizabeth your relative has also conceived a son in her old age; and this is now the sixth month for her who was called barren. ³⁷For with God nothing will be impossible."

³⁸Then Mary said, "Behold the maidservant of the Lord! Let it be to me according to your word." And the angel departed from her.

Mary Visits Elizabeth

³⁹Now Mary arose in those days and went into the hill country with haste, to a city of Judah, ⁴⁰and entered the house of Zacharias and greeted Elizabeth. ⁴¹And it happened, when Elizabeth heard the greeting of Mary, that the babe leaped in her womb; and Elizabeth was filled with the Holy Spirit. ⁴²Then she spoke out with a loud voice and said, "Blessed *are* you among women, and blessed *is* the fruit of your womb! ⁴³But why *is* this *granted* to me, that the mother of my Lord should come to me? ⁴⁴For indeed, as soon as the voice of your greeting sounded in my ears, the babe leaped in my womb for joy. ⁴⁵Blessed *is* she who believed, for there will be a fulfillment of those things which were told her from the Lord."

The Song of Mary

⁴⁶And Mary said:

"My soul magnifies the Lord,
⁴⁷And my spirit has rejoiced in God my
    Savior.
⁴⁸For He has regarded the lowly state of His
    maidservant;
  For behold, henceforth all generations
    will call me blessed.
⁴⁹For He who is mighty has done great
    things for me,
  And holy *is* His name.
⁵⁰And His mercy *is* on those who fear
    Him
  From generation to generation.
⁵¹He has shown strength with His arm;
  He has scattered *the* proud in the
    imagination of their hearts.
⁵²He has put down the mighty from *their*
    thrones,
  And exalted *the* lowly.
⁵³He has filled *the* hungry with good
    things,
  And *the* rich He has sent away empty.
⁵⁴He has helped His servant Israel,
  In remembrance of *His* mercy,
⁵⁵As He spoke to our fathers,
  To Abraham and to his seed forever."

⁵⁶And Mary remained with her about three months, and returned to her house.

↓ KNOW (LUKE 1:34)

The Lord chose to send His Son into the world through a virgin, as prophesied by Isaiah (7:14). Some people struggle with this idea. "I believe in Jesus," they'll say, "but I don't know if I believe in the virgin birth." The problem here is that you cannot really be a Christian without believing in the virgin birth. If He was not supernaturally conceived in the womb of a virgin, then He was not God. And if He was not God, then His death on the Cross might have been tragic, but it was of no great historical significance. A lot of men died on Roman crosses 2,000 years ago. The key difference is that only one, Jesus Christ, died as God in human form, thus atoning for the sin of the world. Three days later, He bodily rose from the dead, proving His claim to deity (see Rom. 1:4). *For more about* Jesus' Life, *see Luke 2:52.*

Birth of John the Baptist

[57]Now Elizabeth's full time came for her to be delivered, and she brought forth a son. [58]When her neighbors and relatives heard how the Lord had shown great mercy to her, they rejoiced with her.

Circumcision of John the Baptist

[59]So it was, on the eighth day, that they came to circumcise the child; and they would have called him by the name of his father, Zacharias. [60]His mother answered and said, "No; he shall be called John."

[61]But they said to her, "There is no one among your relatives who is called by this name." [62]So they made signs to his father—what he would have him called. [63]And he asked for a writing tablet, and wrote, saying, "His name is John." So they all marveled. [64]Immediately his mouth was opened and his tongue *loosed,* and he spoke, praising God. [65]Then fear came on all who dwelt around them; and all these sayings were discussed throughout all the hill country of Judea. [66]And all those who heard *them* kept *them* in their hearts, saying, "What kind of child will this be?" And the hand of the Lord was with him.

Zacharias' Prophecy

[67]Now his father Zacharias was filled with the Holy Spirit, and prophesied, saying:

[68]"Blessed *is* the Lord God of Israel,
   For He has visited and redeemed His
      people,
[69]And has raised up a horn of salvation
      for us
   In the house of His servant David,
[70]As He spoke by the mouth of His holy
      prophets,
   Who *have been* since the world began,
[71]That we should be saved from our
      enemies
   And from the hand of all who hate us,
[72]To perform the mercy *promised* to our
      fathers
   And to remember His holy covenant,
[73]The oath which He swore to our father
      Abraham:
[74]To grant us that we,

   Being delivered from the hand of our
      enemies,
   Might serve Him without fear,
[75]In holiness and righteousness before Him
      all the days of our life.

[76]"And you, child, will be called the prophet
      of the Highest;
   For you will go before the face of the Lord
      to prepare His ways,
[77]To give knowledge of salvation to His
      people
   By the remission of their sins,
[78]Through the tender mercy of our God,
   With which the Dayspring from on high
      has visited[a] us;
[79]To give light to those who sit in darkness
      and the shadow of death,
   To guide our feet into the way of peace."

[80]So the child grew and became strong in spirit, and was in the deserts till the day of his manifestation to Israel.

Christ Born of Mary

2 And it came to pass in those days *that* a decree went out from Caesar Augustus that all the world should be registered. [2]This census first took place while Quirinius was governing Syria. [3]So all went to be registered, everyone to his own city.

[4]Joseph also went up from Galilee, out of the city of Nazareth, into Judea, to the city of David, which is called Bethlehem, because he was of the house and lineage of David, [5]to be registered with Mary, his betrothed wife,[a] who was with child. [6]So it was, that while they were there, the days were completed for her to be delivered. [7]And she brought forth her firstborn Son, and wrapped Him in swaddling cloths, and laid Him in a manger, because there was no room for them in the inn.

Glory in the Highest

[8]Now there were in the same country shepherds living out in the fields, keeping watch over their flock by night. [9]And behold,[a] an angel of the Lord stood before them, and the glory of the Lord shone around them, and they were greatly afraid. [10]Then the angel said to them, "Do not be afraid, for behold, I

1:78 [a]NU-Text reads *shall visit.*   2:5 [a]NU-Text omits *wife.*   2:9 [a]NU-Text omits *behold.*

bring you good tidings of great joy which will be to all people. ¹¹For there is born to you this day in the city of David a Savior, who is Christ the Lord. ¹²And this *will be* the sign to you: You will find a Babe wrapped in swaddling cloths, lying in a manger."

¹³And suddenly there was with the angel a multitude of the heavenly host praising God and saying:

¹⁴"Glory to God in the highest,
    And on earth peace, goodwill toward
        men!"ᵃ

¹⁵So it was, when the angels had gone away from them into heaven, that the shepherds said to one another, "Let us now go to Bethlehem and see this thing that has come to pass, which the Lord has made known to us." ¹⁶And they came with haste and found Mary and Joseph, and the Babe lying in a manger. ¹⁷Now when they had seen *Him,* they made widelyᵃ known the saying which was told them concerning this Child. ¹⁸And all those who heard *it* marveled at those things which were told them by the shepherds. ¹⁹But Mary kept all these things and pondered *them* in her heart.

> ↘ **LEARN**
> • • • • • • • • • • • • • • • • •
> 2:19 • A growing Christian is a thinking Christian. Much of the process of spiritual maturity involves thinking, pondering, meditating, considering, contemplating. It surely is no accident that Mary, the young woman chosen to give birth to the Son of God, is described as a very thoughtful person. When the shepherds declared marvelous things about her baby boy, Luke says Mary "kept all these things and pondered them in her heart." A dozen years later, after Mary found Jesus in Jerusalem discussing God's law with temple scholars, Luke again says she "kept all these things in her heart" (2:51). Thought spurs growth. *For more about* Growing in Christ, *see Luke 24:47.*

²⁰Then the shepherds returned, glorifying and praising God for all the things that they had heard and seen, as it was told them.

Circumcision of Jesus

²¹And when eight days were completed for the circumcision of the Child,ᵃ His name was called JESUS, the name given by the angel before He was conceived in the womb.

Jesus Presented in the Temple

²²Now when the days of her purification according to the law of Moses were completed, they brought Him to Jerusalem to present *Him* to the Lord ²³(as it is written in the law of the Lord, *"Every male who opens the womb shall be called holy to the LORD"*),ᵃ ²⁴and to offer a sacrifice according to what is said in the law of the Lord, *"A pair of turtledoves or two young pigeons."*ᵃ

Simeon Sees God's Salvation

²⁵And behold, there was a man in Jerusalem whose name *was* Simeon, and this man *was* just and devout, waiting for the Consolation of Israel, and the Holy Spirit was upon him. ²⁶And it had been revealed to him by the Holy Spirit that he would not see death before he had seen the Lord's Christ. ²⁷So he came by the Spirit into the temple. And when the parents brought in the Child Jesus, to do for Him according to the custom of the law, ²⁸he took Him up in his arms and blessed God and said:

²⁹"Lord, now You are letting Your servant
        depart in peace,
    According to Your word;
³⁰For my eyes have seen Your salvation
³¹Which You have prepared before the face
        of all peoples,
³²A light to *bring* revelation to the Gentiles,
    And the glory of Your people Israel."

³³And Joseph and His motherᵃ marveled at those things which were spoken of Him. ³⁴Then Simeon blessed them, and said to Mary His mother, "Behold, this *Child* is destined for the fall and rising of many in Israel, and for a sign which will be spoken against ³⁵(yes, a sword will pierce through your own soul also), that the thoughts of many hearts may be revealed."

Anna Bears Witness to the Redeemer

³⁶Now there was one, Anna, a prophetess, the daughter of Phanuel, of the tribe of

---

2:14 ᵃNU-Text reads *toward men of goodwill.*   2:17 ᵃNU-Text omits *widely.*   2:21 ᵃNU-Text reads *for His circumcision.*
2:23 ᵃExodus 13:2, 12, 15   2:24 ᵃLeviticus 12:8   2:33 ᵃNU-Text reads *And His father and mother.*

Asher. She was of a great age, and had lived with a husband seven years from her virginity; [37]and this woman *was* a widow of about eighty-four years,[a] who did not depart from the temple, but served *God* with fastings and prayers night and day. [38]And coming in that instant she gave thanks to the Lord,[a] and spoke of Him to all those who looked for redemption in Jerusalem.

The Family Returns to Nazareth

[39]So when they had performed all things according to the law of the Lord, they returned to Galilee, to their *own* city, Nazareth. [40]And the Child grew and became strong in spirit,[a] filled with wisdom; and the grace of God was upon Him.

The Boy Jesus Amazes the Scholars

[41]His parents went to Jerusalem every year at the Feast of the Passover. [42]And when He was twelve years old, they went up to Jerusalem according to the custom of the feast. [43]When they had finished the days, as they returned, the Boy Jesus lingered behind in Jerusalem. And Joseph and His mother[a] did not know *it;* [44]but supposing Him to have been in the company, they went a day's journey, and sought Him among *their* relatives and acquaintances. [45]So when they did not find Him, they returned to Jerusalem, seeking Him. [46]Now so it was *that* after three days they found Him in the temple, sitting in the midst of the teachers, both listening to them and asking them questions. [47]And all who heard Him were astonished at His understanding and answers. [48]So when they saw Him, they were amazed; and His mother said to Him, "Son, why have You done this to us? Look, Your father and I have sought You anxiously."

[49]And He said to them, "Why did you seek Me? Did you not know that I must be about My Father's business?" [50]But they did not understand the statement which He spoke to them.

Jesus Advances in Wisdom and Favor

[51]Then He went down with them and came to Nazareth, and was subject to them, but His mother kept all these things in her heart. [52]And Jesus increased in wisdom and stature, and in favor with God and men.

John the Baptist Prepares the Way

3 Now in the fifteenth year of the reign of Tiberius Caesar, Pontius Pilate being governor of Judea, Herod being tetrarch of Galilee, his brother Philip tetrarch of Iturea and the region of Trachonitis, and Lysanias tetrarch of Abilene, [2]while Annas and Caiaphas were high priests,[a] the word of God came to John the son of Zacharias in the wilderness. [3]And he went into all the region around the Jordan, preaching a baptism of repentance for the remission of sins, [4]as it is written in the book of the words of Isaiah the prophet, saying:

> "The voice of one crying in the wilderness:
> 'Prepare the way of the LORD;
> Make His paths straight.

2:37 [a]NU-Text reads *a widow until she was eighty-four.*   2:38 [a]NU-Text reads *to God.*   2:40 [a]NU-Text omits *in spirit.*
2:43 [a]NU-Text reads *And His parents.*   3:2 [a]NU-Text and M-Text read *in the high priesthood of Annas and Caiaphas.*

↓ KNOW (LUKE 2:52)

The eternal Son of God, Jesus, actually became a baby. God became an embryo. Deity in diapers! Once Jesus arrived on earth, He went through a learning process, just like anybody else. Luke tells us that, "Jesus increased in wisdom and stature." (Luke 2:52). Some hear this and say, "Hold on! If you are God, then you're omniscient, which means you know all things. So how can you learn anything?" That's a valid question. And here's the biblical answer: Jesus continued to possess His divine attributes *without choosing to use them.* In the words of Scripture, He "emptied" Himself and "humbled" Himself. But self-emptying is not self-extinction. In coming to earth He did *not* lay aside His deity—that was impossible—but rather the privileges of deity. He emptied Himself, not of His essential being or character, but of His right to draw upon the staggering privileges of His deity. *For more about* Jesus' Life, *see Luke 4:1.*

5 *Every valley shall be filled*
  And every mountain and hill brought
      low;
  The crooked places shall be made
      straight
  And the rough ways smooth;
6 *And all flesh shall see the salvation of*
      *God.' "*a

John Preaches to the People

7 Then he said to the multitudes that came out to be baptized by him, "Brood of vipers! Who warned you to flee from the wrath to come? 8 Therefore bear fruits worthy of repentance, and do not begin to say to yourselves, 'We have Abraham as *our* father.' For I say to you that God is able to raise up children to Abraham from these stones. 9 And even now the ax is laid to the root of the trees. Therefore every tree which does not bear good fruit is cut down and thrown into the fire."

10 So the people asked him, saying, "What shall we do then?"

11 He answered and said to them, "He who has two tunics, let him give to him who has none; and he who has food, let him do likewise."

12 Then tax collectors also came to be baptized, and said to him, "Teacher, what shall we do?"

13 And he said to them, "Collect no more than what is appointed for you."

14 Likewise the soldiers asked him, saying, "And what shall we do?"

So he said to them, "Do not intimidate anyone or accuse falsely, and be content with your wages."

15 Now as the people were in expectation, and all reasoned in their hearts about John, whether he was the Christ *or* not, 16 John answered, saying to all, "I indeed baptize you with water; but One mightier than I is coming, whose sandal strap I am not worthy to loose. He will baptize you with the Holy Spirit and fire. 17 His winnowing fan *is* in His hand, and He will thoroughly clean out His threshing floor, and gather the wheat into His barn; but the chaff He will burn with unquenchable fire."

18 And with many other exhortations he preached to the people. 19 But Herod the tetrarch, being rebuked by him concerning Herodias, his brother Philip's wife,a and for all the evils which Herod had done, 20 also added this, above all, that he shut John up in prison.

John Baptizes Jesus

21 When all the people were baptized, it came to pass that Jesus also was baptized; and while He prayed, the heaven was opened. 22 And the Holy Spirit descended in bodily form like a dove upon Him, and a voice came from heaven which said, "You are My beloved Son; in You I am well pleased."

The Genealogy of Jesus Christ

23 Now Jesus Himself began *His ministry* at about thirty years of age, being (as was supposed) *the* son of Joseph, *the son* of Heli, 24 *the son* of Matthat,a *the son* of Levi, *the son* of Melchi, *the son* of Janna, *the son* of Joseph, 25 *the son* of Mattathiah, *the son* of Amos, *the son* of Nahum, *the son* of Esli, *the son* of Naggai, 26 *the son* of Maath, *the son* of Mattathiah, *the son* of Semei, *the son* of Joseph, *the son* of Judah, 27 *the son* of Joannas, *the son* of Rhesa, *the son* of Zerubbabel, *the son* of Shealtiel, *the son* of Neri, 28 *the son* of Melchi, *the son* of Addi, *the son* of Cosam, *the son* of Elmodam, *the son* of Er, 29 *the son* of Jose, *the son* of Eliezer, *the son* of Jorim, *the son* of Matthat, *the son* of Levi, 30 *the son* of Simeon, *the son* of Judah, *the son* of Joseph, *the son* of Jonan, *the son* of Eliakim, 31 *the son* of Melea, *the son* of Menan, *the son* of Mattathah, *the son* of Nathan, *the son* of David, 32 *the son* of Jesse, *the son* of Obed, *the son* of Boaz, *the son* of Salmon, *the son* of Nahshon, 33 *the son* of Amminadab, *the son* of Ram, *the son* of Hezron, *the son* of Perez, *the son* of Judah, 34 *the son* of Jacob, *the son* of Isaac, *the son* of Abraham, *the son* of Terah, *the son* of Nahor, 35 *the son* of Serug, *the son* of Reu, *the son* of Peleg, *the son* of Eber, *the son* of Shelah, 36 *the son* of Cainan, *the son* of Arphaxad, *the son* of Shem, *the son* of Noah, *the son* of Lamech, 37 *the son* of Methuselah, *the son* of Enoch, *the son* of Jared, *the son* of Mahalalel, *the son* of Cainan, 38 *the son* of Enosh, *the son* of Seth, *the son* of Adam, *the son* of God.

3:6 aIsaiah 40:3–5   **3:19** aNU-Text reads *his brother's wife.*   **3:24** aThis and several other names in the genealogy are spelled somewhat differently in the NU-Text. Since the New King James Version uses the Old Testament spelling for persons mentioned in the New Testament, these variations, which come from the Greek, have not been footnoted.

Satan Tempts Jesus

4 Then Jesus, being filled with the Holy Spirit, returned from the Jordan and was led by the Spirit into[a] the wilderness, [2]being tempted for forty days by the devil. And in those days He ate nothing, and afterward, when they had ended, He was hungry.

> **↘ LEARN**
>
> 4:1 • Before Jesus officially began His public ministry, He took two very important steps. First He was baptized, and next He faced temptation in the wilderness. He did both things in order to give us an example. Note carefully that Jesus faced Satan *as a man;* He did not use His divine power to be delivered or to run Satan out. Instead, He showed us what to do and how to do it when *we* face temptation. In other words, He occupied ground that we too can occupy—and it all begins with choosing to be "filled with the Holy Spirit." *For more about* Jesus' Life, *see John 4:28, 29;* Satan, *Acts 2:38; the* Holy Spirit, *Luke 24:45.*

[3]And the devil said to Him, "If You are the Son of God, command this stone to become bread."

[4]But Jesus answered him, saying,[a] "It is written, *'Man shall not live by bread alone, but by every word of God.'*"[b]

[5]Then the devil, taking Him up on a high mountain, showed Him[a] all the kingdoms of the world in a moment of time. [6]And the devil said to Him, "All this authority I will give You, and their glory; for *this* has been delivered to me, and I give it to whomever I wish. [7]Therefore, if You will worship before me, all will be Yours."

[8]And Jesus answered and said to him, "Get behind Me, Satan![a] For[b] it is written, *'You shall worship the LORD your God, and Him only you shall serve.'*"[c]

[9]Then he brought Him to Jerusalem, set Him on the pinnacle of the temple, and said to Him, "If You are the Son of God, throw Yourself down from here. [10]For it is written:

'He shall give His angels charge over you,
To keep you,'

[11]and,

'In their hands they shall bear you up,
Lest you dash your foot against a
stone.'"[a]

[12]And Jesus answered and said to him, "It has been said, *'You shall not tempt the LORD your God.'*"[a]

[13]Now when the devil had ended every temptation, he departed from Him until an opportune time.

Jesus Begins His Galilean Ministry

[14]Then Jesus returned in the power of the Spirit to Galilee, and news of Him went out through all the surrounding region. [15]And He taught in their synagogues, being glorified by all.

Jesus Rejected at Nazareth

[16]So He came to Nazareth, where He had been brought up. And as His custom was, He went into the synagogue on the Sabbath day,

4:1 [a]NU-Text reads *in.*   4:4 [a]Deuteronomy 8:3 [b]NU-Text omits *but by every word of God.*   4:5 [a]NU-Text reads *And taking Him up, he showed Him.*   4:8 [a]NU-Text omits *Get behind Me, Satan.* [b]NU-Text and M-Text omit *For.* [c]Deuteronomy 6:13
4:11 [a]Psalm 91:11, 12   4:12 [a]Deuteronomy 6:16

↑ GROW (LUKE 4:2)

What is our primary weapon for resisting temptation? Answer: the Word of God. While it's great to carry a Bible in your briefcase or in your purse, the best place to carry the Word of God is in your heart. You need to know the Word of God, to memorize good chunks of it. Are you memorizing the Bible? You might say, "It's just too hard. I am not good with remembering things." It's amazing how much information our brains can retain. I know sports fanatics who can instantly recall the scores of their favorite teams, going back twenty years. You probably know someone who quotes lines out of movies, even if the film came out decades ago. And yet we say we can't memorize the Word of God? It is doable; it just takes some discipline. And nothing will help you more when you find yourself under spiritual attack. *For more about* Spiritual Disciplines, *see Acts 6:6;* God's Word, *Luke 21:6.*

and stood up to read. [17]And He was handed the book of the prophet Isaiah. And when He had opened the book, He found the place where it was written:

[18] *"The Spirit of the LORD is upon Me,*
   Because He has anointed Me
   To preach the gospel to the poor;
   He has sent Me to heal the
      brokenhearted,[a]
   To proclaim liberty to the captives
   And recovery of sight to the blind,
   To set at liberty those who are oppressed;
[19] *To proclaim the acceptable year of the*
      LORD. "[a]

[20]Then He closed the book, and gave *it* back to the attendant and sat down. And the eyes of all who were in the synagogue were fixed on Him. [21]And He began to say to them, "Today this Scripture is fulfilled in your hearing." [22]So all bore witness to Him, and marveled at the gracious words which proceeded out of His mouth. And they said, "Is this not Joseph's son?"

[23]He said to them, "You will surely say this proverb to Me, 'Physician, heal yourself! Whatever we have heard done in Capernaum,[a] do also here in Your country.'" [24]Then He said, "Assuredly, I say to you, no prophet is accepted in his own country. [25]But I tell you truly, many widows were in Israel in the days of Elijah, when the heaven was shut up three years and six months, and there was a great famine throughout all the land; [26]but to none of them was Elijah sent except to Zarephath,[a] *in the region* of Sidon, to a woman *who was* a widow. [27]And many lepers were in Israel in the time of Elisha the prophet, and none of them was cleansed except Naaman the Syrian."

[28]So all those in the synagogue, when they heard these things, were filled with wrath, [29]and rose up and thrust Him out of the city; and they led Him to the brow of the hill on which their city was built, that they might throw Him down over the cliff. [30]Then passing through the midst of them, He went His way.

Jesus Casts Out an Unclean Spirit

[31]Then He went down to Capernaum, a city of Galilee, and was teaching them on the Sabbaths. [32]And they were astonished at His teaching, for His word was with authority. [33]Now in the synagogue there was a man who had a spirit of an unclean demon. And he cried out with a loud voice, [34]saying, "Let *us* alone! What have we to do with You, Jesus of Nazareth? Did You come to destroy us? I know who You are—the Holy One of God!"

[35]But Jesus rebuked him, saying, "Be quiet, and come out of him!" And when the demon had thrown him in *their* midst, it came out of him and did not hurt him. [36]Then they were all amazed and spoke among themselves, saying, "What a word this *is!* For with authority and power He commands the unclean spirits, and they come out." [37]And the report about Him went out into every place in the surrounding region.

Peter's Mother-in-Law Healed

[38]Now He arose from the synagogue and entered Simon's house. But Simon's wife's mother was sick with a high fever, and they made request of Him concerning her. [39]So He stood over her and rebuked the fever, and it left her. And immediately she arose and served them.

Many Healed After Sabbath Sunset

[40]When the sun was setting, all those who had any that were sick with various diseases brought them to Him; and He laid His hands on every one of them and healed them. [41]And demons also came out of many, crying out and saying, "You are the Christ,[a] the Son of God!"

And He, rebuking *them,* did not allow them to speak, for they knew that He was the Christ.

Jesus Preaches in Galilee

[42]Now when it was day, He departed and went into a deserted place. And the crowd sought Him and came to Him, and tried to keep Him from leaving them; [43]but He said to them, "I must preach the kingdom of God to the other cities also, because for this purpose I have been sent." [44]And He was preaching in the synagogues of Galilee.[a]

4:18 [a]NU-Text omits *to heal the brokenhearted.*   **4:19** [a]Isaiah 61:1, 2   **4:23** [a]Here and elsewhere the NU-Text spelling is *Capharnaum.*
4:26 [a]Greek *Sarepta*   **4:41** [a]NU-Text omits *the Christ.*   **4:44** [a]NU-Text reads *Judea.*

Four Fishermen Called as Disciples

5 So it was, as the multitude pressed about Him to hear the word of God, that He stood by the Lake of Gennesaret, [2]and saw two boats standing by the lake; but the fishermen had gone from them and were washing *their* nets. [3]Then He got into one of the boats, which was Simon's, and asked him to put out a little from the land. And He sat down and taught the multitudes from the boat.

[4]When He had stopped speaking, He said to Simon, "Launch out into the deep and let down your nets for a catch."

[5]But Simon answered and said to Him, "Master, we have toiled all night and caught nothing; nevertheless at Your word I will let down the net." [6]And when they had done this, they caught a great number of fish, and their net was breaking. [7]So they signaled to *their* partners in the other boat to come and help them. And they came and filled both the boats, so that they began to sink. [8]When Simon Peter saw *it*, he fell down at Jesus' knees, saying, "Depart from me, for I am a sinful man, O Lord!"

[9]For he and all who were with him were astonished at the catch of fish which they had taken; [10]and so also *were* James and John, the sons of Zebedee, who were partners with Simon. And Jesus said to Simon, "Do not be afraid. From now on you will catch men." [11]So when they had brought their boats to land, they forsook all and followed Him.

Jesus Cleanses a Leper

[12]And it happened when He was in a certain city, that behold, a man who was full of leprosy saw Jesus; and he fell on *his* face and implored Him, saying, "Lord, if You are willing, You can make me clean."

[13]Then He put out *His* hand and touched him, saying, "I am willing; be cleansed." Immediately the leprosy left him. [14]And He charged him to tell no one, "But go and show yourself to the priest, and make an offering for your cleansing, as a testimony to them, just as Moses commanded."

[15]However, the report went around concerning Him all the more; and great multitudes came together to hear, and to be healed by Him of their infirmities. [16]So He Himself *often* withdrew into the wilderness and prayed.

Jesus Forgives and Heals a Paralytic

[17]Now it happened on a certain day, as He was teaching, that there were Pharisees and teachers of the law sitting by, who had come out of every town of Galilee, Judea, and Jerusalem. And the power of the Lord was *present* to heal them.[a] [18]Then behold, men brought on a bed a man who was paralyzed, whom they sought to bring in and lay before Him. [19]And when they could not find how they might bring him in, because of the crowd, they went up on the housetop and let him down with *his* bed through the tiling into the midst before Jesus.

[20]When He saw their faith, He said to him, "Man, your sins are forgiven you."

[21]And the scribes and the Pharisees began to reason, saying, "Who is this who speaks blasphemies? Who can forgive sins but God alone?"

[22]But when Jesus perceived their thoughts, He answered and said to them, "Why are you reasoning in your hearts? [23]Which is easier, to say, 'Your sins are forgiven you,' or to say, 'Rise up and walk'? [24]But that you may know that the Son of Man has power on earth to forgive sins"—He said to the man who was paralyzed, "I say to you, arise, take up your bed, and go to your house."

[25]Immediately he rose up before them, took up what he had been lying on, and departed to his own house, glorifying God. [26]And they were all amazed, and they glorified God and were filled with fear, saying, "We have seen strange things today!"

Matthew the Tax Collector

[27]After these things He went out and saw a tax collector named Levi, sitting at the tax office. And He said to him, "Follow Me." [28]So he left all, rose up, and followed Him.

[29]Then Levi gave Him a great feast in his own house. And there were a great number of tax collectors and others who sat down with them. [30]And their scribes and the Pharisees[a] complained against His disciples, saying, "Why do You eat and drink with tax collectors and sinners?"

5:17 [a]NU-Text reads *present with Him to heal.*   **5:30** [a]NU-Text reads *But the Pharisees and their scribes.*

[31]Jesus answered and said to them, "Those who are well have no need of a physician, but those who are sick. [32]I have not come to call *the* righteous, but sinners, to repentance."

➤ *Those who are well have no need of a physician, but those who are sick. I have not come to call the righteous, but sinners, to repentance.* Luke 5:31, 32

Jesus Is Questioned About Fasting

[33]Then they said to Him, "Why do[a] the disciples of John fast often and make prayers, and likewise those of the Pharisees, but Yours eat and drink?"

[34]And He said to them, "Can you make the friends of the bridegroom fast while the bridegroom is with them? [35]But the days will come when the bridegroom will be taken away from them; then they will fast in those days."

[36]Then He spoke a parable to them: "No one puts a piece from a new garment on an old one;[a] otherwise the new makes a tear, and also the piece that was *taken* out of the new does not match the old. [37]And no one puts new wine into old wineskins; or else the new wine will burst the wineskins and be spilled, and the wineskins will be ruined. [38]But new wine must be put into new wineskins, and both are preserved.[a] [39]And no one, having drunk old *wine,* immediately[a] desires new; for he says, 'The old is better.' "[b]

Jesus Is Lord of the Sabbath

6 Now it happened on the second Sabbath after the first[a] that He went through the grainfields. And His disciples plucked the heads of grain and ate *them,* rubbing *them* in *their* hands. [2]And some of the Pharisees said to them, "Why are you doing what is not lawful to do on the Sabbath?"

[3]But Jesus answering them said, "Have you not even read this, what David did when he was hungry, he and those who were with him: [4]how he went into the house of God, took and ate the showbread, and also gave some to those with him, which is not lawful for any but the priests to eat?" [5]And He said to them, "The Son of Man is also Lord of the Sabbath."

Healing on the Sabbath

[6]Now it happened on another Sabbath, also, that He entered the synagogue and taught. And ˌa man was there whose right hand was withered. [7]So the scribes and Pharisees watched Him closely, whether He would heal on the Sabbath, that they might find an accusation against Him. [8]But He knew their thoughts, and said to the man who had the withered hand, "Arise and stand here." And he arose and stood. [9]Then Jesus said to them, "I will ask you one ˌthing: Is it lawful on the Sabbath to do good or to do evil, to save life or to destroy?"[a] [10]And when He had looked around at them all, He said to the man,[a] "Stretch out your hand." And he did so, and his hand was restored as whole as the other.[b] [11]But they were filled with rage, and discussed with one another what they might do to Jesus.

The Twelve Apostles

[12]Now it came to pass in those days that He went out to the mountain to pray, and continued all night in prayer to God. [13]And when it was day, He called His disciples to *Himself;* and from them He chose twelve whom He also named apostles: [14]Simon, whom He also named Peter, and Andrew his brother; James and John; Philip and Bartholomew; [15]Matthew and Thomas; James the *son* of Alphaeus, and Simon called the Zealot; [16]Judas the *son* of James, and Judas Iscariot who also became a traitor.

Jesus Heals a Great Multitude

[17]And He came down with them and stood on a level place with a crowd of His disciples and a great multitude of people from all Judea and Jerusalem, and from the

---

5:33 [a]NU-Text omits *Why do,* making the verse a statement.   **5:36** [a]NU-Text reads *No one tears a piece from a new garment and puts it on an old one.*   **5:38** [a]NU-Text omits *and both are preserved.*   **5:39** [a]NU-Text omits *immediately.* [b]NU-Text reads *good.*   **6:1** [a]NU-Text reads *on a Sabbath.*   **6:9** [a]M-Text reads *to kill.*   **6:10** [a]NU-Text and M-Text read *to him.* [b]NU-Text omits *as whole as the other.*

seacoast of Tyre and Sidon, who came to hear Him and be healed of their diseases, [18]as well as those who were tormented with unclean spirits. And they were healed. [19]And the whole multitude sought to touch Him, for power went out from Him and healed *them* all.

The Beatitudes

[20]Then He lifted up His eyes toward His disciples, and said:

"Blessed *are you* poor,
    For yours is the kingdom of God.
[21]Blessed *are you* who hunger now,
    For you shall be filled.
Blessed *are you* who weep now,
    For you shall laugh.
[22]Blessed are you when men hate you,
    And when they exclude you,
    And revile *you,* and cast out your name
        as evil,
    For the Son of Man's sake.
[23]Rejoice in that day and leap for joy!
    For indeed your reward *is* great in
        heaven,
    For in like manner their fathers did to
        the prophets.

Jesus Pronounces Woes

[24]"But woe to you who are rich,
    For you have received your
        consolation.
[25]Woe to you who are full,
    For you shall hunger.
Woe to you who laugh now,
    For you shall mourn and weep.
[26]Woe to you[a] when all[b] men speak well of
        you,
    For so did their fathers to the false
        prophets.

Love Your Enemies

[27]"But I say to you who hear: Love your enemies, do good to those who hate you, [28]bless those who curse you, and pray for those who spitefully use you. [29]To him who strikes you on the *one* cheek, offer the other also. And from him who takes away your cloak, do not withhold *your* tunic either.

[30]Give to everyone who asks of you. And from him who takes away your goods do not ask *them* back. [31]And just as you want men to do to you, you also do to them likewise.

[32]"But if you love those who love you, what credit is that to you? For even sinners love those who love them. [33]And if you do good to those who do good to you, what credit is that to you? For even sinners do the same. [34]And if you lend *to those* from whom you hope to receive back, what credit is that to you? For even sinners lend to sinners to receive as much back. [35]But love your enemies, do good, and lend, hoping for nothing in return; and your reward will be great, and you will be sons of the Most High. For He is kind to the unthankful and evil. [36]Therefore be merciful, just as your Father also is merciful.

Do Not Judge

[37]"Judge not, and you shall not be judged. Condemn not, and you shall not be condemned. Forgive, and you will be forgiven. [38]Give, and it will be given to you: good measure, pressed down, shaken together, and running over will be put into your bosom. For with the same measure that you use, it will be measured back to you."

[39]And He spoke a parable to them: "Can the blind lead the blind? Will they not both fall into the ditch? [40]A disciple is not above his teacher, but everyone who is perfectly trained will be like his teacher. [41]And why do you look at the speck in your brother's eye, but do not perceive the plank in your own eye? [42]Or how can you say to your brother, 'Brother, let me remove the speck that *is* in your eye,' when you yourself do not see the plank that *is* in your own eye? Hypocrite! First remove the plank from your own eye, and then you will see clearly to remove the speck that is in your brother's eye.

A Tree Is Known by Its Fruit

[43]"For a good tree does not bear bad fruit, nor does a bad tree bear good fruit. [44]For every tree is known by its own fruit. For *men* do not gather figs from thorns, nor do they gather grapes from a bramble bush. [45]A good man out of the good treasure of his heart brings forth good; and an evil man out of the

6:26 [a]NU-Text and M-Text omit *to you.* [b]M-Text omits *all.*

evil treasure of his heart[a] brings forth evil. For out of the abundance of the heart his mouth speaks.

Build on the Rock

[46]"But why do you call Me 'Lord, Lord,' and not do the things which I say? [47]Whoever comes to Me, and hears My sayings and does them, I will show you whom he is like: [48]He is like a man building a house, who dug deep and laid the foundation on the rock. And when the flood arose, the stream beat vehemently against that house, and could not shake it, for it was founded on the rock.[a] [49]But he who heard and did nothing is like a man who built a house on the earth without a foundation, against which the stream beat vehemently; and immediately it fell.[a] And the ruin of that house was great."

Jesus Heals a Centurion's Servant

7 Now when He concluded all His sayings in the hearing of the people, He entered Capernaum. [2]And a certain centurion's servant, who was dear to him, was sick and ready to die. [3]So when he heard about Jesus, he sent elders of the Jews to Him, pleading with Him to come and heal his servant. [4]And when they came to Jesus, they begged Him earnestly, saying that the one for whom He should do this was deserving, [5]"for he loves our nation, and has built us a synagogue." [6]Then Jesus went with them. And when He was already not far from the house, the centurion sent friends to Him, saying to Him, "Lord, do not trouble Yourself, for I am not worthy that You should enter under my roof. [7]Therefore I did not even think myself worthy to come to You. But say the word, and my servant will be healed. [8]For I also am a man placed under authority, having soldiers under me. And I say to one, 'Go,' and he goes; and to another, 'Come,' and he comes; and to my servant, 'Do this,' and he does it."

[9]When Jesus heard these things, He marveled at him, and turned around and said to the crowd that followed Him, "I say to you, I have not found such great faith, not even in Israel!" [10]And those who were sent, returning to the house, found the servant well who had been sick.[a]

Jesus Raises the Son of the Widow of Nain

[11]Now it happened, the day after, that He went into a city called Nain; and many of His disciples went with Him, and a large crowd. [12]And when He came near the gate of the city, behold, a dead man was being carried out, the only son of his mother; and she was a widow. And a large crowd from the city was with her. [13]When the Lord saw her, He had compassion on her and said to her, "Do not weep." [14]Then He came and touched the open coffin, and those who carried him stood still. And He said, "Young man, I say to you, arise." [15]So he who was dead sat up and began to speak. And He presented him to his mother.

[16]Then fear came upon all, and they glorified God, saying, "A great prophet has risen up among us"; and, "God has visited His people." [17]And this report about Him went throughout all Judea and all the surrounding region.

John the Baptist Sends Messengers to Jesus

[18]Then the disciples of John reported to him concerning all these things. [19]And John, calling two of his disciples to him, sent them to Jesus,[a] saying, "Are You the Coming One, or do we look for another?"

↘ LEARN

7:19 • If you have ever doubted your faith, know that you're not alone. In fact, the greatest of all prophets, John, had the same problem. While he did not question the truthfulness of God's Word, he felt *very* unclear in his understanding of those truths. And the uncertainty rocked him. So if you've ever had doubts—or are having them right now—take heart! Don't feel you've failed God or have gone apostate if the working (or lack thereof) of God has confused you. John felt perplexed, too. Note, however, that he called out to Jesus with his doubt. We should do the same. *For more about* Faith, *see Luke 23:42;* Adversity, *John 6:6.*

[20]When the men had come to Him, they said, "John the Baptist has sent us to You, saying, 'Are You the Coming One, or do we look for another?'" [21]And that very hour He cured many of infirmities, afflictions, and evil spirits; and to many blind He gave sight.

[22]Jesus answered and said to them, "Go and tell John the things you have seen and

heard: that *the* blind see, *the* lame walk, *the* lepers are cleansed, *the* deaf hear, *the* dead are raised, *the* poor have the gospel preached to them. ²³And blessed is *he* who is not offended because of Me."

²⁴When the messengers of John had departed, He began to speak to the multitudes concerning John: "What did you go out into the wilderness to see? A reed shaken by the wind? ²⁵But what did you go out to see? A man clothed in soft garments? Indeed those who are gorgeously appareled and live in luxury are in kings' courts. ²⁶But what did you go out to see? A prophet? Yes, I say to you, and more than a prophet. ²⁷This is *he* of whom it is written:

'Behold, I send My messenger before Your
    face,
Who will prepare Your way before You.'ᵃ

²⁸For I say to you, among those born of women there is not a greater prophet than John the Baptist;ᵃ but he who is least in the kingdom of God is greater than he." ²⁹And when all the people heard *Him*, even the tax collectors justified God, having been baptized with the baptism of John. ³⁰But the Pharisees and lawyers rejected the will of God for themselves, not having been baptized by him.

³¹And the Lord said,ᵃ "To what then shall I liken the men of this generation, and what are they like? ³²They are like children sitting in the marketplace and calling to one another, saying:

'We played the flute for you,
    And you did not dance;
We mourned to you,
    And you did not weep.'

³³For John the Baptist came neither eating bread nor drinking wine, and you say, 'He has a demon.' ³⁴The Son of Man has come eating and drinking, and you say, 'Look, a glutton and a winebibber, a friend of tax collectors and sinners!' ³⁵But wisdom is justified by all her children."

A Sinful Woman Forgiven

³⁶Then one of the Pharisees asked Him to eat with him. And He went to the Pharisee's house, and sat down to eat. ³⁷And behold, a woman in the city who was a sinner, when she knew that *Jesus* sat at the table in the Pharisee's house, brought an alabaster flask of fragrant oil, ³⁸and stood at His feet behind *Him* weeping; and she began to wash His feet with her tears, and wiped *them* with the hair of her head; and she kissed His feet and anointed *them* with the fragrant oil. ³⁹Now when the Pharisee who had invited Him saw *this*, he spoke to himself, saying, "This Man, if He were a prophet, would know who and what manner of woman *this is* who is touching Him, for she is a sinner."

→LIVE

7:39 ● All of us are sinful through and through. Granted, some are worse than others. Some have a degree of self-control while others have none. Some try to do the right thing, while others are hell-bent on evil. But none reach God's standards. Sure, the prostitute and murderer fall short—but so do you! Perhaps they stand at the bottom of a mine and you stand at the top of the Alps. But you are no closer to touching the stars than they are. And we want to touch the Creator of the stars, who reigns in heaven in absolute perfection and holiness! *For more about* Sin, *see Luke 12:5.*

⁴⁰And Jesus answered and said to him, "Simon, I have something to say to you."

So he said, "Teacher, say it."

⁴¹"There was a certain creditor who had two debtors. One owed five hundred denarii, and the other fifty. ⁴²And when they had nothing with which to repay, he freely forgave them both. Tell Me, therefore, which of them will love him more?"

⁴³Simon answered and said, "I suppose the *one* whom he forgave more."

And He said to him, "You have rightly judged." ⁴⁴Then He turned to the woman and said to Simon, "Do you see this woman? I entered your house; you gave Me no water for My feet, but she has washed My feet with her tears and wiped *them* with the hair of her head. ⁴⁵You gave Me no kiss, but this woman has not ceased to kiss My feet since the time I came in. ⁴⁶You did not anoint My head with oil, but this woman has anointed My feet with fragrant oil. ⁴⁷Therefore I say to you, her sins, which *are* many, are forgiven, for she

---

7:27 ᵃMalachi 3:1   **7:28** ᵃNU-Text reads *there is none greater than John.*   **7:31** ᵃNU-Text and M-Text omit *And the Lord said.*

loved much. But to whom little is forgiven, *the same* loves little."

⁴⁸Then He said to her, "Your sins are forgiven."

⁴⁹And those who sat at the table with Him began to say to themselves, "Who is this who even forgives sins?"

⁵⁰Then He said to the woman, "Your faith has saved you. Go in peace."

Many Women Minister to Jesus

8 Now it came to pass, afterward, that He went through every city and village, preaching and bringing the glad tidings of the kingdom of God. And the twelve *were* with Him, ²and certain women who had been healed of evil spirits and infirmities—Mary called Magdalene, out of whom had come seven demons, ³and Joanna the wife of Chuza, Herod's steward, and Susanna, and many others who provided for Himᵃ from their substance.

The Parable of the Sower

⁴And when a great multitude had gathered, and they had come to Him from every city, He spoke by a parable: ⁵"A sower went out to sow his seed. And as he sowed, some fell by the wayside; and it was trampled down, and the birds of the air devoured it. ⁶Some fell on rock; and as soon as it sprang up, it withered away because it lacked moisture. ⁷And some fell among thorns, and the thorns sprang up with it and choked it. ⁸But others fell on good ground, sprang up, and yielded a crop a hundredfold." When He had said these things He cried, "He who has ears to hear, let him hear!"

The Purpose of Parables

⁹Then His disciples asked Him, saying, "What does this parable mean?"

¹⁰And He said, "To you it has been given to know the mysteries of the kingdom of God, but to the rest *it is given* in parables, that

'Seeing they may not see,
And hearing they may not understand.'ᵃ

The Parable of the Sower Explained

¹¹"Now the parable is this: The seed is the word of God. ¹²Those by the wayside are the ones who hear; then the devil comes and takes away the word out of their hearts, lest they should believe and be saved. ¹³But the ones on the rock *are those* who, when they hear, receive the word with joy; and these have no root, who believe for a while and in time of temptation fall away. ¹⁴Now the ones *that* fell among thorns are those who, when they have heard, go out and are choked with cares, riches, and pleasures of life, and bring no fruit to maturity. ¹⁵But the ones *that* fell on the good ground are those who, having heard the word with a noble and good heart, keep *it* and bear fruit with patience.

The Parable of the Revealed Light

¹⁶"No one, when he has lit a lamp, covers it with a vessel or puts *it* under a bed, but sets *it* on a lampstand, that those who enter may see the light. ¹⁷For nothing is secret that will not be revealed, nor *anything* hidden that will not be known and come to light. ¹⁸Therefore take heed how you hear. For whoever has, to him *more* will be given; and whoever does not have, even what he seems to have will be taken from him."

Jesus' Mother and Brothers Come to Him

¹⁹Then His mother and brothers came to Him, and could not approach Him because of the crowd. ²⁰And it was told Him *by some,* who said, "Your mother and Your brothers are standing outside, desiring to see You."

²¹But He answered and said to them, "My mother and My brothers are these who hear the word of God and do it."

Wind and Wave Obey Jesus

²²Now it happened, on a certain day, that He got into a boat with His disciples. And He said to them, "Let us cross over to the other side of the lake." And they launched out. ²³But as they sailed He fell asleep. And a windstorm came down on the lake, and they were filling *with water,* and were in jeopardy. ²⁴And they came to Him and awoke Him, saying, "Master, Master, we are perishing!"

8:3 ᵃNU-Text and M-Text read *them.*   **8:10** ᵃIsaiah 6:9

Then He arose and rebuked the wind and the raging of the water. And they ceased, and there was a calm. ²⁵But He said to them, "Where is your faith?"

And they were afraid, and marveled, saying to one another, "Who can this be? For He commands even the winds and water, and they obey Him!"

A Demon-Possessed Man Healed

²⁶Then they sailed to the country of the Gadarenes,ᵃ which is opposite Galilee. ²⁷And when He stepped out on the land, there met Him a certain man from the city who had demons for a long time. And he wore no clothes,ᵃ nor did he live in a house but in the tombs. ²⁸When he saw Jesus, he cried out, fell down before Him, and with a loud voice said, "What have I to do with You, Jesus, Son of the Most High God? I beg You, do not torment me!" ²⁹For He had commanded the unclean spirit to come out of the man. For it had often seized him, and he was kept under guard, bound with chains and shackles; and he broke the bonds and was driven by the demon into the wilderness.

³⁰Jesus asked him, saying, "What is your name?"

And he said, "Legion," because many demons had entered him. ³¹And they begged Him that He would not command them to go out into the abyss.

³²Now a herd of many swine was feeding there on the mountain. So they begged Him that He would permit them to enter them. And He permitted them. ³³Then the demons went out of the man and entered the swine, and the herd ran violently down the steep place into the lake and drowned.

³⁴When those who fed *them* saw what had happened, they fled and told *it* in the city and in the country. ³⁵Then they went out to see what had happened, and came to Jesus, and found the man from whom the demons had departed, sitting at the feet of Jesus, clothed and in his right mind. And they were afraid. ³⁶They also who had seen *it* told them by what means he who had been demon-possessed was healed. ³⁷Then the whole multitude of the surrounding region of the Gadarenesᵃ asked Him to depart from them, for they were seized with great fear. And He got into the boat and returned.

³⁸Now the man from whom the demons had departed begged Him that he might be with Him. But Jesus sent him away, saying, ³⁹"Return to your own house, and tell what great things God has done for you." And he went his way and proclaimed throughout the whole city what great things Jesus had done for him.

A Girl Restored to Life and a Woman Healed

⁴⁰So it was, when Jesus returned, that the multitude welcomed Him, for they were all waiting for Him. ⁴¹And behold, there came a man named Jairus, and he was a ruler of the synagogue. And he fell down at Jesus' feet and begged Him to come to his house, ⁴²for he had an only daughter about twelve years of age, and she was dying.

But as He went, the multitudes thronged Him. ⁴³Now a woman, having a flow of blood for twelve years, who had spent all her livelihood on physicians and could not be healed by any, ⁴⁴came from behind and touched the border of His garment. And immediately her flow of blood stopped.

⁴⁵And Jesus said, "Who touched Me?"

When all denied it, Peter and those with himᵃ said, "Master, the multitudes throng and press You, and You say, 'Who touched Me?' "ᵇ

⁴⁶But Jesus said, "Somebody touched Me, for I perceived power going out from Me." ⁴⁷Now when the woman saw that she was not hidden, she came trembling; and falling down before Him, she declared to Him in the presence of all the people the reason she had touched Him and how she was healed immediately.

⁴⁸And He said to her, "Daughter, be of good cheer;ᵃ your faith has made you well. Go in peace."

⁴⁹While He was still speaking, someone came from the ruler of the synagogue's *house,* saying to him, "Your daughter is dead. Do not trouble the Teacher."ᵃ

⁵⁰But when Jesus heard *it,* He answered him, saying, "Do not be afraid; only believe, and she will be made well." ⁵¹When He came into the house, He permitted no one to go inᵃ

<hr>

8:26 ᵃNU-Text reads *Gerasenes.*   8:27 ᵃNU-Text reads *who had demons and for a long time wore no clothes.*   8:37 ᵃNU-Text reads *Gerasenes.*
8:45 ᵃNU-Text omits *and those with him.*   ᵇNU-Text omits *And you say, 'Who touched Me?'*   8:48 ᵃNU-Text omits *be of good cheer.*
8:49 ᵃNU-Text adds *anymore.*   8:51 ᵃNU-Text adds *with Him.*

except Peter, James, and John,[b] and the father and mother of the girl. [52]Now all wept and mourned for her; but He said, "Do not weep; she is not dead, but sleeping." [53]And they ridiculed Him, knowing that she was dead.

[54]But He put them all outside,[a] took her by the hand and called, saying, "Little girl, arise." [55]Then her spirit returned, and she arose immediately. And He commanded that she be given *something* to eat. [56]And her parents were astonished, but He charged them to tell no one what had happened.

Sending Out the Twelve

9 Then He called His twelve disciples together and gave them power and authority over all demons, and to cure diseases. [2]He sent them to preach the kingdom of God and to heal the sick. [3]And He said to them, "Take nothing for the journey, neither staffs nor bag nor bread nor money; and do not have two tunics apiece.

[4]"Whatever house you enter, stay there, and from there depart. [5]And whoever will not receive you, when you go out of that city, shake off the very dust from your feet as a testimony against them."

[6]So they departed and went through the towns, preaching the gospel and healing everywhere.

Herod Seeks to See Jesus

[7]Now Herod the tetrarch heard of all that was done by Him; and he was perplexed, because it was said by some that John had risen from the dead, [8]and by some that Elijah had appeared, and by others that one of the old prophets had risen again. [9]Herod said, "John I have beheaded, but who is this of whom I hear such things?" So he sought to see Him.

Feeding the Five Thousand

[10]And the apostles, when they had returned, told Him all that they had done. Then He took them and went aside privately into a deserted place belonging to the city called Bethsaida. [11]But when the multitudes knew *it*, they followed Him; and He received them and spoke to them about the kingdom of God, and healed those who had need of healing. [12]When the day began to wear away,

the twelve came and said to Him, "Send the multitude away, that they may go into the surrounding towns and country, and lodge and get provisions; for we are in a deserted place here."

[13]But He said to them, "You give them something to eat."

And they said, "We have no more than five loaves and two fish, unless we go and buy food for all these people." [14]For there were about five thousand men.

Then He said to His disciples, "Make them sit down in groups of fifty." [15]And they did so, and made them all sit down.

[16]Then He took the five loaves and the two fish, and looking up to heaven, He blessed and broke them, and gave *them* to the disciples to set before the multitude. [17]So they all ate and were filled, and twelve baskets of the leftover fragments were taken up by them.

Peter Confesses Jesus as the Christ

[18]And it happened, as He was alone praying, *that* His disciples joined Him, and He asked them, saying, "Who do the crowds say that I am?"

[19]So they answered and said, "John the Baptist, but some *say* Elijah; and others *say* that one of the old prophets has risen again."

[20]He said to them, "But who do you say that I am?"

Peter answered and said, "The Christ of God."

Jesus Predicts His Death and Resurrection

[21]And He strictly warned and commanded them to tell this to no one, [22]saying, "The Son of Man must suffer many things, and be rejected by the elders and chief priests and scribes, and be killed, and be raised the third day."

Take Up the Cross and Follow Him

[23]Then He said to *them* all, "If anyone desires to come after Me, let him deny himself, and take up his cross daily,[a] and follow Me. [24]For whoever desires to save his life will lose it, but whoever loses his life for My sake will save it. [25]For what profit is it to a man if he gains the whole world, and is himself destroyed or lost? [26]For whoever is ashamed of

---

8:51 [b]NU-Text and M-Text read *Peter, John, and James.*   **8:54** [a]NU-Text omits *put them all outside.*   **9:23** [a]M-Text omits *daily.*

→ *If anyone desires to come after Me, let him deny himself, and take up his cross daily, and follow Me.* Luke 9:23

Me and My words, of him the Son of Man will be ashamed when He comes in His *own* glory, and *in His* Father's, and of the holy angels. ²⁷But I tell you truly, there are some standing here who shall not taste death till they see the kingdom of God."

Jesus Transfigured on the Mount

²⁸Now it came to pass, about eight days after these sayings, that He took Peter, John, and James and went up on the mountain to pray. ²⁹As He prayed, the appearance of His face was altered, and His robe *became* white *and* glistening. ³⁰And behold, two men talked with Him, who were Moses and Elijah, ³¹who appeared in glory and spoke of His decease which He was about to accomplish at Jerusalem. ³²But Peter and those with him were heavy with sleep; and when they were fully awake, they saw His glory and the two men who stood with Him. ³³Then it happened, as they were parting from Him, *that* Peter said to Jesus, "Master, it is good for us to be here; and let us make three tabernacles: one for You, one for Moses, and one for Elijah"—not knowing what he said.

³⁴While he was saying this, a cloud came and overshadowed them; and they were fearful as they entered the cloud. ³⁵And a voice came out of the cloud, saying, "This is My beloved Son.^a Hear Him!" ³⁶When the voice had ceased, Jesus was found alone. But they kept quiet, and told no one in those days any of the things they had seen.

A Boy Is Healed

³⁷Now it happened on the next day, when they had come down from the mountain, that a great multitude met Him. ³⁸Suddenly a man from the multitude cried out, saying,

"Teacher, I implore You, look on my son, for he is my only child. ³⁹And behold, a spirit seizes him, and he suddenly cries out; it convulses him so that he foams *at the mouth;* and it departs from him with great difficulty, bruising him. ⁴⁰So I implored Your disciples to cast it out, but they could not."

⁴¹Then Jesus answered and said, "O faithless and perverse generation, how long shall I be with you and bear with you? Bring your son here." ⁴²And as he was still coming, the demon threw him down and convulsed *him.* Then Jesus rebuked the unclean spirit, healed the child, and gave him back to his father.

Jesus Again Predicts His Death

⁴³And they were all amazed at the majesty of God.

But while everyone marveled at all the things which Jesus did, He said to His disciples, ⁴⁴"Let these words sink down into your ears, for the Son of Man is about to be betrayed into the hands of men." ⁴⁵But they did not understand this saying, and it was hidden from them so that they did not perceive it; and they were afraid to ask Him about this saying.

Who Is the Greatest?

⁴⁶Then a dispute arose among them as to which of them would be greatest. ⁴⁷And Jesus, perceiving the thought of their heart, took a little child and set him by Him, ⁴⁸and said to them, "Whoever receives this little child in My name receives Me; and whoever receives Me receives Him who sent Me. For he who is least among you all will be great."

Jesus Forbids Sectarianism

⁴⁹Now John answered and said, "Master, we saw someone casting out demons in Your name, and we forbade him because he does not follow with us."

⁵⁰But Jesus said to him, "Do not forbid *him,* for he who is not against us^a is on our^b side."

A Samaritan Village Rejects the Savior

⁵¹Now it came to pass, when the time had come for Him to be received up, that He

---

9:35 ^aNU-Text reads *This is My Son, the Chosen One.*   **9:50** ^aNU-Text reads *you.* ^bNU-Text reads *your.*

steadfastly set His face to go to Jerusalem, [52]and sent messengers before His face. And as they went, they entered a village of the Samaritans, to prepare for Him. [53]But they did not receive Him, because His face was *set* for the journey to Jerusalem. [54]And when His disciples James and John saw *this,* they said, "Lord, do You want us to command fire to come down from heaven and consume them, just as Elijah did?"[a]

[55]But He turned and rebuked them,[a] and said, "You do not know what manner of spirit you are of. [56]For the Son of Man did not come to destroy men's lives but to save *them.*"[a] And they went to another village.

→ *For the Son of Man did not come to destroy men's lives but to save them.* Luke 9:56

The Cost of Discipleship

[57]Now it happened as they journeyed on the road, *that* someone said to Him, "Lord, I will follow You wherever You go."

[58]And Jesus said to him, "Foxes have holes and birds of the air *have* nests, but the Son of Man has nowhere to lay *His* head."

[59]Then He said to another, "Follow Me."

But he said, "Lord, let me first go and bury my father."

→LIVE
• • • • • • • • • • • • • • • •
9:59 • This man made excuses about why he wouldn't follow Jesus. But Jesus simply said, "Follow me." You may say, "But I've tried and failed!" No, you haven't. Jesus doesn't work for some and not for others. He will change anyone, just as they are. But let me ask some questions. After you put your faith in Jesus, did you begin to study and memorize Scripture? Did you get involved in a church? Did you develop a prayer life? Did you keep His commandments? If "it" didn't work, it's you own fault, because we're not dealing with an "it," but a "Him." *For more about* Submitting to God, *see Luke 17:7–10;* How to Live Out Your Faith, *Luke 11:34–36.*

[60]Jesus said to him, "Let the dead bury their own dead, but you go and preach the kingdom of God."

[61]And another also said, "Lord, I will follow You, but let me first go *and* bid them farewell who are at my house."

[62]But Jesus said to him, "No one, having put his hand to the plow, and looking back, is fit for the kingdom of God."

The Seventy Sent Out

10 After these things the Lord appointed seventy others also,[a] and sent them two by two before His face into every city and place where He Himself was about to go. [2]Then He said to them, "The harvest truly *is* great, but the laborers *are* few; therefore pray the Lord of the harvest to send out laborers into His harvest. [3]Go your way; behold, I send you out as lambs among wolves. [4]Carry neither money bag, knapsack, nor sandals; and greet no one along the road. [5]But whatever house you enter, first say, 'Peace to this house.' [6]And if a son of peace is there, your peace will rest on it; if not, it will return to you. [7]And remain in the same house, eating and drinking such things as they give, for the laborer is worthy of his wages. Do not go from house to house. [8]Whatever city you enter, and they receive you, eat such things as are set before you. [9]And heal the sick there, and say to them, 'The kingdom of God has come near to you.' [10]But whatever city you enter, and they do not receive you, go out into its streets and say, [11]'The very dust of your city which clings to us[a] we wipe off against you. Nevertheless know this, that the kingdom of God has come near you.' [12]But[a] I say to you that it will be more tolerable in that Day for Sodom than for that city.

Woe to the Impenitent Cities

[13]"Woe to you, Chorazin! Woe to you, Bethsaida! For if the mighty works which were done in you had been done in Tyre and Sidon, they would have repented long ago, sitting in sackcloth and ashes. [14]But it will be more tolerable for Tyre and Sidon at the judgment than for you. [15]And you, Capernaum, who are exalted to heaven, will be

---

9:54 [a]NU-Text omits *just as Elijah did.* 9:55 [a]NU-Text omits the rest of this verse. 9:56 [a]NU-Text omits the first sentence of this verse.
10:1 [a]NU-Text reads *seventy-two others.* 10:11 [a]NU-Text reads *our feet.* 10:12 [a]NU-Text and M-Text omit *But.*

brought down to Hades.[a] [16]He who hears you hears Me, he who rejects you rejects Me, and he who rejects Me rejects Him who sent Me."

The Seventy Return with Joy

[17]Then the seventy[a] returned with joy, saying, "Lord, even the demons are subject to us in Your name."

[18]And He said to them, "I saw Satan fall like lightning from heaven. [19]Behold, I give you the authority to trample on serpents and scorpions, and over all the power of the enemy, and nothing shall by any means hurt you. [20]Nevertheless do not rejoice in this, that the spirits are subject to you, but rather[a] rejoice because your names are written in heaven."

Jesus Rejoices in the Spirit

[21]In that hour Jesus rejoiced in the Spirit and said, "I thank You, Father, Lord of heaven and earth, that You have hidden these things from *the* wise and prudent and revealed them to babes. Even so, Father, for so it seemed good in Your sight. [22]All[a] things have been delivered to Me by My Father, and no one knows who the Son is except the Father, and who the Father is except the Son, and *the one* to whom the Son wills to reveal *Him*."

[23]Then He turned to *His* disciples and said privately, "Blessed *are* the eyes which see the things you see; [24]for I tell you that many prophets and kings have desired to see what you see, and have not seen *it,* and to hear what you hear, and have not heard *it.*"

The Parable of the Good Samaritan

[25]And behold, a certain lawyer stood up and tested Him, saying, "Teacher, what shall I do to inherit eternal life?"

[26]He said to him, "What is written in the law? What is your reading *of it?*"

[27]So he answered and said, " '*You shall love the* LORD *your God with all your heart, with all your soul, with all your strength, and with all your mind,* '[a] and '*your neighbor as yourself.* ' "[b]

[28]And He said to him, "You have answered rightly; do this and you will live."

[29]But he, wanting to justify himself, said to Jesus, "And who is my neighbor?"

[30]Then Jesus answered and said: "A certain *man* went down from Jerusalem to Jericho, and fell among thieves, who stripped him of his clothing, wounded *him,* and departed, leaving *him* half dead. [31]Now by chance a certain priest came down that road. And when he saw him, he passed by on the other side. [32]Likewise a Levite, when he arrived at the place, came and looked, and passed by on the other side. [33]But a certain Samaritan, as he journeyed, came where he was. And when he saw him, he had compassion. [34]So he went to *him* and bandaged his wounds, pouring on oil and wine; and he set him on his own animal, brought him to an inn, and took care of him. [35]On the next day, when he departed,[a] he took out two denarii, gave *them* to the innkeeper, and said to him, 'Take care of him; and whatever more you spend, when I come again, I will repay you.' [36]So which of these three do you think was neighbor to him who fell among the thieves?"

[37]And he said, "He who showed mercy on him."

Then Jesus said to him, "Go and do likewise."

Mary and Martha Worship and Serve

[38]Now it happened as they went that He entered a certain village; and a certain woman named Martha welcomed Him into her house. [39]And she had a sister called Mary, who also sat at Jesus'[a] feet and heard His word. [40]But Martha was distracted with much serving, and she approached Him and said, "Lord, do You not care that my sister has left me to serve alone? Therefore tell her to help me."

[41]And Jesus[a] answered and said to her, "Martha, Martha, you are worried and troubled about many things. [42]But one thing is needed, and Mary has chosen that good part, which will not be taken away from her."

The Model Prayer

11 Now it came to pass, as He was praying in a certain place, when He ceased, *that* one of His disciples said

---

10:15 [a]NU-Text reads *will you be exalted to heaven? You will be thrust down to Hades!*   **10:17** [a]NU-Text reads *seventy-two.*
10:20 [a]NU-Text and M-Text omit *rather.*   **10:22** [a]M-Text reads *And turning to the disciples He said, "All . . .*   **10:27** [a]Deuteronomy 6:5
[b]Leviticus 19:18   **10:35** [a]NU-Text omits *when he departed.*   **10:39** [a]NU-Text reads *the Lord's.*   **10:41** [a]NU-Text reads *the Lord.*

to Him, "Lord, teach us to pray, as John also taught his disciples."

²So He said to them, "When you pray, say:

Our Father in heaven,ᵃ
Hallowed be Your name.
Your kingdom come.ᵇ
Your will be done
On earth as *it is* in heaven.
³Give us day by day our daily bread.
⁴And forgive us our sins,
    For we also forgive everyone who is
        indebted to us.
    And do not lead us into temptation,
    But deliver us from the evil one."ᵃ

A Friend Comes at Midnight

⁵And He said to them, "Which of you shall have a friend, and go to him at midnight and say to him, 'Friend, lend me three loaves; ⁶for a friend of mine has come to me on his journey, and I have nothing to set before him'; ⁷and he will answer from within and say, 'Do not trouble me; the door is now shut, and my children are with me in bed; I cannot rise and give to you'? ⁸I say to you, though he will not rise and give to him because he is his friend, yet because of his persistence he will rise and give him as many as he needs.

Keep Asking, Seeking, Knocking

⁹"So I say to you, ask, and it will be given to you; seek, and you will find; knock, and it will be opened to you. ¹⁰For everyone who asks receives, and he who seeks finds, and to

> **↘ LEARN**
> • • • • • • • • • • • • • • •
> 11:5–9 • In biblical times, family members tended to share a sleeping area, so if a man got up at night, he'd wake up everyone. That's why the man in Jesus' story doesn't want to get up. But Jesus is *not* comparing God to a grouchy man who wants to sleep. Jesus means that if persistence paid off for a man who beat on the door of a reluctant friend—verse 9 could be translated, "Keep asking, keep seeking, keep knocking"—certainly it will bring us blessing as we pray to a loving heavenly Father. We are His children, with Him in His house! *For more about* Prayer, *see* Acts 3:19; *the* Attributes of God, *Luke 15:19.*

> **➤** *So I say to you, ask, and it will be given to you; seek, and you will find; knock, and it will be opened to you. For everyone who asks receives, and he who seeks finds, and to him who knocks it will be opened.* Luke 11:9, 10

him who knocks it will be opened. ¹¹If a son asks for breadᵃ from any father among you, will he give him a stone? Or if *he asks* for a fish, will he give him a serpent instead of a fish? ¹²Or if he asks for an egg, will he offer him a scorpion? ¹³If you then, being evil, know how to give good gifts to your children, how much more will *your* heavenly Father give the Holy Spirit to those who ask Him!"

A House Divided Cannot Stand

¹⁴And He was casting out a demon, and it was mute. So it was, when the demon had gone out, that the mute spoke; and the multitudes marveled. ¹⁵But some of them said, "He casts out demons by Beelzebub,ᵃ the ruler of the demons."

¹⁶Others, testing *Him,* sought from Him a sign from heaven. ¹⁷But He, knowing their thoughts, said to them: "Every kingdom divided against itself is brought to desolation, and a house *divided* against a house falls. ¹⁸If Satan also is divided against himself, how will his kingdom stand? Because you say I cast out demons by Beelzebub. ¹⁹And if I cast out demons by Beelzebub, by whom do your sons cast *them* out? Therefore they will be your judges. ²⁰But if I cast out demons with the finger of God, surely the kingdom of God has come upon you. ²¹When a strong man, fully armed, guards his own palace, his goods are in peace. ²²But when a stronger than he comes upon him and overcomes him, he takes from him all his armor in which he trusted, and divides his spoils. ²³He who is not with Me is

11:2 ᵃNU-Text omits *Our* and *in heaven.* ᵇNU-Text omits the rest of this verse.   11:4 ᵃNU-Text omits *But deliver us from the evil one.*
11:11 ᵃNU-Text omits the words from *bread* through *for* in the next sentence.   11:15 ᵃNU-Text and M-Text read *Beelzebul.*

against Me, and he who does not gather with Me scatters.

An Unclean Spirit Returns

²⁴"When an unclean spirit goes out of a man, he goes through dry places, seeking rest; and finding none, he says, 'I will return to my house from which I came.' ²⁵And when he comes, he finds *it* swept and put in order. ²⁶Then he goes and takes with *him* seven other spirits more wicked than himself, and they enter and dwell there; and the last *state* of that man is worse than the first."

Keeping the Word

²⁷And it happened, as He spoke these things, that a certain woman from the crowd raised her voice and said to Him, "Blessed *is* the womb that bore You, and *the* breasts which nursed You!"

²⁸But He said, "More than that, blessed *are* those who hear the word of God and keep it!"

Seeking a Sign

²⁹And while the crowds were thickly gathered together, He began to say, "This is an evil generation. It seeks a sign, and no sign will be given to it except the sign of Jonah the prophet.ᵃ ³⁰For as Jonah became a sign to the Ninevites, so also the Son of Man will be to this generation. ³¹The queen of the South will rise up in the judgment with the men of this generation and condemn them, for she came from the ends of the earth to hear the wisdom of Solomon; and indeed a greater than Solomon *is* here. ³²The men of Nineveh will rise up in the judgment with this generation and condemn it, for they repented at the preaching of Jonah; and indeed a greater than Jonah *is* here.

The Lamp of the Body

³³"No one, when he has lit a lamp, puts *it* in a secret place or under a basket, but on a lampstand, that those who come in may see the light. ³⁴The lamp of the body is the eye. Therefore, when your eye is good, your whole body also is full of light. But when *your eye* is bad, your body also *is* full of darkness. ³⁵Therefore take heed that the light which is

in you is not darkness. ³⁶If then your whole body *is* full of light, having no part dark, *the* whole *body* will be full of light, as when the bright shining of a lamp gives you light."

⭢ LEARN
• • • • • • • • • • • • • • •

11:34–36 • Your spiritual eyesight affects everything you do. In Scripture, the eye often corresponds to the heart, so to "set the heart" and to "fix the eye" often refer to the same thing (see Ps. 119:10, 19). Jesus seems to be saying here, "Just as your eye (sight) affects your whole body, so your ambition—wherever you fix your eyes and heart—affects your whole life." A seeing eye gives light to the whole body, and a single-minded ambition to serve God gives your whole life purpose and direction. You know what you're about and you do it (see Phil. 3:13, 14). *For more about* Loving God, *see Luke 14:26;* How to Live Out Your Faith, *Luke 12:31.*

Woe to the Pharisees and Lawyers

³⁷And as He spoke, a certain Pharisee asked Him to dine with him. So He went in and sat down to eat. ³⁸When the Pharisee saw *it,* he marveled that He had not first washed before dinner.

³⁹Then the Lord said to him, "Now you Pharisees make the outside of the cup and dish clean, but your inward part is full of greed and wickedness. ⁴⁰Foolish ones! Did not He who made the outside make the inside also? ⁴¹But rather give alms of such things as you have; then indeed all things are clean to you.

⁴²"But woe to you Pharisees! For you tithe mint and rue and all manner of herbs, and pass by justice and the love of God. These you ought to have done, without leaving the others undone. ⁴³Woe to you Pharisees! For you love the best seats in the synagogues and greetings in the marketplaces. ⁴⁴Woe to you, scribes and Pharisees, hypocrites!ᵃ For you are like graves which are not seen, and the men who walk over *them* are not aware *of them.*"

⁴⁵Then one of the lawyers answered and said to Him, "Teacher, by saying these things You reproach us also."

⁴⁶And He said, "Woe to you also, lawyers! For you load men with burdens hard to bear, and you yourselves do not touch the burdens with one of your fingers. ⁴⁷Woe to you! For

11:29 ᵃNU-Text omits *the prophet.*   **11:44** ᵃNU-Text omits *scribes and Pharisees, hypocrites.*

you build the tombs of the prophets, and your fathers killed them. [48]In fact, you bear witness that you approve the deeds of your fathers; for they indeed killed them, and you build their tombs. [49]Therefore the wisdom of God also said, 'I will send them prophets and apostles, and *some* of them they will kill and persecute,' [50]that the blood of all the prophets which was shed from the foundation of the world may be required of this generation, [51]from the blood of Abel to the blood of Zechariah who perished between the altar and the temple. Yes, I say to you, it shall be required of this generation.

[52]"Woe to you lawyers! For you have taken away the key of knowledge. You did not enter in yourselves, and those who were entering in you hindered."

[53]And as He said these things to them,[a] the scribes and the Pharisees began to assail *Him* vehemently, and to cross-examine Him about many things, [54]lying in wait for Him, and seeking to catch Him in something He might say, that they might accuse Him.[a]

Beware of Hypocrisy

12 In the meantime, when an innumerable multitude of people had gathered together, so that they trampled one another, He began to say to His disciples first *of all,* "Beware of the leaven of the Pharisees, which is hypocrisy. [2]For there is nothing covered that will not be revealed, nor hidden that will not be known. [3]Therefore whatever you have spoken in the dark will be heard in the light, and what you have spoken in the ear in inner rooms will be proclaimed on the housetops.

Jesus Teaches the Fear of God

[4]"And I say to you, My friends, do not be afraid of those who kill the body, and after that have no more that they can do. [5]But I will show you whom you should fear: Fear Him who, after He has killed, has power to cast into hell; yes, I say to you, fear Him! [6]"Are not five sparrows sold for two copper coins?[a] And not one of them is forgotten before God. [7]But the very hairs of your head are all numbered. Do not fear therefore; you are of more value than many sparrows.

Confess Christ Before Men

[8]"Also I say to you, whoever confesses Me before men, him the Son of Man also will confess before the angels of God. [9]But he who denies Me before men will be denied before the angels of God.

[10]"And anyone who speaks a word against the Son of Man, it will be forgiven him; but to him who blasphemes against the Holy Spirit, it will not be forgiven. [11]"Now when they bring you to the synagogues and magistrates and authorities, do not worry about how or what you should answer, or what you should say. [12]For the Holy Spirit will teach you in that very hour what you ought to say."

The Parable of the Rich Fool

[13]Then one from the crowd said to Him, "Teacher, tell my brother to divide the inheritance with me."

[14]But He said to him, "Man, who made Me a judge or an arbitrator over you?" [15]And He said to them, "Take heed and beware of covetousness,[a] for one's life does not consist in the abundance of the things he possesses."

[16]Then He spoke a parable to them, saying: "The ground of a certain rich man yielded plentifully. [17]And he thought within himself, saying, 'What shall I do, since I have no room to store my crops?' [18]So he said, 'I will do this: I will pull down my barns and build greater, and there I will store all my crops and my goods. [19]And I will say to my soul, "Soul, you have many goods laid up for

---

11:53 [a]NU-Text reads *And when He left there.*   11:54 [a]NU-Text omits *and seeking* and *that they might accuse Him.*
12:6 [a]Greek *assarion,* a coin of very small value

many years; take your ease; eat, drink, *and* be merry." ' [20]But God said to him, 'Fool! This night your soul will be required of you; then whose will those things be which you have provided?'

[21]"So *is* he who lays up treasure for himself, and is not rich toward God."

Do Not Worry

[22]Then He said to His disciples, "Therefore I say to you, do not worry about your life, what you will eat; nor about the body, what you will put on. [23]Life is more than food, and the body *is more* than clothing. [24]Consider the ravens, for they neither sow nor reap, which have neither storehouse nor barn; and God feeds them. Of how much more value are you than the birds? [25]And which of you by worrying can add one cubit to his stature? [26]If you then are not able to do *the* least, why are you anxious for the rest? [27]Consider the lilies, how they grow: they neither toil nor spin; and yet I say to you, even Solomon in all his glory was not arrayed like one of these. [28]If then God so clothes the grass, which today is in the field and tomorrow is thrown into the oven, how much more *will He clothe* you, O *you* of little faith?

[29]"And do not seek what you should eat or what you should drink, nor have an anxious mind. [30]For all these things the nations of the world seek after, and your Father knows that you need these things. [31]But seek the kingdom of God, and all these things[a] shall be added to you.

[32]"Do not fear, little flock, for it is your Father's good pleasure to give you the kingdom. [33]Sell what you have and give alms; provide yourselves money bags which do not grow old, a treasure in the heavens that does not fail, where no thief approaches nor moth destroys. [34]For where your treasure is, there your heart will be also.

The Faithful Servant and the Evil Servant

[35]"Let your waist be girded and *your* lamps burning; [36]and you yourselves be like men who wait for their master, when he will return from the wedding, that when he comes and knocks they may open to him immediately. [37]Blessed *are* those servants whom the master, when he comes, will find watching. Assuredly, I say to you that he will gird himself and have them sit down *to eat*, and will come and serve them. [38]And if he should come in the second watch, or come in the third watch, and find *them* so, blessed are those servants. [39]But know this, that if the master of the house had known what hour the thief would come, he would have watched and[a] not allowed his house to be broken into. [40]Therefore you also be ready, for the Son of Man is coming at an hour you do not expect."

[41]Then Peter said to Him, "Lord, do You speak this parable *only* to us, or to all *people?*"

[42]And the Lord said, "Who then is that faithful and wise steward, whom *his* master will make ruler over his household, to give *them their* portion of food in due season? [43]Blessed *is* that servant whom his master will find so doing when he comes. [44]Truly, I say to you that he will make him ruler over all that he has. [45]But if that servant says in his heart, 'My master is delaying his coming,' and begins to beat the male and female servants, and to eat and drink and be drunk, [46]the master of that servant will come on a day when he is not looking for *him*, and at an hour when he is not aware, and will cut him in two and appoint *him* his portion with the unbelievers. [47]And that servant who knew his master's will, and did not prepare *himself* or do according to his will, shall be beaten with many *stripes*. [48]But he who did not know, yet committed things deserving of stripes, shall be beaten with few. For everyone to whom much is given, from him much will be required; and to whom much has been committed, of him they will ask the more.

> ↘ **LEARN**
> • • • • • • • • • • • • • • •
>
> 12:31 • To "seek first" means to give something our primary attention. So what are we to seek? The kingdom of God. And what is that? It is the rule and reign of Jesus Christ in our lives. In Matthew's account of this verse, the promise is given, "And all these things shall be added to you" (Matt. 6:33). What "things"? What we would eat, drink, and wear. When we put God first in every area of our lives, He will provide for all of our needs. So put God first in all you say and do, and let Him take care of the rest. *For more about* How to Live Out Your Faith, *see Luke 17:1–10.*

12:15 [a]NU-Text reads *all covetousness.*
12:31 [a]NU-Text reads *His kingdom, and these things.*   12:39 [a]NU-Text reads *he would not have allowed.*

Christ Brings Division

[49]"I came to send fire on the earth, and how I wish it were already kindled! [50]But I have a baptism to be baptized with, and how distressed I am till it is accomplished! [51]Do *you* suppose that I came to give peace on earth? I tell you, not at all, but rather division. [52]For from now on five in one house will be divided: three against two, and two against three. [53]Father will be divided against son and son against father, mother against daughter and daughter against mother, mother-in-law against her daughter-in-law and daughter-in-law against her mother-in-law."

Discern the Time

[54]Then He also said to the multitudes, "Whenever you see a cloud rising out of the west, immediately you say, 'A shower is coming'; and so it is. [55]And when *you see* the south wind blow, you say, 'There will be hot weather'; and there is. [56]Hypocrites! You can discern the face of the sky and of the earth, but how *is it* you do not discern this time?

Make Peace with Your Adversary

[57]"Yes, and why, even of yourselves, do you not judge what is right? [58]When you go with your adversary to the magistrate, make every effort along the way to settle with him, lest he drag you to the judge, the judge deliver you to the officer, and the officer throw you into prison. [59]I tell you, you shall not depart from there till you have paid the very last mite."

Repent or Perish

13 There were present at that season some who told Him about the Galileans whose blood Pilate had mingled with their sacrifices. [2]And Jesus answered and said to them, "Do you suppose that these Galileans were worse sinners than all *other* Galileans, because they suffered such things? [3]I tell you, no; but unless you repent you will all likewise perish. [4]Or those eighteen on whom the tower in Siloam fell and killed them, do you think that they were worse sinners than all *other* men who dwelt in Jerusalem? [5]I tell you, no; but unless you repent you will all likewise perish."

The Parable of the Barren Fig Tree

[6]He also spoke this parable: "A certain *man* had a fig tree planted in his vineyard, and he came seeking fruit on it and found none. [7]Then he said to the keeper of his vineyard, 'Look, for three years I have come seeking fruit on this fig tree and find none. Cut it down; why does it use up the ground?' [8]But he answered and said to him, 'Sir, let it alone this year also, until I dig around it and fertilize *it*. [9]And if it bears fruit, *well*. But if not, after that[a] you can cut it down.' "

A Spirit of Infirmity

[10]Now He was teaching in one of the synagogues on the Sabbath. [11]And behold, there was a woman who had a spirit of infirmity eighteen years, and was bent over and could in no way raise *herself* up. [12]But when Jesus saw her, He called *her* to *Him* and said to her, "Woman, you are loosed from your infirmity." [13]And He laid *His* hands on her, and immediately she was made straight, and glorified God.

[14]But the ruler of the synagogue answered with indignation, because Jesus had healed on the Sabbath; and he said to the crowd, "There are six days on which men ought to work; therefore come and be healed on them, and not on the Sabbath day."

[15]The Lord then answered him and said, "Hypocrite![a] Does not each one of you on the Sabbath loose his ox or donkey from the stall, and lead *it* away to water it? [16]So ought not this woman, being a daughter of Abraham, whom Satan has bound—think of it—for eighteen years, be loosed from this bond on the Sabbath?" [17]And when He said these things, all His adversaries were put to shame; and all the multitude rejoiced for all the glorious things that were done by Him.

The Parable of the Mustard Seed

[18]Then He said, "What is the kingdom of God like? And to what shall I compare it? [19]It is like a mustard seed, which a man took and put in his garden; and it grew and became a

---

13:9 [a]NU-Text reads *And if it bears fruit after that, well. But if not, you can cut it down.*   **13:15** [a]NU-Text and M-Text read *Hypocrites.*

large[a] tree, and the birds of the air nested in its branches."

The Parable of the Leaven

²⁰And again He said, "To what shall I liken the kingdom of God? ²¹It is like leaven, which a woman took and hid in three measures[a] of meal till it was all leavened."

The Narrow Way

²²And He went through the cities and villages, teaching, and journeying toward Jerusalem. ²³Then one said to Him, "Lord, are there few who are saved?"

And He said to them, ²⁴"Strive to enter through the narrow gate, for many, I say to you, will seek to enter and will not be able. ²⁵When once the Master of the house has risen up and shut the door, and you begin to stand outside and knock at the door, saying, 'Lord, Lord, open for us,' and He will answer and say to you, 'I do not know you, where you are from,' ²⁶then you will begin to say, 'We ate and drank in Your presence, and You taught in our streets.' ²⁷But He will say, 'I tell you I do not know you, where you are from. Depart from Me, all you workers of iniquity.' ²⁸There will be weeping and gnashing of teeth, when you see Abraham and Isaac and Jacob and all the prophets in the kingdom of God, and yourselves thrust out. ²⁹They will come from the east and the west, from the north and the south, and sit down in the kingdom of God. ³⁰And indeed there are last who will be first, and there are first who will be last."

³¹On that very day[a] some Pharisees came, saying to Him, "Get out and depart from here, for Herod wants to kill You."

³²And He said to them, "Go, tell that fox, 'Behold, I cast out demons and perform cures today and tomorrow, and the third day I shall be perfected.' ³³Nevertheless I must journey today, tomorrow, and the day following; for it cannot be that a prophet should perish outside of Jerusalem.

Jesus Laments over Jerusalem

³⁴"O Jerusalem, Jerusalem, the one who kills the prophets and stones those who are sent to her! How often I wanted to gather your children together, as a hen gathers her brood under her wings, but you were not willing! ³⁵See! Your house is left to you desolate; and assuredly,[a] I say to you, you shall not see Me until the time comes when you say, 'Blessed is He who comes in the name of the LORD!' "[b]

A Man with Dropsy Healed on the Sabbath

14 Now it happened, as He went into the house of one of the rulers of the Pharisees to eat bread on the Sabbath, that they watched Him closely. ²And behold, there was a certain man before Him who had dropsy. ³And Jesus, answering, spoke to the lawyers and Pharisees, saying, "Is it lawful to heal on the Sabbath?"[a]

⁴But they kept silent. And He took him and healed him, and let him go. ⁵Then He answered them, saying, "Which of you, having a donkey[a] or an ox that has fallen into a pit, will not immediately pull him out on the Sabbath day?" ⁶And they could not answer Him regarding these things.

Take the Lowly Place

⁷So He told a parable to those who were invited, when He noted how they chose the best places, saying to them: ⁸"When you are invited by anyone to a wedding feast, do not sit down in the best place, lest one more honorable than you be invited by him; ⁹and he who invited you and him come and say to you, 'Give place to this man,' and then you begin with shame to take the lowest place. ¹⁰But when you are invited, go and sit down in the lowest place, so that when he who invited you comes he may say to you, 'Friend, go up higher.' Then you will have glory in the presence of those who sit at the table with you. ¹¹For whoever exalts himself will be humbled, and he who humbles himself will be exalted."

¹²Then He also said to him who invited Him, "When you give a dinner or a supper, do not ask your friends, your brothers, your relatives, nor rich neighbors, lest they also invite you back, and you be repaid. ¹³But when you give a feast, invite the poor, the maimed, the lame, the blind. ¹⁴And you will be blessed,

13:19 ªNU-Text omits large.   13:21 ªGreek sata, approximately two pecks in all   13:31 ªNU-Text reads In that very hour.
13:35 ªNU-Text and M-Text omit assuredly.   ᵇPsalm 118:26   14:3 ªNU-Text adds or not.   14:5 ªNU-Text and M-Text read son.

because they cannot repay you; for you shall be repaid at the resurrection of the just."

The Parable of the Great Supper

[15]Now when one of those who sat at the table with Him heard these things, he said to Him, "Blessed *is* he who shall eat bread[a] in the kingdom of God!"

[16]Then He said to him, "A certain man gave a great supper and invited many, [17]and sent his servant at supper time to say to those who were invited, 'Come, for all things are now ready.' [18]But they all with one *accord* began to make excuses. The first said to him, 'I have bought a piece of ground, and I must go and see it. I ask you to have me excused.' [19]And another said, 'I have bought five yoke of oxen, and I am going to test them. I ask you to have me excused.' [20]Still another said, 'I have married a wife, and therefore I cannot come.' [21]So that servant came and reported these things to his master. Then the master of the house, being angry, said to his servant, 'Go out quickly into the streets and lanes of the city, and bring in here *the* poor and *the* maimed and *the* lame and *the* blind.' [22]And the servant said, 'Master, it is done as you commanded, and still there is room.' [23]Then the master said to the servant, 'Go out into the highways and hedges, and compel *them* to come in, that my house may be filled. [24]For I say to you that none of those men who were invited shall taste my supper.' "

Leaving All to Follow Christ

[25]Now great multitudes went with Him. And He turned and said to them, [26]"If anyone comes to Me and does not hate his father and mother, wife and children, brothers and sisters, yes, and his own life also, he cannot be My disciple. [27]And whoever does not bear his cross and come after Me cannot be My disciple. [28]For which of you, intending to build a tower, does not sit down first and count the cost, whether he has *enough* to finish *it*—

→LIVE

14:28 • While there is a cost to following Jesus, there is an even greater cost in not following Him. Whatever you give up to follow Christ will be more than made up in this life and certainly in the life to come. Jesus is saying, "Don't do this on the impulse of the moment. Count the cost." Sometimes someone will say impulsively, "I will follow Jesus," but he or she doesn't follow through on that commitment, and such a false start makes it more difficult to make a real commitment later on. Jesus is saying, "Count the cost of following Me." *For more about* Following Christ, *see John 5:6.*

[29]lest, after he has laid the foundation, and is not able to finish, all who see *it* begin to mock him, [30]saying, 'This man began to build and was not able to finish'? [31]Or what king, going to make war against another king, does not sit down first and consider whether he is able with ten thousand to meet him who comes against him with twenty thousand? [32]Or else, while the other is still a great way off, he sends a delegation and asks conditions of peace. [33]So likewise, whoever of you does not forsake all that he has cannot be My disciple.

14:15 [a]M-Text reads *dinner.*

↑GROW (LUKE 14:26)

If you want to be a fully devoted disciple of the Lord—and if you desire to grow spiritually—then you need to love Him more than anything else. Your love for God must grow so strong, so intense, that all other loves seem like hatred by comparison. All else must pale next to Him. Do you want to live your Christian life to its fullest? If so, then you must learn to put God above anyone or anything else. That is the essence of Christ's apparently harsh-sounding words in this sometimes puzzling verse. Love God more than anyone or anything else! Love the Lord Jesus Christ more than your career! Love the Lord more than your possessions! Love the Lord more than your friends! Love the Lord more than your ministry! Love the Lord more than your family! Love the Lord more than *anything in your life*—including yourself. *For more about* Loving God, *see Gal. 5:22;* Following Christ, *Luke 14:28.*

Tasteless Salt Is Worthless

[34]"Salt *is* good; but if the salt has lost its flavor, how shall it be seasoned? [35]It is neither fit for the land nor for the dunghill, *but* men throw it out. He who has ears to hear, let him hear!"

The Parable of the Lost Sheep

15 Then all the tax collectors and the sinners drew near to Him to hear Him. [2]And the Pharisees and scribes complained, saying, "This Man receives sinners and eats with them." [3]So He spoke this parable to them, saying:

[4]"What man of you, having a hundred sheep, if he loses one of them, does not leave the ninety-nine in the wilderness, and go after the one which is lost until he finds it? [5]And when he has found *it*, he lays *it* on his shoulders, rejoicing. [6]And when he comes home, he calls together *his* friends and neighbors, saying to them, 'Rejoice with me, for I have found my sheep which was lost!' [7]I say to you that likewise there will be more joy in heaven over one sinner who repents than over ninety-nine just persons who need no repentance.

The Parable of the Lost Coin

[8]"Or what woman, having ten silver coins,[a] if she loses one coin, does not light a lamp, sweep the house, and search carefully until she finds *it?* [9]And when she has found *it,* she calls *her* friends and neighbors together, saying, 'Rejoice with me, for I have found the piece which I lost!' [10]Likewise, I say to you,

➜ *I say to you that likewise there will be more joy in heaven over one sinner who repents than over ninety-nine just persons who need no repentance.* Luke 15:7

there is joy in the presence of the angels of God over one sinner who repents."

The Parable of the Lost Son

[11]Then He said: "A certain man had two sons. [12]And the younger of them said to *his* father, 'Father, give me the portion of goods that falls *to me.*' So he divided to them *his* livelihood. [13]And not many days after, the younger son gathered all together, journeyed to a far country, and there wasted his possessions with prodigal living. [14]But when he had spent all, there arose a severe famine in that land, and he began to be in want. [15]Then he went and joined himself to a citizen of that country, and he sent him into his fields to feed swine. [16]And he would gladly have filled his stomach with the pods that the swine ate, and no one gave him *anything.*

[17]"But when he came to himself, he said, 'How many of my father's hired servants have bread enough and to spare, and I perish with hunger! [18]I will arise and go to my father, and will say to him, "Father, I have sinned against

15:8 [a]Greek *drachma,* a valuable coin often worn in a ten-piece garland by married women

↓ KNOW (LUKE 15:19)
....

In this parable of the prodigal son, Jesus shows us what God is like. According to Jesus (and who is a more reliable source than Him?), God is like a loving father who misses his wayward son, who welcomes his straying children back into fellowship, as soon as those children turn from that sin. God *wants* to show us His affection, His plan, and His individual purpose. *That* is what God is like. If Jesus Himself had not told this story, it would seem almost irreverent to suggest that God would choose to lose his dignity, if only that's how he can get to his son in a crucial time of need. This all-powerful, all-knowing God *loves you.* And He welcomes you into fellowship with Him. You do not have to go through life alone. God offers you a relationship with Himself, a way to know Him intimately beyond all imagination. *For more about the* Attributes of God, *see John 1:1–5;* God's Love, *John 11:5, 6.*

heaven and before you, ¹⁹and I am no longer worthy to be called your son. Make me like one of your hired servants." '

²⁰"And he arose and came to his father. But when he was still a great way off, his father saw him and had compassion, and ran and fell on his neck and kissed him. ²¹And the son said to him, 'Father, I have sinned against heaven and in your sight, and am no longer worthy to be called your son.'

²²"But the father said to his servants, 'Bringᵃ out the best robe and put *it* on him, and put a ring on his hand and sandals on *his* feet. ²³And bring the fatted calf here and kill *it*, and let us eat and be merry; ²⁴for this my son was dead and is alive again; he was lost and is found.' And they began to be merry.

²⁵"Now his older son was in the field. And as he came and drew near to the house, he heard music and dancing. ²⁶So he called one of the servants and asked what these things meant. ²⁷And he said to him, 'Your brother has come, and because he has received him safe and sound, your father has killed the fatted calf.'

²⁸"But he was angry and would not go in. Therefore his father came out and pleaded with him. ²⁹So he answered and said to *his* father, 'Lo, these many years I have been serving you; I never transgressed your commandment at any time; and yet you never gave me a young goat, that I might make merry with my friends. ³⁰But as soon as this son of yours came, who has devoured your livelihood with harlots, you killed the fatted calf for him.'

³¹"And he said to him, 'Son, you are always with me, and all that I have is yours. ³²It was right that we should make merry and be glad, for your brother was dead and is alive again, and was lost and is found.' "

The Parable of the Unjust Steward

16 He also said to His disciples: "There was a certain rich man who had a steward, and an accusation was brought to him that this man was wasting his goods. ²So he called him and said to him, 'What is this I hear about you? Give an account of your stewardship, for you can no longer be steward.'

³"Then the steward said within himself, 'What shall I do? For my master is taking the stewardship away from me. I cannot dig; I am ashamed to beg. ⁴I have resolved what to do, that when I am put out of the stewardship, they may receive me into their houses.'

⁵"So he called every one of his master's debtors to *him*, and said to the first, 'How much do you owe my master?' ⁶And he said, 'A hundred measuresᵃ of oil.' So he said to him, 'Take your bill, and sit down quickly and write fifty.' ⁷Then he said to another, 'And how much do you owe?' So he said, 'A hundred measuresᵃ of wheat.' And he said to him, 'Take your bill, and write eighty.' ⁸So the master commended the unjust steward because he had dealt shrewdly. For the sons of this world are more shrewd in their generation than the sons of light.

⁹"And I say to you, make friends for yourselves by unrighteous mammon, that when you fail,ᵃ they may receive you into an everlasting home. ¹⁰He who *is* faithful in *what is* least is faithful also in much; and he who is unjust in *what is* least is unjust also in much. ¹¹Therefore if you have not been faithful in the unrighteous mammon, who will commit to your trust the true *riches?* ¹²And if you have not been faithful in what is another man's, who will give you what is your own?

¹³"No servant can serve two masters; for either he will hate the one and love the other, or else he will be loyal to the one and despise the other. You cannot serve God and mammon."

The Law, the Prophets, and the Kingdom

¹⁴Now the Pharisees, who were lovers of money, also heard all these things, and they derided Him. ¹⁵And He said to them, "You are those who justify yourselves before men, but God knows your hearts. For what is highly esteemed among men is an abomination in the sight of God.

¹⁶"The law and the prophets *were* until John. Since that time the kingdom of God has been preached, and everyone is pressing into it. ¹⁷And it is easier for heaven and earth to pass away than for one tittle of the law to fail.

¹⁸"Whoever divorces his wife and marries another commits adultery; and whoever marries her who is divorced from *her* husband commits adultery.

15:22 ᵃNU-Text reads *Quickly bring.* **16:6** ᵃGreek *batos,* eight or nine gallons each (Old Testament *bath*)
16:7 ᵃGreek *koros,* ten or twelve bushels each (Old Testament *kor*) **16:9** ᵃNU-Text reads *it fails.*

The Rich Man and Lazarus

[19]"There was a certain rich man who was clothed in purple and fine linen and fared sumptuously every day. [20]But there was a certain beggar named Lazarus, full of sores, who was laid at his gate, [21]desiring to be fed with the crumbs which fell[a] from the rich man's table. Moreover the dogs came and licked his sores. [22]So it was that the beggar died, and was carried by the angels to Abraham's bosom. The rich man also died and was buried. [23]And being in torments in Hades, he lifted up his eyes and saw Abraham afar off, and Lazarus in his bosom.

[24]"Then he cried and said, 'Father Abraham, have mercy on me, and send Lazarus that he may dip the tip of his finger in water and cool my tongue; for I am tormented in this flame.' [25]But Abraham said, 'Son, remember that in your lifetime you received your good things, and likewise Lazarus evil things; but now he is comforted and you are tormented. [26]And besides all this, between us and you there is a great gulf fixed, so that those who want to pass from here to you cannot, nor can those from there pass to us.'

[27]"Then he said, 'I beg you therefore, father, that you would send him to my father's house, [28]for I have five brothers, that he may testify to them, lest they also come to this place of torment.' [29]Abraham said to him, 'They have Moses and the prophets; let them hear them.' [30]And he said, 'No, father Abraham; but if one goes to them from the dead, they will repent.' [31]But he said to him, 'If they do not hear Moses and the prophets, neither will they be persuaded though one rise from the dead.' "

Jesus Warns of Offenses

17 Then He said to the disciples, "It is impossible that no offenses should come, but woe *to him* through whom they do come! [2]It would be better for him if a millstone were hung around his neck, and he were thrown into the sea, than that he should offend one of these little ones. [3]Take heed to yourselves. If your brother sins against you,[a] rebuke him; and if he repents, forgive him. [4]And if he sins against you seven times in a day, and seven times in a day returns to you,[a] saying, 'I repent,' you shall forgive him."

Faith and Duty

[5]And the apostles said to the Lord, "Increase our faith."

[6]So the Lord said, "If you have faith as a mustard seed, you can say to this mulberry tree, 'Be pulled up by the roots and be planted in the sea,' and it would obey you. [7]And which of you, having a servant plowing or tending sheep, will say to him when he has come in from the field, 'Come at once and sit down to eat'? [8]But will he not rather say to him, 'Prepare something for my supper, and gird yourself and serve me till I have eaten and drunk, and afterward you will eat and drink'? [9]Does he thank that servant because he did the things that were commanded him? I think not.[a] [10]So likewise you, when you have done all those things which you are commanded, say, 'We are unprofitable servants. We have done what was our duty to do.' "

↘ LEARN

· · · · · · · · · · · · · · ·

17:7–10 • The very fact that Jesus would call upon us to do *anything* for Him should thrill our hearts. It means He feels ownership of us. The apostle Paul often opened his letters with the words "Paul, a bondslave of Jesus Christ." He had in mind the ancient custom by which a freed slave indicated he did not want to leave his master, but would stay on to voluntarily serve him. No quibbling or negotiating. The true follower of Jesus *wants* to do His will, and as soon as he knows what it is, he gladly jumps in *and does it! For more about* How to Live Out Your Faith, *see Luke 19:45, 46;* Submitting to God, *John 6:6.*

Ten Lepers Cleansed

[11]Now it happened as He went to Jerusalem that He passed through the midst of Samaria and Galilee. [12]Then as He entered a certain village, there met Him ten men who were lepers, who stood afar off. [13]And they lifted up *their* voices and said, "Jesus, Master, have mercy on us!"

[14]So when He saw *them,* He said to them, "Go, show yourselves to the priests." And so it was that as they went, they were cleansed.

[15]And one of them, when he saw that he

16:21 [a]NU-Text reads *with what fell.*   **17:3** [a]NU-Text omits *against you.*   **17:4** [a]M-Text omits *to you.*
17:9 [a]NU-Text ends verse with *commanded;* M-Text omits *him.*

was healed, returned, and with a loud voice glorified God, [16]and fell down on *his* face at His feet, giving Him thanks. And he was a Samaritan.

[17]So Jesus answered and said, "Were there not ten cleansed? But where *are* the nine? [18]Were there not any found who returned to give glory to God except this foreigner?" [19]And He said to him, "Arise, go your way. Your faith has made you well."

The Coming of the Kingdom

[20]Now when He was asked by the Pharisees when the kingdom of God would come, He answered them and said, "The kingdom of God does not come with observation; [21]nor will they say, 'See here!' or 'See there!'[a] For indeed, the kingdom of God is within you."

[22]Then He said to the disciples, "The days will come when you will desire to see one of the days of the Son of Man, and you will not see *it.* [23]And they will say to you, 'Look here!' or 'Look there!'[a] Do not go after *them* or follow *them.* [24]For as the lightning that flashes out of one *part* under heaven shines to the other *part* under heaven, so also the Son of Man will be in His day. [25]But first He must suffer many things and be rejected by this generation. [26]And as it was in the days of Noah, so it will be also in the days of the Son of Man: [27]They ate, they drank, they married wives, they were given in marriage, until the day that Noah entered the ark, and the flood came and destroyed them all. [28]Likewise as it was also in the days of Lot: They ate, they drank, they bought, they sold, they planted, they built; [29]but on the day that Lot went out of Sodom it rained fire and brimstone from heaven and destroyed *them* all. [30]Even so will it be in the day when the Son of Man is revealed.

[31]"In that day, he who is on the housetop, and his goods *are* in the house, let him not come down to take them away. And likewise the one who is in the field, let him not turn back. [32]Remember Lot's wife. [33]Whoever seeks to save his life will lose it, and whoever loses his life will preserve it. [34]I tell you, in that night there will be two *men* in one bed: the one will be taken and the other will be left. [35]Two *women* will be grinding together: the one will be taken and the other left. [36]Two *men* will be in the field: the one will be taken and the other left."[a]

[37]And they answered and said to Him, "Where, Lord?"

So He said to them, "Wherever the body is, there the eagles will be gathered together."

The Parable of the Persistent Widow

18 Then He spoke a parable to them, that men always ought to pray and not lose heart, [2]saying: "There was in a certain city a judge who did not fear God nor regard man. [3]Now there was a widow in that city; and she came to him, saying, 'Get justice for me from my adversary.' [4]And he would not for a while; but afterward he said within himself, 'Though I do not fear God nor regard man, [5]yet because this widow troubles me I will avenge her, lest by her continual coming she weary me.' "

[6]Then the Lord said, "Hear what the unjust judge said. [7]And shall God not avenge His own elect who cry out day and night to Him, though He bears long with them? [8]I tell you that He will avenge them speedily. Nevertheless, when the Son of Man comes, will He really find faith on the earth?"

The Parable of the Pharisee and the Tax Collector

[9]Also He spoke this parable to some who trusted in themselves that they were righteous, and despised others: [10]"Two men went up to the temple to pray, one a Pharisee and the other a tax collector. [11]The Pharisee stood and prayed thus with himself, 'God, I thank You that I am not like other men—extortioners, unjust, adulterers, or even as this tax collector. [12]I fast twice a week; I give tithes of all that I possess.' [13]And the tax collector, standing afar off, would not so much as raise *his* eyes to heaven, but beat his breast, saying, 'God, be merciful to me a sinner!' [14]I tell you, this man went down to his house justified *rather* than the other; for everyone who exalts himself will be humbled, and he who humbles himself will be exalted."

Jesus Blesses Little Children

[15]Then they also brought infants to Him that He might touch them; but when the disciples saw *it,* they rebuked them. [16]But

17:21 [a]NU-Text reverses *here* and *there.*   17:23 [a]NU-Text reverses *here* and *there.*   17:36 [a]NU-Text and M-Text omit verse 36.

→LIVE
....

18:14 • Jesus suffered and died to provide our forgiveness and justification. To be justified means you are forgiven of every wrong you have done. Justification is a legal act of God declaring the guilty guiltless before God. But it also is a legal term that means, "Just as if it never happened." God forgave you of your debt and then put the riches of Christ in your account! This happens instantaneously to every person who puts his or her faith in Christ, no matter what he or she has done. It is not gradual. It is immediate (2 Cor. 6:2). *For more about New Life in Christ, see John 3:3*; Forgiveness, *Acts 2:38.*

Jesus called them to *Him* and said, "Let the little children come to Me, and do not forbid them; for of such is the kingdom of God. [17]Assuredly, I say to you, whoever does not receive the kingdom of God as a little child will by no means enter it."

Jesus Counsels the Rich Young Ruler

[18]Now a certain ruler asked Him, saying, "Good Teacher, what shall I do to inherit eternal life?"

[19]So Jesus said to him, "Why do you call Me good? No one *is* good but One, *that is,* God. [20]You know the commandments: *'Do not commit adultery,' 'Do not murder,' 'Do not steal,' 'Do not bear false witness,' 'Honor your father and your mother.' "*[a]

[21]And he said, "All these things I have kept from my youth."

[22]So when Jesus heard these things, He said to him, "You still lack one thing. Sell all that you have and distribute to the poor, and you will have treasure in heaven; and come, follow Me."

[23]But when he heard this, he became very sorrowful, for he was very rich.

With God All Things Are Possible

[24]And when Jesus saw that he became very sorrowful, He said, "How hard it is for those who have riches to enter the kingdom of God! [25]For it is easier for a camel to go through the eye of a needle than for a rich man to enter the kingdom of God."

[26]And those who heard it said, "Who then can be saved?"

[27]But He said, "The things which are impossible with men are possible with God."

[28]Then Peter said, "See, we have left all[a] and followed You."

[29]So He said to them, "Assuredly, I say to you, there is no one who has left house or parents or brothers or wife or children, for the sake of the kingdom of God, [30]who shall not receive many times more in this present time, and in the age to come eternal life."

Jesus a Third Time Predicts His Death and Resurrection

[31]Then He took the twelve aside and said to them, "Behold, we are going up to Jerusalem, and all things that are written by the prophets concerning the Son of Man will be accomplished. [32]For He will be delivered to the Gentiles and will be mocked and insulted and spit upon. [33]They will scourge *Him* and kill Him. And the third day He will rise again."

[34]But they understood none of these things; this saying was hidden from them, and they did not know the things which were spoken.

A Blind Man Receives His Sight

[35]Then it happened, as He was coming near Jericho, that a certain blind man sat by the road begging. [36]And hearing a multitude passing by, he asked what it meant. [37]So they told him that Jesus of Nazareth was passing by. [38]And he cried out, saying, "Jesus, Son of David, have mercy on me!"

[39]Then those who went before warned him that he should be quiet; but he cried out all the more, "Son of David, have mercy on me!"

[40]So Jesus stood still and commanded him to be brought to Him. And when he had come near, He asked him, [41]saying, "What do you want Me to do for you?"

He said, "Lord, that I may receive my sight."

[42]Then Jesus said to him, "Receive your sight; your faith has made you well." [43]And immediately he received his sight, and followed Him, glorifying God. And all the people, when they saw *it,* gave praise to God.

18:20 [a]Exodus 20:12–16; Deuteronomy 5:16–20   **18:28** [a]NU-Text reads *our own.*

Jesus Comes to Zacchaeus' House

19 Then *Jesus* entered and passed through Jericho. [2]Now behold, *there was* a man named Zacchaeus who was a chief tax collector, and he was rich. [3]And he sought to see who Jesus was, but could not because of the crowd, for he was of short stature. [4]So he ran ahead and climbed up into a sycamore tree to see Him, for He was going to pass that *way*. [5]And when Jesus came to the place, He looked up and saw him,[a] and said to him, "Zacchaeus, make haste and come down, for today I must stay at your house." [6]So he made haste and came down, and received Him joyfully. [7]But when they saw *it*, they all complained, saying, "He has gone to be a guest with a man who is a sinner."

[8]Then Zacchaeus stood and said to the Lord, "Look, Lord, I give half of my goods to the poor; and if I have taken anything from anyone by false accusation, I restore fourfold."

[9]And Jesus said to him, "Today salvation has come to this house, because he also is a son of Abraham; [10]for the Son of Man has come to seek and to save that which was lost."

The Parable of the Minas

[11]Now as they heard these things, He spoke another parable, because He was near Jerusalem and because they thought the kingdom of God would appear immediately. [12]Therefore He said: "A certain nobleman went into a far country to receive for himself a kingdom and to return. [13]So he called ten of his servants, delivered to them ten minas,[a] and said to them, 'Do business till I come.' [14]But his citizens hated him, and sent a delegation after him, saying, 'We will not have this *man* to reign over us.'

[15]"And so it was that when he returned, having received the kingdom, he then commanded these servants, to whom he had given the money, to be called to him, that he might know how much every man had gained by trading. [16]Then came the first, saying, 'Master, your mina has earned ten minas.' [17]And he said to him, 'Well *done*, good servant; because you were faithful in a very little, have

authority over ten cities.' [18]And the second came, saying, 'Master, your mina has earned five minas.' [19]Likewise he said to him, 'You also be over five cities.'

[20]"Then another came, saying, 'Master, here is your mina, which I have kept put away in a handkerchief. [21]For I feared you, because you are an austere man. You collect what you did not deposit, and reap what you did not sow.' [22]And he said to him, 'Out of your own mouth I will judge you, *you* wicked servant. You knew that I was an austere man, collecting what I did not deposit and reaping what I did not sow. [23]Why then did you not put my money in the bank, that at my coming I might have collected it with interest?'

[24]"And he said to those who stood by, 'Take the mina from him, and give *it* to him who has ten minas.' [25](But they said to him, 'Master, he has ten minas.') [26]'For I say to you, that to everyone who has will be given; and from him who does not have, even what he has will be taken away from him. [27]But bring here those enemies of mine, who did not want me to reign over them, and slay *them* before me.' "

The Triumphal Entry

[28]When He had said this, He went on ahead, going up to Jerusalem. [29]And it came to pass, when He drew near to Bethphage[a] and Bethany, at the mountain called Olivet, *that* He sent two of His disciples, [30]saying, "Go into the village opposite *you*, where as you enter you will find a colt tied, on which no one has ever sat. Loose it and bring *it here*. [31]And if anyone asks you, 'Why are you loosing *it?*' thus you shall say to him, 'Because the Lord has need of it.' "

[32]So those who were sent went their way and found *it* just as He had said to them. [33]But as they were loosing the colt, the owners of it said to them, "Why are you loosing the colt?"

[34]And they said, "The Lord has need of him." [35]Then they brought him to Jesus. And they threw their own clothes on the colt, and they set Jesus on him. [36]And as He went, *many* spread their clothes on the road.

[37]Then, as He was now drawing near the descent of the Mount of Olives, the whole multitude of the disciples began to rejoice

19:5 [a]NU-Text omits *and saw him*.   **19:13** [a]The *mina* (Greek *mna,* Hebrew *minah*) was worth about three months' salary.
19:29 [a]M-Text reads *Bethphage.*

and praise God with a loud voice for all the mighty works they had seen, [38]saying:

> "'Blessed is the King who comes in the
> name of the LORD!'"[a]
> Peace in heaven and glory in the highest!"

[39]And some of the Pharisees called to Him from the crowd, "Teacher, rebuke Your disciples."

[40]But He answered and said to them, "I tell you that if these should keep silent, the stones would immediately cry out."

Jesus Weeps over Jerusalem

[41]Now as He drew near, He saw the city and wept over it, [42]saying, "If you had known, even you, especially in this your day, the things *that make* for your peace! But now they are hidden from your eyes. [43]For days will come upon you when your enemies will build an embankment around you, surround you and close you in on every side, [44]and level you, and your children within you, to the ground; and they will not leave in you one stone upon another, because you did not know the time of your visitation."

Jesus Cleanses the Temple

[45]Then He went into the temple and began to drive out those who bought and sold in it,[a] [46]saying to them, "It is written, *'My house is[a] a house of prayer,'*[b] but you have made it a *'den of thieves.'*"[c]

[47]And He was teaching daily in the temple. But the chief priests, the scribes, and the leaders of the people sought to destroy Him, [48]and were unable to do anything; for all the people were very attentive to hear Him.

Jesus' Authority Questioned

20 Now it happened on one of those days, as He taught the people in the temple and preached the gospel, *that* the chief priests and the scribes, together with the elders, confronted *Him* [2]and spoke to Him, saying, "Tell us, by what authority are You doing these things? Or who is he who gave You this authority?"

[3]But He answered and said to them, "I also will ask you one thing, and answer Me: [4]The baptism of John—was it from heaven or from men?"

[5]And they reasoned among themselves, saying, "If we say, 'From heaven,' He will say, 'Why then[a] did you not believe him?' [6]But if we say, 'From men,' all the people will stone us, for they are persuaded that John was a prophet." [7]So they answered that they did not know where *it was* from.

[8]And Jesus said to them, "Neither will I tell you by what authority I do these things."

The Parable of the Wicked Vinedressers

[9]Then He began to tell the people this parable: "A certain man planted a vineyard, leased it to vinedressers, and went into a far country for a long time. [10]Now at vintagetime he sent a servant to the vinedressers, that they might give him some of the fruit of the vineyard. But the vinedressers beat him and sent *him* away empty-handed. [11]Again he sent another servant; and they beat him also, treated *him* shamefully, and sent *him* away empty-handed. [12]And again he sent a third; and they wounded him also and cast *him* out.

[13]"Then the owner of the vineyard said, 'What shall I do? I will send my beloved son. Probably they will respect *him* when they see him.' [14]But when the vinedressers saw him, they reasoned among themselves, saying, 'This is the heir. Come, let us kill him, that the inheritance may be ours.' [15]So they cast him out of the vineyard and killed *him*. Therefore what will the owner of the vineyard do to them? [16]He will come and destroy those vinedressers and give the vineyard to others."

↘ LEARN

● ● ● ● ● ● ● ● ● ● ● ● ●

19:45, 46 • This passage describes the second time Jesus cleansed the temple. After the first incident, things ran well for a time, but eventually one man set up his table again, another joined him, prices rose, and soon it was as bad as ever. In a similar way, Jesus cleanses our "temple" when we come to faith. He banishes filthy habits and gives us a new purpose and focus. But as time passes, some old things find their way back in. Our lives get cluttered with things that don't belong. Does your temple need cleansing today? If so, let Jesus clean house. *For more about* How to Live Out Your Faith, *see* John 9:4.

19:38 [a]Psalm 118:26   **19:45** [a]NU-Text reads *those who were selling.*   **19:46** [a]NU-Text reads *shall be.* [b]Isaiah 56:7 [c]Jeremiah 7:11
20:5 [a]NU-Text and M-Text omit *then.*

And when they heard *it* they said, "Certainly not!"

[17]Then He looked at them and said, "What then is this that is written:

'The stone which the builders rejected
Has become the chief cornerstone'?[a]

[18]Whoever falls on that stone will be broken; but on whomever it falls, it will grind him to powder."

[19]And the chief priests and the scribes that very hour sought to lay hands on Him, but they feared the people[a]—for they knew He had spoken this parable against them.

The Pharisees: Is It Lawful to Pay Taxes to Caesar?

[20]So they watched *Him,* and sent spies who pretended to be righteous, that they might seize on His words, in order to deliver Him to the power and the authority of the governor. [21]Then they asked Him, saying, "Teacher, we know that You say and teach rightly, and You do not show personal favoritism, but teach the way of God in truth: [22]Is it lawful for us to pay taxes to Caesar or not?"

[23]But He perceived their craftiness, and said to them, "Why do you test Me?[a] [24]Show Me a denarius. Whose image and inscription does it have?"

They answered and said, "Caesar's."

[25]And He said to them, "Render therefore to Caesar the things that are Caesar's, and to God the things that are God's."

[26]But they could not catch Him in His words in the presence of the people. And they marveled at His answer and kept silent.

The Sadducees: What About the Resurrection?

[27]Then some of the Sadducees, who deny that there is a resurrection, came to *Him* and asked Him, [28]saying: "Teacher, Moses wrote to us *that* if a man's brother dies, having a wife, and he dies without children, his brother should take his wife and raise up offspring for his brother. [29]Now there were seven brothers. And the first took a wife, and died without children. [30]And the second[a] took her as wife, and he died childless. [31]Then the third took her, and in like manner the seven also; and they left no children,[a] and died. [32]Last of all the woman died also. [33]Therefore, in the resurrection, whose wife does she become? For all seven had her as wife."

[34]Jesus answered and said to them, "The sons of this age marry and are given in marriage. [35]But those who are counted worthy to attain that age, and the resurrection from the dead, neither marry nor are given in marriage; [36]nor can they die anymore, for they are equal to the angels and are sons of God, being sons of the resurrection. [37]But even Moses showed in the *burning* bush *passage* that the dead are raised, when he called the Lord 'the God of Abraham, the God of Isaac, and the God of Jacob.'[a] [38]For He is not the God of the dead but of the living, for all live to Him."

[39]Then some of the scribes answered and said, "Teacher, You have spoken well." [40]But after that they dared not question Him anymore.

Jesus: How Can David Call His Descendant Lord?

[41]And He said to them, "How can they say that the Christ is the Son of David? [42]Now David himself said in the Book of Psalms:

'The Lord said to my Lord,
"Sit at My right hand,
[43]Till I make Your enemies Your
        footstool." '[a]

[44]Therefore David calls Him 'Lord'; how is He then his Son?"

Beware of the Scribes

[45]Then, in the hearing of all the people, He said to His disciples, [46]"Beware of the scribes, who desire to go around in long robes, love greetings in the marketplaces, the best seats in the synagogues, and the best places at feasts, [47]who devour widows' houses, and for a pretense make long prayers. These will receive greater condemnation."

The Widow's Two Mites

21 And He looked up and saw the rich putting their gifts into the treasury, [2]and He saw also a certain poor

20:17 [a]Psalm 118:22   20:19 [a]M-Text reads *but they were afraid.*   20:23 [a]NU-Text omits *Why do you test Me?*   20:30 [a]NU-Text ends verse 30 here.   20:31 [a]NU-Text and M-Text read *the seven also left no children.*   20:37 [a]Exodus 3:6, 15   20:43 [a]Psalm 110:1

widow putting in two mites. [3]So He said, "Truly I say to you that this poor widow has put in more than all; [4]for all these out of their abundance have put in offerings for God,[a] but she out of her poverty put in all the livelihood that she had."

Jesus Predicts the Destruction of the Temple

[5]Then, as some spoke of the temple, how it was adorned with beautiful stones and donations, He said, [6]"These things which you see—the days will come in which not *one* stone shall be left upon another that shall not be thrown down."

↘ LEARN

• • • • • • • • • • • • • • • •

21:6 • Two thirds of the Bible is prophecy, and half of its prophecies already have come true. That suggests we have no reason to doubt the remaining ones will happen *exactly* as predicted. Around A.D. 30, Jesus declared that not one stone of the temple would be left standing upon another. His words were literally fulfilled in A.D. 70, when the Romans built large wooden scaffolds around the temple complex, piled them high with wood and other flammable items, and set them ablaze. The intense heat caused the stones to crumble. Everything was then dismantled, exactly as Jesus predicted. God's Word is trustworthy! *For more about* God's Word, *see Luke 24:45.*

The Signs of the Times and the End of the Age

[7]So they asked Him, saying, "Teacher, but when will these things be? And what sign *will there be* when these things are about to take place?"

[8]And He said: "Take heed that you not be deceived. For many will come in My name, saying, 'I am *He,*' and, 'The time has drawn near.' Therefore[a] do not go after them. [9]But when you hear of wars and commotions, do not be terrified; for these things must come to pass first, but the end *will* not *come* immediately."

[10]Then He said to them, "Nation will rise against nation, and kingdom against kingdom. [11]And there will be great earthquakes in various places, and famines and pestilences; and there will be fearful sights and great signs from heaven. [12]But before all these things, they will lay their hands on you and persecute *you,* delivering *you* up to the synagogues and prisons. You will be brought before kings and rulers for My name's sake. [13]But it will turn out for you as an occasion for testimony. [14]Therefore settle *it* in your hearts not to meditate beforehand on what you will answer; [15]for I will give you a mouth and wisdom which all your adversaries will not be able to contradict or resist. [16]You will be betrayed even by parents and brothers, relatives and friends; and they will put *some* of you to death. [17]And you will be hated by all for My name's sake. [18]But not a hair of your head shall be lost. [19]By your patience possess your souls.

The Destruction of Jerusalem

[20]"But when you see Jerusalem surrounded by armies, then know that its desolation is near. [21]Then let those who are in Judea flee to the mountains, let those who are in the midst of her depart, and let not those who are in the country enter her. [22]For these are the days of vengeance, that all things which are written may be fulfilled. [23]But woe to those who are pregnant and to those who are nursing babies in those days! For there will be great distress in the land and wrath upon this people. [24]And they will fall by the edge of the sword, and be led away captive into all nations. And Jerusalem will be trampled by Gentiles until the times of the Gentiles are fulfilled.

The Coming of the Son of Man

[25]"And there will be signs in the sun, in the moon, and in the stars; and on the earth distress of nations, with perplexity, the sea and the waves roaring; [26]men's hearts failing them from fear and the expectation of those things which are coming on the earth, for the powers of the heavens will be shaken. [27]Then they will see the Son of Man coming in a cloud with power and great glory. [28]Now when these things begin to happen, look up and lift up your heads, because your redemption draws near."

The Parable of the Fig Tree

[29]Then He spoke to them a parable: "Look at the fig tree, and all the trees. [30]When they

21:4 [a]NU-Text omits *for God.*   21:8 [a]NU-Text omits *Therefore.*

are already budding, you see and know for yourselves that summer is now near. [31]So you also, when you see these things happening, know that the kingdom of God is near. [32]Assuredly, I say to you, this generation will by no means pass away till all things take place. [33]Heaven and earth will pass away, but My words will by no means pass away.

The Importance of Watching

[34]"But take heed to yourselves, lest your hearts be weighed down with carousing, drunkenness, and cares of this life, and that Day come on you unexpectedly. [35]For it will come as a snare on all those who dwell on the face of the whole earth. [36]Watch therefore, and pray always that you may be counted worthy[a] to escape all these things that will come to pass, and to stand before the Son of Man."

[37]And in the daytime He was teaching in the temple, but at night He went out and stayed on the mountain called Olivet. [38]Then early in the morning all the people came to Him in the temple to hear Him.

The Plot to Kill Jesus

22 Now the Feast of Unleavened Bread drew near, which is called Passover. [2]And the chief priests and the scribes sought how they might kill Him, for they feared the people.

[3]Then Satan entered Judas, surnamed Iscariot, who was numbered among the twelve. [4]So he went his way and conferred with the chief priests and captains, how he might betray Him to them. [5]And they were glad, and agreed to give him money. [6]So he promised and sought opportunity to betray Him to them in the absence of the multitude.

Jesus and His Disciples Prepare the Passover

[7]Then came the Day of Unleavened Bread, when the Passover must be killed. [8]And He sent Peter and John, saying, "Go and prepare the Passover for us, that we may eat." [9]So they said to Him, "Where do You want us to prepare?"

[10]And He said to them, "Behold, when you have entered the city, a man will meet you carrying a pitcher of water; follow him into the house which he enters. [11]Then you shall say to the master of the house, 'The Teacher says to you, "Where is the guest room where I may eat the Passover with My disciples?" ' [12]Then he will show you a large, furnished upper room; there make ready."

[13]So they went and found it just as He had said to them, and they prepared the Passover.

Jesus Institutes the Lord's Supper

[14]When the hour had come, He sat down, and the twelve[a] apostles with Him. [15]Then He said to them, "With *fervent* desire I have desired to eat this Passover with you before I suffer; [16]for I say to you, I will no longer eat of it until it is fulfilled in the kingdom of God."

[17]Then He took the cup, and gave thanks, and said, "Take this and divide *it* among yourselves; [18]for I say to you,[a] I will not drink of the fruit of the vine until the kingdom of God comes."

[19]And He took bread, gave thanks and broke *it*, and gave *it* to them, saying, "This is My body which is given for you; do this in remembrance of Me."

[20]Likewise He also *took* the cup after supper, saying, "This cup *is* the new covenant in My blood, which is shed for you. [21]But behold, the hand of My betrayer *is* with Me on the table. [22]And truly the Son of Man goes as it has been determined, but woe to that man by whom He is betrayed!"

[23]Then they began to question among themselves, which of them it was who would do this thing.

The Disciples Argue About Greatness

[24]Now there was also a dispute among them, as to which of them should be considered the greatest. [25]And He said to them, "The kings of the Gentiles exercise lordship over them, and those who exercise authority over them are called 'benefactors.' [26]But not so *among* you; on the contrary, he who is greatest among you, let him be as the younger, and he who governs as he who serves. [27]For who *is* greater, he who sits at the table, or he who serves? *Is* it not he who sits at the table? Yet I am among you as the One who serves.

[28]"But you are those who have continued with Me in My trials. [29]And I bestow upon

21:36 [a]NU-Text reads *may have strength.*   22:14 [a]NU-Text omits *twelve.*   22:18 [a]NU-Text adds *from now on.*

you a kingdom, just as My Father bestowed *one* upon Me, [30]that you may eat and drink at My table in My kingdom, and sit on thrones judging the twelve tribes of Israel."

Jesus Predicts Peter's Denial

[31]And the Lord said,[a] "Simon, Simon! Indeed, Satan has asked for you, that he may sift *you* as wheat. [32]But I have prayed for you, that your faith should not fail; and when you have returned to *Me,* strengthen your brethren."

[33]But he said to Him, "Lord, I am ready to go with You, both to prison and to death."

[34]Then He said, "I tell you, Peter, the rooster shall not crow this day before you will deny three times that you know Me."

Supplies for the Road

[35]And He said to them, "When I sent you without money bag, knapsack, and sandals, did you lack anything?"

So they said, "Nothing."

[36]Then He said to them, "But now, he who has a money bag, let him take *it,* and likewise a knapsack; and he who has no sword, let him sell his garment and buy one. [37]For I say to you that this which is written must still be accomplished in Me: *'And He was numbered with the transgressors.'*[a] For the things concerning Me have an end."

[38]So they said, "Lord, look, here *are* two swords."

And He said to them, "It is enough."

The Prayer in the Garden

[39]Coming out, He went to the Mount of Olives, as He was accustomed, and His disciples also followed Him. [40]When He came to the place, He said to them, "Pray that you may not enter into temptation."

[41]And He was withdrawn from them about a stone's throw, and He knelt down and prayed, [42]saying, "Father, if it is Your will, take this cup away from Me; nevertheless not My will, but Yours, be done." [43]Then an angel appeared to Him from heaven, strengthening Him. [44]And being in agony, He prayed more earnestly. Then His sweat became like great drops of blood falling down to the ground.[a]

[45]When He rose up from prayer, and had come to His disciples, He found them sleeping from sorrow. [46]Then He said to them, "Why do you sleep? Rise and pray, lest you enter into temptation."

Betrayal and Arrest in Gethsemane

[47]And while He was still speaking, behold, a multitude; and he who was called Judas, one of the twelve, went before them and drew near to Jesus to kiss Him. [48]But Jesus said to him, "Judas, are you betraying the Son of Man with a kiss?"

[49]When those around Him saw what was going to happen, they said to Him, "Lord, shall we strike with the sword?" [50]And one of them struck the servant of the high priest and cut off his right ear.

[51]But Jesus answered and said, "Permit even this." And He touched his ear and healed him.

[52]Then Jesus said to the chief priests, captains of the temple, and the elders who had come to Him, "Have you come out, as against a robber, with swords and clubs? [53]When I was with you daily in the temple, you did not try to seize Me. But this is your hour, and the power of darkness."

Peter Denies Jesus, and Weeps Bitterly

[54]Having arrested Him, they led *Him* and brought Him into the high priest's house. But Peter followed at a distance. [55]Now when they had kindled a fire in the midst of the courtyard and sat down together, Peter sat among them. [56]And a certain servant girl, seeing him as he sat by the fire, looked intently at him and said, "This man was also with Him."

[57]But he denied Him,[a] saying, "Woman, I do not know Him."

[58]And after a little while another saw him and said, "You also are of them."

But Peter said, "Man, I am not!"

[59]Then after about an hour had passed, another confidently affirmed, saying, "Surely this *fellow* also was with Him, for he is a Galilean."

[60]But Peter said, "Man, I do not know what you are saying!"

Immediately, while he was still speaking, the rooster[a] crowed. [61]And the Lord turned

---

22:31 [a]NU-Text omits *And the Lord said.*   22:37 [a]Isaiah 53:12   22:44 [a]NU-Text brackets verses 43 and 44 as not in the original text.
22:57 [a]NU-Text reads *denied it.*   22:60 [a]NU-Text and M-Text read *a rooster.*

and looked at Peter. Then Peter remembered the word of the Lord, how He had said to him, "Before the rooster crows,[a] you will deny Me three times." [62]So Peter went out and wept bitterly.

Jesus Mocked and Beaten

[63]Now the men who held Jesus mocked Him and beat Him. [64]And having blindfolded Him, they struck Him on the face and asked Him,[a] saying, "Prophesy! Who is the one who struck You?" [65]And many other things they blasphemously spoke against Him.

Jesus Faces the Sanhedrin

[66]As soon as it was day, the elders of the people, both chief priests and scribes, came together and led Him into their council, saying, [67]"If You are the Christ, tell us."

But He said to them, "If I tell you, you will by no means believe. [68]And if I also ask you, you will by no means answer Me or let Me go.[a] [69]Hereafter the Son of Man will sit on the right hand of the power of God."

[70]Then they all said, "Are You then the Son of God?"

So He said to them, "You rightly say that I am."

[71]And they said, "What further testimony do we need? For we have heard it ourselves from His own mouth."

Jesus Handed Over to Pontius Pilate

23 Then the whole multitude of them arose and led Him to Pilate. [2]And they began to accuse Him, saying, "We found this fellow perverting the[a] nation, and forbidding to pay taxes to Caesar, saying that He Himself is Christ, a King."

[3]Then Pilate asked Him, saying, "Are You the King of the Jews?"

He answered him and said, "It is as you say."

[4]So Pilate said to the chief priests and the crowd, "I find no fault in this Man."

[5]But they were the more fierce, saying, "He stirs up the people, teaching throughout all Judea, beginning from Galilee to this place."

Jesus Faces Herod

[6]When Pilate heard of Galilee,[a] he asked if the Man were a Galilean. [7]And as soon as he knew that He belonged to Herod's jurisdiction, he sent Him to Herod, who was also in Jerusalem at that time. [8]Now when Herod saw Jesus, he was exceedingly glad; for he had desired for a long time to see Him, because he had heard many things about Him, and he hoped to see some miracle done by Him. [9]Then he questioned Him with many words, but He answered him nothing. [10]And the chief priests and scribes stood and vehemently accused Him. [11]Then Herod, with his men of war, treated Him with contempt and mocked Him, arrayed Him in a gorgeous robe, and sent Him back to Pilate. [12]That very day Pilate and Herod became friends with each other, for previously they had been at enmity with each other.

Taking the Place of Barabbas

[13]Then Pilate, when he had called together the chief priests, the rulers, and the people, [14]said to them, "You have brought this Man to me, as one who misleads the people. And indeed, having examined Him in your presence, I have found no fault in this Man concerning those things of which you accuse Him; [15]no, neither did Herod, for I sent you back to him;[a] and indeed nothing deserving of death has been done by Him. [16]I will therefore chastise Him and release Him" [17](for it was necessary for him to release one to them at the feast).[a]

[18]And they all cried out at once, saying, "Away with this Man, and release to us Barabbas"— [19]who had been thrown into prison for a certain rebellion made in the city, and for murder.

[20]Pilate, therefore, wishing to release Jesus, again called out to them. [21]But they shouted, saying, "Crucify Him, crucify Him!"

[22]Then he said to them the third time, "Why, what evil has He done? I have found no reason for death in Him. I will therefore chastise Him and let Him go."

[23]But they were insistent, demanding with loud voices that He be crucified. And the voices of these men and of the chief priests prevailed.[a] [24]So Pilate gave sentence that it

22:61 [a]NU-Text adds today.   22:64 [a]NU-Text reads And having blindfolded Him, they asked Him.   22:68 [a]NU-Text omits also and Me or let Me go.   23:2 [a]NU-Text reads our.   23:6 [a]NU-Text omits of Galilee.   23:15 [a]NU-Text reads for he sent Him back to us. 23:17 [a]NU-Text omits verse 17.   23:23 [a]NU-Text omits and of the chief priests.

should be as they requested. ²⁵And he released to them[a] the one they requested, who for rebellion and murder had been thrown into prison; but he delivered Jesus to their will.

The King on a Cross

²⁶Now as they led Him away, they laid hold of a certain man, Simon a Cyrenian, who was coming from the country, and on him they laid the cross that he might bear *it* after Jesus.

²⁷And a great multitude of the people followed Him, and women who also mourned and lamented Him. ²⁸But Jesus, turning to them, said, "Daughters of Jerusalem, do not weep for Me, but weep for yourselves and for your children. ²⁹For indeed the days are coming in which they will say, 'Blessed *are* the barren, wombs that never bore, and breasts which never nursed!' ³⁰Then they will begin *'to say to the mountains, "Fall on us!" and to the hills, "Cover us!"'* ᵃ ³¹For if they do these things in the green wood, what will be done in the dry?"

³²There were also two others, criminals, led with Him to be put to death. ³³And when they had come to the place called Calvary, there they crucified Him, and the criminals, one on the right hand and the other on the left. ³⁴Then Jesus said, "Father, forgive them, for they do not know what they do."ᵃ

And they divided His garments and cast lots. ³⁵And the people stood looking on. But even the rulers with them sneered, saying, "He saved others; let Him save Himself if He is the Christ, the chosen of God."

³⁶The soldiers also mocked Him, coming and offering Him sour wine, ³⁷and saying, "If You are the King of the Jews, save Yourself."

³⁸And an inscription also was written over Him in letters of Greek, Latin, and Hebrew:ᵃ

THIS IS THE KING OF THE JEWS.

³⁹Then one of the criminals who were hanged blasphemed Him, saying, "If You are the Christ,[a] save Yourself and us."

⁴⁰But the other, answering, rebuked him, saying, "Do you not even fear God, seeing you are under the same condemnation? ⁴¹And we indeed justly, for we receive the due reward of our deeds; but this Man has done nothing wrong." ⁴²Then he said to Jesus, "Lord,[a] remember me when You come into Your kingdom."

⁴³And Jesus said to him, "Assuredly, I say to you, today you will be with Me in Paradise."

→LIVE
. . . .

23:42 • Genuine belief can take place in a flash, a moment. We often think that when someone comes forward in an invitation at church, that is when he becomes a believer. But the actual event of belief may have occurred much earlier. One statement may have sparked it. A sudden realization of God's love washing over a person, where he is genuinely sorry for his sin and, to the best of his ability, reaches out to Jesus and believes. Just like the thief on the cross. One moment he was mocking, the next moment he believed. Belief can come just like that. *For more about* Becoming a Christian, *see* John 1:12; Faith, *John 1:40–46.*

Jesus Dies on the Cross

⁴⁴Now it wasᵃ about the sixth hour, and there was darkness over all the earth until the ninth hour. ⁴⁵Then the sun was darkened,ᵃ and the veil of the temple was torn in two. ⁴⁶And when Jesus had cried out with a loud voice, He said, "Father, *'into Your hands I commit My spirit.'* "ᵃ Having said this, He breathed His last.

⁴⁷So when the centurion saw what had happened, he glorified God, saying, "Certainly this was a righteous Man!"

⁴⁸And the whole crowd who came together to that sight, seeing what had been done, beat their breasts and returned. ⁴⁹But all His acquaintances, and the women who followed Him from Galilee, stood at a distance, watching these things.

Jesus Buried in Joseph's Tomb

⁵⁰Now behold, *there was* a man named Joseph, a council member, a good and just man. ⁵¹He had not consented to their decision and deed. *He was* from Arimathea, a city of the Jews, who himself was also waitingᵃ for

---

23:25 ᵃNU-Text and M-Text omit *to them.*   23:30 ᵃHosea 10:8   23:34 ᵃNU-Text brackets the first sentence as a later addition.
23:38 ᵃNU-Text omits *written* and *in letters of Greek, Latin, and Hebrew.*   23:39 ᵃNU-Text reads *Are You not the Christ?*
23:42 ᵃNU-Text reads *And he said, "Jesus, remember me.*   23:44 ᵃNU-Text adds *already.*   23:45 ᵃNU-Text reads *obscured.*
23:46 ᵃPsalm 31:5   23:51 ᵃNU-Text reads *who was waiting.*

the kingdom of God. [52]This man went to Pilate and asked for the body of Jesus. [53]Then he took it down, wrapped it in linen, and laid it in a tomb *that was* hewn out of the rock, where no one had ever lain before. [54]That day was the Preparation, and the Sabbath drew near.

[55]And the women who had come with Him from Galilee followed after, and they observed the tomb and how His body was laid. [56]Then they returned and prepared spices and fragrant oils. And they rested on the Sabbath according to the commandment.

He Is Risen

24 Now on the first *day* of the week, very early in the morning, they, and certain *other women* with them,[a] came to the tomb bringing the spices which they had prepared. [2]But they found the stone rolled away from the tomb. [3]Then they went in and did not find the body of the Lord Jesus. [4]And it happened, as they were greatly[a] perplexed about this, that behold, two men stood by them in shining garments. [5]Then, as they were afraid and bowed *their* faces to the earth, they said to them, "Why do you seek the living among the dead? [6]He is not here, but is risen! Remember how He spoke to you when He was still in Galilee, [7]saying, 'The Son of Man must be delivered into the hands of sinful men, and be crucified, and the third day rise again.' "

[8]And they remembered His words. [9]Then they returned from the tomb and told all these things to the eleven and to all the rest. [10]It was Mary Magdalene, Joanna, Mary *the mother* of James, and the other *women* with them, who told these things to the apostles. [11]And their words seemed to them like idle tales, and they did not believe them. [12]But Peter arose and ran to the tomb; and stooping down, he saw the linen cloths lying[a] by themselves; and he departed, marveling to himself at what had happened.

The Road to Emmaus

[13]Now behold, two of them were traveling that same day to a village called Emmaus, which was seven miles[a] from Jerusalem. [14]And they talked together of all these things which had happened. [15]So it was, while they conversed and reasoned, that Jesus Himself drew near and went with them. [16]But their eyes were restrained, so that they did not know Him.

[17]And He said to them, "What kind of conversation *is* this that you have with one another as you walk and are sad?"[a]

[18]Then the one whose name was Cleopas answered and said to Him, "Are You the only stranger in Jerusalem, and have You not known the things which happened there in these days?"

[19]And He said to them, "What things?"

So they said to Him, "The things concerning Jesus of Nazareth, who was a Prophet mighty in deed and word before God and all the people, [20]and how the chief priests and our rulers delivered Him to be condemned to death, and crucified Him. [21]But we were hoping that it was He who was going to redeem Israel. Indeed, besides all this, today is the third day since these things happened. [22]Yes, and certain women of our company, who arrived at the tomb early, astonished us. [23]When they did not find His body, they came saying that they had also seen a vision of angels who said He was alive. [24]And certain of those *who were* with us went to the tomb and found *it* just as the women had said; but Him they did not see."

[25]Then He said to them, "O foolish ones, and slow of heart to believe in all that the prophets have spoken! [26]Ought not the Christ to have suffered these things and to enter into His glory?" [27]And beginning at Moses and all the Prophets, He expounded to them in all the Scriptures the things concerning Himself.

The Disciples' Eyes Opened

[28]Then they drew near to the village where they were going, and He indicated that He would have gone farther. [29]But they constrained Him, saying, "Abide with us, for it is toward evening, and the day is far spent." And He went in to stay with them.

[30]Now it came to pass, as He sat at the table with them, that He took bread, blessed and broke *it*, and gave it to them. [31]Then their eyes were opened and they knew Him; and He vanished from their sight.

[32]And they said to one another, "Did not our heart burn within us while He talked with us on the road, and while He opened the Scriptures to us?" [33]So they rose up that very hour and returned to Jerusalem, and found the eleven and those *who were* with them

24:1 [a]NU-Text omits *and certain other women with them.*   24:4 [a]NU-Text omits *greatly.*   24:12 [a]NU-Text omits *lying.*
24:13 [a]Literally *sixty stadia*   24:17 [a]NU-Text reads *as you walk? And they stood still, looking sad.*

gathered together, [34]saying, "The Lord is risen indeed, and has appeared to Simon!" [35]And they told about the things *that had happened* on the road, and how He was known to them in the breaking of bread.

Jesus Appears to His Disciples

[36]Now as they said these things, Jesus Himself stood in the midst of them, and said to them, "Peace to you." [37]But they were terrified and frightened, and supposed they had seen a spirit. [38]And He said to them, "Why are you troubled? And why do doubts arise in your hearts? [39]Behold My hands and My feet, that it is I Myself. Handle Me and see, for a spirit does not have flesh and bones as you see I have."

[40]When He had said this, He showed them His hands and His feet.[a] [41]But while they still did not believe for joy, and marveled, He said to them, "Have you any food here?" [42]So they gave Him a piece of a broiled fish and some honeycomb.[a] [43]And He took *it* and ate in their presence.

The Scriptures Opened

[44]Then He said to them, "These *are* the words which I spoke to you while I was still with you, that all things must be fulfilled which were written in the Law of Moses and *the* Prophets and *the* Psalms concerning Me." [45]And He opened their understanding, that they might comprehend the Scriptures. [46]Then He said to them, "Thus it is written, and thus it was necessary for the Christ

to suffer and to rise[a] from the dead the third day, [47]and that repentance and remission of sins should be preached in His name to all nations, beginning at Jerusalem. [48]And you are witnesses of these things. [49]Behold, I send the Promise of My Father upon you; but tarry in the city of Jerusalem[a] until you are endued with power from on high."

↘ LEARN

24:45 • Have you ever wondered why so many intelligent and even brilliant men, scholars who have mastered biblical languages and thoroughly studied biblical history, seem not to comprehend the central message of the Bible? They are "always learning and never able to come to the knowledge of the truth" (2 Tim. 3:7). Why? For one thing, the fact is that God not only inspired the writing of the Bible, He continues to give us understanding into its meaning. If the Spirit does not open our minds, we will never fully comprehend the Scriptures. So we must continually ask for His aid. *For more about* God's Word, *see Acts 1:1; the* Holy Spirit, *John 3:8.*

The Ascension

[50]And He led them out as far as Bethany, and He lifted up His hands and blessed them. [51]Now it came to pass, while He blessed them, that He was parted from them and carried up into heaven. [52]And they worshiped Him, and returned to Jerusalem with great joy, [53]and were continually in the temple praising and[a] blessing God. Amen.[b]

24:40 [a]Some printed New Testaments omit this verse. It is found in nearly all Greek manuscripts.   24:42 [a]NU-Text omits *and some honeycomb.*   24:46 [a]NU-Text reads *written, that the Christ should suffer and rise.*   24:49 [a]NU-Text omits *of Jerusalem.* 24:53 [a]NU-Text omits *praising and.* [b]NU-Text omits *Amen.*

↑ GROW (LUKE 24:47)

Jesus says we are to preach the gospel everywhere. But notice that we are to do more than preach who Jesus is and what He did. We are also to teach new converts to obey whatever He has commanded us. This is the endgame of our preaching. Our objective is to share the gospel with others, lead them to Christ by God's call, and then help them to get up on their feet spiritually. And then we are to go out and repeat the process. And then do it again. And again. I can tell you from long experience that when you actively help others to come to Christ and then grow spiritually, you will soon see revolutionary changes come to your own Christian life. Sharing your faith and helping others grow spiritually will help to revitalize your faith. We have a choice as Christians: evangelize or fossilize! *For more about* Sharing Your Faith, *see John 1:5;* Growing in Christ, *John 15:8.*

JOHN

INTRODUCTION//

The apostle John wrote the fourth Gospel sometime between A.D. 85–90, in order that "you may believe that Jesus is the Christ, the Son of God, and that believing you may have life in His name" (20:31). Although John's Gospel is a very personal, eyewitness account of who Jesus is and what He came to do, John does not identify himself by name. Instead, he consistently describes himself by using some form of the phrase, "the disciple whom Jesus loved."

John uses very simple language to convey his message, but the truth he presents is as rich and deep as anything in the Bible. While the other three Gospels center on key events in Jesus' life, John often focuses upon the *meaning* of those events. Consider the miracle of the feeding of the five thousand, which all four Gospels record (Matt. 14:15–21; Mark 6:31–44; Luke 9:11–17; John 6:1–13). Only John gives us Jesus' message on the "Bread of Life," which follows that miracle. Here, as elsewhere, John puts special emphasis on the deity of Jesus; so he reports Jesus' words, "I am the bread of life. He who comes to Me shall never hunger, and he who believes in Me shall never thirst" (6:35).

John does not always order his Gospel in a chronological way, but instead highlights seven miracles that Jesus performed and seven "I am" statements that the Savior made. In following this plan, John gives us a unique perspective; in fact, 90 percent of the material found in his Gospel appears nowhere else. John selected what he did in order to lead his readers to put their faith in Jesus Christ as the Messiah, the Savior of the world. For this reason, the word "believe" plays a critical role in the Gospel of John.

The Eternal Word

1 In the beginning was the Word, and the Word was with God, and the Word was God. [2]He was in the beginning with God. [3]All things were made through Him, and without Him nothing was made that was made. [4]In Him was life, and the life was the light of men. [5]And the light shines in the darkness, and the darkness did not comprehend[a] it.

⤵ LEARN
. . . .

1:5 • Those who live in darkness just don't get Christians. It mystifies them how anyone could be so committed to their faith. Even two millennia ago, when Jesus' light first shined in the darkness, the darkness could not comprehend it. In the original language, the word translated "comprehend" carries the meaning of "understood." Although you try to relate to unbelievers and don't want to be considered a fanatic, they plainly see something different about you—something major. Try as you might, unbelievers simply will not understand your faith and commitment to Christ . . . until their spiritual eyes are opened. *For more about* Sharing Your Faith, *see John 4:28, 29.*

John's Witness: The True Light

[6]There was a man sent from God, whose name *was* John. [7]This man came for a witness, to bear witness of the Light, that all through him might believe. [8]He was not that Light, but *was sent* to bear witness of that Light. [9]That was the true Light which gives light to every man coming into the world.[a]

> ➡ *But as many as received Him, to them He gave the right to become children of God, to those who believe in His name . . .* John 1:12

[10]He was in the world, and the world was made through Him, and the world did not know Him. [11]He came to His own,[a] and His own[b] did not receive Him. [12]But as many as received Him, to them He gave the right to become children of God, to those who believe in His name: [13]who were born, not of blood, nor of the will of the flesh, nor of the will of man, but of God.

➡ LIVE
. . . .

1:12 • Jesus Christ stands at the door of the human heart and knocks. We must open that door and ask Him to come into our lives. "God," you may say, "I know I am a sinner. You have exposed my spiritual nakedness. I know I can't become a Christian in my own strength—so I am coming to You on Your terms. I turn from my sin. I believe that Jesus became a man and walked among us. I believe that He died on a Cross for my sin. I put my faith in You. I choose to follow You." *For more about* Becoming a Christian, *see John 1:40–46.*

1:5 [a]Or *overcome*   1:9 [a]Or *That was the true Light which, coming into the world, gives light to every man.*
1:11 [a]That is, His own things or domain   [b]That is, His own people

↓ KNOW (JOHN 1:1–5)
. . . .

Sometimes we speak of God by describing His attributes: omniscience, omnipotence, omnipresence, sovereignty, truth, righteousness, holiness, and love. While these descriptions can help, if you *really* want to know what God is like, then look at Jesus—because He is God in human form. Jesus did not merely represent God as a glorified man; He was God Himself among us, the Messiah in human flesh, God with skin on. Jesus, who embodied all of God's attributes, walked our planet as a man and breathed our air and felt our pain. He was so knowledgeable He could predict future events; so humble He could get on His knees and wash a friend's dirty feet; so powerful He could calm the wind and waves with just a word; so approachable that children laughingly climbed into His arms. In Jesus, God spelled Himself out in language that every one of us can understand. *For more about the* Attributes of God, *see Acts 7:51.*

The Word Becomes Flesh

¹⁴And the Word became flesh and dwelt among us, and we beheld His glory, the glory as of the only begotten of the Father, full of grace and truth.

¹⁵John bore witness of Him and cried out, saying, "This was He of whom I said, 'He who comes after me is preferred before me, for He was before me.' "

¹⁶And[a] of His fullness we have all received, and grace for grace. ¹⁷For the law was given through Moses, *but* grace and truth came through Jesus Christ. ¹⁸No one has seen God at any time. The only begotten Son,[a] who is in the bosom of the Father, He has declared *Him.*

A Voice in the Wilderness

¹⁹Now this is the testimony of John, when the Jews sent priests and Levites from Jerusalem to ask him, "Who are you?"

²⁰He confessed, and did not deny, but confessed, "I am not the Christ."

²¹And they asked him, "What then? Are you Elijah?"

He said, "I am not."

"Are you the Prophet?"

And he answered, "No."

²²Then they said to him, "Who are you, that we may give an answer to those who sent us? What do you say about yourself?"

²³He said: "I *am*

'The voice of one crying in the wilderness:
"Make straight the way of the LORD," '[a]

as the prophet Isaiah said."

²⁴Now those who were sent were from the Pharisees. ²⁵And they asked him, saying, "Why then do you baptize if you are not the Christ, nor Elijah, nor the Prophet?"

²⁶John answered them, saying, "I baptize with water, but there stands One among you whom you do not know. ²⁷It is He who, coming after me, is preferred before me, whose sandal strap I am not worthy to loose."

²⁸These things were done in Bethabara[a] beyond the Jordan, where John was baptizing.

The Lamb of God

²⁹The next day John saw Jesus coming toward him, and said, "Behold! The Lamb of God who takes away the sin of the world! ³⁰This is He of whom I said, 'After me comes a Man who is preferred before me, for He was before me.' ³¹I did not know Him; but that He should be revealed to Israel, therefore I came baptizing with water."

³²And John bore witness, saying, "I saw the Spirit descending from heaven like a dove, and He remained upon Him. ³³I did not know Him, but He who sent me to baptize with water said to me, 'Upon whom you see the Spirit descending, and remaining on Him, this is He who baptizes with the Holy Spirit.' ³⁴And I have seen and testified that this is the Son of God."

The First Disciples

³⁵Again, the next day, John stood with two of his disciples. ³⁶And looking at Jesus as He walked, he said, "Behold the Lamb of God!"

³⁷The two disciples heard him speak, and they followed Jesus. ³⁸Then Jesus turned, and seeing them following, said to them, "What do you seek?"

They said to Him, "Rabbi" (which is to say, when translated, Teacher), "where are You staying?"

³⁹He said to them, "Come and see." They came and saw where He was staying, and remained with Him that day (now it was about the tenth hour).

⁴⁰One of the two who heard John *speak,* and followed Him, was Andrew, Simon Peter's brother. ⁴¹He first found his own brother Simon, and said to him, "We have found the Messiah" (which is translated, the Christ). ⁴²And he brought him to Jesus.

Now when Jesus looked at him, He said, "You are Simon the son of Jonah.[a] You shall be called Cephas" (which is translated, A Stone).

Philip and Nathanael

⁴³The following day Jesus wanted to go to Galilee, and He found Philip and said to him, "Follow Me." ⁴⁴Now Philip was from Bethsaida, the city of Andrew and Peter. ⁴⁵Philip found Nathanael and said to him, "We have found Him of whom Moses in the law, and also the prophets, wrote—Jesus of Nazareth, the son of Joseph."

1:16 [a]NU-Text reads *For.*   1:18 [a]NU-Text reads *only begotten God.*   1:23 [a]Isaiah 40:3   1:28 [a]NU-Text and M-Text read *Bethany.*
1:42 [a]NU-Text reads *John.*

⁴⁶And Nathanael said to him, "Can anything good come out of Nazareth?"

Philip said to him, "Come and see."

⁴⁷Jesus saw Nathanael coming toward Him, and said of him, "Behold, an Israelite indeed, in whom is no deceit!"

⁴⁸Nathanael said to Him, "How do You know me?"

Jesus answered and said to him, "Before Philip called you, when you were under the fig tree, I saw you."

⁴⁹Nathanael answered and said to Him, "Rabbi, You are the Son of God! You are the King of Israel!"

⁵⁰Jesus answered and said to him, "Because I said to you, 'I saw you under the fig tree,' do you believe? You will see greater things than these." ⁵¹And He said to him, "Most assuredly, I say to you, hereafter[a] you shall see heaven open, and the angels of God ascending and descending upon the Son of Man."

Water Turned to Wine

2 On the third day there was a wedding in Cana of Galilee, and the mother of Jesus was there. ²Now both Jesus and His disciples were invited to the wedding. ³And when they ran out of wine, the mother of Jesus said to Him, "They have no wine."

⁴Jesus said to her, "Woman, what does your concern have to do with Me? My hour has not yet come."

⁵His mother said to the servants, "Whatever He says to you, do *it*."

⁶Now there were set there six waterpots of stone, according to the manner of purification of the Jews, containing twenty or thirty gallons apiece. ⁷Jesus said to them, "Fill the waterpots with water." And they filled them up to the brim. ⁸And He said to them, "Draw *some* out now, and take *it* to the master of the feast." And they took *it.* ⁹When the master of the feast had tasted the water that was made wine, and did not know where it came from (but the servants who had drawn the water knew), the master of the feast called the bridegroom. ¹⁰And he said to him, "Every man at the beginning sets out the good wine, and when the *guests* have well drunk, then the inferior. You have kept the good wine until now!"

¹¹This beginning of signs Jesus did in Cana of Galilee, and manifested His glory; and His disciples believed in Him.

¹²After this He went down to Capernaum, He, His mother, His brothers, and His disciples; and they did not stay there many days.

Jesus Cleanses the Temple

¹³Now the Passover of the Jews was at hand, and Jesus went up to Jerusalem. ¹⁴And He found in the temple those who sold oxen and sheep and doves, and the money changers doing business. ¹⁵When He had made a whip of cords, He drove them all out of the temple, with the sheep and the oxen, and poured out the changers' money and overturned the tables. ¹⁶And He said to those who sold doves, "Take these things away! Do not make My Father's house a house of merchandise!" ¹⁷Then His disciples remembered that it was written, *"Zeal for Your house has eaten[a] Me up."*[b]

1:51 [a]NU-Text omits *hereafter.*   **2:17** [a]NU-Text and M-Text read *will eat.*   [b]Psalm 69:9

↑ GROW (JOHN 1:40–46)
· ·

Just as all of us have differing personalities and temperaments, so we all come to faith in different ways. Some have a tremendous emotional experience at conversion, while others may not. I didn't. When I asked the Lord to come into my life, I didn't feel a thing; so I wrongly concluded that perhaps I wasn't even converted. Emotions are not bad, of course; when you come to faith in Christ, you may experience God in a very real and profound way. But this does not happen with everyone. God wants us to live not by feeling, but by faith (see Rom. 1:17). Andrew and John found Jesus through a preacher's message. Simon Peter and Nathanael came to Jesus as the result of the personal efforts of a believer. God used no human instrument in the case of Philip—which, by the way, is the exception rather than the rule. *For more about* Faith, *see John 5:6;* Becoming a Christian, *John 3:3.*

[18]So the Jews answered and said to Him, "What sign do You show to us, since You do these things?"

[19]Jesus answered and said to them, "Destroy this temple, and in three days I will raise it up."

[20]Then the Jews said, "It has taken forty-six years to build this temple, and will You raise it up in three days?"

[21]But He was speaking of the temple of His body. [22]Therefore, when He had risen from the dead, His disciples remembered that He had said this to them;[a] and they believed the Scripture and the word which Jesus had said.

The Discerner of Hearts

[23]Now when He was in Jerusalem at the Passover, during the feast, many believed in His name when they saw the signs which He did. [24]But Jesus did not commit Himself to them, because He knew all *men*, [25]and had no need that anyone should testify of man, for He knew what was in man.

The New Birth

3 There was a man of the Pharisees named Nicodemus, a ruler of the Jews. [2]This man came to Jesus by night and said to Him, "Rabbi, we know that You are a teacher come from God; for no one can do these signs that You do unless God is with him."

[3]Jesus answered and said to him, "Most assuredly, I say to you, unless one is born again, he cannot see the kingdom of God."

[4]Nicodemus said to Him, "How can a

> **→LIVE**
>
> 3:3 • Many people today do not understand what it means to be born again, a term Jesus Himself originated. To be born again means to be "born from above." Today, the term has been pirated, emptied of meaning, dragged through the gutter, and then given back to us, minus its power. Some people say, "I am a Christian, but I am not one of those 'born agains.'" Listen! There is no such thing as a Christian who is not born again. We need a spiritual rebirth because according to Jesus, unless one is born again, he cannot see the kingdom of God. *For more about* New Life in Christ, *see John 17:21;* Becoming a Christian, *John 3:8.*

man be born when he is old? Can he enter a second time into his mother's womb and be born?"

[5]Jesus answered, "Most assuredly, I say to you, unless one is born of water and the Spirit, he cannot enter the kingdom of God. [6]That which is born of the flesh is flesh, and that which is born of the Spirit is spirit. [7]Do not marvel that I said to you, 'You must be born again.' [8]The wind blows where it wishes, and you hear the sound of it, but cannot tell where it comes from and where it goes. So is everyone who is born of the Spirit."

[9]Nicodemus answered and said to Him, "How can these things be?"

[10]Jesus answered and said to him, "Are you the teacher of Israel, and do not know these things? [11]Most assuredly, I say to you, We speak what We know and testify what We have seen, and you do not receive Our witness. [12]If I have told you earthly things and you do not believe, how will you believe if

2:22 [a]NU-Text and M-Text omit *to them.*

↓ KNOW (JOHN 3:8)

How did you become a Christian? Yes, you chose to believe in Jesus—but did you realize that something happened even before you made your decision? When you placed your faith in Christ, you did so in response to the moving of the Holy Spirit, not merely by an act of your will. The Spirit of God alone brings about the work of conversion! The Holy Spirit convicted you of your sin and showed you your need for Jesus. None of us can save ourselves, any more than a drowning man can save himself. A person about to slip under the waves has no choice but to call for help—and we must do the same. As the Holy Spirit moves in our hearts, revealing our desperate spiritual need and offering to us the forgiveness that comes from Jesus Christ, we cry out to the Lord for salvation. And He rescues us. *For more about the* Holy Spirit, *see John 16:8;* Becoming a Christian, *Acts 3:19.*

I tell you heavenly things? [13]No one has ascended to heaven but He who came down from heaven, *that is,* the Son of Man who is in heaven.[a] [14]And as Moses lifted up the serpent in the wilderness, even so must the Son of Man be lifted up, [15]that whoever believes in Him should not perish but[a] have eternal life. [16]For God so loved the world that He gave His only begotten Son, that whoever believes in Him should not perish but have everlasting life. [17]For God did not send His Son into

> **→ *For God so loved the world that He gave His only begotten Son, that whoever believes in Him should not perish but have everlasting life.* John 3:16**

the world to condemn the world, but that the world through Him might be saved. [18]"He who believes in Him is not condemned; but he who does not believe is condemned already, because he has not believed in the name of the only begotten Son of God. [19]And this is the condemnation, that the light has come into the world, and men loved darkness rather than light, because their deeds were evil. [20]For everyone practicing evil hates the light and does not come to the light, lest his deeds should be exposed. [21]But he who does the truth comes to the light, that his deeds may be clearly seen, that they have been done in God."

John the Baptist Exalts Christ

[22]After these things Jesus and His disciples came into the land of Judea, and there He remained with them and baptized. [23]Now John also was baptizing in Aenon near Salim, because there was much water there. And they came and were baptized. [24]For John had not yet been thrown into prison. [25]Then there arose a dispute between *some* of John's disciples and the Jews about purification. [26]And they came to John and said to him, "Rabbi, He who was with you beyond the Jordan, to whom you have

testified—behold, He is baptizing, and all are coming to Him!"

[27]John answered and said, "A man can receive nothing unless it has been given to him from heaven. [28]You yourselves bear me witness, that I said, 'I am not the Christ,' but, 'I have been sent before Him.' [29]He who has the bride is the bridegroom; but the friend of the bridegroom, who stands and hears him, rejoices greatly because of the bridegroom's voice. Therefore this joy of mine is fulfilled. [30]He must increase, but I *must* decrease. [31]He who comes from above is above all; he who is of the earth is earthly and speaks of the earth. He who comes from heaven is above all. [32]And what He has seen and heard, that He testifies; and no one receives His testimony. [33]He who has received His testimony has certified that God is true. [34]For He whom God has sent speaks the words of God, for God does not give the Spirit by measure. [35]The Father loves the Son, and has given all things into His hand. [36]He who believes in the Son has everlasting life; and he who does not believe the Son shall not see life, but the wrath of God abides on him."

A Samaritan Woman Meets Her Messiah

4 Therefore, when the Lord knew that the Pharisees had heard that Jesus made and baptized more disciples than John [2](though Jesus Himself did not baptize, but His disciples), [3]He left Judea and departed again to Galilee. [4]But He needed to go through Samaria.

[5]So He came to a city of Samaria which is called Sychar, near the plot of ground that Jacob gave to his son Joseph. [6]Now Jacob's well was there. Jesus therefore, being wearied from *His* journey, sat thus by the well. It was about the sixth hour.

[7]A woman of Samaria came to draw water. Jesus said to her, "Give Me a drink." [8]For His disciples had gone away into the city to buy food.

[9]Then the woman of Samaria said to Him, "How is it that You, being a Jew, ask a drink from me, a Samaritan woman?" For Jews have no dealings with Samaritans.

[10]Jesus answered and said to her, "If you knew the gift of God, and who it is who says to you, 'Give Me a drink,' you would have

---

3:13 [a]NU-Text omits *who is in heaven.*   **3:15** [a]NU-Text omits *not perish but.*

asked Him, and He would have given you living water."

¹¹The woman said to Him, "Sir, You have nothing to draw with, and the well is deep. Where then do You get that living water? ¹²Are You greater than our father Jacob, who gave us the well, and drank from it himself, as well as his sons and his livestock?"

¹³Jesus answered and said to her, "Whoever drinks of this water will thirst again,

➤ *. . . but whoever drinks of the water that I shall give him will never thirst. But the water that I shall give him will become in him a fountain of water springing up into everlasting life.* John 4:14

¹⁴but whoever drinks of the water that I shall give him will never thirst. But the water that I shall give him will become in him a fountain of water springing up into everlasting life."

¹⁵The woman said to Him, "Sir, give me this water, that I may not thirst, nor come here to draw."

¹⁶Jesus said to her, "Go, call your husband, and come here."

¹⁷The woman answered and said, "I have no husband."

Jesus said to her, "You have well said, 'I have no husband,' ¹⁸for you have had five husbands, and the one whom you now have is not your husband; in that you spoke truly."

¹⁹The woman said to Him, "Sir, I perceive that You are a prophet. ²⁰Our fathers worshiped on this mountain, and you *Jews* say that in Jerusalem is the place where one ought to worship."

²¹Jesus said to her, "Woman, believe Me, the hour is coming when you will neither on this mountain, nor in Jerusalem, worship the Father. ²²You worship what you do not know; we know what we worship, for salvation is of the Jews. ²³But the hour is coming, and now is, when the true worshipers will worship the Father in spirit and truth; for the Father is seeking such to worship Him. ²⁴God *is* Spirit,

and those who worship Him must worship in spirit and truth."

²⁵The woman said to Him, "I know that Messiah is coming" (who is called Christ). "When He comes, He will tell us all things."

²⁶Jesus said to her, "I who speak to you am *He.*"

The Whitened Harvest

²⁷And at this *point* His disciples came, and they marveled that He talked with a woman;

➤LIVE

4:28, 29 • As a social outcast, this woman came to the well at noon (v. 6). Jesus had an appointment with her. He came not to condemn her, but instead to lovingly interact with her—a serial adulterer whom no one else cared to talk to. He spoke of her deepest need, the one that drove her to sin. He refused to get sidetracked by unnecessary religious or political discussions. He kept to the subject. And so a lonely Samaritan woman became the first female evangelist of the New Testament. Despite being just moments old in her faith, she simply *had* to tell others. *For more about* Sharing Your Faith, *see John 9:4;* Jesus' Life, *John 19:26, 27.*

yet no one said, "What do You seek?" or, "Why are You talking with her?"

²⁸The woman then left her waterpot, went her way into the city, and said to the men, ²⁹"Come, see a Man who told me all things that I ever did. Could this be the Christ?" ³⁰Then they went out of the city and came to Him.

³¹In the meantime His disciples urged Him, saying, "Rabbi, eat."

³²But He said to them, "I have food to eat of which you do not know."

³³Therefore the disciples said to one another, "Has anyone brought Him *anything* to eat?"

³⁴Jesus said to them, "My food is to do the will of Him who sent Me, and to finish His work. ³⁵Do you not say, 'There are still four months and *then* comes the harvest'? Behold, I say to you, lift up your eyes and look at the fields, for they are already white for harvest! ³⁶And he who reaps receives wages, and gathers fruit for eternal life, that both he who sows and he who reaps may rejoice together. ³⁷For in this the saying is true: 'One sows and another reaps.' ³⁸I sent you to reap

that for which you have not labored; others have labored, and you have entered into their labors."

The Savior of the World

[39]And many of the Samaritans of that city believed in Him because of the word of the woman who testified, "He told me all that I *ever* did." [40]So when the Samaritans had come to Him, they urged Him to stay with them; and He stayed there two days. [41]And many more believed because of His own word.

[42]Then they said to the woman, "Now we believe, not because of what you said, for we ourselves have heard *Him* and we know that this is indeed the Christ,[a] the Savior of the world."

Welcome at Galilee

[43]Now after the two days He departed from there and went to Galilee. [44]For Jesus Himself testified that a prophet has no honor in his own country. [45]So when He came to Galilee, the Galileans received Him, having seen all the things He did in Jerusalem at the feast; for they also had gone to the feast.

A Nobleman's Son Healed

[46]So Jesus came again to Cana of Galilee where He had made the water wine. And there was a certain nobleman whose son was sick at Capernaum. [47]When he heard that Jesus had come out of Judea into Galilee, he went to Him and implored Him to come down and heal his son, for he was at the point of death. [48]Then Jesus said to him, "Unless you *people* see signs and wonders, you will by no means believe."

[49]The nobleman said to Him, "Sir, come down before my child dies!"

[50]Jesus said to him, "Go your way; your son lives." So the man believed the word that Jesus spoke to him, and he went his way. [51]And as he was now going down, his servants met him and told *him,* saying, "Your son lives!"

[52]Then he inquired of them the hour when he got better. And they said to him, "Yesterday at the seventh hour the fever left him." [53]So the father knew that *it was* at the same hour in which Jesus said to him, "Your

son lives." And he himself believed, and his whole household.

[54]This again *is* the second sign Jesus did when He had come out of Judea into Galilee.

A Man Healed at the Pool of Bethesda

5 After this there was a feast of the Jews, and Jesus went up to Jerusalem. [2]Now there is in Jerusalem by the Sheep *Gate* a pool, which is called in Hebrew, Bethesda,[a] having five porches. [3]In these lay a great multitude of sick people, blind, lame, paralyzed, waiting for the moving of the water. [4]For an angel went down at a certain time into the pool and stirred up the water; then whoever stepped in first, after the stirring of the water, was made well of whatever disease he had.[a] [5]Now a certain man was there who had an infirmity thirty-eight years. [6]When Jesus saw him lying there, and knew that he already had been *in that condition* a long time, He said to him, "Do you want to be made well?"

> ↘ **LEARN**
> . . . .
> 5:6 • Where are you in life? Do you need a change spiritually? Jesus asked the lame man, "Do you want to be made well?" In other words, "Are you willing to place yourself, just as you are, in My hands? Are you ready for Me to do for you what you cannot do for yourself?" So long as we think we can work it out on our own, we'll never get anywhere. But if you are willing to make a break with the past and follow Him, then you will see things happen in your life that you never thought possible. *For more about* Faith, *see John 6:6;* Following Christ, *Acts 26:19, 20.*

[7]The sick man answered Him, "Sir, I have no man to put me into the pool when the water is stirred up; but while I am coming, another steps down before me."

[8]Jesus said to him, "Rise, take up your bed and walk." [9]And immediately the man was made well, took up his bed, and walked.

And that day was the Sabbath. [10]The Jews therefore said to him who was cured, "It is the Sabbath; it is not lawful for you to carry your bed."

[11]He answered them, "He who made me well said to me, 'Take up your bed and walk.' "

4:42 [a]NU-Text omits *the Christ.*   5:2 [a]NU-Text reads *Bethzatha.*
5:4 [a]NU-Text omits *waiting for the moving of the water* at the end of verse 3, and all of verse 4.

[12]Then they asked him, "Who is the Man who said to you, 'Take up your bed and walk'?" [13]But the one who was healed did not know who it was, for Jesus had withdrawn, a multitude being in *that* place. [14]Afterward Jesus found him in the temple, and said to him, "See, you have been made well. Sin no more, lest a worse thing come upon you."

[15]The man departed and told the Jews that it was Jesus who had made him well.

Honor the Father and the Son

[16]For this reason the Jews persecuted Jesus, and sought to kill Him,[a] because He had done these things on the Sabbath. [17]But Jesus answered them, "My Father has been working until now, and I have been working."

[18]Therefore the Jews sought all the more to kill Him, because He not only broke the Sabbath, but also said that God was His Father, making Himself equal with God. [19]Then Jesus answered and said to them, "Most assuredly, I say to you, the Son can do nothing of Himself, but what He sees the Father do; for whatever He does, the Son also does in like manner. [20]For the Father loves the Son, and shows Him all things that He Himself does; and He will show Him greater works than these, that you may marvel. [21]For as the Father raises the dead and gives life to *them,* even so the Son gives life to whom He will. [22]For the Father judges no one, but has committed all judgment to the Son, [23]that all should honor the Son just as they honor the Father. He who does not honor the Son does not honor the Father who sent Him.

Life and Judgment Are Through the Son

[24]"Most assuredly, I say to you, he who hears My word and believes in Him who sent Me has everlasting life, and shall not come into judgment, but has passed from death into life. [25]Most assuredly, I say to you, the hour is coming, and now is, when the dead will hear the voice of the Son of God; and those who hear will live. [26]For as the Father has life in Himself, so He has granted the Son to have life in Himself, [27]and has given Him authority to execute judgment also, because He is the Son of Man. [28]Do not marvel at this; for the hour is coming in which all who are in the graves will hear His voice [29]and come

> ➡ *Most assuredly, I say to you, he who hears My word and believes in Him who sent Me has everlasting life, and shall not come into judgment, but has passed from death into life.* John 5:24

forth—those who have done good, to the resurrection of life, and those who have done evil, to the resurrection of condemnation. [30]I can of Myself do nothing. As I hear, I judge; and My judgment is righteous, because I do not seek My own will but the will of the Father who sent Me.

The Fourfold Witness

[31]"If I bear witness of Myself, My witness is not true. [32]There is another who bears witness of Me, and I know that the witness which He witnesses of Me is true. [33]You have sent to John, and he has borne witness to the truth. [34]Yet I do not receive testimony from man, but I say these things that you may be saved. [35]He was the burning and shining lamp, and you were willing for a time to rejoice in his light. [36]But I have a greater witness than John's; for the works which the Father has given Me to finish—the very works that I do—bear witness of Me, that the Father has sent Me. [37]And the Father Himself, who sent Me, has testified of Me. You have neither heard His voice at any time, nor seen His form. [38]But you do not have His word abiding in you, because whom He sent, Him you do not believe. [39]You search the Scriptures, for in them you think you have eternal life; and these are they which testify of Me. [40]But you are not willing to come to Me that you may have life.

[41]"I do not receive honor from men. [42]But I know you, that you do not have the love of God in you. [43]I have come in My Father's name, and you do not receive Me; if another comes in his own name, him you will receive. [44]How can you believe, who receive honor from one another, and do not seek the honor that *comes* from the only God? [45]Do not think

5:16 [a]NU-Text omits *and sought to kill Him.*

that I shall accuse you to the Father; there is *one* who accuses you—Moses, in whom you trust. [46]For if you believed Moses, you would believe Me; for he wrote about Me. [47]But if you do not believe his writings, how will you believe My words?"

Feeding the Five Thousand

6 After these things Jesus went over the Sea of Galilee, which is *the Sea* of Tiberias. [2]Then a great multitude followed Him, because they saw His signs which He performed on those who were diseased. [3]And Jesus went up on the mountain, and there He sat with His disciples.

[4]Now the Passover, a feast of the Jews, was near. [5]Then Jesus lifted up *His* eyes, and seeing a great multitude coming toward Him, He said to Philip, "Where shall we buy bread, that these may eat?" [6]But this He said to test him, for He Himself knew what He would do.

> **↘ LEARN**
> • • • • • • • • • • • • • • • • • •
> 6:6 • The only way to pass divine tests is to recognize your utter inability to solve them on your own. Instead, you are to cast yourself on God and on Him alone. No backup plan—just trust in the Lord. When that unexpected bill comes in the mail and you wonder, *How will we ever pay this?* When a problem causes you to say, "I don't think I can make it another day"—can you trust God? You must. God *will* allow you to enter situations in which the only way out is Him. Then He will get the glory. *For more about* Adversity, *see John 11:5, 6;* Submitting to God, *John 12:24, 25;* Faith, *John 12:24, 25.*

[7]Philip answered Him, "Two hundred denarii worth of bread is not sufficient for them, that every one of them may have a little."

[8]One of His disciples, Andrew, Simon Peter's brother, said to Him, [9]"There is a lad here who has five barley loaves and two small fish, but what are they among so many?"

[10]Then Jesus said, "Make the people sit down." Now there was much grass in the place. So the men sat down, in number about five thousand. [11]And Jesus took the loaves, and when He had given thanks He distributed *them* to the disciples, and the disciples[a] to those sitting down; and likewise the fish,

as much as they wanted. [12]So when they were filled, He said to His disciples, "Gather up the fragments that remain, so that nothing is lost." [13]Therefore they gathered *them* up, and filled twelve baskets with the fragments of the five barley loaves which were left over by those who had eaten. [14]Then those men, when they had seen the sign that Jesus did, said, "This is truly the Prophet who is to come into the world."

Jesus Walks on the Sea

[15]Therefore when Jesus perceived that they were about to come and take Him by force to make Him king, He departed again to the mountain by Himself alone.

[16]Now when evening came, His disciples went down to the sea, [17]got into the boat, and went over the sea toward Capernaum. And it was already dark, and Jesus had not come to them. [18]Then the sea arose because a great wind was blowing. [19]So when they had rowed about three or four miles,[a] they saw Jesus walking on the sea and drawing near the boat; and they were afraid. [20]But He said to them, "It is I; do not be afraid." [21]Then they willingly received Him into the boat, and immediately the boat was at the land where they were going.

The Bread from Heaven

[22]On the following day, when the people who were standing on the other side of the sea saw that there was no other boat there, except that one which His disciples had entered,[a] and that Jesus had not entered the boat with His disciples, but His disciples had gone away alone— [23]however, other boats came from Tiberias, near the place where they ate bread after the Lord had given thanks— [24]when the people therefore saw that Jesus was not there, nor His disciples, they also got into boats and came to Capernaum, seeking Jesus. [25]And when they found Him on the other side of the sea, they said to Him, "Rabbi, when did You come here?"

[26]Jesus answered them and said, "Most assuredly, I say to you, you seek Me, not because you saw the signs, but because you ate of the loaves and were filled. [27]Do not labor for the food which perishes, but for the food which endures to everlasting life, which the

6:11 [a]NU-Text omits *to the disciples, and the disciples.*   **6:19** [a]Literally *twenty-five or thirty stadia*
6:22 [a]NU-Text omits *that* and *which His disciples had entered.*

Son of Man will give you, because God the Father has set His seal on Him."

²⁸Then they said to Him, "What shall we do, that we may work the works of God?"

²⁹Jesus answered and said to them, "This is the work of God, that you believe in Him whom He sent."

³⁰Therefore they said to Him, "What sign will You perform then, that we may see it and believe You? What work will You do? ³¹Our fathers ate the manna in the desert; as it is written, '*He gave them bread from heaven to eat.*'"ᵃ

³²Then Jesus said to them, "Most assuredly, I say to you, Moses did not give you the bread from heaven, but My Father gives you the true bread from heaven. ³³For the bread of God is He who comes down from heaven and gives life to the world."

³⁴Then they said to Him, "Lord, give us this bread always."

³⁵And Jesus said to them, "I am the bread of life. He who comes to Me shall never hunger, and he who believes in Me shall never thirst. ³⁶But I said to you that you have seen Me and yet do not believe. ³⁷All that the Father gives Me will come to Me, and the one who comes to Me I will by no means cast out. ³⁸For I have come down from heaven, not to do My own will, but the will of Him who sent Me. ³⁹This is the will of the Father who sent Me, that of all He has given Me I should lose nothing, but should raise it up at the last day. ⁴⁰And this is the will of Him who sent Me, that everyone who sees the Son and believes in Him may have everlasting life; and I will raise him up at the last day."

Rejected by His Own

⁴¹The Jews then complained about Him, because He said, "I am the bread which came down from heaven." ⁴²And they said, "Is not this Jesus, the son of Joseph, whose father and mother we know? How is it then that He says, 'I have come down from heaven'?"

⁴³Jesus therefore answered and said to them, "Do not murmur among yourselves. ⁴⁴No one can come to Me unless the Father who sent Me draws him; and I will raise him up at the last day. ⁴⁵It is written in the prophets, '*And they shall all be taught by God.*'ᵃ Therefore everyone who has heard

and learnedᵇ from the Father comes to Me. ⁴⁶Not that anyone has seen the Father, except He who is from God; He has seen the Father. ⁴⁷Most assuredly, I say to you, he who believes in Meᵃ has everlasting life. ⁴⁸I am the bread of life. ⁴⁹Your fathers ate the manna in the wilderness, and are dead. ⁵⁰This is the bread which comes down from heaven, that one may eat of it and not die. ⁵¹I am the living bread which came down from heaven. If anyone eats of this bread, he will live forever; and the bread that I shall give is My flesh, which I shall give for the life of the world."

⁵²The Jews therefore quarreled among themselves, saying, "How can this Man give us *His* flesh to eat?"

⁵³Then Jesus said to them, "Most assuredly, I say to you, unless you eat the flesh of the Son of Man and drink His blood, you have no life in you. ⁵⁴Whoever eats My flesh and drinks My blood has eternal life, and I will raise him up at the last day. ⁵⁵For My flesh is food indeed,ᵃ and My blood is drink indeed. ⁵⁶He who eats My flesh and drinks My blood abides in Me, and I in him. ⁵⁷As the living Father sent Me, and I live because of the Father, so he who feeds on Me will live because of Me. ⁵⁸This is the bread which came down from heaven—not as your fathers ate the manna, and are dead. He who eats this bread will live forever."

⁵⁹These things He said in the synagogue as He taught in Capernaum.

Many Disciples Turn Away

⁶⁰Therefore many of His disciples, when they heard *this,* said, "This is a hard saying; who can understand it?"

⁶¹When Jesus knew in Himself that His disciples complained about this, He said to them, "Does this offend you? ⁶²*What* then if you should see the Son of Man ascend where He was before? ⁶³It is the Spirit who gives life; the flesh profits nothing. The words that I speak to you are spirit, and *they* are life. ⁶⁴But there are some of you who do not believe." For Jesus knew from the beginning who they were who did not believe, and who would betray Him. ⁶⁵And He said, "Therefore I have said to you that no one can come to Me unless it has been granted to him by My Father."

⁶⁶From that *time* many of His disciples

6:31 ᵃExodus 16:4; Nehemiah 9:15; Psalm 78:24   **6:45** ᵃIsaiah 54:13   ᵇM-Text reads *hears and has learned.*
6:47 ᵃNU-Text omits *in Me.*   **6:55** ᵃNU-Text reads *true food* and *true drink.*

went back and walked with Him no more. [67]Then Jesus said to the twelve, "Do you also want to go away?"

[68]But Simon Peter answered Him, "Lord, to whom shall we go? You have the words of eternal life. [69]Also we have come to believe and know that You are the Christ, the Son of the living God."[a]

[70]Jesus answered them, "Did I not choose you, the twelve, and one of you is a devil?" [71]He spoke of Judas Iscariot, *the son* of Simon, for it was he who would betray Him, being one of the twelve.

Jesus' Brothers Disbelieve

7 After these things Jesus walked in Galilee; for He did not want to walk in Judea, because the Jews[a] sought to kill Him. [2]Now the Jews' Feast of Tabernacles was at hand. [3]His brothers therefore said to Him, "Depart from here and go into Judea, that Your disciples also may see the works that You are doing. [4]For no one does anything in secret while he himself seeks to be known openly. If You do these things, show Yourself to the world." [5]For even His brothers did not believe in Him.

[6]Then Jesus said to them, "My time has not yet come, but your time is always ready. [7]The world cannot hate you, but it hates Me because I testify of it that its works are evil. [8]You go up to this feast. I am not yet[a] going up to this feast, for My time has not yet fully come." [9]When He had said these things to them, He remained in Galilee.

The Heavenly Scholar

[10]But when His brothers had gone up, then He also went up to the feast, not openly, but as it were in secret. [11]Then the Jews sought Him at the feast, and said, "Where is He?" [12]And there was much complaining among the people concerning Him. Some said, "He is good"; others said, "No, on the contrary, He deceives the people." [13]However, no one spoke openly of Him for fear of the Jews.

[14]Now about the middle of the feast Jesus went up into the temple and taught. [15]And the Jews marveled, saying, "How does this Man know letters, having never studied?"

[16]Jesus[a] answered them and said, "My doctrine is not Mine, but His who sent Me. [17]If anyone wills to do His will, he shall know concerning the doctrine, whether it is from God or *whether* I speak on My own *authority.* [18]He who speaks from himself seeks his own glory; but He who seeks the glory of the One who sent Him is true, and no unrighteousness is in Him. [19]Did not Moses give you the law, yet none of you keeps the law? Why do you seek to kill Me?"

[20]The people answered and said, "You have a demon. Who is seeking to kill You?"

[21]Jesus answered and said to them, "I did one work, and you all marvel. [22]Moses therefore gave you circumcision (not that it is from Moses, but from the fathers), and you circumcise a man on the Sabbath. [23]If a man receives circumcision on the Sabbath, so that the law of Moses should not be broken, are you angry with Me because I made a man completely well on the Sabbath? [24]Do not judge according to appearance, but judge with righteous judgment."

Could This Be the Christ?

[25]Now some of them from Jerusalem said, "Is this not He whom they seek to kill? [26]But look! He speaks boldly, and they say nothing to Him. Do the rulers know indeed that this is truly[a] the Christ? [27]However, we know where this Man is from; but when the Christ comes, no one knows where He is from."

[28]Then Jesus cried out, as He taught in the temple, saying, "You both know Me, and you know where I am from; and I have not come of Myself, but He who sent Me is true, whom you do not know. [29]But[a] I know Him, for I am from Him, and He sent Me."

[30]Therefore they sought to take Him; but no one laid a hand on Him, because His hour had not yet come. [31]And many of the people believed in Him, and said, "When the Christ comes, will He do more signs than these which this *Man* has done?"

Jesus and the Religious Leaders

[32]The Pharisees heard the crowd murmuring these things concerning Him, and the Pharisees and the chief priests sent officers to take Him. [33]Then Jesus said to them,[a] "I shall

6:69 [a]NU-Text reads *You are the Holy One of God.*   **7:1** [a]That is, the ruling authorities   **7:8** [a]NU-Text omits *yet.*   **7:16** [a]NU-Text and M-Text read *So Jesus.*   **7:26** [a]NU-Text omits *truly.*   **7:29** [a]NU-Text and M-Text omit *But.*   **7:33** [a]NU-Text and M-Text omit *to them.*

be with you a little while longer, and *then* I go to Him who sent Me. [34]You will seek Me and not find *Me,* and where I am you cannot come."

[35]Then the Jews said among themselves, "Where does He intend to go that we shall not find Him? Does He intend to go to the Dispersion among the Greeks and teach the Greeks? [36]What is this thing that He said, 'You will seek Me and not find Me, and where I am you cannot come'?"

The Promise of the Holy Spirit

[37]On the last day, that great *day* of the feast, Jesus stood and cried out, saying, "If anyone thirsts, let him come to Me and drink. [38]He who believes in Me, as the Scripture has said, out of his heart will flow rivers of living water." [39]But this He spoke concerning the Spirit, whom those believing[a] in Him would receive; for the Holy[b] Spirit was not yet *given,* because Jesus was not yet glorified.

> ➤ *If anyone thirsts, let him come to Me and drink. He who believes in Me, as the Scripture has said, out of his heart will flow rivers of living water.* John 7:37, 38

Who Is He?

[40]Therefore many[a] from the crowd, when they heard this saying, said, "Truly this is the Prophet." [41]Others said, "This is the Christ."

But some said, "Will the Christ come out of Galilee? [42]Has not the Scripture said that the Christ comes from the seed of David and from the town of Bethlehem, where David was?" [43]So there was a division among the people because of Him. [44]Now some of them wanted to take Him, but no one laid hands on Him.

Rejected by the Authorities

[45]Then the officers came to the chief priests and Pharisees, who said to them, "Why have you not brought Him?"

[46]The officers answered, "No man ever spoke like this Man!"

[47]Then the Pharisees answered them, "Are you also deceived? [48]Have any of the rulers or the Pharisees believed in Him? [49]But this crowd that does not know the law is accursed."

[50]Nicodemus (he who came to Jesus by night,[a] being one of them) said to them, [51]"Does our law judge a man before it hears him and knows what he is doing?"

[52]They answered and said to him, "Are you also from Galilee? Search and look, for no prophet has arisen[a] out of Galilee."

An Adulteress Faces the Light of the World

[53]And everyone went to his *own* house.[a]

8 But Jesus went to the Mount of Olives. [2]Now early[a] in the morning He came again into the temple, and all the people came to Him; and He sat down and taught them. [3]Then the scribes and Pharisees brought to Him a woman caught in adultery. And when they had set her in the midst, [4]they said to Him, "Teacher, this woman was caught[a] in adultery, in the very act. [5]Now Moses, in the law, commanded[a] us that such should be stoned.[b] But what do You say?"[c] [6]This they said, testing Him, that they might have *something* of which to accuse Him. But Jesus stooped down and wrote on the ground with *His* finger, as though He did not hear.[a]

[7]So when they continued asking Him, He raised Himself up[a] and said to them, "He who is without sin among you, let him throw a stone at her first." [8]And again He stooped down and wrote on the ground. [9]Then those who heard *it,* being convicted by *their* conscience,[a] went out one by one, beginning with the oldest *even* to the last. And Jesus was left alone, and the woman standing in the midst. [10]When Jesus had raised Himself up and saw no one but the woman, He said to her,[a] "Woman, where are those accusers of yours?[b] Has no one condemned you?"

7:39 [a]NU-Text reads *who believed.* [b]NU-Text omits Holy.   7:40 [a]NU-Text reads *some.*   7:50 [a]NU-Text reads *before.*   7:52 [a]NU-Text reads *is to rise.*   7:53 [a]The words *And everyone* through *sin no more* (8:11) are bracketed by NU-Text as not original. They are present in over 900 manuscripts.   8:2 [a]M-Text reads *very early.*   8:4 [a]M-Text reads *we found this woman.*   8:5 [a]M-Text reads *in our law Moses commanded.* [b]NU-Text and M-Text read *to stone such.* [c]M-Text adds *about her.*   8:6 [a]NU-Text and M-Text omit *as though He did not hear.* 8:7 [a]M-Text reads *He looked up.*   8:9 [a]NU-Text and M-Text omit *being convicted by their conscience.*   8:10 [a]NU-Text omits *and saw no one but the woman;* M-Text reads *He saw her and said.* [b]NU-Text and M-Text omit *of yours.*

[11]She said, "No one, Lord."

And Jesus said to her, "Neither do I condemn you; go and[a] sin no more."

[12]Then Jesus spoke to them again, saying, "I am the light of the world. He who follows Me shall not walk in darkness, but have the light of life."

Jesus Defends His Self-Witness

[13]The Pharisees therefore said to Him, "You bear witness of Yourself; Your witness is not true."

[14]Jesus answered and said to them, "Even if I bear witness of Myself, My witness is true, for I know where I came from and where I am going; but you do not know where I come from and where I am going. [15]You judge according to the flesh; I judge no one. [16]And yet if I do judge, My judgment is true; for I am not alone, but I *am* with the Father who sent Me. [17]It is also written in your law that the testimony of two men is true. [18]I am One who bears witness of Myself, and the Father who sent Me bears witness of Me."

[19]Then they said to Him, "Where is Your Father?"

Jesus answered, "You know neither Me nor My Father. If you had known Me, you would have known My Father also."

[20]These words Jesus spoke in the treasury, as He taught in the temple; and no one laid hands on Him, for His hour had not yet come.

Jesus Predicts His Departure

[21]Then Jesus said to them again, "I am going away, and you will seek Me, and will die in your sin. Where I go you cannot come."

[22]So the Jews said, "Will He kill Himself, because He says, 'Where I go you cannot come'?"

[23]And He said to them, "You are from beneath; I am from above. You are of this world; I am not of this world. [24]Therefore I said to you that you will die in your sins; for if you do not believe that I am *He,* you will die in your sins."

[25]Then they said to Him, "Who are You?"

And Jesus said to them, "Just what I have been saying to you from the beginning. [26]I have many things to say and to judge concerning you; but He who sent Me is true;

and I speak to the world those things which I heard from Him."

[27]They did not understand that He spoke to them of the Father.

[28]Then Jesus said to them, "When you lift up the Son of Man, then you will know that I am *He,* and *that* I do nothing of Myself; but as My Father taught Me, I speak these things. [29]And He who sent Me is with Me. The Father has not left Me alone, for I always do those things that please Him." [30]As He spoke these words, many believed in Him.

The Truth Shall Make You Free

[31]Then Jesus said to those Jews who believed Him, "If you abide in My word, you are My disciples indeed. [32]And you shall know the truth, and the truth shall make you free."

> ➤ *And you shall know the truth, and the truth shall make you free.* John 8:32

[33]They answered Him, "We are Abraham's descendants, and have never been in bondage to anyone. How *can* You say, 'You will be made free'?"

[34]Jesus answered them, "Most assuredly, I say to you, whoever commits sin is a slave of sin. [35]And a slave does not abide in the house forever, *but* a son abides forever. [36]Therefore if the Son makes you free, you shall be free indeed.

Abraham's Seed and Satan's

[37]"I know that you are Abraham's descendants, but you seek to kill Me, because My word has no place in you. [38]I speak what I have seen with My Father, and you do what you have seen with[a] your father."

[39]They answered and said to Him, "Abraham is our father."

Jesus said to them, "If you were Abraham's children, you would do the works of Abraham. [40]But now you seek to kill Me, a Man who has told you the truth which I heard from God. Abraham did not do this. [41]You do the deeds of your father."

8:11 [a]NU-Text and M-Text add *from now on.*   **8:38** [a]NU-Text reads *heard from.*

Then they said to Him, "We were not born of fornication; we have one Father—God."

⁴²Jesus said to them, "If God were your Father, you would love Me, for I proceeded forth and came from God; nor have I come of Myself, but He sent Me. ⁴³Why do you not understand My speech? Because you are not able to listen to My word. ⁴⁴You are of *your* father the devil, and the desires of your father you want to do. He was a murderer from the beginning, and does not stand in the truth, because there is no truth in him. When he speaks a lie, he speaks from his own *resources,* for he is a liar and the father of it. ⁴⁵But because I tell the truth, you do not believe Me. ⁴⁶Which of you convicts Me of sin? And if I tell the truth, why do you not believe Me? ⁴⁷He who is of God hears God's words; therefore you do not hear, because you are not of God."

Before Abraham Was, I AM

⁴⁸Then the Jews answered and said to Him, "Do we not say rightly that You are a Samaritan and have a demon?"

⁴⁹Jesus answered, "I do not have a demon; but I honor My Father, and you dishonor Me. ⁵⁰And I do not seek My *own* glory; there is One who seeks and judges. ⁵¹Most assuredly, I say to you, if anyone keeps My word he shall never see death."

⁵²Then the Jews said to Him, "Now we know that You have a demon! Abraham is dead, and the prophets; and You say, 'If anyone keeps My word he shall never taste death.' ⁵³Are You greater than our father Abraham, who is dead? And the prophets are dead. Who do You make Yourself out to be?"

⁵⁴Jesus answered, "If I honor Myself, My honor is nothing. It is My Father who honors Me, of whom you say that He is yourᵃ God. ⁵⁵Yet you have not known Him, but I know Him. And if I say, 'I do not know Him,' I shall be a liar like you; but I do know Him and keep His word. ⁵⁶Your father Abraham rejoiced to see My day, and he saw *it* and was glad."

⁵⁷Then the Jews said to Him, "You are not yet fifty years old, and have You seen Abraham?"

⁵⁸Jesus said to them, "Most assuredly, I say to you, before Abraham was, I AM."

⁵⁹Then they took up stones to throw at Him; but Jesus hid Himself and went out of the temple,ᵃ going through the midst of them, and so passed by.

A Man Born Blind Receives Sight

9 Now as *Jesus* passed by, He saw a man who was blind from birth. ²And His disciples asked Him, saying, "Rabbi, who sinned, this man or his parents, that he was born blind?"

³Jesus answered, "Neither this man nor his parents sinned, but that the works of God should be revealed in him. ⁴Iᵃ must work the works of Him who sent Me while it is day; *the* night is coming when no one can work. ⁵As long as I am in the world, I am the light of the world."

↘ LEARN

9:4 • Life is short. The Bible describes it as a "vapor that appears for a little time and then vanishes away" (James 4:14). We're here, and then we're gone. We live in the blip between now and eternity, and in that brief period God blesses us with significant things to do. Every day the Lord gives us new opportunities to serve and honor Him and share the gospel with others. We are to work for God today, while the daylight endures, for the night fast approaches when no one can work—and none of us knows when that dark curtain will drop. *For more about* Sharing Your Faith, *see Acts 1:8;* How to Live Out Your Faith, *Acts 2:42.*

⁶When He had said these things, He spat on the ground and made clay with the saliva; and He anointed the eyes of the blind man with the clay. ⁷And He said to him, "Go, wash in the pool of Siloam" (which is translated, Sent). So he went and washed, and came back seeing.

⁸Therefore the neighbors and those who previously had seen that he was blindᵃ said, "Is not this he who sat and begged?"

⁹Some said, "This is he." Others *said,* "He is like him."ᵃ

He said, "I am *he.*"

¹⁰Therefore they said to him, "How were your eyes opened?"

¹¹He answered and said, "A Man called Jesus made clay and anointed my eyes and said

8:54 ᵃNU-Text and M-Text read *our.*   **8:59** ᵃNU-Text omits the rest of this verse.   **9:4** ᵃNU-Text reads *We.*
9:8 ᵃNU-Text reads *a beggar.*   **9:9** ᵃNU-Text reads *"No, but he is like him."*

to me, 'Go to the pool of[a] Siloam and wash.' So I went and washed, and I received sight."

¹²Then they said to him, "Where is He?" He said, "I do not know."

The Pharisees Excommunicate the Healed Man

¹³They brought him who formerly was blind to the Pharisees. ¹⁴Now it was a Sabbath when Jesus made the clay and opened his eyes. ¹⁵Then the Pharisees also asked him again how he had received his sight. He said to them, "He put clay on my eyes, and I washed, and I see."

¹⁶Therefore some of the Pharisees said, "This Man is not from God, because He does not keep the Sabbath."

Others said, "How can a man who is a sinner do such signs?" And there was a division among them.

¹⁷They said to the blind man again, "What do you say about Him because He opened your eyes?"

He said, "He is a prophet."

¹⁸But the Jews did not believe concerning him, that he had been blind and received his sight, until they called the parents of him who had received his sight. ¹⁹And they asked them, saying, "Is this your son, who you say was born blind? How then does he now see?"

²⁰His parents answered them and said, "We know that this is our son, and that he was born blind; ²¹but by what means he now sees we do not know, or who opened his eyes we do not know. He is of age; ask him. He will speak for himself." ²²His parents said these *things* because they feared the Jews, for the Jews had agreed already that if anyone confessed *that* He *was* Christ, he would be put out of the synagogue. ²³Therefore his parents said, "He is of age; ask him."

²⁴So they again called the man who was blind, and said to him, "Give God the glory! We know that this Man is a sinner."

²⁵He answered and said, "Whether He is a sinner *or not* I do not know. One thing I know: that though I was blind, now I see."

²⁶Then they said to him again, "What did He do to you? How did He open your eyes?"

²⁷He answered them, "I told you already, and you did not listen. Why do you want to hear *it* again? Do you also want to become His disciples?"

²⁸Then they reviled him and said, "You are His disciple, but we are Moses' disciples. ²⁹We know that God spoke to Moses; *as for* this *fellow,* we do not know where He is from."

³⁰The man answered and said to them, "Why, this is a marvelous thing, that you do not know where He is from; yet He has opened my eyes! ³¹Now we know that God does not hear sinners; but if anyone is a worshiper of God and does His will, He hears him. ³²Since the world began it has been unheard of that anyone opened the eyes of one who was born blind. ³³If this Man were not from God, He could do nothing."

³⁴They answered and said to him, "You were completely born in sins, and are you teaching us?" And they cast him out.

True Vision and True Blindness

³⁵Jesus heard that they had cast him out; and when He had found him, He said to him, "Do you believe in the Son of God?"[a]

³⁶He answered and said, "Who is He, Lord, that I may believe in Him?"

³⁷And Jesus said to him, "You have both seen Him and it is He who is talking with you."

³⁸Then he said, "Lord, I believe!" And he worshiped Him.

³⁹And Jesus said, "For judgment I have come into this world, that those who do not see may see, and that those who see may be made blind."

⁴⁰Then *some* of the Pharisees who were with Him heard these words, and said to Him, "Are we blind also?"

⁴¹Jesus said to them, "If you were blind, you would have no sin; but now you say, 'We see.' Therefore your sin remains.

Jesus the True Shepherd

10 "Most assuredly, I say to you, he who does not enter the sheepfold by the door, but climbs up some other way, the same is a thief and a robber. ²But he who enters by the door is the shepherd of the sheep. ³To him the doorkeeper opens, and the sheep hear his voice; and he calls his own sheep by name and leads them out. ⁴And when he brings out his own sheep, he goes before them; and the sheep follow him, for they know his voice. ⁵Yet they will by no means follow a stranger, but will flee

9:11 [a]NU-Text omits *the pool of.*   **9:35** [a]NU-Text reads *Son of Man.*

from him, for they do not know the voice of strangers." [6]Jesus used this illustration, but they did not understand the things which He spoke to them.

Jesus the Good Shepherd

[7]Then Jesus said to them again, "Most assuredly, I say to you, I am the door of the sheep. [8]All who *ever* came before Me[a] are thieves and robbers, but the sheep did not hear them. [9]I am the door. If anyone enters by Me, he will be saved, and will go in and out and find pasture. [10]The thief does not come except to steal, and to kill, and to destroy. I have come that they may have life, and that they may have *it* more abundantly.

➤ *The thief does not come except to steal, and to kill, and to destroy. I have come that they may have life, and that they may have it more abundantly.* John 10:10

[11]"I am the good shepherd. The good shepherd gives His life for the sheep. [12]But a hireling, *he who is* not the shepherd, one who does not own the sheep, sees the wolf coming and leaves the sheep and flees; and the wolf catches the sheep and scatters them. [13]The hireling flees because he is a hireling and does not care about the sheep. [14]I am the good shepherd; and I know My *sheep,* and am known by My own. [15]As the Father knows Me, even so I know the Father; and I lay down My life for the sheep. [16]And other sheep I have which are not of this fold; them also I must bring, and they will hear My voice; and there will be one flock *and* one shepherd.

[17]"Therefore My Father loves Me, because I lay down My life that I may take it again. [18]No one takes it from Me, but I lay it down of Myself. I have power to lay it down, and I have power to take it again. This command I have received from My Father."

[19]Therefore there was a division again among the Jews because of these sayings.

[20]And many of them said, "He has a demon and is mad. Why do you listen to Him?"

[21]Others said, "These are not the words of one who has a demon. Can a demon open the eyes of the blind?"

The Shepherd Knows His Sheep

[22]Now it was the Feast of Dedication in Jerusalem, and it was winter. [23]And Jesus walked in the temple, in Solomon's porch. [24]Then the Jews surrounded Him and said to Him, "How long do You keep us in doubt? If You are the Christ, tell us plainly."

[25]Jesus answered them, "I told you, and you do not believe. The works that I do in My Father's name, they bear witness of Me. [26]But you do not believe, because you are not of My sheep, as I said to you.[a] [27]My sheep hear My voice, and I know them, and they follow Me. [28]And I give them eternal life, and they shall never perish; neither shall anyone snatch them out of My hand. [29]My Father, who has given *them* to Me, is greater than all; and no one is able to snatch *them* out of My Father's hand. [30]I and *My* Father are one."

➤ *And I give them eternal life, and they shall never perish; neither shall anyone snatch them out of My hand.* John 10:28

Renewed Efforts to Stone Jesus

[31]Then the Jews took up stones again to stone Him. [32]Jesus answered them, "Many good works I have shown you from My Father. For which of those works do you stone Me?"

[33]The Jews answered Him, saying, "For a good work we do not stone You, but for blasphemy, and because You, being a Man, make Yourself God."

[34]Jesus answered them, "Is it not written in your law, *'I said, "You are gods"* '?[a] [35]If He called them gods, to whom the word of God came (and the Scripture cannot be broken), [36]do you say of Him whom the Father sanctified and sent into the world, 'You are blaspheming,' because I said, 'I am the Son of God'? [37]If I do not do the works of My Father,

10:8 [a]M-Text omits *before Me.*   10:26 [a]NU-Text omits *as I said to you.*   10:34 [a]Psalm 82:6

do not believe Me; [38]but if I do, though you do not believe Me, believe the works, that you may know and believe[a] that the Father *is* in Me, and I in Him." [39]Therefore they sought again to seize Him, but He escaped out of their hand.

The Believers Beyond Jordan

[40]And He went away again beyond the Jordan to the place where John was baptizing at first, and there He stayed. [41]Then many came to Him and said, "John performed no sign, but all the things that John spoke about this Man were true." [42]And many believed in Him there.

The Death of Lazarus

11 Now a certain *man* was sick, Lazarus of Bethany, the town of Mary and her sister Martha. [2]It was *that* Mary who anointed the Lord with fragrant oil and wiped His feet with her hair, whose brother Lazarus was sick. [3]Therefore the sisters sent to Him, saying, "Lord, behold, he whom You love is sick."

[4]When Jesus heard *that,* He said, "This sickness is not unto death, but for the glory of God, that the Son of God may be glorified through it."

[5]Now Jesus loved Martha and her sister and Lazarus. [6]So, when He heard that he was sick, He stayed two more days in the place where He was. [7]Then after this He said to *the* disciples, "Let us go to Judea again."

> ↘ **LEARN**
> • • • • • • • • • • • • • • • • •
>
> 11:5, 6 • If Jesus really loved Lazarus, then why didn't He immediately go to heal him when He heard he was sick? When hardship, tragedy, or even death comes into our lives, we often ask the same. It is hard to see through eyes filled with tears! But even though we cannot see how a situation will end or why it has happened to us, we can know that it flows from the love of God and is controlled by Him. That is why we should always interpret His delays in the light of His love—and not the other way around. *For more about* God at Work, *see Acts 16:23, 24;* Adversity, *John 16:33;* God's Love, *John 13:9–14.*

[8]*The* disciples said to Him, "Rabbi, lately the Jews sought to stone You, and are You going there again?"

[9]Jesus answered, "Are there not twelve hours in the day? If anyone walks in the day, he does not stumble, because he sees the light of this world. [10]But if one walks in the night, he stumbles, because the light is not in him." [11]These things He said, and after that He said to them, "Our friend Lazarus sleeps, but I go that I may wake him up."

[12]Then His disciples said, "Lord, if he sleeps he will get well." [13]However, Jesus spoke of his death, but they thought that He was speaking about taking rest in sleep.

[14]Then Jesus said to them plainly, "Lazarus is dead. [15]And I am glad for your sakes that I was not there, that you may believe. Nevertheless let us go to him."

[16]Then Thomas, who is called the Twin, said to his fellow disciples, "Let us also go, that we may die with Him."

I Am the Resurrection and the Life

[17]So when Jesus came, He found that he had already been in the tomb four days. [18]Now Bethany was near Jerusalem, about two miles[a] away. [19]And many of the Jews had joined the women around Martha and Mary, to comfort them concerning their brother.

[20]Now Martha, as soon as she heard that Jesus was coming, went and met Him, but Mary was sitting in the house. [21]Now Martha said to Jesus, "Lord, if You had been here, my brother would not have died. [22]But even now I know that whatever You ask of God, God will give You."

[23]Jesus said to her, "Your brother will rise again."

[24]Martha said to Him, "I know that he will rise again in the resurrection at the last day."

[25]Jesus said to her, "I am the resurrection and the life. He who believes in Me, though

> **➤ *I am the resurrection and the life. He who believes in Me, though he may die, he shall live. And whoever lives and believes in Me shall never die. Do you believe this?*** John 11:25, 26

10:38 [a]NU-Text reads *understand.*   **11:18** [a]Literally *fifteen stadia*

he may die, he shall live. ²⁶And whoever lives and believes in Me shall never die. Do you believe this?"

²⁷She said to Him, "Yes, Lord, I believe that You are the Christ, the Son of God, who is to come into the world."

Jesus and Death, the Last Enemy

²⁸And when she had said these things, she went her way and secretly called Mary her sister, saying, "The Teacher has come and is calling for you." ²⁹As soon as she heard *that,* she arose quickly and came to Him. ³⁰Now Jesus had not yet come into the town, but wasᵃ in the place where Martha met Him. ³¹Then the Jews who were with her in the house, and comforting her, when they saw that Mary rose up quickly and went out, followed her, saying, "She is going to the tomb to weep there."ᵃ

³²Then, when Mary came where Jesus was, and saw Him, she fell down at His feet, saying to Him, "Lord, if You had been here, my brother would not have died."

³³Therefore, when Jesus saw her weeping, and the Jews who came with her weeping, He groaned in the spirit and was troubled. ³⁴And He said, "Where have you laid him?"

They said to Him, "Lord, come and see."

³⁵Jesus wept. ³⁶Then the Jews said, "See how He loved him!"

³⁷And some of them said, "Could not this Man, who opened the eyes of the blind, also have kept this man from dying?"

Lazarus Raised from the Dead

³⁸Then Jesus, again groaning in Himself, came to the tomb. It was a cave, and a stone lay against it. ³⁹Jesus said, "Take away the stone."

Martha, the sister of him who was dead, said to Him, "Lord, by this time there is a stench, for he has been *dead* four days."

⁴⁰Jesus said to her, "Did I not say to you that if you would believe you would see the glory of God?" ⁴¹Then they took away the stone *from the place* where the dead man was lying.ᵃ And Jesus lifted up *His* eyes and said, "Father, I thank You that You have heard Me. ⁴²And I know that You always hear Me, but because of the people who are standing by I said *this,* that they may believe that You sent Me." ⁴³Now when He had said these things, He cried with a loud voice, "Lazarus, come forth!" ⁴⁴And he who had died came out bound hand and foot with graveclothes, and his face was wrapped with a cloth. Jesus said to them, "Loose him, and let him go."

The Plot to Kill Jesus

⁴⁵Then many of the Jews who had come to Mary, and had seen the things Jesus did, believed in Him. ⁴⁶But some of them went away to the Pharisees and told them the things Jesus did. ⁴⁷Then the chief priests and the Pharisees gathered a council and said, "What shall we do? For this Man works many signs. ⁴⁸If we let Him alone like this, everyone will believe in Him, and the Romans will come and take away both our place and nation."

⁴⁹And one of them, Caiaphas, being high priest that year, said to them, "You know nothing at all, ⁵⁰nor do you consider that it is expedient for usᵃ that one man should die for the people, and not that the whole nation should perish." ⁵¹Now this he did not say on his own *authority;* but being high priest that year he prophesied that Jesus would die for the nation, ⁵²and not for that nation only, but also that He would gather together in one the children of God who were scattered abroad.

⁵³Then, from that day on, they plotted to put Him to death. ⁵⁴Therefore Jesus no longer walked openly among the Jews, but went from there into the country near the wilderness, to a city called Ephraim, and there remained with His disciples.

⁵⁵And the Passover of the Jews was near, and many went from the country up to Jerusalem before the Passover, to purify themselves. ⁵⁶Then they sought Jesus, and spoke among themselves as they stood in the temple, "What do you think—that He will not come to the feast?" ⁵⁷Now both the chief priests and the Pharisees had given a command, that if anyone knew where He was, he should report *it,* that they might seize Him.

The Anointing at Bethany

12 Then, six days before the Passover, Jesus came to Bethany, where Lazarus was who had been dead,ᵃ whom

---

11:30 ᵃNU-Text adds *still.*   **11:31** ᵃNU-Text reads *supposing that she was going to the tomb to weep there.*   **11:41** ᵃNU-Text omits *from the place where the dead man was lying.*   **11:50** ᵃNU-Text reads *you.*   **12:1** ᵃNU-Text omits *who had been dead.*

He had raised from the dead. [2]There they made Him a supper; and Martha served, but Lazarus was one of those who sat at the table with Him. [3]Then Mary took a pound of very costly oil of spikenard, anointed the feet of Jesus, and wiped His feet with her hair. And the house was filled with the fragrance of the oil.

[4]But one of His disciples, Judas Iscariot, Simon's *son*, who would betray Him, said, [5]"Why was this fragrant oil not sold for three hundred denarii[a] and given to the poor?" [6]This he said, not that he cared for the poor, but because he was a thief, and had the money box; and he used to take what was put in it. [7]But Jesus said, "Let her alone; she has kept[a] this for the day of My burial. [8]For the poor you have with you always, but Me you do not have always."

The Plot to Kill Lazarus

[9]Now a great many of the Jews knew that He was there; and they came, not for Jesus' sake only, but that they might also see Lazarus, whom He had raised from the dead. [10]But the chief priests plotted to put Lazarus to death also, [11]because on account of him many of the Jews went away and believed in Jesus.

The Triumphal Entry

[12]The next day a great multitude that had come to the feast, when they heard that Jesus was coming to Jerusalem, [13]took branches of palm trees and went out to meet Him, and cried out:

"Hosanna!
 'Blessed is He who comes in the name of the LORD!'[a]
 The King of Israel!"

[14]Then Jesus, when He had found a young donkey, sat on it; as it is written:

[15] *"Fear not, daughter of Zion;*
 Behold, your King is coming,
 Sitting on a donkey's colt."[a]

[16]His disciples did not understand these things at first; but when Jesus was glorified, then they remembered that these things were written about Him and *that* they had done these things to Him.
[17]Therefore the people, who were with Him when He called Lazarus out of his tomb

and raised him from the dead, bore witness. [18]For this reason the people also met Him, because they heard that He had done this sign. [19]The Pharisees therefore said among themselves, "You see that you are accomplishing nothing. Look, the world has gone after Him!"

The Fruitful Grain of Wheat

[20]Now there were certain Greeks among those who came up to worship at the feast. [21]Then they came to Philip, who was from Bethsaida of Galilee, and asked him, saying, "Sir, we wish to see Jesus."

[22]Philip came and told Andrew, and in turn Andrew and Philip told Jesus.

[23]But Jesus answered them, saying, "The hour has come that the Son of Man should be glorified. [24]Most assuredly, I say to you, unless a grain of wheat falls into the ground and dies, it remains alone; but if it dies, it produces much grain. [25]He who loves his life will lose it, and he who hates his life in this world will keep it for eternal life. [26]If anyone serves Me, let him follow Me; and where I am, there My servant will be also. If anyone serves Me, him *My* Father will honor.

↘ LEARN

12:24, 25 • Consider God's plan for finding meaning, purpose, and happiness: *lose your life to find it.* Let go and submit to the will of God. Scary? In fact, you needn't fear to place an unknown future into the hands of a known God. D. L. Moody once said, "Spread out your petition before God, and then say, 'Thy will, not mine, be done.' The sweetest lesson I have learned in God's school is to let the Lord choose for me." Are you willing to "let the Lord choose for you"? If so, you will discover riches off limits to the fearful. *For more about* Faith, *see* John 15:8; God's Will, *Acts 16:6–10;* Submitting to God, *1 Thess. 4:3.*

Jesus Predicts His Death on the Cross

[27]"Now My soul is troubled, and what shall I say? 'Father, save Me from this hour'? But for this purpose I came to this hour. [28]Father, glorify Your name."

Then a voice came from heaven, *saying,* "I have both glorified *it* and will glorify *it* again."

12:5 [a]About one year's wages for a worker   12:7 [a]NU-Text reads *that she may keep.*   12:13 [a]Psalm 118:26   12:15 [a]Zechariah 9:9

²⁹Therefore the people who stood by and heard *it* said that it had thundered. Others said, "An angel has spoken to Him."

³⁰Jesus answered and said, "This voice did not come because of Me, but for your sake. ³¹Now is the judgment of this world; now the ruler of this world will be cast out. ³²And I, if I am lifted up from the earth, will draw all *peoples* to Myself." ³³This He said, signifying by what death He would die.

³⁴The people answered Him, "We have heard from the law that the Christ remains forever; and how *can* You say, 'The Son of Man must be lifted up'? Who is this Son of Man?"

³⁵Then Jesus said to them, "A little while longer the light is with you. Walk while you have the light, lest darkness overtake you; he who walks in darkness does not know where he is going. ³⁶While you have the light, believe in the light, that you may become sons of light." These things Jesus spoke, and departed, and was hidden from them.

Who Has Believed Our Report?

³⁷But although He had done so many signs before them, they did not believe in Him, ³⁸that the word of Isaiah the prophet might be fulfilled, which he spoke:

"Lord, who has believed our report?
And to whom has the arm of the LORD
    been revealed?"ᵃ

³⁹Therefore they could not believe, because Isaiah said again:

⁴⁰ "He has blinded their eyes and hardened
    their hearts,
Lest they should see with their eyes,
Lest they should understand with their
    hearts and turn,
So that I should heal them."ᵃ

⁴¹These things Isaiah said whenᵃ he saw His glory and spoke of Him.

Walk in the Light

⁴²Nevertheless even among the rulers many believed in Him, but because of the Pharisees they did not confess *Him,* lest they should be put out of the synagogue; ⁴³for they loved the praise of men more than the praise of God.

⁴⁴Then Jesus cried out and said, "He who believes in Me, believes not in Me but in Him who sent Me. ⁴⁵And he who sees Me sees Him who sent Me. ⁴⁶I have come *as* a light into the world, that whoever believes in Me should not abide in darkness. ⁴⁷And if anyone hears My words and does not believe,ᵃ I do not judge him; for I did not come to judge the world but to save the world. ⁴⁸He who rejects Me, and does not receive My words, has that which judges him—the word that I have spoken will judge him in the last day. ⁴⁹For I have not spoken on My own *authority;* but the Father who sent Me gave Me a command, what I should say and what I should speak. ⁵⁰And I know that His command is everlasting life. Therefore, whatever I speak, just as the Father has told Me, so I speak."

➤ *I have come as a light into the world, that whoever believes in Me should not abide in darkness.* John 12:46

Jesus Washes the Disciples' Feet

13 Now before the Feast of the Passover, when Jesus knew that His hour had come that He should depart from this world to the Father, having loved His own who were in the world, He loved them to the end.

²And supper being ended,ᵃ the devil having already put it into the heart of Judas Iscariot, Simon's *son,* to betray Him, ³Jesus, knowing that the Father had given all things into His hands, and that He had come from God and was going to God, ⁴rose from supper and laid aside His garments, took a towel and girded Himself. ⁵After that, He poured water into a basin and began to wash the disciples' feet, and to wipe *them* with the towel with which He was girded. ⁶Then He came to Simon Peter. And *Peter* said to Him, "Lord, are You washing my feet?"

12:38 ᵃIsaiah 53:1   12:40 ᵃIsaiah 6:10   12:41 ᵃNU-Text reads *because.*   12:47 ᵃNU-Text reads *keep them.*
13:2 ᵃNU-Text reads *And during supper.*

[7]Jesus answered and said to him, "What I am doing you do not understand now, but you will know after this."

[8]Peter said to Him, "You shall never wash my feet!"

Jesus answered him, "If I do not wash you, you have no part with Me."

[9]Simon Peter said to Him, "Lord, not my feet only, but also *my* hands and *my* head!"

[10]Jesus said to him, "He who is bathed needs only to wash *his* feet, but is completely clean; and you are clean, but not all of you." [11]For He knew who would betray Him; therefore He said, "You are not all clean."

[12]So when He had washed their feet, taken His garments, and sat down again, He said to them, "Do you know what I have done to you? [13]You call Me Teacher and Lord, and you say well, for *so* I am. [14]If I then, *your* Lord and Teacher, have washed your feet, you also ought to wash one another's feet. [15]For I have given you an example, that you should do as I have done to you. [16]Most assuredly, I say to you, a servant is not greater than his master; nor is he who is sent greater than he who sent him. [17]If you know these things, blessed are you if you do them.

Jesus Identifies His Betrayer

[18]"I do not speak concerning all of you. I know whom I have chosen; but that the Scripture may be fulfilled, *'He who eats bread with Me[a] has lifted up his heel against Me.'[b]* [19]Now I tell you before it comes, that when it does come to pass, you may believe that I am *He.* [20]Most assuredly, I say to you, he who receives whomever I send receives Me; and he who receives Me receives Him who sent Me."

[21]When Jesus had said these things, He was troubled in spirit, and testified and said, "Most assuredly, I say to you, one of you will betray Me." [22]Then the disciples looked at one another, perplexed about whom He spoke.

[23]Now there was leaning on Jesus' bosom one of His disciples, whom Jesus loved. [24]Simon Peter therefore motioned to him to ask who it was of whom He spoke.

[25]Then, leaning back[a] on Jesus' breast, he said to Him, "Lord, who is it?"

[26]Jesus answered, "It is he to whom I shall give a piece of bread when I have dipped *it.*" And having dipped the bread, He gave *it* to Judas Iscariot, *the son* of Simon. [27]Now after the piece of bread, Satan entered him. Then Jesus said to him, "What you do, do quickly." [28]But no one at the table knew for what reason He said this to him. [29]For some thought, because Judas had the money box, that Jesus had said to him, "Buy *those things* we need for the feast," or that he should give something to the poor.

[30]Having received the piece of bread, he then went out immediately. And it was night.

The New Commandment

[31]So, when he had gone out, Jesus said, "Now the Son of Man is glorified, and God is glorified in Him. [32]If God is glorified in Him, God will also glorify Him in Himself, and glorify Him immediately. [33]Little children, I shall be with you a little while longer. You will seek Me; and as I said to the Jews, 'Where I am going, you cannot come,' so now I say to you. [34]A new commandment I give to you, that you love one another; as I have loved

13:18 [a]NU-Text reads *My bread.* [b]Psalm 41:9   **13:25** [a]NU-Text and M-Text add *thus.*

↑ GROW (JOHN 13:9–14)

Object lessons sometimes have more punch *after* they're explained. Peter made this discovery on the night Jesus washed his feet. At first the big fisherman voiced his strong objection, and next he wanted Jesus to give him a bath. It's kind of humorous, really. In fact, Jesus intended to provide his men with an example. By washing their feet, He demonstrated that becoming great in the kingdom of God meant becoming the servant of all (see Mark 9:35). After finishing the object lesson, Jesus explicitly told His disciples that they were to serve one another, help one another, and give preference to one another. No doubt Jesus had in mind the time an argument broke out in His presence as to who would be greatest in the kingdom (see Luke 9:24–27). Talk about missing the point! They were willing to fight for the throne—but no one wanted the towel. *For more about* Loving Others, *see* Acts 2:42; God's Love, *John 17:11, 12.*

you, that you also love one another. [35]By this all will know that you are My disciples, if you have love for one another."

→ *A new commandment I give to you, that you love one another; as I have loved you, that you also love one another. By this all will know that you are My disciples, if you have love for one another.* John 13:34, 35

Jesus Predicts Peter's Denial

[36]Simon Peter said to Him, "Lord, where are You going?"

Jesus answered him, "Where I am going you cannot follow Me now, but you shall follow Me afterward."

[37]Peter said to Him, "Lord, why can I not follow You now? I will lay down my life for Your sake."

[38]Jesus answered him, "Will you lay down your life for My sake? Most assuredly, I say to you, the rooster shall not crow till you have denied Me three times.

The Way, the Truth, and the Life

14 "Let not your heart be troubled; you believe in God, believe also in Me. [2]In My Father's house are many mansions;[a] if *it were* not *so,* I would have told you. I go to prepare a place for you.[b] [3]And if I go and prepare a place for you, I will come again and receive you to Myself; that where I am, *there* you may be also. [4]And where I go you know, and the way you know."

[5]Thomas said to Him, "Lord, we do not know where You are going, and how can we know the way?"

[6]Jesus said to him, "I am the way, the truth, and the life. No one comes to the Father except through Me.

> **↘ LEARN**
>
> **14:2** • When you're expecting the arrival of a house-guest, you generally prepare a room ahead of time. Perhaps the individual likes certain books or treats, so you customize the room to suit your friend's preferences. That way, when your guest arrives, he or she will feel right at home. In a similar way, Jesus has gone to prepare a place for us. He is working to make it a place just right for us, a place to call home like nothing we've ever known. What are *your* likes? Whatever the details, heaven will be great. It will surpass your wildest dreams. *For more about* Heaven, *see* Rom. 14:10.

The Father Revealed

[7]"If you had known Me, you would have known My Father also; and from now on you know Him and have seen Him."

[8]Philip said to Him, "Lord, show us the Father, and it is sufficient for us."

[9]Jesus said to him, "Have I been with you so long, and yet you have not known Me, Philip? He who has seen Me has seen the Father; so how can you say, 'Show us the Father'? [10]Do you not believe that I am in the Father, and the Father in Me? The words that I speak to you I do not speak on My own *authority;* but the Father who dwells in Me does the works. [11]Believe Me that I *am* in the Father and the Father in Me, or else believe Me for the sake of the works themselves.

The Answered Prayer

[12]"Most assuredly, I say to you, he who believes in Me, the works that I do he will do also; and greater *works* than these he will do, because I go to My Father. [13]And whatever you ask in My name, that I will do, that the Father may be glorified in the Son. [14]If you ask[a] anything in My name, I will do *it.*

Jesus Promises Another Helper

[15]"If you love Me, keep[a] My commandments. [16]And I will pray the Father, and He will give you another Helper, that He may abide with you forever— [17]the Spirit of truth, whom the world cannot receive, because it neither sees Him nor knows Him; but you

---

14:2 [a]Literally *dwellings* [b]NU-Text adds a word which would cause the text to read either *if it were not so, would I have told you that I go to prepare a place for you?* or *if it were not so I would have told you; for I go to prepare a place for you.*   **14:14** [a]NU-Text adds *Me.*
14:15 [a]NU-Text reads *you will keep.*

know Him, for He dwells with you and will be in you. [18]I will not leave you orphans; I will come to you.

Indwelling of the Father and the Son

[19]"A little while longer and the world will see Me no more, but you will see Me. Because I live, you will live also. [20]At that day you will know that I *am* in My Father, and you in Me, and I in you. [21]He who has My commandments and keeps them, it is he who loves Me. And he who loves Me will be loved by My Father, and I will love him and manifest Myself to him."

➤ *He who has My commandments and keeps them, it is he who loves Me. And he who loves Me will be loved by My Father, and I will love him and manifest Myself to him.* John 14:21

[22]Judas (not Iscariot) said to Him, "Lord, how is it that You will manifest Yourself to us, and not to the world?"

[23]Jesus answered and said to him, "If anyone loves Me, he will keep My word; and My Father will love him, and We will come to him and make Our home with him. [24]He who does not love Me does not keep My words; and the word which you hear is not Mine but the Father's who sent Me.

The Gift of His Peace

[25]"These things I have spoken to you while being present with you. [26]But the Helper, the Holy Spirit, whom the Father will send in My name, He will teach you all things, and bring to your remembrance all things that I said to you. [27]Peace I leave with you, My peace I give to you; not as the world gives do I give to you. Let not your heart be troubled, neither let it be afraid. [28]You have heard Me say to you, 'I am going away and coming *back* to

you.' If you loved Me, you would rejoice because I said,[a] 'I am going to the Father,' for My Father is greater than I.

[29]"And now I have told you before it comes, that when it does come to pass, you may believe. [30]I will no longer talk much with you, for the ruler of this world is coming, and he has nothing in Me. [31]But that the world may know that I love the Father, and as the Father gave Me commandment, so I do. Arise, let us go from here.

The True Vine

15 "I am the true vine, and My Father is the vinedresser. [2]Every branch in Me that does not bear fruit He takes away;[a] and every *branch* that bears fruit He prunes, that it may bear more fruit. [3]You are already clean because of the word which I have spoken to you. [4]Abide in Me, and I in you. As the branch cannot bear fruit of itself, unless it abides in the vine, neither can you, unless you abide in Me.

[5]"I am the vine, you *are* the branches. He who abides in Me, and I in him, bears much fruit; for without Me you can do nothing. [6]If anyone does not abide in Me, he is cast out as a branch and is withered; and they gather them and throw *them* into the fire, and they are burned. [7]If you abide in Me, and My words abide in you, you will[a] ask what you desire, and it shall be done for you. [8]By this My Father is glorified, that you bear much fruit; so you will be My disciples.

➤ *If you abide in Me, and My words abide in you, you will ask what you desire, and it shall be done for you.* John 15:7

Love and Joy Perfected

[9]"As the Father loved Me, I also have loved you; abide in My love. [10]If you keep My commandments, you will abide in My love, just as I have kept My Father's commandments and abide in His love.

[11]"These things I have spoken to you, that

14:28 [a]NU-Text omits *I said.*   15:2 [a]Or *lifts up*   15:7 [a]NU-Text omits *you will.*

My joy may remain in you, and *that* your joy may be full. [12]This is My commandment, that you love one another as I have loved you. [13]Greater love has no one than this, than to lay down one's life for his friends. [14]You are My friends if you do whatever I command you. [15]No longer do I call you servants, for a servant does not know what his master is doing; but I have called you friends, for all things that I heard from My Father I have made known to you. [16]You did not choose Me, but I chose you and appointed you that you should go and bear fruit, and *that* your fruit should remain, that whatever you ask the Father in My name He may give you. [17]These things I command you, that you love one another.

The World's Hatred

[18]"If the world hates you, you know that it hated Me before *it hated* you. [19]If you were of the world, the world would love its own. Yet because you are not of the world, but I chose you out of the world, therefore the world hates you. [20]Remember the word that I said to you, 'A servant is not greater than his master.' If they persecuted Me, they will also persecute you. If they kept My word, they will keep yours also. [21]But all these things they will do to you for My name's sake, because they do not know Him who sent Me. [22]If I had not come and spoken to them, they would have no sin, but now they have no excuse for their sin. [23]He who hates Me hates My Father also. [24]If I had not done among them the works which no one else did, they would have no sin; but now they have seen and also hated both Me and My Father. [25]But

this happened that the word might be fulfilled which is written in their law, *'They hated Me without a cause.'*[a]

The Coming Rejection

[26]"But when the Helper comes, whom I shall send to you from the Father, the Spirit of truth who proceeds from the Father, He will testify of Me. [27]And you also will bear witness, because you have been with Me from the beginning.

16 "These things I have spoken to you, that you should not be made to stumble. [2]They will put you out of the synagogues; yes, the time is coming that whoever kills you will think that he offers God service. [3]And these things they will do to you[a] because they have not known the Father nor Me. [4]But these things I have told you, that when the[a] time comes, you may remember that I told you of them.

"And these things I did not say to you at the beginning, because I was with you.

The Work of the Holy Spirit

[5]"But now I go away to Him who sent Me, and none of you asks Me, 'Where are You going?' [6]But because I have said these things to you, sorrow has filled your heart. [7]Nevertheless I tell you the truth. It is to your advantage that I go away; for if I do not go away, the Helper will not come to you; but if I depart, I will send Him to you. [8]And when He has come, He will convict the world of sin, and of righteousness, and of judgment: [9]of sin, because they do not believe in Me; [10]of righteousness, because I go to My Father and

15:25 [a]Psalm 69:4   **16:3** [a]NU-Text and M-Text omit *to you.*   **16:4** [a]NU-Text reads *their.*

↑ GROW (JOHN 15:8)

How do I know if you are a Christian? For that matter, how do you know if I am a Christian? Obviously, we can't see each other's faith—but we *can* see the results of growing, genuine faith. As we walk with Jesus day by day, as we abide in Him and obey His Word and make it a habit to serve Him through the power of His Spirit, we begin to bear spiritual fruit. Spiritual fruit doesn't appear overnight, of course. It takes time to blossom and grow, and you might miss the subtle changes that accompany such fruit. That can feel discouraging! You might not see any growth at all when you look at your life—but listen to others when they say, "You have really changed! You must be abiding in Jesus because I see you becoming more like Him. I see spiritual fruit in your life!" *For more about* Growing in Christ, *see Rom. 3:18;* Faith, *2 Cor. 5:7.*

→LIVE
• • • • • • • • • • • • • • • •

16:8 • The Holy Spirit came both to convict us and to convince us of our sin. He reveals the truth of the message of Jesus' death and resurrection and then convinces us that we need to turn to God. Without His convicting power, none of us would come to faith in Jesus. Nothing that I can say will ever convince anyone of his or her need for Jesus. The Spirit convicts us of our sin, not to drive us to despair, but to send us into the open, loving arms of Jesus. No man comes to the Father unless the Holy Spirit brings him. *For more about the Holy Spirit, see John 17:21; Sin, Acts 2:38.*

you see Me no more; [11]of judgment, because the ruler of this world is judged.

[12]"I still have many things to say to you, but you cannot bear *them* now. [13]However, when He, the Spirit of truth, has come, He will guide you into all truth; for He will not speak on His own *authority,* but whatever He hears He will speak; and He will tell you things to come. [14]He will glorify Me, for He will take of what is Mine and declare *it* to you. [15]All things that the Father has are Mine. Therefore I said that He will take of Mine and declare *it* to you.[a]

Sorrow Will Turn to Joy

[16]"A little while, and you will not see Me; and again a little while, and you will see Me, because I go to the Father."

[17]Then *some* of His disciples said among themselves, "What is this that He says to us, 'A little while, and you will not see Me; and again a little while, and you will see Me'; and, 'because I go to the Father'?" [18]They said therefore, "What is this that He says, 'A little while'? We do not know what He is saying."

[19]Now Jesus knew that they desired to ask Him, and He said to them, "Are you inquiring among yourselves about what I said, 'A little while, and you will not see Me; and again a little while, and you will see Me'? [20]Most assuredly, I say to you that you will weep and lament, but the world will rejoice; and you will be sorrowful, but your sorrow will be turned into joy. [21]A woman, when she is in labor, has sorrow because her hour has come; but as soon as she has given birth to the child, she no longer remembers the anguish, for joy that a human being has been

born into the world. [22]Therefore you now have sorrow; but I will see you again and your heart will rejoice, and your joy no one will take from you.

[23]"And in that day you will ask Me nothing. Most assuredly, I say to you, whatever you ask the Father in My name He will give you. [24]Until now you have asked nothing in My name. Ask, and you will receive, that your joy may be full.

Jesus Christ Has Overcome the World

[25]"These things I have spoken to you in figurative language; but the time is coming when I will no longer speak to you in figurative language, but I will tell you plainly about the Father. [26]In that day you will ask in My name, and I do not say to you that I shall pray the Father for you; [27]for the Father Himself loves you, because you have loved Me, and have believed that I came forth from God. [28]I came forth from the Father and have come into the world. Again, I leave the world and go to the Father."

[29]His disciples said to Him, "See, now You are speaking plainly, and using no figure of speech! [30]Now we are sure that You know all things, and have no need that anyone should question You. By this we believe that You came forth from God."

[31]Jesus answered them, "Do you now believe? [32]Indeed the hour is coming, yes, has now come, that you will be scattered, each to his own, and will leave Me alone. And yet I am not alone, because the Father is with Me. [33]These things I have spoken to you, that in Me you may have peace. In the world you will[a]

⭲LEARN
• • • • • • • • • • • • • • •

16:33 • A conflict-free life is overrated. Think about the most important lessons you have learned. Did they come when things were going well, or through hardship or difficulty? Tragedy reminds us we can't do life on our own. Sometimes we get arrogant and forget who gives us the strength to succeed. Remember that what you see as bad today, you may later regard as something incredibly good. We tend to see the small picture, God sees the big one. We focus on the temporal, God on the eternal. We camp on the here and now, God on the by and by. *For more about Adversity, see Acts 4:29.*

16:15 [a]NU-Text and M-Text read *He takes of Mine and will declare it to you.*   16:33 [a]NU-Text and M-Text omit *will.*

have tribulation; but be of good cheer, I have overcome the world."

Jesus Prays for Himself

17 Jesus spoke these words, lifted up His eyes to heaven, and said: "Father, the hour has come. Glorify Your Son, that Your Son also may glorify You, ²as You have given Him authority over all flesh, that He should[a] give eternal life to as many as You have given Him. ³And this is eternal life, that they may know You, the only true God, and Jesus Christ whom You have sent. ⁴I have glorified You on the earth. I have finished the work which You have given Me to do. ⁵And now, O Father, glorify Me together with Yourself, with the glory which I had with You before the world was.

Jesus Prays for His Disciples

⁶"I have manifested Your name to the men whom You have given Me out of the world. They were Yours, You gave them to Me, and they have kept Your word. ⁷Now they have known that all things which You have given Me are from You. ⁸For I have given to them the words which You have given Me; and they have received *them*, and have known surely that I came forth from You; and they have believed that You sent Me.

⁹"I pray for them. I do not pray for the world but for those whom You have given Me, for they are Yours. ¹⁰And all Mine are Yours, and Yours are Mine, and I am glorified in them. ¹¹Now I am no longer in the world, but these are in the world, and I come to You.

↘ LEARN

17:11, 12 • Although God will keep us, we must *want* to be kept. So Jesus mentions Judas Iscariot, who had left to betray Him. Jesus kept everyone, "except the son of perdition, that the Scripture might be fulfilled." Judas was not a believer who fell away; Judas was never a believer to begin with. Jesus *keeps* all whom the Father has given to Him. Even so, the Bible tells us, "Keep yourselves in the love of God" (Jude 21), showing us that God has a part, and we have a part. We don't keep ourselves *saved*, but we do keep ourselves *safe*. *For more about God's Love and* Assurance of Salvation, *see Rom. 5:1.*

Holy Father, keep through Your name those whom You have given Me,[a] that they may be one as We *are*. ¹²While I was with them in the world,[a] I kept them in Your name. Those whom You gave Me I have kept;[b] and none of them is lost except the son of perdition, that the Scripture might be fulfilled. ¹³But now I come to You, and these things I speak in the world, that they may have My joy fulfilled in themselves. ¹⁴I have given them Your word; and the world has hated them because they are not of the world, just as I am not of the world. ¹⁵I do not pray that You should take them out of the world, but that You should keep them from the evil one. ¹⁶They are not of the world, just as I am not of the world. ¹⁷Sanctify them by Your truth. Your word is truth. ¹⁸As You sent Me into the world, I also have sent them into the world. ¹⁹And for their sakes I sanctify Myself, that they also may be sanctified by the truth.

Jesus Prays for All Believers

²⁰"I do not pray for these alone, but also for those who will[a] believe in Me through their word; ²¹that they all may be one, as You, Father, *are* in Me, and I in You; that they also may be one in Us, that the world may believe that You sent Me. ²²And the glory which You gave Me I have given them, that they may be one just as We are one: ²³I in them, and You in Me; that they may be made perfect in one, and that the world may know that You have sent Me, and have loved them as You have loved Me.

²⁴"Father, I desire that they also whom You gave Me may be with Me where I am, that they may behold My glory which You have given Me; for You loved Me before the foundation of the world. ²⁵O righteous Father! The world has not known You, but I have known You; and these have known that You sent Me. ²⁶And I have declared to them Your name, and will declare *it,* that the love with which You loved Me may be in them, and I in them."

Betrayal and Arrest in Gethsemane

18 When Jesus had spoken these words, He went out with His disciples over the Brook Kidron, where there was

---

17:2 [a]M-Text reads *shall.*   **17:11** [a]NU-Text and M-Text read *keep them through Your name which You have given Me.*   **17:12** [a]NU-Text omits *in the world.* [b]NU-Text reads *in Your name which You gave Me. And I guarded them;* (or *it;*).   **17:20** [a]NU-Text and M-Text omit *will.*

a garden, which He and His disciples entered. ²And Judas, who betrayed Him, also knew the place; for Jesus often met there with His disciples. ³Then Judas, having received a detachment *of troops,* and officers from the chief priests and Pharisees, came there with lanterns, torches, and weapons. ⁴Jesus therefore, knowing all things that would come upon Him, went forward and said to them, "Whom are you seeking?"

⁵They answered Him, "Jesus of Nazareth."

Jesus said to them, "I am *He.*" And Judas, who betrayed Him, also stood with them. ⁶Now when He said to them, "I am *He,*" they drew back and fell to the ground.

⁷Then He asked them again, "Whom are you seeking?"

And they said, "Jesus of Nazareth."

⁸Jesus answered, "I have told you that I am *He.* Therefore, if you seek Me, let these go their way," ⁹that the saying might be fulfilled which He spoke, "Of those whom You gave Me I have lost none."

¹⁰Then Simon Peter, having a sword, drew it and struck the high priest's servant, and cut off his right ear. The servant's name was Malchus.

¹¹So Jesus said to Peter, "Put your sword into the sheath. Shall I not drink the cup which My Father has given Me?"

Before the High Priest

¹²Then the detachment *of troops* and the captain and the officers of the Jews arrested Jesus and bound Him. ¹³And they led Him away to Annas first, for he was the father-in-law of Caiaphas who was high priest that year. ¹⁴Now it was Caiaphas who advised the Jews that it was expedient that one man should die for the people.

Peter Denies Jesus

¹⁵And Simon Peter followed Jesus, and so *did* another[a] disciple. Now that disciple was known to the high priest, and went with Jesus into the courtyard of the high priest. ¹⁶But Peter stood at the door outside. Then the other disciple, who was known to the high priest, went out and spoke to her who kept the door, and brought Peter in. ¹⁷Then the servant girl who kept the door said to Peter, "You are not also *one* of this Man's disciples, are you?"

He said, "I am not."

¹⁸Now the servants and officers who had made a fire of coals stood there, for it was cold, and they warmed themselves. And Peter stood with them and warmed himself.

Jesus Questioned by the High Priest

¹⁹The high priest then asked Jesus about His disciples and His doctrine. ²⁰Jesus answered him, "I spoke openly to the world. I always taught in synagogues and in the temple, where the Jews always meet,[a] and in secret I have said nothing. ²¹Why do you ask Me? Ask those who have heard Me what I said to them. Indeed they know what I said."

²²And when He had said these things, one of the officers who stood by struck Jesus with the palm of his hand, saying, "Do You answer the high priest like that?"

²³Jesus answered him, "If I have spoken evil, bear witness of the evil; but if well, why do you strike Me?"

18:15 [a]M-Text reads *the other.*   **18:20** [a]NU-Text reads *where all the Jews meet.*

↓ KNOW (JOHN 17:21)

. . . .

Without question, one of the most remarkable teachings in the Bible is that Jesus Christ makes His home in every human heart that welcomes Him. This means that through the ministry of the Holy Spirit, none of us is ever alone. Just as Jesus is in the Father and the Father is in Him, so God wants to make His home with *you.* He doesn't want just to stop by as a houseguest or pay you a visit or have a nice little chat. He wants to move in, indwell you, transform you. He wants you to know that you are one in Him and united in spirit with other believers across the globe. You are never alone! And when your life reflects this truth, Jesus says the world takes notice . . . and many people who don't yet know Jesus will long to get what you already have. *For more about the Holy Spirit, see Acts 1:1;* New Life in Christ, *Acts 13:39.*

²⁴Then Annas sent Him bound to Caiaphas the high priest.

Peter Denies Twice More

²⁵Now Simon Peter stood and warmed himself. Therefore they said to him, "You are not also *one* of His disciples, are you?"

He denied *it* and said, "I am not!"

²⁶One of the servants of the high priest, a relative *of him* whose ear Peter cut off, said, "Did I not see you in the garden with Him?" ²⁷Peter then denied again; and immediately a rooster crowed.

In Pilate's Court

²⁸Then they led Jesus from Caiaphas to the Praetorium, and it was early morning. But they themselves did not go into the Praetorium, lest they should be defiled, but that they might eat the Passover. ²⁹Pilate then went out to them and said, "What accusation do you bring against this Man?"

³⁰They answered and said to him, "If He were not an evildoer, we would not have delivered Him up to you."

³¹Then Pilate said to them, "You take Him and judge Him according to your law."

Therefore the Jews said to him, "It is not lawful for us to put anyone to death," ³²that the saying of Jesus might be fulfilled which He spoke, signifying by what death He would die.

³³Then Pilate entered the Praetorium again, called Jesus, and said to Him, "Are You the King of the Jews?"

³⁴Jesus answered him, "Are you speaking for yourself about this, or did others tell you this concerning Me?"

³⁵Pilate answered, "Am I a Jew? Your own nation and the chief priests have delivered You to me. What have You done?"

³⁶Jesus answered, "My kingdom is not of this world. If My kingdom were of this world, My servants would fight, so that I should not be delivered to the Jews; but now My kingdom is not from here."

³⁷Pilate therefore said to Him, "Are You a king then?"

Jesus answered, "You say *rightly* that I am a king. For this cause I was born, and for this cause I have come into the world, that I should bear witness to the truth. Everyone who is of the truth hears My voice."

³⁸Pilate said to Him, "What is truth?" And when he had said this, he went out again to the Jews, and said to them, "I find no fault in Him at all.

Taking the Place of Barabbas

³⁹"But you have a custom that I should release someone to you at the Passover. Do you therefore want me to release to you the King of the Jews?"

⁴⁰Then they all cried again, saying, "Not this Man, but Barabbas!" Now Barabbas was a robber.

The Soldiers Mock Jesus

19 So then Pilate took Jesus and scourged *Him.* ²And the soldiers twisted a crown of thorns and put *it* on His head, and they put on Him a purple robe. ³Then they said,ᵃ "Hail, King of the Jews!" And they struck Him with their hands.

⁴Pilate then went out again, and said to them, "Behold, I am bringing Him out to you, that you may know that I find no fault in Him."

Pilate's Decision

⁵Then Jesus came out, wearing the crown of thorns and the purple robe. And *Pilate* said to them, "Behold the Man!"

⁶Therefore, when the chief priests and officers saw Him, they cried out, saying, "Crucify *Him,* crucify *Him!*"

Pilate said to them, "You take Him and crucify *Him,* for I find no fault in Him."

⁷The Jews answered him, "We have a law, and according to ourᵃ law He ought to die, because He made Himself the Son of God."

⁸Therefore, when Pilate heard that saying, he was the more afraid, ⁹and went again into the Praetorium, and said to Jesus, "Where are You from?" But Jesus gave him no answer.

¹⁰Then Pilate said to Him, "Are You not speaking to me? Do You not know that I have power to crucify You, and power to release You?"

¹¹Jesus answered, "You could have no power at all against Me unless it had been given you from above. Therefore the one who delivered Me to you has the greater sin."

19:3 ᵃNU-Text reads *And they came up to Him and said.*   19:7 ᵃNU-Text reads *the law.*

[12]From then on Pilate sought to release Him, but the Jews cried out, saying, "If you let this Man go, you are not Caesar's friend. Whoever makes himself a king speaks against Caesar."

[13]When Pilate therefore heard that saying, he brought Jesus out and sat down in the judgment seat in a place that is called *The* Pavement, but in Hebrew, Gabbatha. [14]Now it was the Preparation Day of the Passover, and about the sixth hour. And he said to the Jews, "Behold your King!"

[15]But they cried out, "Away with *Him,* away with *Him!* Crucify Him!"

Pilate said to them, "Shall I crucify your King?"

The chief priests answered, "We have no king but Caesar!"

[16]Then he delivered Him to them to be crucified. Then they took Jesus and led *Him* away.[a]

The King on a Cross

[17]And He, bearing His cross, went out to a place called *the Place* of a Skull, which is called in Hebrew, Golgotha, [18]where they crucified Him, and two others with Him, one on either side, and Jesus in the center. [19]Now Pilate wrote a title and put *it* on the cross. And the writing was:

JESUS OF NAZARETH,
THE KING OF THE JEWS.

[20]Then many of the Jews read this title, for the place where Jesus was crucified was near the city; and it was written in Hebrew, Greek, *and* Latin.

[21]Therefore the chief priests of the Jews said to Pilate, "Do not write, 'The King of the Jews,' but, 'He said, "I am the King of the Jews." ' "

[22]Pilate answered, "What I have written, I have written."

[23]Then the soldiers, when they had crucified Jesus, took His garments and made four parts, to each soldier a part, and also the tunic. Now the tunic was without seam, woven from the top in one piece. [24]They said therefore among themselves, "Let us not tear it, but cast lots for it, whose it shall be," that the Scripture might be fulfilled which says:

"They divided My garments among them,
    And for My clothing they cast lots."[a]

Therefore the soldiers did these things.

Behold Your Mother

[25]Now there stood by the cross of Jesus His mother, and His mother's sister, Mary the *wife* of Clopas, and Mary Magdalene. [26]When Jesus therefore saw His mother, and the disciple whom He loved standing by, He said to His mother, "Woman, behold your son!" [27]Then He said to the disciple, "Behold your mother!" And from that hour that disciple took her to his own *home.*

↘ LEARN
• • • • • • • • • • • • • • • • •

19:26, 27 • It is fascinating to recognize how much of His earthly ministry Jesus devoted to providing for the physical needs of men, women, and children. He healed their blindness, filled their stomachs, calmed their fears, cast out their demons, cured their illness, raised their dead, all in addition to saving their souls. After His resurrection, He continued to meet the physical needs of His followers. And even on the Cross, despite His own cruel suffering, Jesus remembered that His mother needed a roof over her head and food to eat—and so He charged the apostle John with that crucial responsibility. *For more about* Jesus' Life, *see John 20:29.*

It Is Finished

[28]After this, Jesus, knowing[a] that all things were now accomplished, that the Scripture might be fulfilled, said, "I thirst!" [29]Now a vessel full of sour wine was sitting there; and they filled a sponge with sour wine, put *it* on hyssop, and put *it* to His mouth. [30]So when Jesus had received the sour wine, He said, "It is finished!" And bowing His head, He gave up His spirit.

Jesus' Side Is Pierced

[31]Therefore, because it was the Preparation *Day,* that the bodies should not remain on the cross on the Sabbath (for that Sabbath was a high day), the Jews asked Pilate that their legs might be broken, and *that* they might be taken away. [32]Then the soldiers came and broke the legs of the first and of

the other who was crucified with Him. ³³But when they came to Jesus and saw that He was already dead, they did not break His legs. ³⁴But one of the soldiers pierced His side with a spear, and immediately blood and water came out. ³⁵And he who has seen has testified, and his testimony is true; and he knows that he is telling the truth, so that you may believe. ³⁶For these things were done that the Scripture should be fulfilled, *"Not one of His bones shall be broken."*ᵃ ³⁷And again another Scripture says, *"They shall look on Him whom they pierced."*ᵃ

Jesus Buried in Joseph's Tomb

³⁸After this, Joseph of Arimathea, being a disciple of Jesus, but secretly, for fear of the Jews, asked Pilate that he might take away the body of Jesus; and Pilate gave *him* permission. So he came and took the body of Jesus. ³⁹And Nicodemus, who at first came to Jesus by night, also came, bringing a mixture of myrrh and aloes, about a hundred pounds. ⁴⁰Then they took the body of Jesus, and bound it in strips of linen with the spices, as the custom of the Jews is to bury. ⁴¹Now in the place where He was crucified there was a garden, and in the garden a new tomb in which no one had yet been laid. ⁴²So there they laid Jesus, because of the Jews' Preparation *Day,* for the tomb was nearby.

The Empty Tomb

20 Now the first *day* of the week Mary Magdalene went to the tomb early, while it was still dark, and saw *that* the stone had been taken away from the tomb. ²Then she ran and came to Simon Peter, and to the other disciple, whom Jesus loved, and said to them, "They have taken away the Lord out of the tomb, and we do not know where they have laid Him."

³Peter therefore went out, and the other disciple, and were going to the tomb. ⁴So they both ran together, and the other disciple outran Peter and came to the tomb first. ⁵And he, stooping down and looking in, saw the linen cloths lying *there;* yet he did not go in. ⁶Then Simon Peter came, following him, and went into the tomb; and he saw the linen cloths lying *there,* ⁷and the handkerchief that

had been around His head, not lying with the linen cloths, but folded together in a place by itself. ⁸Then the other disciple, who came to the tomb first, went in also; and he saw and believed. ⁹For as yet they did not know the Scripture, that He must rise again from the dead. ¹⁰Then the disciples went away again to their own homes.

Mary Magdalene Sees the Risen Lord

¹¹But Mary stood outside by the tomb weeping, and as she wept she stooped down *and looked* into the tomb. ¹²And she saw two angels in white sitting, one at the head and the other at the feet, where the body of Jesus had lain. ¹³Then they said to her, "Woman, why are you weeping?"

She said to them, "Because they have taken away my Lord, and I do not know where they have laid Him."

¹⁴Now when she had said this, she turned around and saw Jesus standing *there,* and did not know that it was Jesus. ¹⁵Jesus said to her, "Woman, why are you weeping? Whom are you seeking?"

She, supposing Him to be the gardener, said to Him, "Sir, if You have carried Him away, tell me where You have laid Him, and I will take Him away."

¹⁶Jesus said to her, "Mary!"

She turned and said to Him,ᵃ "Rabboni!" (which is to say, Teacher).

¹⁷Jesus said to her, "Do not cling to Me, for I have not yet ascended to My Father; but go to My brethren and say to them, 'I am ascending to My Father and your Father, and *to* My God and your God.' "

¹⁸Mary Magdalene came and told the disciples that she had seen the Lord,ᵃ and *that* He had spoken these things to her.

The Apostles Commissioned

¹⁹Then, the same day at evening, being the first *day* of the week, when the doors were shut where the disciples were assembled,ᵃ for fear of the Jews, Jesus came and stood in the midst, and said to them, "Peace *be* with you." ²⁰When He had said this, He showed them *His* hands and His side. Then the disciples were glad when they saw the Lord.

19:36 ᵃExodus 12:46; Numbers 9:12; Psalm 34:20   **19:37** ᵃZechariah 12:10   **20:16** ᵃNU-Text adds *in Hebrew.*
20:18 ᵃNU-Text reads *disciples, "I have seen the Lord," . . .*   **20:19** ᵃNU-Text omits *assembled.*

[21]So Jesus said to them again, "Peace to you! As the Father has sent Me, I also send you." [22]And when He had said this, He breathed on *them,* and said to them, "Receive the Holy Spirit. [23]If you forgive the sins of any, they are forgiven them; if you retain the *sins* of any, they are retained."

Seeing and Believing

[24]Now Thomas, called the Twin, one of the twelve, was not with them when Jesus came. [25]The other disciples therefore said to him, "We have seen the Lord."

So he said to them, "Unless I see in His hands the print of the nails, and put my finger into the print of the nails, and put my hand into His side, I will not believe."

[26]And after eight days His disciples were again inside, and Thomas with them. Jesus came, the doors being shut, and stood in the midst, and said, "Peace to you!" [27]Then He said to Thomas, "Reach your finger here, and look at My hands; and reach your hand *here,* and put *it* into My side. Do not be unbelieving, but believing."

[28]And Thomas answered and said to Him, "My Lord and my God!"

[29]Jesus said to him, "Thomas,[a] because you have seen Me, you have believed. Blessed *are* those who have not seen and *yet* have believed."

→ LIVE
. . . .

20:29 • Did you know that Jesus both began and concluded His earthly ministry with blessing people? In the greatest gift of all, God blesses us with Himself. As A. B. Simpson wrote,

Once it was the blessing,
Now it is the Lord;
Once it was the feeling,
Now it is His Word.
Once His gifts I wanted,
Now the Giver own;
Once I sought for healing,
Now Himself alone.

While we have yet to see Jesus physically, the day is coming soon when every eye shall see Him. On that day, every knee shall bow. Until that day, we are to believe. *For more about* Jesus' Return, *see 2 Thess. 1:7;* Jesus' Life, *1 Cor. 5:4.*

That You May Believe

[30]And truly Jesus did many other signs in the presence of His disciples, which are not written in this book; [31]but these are written that you may believe that Jesus is the Christ, the Son of God, and that believing you may have life in His name.

Breakfast by the Sea

21 After these things Jesus showed Himself again to the disciples at the Sea of Tiberias, and in this way He showed *Himself:* [2]Simon Peter, Thomas called the Twin, Nathanael of Cana in Galilee, the *sons* of Zebedee, and two others of His disciples were together. [3]Simon Peter said to them, "I am going fishing."

They said to him, "We are going with you also." They went out and immediately[a] got into the boat, and that night they caught nothing. [4]But when the morning had now come, Jesus stood on the shore; yet the disciples did not know that it was Jesus. [5]Then Jesus said to them, "Children, have you any food?"

They answered Him, "No."

[6]And He said to them, "Cast the net on the right side of the boat, and you will find *some.*" So they cast, and now they were not able to draw it in because of the multitude of fish.

[7]Therefore that disciple whom Jesus loved said to Peter, "It is the Lord!" Now when Simon Peter heard that it was the Lord, he put on *his* outer garment (for he had removed it), and plunged into the sea. [8]But the other disciples came in the little boat (for they were not far from land, but about two hundred cubits), dragging the net with fish. [9]Then, as soon as they had come to land, they saw a fire of coals there, and fish laid on it, and bread. [10]Jesus said to them, "Bring some of the fish which you have just caught."

[11]Simon Peter went up and dragged the net to land, full of large fish, one hundred and fifty-three; and although there were so many, the net was not broken. [12]Jesus said to them, "Come *and* eat breakfast." Yet none of the disciples dared ask Him, "Who are You?"—knowing that it was the Lord. [13]Jesus then came and took the bread and gave it to them, and likewise the fish.

20:29 [a]NU-Text and M-Text omit *Thomas.*   21:3 [a]NU-Text omits *immediately.*

¹⁴This *is* now the third time Jesus showed Himself to His disciples after He was raised from the dead.

Jesus Restores Peter

¹⁵So when they had eaten breakfast, Jesus said to Simon Peter, "Simon, *son* of Jonah,^a do you love Me more than these?"

He said to Him, "Yes, Lord; You know that I love You."

He said to him, "Feed My lambs."

¹⁶He said to him again a second time, "Simon, *son* of Jonah,^a do you love Me?"

He said to Him, "Yes, Lord; You know that I love You."

He said to him, "Tend My sheep."

¹⁷He said to him the third time, "Simon, *son* of Jonah,^a do you love Me?" Peter was grieved because He said to him the third time, "Do you love Me?"

And he said to Him, "Lord, You know all things; You know that I love You."

Jesus said to him, "Feed My sheep. ¹⁸Most assuredly, I say to you, when you were younger, you girded yourself and walked where you wished; but when you are old, you will stretch out your hands, and another will gird you and carry *you* where you do not wish." ¹⁹This He spoke, signifying by what death he would glorify God. And when He had spoken this, He said to him, "Follow Me."

The Beloved Disciple and His Book

²⁰Then Peter, turning around, saw the disciple whom Jesus loved following, who also had leaned on His breast at the supper, and said, "Lord, who is the one who betrays You?" ²¹Peter, seeing him, said to Jesus, "But Lord, what *about* this man?"

²²Jesus said to him, "If I will that he remain till I come, what *is that* to you? You follow Me."

²³Then this saying went out among the brethren that this disciple would not die. Yet Jesus did not say to him that he would not die, but, "If I will that he remain till I come, what *is that* to you?"

²⁴This is the disciple who testifies of these things, and wrote these things; and we know that his testimony is true.

²⁵And there are also many other things that Jesus did, which if they were written one by one, I suppose that even the world itself could not contain the books that would be written. Amen.

21:15, 16, 17 ^aNU-Text reads *John.*

ACTS

INTRODUCTION//

L uke wrote the Book of Acts as a sequel to his Gospel in order to show the church's early development and rapid growth. It reveals how the dynamic power of the Holy Spirit transforms a diverse group of fishermen, tax collectors, and other ordinary folks into bold witnesses who radically alter their world. The book demonstrates the transformative power of Christ, not only in individual lives, but in entire nations. Beginning with the ascension of Jesus and the giving of the Holy Spirit at Pentecost, the first half of the book describes the ministry of the apostles, especially Peter. At this time the church began its missionary work, spreading the gospel around the Greek and Roman world. The second half of the book describes the conversion and ministry of Paul, one of the early church's greatest leaders and formerly one of its worst persecutors.

In Acts we see many amazing incidents, such as tongues of fire alighting on the disciples' heads, miracles of healing, unlikely conversions, and powerful sermons and testimonies; but we also see great tragedies. Shortly after the establishment of the church, various groups began a relentless persecution of Christians. Many believers were imprisoned or killed, including most of the apostles and first leaders of the church. These spiritual forebears provide us with a rich heritage and example. We can learn much from studying the sermons, prayers, and actions of the individuals profiled in Acts. Acts also gives the background and setting for most of the New Testament's letters, so that we can better understand the context of many of its great teachings. These first-century believers, without the benefit of modern technology, turned their world upside down (Acts 17:6). In Acts we have a template to follow for the church today. We are wise to emulate it.

Prologue

1 The former account I made, O Theophilus, of all that Jesus began both to do and teach, [2]until the day in which He was taken up, after He through the Holy Spirit had given commandments to the apostles whom He had chosen, [3]to whom He also presented Himself alive after His suffering by many infallible proofs, being seen by them during forty days and speaking of the things pertaining to the kingdom of God.

↘ LEARN

1:1 • The Book of Acts gives us an overview of the infant church's activity from about A.D. 33 to A.D. 63. During those three decades, outsiders said the church had turned the world upside down (Acts 17:6). Sounds impressive, doesn't it? But in fact, the Book of Acts is simply a picture of normal Christianity. If it seems radical to us, that's only because we are not radical enough. The good news is that the same Holy Spirit who set the early church into motion is alive and well today and ready to use *us* . . . if we will open ourselves to Him. *For more about the* Holy Spirit, *see Acts 2:3;* God's Word, *1 Cor. 10:11.*

The Holy Spirit Promised

[4]And being assembled together with *them,* He commanded them not to depart from Jerusalem, but to wait for the Promise of the Father, "which," *He said,* "you have heard from Me; [5]for John truly baptized with water, but you shall be baptized with the Holy Spirit not many days from now." [6]Therefore, when they had come together, they asked Him, saying, "Lord, will You at this time restore the

1:8 [a]NU-Text reads *My witnesses.*

> ➤ *But you shall receive power when the Holy Spirit has come upon you; and you shall be witnesses to Me in Jerusalem, and in all Judea and Samaria, and to the end of the earth.* Acts 1:8

kingdom to Israel?" [7]And He said to them, "It is not for you to know times or seasons which the Father has put in His own authority. [8]But you shall receive power when the Holy Spirit has come upon you; and you shall be witnesses to Me[a] in Jerusalem, and in all Judea and Samaria, and to the end of the earth."

↘ LEARN

1:8 • Jesus told His followers they would receive power to share their faith, to speak up and be counted. The word used for "power" is the Greek term *dunamis,* reflected in our English words *dynamic* and *dynamite.* The same power that set the early church into motion is available to us—and to you—right now. And what is that power for? "To be witnesses." God wants to empower you to be His representative. By tapping into this power, we can send into our culture the same kind of shockwaves that the early church used to rock the entire Roman Empire! *For more about* Sharing Your Faith, *see Acts 3:19.*

↑ GROW (ACTS 1:8)

After the Spirit was poured out, Peter said, "For the promise is to you and to your children, and to all who are afar off, as many as the Lord our God will call" (2:39). The promise was, "You shall receive power . . . and you shall be witnesses." The word translated "power" comes from the Greek term *dunamis,* from which we get the words "dynamite" and "dynamic." So in a sense, Jesus said, "I am going to give you explosive, dynamic, dynamite power!" Not political power to overthrow Rome, but spiritual power to overcome sin, preach the gospel, change the world. This verse also gives us a strategy for evangelism: "in Jerusalem, and in all Judea and Samaria, and to the end of the earth." The order here is significant. It all started in their own backyard! We should start by being witnesses to those around us, whether family, friends, coworkers, or others. *For more about* Sharing Your Faith, *see Acts 3:19.*

Jesus Ascends to Heaven

[9]Now when He had spoken these things, while they watched, He was taken up, and a cloud received Him out of their sight. [10]And while they looked steadfastly toward heaven as He went up, behold, two men stood by them in white apparel, [11]who also said, "Men of Galilee, why do you stand gazing up into heaven? This *same* Jesus, who was taken up from you into heaven, will so come in like manner as you saw Him go into heaven."

The Upper Room Prayer Meeting

[12]Then they returned to Jerusalem from the mount called Olivet, which is near Jerusalem, a Sabbath day's journey. [13]And when they had entered, they went up into the upper room where they were staying: Peter, James, John, and Andrew; Philip and Thomas; Bartholomew and Matthew; James *the son* of Alphaeus and Simon the Zealot; and Judas *the son* of James. [14]These all continued with one accord in prayer and supplication,[a] with the women and Mary the mother of Jesus, and with His brothers.

Matthias Chosen

[15]And in those days Peter stood up in the midst of the disciples[a] (altogether the number of names was about a hundred and twenty), and said, [16]"Men *and* brethren, this Scripture had to be fulfilled, which the Holy Spirit spoke before by the mouth of David concerning Judas, who became a guide to those who arrested Jesus; [17]for he was numbered with us and obtained a part in this ministry."

[18](Now this man purchased a field with the wages of iniquity; and falling headlong, he burst open in the middle and all his entrails gushed out. [19]And it became known to all those dwelling in Jerusalem; so that field is called in their own language, Akel Dama, that is, Field of Blood.)

[20]"For it is written in the Book of Psalms:

'Let his dwelling place be desolate,
    And let no one live in it';[a]

and,

'Let[b] another take his office.'[c]

[21]"Therefore, of these men who have accompanied us all the time that the Lord Jesus went in and out among us, [22]beginning from the baptism of John to that day when He was taken up from us, one of these must become a witness with us of His resurrection."

[23]And they proposed two: Joseph called Barsabas, who was surnamed Justus, and Matthias. [24]And they prayed and said, "You, O Lord, who know the hearts of all, show which of these two You have chosen [25]to take part in this ministry and apostleship from which Judas by transgression fell, that he might go to his own place." [26]And they cast their lots, and the lot fell on Matthias. And he was numbered with the eleven apostles.

Coming of the Holy Spirit

2 When the Day of Pentecost had fully come, they were all with one accord[a] in one place. [2]And suddenly there came a sound from heaven, as of a rushing mighty wind, and it filled the whole house where they were sitting. [3]Then there appeared to them divided tongues, as of fire, and *one* sat upon

1:14 [a]NU-Text omits *and supplication.*   1:15 [a]NU-Text reads *brethren.*   1:20 [a]Psalm 69:25 [b]Psalm 109:8 [c]Greek *episkopen,* position of overseer   2:1 [a]NU-Text reads *together.*

↓ KNOW (ACTS 2:3)

The Holy Spirit is a *Him,* not an *it.* Jesus says, "When *He* has come *He* will convict." Some object, "How can the Spirit be a Him when the Bible uses terms like 'wind' and 'fire' and 'dove' as descriptions?" Consider that Jesus is called both the Bread of Life and the Door (John 6:48, 10:7). And the Bible describes the Father as a consuming fire and a refuge (Heb. 12:29; Ps. 62:8). We can even hide under the shadow of His wings (Ps. 91:4). Does this mean Jesus is a loaf of rye or a gate, or that the Father is an inferno, a castle, or a giant bird? Of course not. The Bible uses these metaphors to help us better understand God. The Spirit is a Person who has emotion. And the Person of the Spirit has a specific work He wants to do in each of our lives. *For more about the* Holy Spirit, *see Acts 2:16–21.*

each of them. [4]And they were all filled with the Holy Spirit and began to speak with other tongues, as the Spirit gave them utterance.

The Crowd's Response

[5]And there were dwelling in Jerusalem Jews, devout men, from every nation under heaven. [6]And when this sound occurred, the multitude came together, and were confused, because everyone heard them speak in his own language. [7]Then they were all amazed and marveled, saying to one another, "Look, are not all these who speak Galileans? [8]And how *is it that* we hear, each in our own language in which we were born? [9]Parthians and Medes and Elamites, those dwelling in Mesopotamia, Judea and Cappadocia, Pontus and Asia, [10]Phrygia and Pamphylia, Egypt and the parts of Libya adjoining Cyrene, visitors from Rome, both Jews and proselytes, [11]Cretans and Arabs—we hear them speaking in our own tongues the wonderful works of God." [12]So they were all amazed and perplexed, saying to one another, "Whatever could this mean?" [13]Others mocking said, "They are full of new wine."

Peter's Sermon

[14]But Peter, standing up with the eleven, raised his voice and said to them, "Men of Judea and all who dwell in Jerusalem, let this be known to you, and heed my words. [15]For these are not drunk, as you suppose, since it is *only* the third hour of the day. [16]But this is what was spoken by the prophet Joel:

[17] '*And it shall come to pass in the last days,*
    says God,
    That I will pour out of My Spirit on all
        flesh;
    Your sons and your daughters shall
        prophesy,
    Your young men shall see visions,
    Your old men shall dream dreams.
[18] *And on My menservants and on My*
        maidservants
    I will pour out My Spirit in those days;
    And they shall prophesy.
[19] *I will show wonders in heaven above*
    And signs in the earth beneath:
    Blood and fire and vapor of smoke.
[20] *The sun shall be turned into darkness,*

> ### ↘ LEARN
> • • • • • • • • • • • • • • • • •
> 2:16–21 • What occurred at Pentecost? Should we expect it to happen again today? The answer is both yes and no. No, we don't need another day of Pentecost any more than we need another Calvary. At no other time did a "rushing mighty wind" come on the disciples, with the Spirit appearing in the form of flames (vv. 2, 3). But yes, we need to personally appropriate what God made available to them. That's why we read frequently of the Holy Spirit empowering, filling, and using believers. Pentecost was a never-to-be-repeated event. But the power poured out back then remains available to all believers today. *For more about the* Holy Spirit, *see Acts 2:38.*

    And the moon into blood,
    Before the coming of the great and
        awesome day of the LORD.
[21] *And it shall come to pass*
    That whoever calls on the name of the
        LORD
    Shall be saved.'[a]

[22]"Men of Israel, hear these words: Jesus of Nazareth, a Man attested by God to you by miracles, wonders, and signs which God did through Him in your midst, as you yourselves also know— [23]Him, being delivered by the determined purpose and foreknowledge of God, you have taken[a] by lawless hands, have crucified, and put to death; [24]whom God raised up, having loosed the pains of death, because it was not possible that He should be held by it. [25]For David says concerning Him:

    '*I foresaw the LORD always before my face,*
    For He is at my right hand, that I may not
        be shaken.
[26] *Therefore my heart rejoiced, and my*
        tongue was glad;
    Moreover my flesh also will rest in hope.
[27] *For You will not leave my soul in Hades,*
    Nor will You allow Your Holy One to see
        corruption.
[28] *You have made known to me the ways*
        of life;
    You will make me full of joy in Your
        presence.'[a]

[29]"Men *and* brethren, let *me* speak freely to you of the patriarch David, that he is both dead and buried, and his tomb is with us to

2:21 [a]Joel 2:28–32   2:23 [a]NU-Text omits *have taken.*   2:28 [a]Psalm 16:8–11

this day. [30]Therefore, being a prophet, and knowing that God had sworn with an oath to him that of the fruit of his body, according to the flesh, He would raise up the Christ to sit on his throne,[a] [31]he, foreseeing this, spoke concerning the resurrection of the Christ, that His soul was not left in Hades, nor did His flesh see corruption. [32]This Jesus God has raised up, of which we are all witnesses. [33]Therefore being exalted to the right hand of God, and having received from the Father the promise of the Holy Spirit, He poured out this which you now see and hear.

[34]"For David did not ascend into the heavens, but he says himself:

> 'The LORD said to my Lord,
> "Sit at My right hand,
> [35]Till I make Your enemies Your
>   footstool." '[a]

[36]"Therefore let all the house of Israel know assuredly that God has made this Jesus, whom you crucified, both Lord and Christ."

[37]Now when they heard *this,* they were cut to the heart, and said to Peter and the rest of the apostles, "Men *and* brethren, what shall we do?"

[38]Then Peter said to them, "Repent, and let every one of you be baptized in the name of Jesus Christ for the remission of sins; and

→LIVE

2:38 • When you sin and you know it, the Spirit convicts your heart, saying to you, "Repent now. Turn from your sin and turn to God. Believe that Jesus died and rose again for the forgiveness of your sins." In other words, He tells you to go straight to the Cross! But the devil says, "No! Don't make a fool of yourself. God would never hear your prayers, you hypocrite!" Satan knows that when you are forgiven, you are right with God. The Holy Spirit will always seek to draw you to the Cross; Satan will always attempt to drive you from it. *For more about the* Holy Spirit, *see Acts 7:51;* Forgiveness, *Acts 13:39;* Satan, *Acts 16:6–10;* Sin, *Acts 3:19.*

you shall receive the gift of the Holy Spirit. [39]For the promise is to you and to your children, and to all who are afar off, as many as the Lord our God will call."

A Vital Church Grows

[40]And with many other words he testified and exhorted them, saying, "Be saved from this perverse generation." [41]Then those who gladly[a] received his word were baptized; and that day about three thousand souls were added *to them.* [42]And they continued steadfastly in the apostles' doctrine and fellowship, in the breaking of bread, and in prayers. [43]Then fear came upon every soul, and many wonders and signs were done through the apostles. [44]Now all who believed were together, and had all things in common, [45]and sold their possessions and goods, and divided them among all, as anyone had need.

↘LEARN

2:42 • The kind of church that transforms its members, its neighborhood, and its world is WELL: **W**orshiping, **E**vangelizing, **L**earning, **L**oving. We worship God and He "inhabits the praises of His people." We proclaim Christ and outsiders place their faith in Him. We hear God's Word preached and immediately sense the freshness of His Spirit. We love one another and our fellowship grows in both depth and size. In a WELL church, people talk together about the things of God. They serve together. They pray together. They sing and speak and study and are smitten with each other. And so things go WELL. *For more about* Worship, *see Acts 24:14;* Fellowship, *1 Cor. 1:10;* How to Live Out Your Faith, *Rom. 3:18;* Loving Others, *Rom. 14:19.*

[46]So continuing daily with one accord in the temple, and breaking bread from house to house, they ate their food with gladness and simplicity of heart, [47]praising God and having favor with all the people. And the Lord added to the church[a] daily those who were being saved.

A Lame Man Healed

3 Now Peter and John went up together to the temple at the hour of prayer, the ninth *hour.* [2]And a certain man lame from his mother's womb was carried, whom they laid daily at the gate of the temple which is called Beautiful, to ask alms from those who entered the temple; [3]who, seeing Peter and John about to go into the temple, asked for alms. [4]And fixing his eyes on him, with John,

2:30 [a]NU-Text omits *according to the flesh, He would raise up the Christ* and completes the verse with *He would seat one on his throne.*
2:35 [a]Psalm 110:1   **2:41** [a]NU-Text omits *gladly.*   **2:47** [a]NU-Text omits *to the church.*

Peter said, "Look at us." [5]So he gave them his attention, expecting to receive something from them. [6]Then Peter said, "Silver and gold I do not have, but what I do have I give you: In the name of Jesus Christ of Nazareth, rise up and walk." [7]And he took him by the right hand and lifted *him* up, and immediately his feet and ankle bones received strength. [8]So he, leaping up, stood and walked and entered the temple with them—walking, leaping, and praising God. [9]And all the people saw him walking and praising God. [10]Then they knew that it was he who sat begging alms at the Beautiful Gate of the temple; and they were filled with wonder and amazement at what had happened to him.

Preaching in Solomon's Portico

[11]Now as the lame man who was healed held on to Peter and John, all the people ran together to them in the porch which is called Solomon's, greatly amazed. [12]So when Peter saw *it*, he responded to the people: "Men of Israel, why do you marvel at this? Or why look so intently at us, as though by our own power or godliness we had made this man walk? [13]The God of Abraham, Isaac, and Jacob, the God of our fathers, glorified His Servant Jesus, whom you delivered up and denied in the presence of Pilate, when he was determined to let *Him* go. [14]But you denied the Holy One and the Just, and asked for a murderer to be granted to you, [15]and killed the Prince of life, whom God raised from the dead, of which we are witnesses. [16]And His name, through faith in His name, has made this man strong, whom you see and know. Yes, the faith which *comes* through Him has

given him this perfect soundness in the presence of you all.

[17]"Yet now, brethren, I know that you did *it* in ignorance, as *did* also your rulers. [18]But those things which God foretold by the mouth of all His prophets, that the Christ would suffer, He has thus fulfilled. [19]Repent therefore and be converted, that your sins may be blotted out, so that times of refreshing may come from the presence of the Lord, [20]and that He may send Jesus Christ,

→LIVE

3:19 • As we call people to believe in Jesus Christ, we also need to call them to repent of their sin. The problem with some preaching today is there is no mention of repentance. "Hey, just believe in Jesus and He will make your life fuller and better." The problem? That is not the whole gospel. When someone believes, explain that he needs to repent of his sin as well. To believe in Jesus involves both taking hold and letting go. Through believing, you take hold of Christ. Through repentance, you let go of sin. You can't have it both ways. *For more about* Sharing Your Faith, *see Acts 4:29;* Sin, *Rom. 7:15;* Becoming a Christian, *Acts 15:3.*

who was preached to you before,[a] [21]whom heaven must receive until the times of restoration of all things, which God has spoken by the mouth of all His holy prophets since the world began. [22]For Moses truly said to the fathers, *'The* LORD *your God will raise up for you a Prophet like me from your brethren. Him you shall hear in all things, whatever He says to you.* [23]*And it shall be that every soul who will not hear that Prophet shall be utterly destroyed from among the people.'*[a]

3:20 [a]NU-Text and M-Text read *Christ Jesus, who was ordained for you before.*   3:23 [a]Deuteronomy 18:15, 18, 19

↑ GROW (ACTS 3:19)

"Repent therefore and be converted." We don't hear these words nearly enough today. Repentance and belief are like two sides of a coin or two wings on an aircraft. Both are vitally important. To believe is to take hold of something, whereas to repent is to let go. Repentance is not just feeling bad about your sin, but turning from it, hanging a U-turn in the road of life. Once you were running away from God; now you are running toward Him. Confession of sin is an important part of growing in Christ because sin means falling short of a mark, failing to live up to God's perfect standard. All of us sin more than we probably realize; that is why we need to pray regularly, "Lord, forgive me of my sins." If we don't confess our sins, then our prayers won't go any higher than the ceiling. Sin cripples an effective prayer life. *For more about* Prayer, *see Acts 4:29;* Sin, *Rom. 7:15;* Becoming a Christian, *Acts 15:3.*

²⁴Yes, and all the prophets, from Samuel and those who follow, as many as have spoken, have also foretold[a] these days. ²⁵You are sons of the prophets, and of the covenant which God made with our fathers, saying to Abraham, *'And in your seed all the families of the earth shall be blessed.'*[a] ²⁶To you first, God, having raised up His Servant Jesus, sent Him to bless you, in turning away every one *of you* from your iniquities."

Peter and John Arrested

4 Now as they spoke to the people, the priests, the captain of the temple, and the Sadducees came upon them, ²being greatly disturbed that they taught the people and preached in Jesus the resurrection from the dead. ³And they laid hands on them, and put *them* in custody until the next day, for it was already evening. ⁴However, many of those who heard the word believed; and the number of the men came to be about five thousand.

Addressing the Sanhedrin

⁵And it came to pass, on the next day, that their rulers, elders, and scribes, ⁶as well as Annas the high priest, Caiaphas, John, and Alexander, and as many as were of the family of the high priest, were gathered together at Jerusalem. ⁷And when they had set them in the midst, they asked, "By what power or by what name have you done this?"

⁸Then Peter, filled with the Holy Spirit, said to them, "Rulers of the people and elders of Israel: ⁹If we this day are judged for a good deed *done* to a helpless man, by what means he has been made well, ¹⁰let it be known to you all, and to all the people of Israel, that by the name of Jesus Christ of Nazareth, whom you crucified, whom God raised from the dead, by Him this man stands here before you whole. ¹¹This is the *'stone which was rejected by you builders, which has become the chief cornerstone.'*[a] ¹²Nor is there salvation in any other, for there is no other name under heaven given among men by which we must be saved."

The Name of Jesus Forbidden

¹³Now when they saw the boldness of Peter and John, and perceived that they were uneducated and untrained men, they marveled. And they realized that they had been with Jesus. ¹⁴And seeing the man who had been healed standing with them, they could say nothing against it. ¹⁵But when they had commanded them to go aside out of the council, they conferred among themselves, ¹⁶saying, "What shall we do to these men? For, indeed, that a notable miracle has been done through them *is* evident to all who dwell in Jerusalem, and we cannot deny *it.* ¹⁷But so that it spreads no further among the people, let us severely threaten them, that from now on they speak to no man in this name."

¹⁸So they called them and commanded them not to speak at all nor teach in the name of Jesus. ¹⁹But Peter and John answered and said to them, "Whether it is right in the sight of God to listen to you more than to God, you judge. ²⁰For we cannot but speak the things which we have seen and heard." ²¹So when they had further threatened them, they let them go, finding no way of punishing them, because of the people, since they all glorified God for what had been done. ²²For the man was over forty years old on whom this miracle of healing had been performed.

Prayer for Boldness

²³And being let go, they went to their own *companions* and reported all that the chief priests and elders had said to them. ²⁴So when they heard that, they raised their voice to God with one accord and said: "Lord, You *are* God, who made heaven and earth and the sea, and all that is in them, ²⁵who by the mouth of Your servant David[a] have said:

> *'Why did the nations rage,*
>   *And the people plot vain things?*
> ²⁶ *The kings of the earth took their stand,*
>   *And the rulers were gathered together*
>   *Against the LORD and against His Christ.'*[a]

²⁷"For truly against Your holy Servant Jesus, whom You anointed, both Herod and Pontius Pilate, with the Gentiles and the people of Israel, were gathered together ²⁸to do whatever Your hand and Your purpose determined before to be done. ²⁹Now, Lord, look on their threats, and grant to Your servants that with all boldness they may speak Your word, ³⁰by stretching out Your hand

---

3:24 [a]NU-Text and M-Text read *proclaimed.*   **3:25** [a]Genesis 22:18; 26:4; 28:14   **4:11** [a]Psalm 118:22
4:25 [a]NU-Text reads *who through the Holy Spirit, by the mouth of our father, Your servant David.*   **4:26** [a]Psalm 2:1, 2

➔LIVE

4:27, 28 • Who is responsible for the death of Jesus? Throughout history, some speakers and writers have falsely laid the claim at the feet of the Jews, but the Bible clearly teaches that although the Jewish religious leaders of the day, along with the occupying Romans, technically arranged for the crucifixion of Jesus, it was God Himself who directed the whole thing behind the scenes (Is. 53:10). It was *our* sins that put Jesus on the Cross, so if you must blame someone, I suppose you could blame me; but then again, don't forget to also include your own responsibility. *For more about* Jesus' Life, *see 1 Cor. 5:4;* The Cross, *Rom. 5:18.*

to heal, and that signs and wonders may be done through the name of Your holy Servant Jesus."

[31]And when they had prayed, the place where they were assembled together was shaken; and they were all filled with the Holy Spirit, and they spoke the word of God with boldness.

↘LEARN

4:29 • The apostles had a very interesting reaction to the threats breathed against them by the authorities who objected to their witness for Christ. We'd probably pray, "Lord, deliver us! Protect us and bring their threats to nothing." But that's not how they prayed at all. Instead they said to God, "Lord, You've heard their threats. So have we. So make us even bolder as we tell others about You." They asked for the blessing of boldness, not the security of safety. Their primary concern was to get the word out about Jesus. Maybe that's why they were so successful at it! *For more about* Prayer, *see Acts 6:6;* Sharing Your Faith, *Acts 8:4;* Adversity, *Acts 5:41.*

Sharing in All Things

[32]Now the multitude of those who believed were of one heart and one soul; neither did anyone say that any of the things he possessed was his own, but they had all things in common. [33]And with great power the apostles gave witness to the resurrection of the Lord Jesus. And great grace was upon them all. [34]Nor was there anyone among them who lacked; for all who were possessors of lands or houses sold them, and brought the proceeds of the things that were sold, [35]and laid *them*

at the apostles' feet; and they distributed to each as anyone had need.

[36]And Joses,[a] who was also named Barnabas by the apostles (which is translated Son of Encouragement), a Levite of the country of Cyprus, [37]having land, sold *it,* and brought the money and laid *it* at the apostles' feet.

Lying to the Holy Spirit

5 But a certain man named Ananias, with Sapphira his wife, sold a possession. [2]And he kept back *part* of the proceeds, his wife also being aware *of it,* and brought a certain part and laid *it* at the apostles' feet. [3]But Peter said, "Ananias, why has Satan filled your heart to lie to the Holy Spirit and keep back *part* of the price of the land for yourself? [4]While it remained, was it not your own? And after it was sold, was it not in your own control? Why have you conceived this thing in your heart? You have not lied to men but to God."

[5]Then Ananias, hearing these words, fell down and breathed his last. So great fear came upon all those who heard these things. [6]And the young men arose and wrapped him up, carried *him* out, and buried *him.*

[7]Now it was about three hours later when his wife came in, not knowing what had happened. [8]And Peter answered her, "Tell me whether you sold the land for so much?"

She said, "Yes, for so much."

[9]Then Peter said to her, "How is it that you have agreed together to test the Spirit of the Lord? Look, the feet of those who have buried your husband *are* at the door, and they will carry you out." [10]Then immediately she fell down at his feet and breathed her last. And the young men came in and found her dead, and carrying *her* out, buried *her* by her husband. [11]So great fear came upon all the church and upon all who heard these things.

Continuing Power in the Church

[12]And through the hands of the apostles many signs and wonders were done among the people. And they were all with one accord in Solomon's Porch. [13]Yet none of the rest dared join them, but the people esteemed them highly. [14]And believers were increasingly added to the Lord, multitudes of both

4:36 [a]NU-Text reads *Joseph.*

men and women, [15]so that they brought the sick out into the streets and laid *them* on beds and couches, that at least the shadow of Peter passing by might fall on some of them. [16]Also a multitude gathered from the surrounding cities to Jerusalem, bringing sick people and those who were tormented by unclean spirits, and they were all healed.

Imprisoned Apostles Freed

[17]Then the high priest rose up, and all those who *were* with him (which is the sect of the Sadducees), and they were filled with indignation, [18]and laid their hands on the apostles and put them in the common prison. [19]But at night an angel of the Lord opened the prison doors and brought them out, and said, [20]"Go, stand in the temple and speak to the people all the words of this life."

[21]And when they heard *that,* they entered the temple early in the morning and taught. But the high priest and those with him came and called the council together, with all the elders of the children of Israel, and sent to the prison to have them brought.

Apostles on Trial Again

[22]But when the officers came and did not find them in the prison, they returned and reported, [23]saying, "Indeed we found the prison shut securely, and the guards standing outside[a] before the doors; but when we opened them, we found no one inside!" [24]Now when the high priest,[a] the captain of the temple, and the chief priests heard these things, they wondered what the outcome would be. [25]So one came and told them, saying,[a] "Look, the men whom you put in prison are standing in the temple and teaching the people!"

[26]Then the captain went with the officers and brought them without violence, for they feared the people, lest they should be stoned. [27]And when they had brought them, they set *them* before the council. And the high priest asked them, [28]saying, "Did we not strictly command you not to teach in this name? And look, you have filled Jerusalem with your doctrine, and intend to bring this Man's blood on us!"

[29]But Peter and the *other* apostles answered and said: "We ought to obey God rather than men. [30]The God of our fathers raised up Jesus whom you murdered by hanging on a tree. [31]Him God has exalted to His right hand *to be* Prince and Savior, to give repentance to Israel and forgiveness of sins. [32]And we are His witnesses to these things, and *so* also *is* the Holy Spirit whom God has given to those who obey Him."

Gamaliel's Advice

[33]When they heard *this,* they were furious and plotted to kill them. [34]Then one in the council stood up, a Pharisee named Gamaliel, a teacher of the law held in respect by all the people, and commanded them to put the apostles outside for a little while. [35]And he said to them: "Men of Israel, take heed to yourselves what you intend to do regarding these men. [36]For some time ago Theudas rose up, claiming to be somebody. A number of men, about four hundred, joined him. He was slain, and all who obeyed him were scattered and came to nothing. [37]After this man, Judas of Galilee rose up in the days of the census, and drew away many people after him. He also perished, and all who obeyed him were dispersed. [38]And now I say to you, keep away from these men and let them alone; for if this plan or this work is of men, it will come to nothing; [39]but if it is of God, you cannot overthrow it—lest you even be found to fight against God."

[40]And they agreed with him, and when they had called for the apostles and beaten *them,* they commanded that they should not speak in the name of Jesus, and let them go. [41]So they departed from the presence of the

↘ LEARN

5:41 • None of us likes to feel ashamed. We don't like to be ridiculed, scorned, or mocked. Rather than bear someone's contempt, often we go silent, try to slip away unnoticed, or distance ourselves from the one being jeered. That's a very human reaction—and it's exactly the opposite of how the disciples responded when their relationship with Jesus brought them public shame. Instead, they rejoiced that they were "counted worthy to suffer shame for His name." To be connected to Jesus is a privilege worth any amount of shame—and in fact, it transforms the shame into a blessing. *For more about* Adversity, *see Acts 16:6–10.*

5:23 [a]NU-Text and M-Text omit *outside.*   5:24 [a]NU-Text omits *the high priest.*   5:25 [a]NU-Text and M-Text omit *saying.*

council, rejoicing that they were counted worthy to suffer shame for His[a] name. [42]And daily in the temple, and in every house, they did not cease teaching and preaching Jesus *as* the Christ.

Seven Chosen to Serve

6 Now in those days, when *the number of* the disciples was multiplying, there arose a complaint against the Hebrews by the Hellenists,[a] because their widows were neglected in the daily distribution. [2]Then the twelve summoned the multitude of the disciples and said, "It is not desirable that we should leave the word of God and serve tables. [3]Therefore, brethren, seek out from among you seven men of *good* reputation, full of the Holy Spirit and wisdom, whom we may appoint over this business; [4]but we will give ourselves continually to prayer and to the ministry of the word."

[5]And the saying pleased the whole multitude. And they chose Stephen, a man full of faith and the Holy Spirit, and Philip, Prochorus, Nicanor, Timon, Parmenas, and Nicolas, a proselyte from Antioch, [6]whom they set before the apostles; and when they had prayed, they laid hands on them.

[7]Then the word of God spread, and the number of the disciples multiplied greatly in Jerusalem, and a great many of the priests were obedient to the faith.

Stephen Accused of Blasphemy

[8]And Stephen, full of faith[a] and power, did great wonders and signs among the people. [9]Then there arose some from what is called the Synagogue of the Freedmen (Cyrenians, Alexandrians, and those from Cilicia and Asia), disputing with Stephen. [10]And they were not able to resist the wisdom and the Spirit by which he spoke. [11]Then they secretly induced men to say, "We have heard him speak blasphemous words against Moses and God." [12]And they stirred up the people, the elders, and the scribes; and they came upon *him,* seized him, and brought *him* to the council. [13]They also set up false witnesses who said, "This man does not cease to speak blasphemous[a] words against this holy place and the law; [14]for we have heard him say that this Jesus of Nazareth will destroy this place and change the customs which Moses delivered to us." [15]And all who sat in the council, looking steadfastly at him, saw his face as the face of an angel.

Stephen's Address: The Call of Abraham

7 Then the high priest said, "Are these things so?"

[2]And he said, "Brethren and fathers, listen: The God of glory appeared to our father Abraham when he was in Mesopotamia, before he dwelt in Haran, [3]and said to him, *'Get out of your country and from your relatives, and come to a land that I will show you.'*[a] [4]Then he came out of the land of the Chaldeans and dwelt in Haran. And from there, when his father was dead, He moved him to this land in which you now dwell. [5]And *God* gave him no inheritance in it, not even *enough* to set his foot on. But even when *Abraham* had no child, He promised to give

5:41 [a]NU-Text reads *the name;* M-Text reads *the name of Jesus.*   **6:1** [a]That is, Greek-speaking Jews   **6:8** [a]NU-Text reads *grace.*
6:13 [a]NU-Text omits *blasphemous.*   **7:3** [a]Genesis 12:1

↑ GROW (ACTS 6:6)

Why is it we often pray longer prayers in public and shorter ones in private? This is not the pattern Jesus modeled, but rather the very opposite. We pray long prayers in public and short prayers in private. In the presence of others, we may go on and on, but when the audience is God alone (which, in fact, is always true), we offer clipped, thirty-second prayers that merely rattle off our needs. It ought to be the other way around! When you pray in private, spend some extended, unhurried time with God. Tell Him how much He means to you, thank Him for what He's done for you, and praise Him for who He is to you—and also make your requests. As Scripture reminds us, "Be still, and know that I am God" (Ps. 46:10). *For more about* Prayer, *see Acts 8:22;* Spiritual Disciplines, *Acts 13:2.*

it to him for a possession, and to his descendants after him. [6]But God spoke in this way: that his descendants would dwell in a foreign land, and that they would bring them into bondage and oppress *them* four hundred years. [7]*'And the nation to whom they will be in bondage I will judge,'*[a] said God, *'and after that they shall come out and serve Me in this place.'*[b] [8]Then He gave him the covenant of circumcision; and so *Abraham* begot Isaac and circumcised him on the eighth day; and Isaac *begot* Jacob, and Jacob *begot* the twelve patriarchs.

The Patriarchs in Egypt

[9]"And the patriarchs, becoming envious, sold Joseph into Egypt. But God was with him [10]and delivered him out of all his troubles, and gave him favor and wisdom in the presence of Pharaoh, king of Egypt; and he made him governor over Egypt and all his house. [11]Now a famine and great trouble came over all the land of Egypt and Canaan, and our fathers found no sustenance. [12]But when Jacob heard that there was grain in Egypt, he sent out our fathers first. [13]And the second *time* Joseph was made known to his brothers, and Joseph's family became known to the Pharaoh. [14]Then Joseph sent and called his father Jacob and all his relatives to *him*, seventy-five[a] people. [15]So Jacob went down to Egypt; and he died, he and our fathers. [16]And they were carried back to Shechem and laid in the tomb that Abraham bought for a sum of money from the sons of Hamor, *the father* of Shechem.

God Delivers Israel by Moses

[17]"But when the time of the promise drew near which God had sworn to Abraham, the people grew and multiplied in Egypt [18]till another king arose who did not know Joseph. [19]This man dealt treacherously with our people, and oppressed our forefathers, making them expose their babies, so that they might not live. [20]At this time Moses was born, and was well pleasing to God; and he was brought up in his father's house for three months. [21]But when he was set out, Pharaoh's daughter took him away and brought him up as her own son. [22]And Moses was learned in all the wisdom of the Egyptians, and was mighty in words and deeds.

[23]"Now when he was forty years old, it came into his heart to visit his brethren, the children of Israel. [24]And seeing one of *them* suffer wrong, he defended and avenged him who was oppressed, and struck down the Egyptian. [25]For he supposed that his brethren would have understood that God would deliver them by his hand, but they did not understand. [26]And the next day he appeared to *two of* them as they were fighting, and *tried to* reconcile them, saying, 'Men, you are brethren; why do you wrong one another?' [27]But he who did his neighbor wrong pushed him away, saying, *'Who made you a ruler and a judge over us? [28]Do you want to kill me as you did the Egyptian yesterday?'*[a] [29]Then, at this saying, Moses fled and became a dweller in the land of Midian, where he had two sons.

[30]"And when forty years had passed, an Angel of the Lord[a] appeared to him in a flame of fire in a bush, in the wilderness of Mount Sinai. [31]When Moses saw *it*, he marveled at the sight; and as he drew near to observe, the voice of the Lord came to him, [32]*saying, 'I am the God of your fathers—the God of Abraham, the God of Isaac, and the God of Jacob.'*[a] And Moses trembled and dared not look. [33]*'Then the Lord said to him, "Take your sandals off your feet, for the place where you stand is holy ground. [34]I have surely seen the oppression of My people who are in Egypt; I have heard their groaning and have come down to deliver them. And now come, I will send you to Egypt."'*[a]

[35]"This Moses whom they rejected, saying, *'Who made you a ruler and a judge?'*[a] is the one God sent *to be* a ruler and a deliverer by the hand of the Angel who appeared to him in the bush. [36]He brought them out, after he had shown wonders and signs in the land of Egypt, and in the Red Sea, and in the wilderness forty years.

Israel Rebels Against God

[37]"This is that Moses who said to the children of Israel,[a] *'The Lord your God will raise up for you a Prophet like me from your brethren. Him you shall hear.'*[b] [38]"This is he who was in the congregation in the wilderness with the Angel who spoke

7:7 [a]Genesis 15:14 [b]Exodus 3:12   **7:14** [a]Or *seventy* (compare Exodus 1:5)   **7:28, 35** [a]Exodus 2:14   **7:30** [a]NU-Text omits *of the Lord.*
7:32 [a]Exodus 3:6, 15   **7:34** [a]Exodus 3:5, 7, 8, 10   **7:37** [a]Deuteronomy 18:15   [b]NU-Text and M-Text omit *Him you shall hear.*

to him on Mount Sinai, and *with* our fathers, the one who received the living oracles to give to us, [39]whom our fathers would not obey, but rejected. And in their hearts they turned back to Egypt, [40]saying to Aaron, *'Make us gods to go before us; as for this Moses who brought us out of the land of Egypt, we do not know what has become of him.'* [41]And they made a calf in those days, offered sacrifices to the idol, and rejoiced in the works of their own hands. [42]Then God turned and gave them up to worship the host of heaven, as it is written in the book of the Prophets:

> *'Did you offer Me slaughtered animals and*
>   *sacrifices during forty years in the*
>   *wilderness,*
> *O house of Israel?*
> [43]*You also took up the tabernacle of Moloch,*
>   *And the star of your god Remphan,*
>   *Images which you made to worship;*
>   *And I will carry you away beyond*
>   *Babylon.'*[a]

God's True Tabernacle

[44]"Our fathers had the tabernacle of witness in the wilderness, as He appointed, instructing Moses to make it according to the pattern that he had seen, [45]which our fathers, having received it in turn, also brought with Joshua into the land possessed by the Gentiles, whom God drove out before the face of our fathers until the days of David, [46]who found favor before God and asked to find a dwelling for the God of Jacob. [47]But Solomon built Him a house.

[48]"However, the Most High does not dwell in temples made with hands, as the prophet says:

> [49]*'Heaven is My throne,*
>   *And earth is My footstool.*
>   *What house will you build for Me? says*
>   *the LORD,*
>   *Or what is the place of My rest?*
> [50]*Has My hand not made all these things?'*[a]

Israel Resists the Holy Spirit

[51]"*You* stiff-necked and uncircumcised in heart and ears! You always resist the Holy Spirit; as your fathers *did,* so *do* you. [52]Which of the prophets did your fathers not persecute? And they killed those who foretold the coming of the Just One, of whom you now have become the betrayers and murderers, [53]who have received the law by the direction of angels and have not kept *it.*"

Stephen the Martyr

[54]When they heard these things they were cut to the heart, and they gnashed at him with *their* teeth. [55]But he, being full of the Holy Spirit, gazed into heaven and saw the glory of God, and Jesus standing at the right hand of God, [56]and said, "Look! I see the heavens opened and the Son of Man standing at the right hand of God!"

[57]Then they cried out with a loud voice, stopped their ears, and ran at him with one accord; [58]and they cast *him* out of the city and stoned *him.* And the witnesses laid down their clothes at the feet of a young man named Saul. [59]And they stoned Stephen as he

7:40 [a]Exodus 32:1, 23   7:43 [a]Amos 5:25–27   7:50 [a]Isaiah 66:1, 2

↓ KNOW (ACTS 7:51)

The Holy Spirit is both patient and persistent. He wants to speak to unbelievers and lead them to God. But the Bible warns that it is possible to resist all of His pleadings. God says in Genesis 6:3, "My Spirit shall not strive with man forever." Apparently, the spiritual leaders of Israel to whom Stephen was speaking had firmly rejected the truth. The implication here is that they believed Stephen was speaking the truth, but they refused to accept it. Thus, they were guilty of resisting the Spirit. This is very different from simply not believing. It is more like, "Yes, I know it's true, but there is *no way* I am ever going to admit this. I refuse to accept what you are saying." When a man or woman reaches that point, he or she is resisting the Spirit. And it is a very, very dangerous place to be. *For more about the* Holy Spirit, *see Acts 9:31; the* Attributes of God, *Rom. 8:28.*

was calling on *God* and saying, "Lord Jesus, receive my spirit." [60]Then he knelt down and cried out with a loud voice, "Lord, do not charge them with this sin." And when he had said this, he fell asleep.

Saul Persecutes the Church

8 Now Saul was consenting to his death. At that time a great persecution arose against the church which was at Jerusalem; and they were all scattered throughout the regions of Judea and Samaria, except the apostles. [2]And devout men carried Stephen *to his burial,* and made great lamentation over him.

[3]As for Saul, he made havoc of the church, entering every house, and dragging off men and women, committing *them* to prison.

Christ Is Preached in Samaria

[4]Therefore those who were scattered went everywhere preaching the word. [5]Then Philip went down to the[a] city of Samaria and preached Christ to them. [6]And the multitudes with one accord heeded the things spoken by Philip, hearing and seeing the miracles which he did. [7]For unclean spirits, crying with a loud voice, came out of many who were possessed; and many who were paralyzed and lame were healed. [8]And there was great joy in that city.

↘ LEARN

8:4 • Wherever you go, does Jesus go with you? At home, at work, in your neighborhood, in the grocery store, at the park—is Jesus in some way on your mind and often on your lips? God used the first major persecution of the church to spread the Good News. Scattered believers "went everywhere preaching the word" about salvation in Jesus Christ. They were ready to talk about the Lord whenever they found someone ready to listen. If God should bring someone in spiritual need across your path today, are *you* ready to point him to Jesus and to eternal life? *For more about* Sharing Your Faith, *see Acts 10:34, 35.*

The Sorcerer's Profession of Faith

[9]But there was a certain man called Simon, who previously practiced sorcery in the city and astonished the people of Samaria, claiming that he was someone great, [10]to whom they all gave heed, from the least to the greatest, saying, "This man is the great power of God." [11]And they heeded him because he had astonished them with his sorceries for a long time. [12]But when they believed Philip as he preached the things concerning the kingdom of God and the name of Jesus Christ, both men and women were baptized. [13]Then Simon himself also believed; and when he was baptized he continued with Philip, and was amazed, seeing the miracles and signs which were done.

The Sorcerer's Sin

[14]Now when the apostles who were at Jerusalem heard that Samaria had received the word of God, they sent Peter and John to them, [15]who, when they had come down, prayed for them that they might receive the Holy Spirit. [16]For as yet He had fallen upon none of them. They had only been baptized in the name of the Lord Jesus. [17]Then they laid hands on them, and they received the Holy Spirit.

[18]And when Simon saw that through the laying on of the apostles' hands the Holy Spirit was given, he offered them money, [19]saying, "Give me this power also, that anyone on whom I lay hands may receive the Holy Spirit."

[20]But Peter said to him, "Your money perish with you, because you thought that the gift of God could be purchased with money! [21]You have neither part nor portion in this matter, for your heart is not right in the sight of God. [22]Repent therefore of this

→ LIVE

8:22 • A nonbeliever can offer up prayers, but only a Christian can truly pray. Prayer is a privilege given to those with a relationship to God. Many people offer their little prayers, maybe ones learned as children, and they pull them out here and there. But that's not how it works. Prayer is communication for the believer. Until you have a relationship with God, a wall called sin separates you from Him and your prayers will not go far. You need to get that barrier removed so you can communicate with the Lord and start talking to Him and hearing from Him (Is. 59:1, 2). *For more about* Prayer, *see Rom. 8:26.*

8:5 [a]Or *a*

your wickedness, and pray God if perhaps the thought of your heart may be forgiven you. ²³For I see that you are poisoned by bitterness and bound by iniquity."

²⁴Then Simon answered and said, "Pray to the Lord for me, that none of the things which you have spoken may come upon me."

²⁵So when they had testified and preached the word of the Lord, they returned to Jerusalem, preaching the gospel in many villages of the Samaritans.

Christ Is Preached to an Ethiopian

²⁶Now an angel of the Lord spoke to Philip, saying, "Arise and go toward the south along the road which goes down from Jerusalem to Gaza." This is desert. ²⁷So he arose and went. And behold, a man of Ethiopia, a eunuch of great authority under Candace the queen of the Ethiopians, who had charge of all her treasury, and had come to Jerusalem to worship, ²⁸was returning. And sitting in his chariot, he was reading Isaiah the prophet. ²⁹Then the Spirit said to Philip, "Go near and overtake this chariot."

³⁰So Philip ran to him, and heard him reading the prophet Isaiah, and said, "Do you understand what you are reading?"

³¹And he said, "How can I, unless someone guides me?" And he asked Philip to come up and sit with him. ³²The place in the Scripture which he read was this:

"He was led as a sheep to the slaughter;
And as a lamb before its shearer is silent,
So He opened not His mouth.
³³In His humiliation His justice was taken
away,
And who will declare His generation?
For His life is taken from the earth."ª

³⁴So the eunuch answered Philip and said, "I ask you, of whom does the prophet say this, of himself or of some other man?" ³⁵Then Philip opened his mouth, and beginning at this Scripture, preached Jesus to him. ³⁶Now as they went down the road, they came to some water. And the eunuch said, "See, here is water. What hinders me from being baptized?"

³⁷Then Philip said, "If you believe with all your heart, you may."

And he answered and said, "I believe that Jesus Christ is the Son of God."ª

³⁸So he commanded the chariot to stand still. And both Philip and the eunuch went down into the water, and he baptized him. ³⁹Now when they came up out of the water, the Spirit of the Lord caught Philip away, so that the eunuch saw him no more; and he went on his way rejoicing. ⁴⁰But Philip was found at Azotus. And passing through, he preached in all the cities till he came to Caesarea.

The Damascus Road: Saul Converted

9 Then Saul, still breathing threats and murder against the disciples of the Lord, went to the high priest ²and asked letters from him to the synagogues of Damascus, so that if he found any who were of the Way, whether men or women, he might bring them bound to Jerusalem.

³As he journeyed he came near Damascus, and suddenly a light shone around him from heaven. ⁴Then he fell to the ground, and heard a voice saying to him, "Saul, Saul, why are you persecuting Me?"

⁵And he said, "Who are You, Lord?"

Then the Lord said, "I am Jesus, whom you are persecuting.ª It is hard for you to kick against the goads."

⁶So he, trembling and astonished, said, "Lord, what do You want me to do?"

Then the Lord said to him, "Arise and go into the city, and you will be told what you must do."

⁷And the men who journeyed with him stood speechless, hearing a voice but seeing no one. ⁸Then Saul arose from the ground, and when his eyes were opened he saw no one. But they led him by the hand and brought him into Damascus. ⁹And he was three days without sight, and neither ate nor drank.

Ananias Baptizes Saul

¹⁰Now there was a certain disciple at Damascus named Ananias; and to him the Lord said in a vision, "Ananias."

And he said, "Here I am, Lord."

¹¹So the Lord said to him, "Arise and go to the street called Straight, and inquire at the house of Judas for one called Saul of Tarsus, for behold, he is praying. ¹²And in a vision

8:33 ªIsaiah 53:7, 8   8:37 ªNU-Text and M-Text omit this verse. It is found in Western texts, including the Latin tradition.
9:5 ªNU-Text and M-Text omit the last sentence of verse 5 and begin verse 6 with *But arise and go.*

he has seen a man named Ananias coming in and putting *his* hand on him, so that he might receive his sight."

[13]Then Ananias answered, "Lord, I have heard from many about this man, how much harm he has done to Your saints in Jerusalem. [14]And here he has authority from the chief priests to bind all who call on Your name."

[15]But the Lord said to him, "Go, for he is a chosen vessel of Mine to bear My name before Gentiles, kings, and the children of Israel. [16]For I will show him how many things he must suffer for My name's sake."

[17]And Ananias went his way and entered the house; and laying his hands on him he said, "Brother Saul, the Lord Jesus,[a] who appeared to you on the road as you came, has sent me that you may receive your sight and be filled with the Holy Spirit." [18]Immediately there fell from his eyes *something* like scales, and he received his sight at once; and he arose and was baptized.

[19]So when he had received food, he was strengthened. Then Saul spent some days with the disciples at Damascus.

Saul Preaches Christ

[20]Immediately he preached the Christ[a] in the synagogues, that He is the Son of God.

[21]Then all who heard were amazed, and said, "Is this not he who destroyed those who called on this name in Jerusalem, and has come here for that purpose, so that he might bring them bound to the chief priests?"

[22]But Saul increased all the more in strength, and confounded the Jews who dwelt in Damascus, proving that this *Jesus* is the Christ.

Saul Escapes Death

[23]Now after many days were past, the Jews plotted to kill him. [24]But their plot became known to Saul. And they watched the gates day and night, to kill him. [25]Then the disciples took him by night and let *him* down through the wall in a large basket.

Saul at Jerusalem

[26]And when Saul had come to Jerusalem, he tried to join the disciples; but they were all afraid of him, and did not believe that he

was a disciple. [27]But Barnabas took him and brought *him* to the apostles. And he declared to them how he had seen the Lord on the road, and that He had spoken to him, and how he had preached boldly at Damascus in the name of Jesus. [28]So he was with them at Jerusalem, coming in and going out. [29]And he spoke boldly in the name of the Lord Jesus and disputed against the Hellenists, but they attempted to kill him. [30]When the brethren found out, they brought him down to Caesarea and sent him out to Tarsus.

The Church Prospers

[31]Then the churches[a] throughout all Judea, Galilee, and Samaria had peace and were edified. And walking in the fear of the Lord and in the comfort of the Holy Spirit, they were multiplied.

↘ LEARN

. . . .

9:31 • Fear and comfort don't seem to go together, do they? When you fear something, normally you feel very little comfort about it. And when you feel comfortable, you don't generally feel afraid. Yet Luke tells us that the early church walked "in the fear of the Lord" at the same time it walked "in the comfort of the Holy Spirit." In other words, early believers rejoiced in God's holiness as much as they did in His love. Their balanced view of God allowed them to fear God—reverence Him, respect Him—*and* delight in Him. The result? The church grew quickly in number. *For more about the* Holy Spirit, *see Rom. 7:15.*

Aeneas Healed

[32]Now it came to pass, as Peter went through all *parts of the country,* that he also came down to the saints who dwelt in Lydda. [33]There he found a certain man named Aeneas, who had been bedridden eight years and was paralyzed. [34]And Peter said to him, "Aeneas, Jesus the Christ heals you. Arise and make your bed." Then he arose immediately. [35]So all who dwelt at Lydda and Sharon saw him and turned to the Lord.

Dorcas Restored to Life

[36]At Joppa there was a certain disciple named Tabitha, which is translated Dorcas.

9:17 [a]M-Text omits *Jesus.* 9:20 [a]NU-Text reads *Jesus.* 9:31 [a]NU-Text reads *church . . . was edified.*

This woman was full of good works and charitable deeds which she did. ³⁷But it happened in those days that she became sick and died. When they had washed her, they laid *her* in an upper room. ³⁸And since Lydda was near Joppa, and the disciples had heard that Peter was there, they sent two men to him, imploring *him* not to delay in coming to them. ³⁹Then Peter arose and went with them. When he had come, they brought *him* to the upper room. And all the widows stood by him weeping, showing the tunics and garments which Dorcas had made while she was with them. ⁴⁰But Peter put them all out, and knelt down and prayed. And turning to the body he said, "Tabitha, arise." And she opened her eyes, and when she saw Peter she sat up. ⁴¹Then he gave her *his* hand and lifted her up; and when he had called the saints and widows, he presented her alive. ⁴²And it became known throughout all Joppa, and many believed on the Lord. ⁴³So it was that he stayed many days in Joppa with Simon, a tanner.

Cornelius Sends a Delegation

10 There was a certain man in Caesarea called Cornelius, a centurion of what was called the Italian Regiment, ²a devout *man* and one who feared God with all his household, who gave alms generously to the people, and prayed to God always. ³About the ninth hour of the day he saw clearly in a vision an angel of God coming in and saying to him, "Cornelius!"

⁴And when he observed him, he was afraid, and said, "What is it, lord?"

So he said to him, "Your prayers and your alms have come up for a memorial before God. ⁵Now send men to Joppa, and send for Simon whose surname is Peter. ⁶He is lodging with Simon, a tanner, whose house is by the sea.ᵃ He will tell you what you must do." ⁷And when the angel who spoke to him had departed, Cornelius called two of his household servants and a devout soldier from among those who waited on him continually. ⁸So when he had explained all *these* things to them, he sent them to Joppa.

Peter's Vision

⁹The next day, as they went on their journey and drew near the city, Peter went up on the housetop to pray, about the sixth hour. ¹⁰Then he became very hungry and wanted to eat; but while they made ready, he fell into a trance ¹¹and saw heaven opened and an object like a great sheet bound at the four corners, descending to him and let down to the earth. ¹²In it were all kinds of four-footed animals of the earth, wild beasts, creeping things, and birds of the air. ¹³And a voice came to him, "Rise, Peter; kill and eat."

¹⁴But Peter said, "Not so, Lord! For I have never eaten anything common or unclean."

¹⁵And a voice *spoke* to him again the second time, "What God has cleansed you must not call common." ¹⁶This was done three times. And the object was taken up into heaven again.

Summoned to Caesarea

¹⁷Now while Peter wondered within himself what this vision which he had seen meant, behold, the men who had been sent from Cornelius had made inquiry for Simon's house, and stood before the gate. ¹⁸And they called and asked whether Simon, whose surname was Peter, was lodging there.

¹⁹While Peter thought about the vision, the Spirit said to him, "Behold, three men are seeking you. ²⁰Arise therefore, go down and go with them, doubting nothing; for I have sent them."

²¹Then Peter went down to the men who had been sent to him from Cornelius,ᵃ and said, "Yes, I am he whom you seek. For what reason have you come?"

²²And they said, "Cornelius *the* centurion, a just man, one who fears God and has a good reputation among all the nation of the Jews, was divinely instructed by a holy angel to summon you to his house, and to hear words from you." ²³Then he invited them in and lodged *them*.

On the next day Peter went away with them, and some brethren from Joppa accompanied him.

Peter Meets Cornelius

²⁴And the following day they entered Caesarea. Now Cornelius was waiting for them, and had called together his relatives and close friends. ²⁵As Peter was coming in, Cornelius met him and fell down at his feet

---

10:6 ᵃNU-Text and M-Text omit the last sentence of this verse.   10:21 ᵃNU-Text and M-Text omit *who had been sent to him from Cornelius*.

and worshiped *him*. ²⁶But Peter lifted him up, saying, "Stand up; I myself am also a man." ²⁷And as he talked with him, he went in and found many who had come together. ²⁸Then he said to them, "You know how unlawful it is for a Jewish man to keep company with or go to one of another nation. But God has shown me that I should not call any man common or unclean. ²⁹Therefore I came without objection as soon as I was sent for. I ask, then, for what reason have you sent for me?"

³⁰So Cornelius said, "Four days ago I was fasting until this hour; and at the ninth hourᵃ I prayed in my house, and behold, a man stood before me in bright clothing, ³¹and said, 'Cornelius, your prayer has been heard, and your alms are remembered in the sight of God. ³²Send therefore to Joppa and call Simon here, whose surname is Peter. He is lodging in the house of Simon, a tanner, by the sea.ᵃ When he comes, he will speak to you.' ³³So I sent to you immediately, and you have done well to come. Now therefore, we are all present before God, to hear all the things commanded you by God."

Preaching to Cornelius' Household

³⁴Then Peter opened *his* mouth and said: "In truth I perceive that God shows no partiality. ³⁵But in every nation whoever fears Him and works righteousness is accepted by Him. ³⁶The word which *God* sent to the children of Israel, preaching peace through Jesus Christ—He is Lord of all— ³⁷that word you know, which was proclaimed throughout all Judea, and began from Galilee after the baptism which John preached: ³⁸how God anointed Jesus of Nazareth with the Holy Spirit and with power, who went about doing good and healing all who were oppressed by the devil, for God was with Him. ³⁹And we are witnesses of all things which He did both in the land of the Jews and in Jerusalem, whom theyᵃ killed by hanging on a tree. ⁴⁰Him God raised up on the third day, and showed Him openly, ⁴¹not to all the people, but to witnesses chosen before by God, *even* to us who ate and drank with Him after He arose from the dead. ⁴²And He commanded us to preach to the people, and to testify that it is He who was ordained by God *to be* Judge

of the living and the dead. ⁴³To Him all the prophets witness that, through His name, whoever believes in Him will receive remission of sins."

➔ *To Him all the prophets witness that, through His name, whoever believes in Him will receive remission of sins.* Acts 10:43

The Holy Spirit Falls on the Gentiles

⁴⁴While Peter was still speaking these words, the Holy Spirit fell upon all those who heard the word. ⁴⁵And those of the circumcision who believed were astonished, as many as came with Peter, because the gift of the Holy Spirit had been poured out on the Gentiles also. ⁴⁶For they heard them speak with tongues and magnify God.

Then Peter answered, ⁴⁷"Can anyone forbid water, that these should not be baptized who have received the Holy Spirit just as we *have*?" ⁴⁸And he commanded them to be baptized in the name of the Lord. Then they asked him to stay a few days.

Peter Defends God's Grace

11 Now the apostles and brethren who were in Judea heard that the Gentiles had also received the word of God. ²And when Peter came up to Jerusalem, those of the circumcision contended with him, ³saying, "You went in to uncircumcised men and ate with them!"

⁴But Peter explained *it* to them in order from the beginning, saying: ⁵"I was in the city of Joppa praying; and in a trance I saw a vision, an object descending like a great sheet, let down from heaven by four corners; and it came to me. ⁶When I observed it intently and considered, I saw four-footed animals of the earth, wild beasts, creeping things, and birds of the air. ⁷And I heard a voice saying to me, 'Rise, Peter; kill and eat.' ⁸But I said, 'Not so, Lord! For nothing common or unclean has at any time entered my mouth.' ⁹But the voice answered me again from heaven, 'What God has cleansed you must not call common.' ¹⁰Now this was done three times, and all were drawn up again into heaven. ¹¹At that very moment, three men stood before the house where I was, having been sent to me from Caesarea. ¹²Then the Spirit told me to go with them, doubting nothing. Moreover these six brethren accompanied me, and we entered the man's house. ¹³And he told us how he had seen an angel standing in his house, who said to him, 'Send men to Joppa, and call for Simon whose surname is Peter, ¹⁴who will tell you words by which you and all your household will be saved.' ¹⁵And as I began to speak, the Holy Spirit fell upon them, as upon us at the beginning. ¹⁶Then I remembered the word of the Lord, how He said, 'John indeed baptized with water, but you shall be baptized with the Holy Spirit.' ¹⁷If therefore God gave them the same gift as *He gave* us when we believed on the Lord Jesus Christ, who was I that I could withstand God?"

¹⁸When they heard these things they became silent; and they glorified God, saying, "Then God has also granted to the Gentiles repentance to life."

Barnabas and Saul at Antioch

¹⁹Now those who were scattered after the persecution that arose over Stephen traveled as far as Phoenicia, Cyprus, and Antioch, preaching the word to no one but the Jews only. ²⁰But some of them were men from Cyprus and Cyrene, who, when they had come to Antioch, spoke to the Hellenists, preaching the Lord Jesus. ²¹And the hand of the Lord

was with them, and a great number believed and turned to the Lord.

²²Then news of these things came to the ears of the church in Jerusalem, and they sent out Barnabas to go as far as Antioch. ²³When he came and had seen the grace of God, he was glad, and encouraged them all that with purpose of heart they should continue with the Lord. ²⁴For he was a good man, full of the Holy Spirit and of faith. And a great many people were added to the Lord.

²⁵Then Barnabas departed for Tarsus to seek Saul. ²⁶And when he had found him, he brought him to Antioch. So it was that for a whole year they assembled with the church and taught a great many people. And the disciples were first called Christians in Antioch.

Relief to Judea

²⁷And in these days prophets came from Jerusalem to Antioch. ²⁸Then one of them, named Agabus, stood up and showed by the Spirit that there was going to be a great famine throughout all the world, which also happened in the days of Claudius Caesar. ²⁹Then the disciples, each according to his ability, determined to send relief to the brethren dwelling in Judea. ³⁰This they also did, and sent it to the elders by the hands of Barnabas and Saul.

Herod's Violence to the Church

12 Now about that time Herod the king stretched out *his* hand to harass some from the church. ²Then he killed James the brother of John with the sword. ³And because he saw that it pleased the Jews, he proceeded further to seize Peter also. Now it was *during* the Days of Unleavened Bread. ⁴So when he had arrested him, he put *him* in prison, and delivered *him* to four squads of soldiers to keep him, intending to bring him before the people after Passover.

Peter Freed from Prison

⁵Peter was therefore kept in prison, but constant[a] prayer was offered to God for him by the church. ⁶And when Herod was about to bring him out, that night Peter was sleeping, bound with two chains between two soldiers; and the guards before the door were keeping the prison. ⁷Now behold, an angel

12:5 ᵃNU-Text reads *constantly* (or *earnestly*).

of the Lord stood by *him,* and a light shone in the prison; and he struck Peter on the side and raised him up, saying, "Arise quickly!" And his chains fell off *his* hands. [8]Then the angel said to him, "Gird yourself and tie on your sandals"; and so he did. And he said to him, "Put on your garment and follow me." [9]So he went out and followed him, and did not know that what was done by the angel was real, but thought he was seeing a vision. [10]When they were past the first and the second guard posts, they came to the iron gate that leads to the city, which opened to them of its own accord; and they went out and went down one street, and immediately the angel departed from him.

[11]And when Peter had come to himself, he said, "Now I know for certain that the Lord has sent His angel, and has delivered me from the hand of Herod and *from* all the expectation of the Jewish people."

[12]So, when he had considered *this,* he came to the house of Mary, the mother of John whose surname was Mark, where many were gathered together praying. [13]And as Peter knocked at the door of the gate, a girl named Rhoda came to answer. [14]When she recognized Peter's voice, because of *her* gladness she did not open the gate, but ran in and announced that Peter stood before the gate. [15]But they said to her, "You are beside yourself!" Yet she kept insisting that it was so. So they said, "It is his angel."

[16]Now Peter continued knocking; and when they opened *the door* and saw him, they were astonished. [17]But motioning to them with his hand to keep silent, he declared to them how the Lord had brought him out of the prison. And he said, "Go, tell these things to James and to the brethren." And he departed and went to another place.

[18]Then, as soon as it was day, there was no small stir among the soldiers about what had become of Peter. [19]But when Herod had searched for him and not found him, he examined the guards and commanded that *they* should be put to death.

And he went down from Judea to Caesarea, and stayed *there.*

Herod's Violent Death

[20]Now Herod had been very angry with the people of Tyre and Sidon; but they came to him with one accord, and having made Blastus the king's personal aide their friend, they asked for peace, because their country was supplied with food by the king's *country.* [21]So on a set day Herod, arrayed in royal apparel, sat on his throne and gave an oration to them. [22]And the people kept shouting, "The voice of a god and not of a man!" [23]Then immediately an angel of the Lord struck him, because he did not give glory to God. And he was eaten by worms and died. [24]But the word of God grew and multiplied.

Barnabas and Saul Appointed

[25]And Barnabas and Saul returned from[a] Jerusalem when they had fulfilled *their* ministry, and they also took with them John whose surname was Mark.

13 Now in the church that was at Antioch there were certain prophets and teachers: Barnabas, Simeon who was called Niger, Lucius of Cyrene, Manaen who had been brought up with Herod the tetrarch, and Saul. [2]As they ministered to the Lord and fasted, the Holy Spirit said, "Now separate to Me Barnabas and Saul for the work to which I have called them." [3]Then, having fasted and prayed, and laid hands on them, they sent *them* away.

↘ LEARN
• • • • • • • • • • • • • • • • •

13:2 • Fasting is a spiritual discipline that, unfortunately, has gone out of style among many Christians today. Yet the truth is that the Lord Jesus Himself fasted, the apostles fasted, and the early church fasted. Why? They didn't fast because they got spiritual brownie points for it; its value lies in something else. The purpose of fasting—giving up food or drink for a specific period of time—is to focus your attention on some issue, to help you better grasp God's perspective or direction on it. Through fasting, God has another channel through which He can communicate His mind to you. *For more about* Spiritual Disciplines, *see Rom. 4:2.*

Preaching in Cyprus

[4]So, being sent out by the Holy Spirit, they went down to Seleucia, and from there they sailed to Cyprus. [5]And when they arrived in

Salamis, they preached the word of God in the synagogues of the Jews. They also had John as *their* assistant.

⁶Now when they had gone through the island[a] to Paphos, they found a certain sorcerer, a false prophet, a Jew whose name *was* Bar-Jesus, ⁷who was with the proconsul, Sergius Paulus, an intelligent man. This man called for Barnabas and Saul and sought to hear the word of God. ⁸But Elymas the sorcerer (for so his name is translated) withstood them, seeking to turn the proconsul away from the faith. ⁹Then Saul, who also *is called* Paul, filled with the Holy Spirit, looked intently at him ¹⁰and said, "O full of all deceit and all fraud, *you* son of the devil, *you* enemy of all righteousness, will you not cease perverting the straight ways of the Lord? ¹¹And now, indeed, the hand of the Lord *is* upon you, and you shall be blind, not seeing the sun for a time."

And immediately a dark mist fell on him, and he went around seeking someone to lead him by the hand. ¹²Then the proconsul believed, when he saw what had been done, being astonished at the teaching of the Lord.

At Antioch in Pisidia

¹³Now when Paul and his party set sail from Paphos, they came to Perga in Pamphylia; and John, departing from them, returned to Jerusalem. ¹⁴But when they departed from Perga, they came to Antioch in Pisidia, and went into the synagogue on the Sabbath day and sat down. ¹⁵And after the reading of the Law and the Prophets, the rulers of the synagogue sent to them, saying, "Men *and* brethren, if you have any word of exhortation for the people, say on."

¹⁶Then Paul stood up, and motioning with *his* hand said, "Men of Israel, and you who fear God, listen: ¹⁷The God of this people Israel[a] chose our fathers, and exalted the people when they dwelt as strangers in the land of Egypt, and with an uplifted arm He brought them out of it. ¹⁸Now for a time of about forty years He put up with their ways in the wilderness. ¹⁹And when He had destroyed seven nations in the land of Canaan, He distributed their land to them by allotment. ²⁰"After that He gave *them* judges for about four hundred and fifty years, until

Samuel the prophet. ²¹And afterward they asked for a king; so God gave them Saul the son of Kish, a man of the tribe of Benjamin, for forty years. ²²And when He had removed him, He raised up for them David as king, to whom also He gave testimony and said, '*I have found David*[a] the *son* of Jesse, *a man after My own heart, who will do all My will.*'[b] ²³From this man's seed, according to *the* promise, God raised up for Israel a Savior—Jesus—[a] ²⁴after John had first preached, before His coming, the baptism of repentance to all the people of Israel. ²⁵And as John was finishing his course, he said, 'Who do you think I am? I am not *He.* But behold, there comes One after me, the sandals of whose feet I am not worthy to loose.'

²⁶"Men *and* brethren, sons of the family of Abraham, and those among you who fear God, to you the word of this salvation has been sent. ²⁷For those who dwell in Jerusalem, and their rulers, because they did not know Him, nor even the voices of the Prophets which are read every Sabbath, have fulfilled *them* in condemning *Him.* ²⁸And though they found no cause for death *in Him,* they asked Pilate that He should be put to death. ²⁹Now when they had fulfilled all that was written concerning Him, they took *Him* down from the tree and laid *Him* in a tomb. ³⁰But God raised Him from the dead. ³¹He was seen for many days by those who came up with Him from Galilee to Jerusalem, who are His witnesses to the people. ³²And we declare to you glad tidings—that promise which was made to the fathers. ³³God has fulfilled this for us their children, in that He has raised up Jesus. As it is also written in the second Psalm:

'You are My Son,
   Today I have begotten You.'[a]

³⁴And that He raised Him from the dead, no more to return to corruption, He has spoken thus:

'I will give you the sure mercies of
   David.'[a]

³⁵Therefore He also says in another *Psalm:*

'You will not allow Your Holy One to see
   corruption.'[a]

13:6 [a]NU-Text reads the whole island.   13:17 [a]M-Text omits Israel.   13:22 [a]Psalm 89:20 [b]1 Samuel 13:14
13:23 [a]M-Text reads for Israel salvation.   13:33 [a]Psalm 2:7   13:34 [a]Isaiah 55:3   13:35 [a]Psalm 16:10

36"For David, after he had served his own generation by the will of God, fell asleep, was buried with his fathers, and saw corruption; 37but He whom God raised up saw no corruption. 38Therefore let it be known to you, brethren, that through this Man is preached to you the forgiveness of sins; 39and by Him

> **→LIVE**
> • • • • • • • • • • • • • • • •
>
> 13:39 • The word *justified* carries a twofold meaning. First, to be justified means that God has forgiven you of all of your sin. When you put your faith in Jesus Christ, all evidence of your sin and guilt is completely wiped out. Let that sink in! When you believe in Jesus *you are forgiven.* Completely. Totally. Immediately. Justification is the answer to the problem of guilt and concerns your legal standing before God. Second, the righteousness of Christ is imputed to your account. God looks at you not in your sin, but as if you are clothed in Jesus' righteousness! *For more about* New Life in Christ, *see Acts 26:18;* Forgiveness, *1 Cor. 1:10.*

everyone who believes is justified from all things from which you could not be justified by the law of Moses. 40Beware therefore, lest what has been spoken in the prophets come upon you:

41 *'Behold, you despisers,*
    Marvel and perish!
    For I work a work in your days,
    A work which you will by no means
        believe,
    *Though one were to declare it to you.' "*a

Blessing and Conflict at Antioch

42So when the Jews went out of the synagogue,a the Gentiles begged that these words might be preached to them the next Sabbath. 43Now when the congregation had broken up, many of the Jews and devout proselytes followed Paul and Barnabas, who, speaking to them, persuaded them to continue in the grace of God.

44On the next Sabbath almost the whole city came together to hear the word of God. 45But when the Jews saw the multitudes, they were filled with envy; and contradicting and blaspheming, they opposed the things spoken by Paul. 46Then Paul and Barnabas grew bold

and said, "It was necessary that the word of God should be spoken to you first; but since you reject it, and judge yourselves unworthy of everlasting life, behold, we turn to the Gentiles. 47For so the Lord has commanded us:

'I have set you as a light to the Gentiles,
    That you should be for salvation to the
        *ends of the earth.' "*a

48Now when the Gentiles heard this, they were glad and glorified the word of the Lord. And as many as had been appointed to eternal life believed.

49And the word of the Lord was being spread throughout all the region. 50But the Jews stirred up the devout and prominent women and the chief men of the city, raised up persecution against Paul and Barnabas, and expelled them from their region. 51But they shook off the dust from their feet against them, and came to Iconium. 52And the disciples were filled with joy and with the Holy Spirit.

At Iconium

14 Now it happened in Iconium that they went together to the synagogue of the Jews, and so spoke that a great multitude both of the Jews and of the Greeks believed. 2But the unbelieving Jews stirred up the Gentiles and poisoned their minds against the brethren. 3Therefore they stayed there a long time, speaking boldly in the Lord, who was bearing witness to the word of His grace, granting signs and wonders to be done by their hands.

4But the multitude of the city was divided: part sided with the Jews, and part with the apostles. 5And when a violent attempt was made by both the Gentiles and Jews, with their rulers, to abuse and stone them, 6they became aware of it and fled to Lystra and Derbe, cities of Lycaonia, and to the surrounding region. 7And they were preaching the gospel there.

Idolatry at Lystra

8And in Lystra a certain man without strength in his feet was sitting, a cripple from his mother's womb, who had never walked. 9*This* man heard Paul speaking.

13:41 aHabakkuk 1:5   13:42 aOr *And when they went out of the synagogue of the Jews;* NU-Text reads *And when they went out, they begged.*
13:47 aIsaiah 49:6

Paul, observing him intently and seeing that he had faith to be healed, [10]said with a loud voice, "Stand up straight on your feet!" And he leaped and walked. [11]Now when the people saw what Paul had done, they raised their voices, saying in the Lycaonian *language,* "The gods have come down to us in the likeness of men!" [12]And Barnabas they called Zeus, and Paul, Hermes, because he was the chief speaker. [13]Then the priest of Zeus, whose temple was in front of their city, brought oxen and garlands to the gates, intending to sacrifice with the multitudes.

[14]But when the apostles Barnabas and Paul heard this, they tore their clothes and ran in among the multitude, crying out [15]and saying, "Men, why are you doing these things? We also are men with the same nature as you, and preach to you that you should turn from these useless things to the living God, who made the heaven, the earth, the sea, and all things that are in them, [16]who in bygone generations allowed all nations to walk in their own ways. [17]Nevertheless He did not leave Himself without witness, in that He did good, gave us rain from heaven and fruitful seasons, filling our hearts with food and gladness." [18]And with these sayings they could scarcely restrain the multitudes from sacrificing to them.

Stoning, Escape to Derbe

[19]Then Jews from Antioch and Iconium came there; and having persuaded the multitudes, they stoned Paul *and* dragged *him* out of the city, supposing him to be dead. [20]However, when the disciples gathered around him, he rose up and went into the city. And the next day he departed with Barnabas to Derbe.

Strengthening the Converts

[21]And when they had preached the gospel to that city and made many disciples, they returned to Lystra, Iconium, and Antioch, [22]strengthening the souls of the disciples, exhorting *them* to continue in the faith, and *saying,* "We must through many tribulations enter the kingdom of God." [23]So when they had appointed elders in every church, and prayed with fasting, they commended them to the Lord in whom they had believed. [24]And after they had passed through Pisidia,

they came to Pamphylia. [25]Now when they had preached the word in Perga, they went down to Attalia. [26]From there they sailed to Antioch, where they had been commended to the grace of God for the work which they had completed.

[27]Now when they had come and gathered the church together, they reported all that God had done with them, and that He had opened the door of faith to the Gentiles. [28]So they stayed there a long time with the disciples.

Conflict over Circumcision

15 And certain *men* came down from Judea and taught the brethren, "Unless you are circumcised according to the custom of Moses, you cannot be saved." [2]Therefore, when Paul and Barnabas had no small dissension and dispute with them, they determined that Paul and Barnabas and certain others of them should go up to Jerusalem, to the apostles and elders, about this question.

[3]So, being sent on their way by the church, they passed through Phoenicia and Samaria, describing the conversion of the Gentiles; and they caused great joy to all the brethren. [4]And when they had come to Jerusalem, they were received by the church and the apostles and the elders; and they reported all things that God had done with them. [5]But some of the sect of the Pharisees who believed rose up, saying, "It is necessary to circumcise them, and to command *them* to keep the law of Moses."

→ LIVE
. . . .

15:3 • Conversion is not a long, drawn-out process. Sometimes you hear people say, "I am converting to Christianity." Maybe they're saying that they are looking into the claims of Christ, pondering them and considering them. That's great! But one is either converted or unconverted. You either believe or you don't believe. Conversion doesn't take hours, days, or months. It takes seconds, perhaps even less. I imagine that a genuine conversion could happen so quickly and instantaneously that we might not even be able to measure the time it takes to occur. Moving from death to life takes only moments. *For more about* Becoming a Christian, *see* Rom. 6:23.

The Jerusalem Council

⁶Now the apostles and elders came together to consider this matter. ⁷And when there had been much dispute, Peter rose up *and* said to them: "Men *and* brethren, you know that a good while ago God chose among us, that by my mouth the Gentiles should hear the word of the gospel and believe. ⁸So God, who knows the heart, acknowledged them by giving them the Holy Spirit, just as *He did* to us, ⁹and made no distinction between us and them, purifying their hearts by faith. ¹⁰Now therefore, why do you test God by putting a yoke on the neck of the disciples which neither our fathers nor we were able to bear? ¹¹But we believe that through the grace of the Lord Jesus Christ[a] we shall be saved in the same manner as they."

¹²Then all the multitude kept silent and listened to Barnabas and Paul declaring how many miracles and wonders God had worked through them among the Gentiles. ¹³And after they had become silent, James answered, saying, "Men *and* brethren, listen to me: ¹⁴Simon has declared how God at the first visited the Gentiles to take out of them a people for His name. ¹⁵And with this the words of the prophets agree, just as it is written:

¹⁶ '*After this I will return*
  And will rebuild the tabernacle of David,
      which has fallen down;
  I will rebuild its ruins,
  And I will set it up;
¹⁷ *So that the rest of mankind may seek the*
      LORD,
  Even all the Gentiles who are called by My
      name,
  Says the LORD *who does all these things.'*[a]

¹⁸"Known to God from eternity are all His works.[a] ¹⁹Therefore I judge that we should not trouble those from among the Gentiles who are turning to God, ²⁰but that we write to them to abstain from things polluted by idols, *from* sexual immorality,[a] *from* things strangled, and *from* blood. ²¹For Moses has had throughout many generations those who preach him in every city, being read in the synagogues every Sabbath."

The Jerusalem Decree

²²Then it pleased the apostles and elders, with the whole church, to send chosen men of their own company to Antioch with Paul and Barnabas, *namely,* Judas who was also named Barsabas,[a] and Silas, leading men among the brethren.

²³They wrote this *letter* by them:

  The apostles, the elders, and the brethren,

  To the brethren who are of the Gentiles in Antioch, Syria, and Cilicia:

  Greetings.

²⁴Since we have heard that some who went out from us have troubled you with words, unsettling your souls, saying, "*You must* be circumcised and keep the law"[a]—to whom we gave no *such* commandment—²⁵it seemed good to us, being assembled with one accord, to send chosen men to you with our beloved Barnabas and Paul, ²⁶men who have risked their lives for the name of our Lord Jesus Christ. ²⁷We have therefore sent Judas and Silas, who will also report the same things by word of mouth. ²⁸For it seemed good to the Holy Spirit, and to us, to lay upon you no greater burden than these necessary things: ²⁹that you abstain from things offered to idols, from blood, from things strangled, and from sexual immorality.[a] If you keep yourselves from these, you will do well.

  Farewell.

Continuing Ministry in Syria

³⁰So when they were sent off, they came to Antioch; and when they had gathered the multitude together, they delivered the letter. ³¹When they had read it, they rejoiced over its encouragement. ³²Now Judas and Silas, themselves being prophets also, exhorted and strengthened the brethren with many words! ³³And after they had stayed *there* for a time,

15:11 [a]NU-Text and M-Text omit *Christ.*   15:17 [a]Amos 9:11, 12   15:18 [a]NU-Text (combining with verse 17) reads *Says the Lord, who makes these things known from eternity (of old).*   15:20, 29 [a]Or *fornication*   15:22 [a]NU-Text and M-Text read *Barsabbas.*
15:24 [a]NU-Text omits *saying, "You must be circumcised and keep the law."*

they were sent back with greetings from the brethren to the apostles.[a]

[34]However, it seemed good to Silas to remain there.[a] [35]Paul and Barnabas also remained in Antioch, teaching and preaching the word of the Lord, with many others also.

Division over John Mark

[36]Then after some days Paul said to Barnabas, "Let us now go back and visit our brethren in every city where we have preached the word of the Lord, *and see* how they are doing." [37]Now Barnabas was determined to take with them John called Mark. [38]But Paul insisted that they should not take with them the one who had departed from them in Pamphylia, and had not gone with them to the work. [39]Then the contention became so sharp that they parted from one another. And so Barnabas took Mark and sailed to Cyprus; [40]but Paul chose Silas and departed, being commended by the brethren to the grace of God. [41]And he went through Syria and Cilicia, strengthening the churches.

Timothy Joins Paul and Silas

16 Then he came to Derbe and Lystra. And behold, a certain disciple was there, named Timothy, *the* son of a certain Jewish woman who believed, but his father *was* Greek. [2]He was well spoken of by the brethren who were at Lystra and Iconium. [3]Paul wanted to have him go on with him. And he took *him* and circumcised him because of the Jews who were in that region, for they all knew that his father was Greek. [4]And as they went through the cities, they delivered to them the decrees to keep, which were determined by the apostles and elders at Jerusalem. [5]So the churches were strengthened in the faith, and increased in number daily.

The Macedonian Call

[6]Now when they had gone through Phrygia and the region of Galatia, they were forbidden by the Holy Spirit to preach the word in Asia. [7]After they had come to Mysia, they tried to go into Bithynia, but the Spirit[a] did not permit them. [8]So passing by Mysia, they came down to Troas. [9]And a vision appeared to Paul in the night. A man of Macedonia stood and pleaded with him, saying, "Come over to Macedonia and help us." [10]Now after he had seen the vision, immediately we sought to go to Macedonia, concluding that the Lord had called us to preach the gospel to them.

> **↘ LEARN**
> • • • • • • • • • • • • • • • • • •
> 16:6–10 • The Christian life is not always smooth sailing. Sometimes God closes doors so we move in another direction. Other times Satan closes them, and we need to push harder. We need to pray for wisdom to know the difference. As I look back over my life, I can't remember a single time God gave me a detailed blueprint of all I was to do. I would take one step, and then He'd show me the next and the next. God's way becomes plain when we start walking in it. Obedience to revealed truth guarantees guidance in matters yet to be revealed. *For more about* God's Will, *see Rom. 12:1;* Adversity, *Acts 16:23, 24;* Satan, *Rom. 1:4.*

Lydia Baptized at Philippi

[11]Therefore, sailing from Troas, we ran a straight course to Samothrace, and the next *day* came to Neapolis, [12]and from there to Philippi, which is the foremost city of that part of Macedonia, a colony. And we were staying in that city for some days. [13]And on the Sabbath day we went out of the city to the riverside, where prayer was customarily made; and we sat down and spoke to the women who met *there*. [14]Now a certain woman named Lydia heard *us*. She was a seller of purple from the city of Thyatira, who worshiped God. The Lord opened her heart to heed the things spoken by Paul. [15]And when she and her household were baptized, she begged *us*, saying, "If you have judged me to be faithful to the Lord, come to my house and stay." So she persuaded us.

Paul and Silas Imprisoned

[16]Now it happened, as we went to prayer, that a certain slave girl possessed with a spirit of divination met us, who brought her masters much profit by fortune-telling. [17]This girl followed Paul and us, and cried out, saying, "These men are the servants of the Most High God, who proclaim to us the way of salvation." [18]And this she did for many days.

15:33 [a]NU-Text reads *to those who had sent them.*   15:34 [a]NU-Text and M-Text omit this verse.   16:7 [a]NU-Text adds *of Jesus.*

But Paul, greatly annoyed, turned and said to the spirit, "I command you in the name of Jesus Christ to come out of her." And he came out that very hour. [19]But when her masters saw that their hope of profit was gone, they seized Paul and Silas and dragged *them* into the marketplace to the authorities.

[20]And they brought them to the magistrates, and said, "These men, being Jews, exceedingly trouble our city; [21]and they teach customs which are not lawful for us, being Romans, to receive or observe." [22]Then the multitude rose up together against them; and the magistrates tore off their clothes and commanded *them* to be beaten with rods. [23]And when they had laid many stripes on them, they threw *them* into prison, commanding the jailer to keep them securely. [24]Having received such a charge, he put them into the inner prison and fastened their feet in the stocks.

↘ LEARN

16:23, 24 • If you are doing God's work, understand you *will* face opposition. But that's not necessarily bad! Years ago merchants shipping codfish from the east coast found that the fish spoiled by the time it arrived out west. Freezing turned the fish mushy. Finally, they added catfish, the codfish's mortal enemy, to the shipping tanks. By the time the codfish arrived, it was alive and well, vigorous (and tasty) from fleeing the catfish. In a similar way, God put catfish in the tank of Paul and Silas to keep them alive and well spiritually—just as He'll do with you. *For more about* Adversity, *see Rom. 8:26;* God at Work, *Rom. 1:4.*

The Philippian Jailer Saved

[25]But at midnight Paul and Silas were praying and singing hymns to God, and the prisoners were listening to them. [26]Suddenly there was a great earthquake, so that the foundations of the prison were shaken; and immediately all the doors were opened and everyone's chains were loosed. [27]And the keeper of the prison, awaking from sleep and seeing the prison doors open, supposing the prisoners had fled, drew his sword and was about to kill himself. [28]But Paul called with a loud voice, saying, "Do yourself no harm, for we are all here."

[29]Then he called for a light, ran in, and fell down trembling before Paul and Silas. [30]And he brought them out and said, "Sirs, what must I do to be saved?"

[31]So they said, "Believe on the Lord Jesus Christ, and you will be saved, you and your household." [32]Then they spoke the word of the Lord to him and to all who were in his house. [33]And he took them the same hour of the night and washed *their* stripes. And immediately he and all his *family* were baptized. [34]Now when he had brought them into his house, he set food before them; and he rejoiced, having believed in God with all his household.

Paul Refuses to Depart Secretly

[35]And when it was day, the magistrates sent the officers, saying, "Let those men go."

[36]So the keeper of the prison reported these words to Paul, saying, "The magistrates have sent to let you go. Now therefore depart, and go in peace."

[37]But Paul said to them, "They have beaten us openly, uncondemned Romans, *and* have thrown *us* into prison. And now do they put us out secretly? No indeed! Let them come themselves and get us out."

[38]And the officers told these words to the magistrates, and they were afraid when they heard that they were Romans. [39]Then they came and pleaded with them and brought *them* out, and asked *them* to depart from the city. [40]So they went out of the prison and entered *the house of* Lydia; and when they had seen the brethren, they encouraged them and departed.

Preaching Christ at Thessalonica

17 Now when they had passed through Amphipolis and Apollonia, they came to Thessalonica, where there was a synagogue of the Jews. [2]Then Paul, as his custom was, went in to them, and for three Sabbaths reasoned with them from the Scriptures, [3]explaining and demonstrating that the Christ had to suffer and rise again from the dead, and *saying,* "This Jesus whom I preach to you is the Christ." [4]And some of them were persuaded; and a great multitude of the devout Greeks, and not a few of the leading women, joined Paul and Silas.

Assault on Jason's House

[5]But the Jews who were not persuaded, becoming envious,[a] took some of the evil men from the marketplace, and gathering a mob, set all the city in an uproar and attacked the house of Jason, and sought to bring them out to the people. [6]But when they did not find them, they dragged Jason and some brethren to the rulers of the city, crying out, "These who have turned the world upside down have come here too. [7]Jason has harbored them, and these are all acting contrary to the decrees of Caesar, saying there is another king—Jesus." [8]And they troubled the crowd and the rulers of the city when they heard these things. [9]So when they had taken security from Jason and the rest, they let them go.

Ministering at Berea

[10]Then the brethren immediately sent Paul and Silas away by night to Berea. When they arrived, they went into the synagogue of the Jews. [11]These were more fair-minded than those in Thessalonica, in that they received the word with all readiness, and searched the Scriptures daily *to find out* whether these things were so. [12]Therefore many of them believed, and also not a few of the Greeks, prominent women as well as men. [13]But when the Jews from Thessalonica learned that the word of God was preached by Paul at Berea, they came there also and stirred up the crowds. [14]Then immediately the brethren sent Paul away, to go to the sea; but both Silas and Timothy remained there. [15]So those who conducted Paul brought him to Athens; and receiving a command for Silas and Timothy to come to him with all speed, they departed.

The Philosophers at Athens

[16]Now while Paul waited for them at Athens, his spirit was provoked within him when he saw that the city was given over to idols. [17]Therefore he reasoned in the synagogue with the Jews and with the *Gentile* worshipers, and in the marketplace daily with those who happened to be there. [18]Then[a] certain Epicurean and Stoic philosophers encountered him. And some said, "What does this babbler want to say?"

Others said, "He seems to be a proclaimer of foreign gods," because he preached to them Jesus and the resurrection.

[19]And they took him and brought him to the Areopagus, saying, "May we know what this new doctrine *is* of which you speak? [20]For you are bringing some strange things to our ears. Therefore we want to know what these things mean." [21]For all the Athenians and the foreigners who were there spent their time in nothing else but either to tell or to hear some new thing.

Addressing the Areopagus

[22]Then Paul stood in the midst of the Areopagus and said, "Men of Athens, I perceive that in all things you are very religious; [23]for as I was passing through and considering the objects of your worship, I even found an altar with this inscription:

TO THE UNKNOWN GOD.

Therefore, the One whom you worship without knowing, Him I proclaim to you: [24]God, who made the world and everything in it, since He is Lord of heaven and earth, does not dwell in temples made with hands. [25]Nor is He worshiped with men's hands, as though He needed anything, since He gives to all life, breath, and all things. [26]And He has made from one blood[a] every nation of men to dwell on all the face of the earth, and has determined their preappointed times and the boundaries of their dwellings, [27]so that they should seek the Lord, in the hope that they might grope for Him and find Him, though He is not far from each one of us; [28]for in Him we live and move and have our being, as also some of your own poets have said, 'For we are also His offspring.' [29]Therefore, since we are the offspring of God, we ought not to think that the Divine Nature is like gold or silver or stone, something shaped by art and man's devising. [30]Truly, these times of ignorance God overlooked, but now commands all men everywhere to repent, [31]because He has appointed a day on which He will judge the world in righteousness by the Man whom He has ordained. He has given assurance of this to all by raising Him from the dead."

[32]And when they heard of the resurrection of the dead, some mocked, while others said,

17:5 [a]NU-Text omits *who were not persuaded;* M-Text omits *becoming envious.*   17:18 [a]NU-Text and M-Text add *also.*
17:26 [a]NU-Text omits *blood.*

"We will hear you again on this *matter*." [33]So Paul departed from among them. [34]However, some men joined him and believed, among them Dionysius the Areopagite, a woman named Damaris, and others with them.

Ministering at Corinth

18 After these things Paul departed from Athens and went to Corinth. [2]And he found a certain Jew named Aquila, born in Pontus, who had recently come from Italy with his wife Priscilla (because Claudius had commanded all the Jews to depart from Rome); and he came to them. [3]So, because he was of the same trade, he stayed with them and worked; for by occupation they were tentmakers. [4]And he reasoned in the synagogue every Sabbath, and persuaded both Jews and Greeks.

[5]When Silas and Timothy had come from Macedonia, Paul was compelled by the Spirit, and testified to the Jews *that* Jesus *is* the Christ. [6]But when they opposed him and blasphemed, he shook *his* garments and said to them, "Your blood *be* upon your *own* heads; I *am* clean. From now on I will go to the Gentiles." [7]And he departed from there and entered the house of a certain *man* named Justus,[a] *one* who worshiped God, whose house was next door to the synagogue. [8]Then Crispus, the ruler of the synagogue, believed on the Lord with all his household. And many of the Corinthians, hearing, believed and were baptized.

[9]Now the Lord spoke to Paul in the night by a vision, "Do not be afraid, but speak, and do not keep silent; [10]for I am with you, and no one will attack you to hurt you; for I have many people in this city." [11]And he continued *there* a year and six months, teaching the word of God among them.

[12]When Gallio was proconsul of Achaia, the Jews with one accord rose up against Paul and brought him to the judgment seat, [13]saying, "This *fellow* persuades men to worship God contrary to the law."

[14]And when Paul was about to open *his* mouth, Gallio said to the Jews, "If it were a matter of wrongdoing or wicked crimes, O Jews, there would be reason why I should bear with you. [15]But if it is a question of words and names and your own law, look *to it* yourselves; for I do not want to be a judge of such *matters*." [16]And he drove them from the judgment seat. [17]Then all the Greeks[a] took Sosthenes, the ruler of the synagogue, and beat *him* before the judgment seat. But Gallio took no notice of these things.

Paul Returns to Antioch

[18]So Paul still remained a good while. Then he took leave of the brethren and sailed for Syria, and Priscilla and Aquila *were* with him. He had *his* hair cut off at Cenchrea, for he had taken a vow. [19]And he came to Ephesus, and left them there; but he himself entered the synagogue and reasoned with the Jews. [20]When they asked *him* to stay a longer time with them, he did not consent, [21]but took leave of them, saying, "I must by all means keep this coming feast in Jerusalem;[a] but I will return again to you, God willing." And he sailed from Ephesus.

[22]And when he had landed at Caesarea, and gone up and greeted the church, he went down to Antioch. [23]After he had spent some time *there*, he departed and went over the region of Galatia and Phrygia in order, strengthening all the disciples.

Ministry of Apollos

[24]Now a certain Jew named Apollos, born at Alexandria, an eloquent man *and* mighty in the Scriptures, came to Ephesus. [25]This man had been instructed in the way of the Lord; and being fervent in spirit, he spoke and taught accurately the things of the Lord, though he knew only the baptism of John. [26]So he began to speak boldly in the synagogue. When Aquila and Priscilla heard him, they took him aside and explained to him the way of God more accurately. [27]And when he desired to cross to Achaia, the brethren wrote, exhorting the disciples to receive him; and when he arrived, he greatly helped those who had believed through grace; [28]for he vigorously refuted the Jews publicly, showing from the Scriptures that Jesus is the Christ.

Paul at Ephesus

19 And it happened, while Apollos was at Corinth, that Paul, having passed through the upper regions, came to Ephesus. And finding some disciples [2]he said

18:7 [a]NU-Text reads *Titius Justus.*   18:17 [a]NU-Text reads *they all.*   18:21 [a]NU-Text omits *I must* through *Jerusalem.*

to them, "Did you receive the Holy Spirit when you believed?"

So they said to him, "We have not so much as heard whether there is a Holy Spirit."

[3]And he said to them, "Into what then were you baptized?"

So they said, "Into John's baptism."

[4]Then Paul said, "John indeed baptized with a baptism of repentance, saying to the people that they should believe on Him who would come after him, that is, on Christ Jesus."

[5]When they heard *this,* they were baptized in the name of the Lord Jesus. [6]And when Paul had laid hands on them, the Holy Spirit came upon them, and they spoke with tongues and prophesied. [7]Now the men were about twelve in all.

[8]And he went into the synagogue and spoke boldly for three months, reasoning and persuading concerning the things of the kingdom of God. [9]But when some were hardened and did not believe, but spoke evil of the Way before the multitude, he departed from them and withdrew the disciples, reasoning daily in the school of Tyrannus. [10]And this continued for two years, so that all who dwelt in Asia heard the word of the Lord Jesus, both Jews and Greeks.

Miracles Glorify Christ

[11]Now God worked unusual miracles by the hands of Paul, [12]so that even handkerchiefs or aprons were brought from his body to the sick, and the diseases left them and the evil spirits went out of them. [13]Then some of the itinerant Jewish exorcists took it upon themselves to call the name of the Lord Jesus over those who had evil spirits, saying, "We[a] exorcise you by the Jesus whom Paul preaches." [14]Also there were seven sons of Sceva, a Jewish chief priest, who did so.

[15]And the evil spirit answered and said, "Jesus I know, and Paul I know; but who are you?"

[16]Then the man in whom the evil spirit was leaped on them, overpowered[a] them, and prevailed against them,[b] so that they fled out of that house naked and wounded. [17]This became known both to all Jews and Greeks dwelling in Ephesus; and fear fell on them all,

and the name of the Lord Jesus was magnified. [18]And many who had believed came confessing and telling their deeds. [19]Also, many of those who had practiced magic brought their books together and burned *them* in the sight of all. And they counted up the value of them, and *it* totaled fifty thousand *pieces* of silver. [20]So the word of the Lord grew mightily and prevailed.

The Riot at Ephesus

[21]When these things were accomplished, Paul purposed in the Spirit, when he had passed through Macedonia and Achaia, to go to Jerusalem, saying, "After I have been there, I must also see Rome." [22]So he sent into Macedonia two of those who ministered to him, Timothy and Erastus, but he himself stayed in Asia for a time.

[23]And about that time there arose a great commotion about the Way. [24]For a certain man named Demetrius, a silversmith, who made silver shrines of Diana,[a] brought no small profit to the craftsmen. [25]He called them together with the workers of similar occupation, and said: "Men, you know that we have our prosperity by this trade. [26]Moreover you see and hear that not only at Ephesus, but throughout almost all Asia, this Paul has persuaded and turned away many people, saying that they are not gods which are made with hands. [27]So not only is this trade of ours in danger of falling into disrepute, but also the temple of the great goddess Diana may be despised and her magnificence destroyed,[a] whom all Asia and the world worship."

[28]Now when they heard *this,* they were full of wrath and cried out, saying, "Great *is* Diana of the Ephesians!" [29]So the whole city was filled with confusion, and rushed into the theater with one accord, having seized Gaius and Aristarchus, Macedonians, Paul's travel companions. [30]And when Paul wanted to go in to the people, the disciples would not allow him. [31]Then some of the officials of Asia, who were his friends, sent to him pleading that he would not venture into the theater. [32]Some therefore cried one thing and some another, for the assembly was confused, and most of them did not know why they had come together. [33]And they drew Alexander out of the multitude, the Jews putting him forward.

19:13 [a]NU-Text reads *I.*   **19:16** [a]M-Text reads *and they overpowered.*   [b]NU-Text reads *both of them.*   **19:24** [a]Greek *Artemis*
19:27 [a]NU-Text reads *she be deposed from her magnificence.*

And Alexander motioned with his hand, and wanted to make his defense to the people. [34]But when they found out that he was a Jew, all with one voice cried out for about two hours, "Great is Diana of the Ephesians!"

[35]And when the city clerk had quieted the crowd, he said: "Men of Ephesus, what man is there who does not know that the city of the Ephesians is temple guardian of the great goddess Diana, and of the *image* which fell down from Zeus? [36]Therefore, since these things cannot be denied, you ought to be quiet and do nothing rashly. [37]For you have brought these men here who are neither robbers of temples nor blasphemers of your[a] goddess. [38]Therefore, if Demetrius and his fellow craftsmen have a case against anyone, the courts are open and there are proconsuls. Let them bring charges against one another. [39]But if you have any other inquiry to make, it shall be determined in the lawful assembly. [40]For we are in danger of being called in question for today's uproar, there being no reason which we may give to account for this disorderly gathering." [41]And when he had said these things, he dismissed the assembly.

Journeys in Greece

20 After the uproar had ceased, Paul called the disciples to *himself,* embraced *them,* and departed to go to Macedonia. [2]Now when he had gone over that region and encouraged them with many words, he came to Greece [3]and stayed three months. And when the Jews plotted against him as he was about to sail to Syria, he decided to return through Macedonia. [4]And Sopater of Berea accompanied him to Asia— also Aristarchus and Secundus of the Thessalonians, and Gaius of Derbe, and Timothy, and Tychicus and Trophimus of Asia. [5]These men, going ahead, waited for us at Troas. [6]But we sailed away from Philippi after the Days of Unleavened Bread, and in five days joined them at Troas, where we stayed seven days.

Ministering at Troas

[7]Now on the first *day* of the week, when the disciples came together to break bread, Paul, ready to depart the next day, spoke to them and continued his message until midnight. [8]There were many lamps in the upper room where they[a] were gathered together. [9]And in a window sat a certain young man named Eutychus, who was sinking into a deep sleep. He was overcome by sleep; and as Paul continued speaking, he fell down from the third story and was taken up dead. [10]But Paul went down, fell on him, and embracing *him* said, "Do not trouble yourselves, for his life is in him." [11]Now when he had come up, had broken bread and eaten, and talked a long while, even till daybreak, he departed. [12]And they brought the young man in alive, and they were not a little comforted.

From Troas to Miletus

[13]Then we went ahead to the ship and sailed to Assos, there intending to take Paul on board; for so he had given orders, intending himself to go on foot. [14]And when he met us at Assos, we took him on board and came to Mitylene. [15]We sailed from there, and the next *day* came opposite Chios. The following *day* we arrived at Samos and stayed at Trogyllium. The next *day* we came to Miletus. [16]For Paul had decided to sail past Ephesus, so that he would not have to spend time in Asia; for he was hurrying to be at Jerusalem, if possible, on the Day of Pentecost.

The Ephesian Elders Exhorted

[17]From Miletus he sent to Ephesus and called for the elders of the church. [18]And when they had come to him, he said to them: "You know, from the first day that I came to Asia, in what manner I always lived among you, [19]serving the Lord with all humility, with many tears and trials which happened to me by the plotting of the Jews; [20]how I kept back nothing that was helpful, but proclaimed it to you, and taught you publicly and from house to house, [21]testifying to Jews, and also to Greeks, repentance toward God and faith toward our Lord Jesus Christ. [22]And see, now I go bound in the spirit to Jerusalem, not knowing the things that will happen to me there, [23]except that the Holy Spirit testifies in every city, saying that chains and tribulations await me. [24]But none of these things move me; nor do I count my life dear to myself,[a]

19:37 [a]NU-Text reads *our.*   **20:8** [a]NU-Text and M-Text read *we.*
20:24 [a]NU-Text reads *But I do not count my life of any value or dear to myself.*

so that I may finish my race with joy, and the ministry which I received from the Lord Jesus, to testify to the gospel of the grace of God.

25"And indeed, now I know that you all, among whom I have gone preaching the kingdom of God, will see my face no more. 26Therefore I testify to you this day that I *am* innocent of the blood of all *men*. 27For I have not shunned to declare to you the whole counsel of God. 28Therefore take heed to yourselves and to all the flock, among which the Holy Spirit has made you overseers, to shepherd the church of Goda which He purchased with His own blood. 29For I know this, that after my departure savage wolves will come in among you, not sparing the flock. 30Also from among yourselves men will rise up, speaking perverse things, to draw away the disciples after themselves. 31Therefore watch, and remember that for three years I did not cease to warn everyone night and day with tears.

32"So now, brethren, I commend you to God and to the word of His grace, which is able to build you up and give you an inheritance among all those who are sanctified. 33I have coveted no one's silver or gold or apparel. 34Yes,a you yourselves know that these hands have provided for my necessities, and for those who were with me. 35I have shown you in every way, by laboring like this, that you must support the weak. And remember the words of the Lord Jesus, that He said, 'It is more blessed to give than to receive.' "

36And when he had said these things, he knelt down and prayed with them all. 37Then they all wept freely, and fell on Paul's neck and kissed him, 38sorrowing most of all for the words which he spoke, that they would see his face no more. And they accompanied him to the ship.

Warnings on the Journey to Jerusalem

21 Now it came to pass, that when we had departed from them and set sail, running a straight course we came to Cos, the following *day* to Rhodes, and from there to Patara. 2And finding a ship sailing over to Phoenicia, we went aboard and set sail. 3When we had sighted Cyprus, we passed it on the left, sailed to Syria, and landed at Tyre; for there the ship was to

unload her cargo. 4And finding disciples,a we stayed there seven days. They told Paul through the Spirit not to go up to Jerusalem. 5When we had come to the end of those days, we departed and went on our way; and they all accompanied us, with wives and children, till *we were* out of the city. And we knelt down on the shore and prayed. 6When we had taken our leave of one another, we boarded the ship, and they returned home.

7And when we had finished *our* voyage from Tyre, we came to Ptolemais, greeted the brethren, and stayed with them one day. 8On the next *day* we who were Paul's companionsa departed and came to Caesarea, and entered the house of Philip the evangelist, who was *one* of the seven, and stayed with him. 9Now this man had four virgin daughters who prophesied. 10And as we stayed many days, a certain prophet named Agabus came down from Judea. 11When he had come to us, he took Paul's belt, bound his *own* hands and feet, and said, "Thus says the Holy Spirit, 'So shall the Jews at Jerusalem bind the man who owns this belt, and deliver *him* into the hands of the Gentiles.' "

12Now when we heard these things, both we and those from that place pleaded with him not to go up to Jerusalem. 13Then Paul answered, "What do you mean by weeping and breaking my heart? For I am ready not only to be bound, but also to die at Jerusalem for the name of the Lord Jesus."

14So when he would not be persuaded, we ceased, saying, "The will of the Lord be done."

Paul Urged to Make Peace

15And after those days we packed and went up to Jerusalem. 16Also some of the disciples from Caesarea went with us and brought with them a certain Mnason of Cyprus, an early disciple, with whom we were to lodge.

17And when we had come to Jerusalem, the brethren received us gladly. 18On the following *day* Paul went in with us to James, and all the elders were present. 19When he had greeted them, he told in detail those things which God had done among the Gentiles through his ministry. 20And when they heard *it*, they glorified the Lord. And they said to him, "You see, brother, how many myriads of Jews there are who have believed, and they are all zealous for

20:28 aM-Text reads *of the Lord and God.*   20:34 aNU-Text and M-Text omit *Yes.*   21:4 aNU-Text reads *the disciples.*
21:8 aNU-Text omits *who were Paul's companions.*

the law; ²¹but they have been informed about you that you teach all the Jews who are among the Gentiles to forsake Moses, saying that they ought not to circumcise *their* children nor to walk according to the customs. ²²What then? The assembly must certainly meet, for they will^a hear that you have come. ²³Therefore do what we tell you: We have four men who have taken a vow. ²⁴Take them and be purified with them, and pay their expenses so that they may shave *their* heads, and that all may know that those things of which they were informed concerning you are nothing, but *that* you yourself also walk orderly and keep the law. ²⁵But concerning the Gentiles who believe, we have written *and* decided that they should observe no such thing, except^a that they should keep themselves from *things* offered to idols, from blood, from things strangled, and from sexual immorality."

Arrested in the Temple

²⁶Then Paul took the men, and the next day, having been purified with them, entered the temple to announce the expiration of the days of purification, at which time an offering should be made for each one of them.

²⁷Now when the seven days were almost ended, the Jews from Asia, seeing him in the temple, stirred up the whole crowd and laid hands on him, ²⁸crying out, "Men of Israel, help! This is the man who teaches all *men* everywhere against the people, the law, and this place; and furthermore he also brought Greeks into the temple and has defiled this holy place." ²⁹(For they had previously^a seen Trophimus the Ephesian with him in the city, whom they supposed that Paul had brought into the temple.)

³⁰And all the city was disturbed; and the people ran together, seized Paul, and dragged him out of the temple; and immediately the doors were shut. ³¹Now as they were seeking to kill him, news came to the commander of the garrison that all Jerusalem was in an uproar. ³²He immediately took soldiers and centurions, and ran down to them. And when they saw the commander and the soldiers, they stopped beating Paul. ³³Then the commander came near and took him, and commanded *him* to be bound with two chains; and he asked who he was and what he had done. ³⁴And some among the multitude cried one thing and some another.

So when he could not ascertain the truth because of the tumult, he commanded him to be taken into the barracks. ³⁵When he reached the stairs, he had to be carried by the soldiers because of the violence of the mob. ³⁶For the multitude of the people followed after, crying out, "Away with him!"

Addressing the Jerusalem Mob

³⁷Then as Paul was about to be led into the barracks, he said to the commander, "May I speak to you?"

He replied, "Can you speak Greek? ³⁸Are you not the Egyptian who some time ago stirred up a rebellion and led the four thousand assassins out into the wilderness?"

³⁹But Paul said, "I am a Jew from Tarsus, in Cilicia, a citizen of no mean city; and I implore you, permit me to speak to the people."

⁴⁰So when he had given him permission, Paul stood on the stairs and motioned with his hand to the people. And when there was a great silence, he spoke to *them* in the Hebrew language, saying,

22 "Brethren and fathers, hear my defense before you now." ²And when they heard that he spoke to them in the Hebrew language, they kept all the more silent.

Then he said: ³"I am indeed a Jew, born in Tarsus of Cilicia, but brought up in this city at the feet of Gamaliel, taught according to the strictness of our fathers' law, and was zealous toward God as you all are today. ⁴I persecuted this Way to the death, binding and delivering into prisons both men and women, ⁵as also the high priest bears me witness, and all the council of the elders, from whom I also received letters to the brethren, and went to Damascus to bring in chains even those who were there to Jerusalem to be punished.

⁶"Now it happened, as I journeyed and came near Damascus at about noon, suddenly a great light from heaven shone around me. ⁷And I fell to the ground and heard a voice saying to me, 'Saul, Saul, why are you persecuting Me?' ⁸So I answered, 'Who are You, Lord?' And He said to me, 'I am Jesus of Nazareth, whom you are persecuting.'

⁹"And those who were with me indeed saw the light and were afraid,ᵃ but they did not hear the voice of Him who spoke to me. ¹⁰So I said, 'What shall I do, Lord?' And the Lord said to me, 'Arise and go into Damascus, and there you will be told all things which are appointed for you to do.' ¹¹And since I could not see for the glory of that light, being led by the hand of those who were with me, I came into Damascus.

¹²"Then a certain Ananias, a devout man according to the law, having a good testimony with all the Jews who dwelt *there,* ¹³came to me; and he stood and said to me, 'Brother Saul, receive your sight.' And at that same hour I looked up at him. ¹⁴Then he said, 'The God of our fathers has chosen you that you should know His will, and see the Just One, and hear the voice of His mouth. ¹⁵For you will be His witness to all men of what you have seen and heard. ¹⁶And now why are you waiting? Arise and be baptized, and wash away your sins, calling on the name of the Lord.'

¹⁷"Now it happened, when I returned to Jerusalem and was praying in the temple, that I was in a trance ¹⁸and saw Him saying to me, 'Make haste and get out of Jerusalem quickly, for they will not receive your testimony concerning Me.' ¹⁹So I said, 'Lord, they know that in every synagogue I imprisoned and beat those who believe on You. ²⁰And when the blood of Your martyr Stephen was shed, I also was standing by consenting to his death,ᵃ and guarding the clothes of those who were killing him.' ²¹Then He said to me, 'Depart, for I will send you far from here to the Gentiles.' "

Paul's Roman Citizenship

²²And they listened to him until this word, and *then* they raised their voices and said, "Away with such a *fellow* from the earth, for he is not fit to live!" ²³Then, as they cried out and tore off *their* clothes and threw dust into the air, ²⁴the commander ordered him to be brought into the barracks, and said that he should be examined under scourging, so that he might know why they shouted so against him. ²⁵And as they bound him with thongs, Paul said to the centurion who stood by, "Is it lawful for you to scourge a man who is a Roman, and uncondemned?"

²⁶When the centurion heard *that,* he went and told the commander, saying, "Take care what you do, for this man is a Roman."

²⁷Then the commander came and said to him, "Tell me, are you a Roman?"

He said, "Yes."

²⁸The commander answered, "With a large sum I obtained this citizenship."

And Paul said, "But I was born *a citizen.*"

²⁹Then immediately those who were about to examine him withdrew from him; and the commander was also afraid after he found out that he was a Roman, and because he had bound him.

The Sanhedrin Divided

³⁰The next day, because he wanted to know for certain why he was accused by the Jews, he released him from *his* bonds, and commanded the chief priests and all their council to appear, and brought Paul down and set him before them.

23 Then Paul, looking earnestly at the council, said, "Men *and* brethren, I have lived in all good conscience before God until this day." ²And the high priest Ananias commanded those who stood by him to strike him on the mouth. ³Then Paul said to him, "God will strike you, *you* whitewashed wall! For you sit to judge me according to the law, and do you command me to be struck contrary to the law?"

⁴And those who stood by said, "Do you revile God's high priest?"

⁵Then Paul said, "I did not know, brethren, that he was the high priest; for it is written, *'You shall not speak evil of a ruler of your people.'* "ᵃ

⁶But when Paul perceived that one part were Sadducees and the other Pharisees, he cried out in the council, "Men *and* brethren, I am a Pharisee, the son of a Pharisee; concerning the hope and resurrection of the dead I am being judged!"

⁷And when he had said this, a dissension arose between the Pharisees and the Sadducees; and the assembly was divided. ⁸For Sadducees say that there is no resurrection—and no angel or spirit; but the Pharisees confess both. ⁹Then there arose a loud outcry. And the scribes of the Pharisees' party arose and protested, saying, "We find no evil in this

22:9 ᵃNU-Text omits *and were afraid.*   22:20 ᵃNU-Text omits *to his death.*   23:5 ᵃExodus 22:28

man; but if a spirit or an angel has spoken to him, let us not fight against God."ᵃ

¹⁰Now when there arose a great dissension, the commander, fearing lest Paul might be pulled to pieces by them, commanded the soldiers to go down and take him by force from among them, and bring him into the barracks.

The Plot Against Paul

¹¹But the following night the Lord stood by him and said, "Be of good cheer, Paul; for as you have testified for Me in Jerusalem, so you must also bear witness at Rome."

¹²And when it was day, some of the Jews banded together and bound themselves under an oath, saying that they would neither eat nor drink till they had killed Paul. ¹³Now there were more than forty who had formed this conspiracy. ¹⁴They came to the chief priests and elders, and said, "We have bound ourselves under a great oath that we will eat nothing until we have killed Paul. ¹⁵Now you, therefore, together with the council, suggest to the commander that he be brought down to you tomorrow,ᵃ as though you were going to make further inquiries concerning him; but we are ready to kill him before he comes near."

¹⁶So when Paul's sister's son heard of their ambush, he went and entered the barracks and told Paul. ¹⁷Then Paul called one of the centurions to him and said, "Take this young man to the commander, for he has something to tell him." ¹⁸So he took him and brought him to the commander and said, "Paul the prisoner called me to him and asked me to bring this young man to you. He has something to say to you."

¹⁹Then the commander took him by the hand, went aside, and asked privately, "What is it that you have to tell me?"

²⁰And he said, "The Jews have agreed to ask that you bring Paul down to the council tomorrow, as though they were going to inquire more fully about him. ²¹But do not yield to them, for more than forty of them lie in wait for him, men who have bound themselves by an oath that they will neither eat nor drink till they have killed him; and now they are ready, waiting for the promise from you."

²²So the commander let the young man depart, and commanded him, "Tell no one that you have revealed these things to me."

Sent to Felix

²³And he called for two centurions, saying, "Prepare two hundred soldiers, seventy horsemen, and two hundred spearmen to go to Caesarea at the third hour of the night; ²⁴and provide mounts to set Paul on, and bring him safely to Felix the governor." ²⁵He wrote a letter in the following manner:

²⁶Claudius Lysias,

To the most excellent governor Felix:

Greetings.

²⁷This man was seized by the Jews and was about to be killed by them. Coming with the troops I rescued him, having learned that he was a Roman. ²⁸And when I wanted to know the reason they accused him, I brought him before their council. ²⁹I found out that he was accused concerning questions of their law, but had nothing charged against him deserving of death or chains. ³⁰And when it was told me that the Jews lay in wait for the man,ᵃ I sent him immediately to you, and also commanded his accusers to state before you the charges against him.

Farewell.

³¹Then the soldiers, as they were commanded, took Paul and brought him by night to Antipatris. ³²The next day they left the horsemen to go on with him, and returned to the barracks. ³³When they came to Caesarea and had delivered the letter to the governor, they also presented Paul to him. ³⁴And when the governor had read it, he asked what province he was from. And when he understood that he was from Cilicia, ³⁵he said, "I will hear you when your accusers also have come." And he commanded him to be kept in Herod's Praetorium.

Accused of Sedition

24 Now after five days Ananias the high priest came down with the elders and a certain orator named

23:9 ᵃNU-Text omits last clause and reads what if a spirit or an angel has spoken to him?   **23:15** ᵃNU-Text omits tomorrow.
23:30 ᵃNU-Text reads there would be a plot against the man.

Tertullus. These gave evidence to the governor against Paul.

2And when he was called upon, Tertullus began his accusation, saying: "Seeing that through you we enjoy great peace, and prosperity is being brought to this nation by your foresight, 3we accept *it* always and in all places, most noble Felix, with all thankfulness. 4Nevertheless, not to be tedious to you any further, I beg you to hear, by your courtesy, a few words from us. 5For we have found this man a plague, a creator of dissension among all the Jews throughout the world, and a ringleader of the sect of the Nazarenes. 6He even tried to profane the temple, and we seized him,[a] and wanted to judge him according to our law. 7But the commander Lysias came by and with great violence took *him* out of our hands, 8commanding his accusers to come to you. By examining him yourself you may ascertain all these things of which we accuse him." 9And the Jews also assented,[a] maintaining that these things were so.

The Defense Before Felix

10Then Paul, after the governor had nodded to him to speak, answered: "Inasmuch as I know that you have been for many years a judge of this nation, I do the more cheerfully answer for myself, 11because you may ascertain that it is no more than twelve days since I went up to Jerusalem to worship. 12And they neither found me in the temple disputing with anyone nor inciting the crowd, either in the synagogues or in the city. 13Nor can they prove the things of which they now accuse me. 14But this I confess to you, that

according to the Way which they call a sect, so I worship the God of my fathers, believing all things which are written in the Law and in the Prophets. 15I have hope in God, which they themselves also accept, that there will be a resurrection of *the* dead,[a] both of *the* just and *the* unjust. 16This *being* so, I myself always strive to have a conscience without offense toward God and men.

17"Now after many years I came to bring alms and offerings to my nation, 18in the midst of which some Jews from Asia found me purified in the temple, neither with a mob nor with tumult. 19They ought to have been here before you to object if they had anything against me. 20Or else let those who are here themselves say if they found any wrongdoing[a] in me while I stood before the council, 21unless *it is* for this one statement which I cried out, standing among them, 'Concerning the resurrection of the dead I am being judged by you this day.' "

Felix Procrastinates

22But when Felix heard these things, having more accurate knowledge of *the* Way, he adjourned the proceedings and said, "When Lysias the commander comes down, I will make a decision on your case." 23So he commanded the centurion to keep Paul and to let *him* have liberty, and told him not to forbid any of his friends to provide for or visit him.

24And after some days, when Felix came with his wife Drusilla, who was Jewish, he sent for Paul and heard him concerning the faith in Christ. 25Now as he reasoned about righteousness, self-control, and the judgment

24:6 [a]NU-Text ends the sentence here and omits the rest of verse 6, all of verse 7, and the first clause of verse 8.   24:9 [a]NU-Text and M-Text read *joined the attack.*   24:15 [a]NU-Text omits *of the dead.*   24:20 [a]NU-Text and M-Text read *say what wrongdoing they found.*

↑ GROW (ACTS 24:14)
· ·

What does God require of us in worship? First, we must worship God in truth. The God we worship must be the true God and not a little god of our own making. The fact is that we have free access to God through the blood of Jesus alone. Because of what He has done for us, God is always worthy of our worship, and not merely when we feel like it. God has invited us to worship and He has everything in control. The Bible speaks of offering to God a "sacrifice of praise" (Heb. 13:15). God is far more interested in our motives than in our talent. When we worship, we stand before an audience of One. If in worship we want people to look at us or we begin thinking about anything other than God, then that is not worship. Remember, God looks on the heart (1 Sam. 16:7). *For more about* Worship, *see Phil. 4:11, 12.*

to come, Felix was afraid and answered, "Go away for now; when I have a convenient time I will call for you." [26]Meanwhile he also hoped that money would be given him by Paul, that he might release him.[a] Therefore he sent for him more often and conversed with him.

[27]But after two years Porcius Festus succeeded Felix; and Felix, wanting to do the Jews a favor, left Paul bound.

Paul Appeals to Caesar

25 Now when Festus had come to the province, after three days he went up from Caesarea to Jerusalem. [2]Then the high priest[a] and the chief men of the Jews informed him against Paul; and they petitioned him, [3]asking a favor against him, that he would summon him to Jerusalem—while *they* lay in ambush along the road to kill him. [4]But Festus answered that Paul should be kept at Caesarea, and that he himself was going *there* shortly. [5]"Therefore," he said, "let those who have authority among you go down with *me* and accuse this man, to see if there is any fault in him."

[6]And when he had remained among them more than ten days, he went down to Caesarea. And the next day, sitting on the judgment seat, he commanded Paul to be brought. [7]When he had come, the Jews who had come down from Jerusalem stood about and laid many serious complaints against Paul, which they could not prove, [8]while he answered for himself, "Neither against the law of the Jews, nor against the temple, nor against Caesar have I offended in anything at all."

[9]But Festus, wanting to do the Jews a favor, answered Paul and said, "Are you willing to go up to Jerusalem and there be judged before me concerning these things?"

[10]So Paul said, "I stand at Caesar's judgment seat, where I ought to be judged. To the Jews I have done no wrong, as you very well know. [11]For if I am an offender, or have committed anything deserving of death, I do not object to dying; but if there is nothing in these things of which these men accuse me, no one can deliver me to them. I appeal to Caesar."

[12]Then Festus, when he had conferred with the council, answered, "You have appealed to Caesar? To Caesar you shall go!"

Paul Before Agrippa

[13]And after some days King Agrippa and Bernice came to Caesarea to greet Festus. [14]When they had been there many days, Festus laid Paul's case before the king, saying: "There is a certain man left a prisoner by Felix, [15]about whom the chief priests and the elders of the Jews informed *me*, when I was in Jerusalem, asking for a judgment against him. [16]To them I answered, 'It is not the custom of the Romans to deliver any man to destruction[a] before the accused meets the accusers face to face, and has opportunity to answer for himself concerning the charge against him.' [17]Therefore when they had come together, without any delay, the next day I sat on the judgment seat and commanded the man to be brought in. [18]When the accusers stood up, they brought no accusation against him of such things as I supposed, [19]but had some questions against him about their own religion and about a certain Jesus, who had died, whom Paul affirmed to be alive. [20]And because I was uncertain of such questions, I asked whether he was willing to go to Jerusalem and there be judged concerning these matters. [21]But when Paul appealed to be reserved for the decision of Augustus, I commanded him to be kept till I could send him to Caesar."

[22]Then Agrippa said to Festus, "I also would like to hear the man myself."

"Tomorrow," he said, "you shall hear him."

[23]So the next day, when Agrippa and Bernice had come with great pomp, and had entered the auditorium with the commanders and the prominent men of the city, at Festus' command Paul was brought in. [24]And Festus said: "King Agrippa and all the men who are here present with us, you see this man about whom the whole assembly of the Jews petitioned me, both at Jerusalem and here, crying out that he was not fit to live any longer. [25]But when I found that he had committed nothing deserving of death, and that he himself had appealed to Augustus, I decided to send him. [26]I have nothing certain to write to my lord concerning him. Therefore I have

24:26 [a]NU-Text omits *that he might release him.*   **25:2** [a]NU-Text reads *chief priests.*
25:16 [a]NU-Text omits *to destruction,* although it is implied.

brought him out before you, and especially before you, King Agrippa, so that after the examination has taken place I may have something to write. [27]For it seems to me unreasonable to send a prisoner and not to specify the charges against him."

Paul's Early Life

26 Then Agrippa said to Paul, "You are permitted to speak for yourself."

So Paul stretched out his hand and answered for himself: [2]"I think myself happy, King Agrippa, because today I shall answer for myself before you concerning all the things of which I am accused by the Jews, [3]especially because you are expert in all customs and questions which have to do with the Jews. Therefore I beg you to hear me patiently.

[4]"My manner of life from my youth, which was spent from the beginning among my own nation at Jerusalem, all the Jews know. [5]They knew me from the first, if they were willing to testify, that according to the strictest sect of our religion I lived a Pharisee. [6]And now I stand and am judged for the hope of the promise made by God to our fathers. [7]To this *promise* our twelve tribes, earnestly serving *God* night and day, hope to attain. For this hope's sake, King Agrippa, I am accused by the Jews. [8]Why should it be thought incredible by you that God raises the dead?

[9]"Indeed, I myself thought I must do many things contrary to the name of Jesus of Nazareth. [10]This I also did in Jerusalem, and many of the saints I shut up in prison, having received authority from the chief priests; and when they were put to death, I cast my vote against *them*. [11]And I punished them often in every synagogue and compelled *them* to blaspheme; and being exceedingly enraged against them, I persecuted *them* even to foreign cities.

Paul Recounts His Conversion

[12]"While thus occupied, as I journeyed to Damascus with authority and commission from the chief priests, [13]at midday, O king, along the road I saw a light from heaven, brighter than the sun, shining around me and those who journeyed with me. [14]And when we all had fallen to the ground, I heard

a voice speaking to me and saying in the Hebrew language, 'Saul, Saul, why are you persecuting Me? *It is* hard for you to kick against the goads.' [15]So I said, 'Who are You, Lord?' And He said, 'I am Jesus, whom you are persecuting. [16]But rise and stand on your feet; for I have appeared to you for this purpose, to make you a minister and a witness both of the things which you have seen and of the things which I will yet reveal to you. [17]I will deliver you from the *Jewish* people, as well as *from* the Gentiles, to whom I now[a] send you, [18]to open their eyes, *in order* to turn *them* from darkness to light, and *from* the power of Satan to God, that they may receive forgiveness of sins and an inheritance among those who are sanctified by faith in Me.'

> **→LIVE**
> • • • • • • • • • • • • • • • • • •
> 26:18 • When you believe in Jesus, you are regenerated. To be saved is to experience regeneration. We often use terms like "born again," "believe in," "saved," and "regenerated," in a nearly interchangeable fashion. The moment you put your faith in Christ, God regenerates you. You pass from darkness to light and from the power of Satan to the kingdom of God. Your eternal residence moves from hell to heaven and you are qualified to become an heir of Christ. Regeneration has to do with what takes place in the believer's heart. Regeneration is God's answer to the problem of spiritual death. *For more about* New Life in Christ, *see Rom. 3:26.*

Paul's Post-Conversion Life

[19]"Therefore, King Agrippa, I was not disobedient to the heavenly vision, [20]but declared first to those in Damascus and in Jerusalem, and throughout all the region of Judea, and *then* to the Gentiles, that they should repent, turn to God, and do works befitting repentance. [21]For these reasons the Jews seized me in the temple and tried to kill *me*. [22]Therefore, having obtained help from God, to this day I stand, witnessing both to small and great, saying no other things than those which the prophets and Moses said would come— [23]that the Christ would suffer, that He would be the first to rise from the dead, and would proclaim light to the *Jewish* people and to the Gentiles."

26:17 [a]NU-Text and M-Text omit *now.*

Agrippa Parries Paul's Challenge

24Now as he thus made his defense, Festus said with a loud voice, "Paul, you are beside yourself! Much learning is driving you mad!" 25But he said, "I am not mad, most noble Festus, but speak the words of truth and reason. 26For the king, before whom I also speak freely, knows these things; for I am convinced that none of these things escapes his attention, since this thing was not done in a corner. 27King Agrippa, do you believe the prophets? I know that you do believe." 28Then Agrippa said to Paul, "You almost persuade me to become a Christian." 29And Paul said, "I would to God that not only you, but also all who hear me today, might become both almost and altogether such as I am, except for these chains." 30When he had said these things, the king stood up, as well as the governor and Bernice and those who sat with them; 31and when they had gone aside, they talked among themselves, saying, "This man is doing nothing deserving of death or chains." 32Then Agrippa said to Festus, "This man might have been set free if he had not appealed to Caesar."

The Voyage to Rome Begins

27 And when it was decided that we should sail to Italy, they delivered Paul and some other prisoners to *one* named Julius, a centurion of the Augustan Regiment. 2So, entering a ship of Adramyttium, we put to sea, meaning to sail along the coasts of Asia. Aristarchus, a Macedonian of Thessalonica, was with us. 3And the next *day* we landed at Sidon. And Julius treated Paul kindly and gave *him* liberty to go to his friends and receive care. 4When we had put to sea from there, we sailed under *the shelter of* Cyprus, because the winds were contrary. 5And when we had sailed over the sea which is off Cilicia and Pamphylia, we came to Myra, *a city* of Lycia. 6There the centurion found an Alexandrian ship sailing to Italy, and he put us on board. 7When we had sailed slowly many days, and arrived with difficulty off Cnidus, the wind not permitting us to proceed, we sailed under *the shelter of* Crete off Salmone. 8Passing it with difficulty, we came to a place called Fair Havens, near the city *of* Lasea.

Paul's Warning Ignored

9Now when much time had been spent, and sailing was now dangerous because the Fast was already over, Paul advised them, 10saying, "Men, I perceive that this voyage will end with disaster and much loss, not only of the cargo and ship, but also our lives." 11Nevertheless the centurion was more persuaded by the helmsman and the owner of the ship than by the things spoken by Paul. 12And because the harbor was not suitable to winter in, the majority advised to set sail from there also, if by any means they could reach Phoenix, a harbor of Crete opening toward the southwest and northwest, *and* winter *there.*

In the Tempest

13When the south wind blew softly, supposing that they had obtained *their* desire, putting out to sea, they sailed close by Crete. 14But not long after, a tempestuous head

---

↑ GROW (ACTS 26:19, 20)

If anyone should ask what you live for, you might immediately reply, "I live for Christ!" And that *is* the correct "spiritual" answer. But the truth is that people *really* know what you live for, not by what you say, but by what you do. If I could follow you around for a day, I would know exactly what you live for. I would note what you talk about, what kind of music you listen to, what you do with your spare time, who your friends are, what websites you visit. I wouldn't have to guess; I would know quickly. What you *really* live for would be reflected in your actions far more than in your words. Of course, all true followers of Jesus Christ should be able to say, "My determined purpose in life is to know Him" (see Phil. 3:10). But their actions should say so even more clearly. *For more about* Following Christ, *see Philem. 5;* Sharing Your Faith, *1 Cor. 1:23.*

wind arose, called Euroclydon.[a] [15]So when the ship was caught, and could not head into the wind, we let *her* drive. [16]And running under *the shelter of* an island called Clauda,[a] we secured the skiff with difficulty. [17]When they had taken it on board, they used cables to undergird the ship; and fearing lest they should run aground on the Syrtis[a] *Sands*, they struck sail and so were driven. [18]And because we were exceedingly tempest-tossed, the next *day* they lightened the ship. [19]On the third *day* we threw the ship's tackle overboard with our own hands. [20]Now when neither sun nor stars appeared for many days, and no small tempest beat on *us*, all hope that we would be saved was finally given up.

[21]But after long abstinence from food, then Paul stood in the midst of them and said, "Men, you should have listened to me, and not have sailed from Crete and incurred this disaster and loss. [22]And now I urge you to take heart, for there will be no loss of life among you, but only of the ship. [23]For there stood by me this night an angel of the God to whom I belong and whom I serve, [24]saying, 'Do not be afraid, Paul; you must be brought before Caesar; and indeed God has granted you all those who sail with you.' [25]Therefore take heart, men, for I believe God that it will be just as it was told me. [26]However, we must run aground on a certain island."

[27]Now when the fourteenth night had come, as we were driven up and down in the Adriatic *Sea*, about midnight the sailors sensed that they were drawing near some land. [28]And they took soundings and found *it* to be twenty fathoms; and when they had gone a little farther, they took soundings again and found *it* to be fifteen fathoms. [29]Then, fearing lest we should run aground on the rocks, they dropped four anchors from the stern, and prayed for day to come. [30]And as the sailors were seeking to escape from the ship, when they had let down the skiff into the sea, under pretense of putting out anchors from the prow, [31]Paul said to the centurion and the soldiers, "Unless these men stay in the ship, you cannot be saved." [32]Then the soldiers cut away the ropes of the skiff and let it fall off.

[33]And as day was about to dawn, Paul implored *them* all to take food, saying, "Today is the fourteenth day you have waited and continued without food, and eaten nothing. [34]Therefore I urge you to take nourishment, for this is for your survival, since not a hair will fall from the head of any of you." [35]And when he had said these things, he took bread and gave thanks to God in the presence of them all; and when he had broken *it* he began to eat. [36]Then they were all encouraged, and also took food themselves. [37]And in all we were two hundred and seventy-six persons on the ship. [38]So when they had eaten enough, they lightened the ship and threw out the wheat into the sea.

Shipwrecked on Malta

[39]When it was day, they did not recognize the land; but they observed a bay with a beach, onto which they planned to run the ship if possible. [40]And they let go the anchors and left *them* in the sea, meanwhile loosing the rudder ropes; and they hoisted the mainsail to the wind and made for shore. [41]But striking a place where two seas met, they ran the ship aground; and the prow stuck fast and remained immovable, but the stern was being broken up by the violence of the waves.

[42]And the soldiers' plan was to kill the prisoners, lest any of them should swim away and escape. [43]But the centurion, wanting to save Paul, kept them from *their* purpose, and commanded that those who could swim should jump *overboard* first and get to land, [44]and the rest, some on boards and some on *parts* of the ship. And so it was that they all escaped safely to land.

Paul's Ministry on Malta

28 Now when they had escaped, they then found out that the island was called Malta. [2]And the natives showed us unusual kindness; for they kindled a fire and made us all welcome, because of the rain that was falling and because of the cold. [3]But when Paul had gathered a bundle of sticks and laid *them* on the fire, a viper came out because of the heat, and fastened on his hand. [4]So when the natives saw the creature hanging from his hand, they said to one another, "No doubt this man is a murderer, whom, though he has escaped the sea, yet justice does not allow to live." [5]But he shook off the creature into the fire and suffered no harm. [6]However, they were expecting that he would swell up or suddenly fall down dead.

27:14 [a]NU-Text reads *Euraquilon*.   27:16 [a]NU-Text reads *Cauda*.   27:17 [a]M-Text reads *Syrtes*.

But after they had looked for a long time and saw no harm come to him, they changed their minds and said that he was a god.

[7]In that region there was an estate of the leading citizen of the island, whose name was Publius, who received us and entertained us courteously for three days. [8]And it happened that the father of Publius lay sick of a fever and dysentery. Paul went in to him and prayed, and he laid his hands on him and healed him. [9]So when this was done, the rest of those on the island who had diseases also came and were healed. [10]They also honored us in many ways; and when we departed, they provided such things as were necessary.

Arrival at Rome

[11]After three months we sailed in an Alexandrian ship whose figurehead was the Twin Brothers, which had wintered at the island. [12]And landing at Syracuse, we stayed three days. [13]From there we circled round and reached Rhegium. And after one day the south wind blew; and the next day we came to Puteoli, [14]where we found brethren, and were invited to stay with them seven days. And so we went toward Rome. [15]And from there, when the brethren heard about us, they came to meet us as far as Appii Forum and Three Inns. When Paul saw them, he thanked God and took courage.

[16]Now when we came to Rome, the centurion delivered the prisoners to the captain of the guard; but Paul was permitted to dwell by himself with the soldier who guarded him.

Paul's Ministry at Rome

[17]And it came to pass after three days that Paul called the leaders of the Jews together. So when they had come together, he said to them: "Men *and* brethren, though I have done nothing against our people or the customs of our fathers, yet I was delivered as a prisoner from Jerusalem into the hands of the Romans, [18]who, when they had examined me, wanted to let *me* go, because there was no cause for putting me to death. [19]But when the Jews[a] spoke against *it*, I was compelled to appeal to Caesar, not that I had anything of which to accuse my nation. [20]For this reason therefore I have called for you, to see *you* and speak with *you*, because for the hope of Israel I am bound with this chain."

[21]Then they said to him, "We neither received letters from Judea concerning you, nor have any of the brethren who came reported or spoken any evil of you. [22]But we desire to hear from you what you think; for concerning this sect, we know that it is spoken against everywhere."

[23]So when they had appointed him a day, many came to him at *his* lodging, to whom he explained and solemnly testified of the kingdom of God, persuading them concerning Jesus from both the Law of Moses and the Prophets, from morning till evening. [24]And some were persuaded by the things which were spoken, and some disbelieved. [25]So when they did not agree among themselves, they departed after Paul had said one word: "The Holy Spirit spoke rightly through Isaiah the prophet to our[a] fathers, [26]saying,

'Go to this people and say:
"Hearing you will hear, and shall not
    understand;
And seeing you will see, and not perceive;
[27] For the hearts of this people have grown
    dull.
Their ears are hard of hearing,
And their eyes they have closed,
Lest they should see with their eyes and
    hear with their ears,
Lest they should understand with their
    hearts and turn,
So that I should heal them." '[a]

[28]"Therefore let it be known to you that the salvation of God has been sent to the Gentiles, and they will hear it!" [29]And when he had said these words, the Jews departed and had a great dispute among themselves.[a]

[30]Then Paul dwelt two whole years in his own rented house, and received all who came to him, [31]preaching the kingdom of God and teaching the things which concern the Lord Jesus Christ with all confidence, no one forbidding him.

28:19 [a]That is, the ruling authorities   **28:25** [a]NU-Text reads *your.*   **28:27** [a]Isaiah 6:9, 10   **28:29** [a]NU-Text omits this verse.

ROMANS

INTRODUCTION//

A brand new life of faith begins when we place our trust in Jesus Christ—and probably no book in the Bible speaks more clearly, passionately, and thoroughly about building a deep relationship with God than does the Book of Romans.

This book, written by the apostle Paul, has been described as "The gospel taught to believers."

In this amazing letter, written to a large church in ancient Rome, Paul set out to explain how the Good News of faith in Jesus Christ—who died on the Cross for our sins and rose again by the power of God—can radically transform our lives on earth even as it prepares us for eternity in heaven. Paul called the gospel "the power of God to salvation for everyone who believes" and declared that in it "the righteousness of God is revealed from faith to faith; as it is written, 'The just shall live by faith'" (1:16, 17).

Romans offers a systematic look at God's plan to rescue us from our sin. It insists that everyone has sinned (3:23) and that our sin separates us from God, resulting in spiritual death—but that God gives us eternal life when we place our faith in Jesus (6:23). Once we invite Jesus to be our Savior, He enables us to live in a way that pleases God, free from all condemnation (8:1).

In Romans Paul clearly tells us *how* to enter into a living relationship with God. He writes, "If you confess with your mouth the Lord Jesus and believe in your heart that God has raised Him from the dead, you will be saved" (10:9). At that point, God immediately adopts us into His family (8:15) and we receive the power, through the Holy Spirit, to live in ways that delight our Lord's heart.

Greeting

1 Paul, a bondservant of Jesus Christ, called *to be* an apostle, separated to the gospel of God [2]which He promised before through His prophets in the Holy Scriptures, [3]concerning His Son Jesus Christ our Lord, who was born of the seed of David according to the flesh, [4]*and* declared *to be* the Son of God with power according to the Spirit of holiness, by the resurrection from the dead. [5]Through Him we have received grace and apostleship for obedience to the faith among all nations for His name, [6]among whom you also are the called of Jesus Christ;

[7]To all who are in Rome, beloved of God, called *to be* saints:

Grace to you and peace from God our Father and the Lord Jesus Christ.

Desire to Visit Rome

[8]First, I thank my God through Jesus Christ for you all, that your faith is spoken of throughout the whole world. [9]For God is my witness, whom I serve with my spirit in the gospel of His Son, that without ceasing I make mention of you always in my prayers, [10]making request if, by some means, now at last I may find a way in the will of God to come to you. [11]For I long to see you, that I may impart to you some spiritual gift, so that you may be established— [12]that is, that I may be encouraged together with you by the mutual faith both of you and me.

[13]Now I do not want you to be unaware, brethren, that I often planned to come to you (but was hindered until now), that I might have some fruit among you also, just as among the other Gentiles. [14]I am a debtor both to Greeks and to barbarians, both to wise and to unwise. [15]So, as much as is in me, *I am* ready to preach the gospel to you who are in Rome also.

The Just Live by Faith

[16]For I am not ashamed of the gospel of Christ,[a] for it is the power of God to salvation for everyone who believes, for the Jew first and also for the Greek. [17]For in it the righteousness of God is revealed from faith to faith; as it is written, *"The just shall live by faith."*[a]

> ➡ *For I am not ashamed of the gospel of Christ, for it is the power of God to salvation for everyone who believes . . .* Rom. 1:16

God's Wrath on Unrighteousness

[18]For the wrath of God is revealed from heaven against all ungodliness and unrighteousness of men, who suppress the truth in unrighteousness, [19]because what may be known of God is manifest in them, for God has shown *it* to them. [20]For since the creation of the world His invisible *attributes* are clearly seen, being understood by the things that are made, *even* His eternal power and Godhead,

1:16 [a]NU-Text omits *of Christ*.   1:17 [a]Habakkuk 2:4

↑ GROW (ROM. 1:4)

God loves to take the greatest tragedies of life and turn them into the greatest of victories. What was more inexplicable and heartbreaking than the Crucifixion of Jesus Christ? And who was behind the Crucifixion? The devil. But the Bible says that, ultimately, God Himself was the behind-the-scenes Director. So for one rare moment, God the Father and the devil were working toward the same goal (although not for the same final outcome!). At the Cross of Jesus, God took the greatest of tragedies and turned it into the greatest of victories. In the same way, God can accomplish His purposes in your life even through the activity of Satan. Demonic trials and even temptations can help you grow stronger spiritually. Paul spoke of a "messenger of Satan to buffet" him, yet He spoke of how God had allowed that for His own purposes (2 Cor. 12:7–9). That doesn't mean that bad becomes good; bad is always bad. But it does mean that God can bring about good in your life despite the bad. *For more about* Satan, *see Rom. 6:6, 9;* God at Work, *2 Cor. 1:3, 4.*

so that they are without excuse, [21]because, although they knew God, they did not glorify *Him* as God, nor were thankful, but became futile in their thoughts, and their foolish hearts were darkened. [22]Professing to be wise, they became fools, [23]and changed the glory of the incorruptible God into an image made like corruptible man—and birds and four-footed animals and creeping things.

[24]Therefore God also gave them up to uncleanness, in the lusts of their hearts, to dishonor their bodies among themselves, [25]who exchanged the truth of God for the lie, and worshiped and served the creature rather than the Creator, who is blessed forever. Amen.

[26]For this reason God gave them up to vile passions. For even their women exchanged the natural use for what is against nature. [27]Likewise also the men, leaving the natural use of the woman, burned in their lust for one another, men with men committing what is shameful, and receiving in themselves the penalty of their error which was due.

[28]And even as they did not like to retain God in *their* knowledge, God gave them over to a debased mind, to do those things which are not fitting; [29]being filled with all unrighteousness, sexual immorality,[a] wickedness, covetousness, maliciousness; full of envy, murder, strife, deceit, evil-mindedness; *they are* whisperers, [30]backbiters, haters of God, violent, proud, boasters, inventors of evil things, disobedient to parents, [31]undiscerning, untrustworthy, unloving, unforgiving,[a] unmerciful; [32]who, knowing the righteous judgment of God, that those who practice such things are deserving of death, not only do the same but also approve of those who practice them.

God's Righteous Judgment

2 Therefore you are inexcusable, O man, whoever you are who judge, for in whatever you judge another you condemn yourself; for you who judge practice the same things. [2]But we know that the judgment of God is according to truth against those who practice such things. [3]And do you think this, O man, you who judge those practicing such things, and doing the same, that you will escape the judgment of God? [4]Or do you despise the riches of His goodness, forbearance, and longsuffering, not knowing that the goodness of God leads you to repentance? [5]But in accordance with your hardness and your impenitent heart you are treasuring up for yourself wrath in the day of wrath and revelation of the righteous judgment of God, [6]who *"will render to each one according to his deeds"*:[a] [7]eternal life to those who by patient continuance in doing good seek for glory, honor, and immortality; [8]but to those who are self-seeking and do not obey the truth, but obey unrighteousness—indignation and wrath, [9]tribulation and anguish, on every soul of man who does evil, of the Jew first and also of the Greek; [10]but glory, honor, and peace to everyone who works what is good, to the Jew first and also to the Greek. [11]For there is no partiality with God.

[12]For as many as have sinned without law will also perish without law, and as many as have sinned in the law will be judged by the law [13](for not the hearers of the law *are* just in the sight of God, but the doers of the law will be justified; [14]for when Gentiles, who do not have the law, by nature do the things in the law, these, although not having the law, are a law to themselves, [15]who show the work of the law written in their hearts, their conscience also bearing witness, and between themselves *their* thoughts accusing or else excusing *them*) [16]in the day when God will judge the secrets of men by Jesus Christ, according to my gospel.

The Jews Guilty as the Gentiles

[17]Indeed[a] you are called a Jew, and rest on the law, and make your boast in God, [18]and know *His* will, and approve the things that are excellent, being instructed out of the law, [19]and are confident that you yourself are a guide to the blind, a light to those who are in darkness, [20]an instructor of the foolish, a teacher of babes, having the form of knowledge and truth in the law. [21]You, therefore, who teach another, do you not teach yourself? You who preach that a man should not steal, do you steal? [22]You who say, "Do not commit adultery," do you commit adultery? You who abhor idols, do you rob temples? [23]You who make your boast in the law, do you dishonor God through breaking the law? [24]For

1:29 [a]NU-Text omits *sexual immorality*.   1:31 [a]NU-Text omits *unforgiving*.   2:6 [a]Psalm 62:12; Proverbs 24:12
2:17 [a]NU-Text reads *But if*.

"the name of God is blasphemed among the Gentiles because of you,"[a] as it is written.

Circumcision of No Avail

[25]For circumcision is indeed profitable if you keep the law; but if you are a breaker of the law, your circumcision has become uncircumcision. [26]Therefore, if an uncircumcised man keeps the righteous requirements of the law, will not his uncircumcision be counted as circumcision? [27]And will not the physically uncircumcised, if he fulfills the law, judge you who, *even* with *your* written *code* and circumcision, *are* a transgressor of the law? [28]For he is not a Jew who *is one* outwardly, nor *is* circumcision that which *is* outward in the flesh; [29]but *he is* a Jew who *is one* inwardly; and circumcision *is that* of the heart, in the Spirit, not in the letter; whose praise *is* not from men but from God.

God's Judgment Defended

3 What advantage then has the Jew, or what *is* the profit of circumcision? [2]Much in every way! Chiefly because to them were committed the oracles of God. [3]For what if some did not believe? Will their unbelief make the faithfulness of God without effect? [4]Certainly not! Indeed, let God be true but every man a liar. As it is written:

> *"That You may be justified in Your words,*
> *And may overcome when You are judged."*[a]

[5]But if our unrighteousness demonstrates the righteousness of God, what shall we say? *Is* God unjust who inflicts wrath? (I speak as a man.) [6]Certainly not! For then how will God judge the world? [7]For if the truth of God has increased through my lie to His glory, why am I also still judged as a sinner? [8]And *why* not *say,* "Let us do evil that good may come"?—as we are slanderously reported and as some affirm that we say. Their condemnation is just.

All Have Sinned

[9]What then? Are we better *than they?* Not at all. For we have previously charged both Jews and Greeks that they are all under sin.

[10]As it is written:

> *"There is none righteous, no, not one;*
> [11]*There is none who understands;*
>   *There is none who seeks after God.*
> [12]*They have all turned aside;*
>   *They have together become unprofitable;*
>   *There is none who does good, no, not one."*[a]
> [13]*"Their throat is an open tomb;*
>   *With their tongues they have practiced deceit";*[a]
>   *"The poison of asps is under their lips";*[b]
> [14]*"Whose mouth is full of cursing and bitterness."*[a]
> [15]*"Their feet are swift to shed blood;*
> [16]*Destruction and misery are in their ways;*
> [17]*And the way of peace they have not known."*[a]
> [18]*"There is no fear of God before their eyes."*[a]

[19]Now we know that whatever the law says, it says to those who are under the law, that every mouth may be stopped, and all the world may become guilty before God. [20]Therefore by the deeds of the law no flesh will be justified in His sight, for by the law *is* the knowledge of sin.

God's Righteousness Through Faith

[21]But now the righteousness of God apart from the law is revealed, being witnessed by the Law and the Prophets, [22]even the righteousness of God, through faith in Jesus Christ, to all and on all[a] who believe. For there is no difference; [23]for all have sinned

2:24 [a]Isaiah 52:5; Ezekiel 36:22   3:4 [a]Psalm 51:4   3:12 [a]Psalms 14:1–3; 53:1–3; Ecclesiastes 7:20   3:13 [a]Psalm 5:9   [b]Psalm 140:3   3:14 [a]Psalm 10:7   3:17 [a]Isaiah 59:7, 8   3:18 [a]Psalm 36:1   3:22 [a]NU-Text omits *and on all.*

and fall short of the glory of God, [24]being justified freely by His grace through the redemption that is in Christ Jesus, [25]whom God set forth *as* a propitiation by His blood, through

➤ *. . . for all have sinned and fall short of the glory of God . . .* Rom. 3:23

faith, to demonstrate His righteousness, because in His forbearance God had passed over the sins that were previously committed, [26]to demonstrate at the present time His righteousness, that He might be just and the justifier of the one who has faith in Jesus.

➤ LIVE
• • • • • • • • • • • • • • • • • •
3:26 • One side of justification is positive and includes what God has done for us and given to us. A technical definition of the word *justified* is "to put to one's account." When God justifies a person, He does so by placing to his or her credit the righteousness of Jesus Christ. This balances the moral and spiritual budget for us, if you will. God removed all of your sin. He forgave all of it. And then He put the righteousness of Christ into your account for the future, the part of justification that a lot of people don't know about. *For more about* New Life in Christ, *see Rom. 4:2.*

Boasting Excluded

[27]Where *is* boasting then? It is excluded. By what law? Of works? No, but by the law of faith. [28]Therefore we conclude that a man is justified by faith apart from the deeds of the law. [29]Or *is* He the God of the Jews only? *Is* He not also the God of the Gentiles? Yes, of the Gentiles also, [30]since *there is* one God who will justify the circumcised by faith and the uncircumcised through faith. [31]Do we then make void the law through faith? Certainly not! On the contrary, we establish the law.

Abraham Justified by Faith

4 What then shall we say that Abraham our father has found according to the flesh?[a] [2]For if Abraham was justified by works, he has *something* to boast about, but not before God. [3]For what does the Scripture

➤ LIVE
• • • • • • • • • • • • • • • • • •
4:2 • Justification, a believer's new and righteous standing before God, does not depend on keeping a physical rite. After all, Abraham's justification took place fourteen years before he was ever circumcised. For this reason, the rite itself had nothing to do with his acceptance before God. Paul is refuting the idea that we must do certain things to gain God's approval. No! It is *because* God has justified you, *because* He loves and accepts you, that you read His Word and spend time in His presence. You do so not to earn His approval, but rather because you already have it! *For more about* New Life in Christ, *see Rom. 5:1;* Spiritual Disciplines, *Rom. 6:6, 9.*

say? *"Abraham believed God, and it was accounted to him for righteousness."*[a] [4]Now to him who works, the wages are not counted as grace but as debt.

David Celebrates the Same Truth

[5]But to him who does not work but believes on Him who justifies the ungodly, his faith is accounted for righteousness, [6]just as David also describes the blessedness of the man to whom God imputes righteousness apart from works:

[7] *"Blessed are those whose lawless deeds are forgiven,*
   And whose sins are covered;
[8] *Blessed is the man to whom the LORD shall not impute sin."*[a]

Abraham Justified Before Circumcision

[9]*Does* this blessedness then *come* upon the circumcised *only,* or upon the uncircumcised also? For we say that faith was accounted to Abraham for righteousness. [10]How then was it accounted? While he was circumcised, or uncircumcised? Not while circumcised, but while uncircumcised. [11]And he received the sign of circumcision, a seal of the righteousness of the faith which *he had while still* uncircumcised, that he might be the father of all those who believe, though they are uncircumcised, that righteousness might be imputed to them also, [12]and the father of circumcision to those who not only *are* of the circumcision, but who also walk in the steps

4:1 [a]*Or Abraham our (fore)father according to the flesh has found?*   4:3 [a]Genesis 15:6   4:8 [a]Psalm 32:1, 2

of the faith which our father Abraham *had* *while still* uncircumcised.

The Promise Granted Through Faith

[13]For the promise that he would be the heir of the world *was* not to Abraham or to his seed through the law, but through the righteousness of faith. [14]For if those who are of the law *are* heirs, faith is made void and the promise made of no effect, [15]because the law brings about wrath; for where there is no law *there is* no transgression.

[16]Therefore *it is* of faith that *it might be* according to grace, so that the promise might be sure to all the seed, not only to those who are of the law, but also to those who are of the faith of Abraham, who is the father of us all [17](as it is written, *"I have made you a father of many nations"*[a]) in the presence of Him whom he believed—God, who gives life to the dead and calls those things which do not exist as though they did; [18]who, contrary to hope, in hope believed, so that he became the father of many nations, according to what was spoken, *"So shall your descendants be."*[a] [19]And not being weak in faith, he did not consider his own body, already dead (since he was about a hundred years old), and the deadness of Sarah's womb. [20]He did not waver at the promise of God through unbelief, but was strengthened in faith, giving glory to God, [21]and being fully convinced that what He had promised He was also able to perform. [22]And therefore *"it was accounted to him for righteousness."*[a]

[23]Now it was not written for his sake alone that it was imputed to him, [24]but also for us. It shall be imputed to us who believe in Him who raised up Jesus our Lord from the dead, [25]who was delivered up because of our offenses, and was raised because of our justification.

Faith Triumphs in Trouble

5 Therefore, having been justified by faith, we have[a] peace with God through our Lord Jesus Christ, [2]through whom also we have access by faith into this grace in which we stand, and rejoice in hope of the glory of God. [3]And not only *that,* but we also glory in tribulations, knowing that tribulation produces perseverance; [4]and perseverance, character; and character, hope. [5]Now hope does not disappoint, because the love of God

↘ LEARN

5:1 • Having spoken of being justified before God, Paul now describes the benefits, results, and fruit of it. Many of our blessings are yet future, such as the hope of heaven or our new resurrection bodies. But this peace with God is ours here and now. I distinctly remember this as one of the first things I experienced as a new Christian; it was as though a huge burden had been lifted from my shoulders. This peace is not subjective, but objective; not a feeling, but a fact. It comes not from what we do but from what He has done. *For more about* New Life in Christ, *see Rom. 5:18.*

→ LIVE

5:1 • I don't have to live in constant fear about what God thinks about me. I don't have to earn His approval. I don't have to worry about where I am going to spend eternity. This is all covered in Christ Jesus, which gives me great confidence and peace that says, "No matter what happens, the big things are covered." I don't have to sweat the small stuff. Sure, we all have our trials and our tribulations in life. But we also know that we are saved and safe in the Lord. As Christians, we know heaven is our future home. *For more about* God's Love, *see Rom. 6:23;* Assurance of Salvation, *Rom. 8:16.*

has been poured out in our hearts by the Holy Spirit who was given to us.

Christ in Our Place

[6]For when we were still without strength, in due time Christ died for the ungodly. [7]For scarcely for a righteous man will one die; yet perhaps for a good man someone would even dare to die. [8]But God demonstrates His own love toward us, in that while we were still sinners, Christ died for us. [9]Much more then, having now been justified by His blood, we shall be saved from wrath through Him. [10]For

> **But God demonstrates His own love toward us, in that while we were still sinners, Christ died for us.** Rom. 5:8

4:17 [a]Genesis 17:5   **4:18** [a]Genesis 15:5   **4:22** [a]Genesis 15:6   **5:1** [a]Another ancient reading is, *let us have peace.*

if when we were enemies we were reconciled to God through the death of His Son, much more, having been reconciled, we shall be saved by His life. [11]And not only *that*, but we also rejoice in God through our Lord Jesus Christ, through whom we have now received the reconciliation.

Death in Adam, Life in Christ

[12]Therefore, just as through one man sin entered the world, and death through sin, and thus death spread to all men, because all sinned— [13](For until the law sin was in the world, but sin is not imputed when there is no law. [14]Nevertheless death reigned from Adam to Moses, even over those who had not sinned according to the likeness of the transgression of Adam, who is a type of Him who was to come. [15]But the free gift *is* not like the offense. For if by the one man's offense many died, much more the grace of God and the gift by the grace of the one Man, Jesus Christ, abounded to many. [16]And the gift *is* not like *that which came* through the one who sinned. For the judgment *which came* from one *offense resulted* in condemnation, but the free gift *which came* from many offenses *resulted* in justification. [17]For if by the one man's offense death reigned through the one, much more those who receive abundance of grace and of the gift of righteousness will reign in life through the One, Jesus Christ.) [18]Therefore, as through one man's offense *judgment came* to all men, resulting in condemnation, even so through one Man's righteous act *the free gift came* to all men, resulting in justification of life. [19]For as by one man's disobedience many were made sinners, so also by one Man's obedience many will be made righteous.

→**LIVE**

5:18 • Justification by faith is a living relationship. It is "justification that brings life" (Rom. 5:18, literal translation). I am in Christ, identified with Him. Therefore, whatever happened to Christ, also happened to me. When He died, I died. When He arose, I arose. Because of this living union with Jesus, I have a new relationship to sin. We don't fight *for* victory, we fight *from* victory. We share in what Christ has done on our behalf! On the Cross, Jesus cried "It is finished!" (John 19:30). Finished means it is completed, it is made an end of, it is accomplished. *For more about* New Life in Christ, *see Rom. 6:6, 9;* The Cross, *Heb. 2:15.*

[20]Moreover the law entered that the offense might abound. But where sin abounded, grace abounded much more, [21]so that as sin reigned in death, even so grace might reign through righteousness to eternal life through Jesus Christ our Lord.

Dead to Sin, Alive to God

6 What shall we say then? Shall we continue in sin that grace may abound? [2]Certainly not! How shall we who died to sin live any longer in it? [3]Or do you not know that as many of us as were baptized into Christ Jesus were baptized into His death? [4]Therefore we were buried with Him through baptism into death, that just as Christ was raised from the dead by the glory of the Father, even so we also should walk in newness of life.

[5]For if we have been united together in the likeness of His death, certainly we also shall be *in the likeness* of *His* resurrection, [6]knowing this, that our old man was crucified with *Him,* that the body of sin might be

↑ **GROW** (ROM. 5:4)

Character counts. In fact, it may be the most important thing about you. Character is not merely what you say, but what you are when no one else is looking. It's what you are in the dark, so to speak. We all put out an image for public consumption: "I am kind. I am considerate. I am a really good person. Everybody likes me. This is who I am." When you sit in church next to someone you don't know, and you converse with that person for a while, in a few moments you both have a sense of the other. But the real you is not necessarily the person who sat so pleasantly in church, chatting amiably. The real you, in fact, is what you are in private, when there is no one to impress, when you are not aware that anyone is watching. *That* is the real you. *For more about* How to Live Out Your Faith, *see Rom. 13:14.*

↘ LEARN

6:6, 9 • Many Christians think the way to overcome sin is to say "No, no, no!" But the apostle Paul taught believers to "Know, know, know!" Christian *living* depends on Christian *learning*. *Duty* is always founded on *doctrine*. If Satan can keep a Christian ignorant, he can keep him impotent. It's like trying to hold back the enemy with no ammunition, while all the time you have more than you'd need for 1,000 battles! Our defeat lies largely in our ignorance of the facts. In Jesus Christ we have the power to live a new life and get free of sin's control. *For more about* Spiritual Disciplines, *see 2 Cor. 8:7;* Satan, *Eph. 6:11, 12;* New Life in Christ, *1 Cor. 1:23.*

done away with, that we should no longer be slaves of sin. [7]For he who has died has been freed from sin. [8]Now if we died with Christ, we believe that we shall also live with Him, [9]knowing that Christ, having been raised from the dead, dies no more. Death no longer has dominion over Him. [10]For *the death* that He died, He died to sin once for all; but *the life* that He lives, He lives to God. [11]Likewise you also, reckon yourselves to be dead indeed to sin, but alive to God in Christ Jesus our Lord.

[12]Therefore do not let sin reign in your mortal body, that you should obey it in its lusts. [13]And do not present your members *as* instruments of unrighteousness to sin, but present yourselves to God as being alive from the dead, and your members *as* instruments of righteousness to God. [14]For sin shall not have dominion over you, for you are not under law but under grace.

From Slaves of Sin to Slaves of God

[15]What then? Shall we sin because we are not under law but under grace? Certainly not! [16]Do you not know that to whom you present yourselves slaves to obey, you are that one's slaves whom you obey, whether of sin *leading* to death, or of obedience *leading* to righteousness? [17]But God be thanked that *though* you were slaves of sin, yet you obeyed from the heart that form of doctrine to which you were delivered. [18]And having been set free from sin, you became slaves of righteousness. [19]I speak in human *terms* because of the weakness of your flesh. For just as you presented your members *as* slaves of uncleanness, and of lawlessness *leading* to *more* lawlessness, so

➔ *For the wages of sin is death, but the gift of God is eternal life in Christ Jesus our Lord.* Rom. 6:23

now present your members *as* slaves *of* righteousness for holiness.

[20]For when you were slaves of sin, you were free in regard to righteousness. [21]What fruit did you have then in the things of which you are now ashamed? For the end of those things *is* death. [22]But now having been set free from sin, and having become slaves of God, you have your fruit to holiness, and the end, everlasting life. [23]For the wages of sin *is* death, but the gift of God *is* eternal life in Christ Jesus our Lord.

➔ LIVE

6:23 • Although many picture God as a cosmic killjoy, the truth is God loves you and wants a relationship with you. While religion declares what you must do to *reach* up to heaven, God reached down from heaven by sending His Son, Jesus Christ, who lived a perfect life, died on the Cross in your place, shed His blood for you, and now offers you the gift of eternal life . . . if you will believe. If you live for sin, you will get your wages: death. But if you trust in Christ, you will receive your gift: eternal life. *For more about* Becoming a Christian, *see Rom. 8:29;* God's Love, *1 Cor. 1:30.*

Freed from the Law

7 Or do you not know, brethren (for I speak to those who know the law), that the law has dominion over a man as long as he lives? [2]For the woman who has a husband is bound by the law to *her* husband as long as he lives. But if the husband dies, she is released from the law of *her* husband. [3]So then if, while *her* husband lives, she marries another man, she will be called an adulteress; but if her husband dies, she is free from that law, so that she is no adulteress, though she has married another man. [4]Therefore, my brethren, you also have become dead to the law through the body of Christ, that you may be married to another—to Him who was raised from the dead, that we should bear fruit to God. [5]For when we were in the flesh, the sinful passions which were aroused by the law were at work in our members to bear fruit to death. [6]But now we have been delivered from the law, having died to what we were held by, so that we should serve in the newness of the Spirit and not *in* the oldness of the letter.

Sin's Advantage in the Law

[7]What shall we say then? *Is* the law sin? Certainly not! On the contrary, I would not have known sin except through the law. For I would not have known covetousness unless the law had said, *"You shall not covet."*[a] [8]But sin, taking opportunity by the commandment, produced in me all *manner of* evil desire. For apart from the law sin *was* dead. [9]I was alive once without the law, but when the commandment came, sin revived and I died. [10]And the commandment, which *was* to *bring* life, I found to *bring* death. [11]For sin, taking occasion by the commandment, deceived me, and by it killed *me.* [12]Therefore the law *is* holy, and the commandment holy and just and good.

Law Cannot Save from Sin

[13]Has then what is good become death to me? Certainly not! But sin, that it might appear sin, was producing death in me through what is good, so that sin through the commandment might become exceedingly sinful. [14]For we know that the law is spiritual, but I am carnal, sold under sin. [15]For what I am doing, I do not understand. For what I will to do, that I do not practice; but what I hate, that I do. [16]If, then, I do what I will not to do, I agree with the law that *it is* good. [17]But now, *it is* no

longer I who do it, but sin that dwells in me. [18]For I know that in me (that is, in my flesh) nothing good dwells; for to will is present with me, but *how* to perform what is good I do not find. [19]For the good that I will *to do,* I do not do; but the evil I will not *to do,* that I practice. [20]Now if I do what I will not *to do,* it is no longer I who do it, but sin that dwells in me.

[21]I find then a law, that evil is present with me, the one who wills to do good. [22]For I delight in the law of God according to the inward man. [23]But I see another law in my members, warring against the law of my mind, and bringing me into captivity to the law of sin which is in my members. [24]O wretched man that I am! Who will deliver me from this body of death? [25]I thank God—through Jesus Christ our Lord!

So then, with the mind I myself serve the law of God, but with the flesh the law of sin.

7:7 [a]Exodus 20:17; Deuteronomy 5:21

↘ LEARN

7:15 • No matter how mature in the Lord you are, no matter how spiritual you may feel, at times your unredeemed flesh will raise its ugly head—and you'll find yourself blurting out things that shock you, doing things that horrify you, and even mentally planning things that appall you. When this happens, repent immediately, but don't act all that surprised. The Bible tells us, "The heart is deceitful above all things, and desperately wicked" (Jer. 17:9). While we live in these fallen bodies, "we all stumble in many things" (James 3:2). Never forget that when you feel tempted to yield to sin's pull, a fall is not far away. So keep up your spiritual guard! *For more about* Sin, *see 1 Cor. 10:13.*

↓ KNOW (ROM. 7:15)

Why do people give in to the most illogical sins? Here is a family whom God has blessed, with a loving husband and a beautiful wife who are raising their children in the way of the Lord. So why did that guy choose to commit adultery against his wife and thus destroy his family? Why did another man take leave of his senses and commit that foolish act? Why did a group of sane people agree to join another group in doing some awful, idiotic thing? It doesn't make any sense. And that is the point. It *doesn't* make sense. Sin has nothing to do with logic. The desire to sin and to violate the loving, wise commandments of God is just our nature—the combustible, evil, sinful nature inside of us. No exceptions. We daily, even hourly, need the Holy Spirit's help to effectively live the Christian life. *For more about* Sin, *see 1 Cor. 10:13; the* Holy Spirit, *Rom. 8:16.*

Free from Indwelling Sin

8 *There* is therefore now no condemnation to those who are in Christ Jesus,[a] who do not walk according to the flesh, but according to the Spirit. [2]For the law of the Spirit of life in Christ Jesus has made me free from the law of sin and death. [3]For what the law could not do in that it was weak through the flesh, God *did* by sending His own Son in the likeness of sinful flesh, on account of sin: He condemned sin in the flesh, [4]that the righteous requirement of the law might be fulfilled in us who do not walk according to the flesh but according to the Spirit. [5]For those who live according to the flesh set their minds on the things of the flesh, but those *who live* according to the Spirit, the things of the Spirit. [6]For to be carnally minded *is* death, but to be spiritually minded *is* life and peace. [7]Because the carnal mind *is* enmity against God; for it is not subject to the law of God, nor indeed can be. [8]So then, those who are in the flesh cannot please God.

[9]But you are not in the flesh but in the Spirit, if indeed the Spirit of God dwells in you. Now if anyone does not have the Spirit of Christ, he is not His. [10]And if Christ *is* in you, the body *is* dead because of sin, but the Spirit *is* life because of righteousness. [11]But if the Spirit of Him who raised Jesus from the dead dwells in you, He who raised Christ from the dead will also give life to your mortal bodies through His Spirit who dwells in you.

Sonship Through the Spirit

[12]Therefore, brethren, we are debtors—not to the flesh, to live according to the flesh. [13]For if you live according to the flesh you will die; but if by the Spirit you put to death the deeds of the body, you will live. [14]For as many as are led by the Spirit of God, these are sons of God. [15]For you did not receive the spirit of bondage again to fear, but you received the Spirit of adoption by whom we cry out, "Abba, Father." [16]The Spirit Himself bears witness with our spirit that we are children of God, [17]and if children, then heirs—heirs of God and joint heirs with Christ, if indeed we suffer with *Him*, that we may also be glorified together.

From Suffering to Glory

[18]For I consider that the sufferings of this present time are not worthy *to be compared*

8:1 [a]NU-Text omits the rest of this verse.

→LIVE
• • • • • • • • • • • • • • • • • •

8:16 • The Holy Spirit personally gives us the assurance that Christ has come into our lives—a wonderful inner conviction. You just know that you know. It is hard to explain, but it is as real as the breath you are drawing right now. I have that conviction in my heart. Do you? The Holy Spirit delights to give you that inner witness that, yes, you are a child of God. And as part of this wonderful miracle of conversion, the Bible teaches that the Holy Spirit indwells us. When you become a Christian, the Spirit comes to live inside you. *For more about the* Holy Spirit, *see Rom. 8:26;* Assurance of Salvation, *2 Cor. 1:22.*

with the glory which shall be revealed in us. [19]For the earnest expectation of the creation eagerly waits for the revealing of the sons of God. [20]For the creation was subjected to futility, not willingly, but because of Him who subjected *it* in hope; [21]because the creation itself also will be delivered from the bondage of corruption into the glorious liberty of the children of God. [22]For we know that the whole creation groans and labors with birth pangs together until now. [23]Not only *that,* but we also who have the firstfruits of the Spirit, even we ourselves groan within ourselves, eagerly waiting for the adoption, the redemption of our body. [24]For we were saved in this hope, but hope that is seen is not hope; for why does one still hope for what he sees? [25]But if we hope for what we do not see, we eagerly wait for *it* with perseverance.

[26]Likewise the Spirit also helps in our weaknesses. For we do not know what we should pray for as we ought, but the Spirit

↘LEARN
• • • • • • • • • • • • • • •

8:26 • At some point in our lives, and usually at many points, we will face circumstances that seem so overwhelming or frightening or confusing that we simply don't know what to do. We want to pray about the situation, but frankly we don't even know what to say. Are we stuck? Not at all. Paul reminds us that God cares for us so deeply that when we have no idea what to pray for, the Holy Spirit Himself intercedes for us according to God's will. God so passionately wants the best for you that God prays to God on your behalf! *For more about* Prayer, *see Phil. 4:6; the* Holy Spirit, *2 Cor. 1:22;* Adversity, *2 Cor. 1:3, 4.*

Himself makes intercession for us[a] with groanings which cannot be uttered. [27]Now He who searches the hearts knows what the mind of the Spirit *is,* because He makes intercession for the saints according to *the will of* God.

[28]And we know that all things work together for good to those who love God, to those who are the called according to *His* purpose. [29]For whom He foreknew, He also predestined *to be* conformed to the image of His Son, that He might be the firstborn among many brethren. [30]Moreover whom He predestined, these He also called; whom He called, these He also justified; and whom He justified, these He also glorified.

God's Everlasting Love

[31]What then shall we say to these things? If God *is* for us, who *can be* against us? [32]He who did not spare His own Son, but delivered Him up for us all, how shall He not with Him also freely give us all things? [33]Who shall bring a charge against God's elect? *It is* God who justifies. [34]Who *is* he who condemns? *It is* Christ who died, and furthermore is also risen, who is even at the right hand of God, who also makes intercession for us. [35]Who shall separate us from the love of Christ? *Shall* tribulation, or distress, or persecution, or famine, or nakedness, or peril, or sword? [36]As it is written:

> *"For Your sake we are killed all day long;*
> *We are accounted as sheep for the*
>   *slaughter."*[a]

[37]Yet in all these things we are more than conquerors through Him who loved us. [38]For I am persuaded that neither death nor life, nor angels nor principalities nor powers, nor things present nor things to come, [39]nor height nor depth, nor any other created thing,

> ➤ *For I am persuaded that neither death nor life, nor angels nor principalities nor powers, nor things present nor things to come, nor height nor depth, nor any other created thing, shall be able to separate us from the love of God which is in Christ Jesus our Lord.* Rom. 8:38, 39

➤ LIVE

8:29 • Does God randomly pick and reject people for salvation? Scripture certainly does not seem to support that idea. Perhaps His choice is based on His foreknowledge of who would choose Him. The real question is, how do you know if *you* are chosen? Commit your life to Jesus Christ and you will confirm that you are. Reject Him and you will confirm that you are not. The main issue is not so much how you were chosen, but what you were chosen for. According to this verse, we were chosen to "be conformed to the image of His Son." *For more about* Becoming a Christian, *see 1 Cor. 5:6–8.*

8:26 [a]NU-Text omits *for us.*   **8:36** [a]Psalm 44:22

↑ GROW (ROM. 8:26)

It's a good thing the Holy Spirit helps us to pray because difficult moments arrive when we simply don't know what or how to pray. Perhaps we feel overwhelmed with a burden. We struggle with discouragement, depression, doubt, or fear. It is then that the Holy Spirit comes to help us. Jesus once referred to the Holy Spirit as the "Helper," a term that in the original Greek means "Comforter, someone called alongside to help" (John 14:16). How wonderful that the Holy Spirit comes to help you, to aid you, to assist you in prayer! The Holy Spirit comes as an advocate and pleads your cause before the Father, interceding for you. In your most difficult and trying times, when you just don't know what words to put to your prayers, the Spirit of the Living God prays for you. *For more about* Prayer, *see Phil. 4:6; the* Holy Spirit, *2 Cor. 1:22;* Adversity, *2 Cor. 1:3, 4.*

shall be able to separate us from the love of God which is in Christ Jesus our Lord.

Israel's Rejection of Christ

9 I tell the truth in Christ, I am not lying, my conscience also bearing me witness in the Holy Spirit, [2]that I have great sorrow and continual grief in my heart. [3]For I could wish that I myself were accursed from Christ for my brethren, my countrymen[a] according to the flesh, [4]who are Israelites, to whom *pertain* the adoption, the glory, the covenants, the giving of the law, the service *of God*, and the promises; [5]of whom *are* the fathers and from whom, according to the flesh, Christ *came*, who is over all, *the* eternally blessed God. Amen.

Israel's Rejection and God's Purpose

[6]But it is not that the word of God has taken no effect. For they *are* not all Israel who *are* of Israel, [7]nor *are they* all children because they are the seed of Abraham; but, *"In Isaac your seed shall be called."*[a] [8]That is, those who *are* the children of the flesh, these *are* not the children of God; but the children of the promise are counted as the seed. [9]For this *is* the word of promise: *"At this time I will come and Sarah shall have a son."*[a]

[10]And not only *this*, but when Rebecca also had conceived by one man, *even* by our father Isaac [11](for *the children* not yet being born, nor having done any good or evil, that the purpose of God according to election might stand, not of works but of Him who calls), [12]it was said to her, *"The older shall serve the younger."*[a] [13]As it is written, *"Jacob I have loved, but Esau I have hated."*[a]

Israel's Rejection and God's Justice

[14]What shall we say then? *Is there* unrighteousness with God? Certainly not! [15]For He says to Moses, *"I will have mercy on whomever I will have mercy, and I will have compassion on whomever I will have compassion."*[a] [16]So then *it is* not of him who wills, nor of him who runs, but of God who shows mercy. [17]For the Scripture says to the Pharaoh, *"For this very purpose I have raised you up, that I may show My power in you, and that My name may be declared in all the earth."*[a] [18]Therefore He has mercy on whom He wills, and whom He wills He hardens.

[19]You will say to me then, "Why does He still find fault? For who has resisted His will?" [20]But indeed, O man, who are you to reply against God? Will the thing formed say to him who formed *it*, "Why have you made me like this?" [21]Does not the potter have power over the clay, from the same lump to make one vessel for honor and another for dishonor? [22]*What* if God, wanting to show *His* wrath and to make His power known, endured with much longsuffering the vessels of wrath prepared for destruction, [23]and that He might make known the riches of His glory on the vessels of mercy, which He had prepared beforehand for glory, [24]even us whom He called, not of the Jews only, but also of the Gentiles?

[25]As He says also in Hosea:

"I will call them My people, who were not My people,
And her beloved, who was not beloved."[a]
[26]*"And it shall come to pass in the place where it was said to them,*

9:3 [a]Or *relatives*   9:7 [a]Genesis 21:12   9:9 [a]Genesis 18:10, 14   9:12 [a]Genesis 25:23   9:13 [a]Malachi 1:2, 3   9:15 [a]Exodus 33:19
9:17 [a]Exodus 9:16   9:25 [a]Hosea 2:23

↓ KNOW (ROM. 8:28)

God is all-knowing, all-powerful, omnipresent, holy, righteous, and true—He is all of those things, perfectly. But He is much more! Beyond all of them, God is good. And when I say good, I mean that God is the final standard of good. All that God is and does is worthy of our heartiest approval. Since God Himself is infinitely good, He not only determines for us what is good, He also tells us what is bad. God has every right to declare something "bad" or "sinful," because He knows without any doubt what is good and right. So remember that regardless of your current circumstances—whether you like them or hate them—the same God who declares Himself to be good promises in Romans 8:28 that He causes all things to work together for *good* to those who love Him and are the called according to His purpose. *For more about the* Attributes of God, *see 2 Cor. 13:14.*

'You are not My people,'
There they shall be called sons of the
    living God.'"ᵃ

²⁷Isaiah also cries out concerning Israel:ᵃ

"Though the number of the children of
    Israel be as the sand of the sea,
The remnant will be saved.
²⁸For He will finish the work and cut it
    short in righteousness,
Because the LORD will make a short work
    upon the earth."ᵃ

²⁹And as Isaiah said before:

"Unless the LORD of Sabaothᵃ had left us
    a seed,
We would have become like Sodom,
And we would have been made like
    Gomorrah."ᵇ

Present Condition of Israel

³⁰What shall we say then? That Gentiles,
who did not pursue righteousness, have
attained to righteousness, even the righteousness of faith; ³¹but Israel, pursuing the
law of righteousness, has not attained to the
law of righteousness.ᵃ ³²Why? Because *they
did* not *seek it* by faith, but as it were, by the
works of the law.ᵃ For they stumbled at that
stumbling stone. ³³As it is written:

"Behold, I lay in Zion a stumbling stone
    and rock of offense,
And whoever believes on Him will not be
    put to shame."ᵃ

Israel Needs the Gospel

10 Brethren, my heart's desire and
prayer to God for Israelᵃ is that they
may be saved. ²For I bear them witness that they have a zeal for God, but not
according to knowledge. ³For they being ignorant of God's righteousness, and seeking
to establish their own righteousness, have not
submitted to the righteousness of God. ⁴For
Christ *is* the end of the law for righteousness
to everyone who believes.
    ⁵For Moses writes about the righteous-
ness which is of the law, "The man who does

those things shall live by them."ᵃ ⁶But the
righteousness of faith speaks in this way, "Do
not say in your heart, 'Who will ascend into
heaven?'"ᵃ (that is, to bring Christ down
from above) ⁷or, "'Who will descend into the
abyss?'"ᵃ (that is, to bring Christ up from the
dead). ⁸But what does it say? "The word is
near you, in your mouth and in your heart"ᵃ
(that is, the word of faith which we preach):
⁹that if you confess with your mouth the Lord
Jesus and believe in your heart that God has
raised Him from the dead, you will be saved.
¹⁰For with the heart one believes unto righteousness, and with the mouth confession is
made unto salvation. ¹¹For the Scripture says,
"Whoever believes on Him will not be put to
shame."ᵃ ¹²For there is no distinction between
Jew and Greek, for the same Lord over all is
rich to all who call upon Him. ¹³For "whoever
calls on the name of the LORD shall be saved."ᵃ

Israel Rejects the Gospel

¹⁴How then shall they call on Him in
whom they have not believed? And how shall
they believe in Him of whom they have not
heard? And how shall they hear without a
preacher? ¹⁵And how shall they preach unless
they are sent? As it is written:

"How beautiful are the feet of those who
    preach the gospel of peace,ᵃ
Who bring glad tidings of good things!"ᵇ

¹⁶But they have not all obeyed the gospel.
For Isaiah says, "LORD, who has believed our
report?"ᵃ ¹⁷So then faith *comes* by hearing, and
hearing by the word of God.
    ¹⁸But I say, have they not heard? Yes in-
deed:

"Their sound has gone out to all the earth,
And their words to the ends of the world."ᵃ

¹⁹But I say, did Israel not know? First Moses says:

"I will provoke you to jealousy by those
    who are not a nation,
I will move you to anger by a foolish
    nation."ᵃ

9:26 ᵃHosea 1:10   **9:27** ᵃIsaiah 10:22, 23   **9:28** ᵃNU-Text reads *For the LORD will finish the work and cut it short upon the earth.*
9:29 ᵃLiterally, in Hebrew, *Hosts* ᵇIsaiah 1:9   **9:31** ᵃNU-Text omits *of righteousness.*   **9:32** ᵃNU-Text reads *by works.*   **9:33** ᵃIsaiah 8:14;
28:16   **10:1** ᵃNU-Text reads *them.*   **10:5** ᵃLeviticus 18:5   **10:6** ᵃDeuteronomy 30:12   **10:7** ᵃDeuteronomy 30:13   **10:8** ᵃDeuteronomy
30:14   **10:11** ᵃIsaiah 28:16   **10:13** ᵃJoel 2:32   **10:15** ᵃNU-Text omits *preach the gospel of peace, Who.* ᵇIsaiah 52:7; Nahum 1:15
10:16 ᵃIsaiah 53:1   **10:18** ᵃPsalm 19:4   **10:19** ᵃDeuteronomy 32:21

²⁰But Isaiah is very bold and says:

"I was found by those who did not seek Me;
I was made manifest to those who did not
*   ask for Me."*^a

²¹But to Israel he says:

"All day long I have stretched out My hands
To a disobedient and contrary people."^a

Israel's Rejection Not Total

11 I say then, has God cast away His people? Certainly not! For I also am an Israelite, of the seed of Abraham, of the tribe of Benjamin. ²God has not cast away His people whom He foreknew. Or do you not know what the Scripture says of Elijah, how he pleads with God against Israel, saying, ³ *"LORD, they have killed Your prophets and torn down Your altars, and I alone am left, and they seek my life"?*^a ⁴But what does the divine response say to him? *"I have reserved for Myself seven thousand men who have not bowed the knee to Baal."*^a ⁵Even so then, at this present time there is a remnant according to the election of grace. ⁶And if by grace, then *it is* no longer of works; otherwise grace is no longer grace.^a But if *it is* of works, it is no longer grace; otherwise work is no longer work.

⁷What then? Israel has not obtained what it seeks; but the elect have obtained it, and the rest were blinded. ⁸Just as it is written:

"God has given them a spirit of stupor,
Eyes that they should not see
And ears that they should not hear,
To this very day."^a

⁹And David says:

"Let their table become a snare and a trap,
A stumbling block and a recompense to
*   them.*
¹⁰ *Let their eyes be darkened, so that they do*
*   not see,*
And bow down their back always."^a

Israel's Rejection Not Final

¹¹I say then, have they stumbled that they should fall? Certainly not! But through their fall, to provoke them to jealousy, salvation *has come* to the Gentiles. ¹²Now if their fall *is* riches for the world, and their failure riches for the Gentiles, how much more their fullness!

¹³For I speak to you Gentiles; inasmuch as I am an apostle to the Gentiles, I magnify my ministry, ¹⁴if by any means I may provoke to jealousy *those who are* my flesh and save some of them. ¹⁵For if their being cast away *is* the reconciling of the world, what *will* their acceptance *be* but life from the dead?

¹⁶For if the firstfruit *is* holy, the lump *is* also *holy;* and if the root *is* holy, so *are* the branches. ¹⁷And if some of the branches were broken off, and you, being a wild olive tree, were grafted in among them, and with them became a partaker of the root and fatness of the olive tree, ¹⁸do not boast against the branches. But if you do boast, *remember that* you do not support the root, but the root *supports* you.

¹⁹You will say then, "Branches were broken off that I might be grafted in." ²⁰Well *said.* Because of unbelief they were broken off, and you stand by faith. Do not be haughty, but fear. ²¹For if God did not spare the natural branches, He may not spare you either. ²²Therefore consider the goodness and severity of God: on those who fell, severity; but toward you, goodness,^a if you continue in *His* goodness. Otherwise you also will be cut off. ²³And they also, if they do not continue in unbelief, will be grafted in, for God is able to graft them in again. ²⁴For if you were cut out of the olive tree which is wild by nature, and were grafted contrary to nature into a cultivated olive tree, how much more will these, who *are* natural *branches,* be grafted into their own olive tree?

²⁵For I do not desire, brethren, that you should be ignorant of this mystery, lest you should be wise in your own opinion, that blindness in part has happened to Israel until the fullness of the Gentiles has come in. ²⁶And so all Israel will be saved,^a as it is written:

"The Deliverer will come out of Zion,
*   And He will turn away ungodliness from*
*   Jacob;*
²⁷ *For this is My covenant with them,*
*   When I take away their sins."*^a

10:20 ^aIsaiah 65:1   **10:21** ^aIsaiah 65:2   **11:3** ^a1 Kings 19:10, 14   **11:4** ^a1 Kings 19:18   **11:6** ^aNU-Text omits the rest of this verse.
11:8 ^aDeuteronomy 29:4; Isaiah 29:10   **11:10** ^aPsalm 69:22, 23   **11:22** ^aNU-Text adds *of God.*   **11:26** ^aOr *delivered*   **11:27** ^aIsaiah 59:20, 21

[28]Concerning the gospel *they are* enemies for your sake, but concerning the election *they are* beloved for the sake of the fathers. [29]For the gifts and the calling of God *are* irrevocable. [30]For as you were once disobedient to God, yet have now obtained mercy through their disobedience, [31]even so these also have now been disobedient, that through the mercy shown you they also may obtain mercy. [32]For God has committed them all to disobedience, that He might have mercy on all.

[33]Oh, the depth of the riches both of the wisdom and knowledge of God! How unsearchable *are* His judgments and His ways past finding out!

[34]*"For who has known the mind of the*
    LORD?
    Or who has become His counselor?"[a]
[35]*"Or who has first given to Him*
    And it shall be repaid to him?"[a]

[36]For of Him and through Him and to Him *are* all things, to whom *be* glory forever. Amen.

Living Sacrifices to God

12 I beseech you therefore, brethren, by the mercies of God, that you present your bodies a living sacrifice, holy, acceptable to God, *which is* your reasonable service. [2]And do not be conformed to this world, but be transformed by the renewing of your mind, that you may prove what *is* that good and acceptable and perfect will of God.

> ⬐ **LEARN**
> • • • • • • • • • • • • • • • •
> 12:1 • I wish I could offer you an easy 1-2-3 method for knowing the will of God, but history teaches me that God's will usually becomes plain in my life as I take steps of faith, trying to live by scriptural principles. At times He clearly speaks to me in a more tangible way, but usually it's a journey of faith. I read Scripture, pray for guidance, and then make decisions. God's will is not an itinerary but an attitude. And remember this: God is more concerned about keeping you in His will than you are to be kept in it! *For more about* God's Will, *see 1 Thess. 4:3.*

➤ *And do not be conformed to this world, but be transformed by the renewing of your mind, that you may prove what is that good and acceptable and perfect will of God.* Rom. 12:2

Serve God with Spiritual Gifts

[3]For I say, through the grace given to me, to everyone who is among you, not to think *of himself* more highly than he ought to think, but to think soberly, as God has dealt to each one a measure of faith. [4]For as we have many members in one body, but all the members do not have the same function, [5]so we, *being* many, are one body in Christ, and individually members of one another. [6]Having then gifts differing according to the grace that is given to us, *let us use them:* if prophecy, *let us prophesy* in proportion to our faith; [7]or ministry, *let us use it* in *our* ministering; he who teaches, in teaching; [8]he who exhorts, in exhortation; he who gives, with liberality; he who leads, with diligence; he who shows mercy, with cheerfulness.

Behave Like a Christian

[9]*Let* love *be* without hypocrisy. Abhor what is evil. Cling to what is good. [10]*Be* kindly affectionate to one another with brotherly love, in honor giving preference to one another; [11]not lagging in diligence, fervent in spirit, serving the Lord; [12]rejoicing in hope, patient in tribulation, continuing steadfastly in prayer; [13]distributing to the needs of the saints, given to hospitality.

[14]Bless those who persecute you; bless and do not curse. [15]Rejoice with those who rejoice, and weep with those who weep. [16]Be of the same mind toward one another. Do not set your mind on high things, but associate with the humble. Do not be wise in your own opinion.

11:34 [a]Isaiah 40:13; Jeremiah 23:18   11:35 [a]Job 41:11

[17]Repay no one evil for evil. Have regard for good things in the sight of all men. [18]If it is possible, as much as depends on you, live peaceably with all men. [19]Beloved, do not avenge yourselves, but *rather* give place to wrath; for it is written, *"Vengeance is Mine, I will repay,"*[a] says the Lord. [20]Therefore

> *"If your enemy is hungry, feed him;*
> *If he is thirsty, give him a drink;*
> *For in so doing you will heap coals of fire*
>   *on his head."*[a]

[21]Do not be overcome by evil, but overcome evil with good.

Submit to Government

13 Let every soul be subject to the governing authorities. For there is no authority except from God, and the authorities that exist are appointed by God. [2]Therefore whoever resists the authority resists the ordinance of God, and those who resist will bring judgment on themselves. [3]For rulers are not a terror to good works, but to evil. Do you want to be unafraid of the authority? Do what is good, and you will have praise from the same. [4]For he is God's minister to you for good. But if you do evil, be afraid; for he does not bear the sword in vain; for he is God's minister, an avenger to *execute* wrath on him who practices evil. [5]Therefore *you* must be subject, not only because of wrath but also for conscience' sake. [6]For because of this you also pay taxes, for they are God's ministers attending continually to this very thing. [7]Render therefore to all their due: taxes to whom taxes *are due,* customs to whom customs, fear to whom fear, honor to whom honor.

Love Your Neighbor

[8]Owe no one anything except to love one another, for he who loves another has fulfilled the law. [9]For the commandments, *"You shall not commit adultery," "You shall not murder," "You shall not steal," "You shall not bear false witness,"*[a] *"You shall not covet,"*[b] and if *there is* any other commandment, are *all* summed up in this saying, namely, *"You shall love your neighbor as yourself."*[c] [10]Love does no harm to a neighbor; therefore love *is* the fulfillment of the law.

Put on Christ

[11]And *do* this, knowing the time, that now *it is* high time to awake out of sleep; for now our salvation *is* nearer than when we *first* believed. [12]The night is far spent, the day is at hand. Therefore let us cast off the works of darkness, and let us put on the armor of light. [13]Let us walk properly, as in the day, not in revelry and drunkenness, not in lewdness and lust, not in strife and envy. [14]But put on the Lord Jesus Christ, and make no provision for the flesh, to *fulfill its* lusts.

The Law of Liberty

14 Receive one who is weak in the faith, *but* not to disputes over doubtful things. [2]For one believes

12:19 [a]Deuteronomy 32:35   **12:20** [a]Proverbs 25:21, 22   **13:9** [a]NU-Text omits *"You shall not bear false witness."*
[b]Exodus 20:13–15, 17; Deuteronomy 5:17–19, 21 [c]Leviticus 19:18

↑ GROW (ROM. 13:14)

To "put on the Lord Jesus Christ" conveys the idea of making Jesus a part of everything you say and do. Like a comfortable piece of clothing that you wear all day, Jesus wants to join your decision-making process. He wants to be Lord over your singleness or your marriage, over your career and free time, over what you hear and watch. By the way you live, you reveal that either He is Lord *of* all, or He is not Lord *at* all. This is especially true when it comes to the lust of the flesh. Some of us play around a little here; we set up our schedules or create certain routes that we *know* will take us past something we have a hard time resisting. And when we fall, we say, "I couldn't help it." Yes, you could. Make no provision for the flesh! That's part of "putting on" Jesus. *For more about* How to Live Out Your Faith, *see Rom. 14:10.*

he may eat all things, but he who is weak eats *only* vegetables. ³Let not him who eats despise him who does not eat, and let not him who does not eat judge him who eats; for God has received him. ⁴Who are you to judge another's servant? To his own master he stands or falls. Indeed, he will be made to stand, for God is able to make him stand.

⁵One person esteems *one* day above another; another esteems every day *alike*. Let each be fully convinced in his own mind. ⁶He who observes the day, observes *it* to the Lord;^a and he who does not observe the day, to the Lord he does not observe *it*. He who eats, eats to the Lord, for he gives God thanks; and he who does not eat, to the Lord he does not eat, and gives God thanks. ⁷For none of us lives to himself, and no one dies to himself. ⁸For if we live, we live to the Lord; and if we die, we die to the Lord. Therefore, whether we live or die, we are the Lord's. ⁹For to this end Christ died and rose^a and lived again, that He might be Lord of both the dead and the living. ¹⁰But why do you judge your brother? Or why do you show contempt for your brother? For we shall all stand before the judgment seat of Christ.^a ¹¹For it is written:

"As I live, says the LORD,
    Every knee shall bow to Me,
    And every tongue shall confess to
        God."^a

¹²So then each of us shall give account of himself to God. ¹³Therefore let us not judge one another anymore, but rather resolve this, not to put a stumbling block or a cause to fall in *our* brother's way.

The Law of Love

¹⁴I know and am convinced by the Lord Jesus that *there is* nothing unclean of itself; but to him who considers anything to be unclean, to him *it is* unclean. ¹⁵Yet if your brother is grieved because of *your* food, you are no longer walking in love. Do not destroy with your food the one for whom Christ died. ¹⁶Therefore do not let your good be spoken of as evil; ¹⁷for the kingdom of God is not eating and drinking, but righteousness and peace and joy in the Holy Spirit. ¹⁸For he who serves Christ in these things^a *is* acceptable to God and approved by men.

¹⁹Therefore let us pursue the things *which make* for peace and the things by which one may edify another. ²⁰Do not destroy the work of God for the sake of food. All things indeed *are* pure, but *it is* evil for the man who eats with offense. ²¹*It is* good neither to eat meat nor drink wine nor *do anything* by which

⤷ LEARN

• • • • • • • • • • • • • • • • •

14:19 • How many arguments and conflicts could we avoid if we followed Paul's simple instruction to "pursue the things which make for peace"? Life sometimes gets very hard for us, and painful, and full of anxiety, simply because we don't ask ourselves, *Is what I'm about to say likely to cause problems or promote peace?* One hallmark of spiritual maturity is the commitment to doing what edifies others, regardless of the potential cost. And most of the time, what spiritually builds up and edifies others also tends to bring peace. A harsh word stirs up anger, but a gentle answer turns away wrath (Prov. 15:1). *For more about* Loving Others, *see 1 Cor. 1:10;* How to Live Out Your Faith, *1 Cor. 10:13.*

14:6 ^aNU-Text omits the rest of this sentence.   **14:9** ^aNU-Text omits *and rose.*   **14:10** ^aNU-Text reads *of God.*   **14:11** ^aIsaiah 45:23
14:18 ^aNU-Text reads *this.*

⤵ KNOW (ROM. 14:10)

• •

When you get to heaven, expect to see some awards given out. The judgment seat of Christ will determine the divine rewards (or lack thereof) for every Christian who ever lived (2 Cor. 5:10, 11). This judgment is not about whether you get to heaven because it takes place in heaven. This is not so much about bad things believers might have done, as about what they did positively. It's coming for you, too. Did you accomplish anything? Did you impact anyone? Did you seek to glorify your own life? Did you spend your days in the pursuit of nothingness? God will give out several special crowns. For starters, there is a crown of rejoicing (1 Thess. 2:19), a crown of life (James 1:12), and a crown of righteousness (2 Tim. 4:8). There is also the crown of glory (1 Pet. 5:4), if you remain faithful to the Lord and finish the race. *For more about* Heaven, *see 1 Cor. 15:35–58;* How to Live Out Your Faith, *Rom. 14:19.*

your brother stumbles or is offended or is made weak.[a] [22]Do you have faith?[a] Have *it* to yourself before God. Happy *is* he who does not condemn himself in what he approves. [23]But he who doubts is condemned if he eats, because *he does* not *eat* from faith; for whatever *is* not from faith is sin.[a]

Bearing Others' Burdens

15 We then who are strong ought to bear with the scruples of the weak, and not to please ourselves. [2]Let each of us please *his* neighbor for *his* good, leading to edification. [3]For even Christ did not please Himself; but as it is written, *"The reproaches of those who reproached You fell on Me."*[a] [4]For whatever things were written before were written for our learning, that we through the patience and comfort of the Scriptures might have hope. [5]Now may the God of patience and comfort grant you to be like-minded toward one another, according to Christ Jesus, [6]that you may with one mind *and* one mouth glorify the God and Father of our Lord Jesus Christ.

Glorify God Together

[7]Therefore receive one another, just as Christ also received us,[a] to the glory of God. [8]Now I say that Jesus Christ has become a servant to the circumcision for the truth of God, to confirm the promises *made* to the fathers, [9]and that the Gentiles might glorify God for *His* mercy, as it is written:

*"For this reason I will confess to You
    among the Gentiles,
And sing to Your name."*[a]

[10]And again he says:

"Rejoice, O Gentiles, with His people!"[a]

[11]And again:

*"Praise the LORD, all you Gentiles!
Laud Him, all you peoples!"*[a]

[12]And again, Isaiah says:

*"There shall be a root of Jesse;
And He who shall rise to reign over the
    Gentiles,
In Him the Gentiles shall hope."*[a]

[13]Now may the God of hope fill you with all joy and peace in believing, that you may abound in hope by the power of the Holy Spirit.

From Jerusalem to Illyricum

[14]Now I myself am confident concerning you, my brethren, that you also are full of goodness, filled with all knowledge, able also to admonish one another.[a] [15]Nevertheless, brethren, I have written more boldly to you on *some* points, as reminding you, because of the grace given to me by God, [16]that I might be a minister of Jesus Christ to the Gentiles, ministering the gospel of God, that the offering of the Gentiles might be acceptable, sanctified by the Holy Spirit. [17]Therefore I have reason to glory in Christ Jesus in the things *which pertain* to God. [18]For I will not dare to speak of any of those things which Christ has not accomplished through me, in word and deed, to make the Gentiles obedient— [19]in mighty signs and wonders, by the power of the Spirit of God, so that from Jerusalem and round about to Illyricum I have fully preached the gospel of Christ. [20]And so I have made it my aim to preach the gospel, not where Christ was named, lest I should build on another man's foundation, [21]but as it is written:

*"To whom He was not announced, they
    shall see;
And those who have not heard shall
    understand."*[a]

Plan to Visit Rome

[22]For this reason I also have been much hindered from coming to you. [23]But now no longer having a place in these parts, and having a great desire these many years to come to you, [24]whenever I journey to Spain, I shall come to you.[a] For I hope to see you on my journey, and to be helped on my way there by you, if first I may enjoy your *company* for a while. [25]But now I am going to Jerusalem to minister to the saints. [26]For it pleased those from Macedonia and Achaia to make a certain contribution for the poor among the saints who are in Jerusalem. [27]It pleased them indeed, and they are their debtors. For if the Gentiles have been partakers of their spiritual things, their duty is also to minister to them in

14:21 [a]NU-Text omits *or is offended or is made weak.*   **14:22** [a]NU-Text reads *The faith which you have—have.*   **14:23** [a]M-Text puts Romans 16:25–27 here.   **15:3** [a]Psalm 69:9   **15:7** [a]NU-Text and M-Text read *you.*   **15:9** [a]2 Samuel 22:50; Psalm 18:49   **15:10** [a]Deuteronomy 32:43   **15:11** [a]Psalm 117:1   **15:12** [a]Isaiah 11:10   **15:14** [a]M-Text reads *others.*   **15:21** [a]Isaiah 52:15   **15:24** [a]NU-Text omits *I shall come to you* (and joins *Spain* with the next sentence).

material things. [28]Therefore, when I have performed this and have sealed to them this fruit, I shall go by way of you to Spain. [29]But I know that when I come to you, I shall come in the fullness of the blessing of the gospel[a] of Christ.

[30]Now I beg you, brethren, through the Lord Jesus Christ, and through the love of the Spirit, that you strive together with me in prayers to God for me, [31]that I may be delivered from those in Judea who do not believe, and that my service for Jerusalem may be acceptable to the saints, [32]that I may come to you with joy by the will of God, and may be refreshed together with you. [33]Now the God of peace *be* with you all. Amen.

Sister Phoebe Commended

16 I commend to you Phoebe our sister, who is a servant of the church in Cenchrea, [2]that you may receive her in the Lord in a manner worthy of the saints, and assist her in whatever business she has need of you; for indeed she has been a helper of many and of myself also.

Greeting Roman Saints

[3]Greet Priscilla and Aquila, my fellow workers in Christ Jesus, [4]who risked their own necks for my life, to whom not only I give thanks, but also all the churches of the Gentiles. [5]Likewise *greet* the church that is in their house.

Greet my beloved Epaenetus, who is the firstfruits of Achaia[a] to Christ. [6]Greet Mary, who labored much for us. [7]Greet Andronicus and Junia, my countrymen and my fellow prisoners, who are of note among the apostles, who also were in Christ before me.

[8]Greet Amplias, my beloved in the Lord. [9]Greet Urbanus, our fellow worker in Christ, and Stachys, my beloved. [10]Greet Apelles, approved in Christ. Greet those who are of the *household* of Aristobulus. [11]Greet Herodion, my countryman.[a] Greet those who are of the *household* of Narcissus who are in the Lord.

[12]Greet Tryphena and Tryphosa, who have labored in the Lord. Greet the beloved Persis, who labored much in the Lord. [13]Greet Rufus, chosen in the Lord, and his mother and

mine. [14]Greet Asyncritus, Phlegon, Hermas, Patrobas, Hermes, and the brethren who are with them. [15]Greet Philologus and Julia, Nereus and his sister, and Olympas, and all the saints who are with them.

[16]Greet one another with a holy kiss. The[a] churches of Christ greet you.

Avoid Divisive Persons

[17]Now I urge you, brethren, note those who cause divisions and offenses, contrary to the doctrine which you learned, and avoid them. [18]For those who are such do not serve our Lord Jesus[a] Christ, but their own belly, and by smooth words and flattering speech deceive the hearts of the simple. [19]For your obedience has become known to all. Therefore I am glad on your behalf; but I want you to be wise in what is good, and simple concerning evil. [20]And the God of peace will crush Satan under your feet shortly.

The grace of our Lord Jesus Christ *be* with you. Amen.

Greetings from Paul's Friends

[21]Timothy, my fellow worker, and Lucius, Jason, and Sosipater, my countrymen, greet you.

[22]I, Tertius, who wrote *this* epistle, greet you in the Lord.

[23]Gaius, my host and *the host* of the whole church, greets you. Erastus, the treasurer of the city, greets you, and Quartus, a brother. [24]The grace of our Lord Jesus Christ *be* with you all. Amen.[a]

Benediction

[25]Now to Him who is able to establish you according to my gospel and the preaching of Jesus Christ, according to the revelation of the mystery kept secret since the world began [26]but now made manifest, and by the prophetic Scriptures made known to all nations, according to the commandment of the everlasting God, for obedience to the faith— [27]to God, alone wise, *be* glory through Jesus Christ forever. Amen.[a]

15:29 [a]NU-Text omits *of the gospel.*   **16:5** [a]NU-Text reads *Asia.*   **16:11** [a]Or *relative*   **16:16** [a]NU-Text reads *All the churches.*
16:18 [a]NU-Text and M-Text omit *Jesus.*   **16:24** [a]NU-Text omits this verse.   **16:27** [a]M-Text puts Romans 16:25–27 after Romans 14:23.

1 CORINTHIANS ↙

INTRODUCTION//

Paul wrote this sometimes sharply-worded letter in response to difficult situations that arose in the ancient Corinthian church. The Corinthians lived in a Greek culture that featured every kind of sin imaginable, and this external pressure quickly influenced and then injured the church. Paul straightforwardly dealt with these errors. He began by rebuking the Corinthians for fostering divisions and cliques in the church. Various groups claimed to follow differing religious celebrities, causing rifts as each group staked out its own territory, each claiming to be superior to the other (1:12–17). Springing out of these divisions, lawsuits began to multiply between members of the church, legal tussles that tainted the reputation of the church within its culture (6:1–11). Paul reminds the Corinthians, and us, that Christ is to be the center of everything we do. He instructs us to focus on Christ and to seek His wisdom whenever fights start to fester and break out in the church.

Paul also addressed sexual immorality that had wormed its way into the church, a kind prevalent in Greek society. Some people had begun to believe that God's grace allowed them to continue to sin; after all, He had forgiven them. Paul confronted this issue strongly, telling his readers to "flee sexual immorality" (6:18). Finally, Paul answered questions on various issues raised earlier by members of the church, including topics about marriage, communion, worship, and the Resurrection. He also provided foundational teaching on the proper use of the gifts of the Spirit. Believers share a wide assortment of gifts, and each gift is needed for the church to function wholly. Finally, the thing that holds all of this together is love—and in the thirteenth chapter Paul gives us a beautiful exposition of love and its centrality to everything in our faith.

Greeting

1 Paul, called *to be* an apostle of Jesus Christ through the will of God, and Sosthenes *our* brother,

[2]To the church of God which is at Corinth, to those who are sanctified in Christ Jesus, called *to be* saints, with all who in every place call on the name of Jesus Christ our Lord, both theirs and ours:

[3]Grace to you and peace from God our Father and the Lord Jesus Christ.

Spiritual Gifts at Corinth

[4]I thank my God always concerning you for the grace of God which was given to you by Christ Jesus, [5]that you were enriched in everything by Him in all utterance and all knowledge, [6]even as the testimony of Christ was confirmed in you, [7]so that you come short in no gift, eagerly waiting for the revelation of our Lord Jesus Christ, [8]who will also confirm you to the end, *that you may be* blameless in the day of our Lord Jesus Christ. [9]God *is* faithful, by whom you were called into the fellowship of His Son, Jesus Christ our Lord.

Sectarianism Is Sin

[10]Now I plead with you, brethren, by the name of our Lord Jesus Christ, that you all speak the same thing, and *that* there be no divisions among you, but *that* you be perfectly joined together in the same mind and in the same judgment. [11]For it has been declared to me concerning you, my brethren, by those of Chloe's *household,* that there are contentions among you. [12]Now I say this, that each of you says, "I am of Paul," or "I am of Apollos," or "I am of Cephas," or "I am of Christ." [13]Is Christ divided? Was Paul crucified for you? Or were you baptized in the name of Paul?

[14]I thank God that I baptized none of you except Crispus and Gaius, [15]lest anyone should say that I had baptized in my own name. [16]Yes, I also baptized the household of Stephanas. Besides, I do not know whether I baptized any other. [17]For Christ did not send me to baptize, but to preach the gospel, not with wisdom of words, lest the cross of Christ should be made of no effect.

↘ LEARN

• • • • • • • • • • • • • • • • •

1:10 • "A house divided against a house falls," Jesus said (Luke 11:17). A church divided against itself— a congregation where sharp divisions exist, where members slander and attack each other—cannot produce healthy, mature believers. We grow up together in Jesus (Eph. 4:15), and all of us belong to each other (Rom. 12:5; 1 Cor. 12:20). In the church, no one lives to himself alone and no one dies to himself alone (Rom. 14:7). As iron sharpens iron, so we help one another grow spiritually (Prov. 27:17). We become fully mature followers of Christ as we learn to live as a family, quick to forgive one another. *For more about* Loving Others, *see 1 Cor. 14:26;* Forgiveness, *1 Cor. 1:30;* Fellowship, *1 Cor. 14:26.*

Christ the Power and Wisdom of God

[18]For the message of the cross is foolishness to those who are perishing, but to us who are being saved it is the power of God. [19]For it is written:

> *"I will destroy the wisdom of the wise,*
> *And bring to nothing the understanding*
> *of the prudent."*[a]

[20]Where *is* the wise? Where *is* the scribe? Where *is* the disputer of this age? Has not God made foolish the wisdom of this world? [21]For since, in the wisdom of God, the world through wisdom did not know God, it pleased God through the foolishness of the message preached to save those who believe. [22]For Jews request a sign, and Greeks seek after wisdom; [23]but we preach Christ crucified, to the Jews a stumbling block and to the Greeks[a] foolishness, [24]but to those who are called, both Jews and Greeks, Christ the power of God and the wisdom of God. [25]Because the foolishness of God is wiser than men, and the weakness of God is stronger than men.

Glory Only in the Lord

[26]For you see your calling, brethren, that not many wise according to the flesh, not many mighty, not many noble, *are called.* [27]But God has chosen the foolish things of the world to put to shame the wise, and God has chosen the weak things of the world to put to shame the things which are mighty; [28]and the base things of the world and the things which

---

1:19 [a]Isaiah 29:14   1:23 [a]NU-Text reads *Gentiles.*

➔ **LIVE**

1:30 • The word *redemption* carries the idea of delivering, especially by means of paying a price. It is a commercial term, borrowed from the marketplace. In the Old Testament it was used of slaves purchased in order to be set free. It was commonly used of paying a ransom to free a prisoner. Thus he was redeemed. Imagine how amazed you would be if the President of the United States offered to trade himself for a group of hostages held by terrorists. God did far more than that when He took upon Himself the wrath that should have fallen on us. *For more about* Forgiveness, *see Gal. 2:16;* God's Love, *2 Cor. 13:14.*

Spiritual Wisdom

6However, we speak wisdom among those who are mature, yet not the wisdom of this age, nor of the rulers of this age, who are coming to nothing. 7But we speak the wisdom of God in a mystery, the hidden *wisdom* which God ordained before the ages for our glory, 8which none of the rulers of this age knew; for had they known, they would not have crucified the Lord of glory.

9But as it is written:

> "Eye has not seen, nor ear heard,
> Nor have entered into the heart of man
> The things which God has prepared for
>   those who love Him."a

10But God has revealed *them* to us through His Spirit. For the Spirit searches all things, yes, the deep things of God. 11For what man knows the things of a man except the spirit of the man which is in him? Even so no one knows the things of God except the Spirit of God. 12Now we have received, not the spirit

are despised God has chosen, and the things which are not, to bring to nothing the things that are, 29that no flesh should glory in His presence. 30But of Him you are in Christ Jesus, who became for us wisdom from God— and righteousness and sanctification and redemption— 31that, as it is written, *"He who glories, let him glory in the LORD."*a

Christ Crucified

2 And I, brethren, when I came to you, did not come with excellence of speech or of wisdom declaring to you the testimonya of God. 2For I determined not to know anything among you except Jesus Christ and Him crucified. 3I was with you in weakness, in fear, and in much trembling. 4And my speech and my preaching *were* not with persuasive words of humana wisdom, but in demonstration of the Spirit and of power, 5that your faith should not be in the wisdom of men but in the power of God.

➔ *Now we have received, not the spirit of the world, but the Spirit who is from God, that we might know the things that have been freely given to us by God.* 1 Cor. 2:12

1:31 aJeremiah 9:24   2:1 aNU-Text reads *mystery.*   2:4 aNU-Text omits *human.*   2:9 aIsaiah 64:4

↑ **GROW** (1 COR. 1:23)

Here is the gospel message—and it starts with bad news. In our natural state, we are separated from God. We can do nothing to earn God's favor. Good morals won't get us to heaven, which means we are in deep trouble. The good news is that God loved us so much that He sent His perfect Son, Jesus, to the Cross to die in our place. Jesus became sin for us, and if we believe in Him, we can be forgiven. Jesus Christ and Him crucified is the primary message of the gospel, the bottom line of every evangelistic proclamation. There is great power in the simple story of the life, death, and resurrection of Jesus! When you tell the story, don't complicate it. Don't add to it. Don't take away from it. Don't apologize for it. Just proclaim it and stand back and watch what God will do. *For more about* Sharing Your Faith, *see 1 Cor. 4:12;* New Life in Christ, *1 Cor. 15:35–58.*

of the world, but the Spirit who is from God, that we might know the things that have been freely given to us by God.

[13]These things we also speak, not in words which man's wisdom teaches but which the Holy[a] Spirit teaches, comparing spiritual things with spiritual. [14]But the natural man does not receive the things of the Spirit of God, for they are foolishness to him; nor can he know *them,* because they are spiritually discerned. [15]But he who is spiritual judges all things, yet he himself is *rightly* judged by no one. [16]For *"who has known the mind of the LORD that he may instruct Him?"*[a] But we have the mind of Christ.

Sectarianism Is Carnal

3 And I, brethren, could not speak to you as to spiritual *people* but as to carnal, as to babes in Christ. [2]I fed you with milk and not with solid food; for until now you were not able *to receive it,* and even now you are still not able; [3]for you are still carnal. For where *there are* envy, strife, and divisions among you, are you not carnal and behaving like *mere* men? [4]For when one says, "I am of Paul," and another, "I *am* of Apollos," are you not carnal?

Watering, Working, Warning

[5]Who then is Paul, and who *is* Apollos, but ministers through whom you believed, as the Lord gave to each one? [6]I planted, Apollos watered, but God gave the increase. [7]So then neither he who plants is anything, nor he who waters, but God who gives the increase. [8]Now he who plants and he who waters are one, and each one will receive his own reward according to his own labor.

[9]For we are God's fellow workers; you are God's field, *you are* God's building. [10]According to the grace of God which was given to me, as a wise master builder I have laid the foundation, and another builds on it. But let each one take heed how he builds on it. [11]For no other foundation can anyone lay than that which is laid, which is Jesus Christ. [12]Now if anyone builds on this foundation *with* gold, silver, precious stones, wood, hay, straw, [13]each one's work will become clear; for the Day will declare it, because it will be revealed by fire; and the fire will test each one's work, of what sort it is. [14]If anyone's work which he

has built on *it* endures, he will receive a reward. [15]If anyone's work is burned, he will suffer loss; but he himself will be saved, yet so as through fire.

[16]Do you not know that you are the temple of God and *that* the Spirit of God dwells in you? [17]If anyone defiles the temple of God, God will destroy him. For the temple of God is holy, which *temple* you are.

> → *Do you not know that you are the temple of God and that the Spirit of God dwells in you?* 1 Cor. 3:16

Avoid Worldly Wisdom

[18]Let no one deceive himself. If anyone among you seems to be wise in this age, let him become a fool that he may become wise. [19]For the wisdom of this world is foolishness with God. For it is written, *"He catches the wise in their own craftiness";*[a] [20]and again, *"The LORD knows the thoughts of the wise, that they are futile."*[a] [21]Therefore let no one boast in men. For all things are yours: [22]whether Paul or Apollos or Cephas, or the world or life or death, or things present or things to come—all are yours. [23]And you *are* Christ's, and Christ *is* God's.

Stewards of the Mysteries of God

4 Let a man so consider us, as servants of Christ and stewards of the mysteries of God. [2]Moreover it is required in stewards that one be found faithful. [3]But with me it is a very small thing that I should be judged by you or by a human court.[a] In fact, I do not even judge myself. [4]For I know of nothing against myself, yet I am not justified by this; but He who judges me is the Lord. [5]Therefore judge nothing before the time, until the Lord comes, who will both bring to light the hidden things of darkness and reveal the counsels of the hearts. Then each one's praise will come from God.

Fools for Christ's Sake

[6]Now these things, brethren, I have figuratively transferred to myself and Apollos

2:13 [a]NU-Text omits *Holy.*   2:16 [a]Isaiah 40:13   3:19 [a]Job 5:13   3:20 [a]Psalm 94:11   4:3 [a]Literally *day*

for your sakes, that you may learn in us not to think beyond what is written, that none of you may be puffed up on behalf of one against the other. [7]For who makes you differ *from another?* And what do you have that you did not receive? Now if you did indeed receive *it,* why do you boast as if you had not received *it?*

[8]You are already full! You are already rich! You have reigned as kings without us—and indeed I could wish you did reign, that we also might reign with you! [9]For I think that God has displayed us, the apostles, last, as men condemned to death; for we have been made a spectacle to the world, both to angels and to men. [10]We *are* fools for Christ's sake, but you *are* wise in Christ! We *are* weak, but you *are* strong! You *are* distinguished, but we *are* dishonored! [11]To the present hour we both hunger and thirst, and we are poorly clothed, and beaten, and homeless. [12]And we labor, working with our own hands. Being reviled, we bless; being persecuted, we endure; [13]being defamed, we entreat. We have been made as the filth of the world, the offscouring of all things until now.

Paul's Paternal Care

[14]I do not write these things to shame you, but as my beloved children I warn *you.* [15]For though you might have ten thousand instructors in Christ, yet *you do* not *have* many fathers; for in Christ Jesus I have begotten you through the gospel. [16]Therefore I urge you, imitate me. [17]For this reason I have sent Timothy to you, who is my beloved and faithful son in the Lord, who will remind you of my ways in Christ, as I teach everywhere in every church.

[18]Now some are puffed up, as though I were not coming to you. [19]But I will come to you shortly, if the Lord wills, and I will know, not the word of those who are puffed up, but the power. [20]For the kingdom of God *is* not in word but in power. [21]What do you want? Shall I come to you with a rod, or in love and a spirit of gentleness?

Immorality Defiles the Church

5 It is actually reported *that there is* sexual immorality among you, and such sexual immorality as is not even named[a] among the Gentiles—that a man has his father's wife! [2]And you are puffed up, and have not rather mourned, that he who has done this deed might be taken away from among you. [3]For I indeed, as absent in body but present in spirit, have already judged (as though I were present) him who has so done this deed. [4]In the name of our Lord Jesus Christ, when you are gathered together, along with my spirit, with the power of our Lord Jesus Christ, [5]deliver such a one to Satan for the destruction of the flesh, that his spirit may be saved in the day of the Lord Jesus.[a]

[6]Your glorying *is* not good. Do you not know that a little leaven leavens the whole lump? [7]Therefore purge out the old leaven, that you may be a new lump, since you truly are unleavened. For indeed Christ, our Passover, was sacrificed for us.[a] [8]Therefore let us keep the feast, not with old leaven, nor with the leaven of malice and wickedness, but with the unleavened *bread* of sincerity and truth.

5:1 [a]NU-Text omits *named.*   5:5 [a]NU-Text omits *Jesus.*   5:7 [a]NU-Text omits *for us.*

↑ **GROW** (1 COR. 4:12)
. . . .

Often, the hardest part about evangelism is getting started. But once you get moving and the Lord starts speaking through you, it can be one of the most joyful things you have ever experienced. To think that God almighty would speak through someone like you or me is indeed a great privilege! It is an honor to tell others about Jesus. This message that God has given us was not designed to be hoarded, but to be shared. You and I were blessed to be a blessing. Next to knowing the Lord Himself, one of the greatest joys you will ever experience is when you have the privilege of praying with someone to accept Christ. And as you bless others with the gospel, you will find that God will bless you even more. Take a step of faith and initiate a conversation about Jesus and see what the Lord will do. *For more about* Sharing Your Faith, *see 2 Cor. 3:2;* God at Work, *2 Cor. 1:3, 4.*

→LIVE

• • • • • • • • • • • • • • •

5:6–8 • We must stop looking within ourselves for the resources and answers we need and instead, in absolute weakness and helplessness, turn to God. Apart from God, we have no ray of hope, no flicker of light, no prospect of rescue. But the Lord intervenes and hope appears! After the long, dark night, the sun rises, a new day dawns, and the world is flooded with light. Against the unrighteousness of some and the self-righteousness of others, we have the righteousness of God! But no one will accept God's remedy for their plight if they don't first accept His diagnosis of their sin. *For more about* Becoming a Christian, *see Gal. 1:8.*

Immorality Must Be Judged

⁹I wrote to you in my epistle not to keep company with sexually immoral people. ¹⁰Yet *I* certainly *did* not *mean* with the sexually immoral people of this world, or with the covetous, or extortioners, or idolaters, since then you would need to go out of the world. ¹¹But now I have written to you not to keep company with anyone named a brother, who is sexually immoral, or covetous, or an idolater, or a reviler, or a drunkard, or an extortioner—not even to eat with such a person.

¹²For what *have* I *to do* with judging those also who are outside? Do you not judge those who are inside? ¹³But those who are outside God judges. Therefore *"put away from yourselves the evil person."*[a]

Do Not Sue the Brethren

6 Dare any of you, having a matter against another, go to law before the unrighteous, and not before the saints? ²Do you not know that the saints will judge the world? And if the world will be judged by you, are you unworthy to judge the smallest matters? ³Do you not know that we shall judge angels? How much more, things that pertain to this life? ⁴If then you have judgments concerning things pertaining to this life, do you appoint those who are least esteemed by the church to judge? ⁵I say this to your shame. Is it so, that there is not a wise man among you, not even one, who will be able to judge between his brethren? ⁶But brother goes to law against brother, and that before unbelievers!

⁷Now therefore, it is already an utter failure for you that you go to law against one another. Why do you not rather accept wrong? Why do you not rather *let yourselves* be cheated? ⁸No, you yourselves do wrong and cheat, and *you do* these things *to your* brethren! ⁹Do you not know that the unrighteous will not inherit the kingdom of God? Do not be deceived. Neither fornicators, nor idolaters, nor adulterers, nor homosexuals,[a] nor sodomites, ¹⁰nor thieves, nor covetous, nor drunkards, nor revilers, nor extortioners will inherit the kingdom of God. ¹¹And such were some of you. But you were washed, but you were sanctified, but you were justified in the name of the Lord Jesus and by the Spirit of our God.

Glorify God in Body and Spirit

¹²All things are lawful for me, but all things are not helpful. All things are lawful for me, but I will not be brought under the power of any. ¹³Foods for the stomach and the stomach for foods, but God will destroy both it and them. Now the body *is* not for sexual

5:13 [a]Deuteronomy 17:7; 19:19; 22:21, 24; 24:7   **6:9** [a]That is, catamites

↓ KNOW (1 COR. 5:4)

• •

No one has ever marched across the human stage quite like Jesus Christ. He stands apart from all others. Even today we mark human time from the date of His appearance on this planet. His very name ripples with power. If you don't believe me, just say it sometime. When you're in a crowded room and people are talking, say the names of various religious leaders, gurus, or prophets—probably, you'll get little or no response. But say the name Jesus, and you *will* get a reaction. A hush will fall over the room. Even an atheist who says there is no God will use Jesus' name to punctuate a point or to utter a profanity. Why? Because even nonbelievers know there is power in the name of Jesus. Jesus is the name above all names (Phil. 2:10), and that amazing name has power above all others. *For more about* Jesus' Life, *see Heb. 1:8.*

immorality but for the Lord, and the Lord for the body. [14]And God both raised up the Lord and will also raise us up by His power.

[15]Do you not know that your bodies are members of Christ? Shall I then take the members of Christ and make *them* members of a harlot? Certainly not! [16]Or do you not know that he who is joined to a harlot is one body *with her*? For *"the two,"* He says, *"shall become one flesh."*[a] [17]But he who is joined to the Lord is one spirit *with Him*.

[18]Flee sexual immorality. Every sin that a man does is outside the body, but he who commits sexual immorality sins against his own body. [19]Or do you not know that your body is the temple of the Holy Spirit *who is* in you, whom you have from God, and you are not your own? [20]For you were bought at a price; therefore glorify God in your body[a] and in your spirit, which are God's.

Principles of Marriage

7 Now concerning the things of which you wrote to me:

It is good for a man not to touch a woman. [2]Nevertheless, because of sexual immorality, let each man have his own wife, and let each woman have her own husband. [3]Let the husband render to his wife the affection due her, and likewise also the wife to her husband. [4]The wife does not have authority over her own body, but the husband *does*. And likewise the husband does not have authority over his own body, but the wife *does*. [5]Do not deprive one another except with consent for a time, that you may give yourselves to fasting and prayer; and come together again so that Satan does not tempt you because of your lack of self-control. [6]But I say this as a concession, not as a commandment. [7]For I wish that all men were even as I myself. But each one has his own gift from God, one in this manner and another in that.

[8]But I say to the unmarried and to the widows: It is good for them if they remain even as I am; [9]but if they cannot exercise self-control, let them marry. For it is better to marry than to burn *with passion*.

Keep Your Marriage Vows

[10]Now to the married I command, *yet* not I but the Lord: A wife is not to depart from

her husband. [11]But even if she does depart, let her remain unmarried or be reconciled to *her* husband. And a husband is not to divorce *his* wife.

[12]But to the rest I, not the Lord, say: If any brother has a wife who does not believe, and she is willing to live with him, let him not divorce her. [13]And a woman who has a husband who does not believe, if he is willing to live with her, let her not divorce him. [14]For the unbelieving husband is sanctified by the wife, and the unbelieving wife is sanctified by the husband; otherwise your children would be unclean, but now they are holy. [15]But if the unbeliever departs, let him depart; a brother or a sister is not under bondage in such *cases*. But God has called us to peace. [16]For how do you know, O wife, whether you will save *your* husband? Or how do you know, O husband, whether you will save *your* wife?

Live as You Are Called

[17]But as God has distributed to each one, as the Lord has called each one, so let him walk. And so I ordain in all the churches. [18]Was anyone called while circumcised? Let him not become uncircumcised. Was anyone called while uncircumcised? Let him not be circumcised. [19]Circumcision is nothing and uncircumcision is nothing, but keeping the commandments of God *is what matters*. [20]Let each one remain in the same calling in which he was called. [21]Were you called *while* a slave? Do not be concerned about it; but if you can be made free, rather use *it*. [22]For he who is called in the Lord *while* a slave is the Lord's freedman. Likewise he who is called *while* free is Christ's slave. [23]You were bought at a price; do not become slaves of men. [24]Brethren, let each one remain with God in that *state* in which he was called.

To the Unmarried and Widows

[25]Now concerning virgins: I have no commandment from the Lord; yet I give judgment as one whom the Lord in His mercy has made trustworthy. [26]I suppose therefore that this is good because of the present distress— that *it is* good for a man to remain as he is: [27]Are you bound to a wife? Do not seek to be loosed. Are you loosed from a wife? Do not seek a wife. [28]But even if you do marry, you

6:16 [a]Genesis 2:24   **6:20** [a]NU-Text ends the verse at *body*.

have not sinned; and if a virgin marries, she has not sinned. Nevertheless such will have trouble in the flesh, but I would spare you.

[29]But this I say, brethren, the time *is* short, so that from now on even those who have wives should be as though they had none, [30]those who weep as though they did not weep, those who rejoice as though they did not rejoice, those who buy as though they did not possess, [31]and those who use this world as not misusing *it.* For the form of this world is passing away.

[32]But I want you to be without care. He who is unmarried cares for the things of the Lord—how he may please the Lord. [33]But he who is married cares about the things of the world—how he may please *his* wife. [34]There is[a] a difference between a wife and a virgin. The unmarried woman cares about the things of the Lord, that she may be holy both in body and in spirit. But she who is married cares about the things of the world—how she may please *her* husband. [35]And this I say for your own profit, not that I may put a leash on you, but for what is proper, and that you may serve the Lord without distraction.

[36]But if any man thinks he is behaving improperly toward his virgin, if she is past the flower of youth, and thus it must be, let him do what he wishes. He does not sin; let them marry. [37]Nevertheless he who stands steadfast in his heart, having no necessity, but has power over his own will, and has so determined in his heart that he will keep his virgin,[a] does well. [38]So then he who gives *her*[a] in marriage does well, but he who does not give *her* in marriage does better.

[39]A wife is bound by law as long as her husband lives; but if her husband dies, she is at liberty to be married to whom she wishes, only in the Lord. [40]But she is happier if she remains as she is, according to my judgment—and I think I also have the Spirit of God.

Be Sensitive to Conscience

8 Now concerning things offered to idols: We know that we all have knowledge. Knowledge puffs up, but love edifies. [2]And if anyone thinks that he knows anything, he knows nothing yet as he ought to know. [3]But if anyone loves God, this one is known by Him.

[4]Therefore concerning the eating of things offered to idols, we know that an idol *is* nothing in the world, and that *there is* no other God but one. [5]For even if there are so-called gods, whether in heaven or on earth (as there are many gods and many lords), [6]yet for us *there is* one God, the Father, of whom *are* all things, and we for Him; and one Lord Jesus Christ, through whom *are* all things, and through whom we *live.*

[7]However, *there is* not in everyone that knowledge; for some, with consciousness of the idol, until now eat *it* as a thing offered to an idol; and their conscience, being weak, is defiled. [8]But food does not commend us to God; for neither if we eat are we the better, nor if we do not eat are we the worse.

[9]But beware lest somehow this liberty of yours become a stumbling block to those who are weak. [10]For if anyone sees you who have knowledge eating in an idol's temple, will not the conscience of him who is weak be emboldened to eat those things offered to idols? [11]And because of your knowledge shall the weak brother perish, for whom Christ died? [12]But when you thus sin against the brethren, and wound their weak conscience, you sin against Christ. [13]Therefore, if food makes my brother stumble, I will never again eat meat, lest I make my brother stumble.

A Pattern of Self-Denial

9 Am I not an apostle? Am I not free? Have I not seen Jesus Christ our Lord? Are you not my work in the Lord? [2]If I am not an apostle to others, yet doubtless I am to you. For you are the seal of my apostleship in the Lord.

[3]My defense to those who examine me is this: [4]Do we have no right to eat and drink? [5]Do we have no right to take along a believing wife, as *do* also the other apostles, the brothers of the Lord, and Cephas? [6]Or *is it* only Barnabas and I *who* have no right to refrain from working? [7]Who ever goes to war at his own expense? Who plants a vineyard and does not eat of its fruit? Or who tends a flock and does not drink of the milk of the flock?

[8]Do I say these things as a *mere* man? Or does not the law say the same also? [9]For it is written in the law of Moses, *"You shall not muzzle an ox while it treads out the grain."*[a] Is it oxen God is concerned about? [10]Or does He say *it* altogether for our sakes?

7:34 [a]M-Text adds *also.*   7:37 [a]Or *virgin daughter*   7:38 [a]NU-Text reads *his own virgin.*   9:9 [a]Deuteronomy 25:4

For our sakes, no doubt, *this* is written, that he who plows should plow in hope, and he who threshes in hope should be partaker of his hope. ¹¹If we have sown spiritual things for you, *is it* a great thing if we reap your material things? ¹²If others are partakers of *this* right over you, *are* we not even more?

Nevertheless we have not used this right, but endure all things lest we hinder the gospel of Christ. ¹³Do you not know that those who minister the holy things eat *of the things* of the temple, and those who serve at the altar partake of *the offerings of* the altar? ¹⁴Even so the Lord has commanded that those who preach the gospel should live from the gospel.

¹⁵But I have used none of these things, nor have I written these things that it should be done so to me; for it *would be* better for me to die than that anyone should make my boasting void. ¹⁶For if I preach the gospel, I have nothing to boast of, for necessity is laid upon me; yes, woe is me if I do not preach the gospel! ¹⁷For if I do this willingly, I have a reward; but if against my will, I have been entrusted with a stewardship. ¹⁸What is my reward then? That when I preach the gospel, I may present the gospel of Christ[a] without charge, that I may not abuse my authority in the gospel.

Serving All Men

¹⁹For though I am free from all *men,* I have made myself a servant to all, that I might win the more; ²⁰and to the Jews I became as a Jew, that I might win Jews; to those *who are* under the law, as under the law,[a] that I might win those *who are* under the law; ²¹to those *who are* without law, as without law (not being without law toward God,[a] but under law toward Christ[b]), that I might win those *who are* without law; ²²to the weak I became as[a] weak, that I might win the weak. I have become all things to all *men,* that I might by all means save some. ²³Now this I do for the gospel's sake, that I may be partaker of it with *you.*

Striving for a Crown

²⁴Do you not know that those who run in a race all run, but one receives the prize? Run in such a way that you may obtain *it.* ²⁵And everyone who competes *for the prize* is temperate in all things. Now they *do it* to obtain

a perishable crown, but we *for* an imperishable *crown.* ²⁶Therefore I run thus: not with uncertainty. Thus I fight: not as *one who* beats the air. ²⁷But I discipline my body and bring *it* into subjection, lest, when I have preached to others, I myself should become disqualified.

Old Testament Examples

10 Moreover, brethren, I do not want you to be unaware that all our fathers were under the cloud, all passed through the sea, ²all were baptized into Moses in the cloud and in the sea, ³all ate the same spiritual food, ⁴and all drank the same spiritual drink. For they drank of that spiritual Rock that followed them, and that Rock was Christ. ⁵But with most of them God was not well pleased, for *their bodies* were scattered in the wilderness.

⁶Now these things became our examples, to the intent that we should not lust after evil things as they also lusted. ⁷And do not become idolaters as *were* some of them. As it is written, *"The people sat down to eat and drink, and rose up to play."*[a] ⁸Nor let us commit sexual immorality, as some of them did, and in one day twenty-three thousand fell; ⁹nor let us tempt Christ, as some of them also tempted, and were destroyed by serpents; ¹⁰nor complain, as some of them also complained, and were destroyed by the destroyer. ¹¹Now all[a] these things happened to them as examples, and they were written for our admonition, upon whom the ends of the ages have come.

↘ LEARN

10:11 • When Paul wrote that "these things" happened to provide us with "examples," he was speaking primarily of the Old Testament. The amazing stories, types, and lessons found there are every bit as inspired as those in the New Testament. "*All* Scripture is given by inspiration of God" (2 Tim. 3:16, italics added). For *our* benefit the Lord inspired men of God to write down the words of the Old Testament so that we might learn by example both how to please God and how a holy God reacts to sin. The Old Testament was Jesus' Bible, and He still uses it to teach us God's ways. As it has been said, "All new news is old news happening to new people." *For more about God's Word, see Gal. 1:8.*

9:18 ªNU-Text omits *of Christ.*   **9:20** ªNU-Text adds *though not being myself under the law.*   **9:21** ªNU-Text reads *God's law.*   ᵇNU-Text reads *Christ's law.*   **9:22** ªNU-Text omits *as.*   **10:7** ªExodus 32:6   **10:11** ªNU-Text omits *all.*

[12]Therefore let him who thinks he stands take heed lest he fall. [13]No temptation has overtaken you except such as is common to man; but God *is* faithful, who will not allow you to be tempted beyond what you are able, but with the temptation will also make the way of escape, that you may be able to bear *it*.

Flee from Idolatry

[14]Therefore, my beloved, flee from idolatry. [15]I speak as to wise men; judge for yourselves what I say. [16]The cup of blessing which we bless, is it not the communion of the blood of Christ? The bread which we break, is it not the communion of the body of Christ? [17]For we, *though* many, are one bread *and* one body; for we all partake of that one bread. [18]Observe Israel after the flesh: Are not those who eat of the sacrifices partakers of the altar? [19]What am I saying then? That an idol is anything, or what is offered to idols is anything? [20]Rather, that the things which the Gentiles sacrifice they sacrifice to demons and not to God, and I do not want you to have fellowship with demons. [21]You cannot drink the cup of the Lord and the cup of demons; you cannot partake of the Lord's table and of the table of demons. [22]Or do we provoke the Lord to jealousy? Are we stronger than He?

All to the Glory of God

[23]All things are lawful for me,[a] but not all things are helpful; all things are lawful for me,[b] but not all things edify. [24]Let no one seek his own, but each one the other's *well-being*. [25]Eat whatever is sold in the meat market, asking no questions for conscience' sake; [26]for *"the earth is the LORD's, and all its fullness."*[a]

[27]If any of those who do not believe invites you *to dinner,* and you desire to go, eat whatever is set before you, asking no question for conscience' sake. [28]But if anyone says to you, "This was offered to idols," do not eat it for the sake of the one who told you, and for conscience' sake;[a] for *"the earth is the LORD's, and all its fullness."*[b] [29]"Conscience," I say, not your own, but that of the other. For why is my liberty judged by another *man's* conscience? [30]But if I partake with thanks, why am I evil spoken of for *the food* over which I give thanks?

[31]Therefore, whether you eat or drink, or whatever you do, do all to the glory of God. [32]Give no offense, either to the Jews or to the Greeks or to the church of God, [33]just as I also please all *men* in all *things,* not seeking my own profit, but the *profit* of many, that they may be saved.

11

Imitate me, just as I also *imitate* Christ.

Head Coverings

[2]Now I praise you, brethren, that you remember me in all things and keep the traditions just as I delivered *them* to you. [3]But I want you to know that the head of every man is Christ, the head of woman *is* man, and the head of Christ *is* God. [4]Every man praying or prophesying, having *his* head covered, dishonors his head. [5]But every woman who prays or prophesies with *her* head uncovered dishonors her head, for that is one and the same as if her head were shaved. [6]For if a

10:23 [a]NU-Text omits *for me.* [b]NU-Text omits *for me.* 10:26 [a]Psalm 24:1 10:28 [a]NU-Text omits the rest of this verse. [b]Psalm 24:1

↑ GROW (1 COR. 10:13)

This is an excellent passage to commit to memory. Sometimes we put ourselves in the way of temptation. We stick our hand in the fire and then feel surprised when it gets burned. One person said, "Lead me not into temptation—I can find it myself." Instead of taking practical steps to stay away from things that could drag us down, we put ourselves directly in their path. Listen, we live in a fallen world. All around us temptations clamor for our attention, trying to entice us. There's not much you can do about that. It is quite another thing, however, to put yourself in a place where you *know* you are weak. God will never give you more than you can handle—but you need to learn to take the way out He so faithfully provides. Sometimes that's as simple as walking out a door or pushing an off button. Flee temptation and don't leave a forwarding address. *For more about* How to Live Out Your Faith *and* Sin, *see 2 Cor. 10:5.*

woman is not covered, let her also be shorn. But if it is shameful for a woman to be shorn or shaved, let her be covered. [7]For a man indeed ought not to cover *his* head, since he is the image and glory of God; but woman is the glory of man. [8]For man is not from woman, but woman from man. [9]Nor was man created for the woman, but woman for the man. [10]For this reason the woman ought to have *a symbol of* authority on *her* head, because of the angels. [11]Nevertheless, neither *is* man independent of woman, nor woman independent of man, in the Lord. [12]For as woman *came* from man, even so man also *comes* through woman; but all things are from God.

[13]Judge among yourselves. Is it proper for a woman to pray to God with her head uncovered? [14]Does not even nature itself teach you that if a man has long hair, it is a dishonor to him? [15]But if a woman has long hair, it is a glory to her; for *her* hair is given to her[a] for a covering. [16]But if anyone seems to be contentious, we have no such custom, nor *do* the churches of God.

Conduct at the Lord's Supper

[17]Now in giving these instructions I do not praise *you,* since you come together not for the better but for the worse. [18]For first of all, when you come together as a church, I hear that there are divisions among you, and in part I believe it. [19]For there must also be factions among you, that those who are approved may be recognized among you. [20]Therefore when you come together in one place, it is not to eat the Lord's Supper. [21]For in eating, each one takes his own supper ahead of *others;* and one is hungry and another is drunk. [22]What! Do you not have houses to eat and drink in? Or do you despise the church of God and shame those who have nothing? What shall I say to you? Shall I praise you in this? I do not praise *you.*

Institution of the Lord's Supper

[23]For I received from the Lord that which I also delivered to you: that the Lord Jesus on the *same* night in which He was betrayed took bread; [24]and when He had given thanks, He broke *it* and said, "Take, eat;[a] this is My body which is broken[b] for you; do this in remembrance of Me." [25]In the same manner He also *took* the cup after supper, saying, "This cup is the new covenant in My blood. This do, as often as you drink *it,* in remembrance of Me."

[26]For as often as you eat this bread and drink this cup, you proclaim the Lord's death till He comes.

Examine Yourself

[27]Therefore whoever eats this bread or drinks *this* cup of the Lord in an unworthy manner will be guilty of the body and blood[a] of the Lord. [28]But let a man examine himself, and so let him eat of the bread and drink of the cup. [29]For he who eats and drinks in an unworthy manner[a] eats and drinks judgment to himself, not discerning the Lord's[b] body. [30]For this reason many *are* weak and sick among you, and many sleep. [31]For if we would judge ourselves, we would not be judged. [32]But when we are judged, we are chastened by the Lord, that we may not be condemned with the world.

[33]Therefore, my brethren, when you come together to eat, wait for one another. [34]But if anyone is hungry, let him eat at home, lest you come together for judgment. And the rest I will set in order when I come.

Spiritual Gifts: Unity in Diversity

12 Now concerning spiritual *gifts,* brethren, I do not want you to be ignorant: [2]You know that[a] you were Gentiles, carried away to these dumb idols, however you were led. [3]Therefore I make known to you that no one speaking by the Spirit of God calls Jesus accursed, and no one can say that Jesus is Lord except by the Holy Spirit.

[4]There are diversities of gifts, but the same Spirit. [5]There are differences of ministries, but the same Lord. [6]And there are diversities of activities, but it is the same God who works all in all. [7]But the manifestation of the Spirit is given to each one for the profit *of all:* [8]for to one is given the word of wisdom through the Spirit, to another the word of knowledge through the same Spirit, [9]to another faith by the same Spirit, to another gifts of healings by the same[a] Spirit, [10]to another the working

---

11:15 [a]M-Text omits *to her.*   11:24 [a]NU-Text omits *Take, eat.* [b]NU-Text omits *broken.*   11:27 [a]NU-Text and M-Text read *the blood.*
11:29 [a]NU-Text omits *in an unworthy manner.* [b]NU-Text omits *Lord's.*   12:2 [a]NU-Text and M-Text add *when.*   12:9 [a]NU-Text reads *one.*

of miracles, to another prophecy, to another discerning of spirits, to another *different* kinds of tongues, to another the interpretation of tongues. [11]But one and the same Spirit works all these things, distributing to each one individually as He wills.

Unity and Diversity in One Body

[12]For as the body is one and has many members, but all the members of that one body, being many, are one body, so also *is* Christ. [13]For by one Spirit we were all baptized into one body—whether Jews or Greeks, whether slaves or free—and have all been made to drink into[a] one Spirit. [14]For in fact the body is not one member but many.

[15]If the foot should say, "Because I am not a hand, I am not of the body," is it therefore not of the body? [16]And if the ear should say, "Because I am not an eye, I am not of the body," is it therefore not of the body? [17]If the whole body *were* an eye, where *would be* the hearing? If the whole *were* hearing, where *would be* the smelling? [18]But now God has set the members, each one of them, in the body just as He pleased. [19]And if they were all one member, where *would* the body *be*?

[20]But now indeed *there are* many members, yet one body. [21]And the eye cannot say to the hand, "I have no need of you"; nor again the head to the feet, "I have no need of you." [22]No, much rather, those members of the body which seem to be weaker are necessary. [23]And those *members* of the body which we think to be less honorable, on these we bestow greater honor; and our unpresentable *parts* have greater modesty, [24]but our presentable *parts* have no need. But God composed the body, having given greater honor to that *part* which lacks it, [25]that there should be no schism in the body, but *that* the members should have the same care for one another. [26]And if one member suffers, all the members suffer with *it;* or if one member is honored, all the members rejoice with *it.*

[27]Now you are the body of Christ, and members individually. [28]And God has appointed these in the church: first apostles, second prophets, third teachers, after that miracles, then gifts of healings, helps, administrations, varieties of tongues. [29]*Are* all apostles? *Are* all prophets? *Are* all teachers? *Are* all workers of miracles? [30]Do all have gifts

of healings? Do all speak with tongues? Do all interpret? [31]But earnestly desire the best[a] gifts. And yet I show you a more excellent way.

The Greatest Gift

13 Though I speak with the tongues of men and of angels, but have not love, I have become sounding brass or a clanging cymbal. [2]And though I have *the gift of* prophecy, and understand all mysteries and all knowledge, and though I have all faith, so that I could remove mountains, but have not love, I am nothing. [3]And though I bestow all my goods to feed *the poor,* and though I give my body to be burned,[a] but have not love, it profits me nothing.

[4]Love suffers long *and* is kind; love does not envy; love does not parade itself, is not puffed up; [5]does not behave rudely, does not seek its own, is not provoked, thinks no evil; [6]does not rejoice in iniquity, but rejoices in the truth; [7]bears all things, believes all things, hopes all things, endures all things.

[8]Love never fails. But whether *there are* prophecies, they will fail; whether *there are* tongues, they will cease; whether *there is* knowledge, it will vanish away. [9]For we know in part and we prophesy in part. [10]But when that which is perfect has come, then that which is in part will be done away.

[11]When I was a child, I spoke as a child, I understood as a child, I thought as a child; but when I became a man, I put away childish things. [12]For now we see in a mirror, dimly, but then face to face. Now I know in part, but then I shall know just as I also am known.

[13]And now abide faith, hope, love, these three; but the greatest of these *is* love.

Prophecy and Tongues

14 Pursue love, and desire spiritual *gifts,* but especially that you may prophesy. [2]For he who speaks in a tongue does not speak to men but to God, for no one understands *him;* however, in the spirit he speaks mysteries. [3]But he who prophesies speaks edification and exhortation and comfort to men. [4]He who speaks in a tongue edifies himself, but he who prophesies edifies the church. [5]I wish you all spoke with tongues, but even more that you prophesied; for[a] he who prophesies *is* greater than he who speaks with tongues, unless indeed he interprets, that the church may receive edification.

Tongues Must Be Interpreted

[6]But now, brethren, if I come to you speaking with tongues, what shall I profit you unless I speak to you either by revelation, by knowledge, by prophesying, or by teaching? [7]Even things without life, whether flute or harp, when they make a sound, unless they make a distinction in the sounds, how will it be known what is piped or played? [8]For if the trumpet makes an uncertain sound, who will prepare for battle? [9]So likewise you, unless you utter by the tongue words easy to understand, how will it be known what is spoken? For you will be speaking into the air. [10]There are, it may be, so many kinds of languages in the world, and none of them *is* without significance. [11]Therefore, if I do not know the meaning of the language, I shall be a foreigner to him who speaks, and he who speaks *will be* a foreigner to me. [12]Even so you, since you are zealous for spiritual *gifts, let it be* for the edification of the church *that* you seek to excel.

[13]Therefore let him who speaks in a tongue pray that he may interpret. [14]For if I pray in a tongue, my spirit prays, but my understanding is unfruitful. [15]What is *the conclusion* then? I will pray with the spirit, and I will also pray with the understanding. I will sing with the spirit, and I will also sing with the understanding. [16]Otherwise, if you bless with the spirit, how will he who occupies the place of the uninformed say "Amen" at your giving of thanks, since he does not understand what you say? [17]For you indeed give thanks well, but the other is not edified.

[18]I thank my God I speak with tongues more than you all; [19]yet in the church I would rather speak five words with my understanding, that I may teach others also, than ten thousand words in a tongue.

Tongues a Sign to Unbelievers

[20]Brethren, do not be children in understanding; however, in malice be babes, but in understanding be mature. [21]In the law it is written:

"With men of other tongues and other lips I will speak to this people;

And yet, for all that, they will not hear Me,"[a]

says the Lord. [22]Therefore tongues are for a sign, not to those who believe but to unbelievers; but prophesying is not for unbelievers but for those who believe. [23]Therefore if the whole church comes together in one place, and all speak with tongues, and there come in *those who are* uninformed or unbelievers, will they not say that you are out of your mind? [24]But if all prophesy, and an unbeliever or an uninformed person comes in, he is convinced by all, he is convicted by all. [25]And thus[a] the secrets of his heart are revealed; and so, falling down on *his* face, he will worship God and report that God is truly among you.

Order in Church Meetings

[26]How is it then, brethren? Whenever you come together, each of you has a psalm, has a teaching, has a tongue, has a revelation, has an interpretation. Let all things be done for edification. [27]If anyone speaks in a tongue, *let there be* two or at the most three, *each* in turn, and let one interpret. [28]But if there is no interpreter, let him keep silent in church, and let him speak to himself and to God. [29]Let two or three prophets speak, and let the others judge. [30]But if *anything* is revealed to another who sits by, let the first keep silent. [31]For you can all prophesy one by one, that all may learn and all may be encouraged. [32]And the spirits of the prophets are subject to the prophets. [33]For God is not *the author* of

> ### ↘ LEARN
> . . . .
> **14:26** • Paul assumes that followers of Jesus will regularly gather together to encourage one another, to teach one another, to build up each other. Some individuals have good singing voices; some are good teachers; some serve more effectively behind the scenes. But how will people benefit from any of these things if they're not somehow together in one place? How can you *give* something to others as well as *receive* something from others if you're not *with* others? Everyone has something to bring to the table when the church comes together. Know this: You need the church, and the church needs you. *For more about* Fellowship, *see 2 Cor. 6:14;* Loving Others, *2 Cor. 1:3, 4.*

14:21 [a]Isaiah 28:11, 12   **14:25** [a]NU-Text omits *And thus.*

confusion but of peace, as in all the churches of the saints.

[34]Let your[a] women keep silent in the churches, for they are not permitted to speak; but *they are* to be submissive, as the law also says. [35]And if they want to learn something, let them ask their own husbands at home; for it is shameful for women to speak in church.

[36]Or did the word of God come *originally* from you? Or *was it* you only that it reached? [37]If anyone thinks himself to be a prophet or spiritual, let him acknowledge that the things which I write to you are the commandments of the Lord. [38]But if anyone is ignorant, let him be ignorant.[a]

[39]Therefore, brethren, desire earnestly to prophesy, and do not forbid to speak with tongues. [40]Let all things be done decently and in order.

The Risen Christ, Faith's Reality

15 Moreover, brethren, I declare to you the gospel which I preached to you, which also you received and in which you stand, [2]by which also you are saved, if you hold fast that word which I preached to you—unless you believed in vain.

[3]For I delivered to you first of all that which I also received: that Christ died for our sins according to the Scriptures, [4]and that He was buried, and that He rose again the third day according to the Scriptures, [5]and that He was seen by Cephas, then by the twelve. [6]After that He was seen by over five hundred brethren at once, of whom the greater part remain to the present, but some have fallen asleep. [7]After that He was seen by James, then by all the apostles. [8]Then last of all He was seen by me also, as by one born out of due time.

[9]For I am the least of the apostles, who am not worthy to be called an apostle, because I persecuted the church of God. [10]But by the grace of God I am what I am, and His grace toward me was not in vain; but I labored more abundantly than they all, yet not I, but the grace of God *which was* with me. [11]Therefore, whether *it was* I or they, so we preach and so you believed.

The Risen Christ, Our Hope

[12]Now if Christ is preached that He has been raised from the dead, how do some among you say that there is no resurrection of the dead? [13]But if there is no resurrection of the dead, then Christ is not risen. [14]And if Christ is not risen, then our preaching *is* empty and your faith *is* also empty. [15]Yes, and we are found false witnesses of God, because we have testified of God that He raised up Christ, whom He did not raise up—if in fact the dead do not rise. [16]For if *the* dead do not rise, then Christ is not risen. [17]And if Christ is not risen, your faith *is* futile; you are still in your sins! [18]Then also those who have fallen asleep in Christ have perished. [19]If in this life only we have hope in Christ, we are of all men the most pitiable.

The Last Enemy Destroyed

[20]But now Christ is risen from the dead, *and* has become the firstfruits of those who have fallen asleep. [21]For since by man *came* death, by Man also *came* the resurrection of the dead. [22]For as in Adam all die, even so in Christ all shall be made alive. [23]But each one in his own order: Christ the firstfruits, afterward those *who are* Christ's at His coming. [24]Then *comes* the end, when He delivers the kingdom to God the Father, when He puts an end to all rule and all authority and power. [25]For He must reign till He has put all enemies under His feet. [26]The last enemy *that* will be destroyed *is* death. [27]For *"He has put all things under His feet."*[a] But when He says "all things are put under *Him*," *it is* evident that He who put all things under Him is excepted. [28]Now when all things are made subject to Him, then the Son Himself will also be subject to Him who put all things under Him, that God may be all in all.

Effects of Denying the Resurrection

[29]Otherwise, what will they do who are baptized for the dead, if the dead do not rise at all? Why then are they baptized for the dead? [30]And why do we stand in jeopardy every hour? [31]I affirm, by the boasting in you which I have in Christ Jesus our Lord, I die daily. [32]If, in the manner of men, I have fought with beasts at Ephesus, what advantage *is it* to me? If *the* dead do not rise, *"Let us eat and drink, for tomorrow we die!"*[a]

[33]Do not be deceived: "Evil company

---

corrupts good habits." [34]Awake to righteousness, and do not sin; for some do not have the knowledge of God. I speak *this* to your shame.

A Glorious Body

[35]But someone will say, "How are the dead raised up? And with what body do they come?" [36]Foolish one, what you sow is not made alive unless it dies. [37]And what you sow, you do not sow that body that shall be, but mere grain—perhaps wheat or some other *grain.* [38]But God gives it a body as He pleases, and to each seed its own body.

[39]All flesh *is* not the same flesh, but *there is* one *kind of* flesh[a] of men, another flesh of animals, another of fish, *and* another of birds.

[40]*There are* also celestial bodies and terrestrial bodies; but the glory of the celestial *is* one, and the *glory* of the terrestrial *is* another. [41]*There is* one glory of the sun, another glory of the moon, and another glory of the stars; for *one* star differs from *another* star in glory.

[42]So also *is* the resurrection of the dead. *The body* is sown in corruption, it is raised in incorruption. [43]It is sown in dishonor, it is raised in glory. It is sown in weakness, it is raised in power. [44]It is sown a natural body, it is raised a spiritual body. There is a natural body, and there is a spiritual body. [45]And so it is written, *"The first man Adam became a living being."*[a] The last Adam *became* a life-giving spirit.

[46]However, the spiritual is not first, but the natural, and afterward the spiritual. [47]The first man *was* of the earth, *made* of dust; the

second Man *is* the Lord[a] from heaven. [48]As *was* the *man* of dust, so also *are* those *who are made* of dust; and as *is* the heavenly *Man,* so also *are* those *who are* heavenly. [49]And as we have borne the image of the *man* of dust, we shall also bear[a] the image of the heavenly *Man.*

Our Final Victory

[50]Now this I say, brethren, that flesh and blood cannot inherit the kingdom of God; nor does corruption inherit incorruption. [51]Behold, I tell you a mystery: We shall not all sleep, but we shall all be changed— [52]in a moment, in the twinkling of an eye, at the last trumpet. For the trumpet will sound, and the dead will be raised incorruptible, and we shall be changed. [53]For this corruptible must put on incorruption, and this mortal *must* put on immortality. [54]So when this corruptible has put on incorruption, and this mortal has put

→ LIVE

15:42 • We have the great hope that God will one day give us a new, glorified resurrection body. The blueprints are already in the bodies we now possess. Heaven is the earthly life of the believer, glorified and perfected. When we pass over to the other side, our minds and memories will be clearer than ever (1 Cor. 15:43, 44). Our new bodies will in some ways be the same as our old bodies, and in other ways different. But without question, radically improved! No more physical disabilities. No signs of age and no sinful tendencies. Our resurrection bodies will resemble His (1 John 3:2). *For more about* Heaven, *see Col. 3:2.*

15:39 [a]NU-Text and M-Text omit *of flesh.*   15:45 [a]Genesis 2:7   15:47 [a]NU-Text omits *the Lord.*   15:49 [a]M-Text reads *let us also bear.*

↓ KNOW (1 COR. 15:35–58)

One day, God is going to give you a brand new body, related in some way to your existing body. And what will that new body be like? The blueprint for your glorified body is contained in the body you currently possess. It's already there. I know this because the Bible promises these bodies of ours will be resurrected. And so some connection will exist between the old and the new. Heaven is the earthly life of faith, glorified and perfected. When we get to the other side, our minds and our memories will be clearer than they ever have been. That means that our new bodies will in some ways be the same as our old bodies, but at the same time will be markedly different. Without question they will be radically improved! No more physical disabilities. No signs of age. And perhaps best of all, no sinful tendencies. *For more about* Heaven, *see 1 Cor. 15:42;* New Life in Christ, *Gal. 2:16.*

on immortality, then shall be brought to pass the saying that is written: *"Death is swallowed up in victory."*[a]

55 *"O Death, where is your sting?*[a]
O Hades, where is your victory?"[b]

[56]The sting of death *is* sin, and the strength of sin *is* the law. [57]But thanks *be* to God, who gives us the victory through our Lord Jesus Christ.

[58]Therefore, my beloved brethren, be steadfast, immovable, always abounding in the work of the Lord, knowing that your labor is not in vain in the Lord.

> → *Therefore, my beloved brethren, be steadfast, immovable, always abounding in the work of the Lord, knowing that your labor is not in vain in the Lord.* 1 Cor. 15:58

Collection for the Saints

16 Now concerning the collection for the saints, as I have given orders to the churches of Galatia, so you must do also: [2]On the first *day* of the week let each one of you lay something aside, storing up as he may prosper, that there be no collections when I come. [3]And when I come, whomever you approve by *your* letters I will send to bear your gift to Jerusalem. [4]But if it is fitting that I go also, they will go with me.

Personal Plans

[5]Now I will come to you when I pass through Macedonia (for I am passing through Macedonia). [6]And it may be that I will remain, or even spend the winter with you, that you may send me on my journey,

wherever I go. [7]For I do not wish to see you now on the way; but I hope to stay a while with you, if the Lord permits.

[8]But I will tarry in Ephesus until Pentecost. [9]For a great and effective door has opened to me, and *there are* many adversaries.

[10]And if Timothy comes, see that he may be with you without fear; for he does the work of the Lord, as I also *do*. [11]Therefore let no one despise him. But send him on his journey in peace, that he may come to me; for I am waiting for him with the brethren.

[12]Now concerning *our* brother Apollos, I strongly urged him to come to you with the brethren, but he was quite unwilling to come at this time; however, he will come when he has a convenient time.

Final Exhortations

[13]Watch, stand fast in the faith, be brave, be strong. [14]Let all *that* you *do* be done with love.

[15]I urge you, brethren—you know the household of Stephanas, that it is the firstfruits of Achaia, and *that* they have devoted themselves to the ministry of the saints— [16]that you also submit to such, and to everyone who works and labors with *us*.

[17]I am glad about the coming of Stephanas, Fortunatus, and Achaicus, for what was lacking on your part they supplied. [18]For they refreshed my spirit and yours. Therefore acknowledge such men.

Greetings and a Solemn Farewell

[19]The churches of Asia greet you. Aquila and Priscilla greet you heartily in the Lord, with the church that is in their house. [20]All the brethren greet you.

Greet one another with a holy kiss.

[21]The salutation with my own hand—Paul's.

[22]If anyone does not love the Lord Jesus Christ, let him be accursed.[a] O Lord, come![b]

[23]The grace of our Lord Jesus Christ *be* with you. [24]My love *be* with you all in Christ Jesus. Amen.

15:54 [a]Isaiah 25:8   15:55 [a]Hosea 13:14   [b]NU-Text reads *O Death, where is your victory? O Death, where is your sting?*
16:22 [a]Greek *anathema*   [b]Aramaic *Maranatha*

2 CORINTHIANS

INTRODUCTION//

Paul wrote this second letter to the Corinthian church in order to deal with some persistent problems within this fractious congregation. Some of the Corinthians continued to live in sin after Paul's first letter arrived, denying his authority to direct their behavior. Many false teachers in the church, along with those who didn't like what Paul had to say in his first letter, tried to discredit him so that they could live as they pleased. In this letter Paul makes a very personal plea for the people to listen to him. All of his words, he says, flow out of love for them and concern for their souls. He reminds them of the glory and righteousness that comes through the ministry of the faith (3:7–18) and of the rewards that God has promised for faithful obedience (4:1—5:10). Though life is difficult and "we are hard-pressed on every side" (4:8), we have been guaranteed a place in heaven. Paul also gives his personal testimony and explains his theological position, in the hopes that his readers will understand his authority and sincerity. He writes of his suffering for Christ and all that he has endured because of his faith in the truth, and that a greater glory will come from it.

In the middle of his argument for the welfare of the Corinthians, Paul gives some wise counsel on giving in the church. The church is sustained through the gracious, sometimes sacrificial, gifts of its members. Generosity is the key not only to a fruitful church, but to a fruitful life. And here as elsewhere, Jesus provides us with the ultimate example of giving: "For you know the grace of our Lord Jesus Christ, that though He was rich, yet for your sakes He became poor, that you through His poverty might become rich" (8:9).

Greeting

1
Paul, an apostle of Jesus Christ by the will of God, and Timothy *our* brother,

To the church of God which is at Corinth, with all the saints who are in all Achaia:

²Grace to you and peace from God our Father and the Lord Jesus Christ.

Comfort in Suffering

³Blessed *be* the God and Father of our Lord Jesus Christ, the Father of mercies and God of all comfort, ⁴who comforts us in all our tribulation, that we may be able to comfort those who are in any trouble, with the comfort with which we ourselves are comforted by God. ⁵For as the sufferings of Christ abound in us, so our consolation also abounds through Christ. ⁶Now if we are afflicted, *it is* for your consolation and salvation, which is effective for enduring the same sufferings which we also suffer. Or if we are comforted, *it is* for your consolation and salvation. ⁷And our hope for you *is* steadfast, because we know that as you are partakers of the sufferings, so also *you will partake* of the consolation.

↘ LEARN
• • • • • • • • • • • • • • •

1:3, 4 • God sometimes allows events in our lives that do not seem to make sense. But the Lord is in control of all circumstances in the life of a believer. He causes all things to work together for good to those who love Him (Rom. 8:28). When we come through difficulties in life, we then can bring comfort to others who need it. You gain greater credibility in the eyes of the person you are ministering to when you yourself are going through something difficult or have come through it. Allow the Lord to use you to bring much needed comfort to others. *For more about* Adversity, *see Eph. 6:11, 12;* God at Work, *Phil. 2:12;* Loving Others, *2 Cor. 8:7.*

Delivered from Suffering

⁸For we do not want you to be ignorant, brethren, of our trouble which came to us in Asia: that we were burdened beyond measure, above strength, so that we despaired even of life. ⁹Yes, we had the sentence of death in ourselves, that we should not trust

in ourselves but in God who raises the dead, ¹⁰who delivered us from so great a death, and doesª deliver us; in whom we trust that He will still deliver *us*, ¹¹you also helping together in prayer for us, that thanks may be given by many persons on ourª behalf for the gift *granted* to us through many.

Paul's Sincerity

¹²For our boasting is this: the testimony of our conscience that we conducted ourselves in the world in simplicity and godly sincerity, not with fleshly wisdom but by the grace of God, and more abundantly toward you. ¹³For we are not writing any other things to you than what you read or understand. Now I trust you will understand, even to the end ¹⁴(as also you have understood us in part), that we are your boast as you also *are* ours, in the day of the Lord Jesus.

Sparing the Church

¹⁵And in this confidence I intended to come to you before, that you might have a second benefit— ¹⁶to pass by way of you to Macedonia, to come again from Macedonia to you, and be helped by you on my way to Judea. ¹⁷Therefore, when I was planning this, did I do it lightly? Or the things I plan, do I plan according to the flesh, that with me there should be Yes, Yes, and No, No? ¹⁸But *as* God *is* faithful, our word to you was not Yes and No. ¹⁹For the Son of God, Jesus Christ, who was preached among you by us—by me, Silvanus, and Timothy—was not Yes and No, but in Him was Yes. ²⁰For all the promises of God in Him *are* Yes, and in Him Amen, to the glory of God through us. ²¹Now He who establishes us with you in Christ and has anointed us *is* God, ²²who also has sealed us and given us the Spirit in our hearts as a guarantee.

²³Moreover I call God as witness against my soul, that to spare you I came no more to Corinth. ²⁴Not that we have dominion over your faith, but are fellow workers for your joy; for by faith you stand.

2
But I determined this within myself, that I would not come again to you in sorrow. ²For if I make you sorrowful, then who is he who makes me glad but the one who is made sorrowful by me?

1:10 ªNU-Text reads *shall.*   1:11 ªM-Text reads *your behalf.*

→ LIVE
• • • • • • • • • • • • • • • •

1:22 • The Holy Spirit is called the guarantee of our inheritance. It's like putting down cash to hold some item. Perhaps you see something you want to purchase and you are told you must put something down to show good faith. Your deposit holds the purchase for you until you make full payment. In the same way, God wants you to know that He is sincere about redeeming you. He intends to complete His transaction. He won't back down or change His mind. So He gives us the deposit of the Holy Spirit to show us that He means business! *For more about the* Holy Spirit, *see Gal. 5:16;* Assurance of Salvation, *Eph. 4:30.*

Forgive the Offender

³And I wrote this very thing to you, lest, when I came, I should have sorrow over those from whom I ought to have joy, having confidence in you all that my joy is *the joy* of you all. ⁴For out of much affliction and anguish of heart I wrote to you, with many tears, not that you should be grieved, but that you might know the love which I have so abundantly for you.

⁵But if anyone has caused grief, he has not grieved me, but all of you to some extent—not to be too severe. ⁶This punishment which *was inflicted* by the majority *is* sufficient for such a man, ⁷so that, on the contrary, you *ought* rather to forgive and comfort *him,* lest perhaps such a one be swallowed up with too much sorrow. ⁸Therefore I urge you to reaffirm *your* love to him. ⁹For to this end I also wrote, that I might put you to the test, whether you are obedient in all things. ¹⁰Now whom you forgive anything, I also *forgive.* For if indeed I have forgiven anything, I have forgiven that one[a] for your sakes in the presence of Christ, ¹¹lest Satan should take advantage of us; for we are not ignorant of his devices.

Triumph in Christ

¹²Furthermore, when I came to Troas to *preach* Christ's gospel, and a door was opened to me by the Lord, ¹³I had no rest in my spirit, because I did not find Titus my brother; but taking my leave of them, I departed for Macedonia.

¹⁴Now thanks *be* to God who always leads us in triumph in Christ, and through us diffuses the fragrance of His knowledge in every place. ¹⁵For we are to God the fragrance of Christ among those who are being saved and among those who are perishing. ¹⁶To the one *we are* the aroma of death *leading* to death, and to the other the aroma of life *leading* to life. And who *is* sufficient for these things? ¹⁷For we are not, as so many,[a] peddling the word of God; but as of sincerity, but as from God, we speak in the sight of God in Christ.

Christ's Epistle

3 Do we begin again to commend ourselves? Or do we need, as some *others,* epistles of commendation to you or *letters* of commendation from you? ²You are our epistle written in our hearts, known and read by all men; ³clearly you are an epistle of Christ, ministered by us, written not with ink but by the Spirit of the living God, not on tablets of stone but on tablets of flesh, *that is,* of the heart.

2:10 [a]NU-Text reads *For indeed, what I have forgiven, if I have forgiven anything, I did it.*   **2:17** [a]M-Text reads *the rest.*

↑ GROW (2 COR. 3:2)
• •

The Bible likens Christians to walking epistles, written by God and read by men. You are the only Bible some people will ever read—and make no mistake, they *will* watch you. Closely. Some just want to see you fail spiritually, but others secretly hope to see some reality in your walk of faith. When the first-century church remembered this and lived like it, its members turned their world upside down; and by not living in this way, the twenty-first-century church is *not* turning its world upside down. Far too often, it seems like our world is turning us upside down. Frankly, we have too many fair-weather followers and too few genuine disciples. Never forget that *your* life speaks volumes to people who as yet have no interest in cracking open a Bible. The question is what are you saying? Make up your mind to be a faithful representative of Jesus Christ in this mixed-up culture. Remember, you are being watched! *For more about* Sharing Your Faith, *see 2 Tim. 1:8.*

The Spirit, Not the Letter

[4]And we have such trust through Christ toward God. [5]Not that we are sufficient of ourselves to think of anything as *being* from ourselves, but our sufficiency *is* from God, [6]who also made us sufficient as ministers of the new covenant, not of the letter but of the Spirit;[a] for the letter kills, but the Spirit gives life.

Glory of the New Covenant

[7]But if the ministry of death, written *and* engraved on stones, was glorious, so that the children of Israel could not look steadily at the face of Moses because of the glory of his countenance, which *glory* was passing away, [8]how will the ministry of the Spirit not be more glorious? [9]For if the ministry of condemnation *had* glory, the ministry of righteousness exceeds much more in glory. [10]For even what was made glorious had no glory in this respect, because of the glory that excels. [11]For if what is passing away *was* glorious, what remains *is* much more glorious.

[12]Therefore, since we have such hope, we use great boldness of speech— [13]unlike Moses, *who* put a veil over his face so that the children of Israel could not look steadily at the end of what was passing away. [14]But their minds were blinded. For until this day the same veil remains unlifted in the reading of the Old Testament, because the *veil* is taken away in Christ. [15]But even to this day, when Moses is read, a veil lies on their heart. [16]Nevertheless when one turns to the Lord, the veil is taken away. [17]Now the Lord is the Spirit; and where the Spirit of the Lord *is,* there *is* liberty. [18]But we all, with unveiled face, beholding as in a mirror the glory of the Lord, are being transformed into the same image from glory to glory, just as by the Spirit of the Lord.

The Light of Christ's Gospel

4 Therefore, since we have this ministry, as we have received mercy, we do not lose heart. [2]But we have renounced the hidden things of shame, not walking in craftiness nor handling the word of God deceitfully, but by manifestation of the truth commending ourselves to every man's conscience in the sight of God. [3]But even if our gospel is veiled, it is veiled to those who are perishing, [4]whose minds the god of this age has blinded, who do not believe, lest the light of the gospel of the glory of Christ, who is the image of God, should shine on them. [5]For we do not preach ourselves, but Christ Jesus the Lord, and ourselves your bondservants for Jesus' sake. [6]For it is the God who commanded light to shine out of darkness, who has shone in our hearts to *give* the light of the knowledge of the glory of God in the face of Jesus Christ.

Cast Down but Unconquered

[7]But we have this treasure in earthen vessels, that the excellence of the power may be of God and not of us. [8]*We are* hard-pressed on every side, yet not crushed; *we are* perplexed, but not in despair; [9]persecuted, but not forsaken; struck down, but not destroyed— [10]always carrying about in the body the dying of the Lord Jesus, that the life of Jesus also may be manifested in our body. [11]For we who live are always delivered to death for Jesus' sake, that the life of Jesus also may be manifested in our mortal flesh. [12]So then death is working in us, but life in you.

[13]And since we have the same spirit of faith, according to what is written, *"I believed and therefore I spoke,"*[a] we also believe and therefore speak, [14]knowing that He who raised up the Lord Jesus will also raise us up with Jesus, and will present *us* with you. [15]For all things *are* for your sakes, that grace, having spread through the many, may cause thanksgiving to abound to the glory of God.

Seeing the Invisible

[16]Therefore we do not lose heart. Even though our outward man is perishing, yet the inward *man* is being renewed day by day. [17]For our light affliction, which is but for a moment, is working for us a far more exceeding *and* eternal weight of glory, [18]while we do not look at the things which are seen, but at the things which are not seen. For the things which are seen *are* temporary, but the things which are not seen *are* eternal.

Assurance of the Resurrection

5 For we know that if our earthly house, *this* tent, is destroyed, we have a building from God, a house not made with hands,

3:6 [a]Or *spirit*   **4:13** [a]Psalm 116:10

eternal in the heavens. [2]For in this we groan, earnestly desiring to be clothed with our habitation which is from heaven, [3]if indeed, having been clothed, we shall not be found naked. [4]For we who are in *this* tent groan, being burdened, not because we want to be unclothed, but further clothed, that mortality may be swallowed up by life. [5]Now He who has prepared us for this very thing *is* God, who also has given us the Spirit as a guarantee.

➤ *For we walk by faith, not by sight.* 2 Cor. 5:7

[6]So *we are* always confident, knowing that while we are at home in the body we are absent from the Lord. [7]For we walk by faith, not by sight. [8]We are confident, yes, well pleased rather to be absent from the body and to be present with the Lord.

> ↘ **LEARN**
> ● ● ● ● ● ● ● ● ● ● ● ● ● ● ● ● ●
>
> 5:7 • What does it mean to "walk by faith, not by sight"? Does it mean you close your eyes to reality? Does it mean you turn off your brain? Hardly. In essence, it means that you entrust your whole life into the hands of Jesus, whom you cannot see. You make your plans, commit them to God in prayer, and then step out in faith, confident that Jesus will be with you, guiding you every step of the way. Just make sure to immerse yourself in the Word of God so you will have a clear biblical grid by which to make your decisions. Never be afraid to commit an unknown future to a known God. *For more about* Faith, *see Gal 3:3.*

The Judgment Seat of Christ

[9]Therefore we make it our aim, whether present or absent, to be well pleasing to Him. [10]For we must all appear before the judgment seat of Christ, that each one may receive the things *done* in the body, according to what he has done, whether good or bad. [11]Knowing, therefore, the terror of the Lord, we persuade men; but we are well known to God, and I also trust are well known in your consciences.

Be Reconciled to God

[12]For we do not commend ourselves again to you, but give you opportunity to boast on our behalf, that you may have *an answer* for those who boast in appearance and not in heart. [13]For if we are beside ourselves, *it is* for God; or if we are of sound mind, *it is* for you. [14]For the love of Christ compels us, because we judge thus: that if One died for all, then all died; [15]and He died for all, that those who live should live no longer for themselves, but for Him who died for them and rose again.

[16]Therefore, from now on, we regard no one according to the flesh. Even though we have known Christ according to the flesh, yet now we know *Him thus* no longer. [17]Therefore, if anyone *is* in Christ, *he is* a new creation; old things have passed away; behold, all things have become new. [18]Now all things *are* of God, who has reconciled us to Himself through Jesus Christ, and has given us the ministry of reconciliation, [19]that is, that God was in Christ reconciling the world to Himself, not imputing their trespasses to them, and has committed to us the word of reconciliation.

➤ *Therefore, if anyone is in Christ, he is a new creation; old things have passed away; behold, all things have become new.* 2 Cor. 5:17

[20]Now then, we are ambassadors for Christ, as though God were pleading through us: we implore *you* on Christ's behalf, be reconciled to God. [21]For He made Him who knew no sin *to be* sin for us, that we might become the righteousness of God in Him.

Marks of the Ministry

6 We then, *as* workers together *with Him* also plead with *you* not to receive the grace of God in vain. [2]For He says:

"In an acceptable time I have heard you,
And in the day of salvation I have helped you."[a]

Behold, now *is* the accepted time; behold, now *is* the day of salvation.

[3]We give no offense in anything, that our ministry may not be blamed. [4]But in all *things* we commend ourselves as ministers of God: in much patience, in tribulations, in needs, in distresses, [5]in stripes, in imprisonments, in tumults, in labors, in sleeplessness, in fastings; [6]by purity, by knowledge, by longsuffering, by kindness, by the Holy Spirit, by sincere love, [7]by the word of truth, by the power of God, by the armor of righteousness on the right hand and on the left, [8]by honor and dishonor, by evil report and good report; as deceivers, and *yet* true; [9]as unknown, and *yet* well known; as dying, and behold we live; as chastened, and *yet* not killed; [10]as sorrowful, yet always rejoicing; as poor, yet making many rich; as having nothing, and *yet* possessing all things.

Be Holy

[11]O Corinthians! We have spoken openly to you, our heart is wide open. [12]You are not restricted by us, but you are restricted by your *own* affections. [13]Now in return for the same (I speak as to children), you also be open.

[14]Do not be unequally yoked together with unbelievers. For what fellowship has righteousness with lawlessness? And what communion has light with darkness? [15]And what accord has Christ with Belial? Or what part has a believer with an unbeliever? [16]And what agreement has the temple of God with idols? For you[a] are the temple of the living God. As God has said:

> "I will dwell in them
> And walk among them.

↘ LEARN
• • • • • • • • • • • • • • •

6:14 • Many of us get into serious trouble when we ignore one of the simplest rules of the Christian life: "Do not be unequally yoked together with unbelievers." A yoke is a steering device used to direct a work animal. If you were to yoke a live animal with a dead one, in what direction do you think the cart would go? Something similar happens when a follower of Christ yokes himself to a nonbeliever (Eph. 2:5). It is far easier for a believer to go backward spiritually (we still have an old nature) than it is for a nonbeliever (without a new nature) to go forward. Avoid this often deadly trap. *For more about Fellowship, see Col. 1:9.*

> I will be their God,
> And they shall be My people."[b]

[17]Therefore

> "Come out from among them
> And be separate, says the Lord.
> Do not touch what is unclean,
> And I will receive you."[a]
> [18]"I will be a Father to you,
> And you shall be My sons and daughters,
> Says the LORD Almighty."[a]

7 Therefore, having these promises, beloved, let us cleanse ourselves from all filthiness of the flesh and spirit, perfecting holiness in the fear of God.

The Corinthians' Repentance

[2]Open *your hearts* to us. We have wronged no one, we have corrupted no one, we have cheated no one. [3]I do not say *this* to condemn; for I have said before that you are in our hearts, to die together and to live together. [4]Great *is* my boldness of speech toward you, great *is* my boasting on your behalf. I am filled with comfort. I am exceedingly joyful in all our tribulation.

[5]For indeed, when we came to Macedonia, our bodies had no rest, but we were troubled on every side. Outside *were* conflicts, inside *were* fears. [6]Nevertheless God, who comforts the downcast, comforted us by the coming of Titus, [7]and not only by his coming, but also by the consolation with which he was comforted in you, when he told us of your earnest desire, your mourning, your zeal for me, so that I rejoiced even more.

[8]For even if I made you sorry with my letter, I do not regret it; though I did regret it. For I perceive that the same epistle made you sorry, though only for a while. [9]Now I rejoice, not that you were made sorry, but that your sorrow led to repentance. For you were made sorry in a godly manner, that you might suffer loss from us in nothing. [10]For godly sorrow produces repentance *leading* to salvation, not to be regretted; but the sorrow of the world produces death. [11]For observe this very thing, that you sorrowed in a godly manner: What diligence it produced in you, *what* clearing *of yourselves, what* indignation, *what* fear, *what* vehement desire, *what* zeal,

what vindication! In all *things* you proved yourselves to be clear in this matter. [12]Therefore, although I wrote to you, *I did* not *do it* for the sake of him who had done the wrong, nor for the sake of him who suffered wrong, but that our care for you in the sight of God might appear to you.

The Joy of Titus

[13]Therefore we have been comforted in your comfort. And we rejoiced exceedingly more for the joy of Titus, because his spirit has been refreshed by you all. [14]For if in anything I have boasted to him about you, I am not ashamed. But as we spoke all things to you in truth, even so our boasting to Titus was found true. [15]And his affections are greater for you as he remembers the obedience of you all, how with fear and trembling you received him. [16]Therefore I rejoice that I have confidence in you in everything.

Excel in Giving

8 Moreover, brethren, we make known to you the grace of God bestowed on the churches of Macedonia: [2]that in a great trial of affliction the abundance of their joy and their deep poverty abounded in the riches of their liberality. [3]For I bear witness that according to *their* ability, yes, and beyond *their* ability, *they were* freely willing, [4]imploring us with much urgency that we would receive[a] the gift and the fellowship of the ministering to the saints. [5]And not *only* as we had hoped, but they first gave themselves to the Lord, and *then* to us by the will of God. [6]So we urged Titus, that as he had begun, so he would also complete this grace in you as well. [7]But as you abound in everything—in faith, in speech, in knowledge, in all diligence, and in your love for us—*see* that you abound in this grace also.

Christ Our Pattern

[8]I speak not by commandment, but I am testing the sincerity of your love by the diligence of others. [9]For you know the grace of our Lord Jesus Christ, that though He was rich, yet for your sakes He became poor, that you through His poverty might become rich.

↘ LEARN

8:7 • God loves it when we use some of the resources He has given us to meet the needs of His people and of His church. That's why Paul wanted his friends in Corinth to "abound" in what he called the "grace" of giving. The apostle did not command them to give, but he did say that their freely-offered gifts amounted to a test of their love for Christ (v. 8). Our checkbooks tend to reflect what's in our hearts. A tight fist generally does not lead to a growing spirit. Remember, you can never out-give God. *For more about* Loving Others, *see Gal. 5:22;* Spiritual Disciplines, *2 Cor. 10:5.*

[10]And in this I give advice: It is to your advantage not only to be doing what you began and were desiring to do a year ago; [11]but now you also must complete the doing *of it;* that as *there was* a readiness to desire *it,* so *there* also *may be* a completion out of what *you* have. [12]For if there is first a willing mind, *it is* accepted according to what one has, *and* not according to what he does not have. [13]For *I do* not *mean* that others should be eased and you burdened; [14]but by an equality, *that* now at this time your abundance *may supply* their lack, that their abundance also may *supply* your lack—that there may be equality. [15]As it is written, *"He who gathered much had nothing left over, and he who gathered little had no lack."*[a]

Collection for the Judean Saints

[16]But thanks *be* to God who puts[a] the same earnest care for you into the heart of Titus. [17]For he not only accepted the exhortation, but being more diligent, he went to you of his own accord. [18]And we have sent with him the brother whose praise *is* in the gospel throughout all the churches, [19]and not only *that,* but who was also chosen by the churches to travel with us with this gift, which is administered by us to the glory of the Lord Himself and *to show* your ready mind, [20]avoiding this: that anyone should blame us in this lavish gift which is administered by us— [21]providing honorable things, not only in the sight of the Lord, but also in the sight of men. [22]And we have sent with them our brother whom we have often proved diligent in many things, but now much more diligent, because

8:4 [a]NU-Text and M-Text omit *that we would receive,* thus changing text to *urgency for the favor and fellowship....*
8:15 [a]Exodus 16:18   8:16 [a]NU-Text reads *has put.*

of the great confidence which *we have* in you. [23]If *anyone inquires* about Titus, *he is* my partner and fellow worker concerning you. Or if our brethren *are inquired about, they are* messengers of the churches, the glory of Christ. [24]Therefore show to them, and[a] before the churches, the proof of your love and of our boasting on your behalf.

Administering the Gift

9 Now concerning the ministering to the saints, it is superfluous for me to write to you; [2]for I know your willingness, about which I boast of you to the Macedonians, that Achaia was ready a year ago; and your zeal has stirred up the majority. [3]Yet I have sent the brethren, lest our boasting of you should be in vain in this respect, that, as I said, you may be ready; [4]lest if *some* Macedonians come with me and find you unprepared, we (not to mention you!) should be ashamed of this confident boasting.[a] [5]Therefore I thought it necessary to exhort the brethren to go to you ahead of time, and prepare your generous gift beforehand, which *you had* previously promised, that it may be ready as *a matter of* generosity and not as a grudging obligation.

The Cheerful Giver

[6]But this *I say:* He who sows sparingly will also reap sparingly, and he who sows bountifully will also reap bountifully. [7]*So let* each one *give* as he purposes in his heart, not grudgingly or of necessity; for God loves a cheerful giver. [8]And God *is* able to make all grace abound toward you, that you, always having all sufficiency in all *things,* may have an abundance for every good work. [9]As it is written:

"He has dispersed abroad,
He has given to the poor;
His righteousness endures forever."[a]

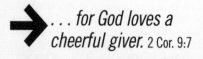

... for God loves a cheerful giver. 2 Cor. 9:7

[10]Now may[a] He who supplies seed to the sower, and bread for food, supply and multiply the seed you have *sown* and increase the fruits of your righteousness, [11]while *you are* enriched in everything for all liberality, which causes thanksgiving through us to God. [12]For the administration of this service not only supplies the needs of the saints, but also is abounding through many thanksgivings to God, [13]while, through the proof of this ministry, they glorify God for the obedience of your confession to the gospel of Christ, and for *your* liberal sharing with them and all *men,* [14]and by their prayer for you, who long for you because of the exceeding grace of God in you. [15]Thanks *be* to God for His indescribable gift!

The Spiritual War

10 Now I, Paul, myself am pleading with you by the meekness and gentleness of Christ—who in presence *am* lowly among you, but being absent am bold toward you. [2]But I beg *you* that when I am present I may not be bold with that confidence by which I intend to be bold against some, who think of us as if we walked according to the flesh. [3]For though we walk in the flesh, we do not war according to the flesh. [4]For the weapons of our warfare *are* not carnal but mighty in God for pulling down strongholds, [5]casting down arguments and every high thing that exalts itself against the knowledge of God, bringing every thought into captivity to the obedience of Christ, [6]and being ready to punish all disobedience when your obedience is fulfilled.

↘ LEARN

10:5 • The mind is the battlefield where we both win and lose spiritual wars. We don't normally just fall off a cliff when we commit some sin; instead we choose to entertain one little impure thought after another until we wind up on a crooked path that ends abruptly at the edge of the Grand Canyon. So Paul instructs us to bring "*every* thought into captivity to the obedience of Christ." It doesn't matter how little the thought may be or how insignificant it seems. Disciplined training of the mind leads away from the canyon and toward the mountaintop of God's best. *For more about* Spiritual Disciplines, *see Eph. 1:17;* Sin, *Gal. 2:16;* How to Live Out Your Faith, *Phil. 2:12.*

8:24 [a]NU-Text and M-Text omit *and.*   9:4 [a]NU-Text reads *this confidence.*   9:9 [a]Psalm 112:9
9:10 [a]NU-Text reads *Now He who supplies . . . will supply. . . .*

Reality of Paul's Authority

[7]Do you look at things according to the outward appearance? If anyone is convinced in himself that he is Christ's, let him again consider this in himself, that just as he *is* Christ's, even so we *are* Christ's.[a] [8]For even if I should boast somewhat more about our authority, which the Lord gave us[a] for edification and not for your destruction, I shall not be ashamed— [9]lest I seem to terrify you by letters. [10]"For *his* letters," they say, "*are* weighty and powerful, but *his* bodily presence *is* weak, and *his* speech contemptible." [11]Let such a person consider this, that what we are in word by letters when we are absent, such *we will* also *be* in deed when we are present.

Limits of Paul's Authority

[12]For we dare not class ourselves or compare ourselves with those who commend themselves. But they, measuring themselves by themselves, and comparing themselves among themselves, are not wise. [13]We, however, will not boast beyond measure, but within the limits of the sphere which God appointed us—a sphere which especially includes you. [14]For we are not overextending ourselves (as though *our authority* did not extend to you), for it was to you that we came with the gospel of Christ; [15]not boasting of things beyond measure, *that is,* in other men's labors, but having hope, *that* as your faith is increased, we shall be greatly enlarged by you in our sphere, [16]to preach the gospel in the *regions* beyond you, *and* not to boast in another man's sphere of accomplishment.

[17]But *"he who glories, let him glory in the* LORD.*"*[a] [18]For not he who commends himself is approved, but whom the Lord commends.

Concern for Their Faithfulness

11 Oh, that you would bear with me in a little folly—and indeed you do bear with me. [2]For I am jealous for you with godly jealousy. For I have betrothed you to one husband, that I may present *you* as a chaste virgin to Christ. [3]But I fear, lest somehow, as the serpent deceived Eve by his craftiness, so your minds may be corrupted from the simplicity[a] that is in Christ. [4]For if he who comes preaches another Jesus whom we have not preached, or *if* you receive a different spirit which you have not received, or a different gospel which you have not accepted—you may well put up with it!

Paul and False Apostles

[5]For I consider that I am not at all inferior to the most eminent apostles. [6]Even though *I am* untrained in speech, yet *I am* not in knowledge. But we have been thoroughly manifested[a] among you in all things.

[7]Did I commit sin in humbling myself that you might be exalted, because I preached the gospel of God to you free of charge? [8]I robbed other churches, taking wages *from them* to minister to you. [9]And when I was present with you, and in need, I was a burden to no one, for what I lacked the brethren who came from Macedonia supplied. And in everything

10:7 [a]NU-Text reads *even as we are.*   **10:8** [a]NU-Text omits *us.*   **10:17** [a]Jeremiah 9:24   **11:3** [a]NU-Text adds *and purity.*
11:6 [a]NU-Text omits *been.*

↑ GROW (2 COR. 10:5)
....

Every day we are barraged with temptations contrary to Scripture. We hear and see things that try to lure us away from Jesus. We must learn how to process information, how to think and live biblically as we develop a Christian worldview. We cannot afford to let our minds and imaginations wander. We must take what we hear and compare it to the clear teaching of Scripture. We have to learn how to think critically in line with the teachings of the Bible. Sometimes, for example, fear and anxiety can put us in their grip, as we foolishly play the "what if" game so popular in our culture: "What if this happens? What if that happens?" We must trust in the Lord, especially as we lie down to sleep at night. He promises to keep us in peace as we do so (Is. 26:3). God works the night shift! *For more about* How to Live Out Your Faith, *see Gal. 6:7, 8.*

I kept myself from being burdensome to you, and so I will keep *myself*. [10]As the truth of Christ is in me, no one shall stop me from this boasting in the regions of Achaia. [11]Why? Because I do not love you? God knows!

[12]But what I do, I will also continue to do, that I may cut off the opportunity from those who desire an opportunity to be regarded just as we are in the things of which they boast. [13]For such *are* false apostles, deceitful workers, transforming themselves into apostles of Christ. [14]And no wonder! For Satan himself transforms himself into an angel of light. [15]Therefore *it is* no great thing if his ministers also transform themselves into ministers of righteousness, whose end will be according to their works.

Reluctant Boasting

[16]I say again, let no one think me a fool. If otherwise, at least receive me as a fool, that I also may boast a little. [17]What I speak, I speak not according to the Lord, but as it were, foolishly, in this confidence of boasting. [18]Seeing that many boast according to the flesh, I also will boast. [19]For you put up with fools gladly, since you *yourselves* are wise! [20]For you put up with it if one brings you into bondage, if one devours *you*, if one takes *from you*, if one exalts himself, if one strikes you on the face. [21]To *our* shame I say that we were too weak for that! But in whatever anyone is bold— I speak foolishly—I am bold also.

Suffering for Christ

[22]Are they Hebrews? So *am* I. Are they Israelites? So *am* I. Are they the seed of Abraham? So *am* I. [23]Are they ministers of Christ?—I speak as a fool—I *am* more: in labors more abundant, in stripes above measure, in prisons more frequently, in deaths often. [24]From the Jews five times I received forty *stripes* minus one. [25]Three times I was beaten with rods; once I was stoned; three times I was shipwrecked; a night and a day I have been in the deep; [26]*in* journeys often, *in* perils of waters, *in* perils of robbers, *in* perils of *my own* countrymen, *in* perils of the Gentiles, *in* perils in the city, *in* perils in the wilderness, *in* perils in the sea, *in* perils among false brethren; [27]in weariness and toil, in sleeplessness often, in hunger and thirst, in fastings often, in cold and nakedness— [28]besides the other things, what comes upon me daily: my deep concern for all the churches. [29]Who is weak, and I am not weak? Who is made to stumble, and I do not burn *with indignation?*

[30]If I must boast, I will boast in the things which concern my infirmity. [31]The God and Father of our Lord Jesus Christ, who is blessed forever, knows that I am not lying. [32]In Damascus the governor, under Aretas the king, was guarding the city of the Damascenes with a garrison, desiring to arrest me; [33]but I was let down in a basket through a window in the wall, and escaped from his hands.

The Vision of Paradise

12 It is doubtless[a] not profitable for me to boast. I will come to visions and revelations of the Lord: [2]I know a man in Christ who fourteen years ago—whether in the body I do not know, or whether out of the body I do not know, God knows—such a one was caught up to the third heaven. [3]And I know such a man— whether in the body or out of the body I do not know, God knows— [4]how he was caught up into Paradise and heard inexpressible words, which it is not lawful for a man to utter. [5]Of such a one I will boast; yet of myself I will not boast, except in my infirmities. [6]For though I might desire to boast, I will not be a fool; for I will speak the truth. But I refrain, lest anyone should think of me above what he sees me *to be* or hears from me.

The Thorn in the Flesh

[7]And lest I should be exalted above measure by the abundance of the revelations, a thorn in the flesh was given to me, a messenger of Satan to buffet me, lest I be exalted above measure. [8]Concerning this thing I pleaded with the Lord three times that it might depart from me. [9]And He said to me, "My grace is sufficient for you, for My strength is made perfect in weakness." Therefore most gladly I will rather boast in my infirmities, that the power of Christ may rest upon me. [10]Therefore I take pleasure in infirmities, in reproaches, in needs, in

12:1 [a]NU-Text reads *necessary, though not profitable, to boast.*

persecutions, in distresses, for Christ's sake. For when I am weak, then I am strong.

Signs of an Apostle

[11]I have become a fool in boasting;[a] you have compelled me. For I ought to have been commended by you; for in nothing was I behind the most eminent apostles, though I am nothing. [12]Truly the signs of an apostle were accomplished among you with all perseverance, in signs and wonders and mighty deeds. [13]For what is it in which you were inferior to other churches, except that I myself was not burdensome to you? Forgive me this wrong!

Love for the Church

[14]Now *for* the third time I am ready to come to you. And I will not be burdensome to you; for I do not seek yours, but you. For the children ought not to lay up for the parents, but the parents for the children. [15]And I will very gladly spend and be spent for your souls; though the more abundantly I love you, the less I am loved.

[16]But be that *as it may,* I did not burden you. Nevertheless, being crafty, I caught you by cunning! [17]Did I take advantage of you by any of those whom I sent to you? [18]I urged Titus, and sent our brother with *him.* Did Titus take advantage of you? Did we not walk in the same spirit? Did *we* not *walk* in the same steps?

[19]Again, do you think[a] that we excuse ourselves to you? We speak before God in Christ. But *we do* all things, beloved, for your edification. [20]For I fear lest, when I come, I shall not find you such as I wish, and *that* I shall be found by you such as you do not wish; lest *there be* contentions, jealousies, outbursts of wrath, selfish ambitions, backbitings, whisperings, conceits, tumults; [21]lest, when I come again, my God will humble me among you, and I shall mourn for many who have sinned before and have not repented of the uncleanness, fornication, and lewdness which they have practiced.

Coming with Authority

13 This *will be* the third *time* I am coming to you. *"By the mouth of two or three witnesses every word shall be established."*[a] [2]I have told you before, and foretell as if I were present the second time, and now being absent I write[a] to those who have sinned before, and to all the rest, that if I come again I will not spare— [3]since you seek a proof of Christ speaking in me, who is not weak toward you, but mighty in you. [4]For though He was crucified in weakness, yet He lives by the power of God. For we also are weak in Him, but we shall live with Him by the power of God toward you.

[5]Examine yourselves *as to* whether you are in the faith. Test yourselves. Do you not know yourselves, that Jesus Christ is in you?—unless indeed you are disqualified. [6]But I trust that you will know that we are not disqualified.

Paul Prefers Gentleness

[7]Now I[a] pray to God that you do no evil, not that we should appear approved, but that

---

12:11 [a]NU-Text omits *in boasting.*   12:19 [a]NU-Text reads *You have been thinking for a long time....*   13:1 [a]Deuteronomy 19:15
13:2 [a]NU-Text omits *I write.*   13:7 [a]NU-Text reads *we.*

↓ KNOW (2 COR. 13:14)
••

Not only is God holy, but He also is loving. "God is love" (1 John 4:8, 16). He does not merely have love, nor is He merely loving, but God is Himself love. He is not the shallow Hollywood version of love; God's love for us is not fickle. It does not depend on how attractive we are or even how well we perform. His love does not change. His love never ends. And God doesn't merely talk about love; He has demonstrated it to us in the most powerful way possible, for the Scripture says, "While we were still sinners, Christ died for us" (Rom. 5:8). There is no greater demonstration of love. Through the dual attributes of holiness and love, we can get glimpses of *all* the attributes of God. In His holiness He is unapproachable. In His love He approaches us. God is holy. And God is love. *For more about the* Attributes of God, *see Eph. 1:5;* God's Love, *Gal. 4:6.*

you should do what is honorable, though we may seem disqualified. [8]For we can do nothing against the truth, but for the truth. [9]For we are glad when we are weak and you are strong. And this also we pray, that you may be made complete. [10]Therefore I write these things being absent, lest being present I should use sharpness, according to the authority which the Lord has given me for edification and not for destruction.

Greetings and Benediction

[11]Finally, brethren, farewell. Become complete. Be of good comfort, be of one mind, live in peace; and the God of love and peace will be with you.

[12]Greet one another with a holy kiss.

[13]All the saints greet you.

[14]The grace of the Lord Jesus Christ, and the love of God, and the communion of the Holy Spirit *be* with you all. Amen.

GALATIANS ↙

INTRODUCTION//

The foundational study of Galatians shows us how the work of Jesus' death on the Cross provides us with everything we need for salvation. Many early Jewish Christians had grown confused about the role of Gentiles in Christianity, and so a radical sect called the Judaizers taught that no Gentile could be saved without also adhering to the Jewish law. Paul counters that by continuing to follow the law, these Judaizers were in fact negating the grace of God. If the law were the most important thing in salvation, Paul insists, then Christ died for nothing and the new covenant is nullified. Rather, the law exists to show us our sin and "to bring us to Christ, that we might be justified by faith. But after faith has come, we are no longer under a tutor," which is the law (3:24, 25). Paul says that we did not receive the Holy Spirit because we followed the law, but because we believed in Christ—so why should we think that we would continue to be saved through keeping the law?

Christ's death freed us from the constraints of the law, something we should celebrate. We are no longer bound to a code that prescribes death, but can live to the full in Christ. Paul reminds us, however, not to waste our freedom on a sinful life, but to use it to glorify the Lord and live according His holy will. If we live in such a way, we will begin to show the fruit of the Spirit (5:22, 23). The grace of God is sufficient for our salvation and bestows upon us the life God meant us to live. Nothing needs to be added to the work of Jesus, nor does it need to be improved. You simply can't improve upon perfection.

Greeting

1
Paul, an apostle (not from men nor through man, but through Jesus Christ and God the Father who raised Him from the dead), [2]and all the brethren who are with me,

To the churches of Galatia:

[3]Grace to you and peace from God the Father and our Lord Jesus Christ, [4]who gave Himself for our sins, that He might deliver us from this present evil age, according to the will of our God and Father, [5]to whom *be* glory forever and ever. Amen.

Only One Gospel

[6]I marvel that you are turning away so soon from Him who called you in the grace of Christ, to a different gospel, [7]which is not another; but there are some who trouble you and want to pervert the gospel of Christ. [8]But even if we, or an angel from heaven, preach any other gospel to you than what we have preached to you, let him be accursed. [9]As we have said before, so now I say again, if anyone preaches any other gospel to you than what you have received, let him be accursed.

↘ LEARN
• • • • • • • • • • • • • •

1:8 • Only one gospel brings eternal life, and that's the one that proclaims the death and resurrection of Jesus Christ as the basis of salvation for all who place their trust in Him. No one who tries to build on a foundation other than this can grow spiritually, let alone find an eternal home in heaven. Paul considered this teaching such an essential truth that he called "accursed" anyone who embraced a different version of the Good News. That's serious business! Times change, people change, opinions change, fashions and fads change—but the gospel of Jesus Christ remains the same forever. *For more about* Becoming a Christian, *see Gal. 3:3;* God's Word, *Eph. 1:17.*

[10]For do I now persuade men, or God? Or do I seek to please men? For if I still pleased men, I would not be a bondservant of Christ.

Call to Apostleship

[11]But I make known to you, brethren, that the gospel which was preached by me is not

according to man. [12]For I neither received it from man, nor was I taught *it,* but *it came* through the revelation of Jesus Christ.

[13]For you have heard of my former conduct in Judaism, how I persecuted the church of God beyond measure and *tried to* destroy it. [14]And I advanced in Judaism beyond many of my contemporaries in my own nation, being more exceedingly zealous for the traditions of my fathers.

[15]But when it pleased God, who separated me from my mother's womb and called *me* through His grace, [16]to reveal His Son in me, that I might preach Him among the Gentiles, I did not immediately confer with flesh and blood, [17]nor did I go up to Jerusalem to those *who were* apostles before me; but I went to Arabia, and returned again to Damascus.

Contacts at Jerusalem

[18]Then after three years I went up to Jerusalem to see Peter,[a] and remained with him fifteen days. [19]But I saw none of the other apostles except James, the Lord's brother. [20](Now *concerning* the things which I write to you, indeed, before God, I do not lie.) [21]Afterward I went into the regions of Syria and Cilicia. [22]And I was unknown by face to the churches of Judea which *were* in Christ. [23]But they were hearing only, "He who formerly persecuted us now preaches the faith which he once *tried to* destroy." [24]And they glorified God in me.

Defending the Gospel

2
Then after fourteen years I went up again to Jerusalem with Barnabas, and also took Titus with *me.* [2]And I went up by revelation, and communicated to them that gospel which I preach among the Gentiles, but privately to those who were of reputation, lest by any means I might run, or had run, in vain. [3]Yet not even Titus who *was* with me, being a Greek, was compelled to be circumcised. [4]And *this occurred* because of false brethren secretly brought in (who came in by stealth to spy out our liberty which we have in Christ Jesus, that they might bring us into bondage), [5]to whom we did not yield submission even for an hour, that the truth of the gospel might continue with you.

[6]But from those who seemed to be

1:18 [a]NU-Text reads *Cephas.*

something—whatever they were, it makes no difference to me; God shows personal favoritism to no man—for those who seemed *to be something* added nothing to me. [7]But on the contrary, when they saw that the gospel for the uncircumcised had been committed to me, as *the gospel* for the circumcised *was* to Peter [8](for He who worked effectively in Peter for the apostleship to the circumcised also worked effectively in me toward the Gentiles), [9]and when James, Cephas, and John, who seemed to be pillars, perceived the grace that had been given to me, they gave me and Barnabas the right hand of fellowship, that we *should go* to the Gentiles and they to the circumcised. [10]*They desired* only that we should remember the poor, the very thing which I also was eager to do.

No Return to the Law

[11]Now when Peter[a] had come to Antioch, I withstood him to his face, because he was to be blamed; [12]for before certain men came from James, he would eat with the Gentiles; but when they came, he withdrew and separated himself, fearing those who were of the circumcision. [13]And the rest of the Jews also played the hypocrite with him, so that even Barnabas was carried away with their hypocrisy.

[14]But when I saw that they were not straightforward about the truth of the gospel, I said to Peter before *them* all, "If you, being a Jew, live in the manner of Gentiles and not as the Jews, why do you[a] compel Gentiles to live as Jews?[b] [15]We *who are* Jews by nature, and not sinners of the Gentiles, [16]knowing that a man is not justified by the works of the law but by faith in Jesus Christ, even we have believed in Christ Jesus, that we might be justified by faith in Christ and not by the works of the law; for by the works of the law no flesh shall be justified.

[17]"But if, while we seek to be justified by Christ, we ourselves also are found sinners, *is* Christ therefore a minister of sin? Certainly not! [18]For if I build again those things which I destroyed, I make myself a transgressor. [19]For I through the law died to the law that I might live to God. [20]I have been crucified with Christ; it is no longer I who live, but Christ lives in me; and the *life* which I now live in

→LIVE
• • • • • • • • • • • • • • • • •

2:16 • God has taken your sins and has cast them to the depths of the sea. They are gone. And they are not just forgiven, they are forgotten. That doesn't mean that God has a lapse in memory! He technically knows, but He has chosen not to remember—and we should not choose to remember what God has chosen to forget. Why do we dredge up old sins? Why do we have to keep reliving those ugly things? Can you accept that when you have salvation in Christ, you are justified? God has taken your sin, forgiven it, and forgotten it. *For more about* Forgiveness, *see Eph. 4:32;* New Life in Christ, *Gal. 4:6;* Sin, *Gal. 6:7, 8.*

the flesh I live by faith in the Son of God, who loved me and gave Himself for me. [21]I do not set aside the grace of God; for if righteousness *comes* through the law, then Christ died in vain."

→ *I have been crucified with Christ; it is no longer I who live, but Christ lives in me; and the life which I now live in the flesh I live by faith in the Son of God, who loved me and gave Himself for me.* Gal. 2:20

Justification by Faith

3 O foolish Galatians! Who has bewitched you that you should not obey the truth,[a] before whose eyes Jesus Christ was clearly portrayed among you[b] as crucified? [2]This only I want to learn from you: Did you receive the Spirit by the works of the law, or by the hearing of faith? [3]Are you so foolish? Having begun in the Spirit, are you now being made perfect by the flesh? [4]Have you suffered so many things in vain—if indeed *it was* in vain?

[5]Therefore He who supplies the Spirit to you and works miracles among you, *does He do it* by the works of the law, or by the

2:11 [a]NU-Text reads *Cephas.*   2:14 [a]NU-Text reads *how can you.*   [b]Some interpreters stop the quotation here.
3:1 [a]NU-Text omits *that you should not obey the truth.*   [b]NU-Text omits *among you.*

↘ LEARN

3:3 • The only way to become a Christian is by grace through faith. And the only way to grow spiritually is by grace through faith. No one can succeed by beginning with faith and then shifting to personal effort. The context of this verse speaks of people, transformed by Jesus Christ, who chose to go back to keeping Old Testament law. Effort is certainly required, but it's the kind of effort empowered by the Holy Spirit. So Paul wrote, "I labored more abundantly than they all, yet not I, but the grace of God which was with me" (1 Cor. 15:10). *For more about Faith, see 1 Thess. 4:3;* Growing in Christ, *Gal. 5:16;* Becoming a Christian, *Phil. 3:18.*

hearing of faith?— [6]just as Abraham *"believed God, and it was accounted to him for righteousness."*[a] [7]Therefore know that *only* those who are of faith are sons of Abraham. [8]And the Scripture, foreseeing that God would justify the Gentiles by faith, preached the gospel to Abraham beforehand, *saying, "In you all the nations shall be blessed."*[a] [9]So then those who *are* of faith are blessed with believing Abraham.

The Law Brings a Curse

[10]For as many as are of the works of the law are under the curse; for it is written, *"Cursed is everyone who does not continue in all things which are written in the book of the law, to do them."*[a] [11]But that no one is justified by the law in the sight of God *is* evident, for *"the just shall live by faith."*[a] [12]Yet the law is not of faith, but *"the man who does them shall live by them."*[a]

[13]Christ has redeemed us from the curse of the law, having become a curse for us (for it is written, *"Cursed is everyone who hangs on a tree"*[a]), [14]that the blessing of Abraham might come upon the Gentiles in Christ Jesus, that we might receive the promise of the Spirit through faith.

The Changeless Promise

[15]Brethren, I speak in the manner of men: Though *it is* only a man's covenant, yet *if it is* confirmed, no one annuls or adds to it. [16]Now to Abraham and his Seed were the promises made. He does not say, "And to

seeds," as of many, but as of one, *"And to your Seed,"*[a] who is Christ. [17]And this I say, *that* the law, which was four hundred and thirty years later, cannot annul the covenant that was confirmed before by God in Christ,[a] that it should make the promise of no effect. [18]For if the inheritance *is* of the law, *it is* no longer of promise; but God gave *it* to Abraham by promise.

Purpose of the Law

[19]What purpose then *does* the law *serve?* It was added because of transgressions, till the Seed should come to whom the promise was made; *and it was* appointed through angels by the hand of a mediator. [20]Now a mediator does not *mediate* for one *only,* but God is one.

[21]*Is* the law then against the promises of God? Certainly not! For if there had been a law given which could have given life, truly righteousness would have been by the law. [22]But the Scripture has confined all under sin, that the promise by faith in Jesus Christ might be given to those who believe. [23]But before faith came, we were kept under guard by the law, kept for the faith which would afterward be revealed. [24]Therefore the law was our tutor *to bring us* to Christ, that we might be justified by faith. [25]But after faith has come, we are no longer under a tutor.

Sons and Heirs

[26]For you are all sons of God through faith in Christ Jesus. [27]For as many of you as were baptized into Christ have put on Christ. [28]There is neither Jew nor Greek, there is neither slave nor free, there is neither male nor female; for you are all one in Christ Jesus. [29]And if you *are* Christ's, then you are Abraham's seed, and heirs according to the promise.

4 Now I say *that* the heir, as long as he is a child, does not differ at all from a slave, though he is master of all, [2]but is under guardians and stewards until the time appointed by the father. [3]Even so we, when we were children, were in bondage under the elements of the world. [4]But when the fullness of the time had come, God sent forth His Son, born[a] of a woman, born under the law, [5]to

3:6 [a]Genesis 15:6   **3:8** [a]Genesis 12:3; 18:18; 22:18; 26:4; 28:14   **3:10** [a]Deuteronomy 27:26   **3:11** [a]Habakkuk 2:4   **3:12** [a]Leviticus 18:5
3:13 [a]Deuteronomy 21:23   **3:16** [a]Genesis 12:7; 13:15; 24:7   **3:17** [a]NU-Text omits *in Christ.*   **4:4** [a]Or *made*

redeem those who were under the law, that we might receive the adoption as sons.

[6]And because you are sons, God has sent forth the Spirit of His Son into your hearts, crying out, "Abba, Father!" [7]Therefore you are no longer a slave but a son, and if a son, then an heir of[a] God through Christ.

→LIVE

● ● ● ● ● ● ● ● ● ● ● ● ● ● ● ● ●

4:6 • If you are a believer in Jesus, God has adopted you into His family. In adoption you become His child, as though you were born into His family. The word *adoption* means, "the placing of a son or a daughter." By adopting you, God is saying, "Don't just stand in awe of me. Come close to me. I want a relationship with you." Through the death and resurrection of Jesus Christ, you come into this adoptive relationship with God where you can cry, "Abba Father." This is the very expression Jesus Himself used when praying to the Father (Mark 14:36). *For more about* God's Love, *see 2 Thess. 3:5;* New Life in Christ, *Phil. 3:18.*

Fears for the Church

[8]But then, indeed, when you did not know God, you served those which by nature are not gods. [9]But now after you have known God, or rather are known by God, how *is it that* you turn again to the weak and beggarly elements, to which you desire again to be in bondage? [10]You observe days and months and seasons and years. [11]I am afraid for you, lest I have labored for you in vain.

[12]Brethren, I urge you to become like me, for I *became* like you. You have not injured me at all. [13]You know that because of physical infirmity I preached the gospel to you at the first. [14]And my trial which was in my flesh you did not despise or reject, but you received me as an angel of God, *even* as Christ Jesus. [15]What[a] then was the blessing you *enjoyed?* For I bear you witness that, if possible, you would have plucked out your own eyes and given them to me. [16]Have I therefore become your enemy because I tell you the truth?

[17]They zealously court you, *but* for no good; yes, they want to exclude you, that you may be zealous for them. [18]But it is good to be zealous in a good thing always, and not only when I am present with you. [19]My little children, for whom I labor in birth again

until Christ is formed in you, [20]I would like to be present with you now and to change my tone; for I have doubts about you.

Two Covenants

[21]Tell me, you who desire to be under the law, do you not hear the law? [22]For it is written that Abraham had two sons: the one by a bondwoman, the other by a freewoman. [23]But he *who was* of the bondwoman was born according to the flesh, and he of the freewoman through promise, [24]which things are symbolic. For these are the[a] two covenants: the one from Mount Sinai which gives birth to bondage, which is Hagar— [25]for this Hagar is Mount Sinai in Arabia, and corresponds to Jerusalem which now is, and is in bondage with her children— [26]but the Jerusalem above is free, which is the mother of us all. [27]For it is written:

> *"Rejoice, O barren,*
> *You who do not bear!*
> *Break forth and shout,*
> *You who are not in labor!*
> *For the desolate has many more children*
> *Than she who has a husband."*[a]

[28]Now we, brethren, as Isaac *was,* are children of promise. [29]But, as he who was born according to the flesh then persecuted him *who was born* according to the Spirit, even so *it is* now. [30]Nevertheless what does the Scripture say? *"Cast out the bondwoman and her son, for the son of the bondwoman shall not be heir with the son of the freewoman."*[a] [31]So then, brethren, we are not children of the bondwoman but of the free.

Christian Liberty

5 Stand fast therefore in the liberty by which Christ has made us free,[a] and do not be entangled again with a yoke of bondage. [2]Indeed I, Paul, say to you that if you become circumcised, Christ will profit you nothing. [3]And I testify again to every man who becomes circumcised that he is a debtor to keep the whole law. [4]You have become estranged from Christ, you who *attempt to* be justified by law; you have fallen from grace. [5]For we through the Spirit eagerly wait for the hope of righteousness by faith. [6]For in

---

4:7 [a]NU-Text reads *through God* and omits *through Christ.*   4:15 [a]NU-Text reads *Where.*   4:24 [a]NU-Text and M-Text omit *the.*
4:27 [a]Isaiah 54:1   4:30 [a]Genesis 21:10   5:1 [a]NU-Text reads *For freedom Christ has made us free; stand fast therefore.*

Christ Jesus neither circumcision nor uncircumcision avails anything, but faith working through love.

Love Fulfills the Law

[7]You ran well. Who hindered you from obeying the truth? [8]This persuasion does not *come* from Him who calls you. [9]A little leaven leavens the whole lump. [10]I have confidence in you, in the Lord, that you will have no other mind; but he who troubles you shall bear his judgment, whoever he is.

[11]And I, brethren, if I still preach circumcision, why do I still suffer persecution? Then the offense of the cross has ceased. [12]I could wish that those who trouble you would even cut themselves off!

[13]For you, brethren, have been called to liberty; only do not *use* liberty as an opportunity for the flesh, but through love serve one another. [14]For all the law is fulfilled in one word, *even* in this: *"You shall love your neighbor as yourself."*[a] [15]But if you bite and devour one another, beware lest you be consumed by one another!

Walking in the Spirit

[16]I say then: Walk in the Spirit, and you shall not fulfill the lust of the flesh. [17]For the flesh lusts against the Spirit, and the Spirit against the flesh; and these are contrary to one another, so that you do not do the things that you wish. [18]But if you are led by the Spirit, you are not under the law.

[19]Now the works of the flesh are evident, which are: adultery,[a] fornication, uncleanness, lewdness, [20]idolatry, sorcery, hatred,

> ↘ **LEARN**
> • • • • • • • • • • • • • • • • • •
> 5:16 • The best way to not go backwards spiritually is to move forward. The key to spiritual growth is positive, not negative; it's learning how to walk in the Spirit, not how to evade the lust of the flesh. It's learning to ask God, moment by moment, to give you the strength and the wisdom to please Him by the way you live, so that more and more you resemble His Son, Jesus. *For more about* Growing in Christ *and the* Holy Spirit, *see Gal. 5:22.*

contentions, jealousies, outbursts of wrath, selfish ambitions, dissensions, heresies, [21]envy, murders,[a] drunkenness, revelries, and the like; of which I tell you beforehand, just as I also told *you* in time past, that those who practice such things will not inherit the kingdom of God.

[22]But the fruit of the Spirit is love, joy, peace, longsuffering, kindness, goodness, faithfulness, [23]gentleness, self-control. Against such there is no law. [24]And those *who are* Christ's have crucified the flesh with its passions and desires. [25]If we live in the Spirit, let us also walk in the Spirit. [26]Let us not become conceited, provoking one another, envying one another.

Bear and Share the Burdens

6 Brethren, if a man is overtaken in any trespass, you who *are* spiritual restore such a one in a spirit of gentleness, considering yourself lest you also be tempted. [2]Bear one another's burdens, and so fulfill the law of Christ. [3]For if anyone thinks himself to

5:14 [a]Leviticus 19:18   **5:19** [a]NU-Text omits *adultery.*   **5:21** [a]NU-Text omits *murders.*

↑ GROW (GAL. 5:22)
• •

When you abide in Christ—when you walk with Him daily, read His Word, keep an open line of communication, seek to please Him above all else—you naturally begin to bear spiritual fruit. In fact, this fruit bearing is one good way to tell if we or others are actually Christians (Matt. 7:20). And what is the "fruit of the Spirit"? The apostle tells us, "The fruit of the Spirit is love." Some people talk about the fruits of the Spirit, plural, but there's really just one fruit, love, that comes in several luscious flavors. When you love God and love others, you express your love in several flavorful ways: with joy, peace, patience, kindness, goodness, faithfulness, gentleness, and self-control. Remember that fruit takes time to grow, however, so be patient with yourself as God brings forth this fruit in your life. *For more about* Growing in Christ, *see Eph. 2:20;* Loving God, *Rev. 2:4;* Loving Others, *Eph. 4:15; the* Holy Spirit, *Eph. 1:17.*

be something, when he is nothing, he deceives himself. ⁴But let each one examine his own work, and then he will have rejoicing in himself alone, and not in another. ⁵For each one shall bear his own load.

Be Generous and Do Good

⁶Let him who is taught the word share in all good things with him who teaches.

⁷Do not be deceived, God is not mocked; for whatever a man sows, that he will also reap. ⁸For he who sows to his flesh will of the flesh reap corruption, but he who sows to the Spirit will of the Spirit reap everlasting life. ⁹And let us not grow weary while doing good, for in due season we shall reap if we do not lose heart. ¹⁰Therefore, as we have opportunity, let us do good to all, especially to those who are of the household of faith.

> ↘ **LEARN**
>
> **6:7, 8** • Just as there is a law of gravity, so is there a spiritual law of sowing and reaping. Grace doesn't mean that because you hold a free ticket to heaven, you can (or would want to) run around on earth as if you were a child of hell. If you live to please your fleshly nature, then expect to suffer some very painful consequences. You can't plant weeds and expect to harvest watermelons! So there is a negative to this: "He who sows to his flesh will of the flesh reap corruption." But there is a positive as well, for "he who sows to the Spirit will of the Spirit reap everlasting life." Someone has summed it up like this: Sow a thought, reap an act. Sow an act, reap a character. Sow a character, reap a destiny. *For more about* How to Live Out Your Faith, *see Phil. 1:4;* Sin, *Eph. 4:30.*

6:14 ªOr *by which* (the cross)

> ➡ *And let us not grow weary while doing good, for in due season we shall reap if we do not lose heart.* Gal. 6:9

Glory Only in the Cross

¹¹See with what large letters I have written to you with my own hand! ¹²As many as desire to make a good showing in the flesh, these *would* compel you to be circumcised, only that they may not suffer persecution for the cross of Christ. ¹³For not even those who are circumcised keep the law, but they desire to have you circumcised that they may boast in your flesh. ¹⁴But God forbid that I should boast except in the cross of our Lord Jesus Christ, by whomª the world has been crucified to me, and I to the world. ¹⁵For in Christ Jesus neither circumcision nor uncircumcision avails anything, but a new creation.

Blessing and a Plea

¹⁶And as many as walk according to this rule, peace and mercy *be* upon them, and upon the Israel of God.

¹⁷From now on let no one trouble me, for I bear in my body the marks of the Lord Jesus.

¹⁸Brethren, the grace of our Lord Jesus Christ *be* with your spirit. Amen.

EPHESIANS

INTRODUCTION//

Every once in a while we need someone to come alongside us, to guide us in our walk with Christ, and to show us the divine tools at our disposal. That is exactly what Paul does in his letter to the church at Ephesus. It can be divided into three sections: the wealth, the walk, and the warfare of the believer.

It surprises some that the Christian life is not a playground, but a battleground. Paul makes this abundantly clear, especially in chapter 6. This letter doesn't condemn the church for misconduct, but instead instructs the people how to grow in their faith, build toward unity, and act as Christians called by God to reflect the glory of Christ. Paul describes our rightful position as children of God "in the heavenly places" with Jesus (2:6) and tells us how to fully appreciate and implement the amazing things God has done for us.

Paul begins by explaining what we have gained in and through Christ. He speaks of spiritual blessings (1:3–14), the new life (2:1–10), and the unity we share through Jesus (2:11–22; 4:1–16). He lists several ways in which we already are unified: we are one in Spirit, in hope, in faith, and in baptism (4:4). Paul then reminds us how to live as redeemed members of the body of Christ, now that we have a new, unified life under Jesus (4:17—6:20). He especially focuses on our speech, insisting that we do not lie, slander, gossip, or speak unwholesomely. In one of the most famous passages in Ephesians, Paul describes proper family conduct (5:22—6:9), emphasizing the complementary roles of husbands and wives. Paul closes by describing the "armor" God gives us to protect us from the devil's furious assaults (6:10–20). And he ends his letter as he frequently begins them, with "grace" (6:24).

Greeting

1 Paul, an apostle of Jesus Christ by the will of God,

To the saints who are in Ephesus, and faithful in Christ Jesus:

²Grace to you and peace from God our Father and the Lord Jesus Christ.

Redemption in Christ

³Blessed *be* the God and Father of our Lord Jesus Christ, who has blessed us with every spiritual blessing in the heavenly *places* in Christ, ⁴just as He chose us in Him before the foundation of the world, that we should be holy and without blame before Him in love, ⁵having predestined us to adoption as sons by Jesus Christ to Himself, according to the good pleasure of His will, ⁶to the praise of the glory of His grace, by which He made us accepted in the Beloved.

→ LIVE

1:5 • As your adoptive Father, God understands you even better than you know your own children. All it takes for us is a look at our kids to know when they are doing well and not so well. We know when they have done something wrong because they get this certain expression on their faces. We understand. Even when our children have failed, we love them unconditionally and care for them. We want the best for them. We pray for them. So if we have compassion on our children, then imagine how much more our heavenly Father has compassion on us! *For more about the* Attributes of God, *see Col. 1:15.*

⁷In Him we have redemption through His blood, the forgiveness of sins, according to the riches of His grace ⁸which He made to abound toward us in all wisdom and prudence, ⁹having made known to us the mystery of His will, according to His good pleasure which He purposed in Himself, ¹⁰that in the dispensation of the fullness of the times He might gather together in one all things in Christ, both^a which are in heaven and which are on earth—in Him. ¹¹In Him also we have obtained an inheritance, being predestined according to the purpose of Him who works all things according to the counsel of His will, ¹²that we who first trusted in Christ should be to the praise of His glory.

¹³In Him you also *trusted,* after you heard the word of truth, the gospel of your salvation; in whom also, having believed, you were sealed with the Holy Spirit of promise, ¹⁴who^a is the guarantee of our inheritance until the redemption of the purchased possession, to the praise of His glory.

Prayer for Spiritual Wisdom

¹⁵Therefore I also, after I heard of your faith in the Lord Jesus and your love for all the saints, ¹⁶do not cease to give thanks for you, making mention of you in my prayers: ¹⁷that the God of our Lord Jesus Christ, the Father of glory, may give to you the spirit of wisdom and revelation in the knowledge of Him, ¹⁸the eyes of your understanding^a being enlightened; that you may know what is the hope of His calling, what are the riches of the glory of His inheritance in the saints, ¹⁹and what *is* the exceeding greatness of His

1:10 ªNU-Text and M-Text omit *both.*   **1:14** ªNU-Text reads *which.*   **1:18** ªNU-Text and M-Text read *hearts.*

↑ GROW (EPH. 1:17)

The Holy Spirit helps you in your study, knowledge, and memorization of Scripture. Have you ever felt down or discouraged or unsure about what to do in some difficult situation, when out of the blue a verse of Scripture just seemed to jump into your mind? And here's the interesting thing: *you don't remember memorizing the verse.* You might have heard the passage quoted in a sermon a month ago, or encountered it somewhere else a decade ago—and suddenly, there it is, vividly flashing in the front of your mind. Where did it come from? It came from the Holy Spirit. He brought to your remembrance exactly what you needed to know. The Spirit of God both inspired the Bible and brings it to life in our consciousness. That is why you should pray before you study the Word, asking that the Holy Spirit might illumine what you're reading. *For more about the* Holy Spirit, *see Eph. 4:30;* God's Word, *Eph. 2:20;* Spiritual Disciplines, *Col. 2:7.*

power toward us who believe, according to the working of His mighty power [20]which He worked in Christ when He raised Him from the dead and seated *Him* at His right hand in the heavenly *places,* [21]far above all principality and power and might and dominion, and every name that is named, not only in this age but also in that which is to come. [22]And He put all *things* under His feet, and gave Him *to be* head over all *things* to the church, [23]which is His body, the fullness of Him who fills all in all.

By Grace Through Faith

2 And you *He made alive,* who were dead in trespasses and sins, [2]in which you once walked according to the course of this world, according to the prince of the power of the air, the spirit who now works in the sons of disobedience, [3]among whom also we all once conducted ourselves in the lusts of our flesh, fulfilling the desires of the flesh and of the mind, and were by nature children of wrath, just as the others. [4]But God, who is rich in mercy, because of His great love with which He loved us, [5]even when we were dead in trespasses, made us alive together with Christ (by grace you have been saved), [6]and raised *us* up together, and made *us* sit together in the heavenly *places* in Christ Jesus, [7]that in the ages to come He might show the exceeding riches of His grace in *His* kindness toward us in Christ Jesus. [8]For by grace you have been saved through faith, and that not of yourselves; *it is* the gift of God, [9]not of works, lest anyone should boast. [10]For we are His workmanship, created in Christ Jesus for good works, which God prepared beforehand that we should walk in them.

→ *For by grace you have been saved through faith, and that not of yourselves; it is the gift of God, not of works, lest anyone should boast.* Eph. 2:8, 9

Brought Near by His Blood

[11]Therefore remember that you, once Gentiles in the flesh—who are called Uncircumcision by what is called the Circumcision made in the flesh by hands— [12]that at that time you were without Christ, being aliens from the commonwealth of Israel and strangers from the covenants of promise, having no hope and without God in the world. [13]But now in Christ Jesus you who once were far off have been brought near by the blood of Christ.

Christ Our Peace

[14]For He Himself is our peace, who has made both one, and has broken down the middle wall of separation, [15]having abolished in His flesh the enmity, *that is,* the law of commandments *contained* in ordinances, so as to create in Himself one new man *from* the two, *thus* making peace, [16]and that He might reconcile them both to God in one body through the cross, thereby putting to death the enmity. [17]And He came and preached peace to you who were afar off and to those who were near. [18]For through Him we both have access by one Spirit to the Father.

Christ Our Cornerstone

[19]Now, therefore, you are no longer strangers and foreigners, but fellow citizens with the saints and members of the household of God, [20]having been built on the foundation of the apostles and prophets, Jesus Christ Himself being the chief corner*stone,*

↘ LEARN
. . . .

2:20 • Strong buildings have strong foundations. You can construct the finest facility known to man, but if it doesn't rest upon a solid foundation, that building will crumble sooner rather than later. That's why Paul says we must build our Christian lives upon the foundation of Scripture, both the New Testament ("the apostles") and the Old Testament ("the prophets"). All of our understanding about a growing relationship with God must flow from our connection to Jesus Christ, the "chief cornerstone." Storms will come to test our foundation, but if have built our faith on Christ, we will stand strong (Matt. 7:24–27). *For more about* Growing in Christ, *see Eph. 4:15; God's Word, Col. 3:16.*

[21]in whom the whole building, being fitted together, grows into a holy temple in the Lord, [22]in whom you also are being built together for a dwelling place of God in the Spirit.

The Mystery Revealed

3 For this reason I, Paul, the prisoner of Christ Jesus for you Gentiles— [2]if indeed you have heard of the dispensation of the grace of God which was given to me for you, [3]how that by revelation He made known to me the mystery (as I have briefly written already, [4]by which, when you read, you may understand my knowledge in the mystery of Christ), [5]which in other ages was not made known to the sons of men, as it has now been revealed by the Spirit to His holy apostles and prophets: [6]that the Gentiles should be fellow heirs, of the same body, and partakers of His promise in Christ through the gospel, [7]of which I became a minister according to the gift of the grace of God given to me by the effective working of His power.

Purpose of the Mystery

[8]To me, who am less than the least of all the saints, this grace was given, that I should preach among the Gentiles the unsearchable riches of Christ, [9]and to make all see what *is* the fellowship[a] of the mystery, which from the beginning of the ages has been hidden in God who created all things through Jesus Christ;[b] [10]to the intent that now the manifold wisdom of God might be made known by the church to the principalities and powers in the heavenly *places,* [11]according to the eternal purpose which He accomplished in Christ Jesus our Lord, [12]in whom we have boldness and access with confidence through faith in Him. [13]Therefore I ask that you do not lose heart at my tribulations for you, which is your glory.

Appreciation of the Mystery

[14]For this reason I bow my knees to the Father of our Lord Jesus Christ,[a] [15]from whom the whole family in heaven and earth is named, [16]that He would grant you, according to the riches of His glory, to be strengthened with might through His Spirit in the inner man, [17]that Christ may dwell in your hearts through faith; that you, being rooted and grounded in love, [18]may be able to comprehend with all the saints what *is* the width and length and depth and height— [19]to know the love of Christ which passes knowledge; that you may be filled with all the fullness of God.

[20]Now to Him who is able to do exceedingly abundantly above all that we ask or think, according to the power that works in us, [21]to Him *be* glory in the church by Christ Jesus to all generations, forever and ever. Amen.

Walk in Unity

4 I, therefore, the prisoner of the Lord, beseech you to walk worthy of the calling with which you were called, [2]with all lowliness and gentleness, with longsuffering, bearing with one another in love, [3]endeavoring to keep the unity of the Spirit in the bond of peace. [4]*There is* one body and one Spirit, just as you were called in one hope of your calling; [5]one Lord, one faith, one baptism; [6]one God and Father of all, who *is* above all, and through all, and in you[a] all.

Spiritual Gifts

[7]But to each one of us grace was given according to the measure of Christ's gift. [8]Therefore He says:

> "When He ascended on high,
> He led captivity captive,
> And gave gifts to men."[a]

[9](Now this, *"He ascended"*—what does it mean but that He also first[a] descended into the lower parts of the earth? [10]He who descended is also the One who ascended far above all the heavens, that He might fill all things.)

[11]And He Himself gave some *to be* apostles, some prophets, some evangelists, and some pastors and teachers, [12]for the equipping of the saints for the work of ministry, for the edifying of the body of Christ, [13]till we all come to the unity of the faith and of the knowledge of the Son of God, to a perfect man, to the measure of the stature of the fullness of Christ; [14]that we should no longer be

---

3:9 [a]NU-Text and M-Text read *stewardship (dispensation).* [b]NU-Text omits *through Jesus Christ.* **3:14** [a]NU-Text omits *of our Lord Jesus Christ.* **4:6** [a]NU-Text omits *you;* M-Text reads *us.* **4:8** [a]Psalm 68:18 **4:9** [a]NU-Text omits *first.*

children, tossed to and fro and carried about with every wind of doctrine, by the trickery of men, in the cunning craftiness of deceitful plotting, [15]but, speaking the truth in love, may grow up in all things into Him who is the head—Christ— [16]from whom the whole body, joined and knit together by what every joint supplies, according to the effective working by which every part does its share, causes growth of the body for the edifying of itself in love.

> ↘ **LEARN**
> . . . .
>
> **4:15** • Truth and love—we need both to leave behind spiritual childhood and grow into mature adults. The goal is not to be child*ish*, but rather child*like*. We need truth—the truth about ourselves, the truth about God, the truth about our failures, our successes, our priorities, and our dreams. And we need love—love for God, love for our families and friends, love for our brothers and sisters in Christ, love for those not yet connected to Jesus. Sometimes we find the truth hard both to hear and to speak. When we wrap it in love, however, the total package yields maturity in Christ. *For more about* Loving Others, *see Phil. 2:3;* Growing in Christ, *Col. 1:9.*

The New Man

[17]This I say, therefore, and testify in the Lord, that you should no longer walk as the rest of[a] the Gentiles walk, in the futility of their mind, [18]having their understanding darkened, being alienated from the life of God, because of the ignorance that is in them, because of the blindness of their heart; [19]who, being past feeling, have given themselves over to lewdness, to work all uncleanness with greediness.

[20]But you have not so learned Christ, [21]if indeed you have heard Him and have been taught by Him, as the truth is in Jesus: [22]that you put off, concerning your former conduct, the old man which grows corrupt according to the deceitful lusts, [23]and be renewed in the spirit of your mind, [24]and that you put on the new man which was created according to God, in true righteousness and holiness.

Do Not Grieve the Spirit

[25]Therefore, putting away lying, *"Let each one of you speak truth with his neighbor,"*[a] for we are members of one another. [26]*"Be angry, and do not sin":*[a] do not let the sun go down on your wrath, [27]nor give place to the devil. [28]Let him who stole steal no longer, but rather let him labor, working with *his* hands what is good, that he may have something to give him who has need. [29]Let no corrupt word proceed out of your mouth, but what is good for necessary edification, that it may impart grace to the hearers. [30]And do not grieve the Holy Spirit of God, by whom you were sealed for the day of redemption. [31]Let all bitterness, wrath, anger, clamor, and evil speaking be put away from you, with all malice. [32]And be kind to one another, tenderhearted, forgiving one another, even as God in Christ forgave you.

Walk in Love

5 Therefore be imitators of God as dear children. [2]And walk in love, as Christ also has loved us and given Himself for us, an offering and a sacrifice to God for a sweet-smelling aroma.

4:17 [a]NU-Text omits the rest of.   4:25 [a]Zechariah 8:16   4:26 [a]Psalm 4:4

↓ **KNOW** (EPH. 4:30)
. . . .
It is possible to grieve the Holy Spirit of God. The word *grieve* means "to make sad or sorrowful." What grieves the Holy Spirit? "Evil speaking" or foul and abusive language makes the Holy Spirit sad (v. 31). The phrase in the original language means "rotten," something that has gone bad. This includes obscene language, profanity, dirty stories, and vulgarity. If God has cleaned up your heart, your speech should change. Bitterness— a resentful spirit that refuses to be reconciled—also makes the Holy Spirit sorrowful. I have found that those who try to cover up their own sin are often the ones trying to uncover sin in the lives of everyone else. Fits of rage and uncontrolled anger also make the Holy Spirit sad. Has someone hurt you? Me, too. We are to forgive them as God in Christ forgave us. And if we don't, we grieve the Holy Spirit. *For more about the* Holy Spirit, *see Eph. 5:18;* Sin, *1 Thess. 5:19.*

→LIVE

• • • • • • • • • • • • • • • • •

4:30 • As part of the great work of conversion, the Holy Spirit seals us. In ancient days, merchants shipping their goods stamped their items with a waxed seal, imprinted with a signet ring that bore a unique mark of ownership. Important documents, as from a king, also would be sealed in wax and imprinted with the royal seal, so no one would dare open it except for the addressee. So when the Bible says that you are sealed with the Spirit, it means that God has put His personal imprint on your life. God has put His own ID tag on you! *For more about* Assurance of Salvation, *see Col. 2:13; the* Holy Spirit, *Eph. 5:18.*

³But fornication and all uncleanness or covetousness, let it not even be named among you, as is fitting for saints; ⁴neither filthiness, nor foolish talking, nor coarse jesting, which are not fitting, but rather giving of thanks. ⁵For this you know,ᵃ that no fornicator, unclean person, nor covetous man, who is an idolater, has any inheritance in the kingdom of Christ and God. ⁶Let no one deceive you with empty words, for because of these things the wrath of God comes upon the sons of disobedience. ⁷Therefore do not be partakers with them.

Walk in Light

⁸For you were once darkness, but now *you are* light in the Lord. Walk as children of light ⁹(for the fruit of the Spiritᵃ *is* in all goodness, righteousness, and truth), ¹⁰finding out what is acceptable to the Lord. ¹¹And have no fellowship with the unfruitful works of darkness, but rather expose *them*. ¹²For it is

5:5 ᵃNU-Text reads *For know this.*   5:9 ᵃNU-Text reads *light.*

shameful even to speak of those things which are done by them in secret. ¹³But all things that are exposed are made manifest by the light, for whatever makes manifest is light. ¹⁴Therefore He says:

> "Awake, you who sleep,
> Arise from the dead,
> And Christ will give you light."

Walk in Wisdom

¹⁵See then that you walk circumspectly, not as fools but as wise, ¹⁶redeeming the time, because the days are evil. ¹⁷Therefore do not be unwise, but understand what the will of the Lord *is*. ¹⁸And do not be drunk with wine, in which is dissipation; but be filled with the Spirit, ¹⁹speaking to one another in psalms and hymns and spiritual songs, singing and making melody in your heart to the Lord, ²⁰giving thanks always for all things to God the Father in the

↘LEARN

• • • • • • • • • • • • • • • •

5:18 • We are to be filled with the Spirit, not the spirits (alcohol). In the original language, this is a command; it is not an option for the believer. The word speaks of something continuous; we are to be filled *daily* with the Spirit. The word also speaks of permeation; ancient peoples rubbed salt in meat, permeating it to preserve it. In a similar way, God's Spirit is to permeate all we say and do. The word also applies to wind that fills sails. So God commands us to be filled continuously with the Holy Spirit, allowing Him to permeate every area of our lives. *For more about the* Holy Spirit, *see Col. 1:15.*

↑ GROW (EPH. 4:32)

• •

If you are a Christian, Jesus requires you to forgive those who hurt you or wrong you. Forgiven people are forgiving people. In fact, an unforgiving Christian is an oxymoron. As one person said, "To not forgive someone is like drinking rat poison and waiting for the rat to die." You *cannot* be an unforgiving Christian. Still, we all have to learn to forgive. Remember that as flawed people, we all sin against others and others sin against us. So we must learn to say, "You know what? I am going to forgive her for that. I am not going to let this keep me from fellowship with God." Do you know who gets hurt the most when you continue to harbor anger and hostility and vengeful thoughts toward someone who hurt you? You. By your action, you cut yourself off from fellowship with God. So give in to God's love and grace, and learn to forgive. When you forgive someone, you set a prisoner free . . . yourself! *For more about* Forgiveness, *see 1 Tim. 1:15.*

name of our Lord Jesus Christ, [21]submitting to one another in the fear of God.[a]

Marriage—Christ and the Church

[22]Wives, submit to your own husbands, as to the Lord. [23]For the husband is head of the wife, as also Christ is head of the church; and He is the Savior of the body. [24]Therefore, just as the church is subject to Christ, so *let* the wives *be* to their own husbands in everything.

[25]Husbands, love your wives, just as Christ also loved the church and gave Himself for her, [26]that He might sanctify and cleanse her with the washing of water by the word, [27]that He might present her to Himself a glorious church, not having spot or wrinkle or any such thing, but that she should be holy and without blemish. [28]So husbands ought to love their own wives as their own bodies; he who loves his wife loves himself. [29]For no one ever hated his own flesh, but nourishes and cherishes it, just as the Lord *does* the church. [30]For we are members of His body,[a] of His flesh and of His bones. [31]*"For this reason a man shall leave his father and mother and be joined to his wife, and the two shall become one flesh."*[a] [32]This is a great mystery, but I speak concerning Christ and the church. [33]Nevertheless let each one of you in particular so love his own wife as himself, and let the wife *see* that she respects *her* husband.

Children and Parents

6 Children, obey your parents in the Lord, for this is right. [2]*"Honor your father and mother,"* which is the first commandment with promise: [3]*"that it may be well with you and you may live long on the earth."*[a]

[4]And you, fathers, do not provoke your children to wrath, but bring them up in the training and admonition of the Lord.

Bondservants and Masters

[5]Bondservants, be obedient to those who are your masters according to the flesh, with fear and trembling, in sincerity of heart, as to Christ; [6]not with eyeservice, as men-pleasers, but as bondservants of Christ, doing the will

of God from the heart, [7]with goodwill doing service, as to the Lord, and not to men, [8]knowing that whatever good anyone does, he will receive the same from the Lord, whether *he is* a slave or free.

[9]And you, masters, do the same things to them, giving up threatening, knowing that your own Master also[a] is in heaven, and there is no partiality with Him.

The Whole Armor of God

[10]Finally, my brethren, be strong in the Lord and in the power of His might. [11]Put on the whole armor of God, that you may be able to stand against the wiles of the devil. [12]For we do not wrestle against flesh and blood, but against principalities, against powers, against the rulers of the darkness of this age,[a] against spiritual *hosts* of wickedness in the heavenly *places.* [13]Therefore take up the whole armor of God, that you may be able to withstand in the evil day, and having done all, to stand.

[14]Stand therefore, having girded your

> ↘ **LEARN**
> . . . .
> 6:11, 12 • The Christian life is not a playground, but a battleground; and in this spiritual battle, we are either winning or losing, gaining ground or losing it. When you became a Christian, you not only became a child of God, you also became a target of the devil. Satan wants to destroy you. That's why God has given you access to strong spiritual armor that can help you defeat your enemy. Like all armor, however, you have to use it if it is to do you any good. So Paul fills his instruction with terms like "take up" and "stand" and "shod" and "quench."
> *For more about* Adversity, *see Phil. 4:6;* Satan, *Col. 2:13.*

waist with truth, having put on the breastplate of righteousness, [15]and having shod your feet with the preparation of the gospel of peace; [16]above all, taking the shield of faith with which you will be able to quench all the fiery darts of the wicked one. [17]And take the helmet of salvation, and the sword of the Spirit, which is the word of God; [18]praying always with all prayer and supplication in the Spirit, being watchful to this end with all perseverance and supplication for all the saints— [19]and for me, that utterance may be given

---

5:21 [a]NU-Text reads *Christ.*   **5:30** [a]NU-Text omits the rest of this verse.   **5:31** [a]Genesis 2:24   **6:3** [a]Deuteronomy 5:16   **6:9** [a]NU-Text reads *He who is both their Master and yours.*   **6:12** [a]NU-Text reads *rulers of this darkness.*

to me, that I may open my mouth boldly to make known the mystery of the gospel, [20]for which I am an ambassador in chains; that in it I may speak boldly, as I ought to speak.

A Gracious Greeting

[21]But that you also may know my affairs *and* how I am doing, Tychicus, a beloved brother and faithful minister in the Lord, will make all things known to you; [22]whom I have sent to you for this very purpose, that you may know our affairs, and *that* he may comfort your hearts.

[23]Peace to the brethren, and love with faith, from God the Father and the Lord Jesus Christ. [24]Grace *be* with all those who love our Lord Jesus Christ in sincerity. Amen.

PHILIPPIANS

INTRODUCTION//

We all want to be happy and we all search for happiness. Many people spend their lives searching for that one thing, that one person, that one job that will make them happy. Some find happiness in positive things, like their family, charity, or even work. Some turn to drugs, sex, and crime to try to fulfill their longings, although they get only fleeting satisfaction—and then the inevitable emptiness that always follows sinful pursuits. In the end, all of these things fall short of fulfilling the lifelong desire for happiness.

Christians have access to the only source of lasting happiness: Christ. In fact, when we become Christians, we gain more than happiness; we get "joy inexpressible and full of glory" (1 Pet. 1:8). Paul writes to the church in Philippi to encourage them in their faith and to describe the many ways they can find this joy of the Lord. This book explains the mindset, attitude, and outlook the believer must have if he or she is going to experience the joy of the Lord in a troubled world. At least nineteen times in these four chapters Paul mentions joy, rejoicing, or gladness.

When he thought of the Philippian believers, it brought a smile to his face (1:3, 4). When he thought of his potential death (which could have taken place in the prison from which he wrote this letter), this joy remained (1:21–25). When he encouraged them to work together in unselfish harmony, his own joy intensified as they envisioned that very thing happening (2:1, 2). When he mentioned sending a friend to visit them, he urged them to receive him joyfully (2:28, 29). The apostle really laid out the bottom line of the letter in 4:4, "Rejoice in the Lord always. Again I will say, rejoice!"

Greeting

1 Paul and Timothy, bondservants of Jesus Christ,

To all the saints in Christ Jesus who are in Philippi, with the bishops[a] and deacons:

[2]Grace to you and peace from God our Father and the Lord Jesus Christ.

Thankfulness and Prayer

[3]I thank my God upon every remembrance of you, [4]always in every prayer of mine making request for you all with joy, [5]for your fellowship in the gospel from the first day until now, [6]being confident of this very thing, that He who has begun a good work in you will complete *it* until the day of Jesus Christ; [7]just as it is right for me to think this of you all, because I have you in my heart, inasmuch as both in my chains and in the defense and confirmation of the gospel, you all are partakers with me of grace. [8]For God is my witness, how greatly I long for you all with the affection of Jesus Christ.

> ### ↘ LEARN
> • • • • • • • • • • • • • • • • •
> 1:4 • Paul had a secret for joyful living, available to anyone who meets the criteria laid out in Philippians. Would you like to know what it is? The secret is found in the word "mind," which appears in this book five times, along with the word "think," which appears another five times. The secret of Christian joy, therefore, is found in the way a believer thinks: his attitude, her outlook. Paul in this book points to the mind, attitude, and outlook a believer must have to experience the joy of the Lord in a troubled world. *For more about* How to Live Out Your Faith, *see Phil. 2:12.*

[9]And this I pray, that your love may abound still more and more in knowledge and all discernment, [10]that you may approve the things that are excellent, that you may be sincere and without offense till the day of Christ, [11]being filled with the fruits of righteousness which *are* by Jesus Christ, to the glory and praise of God.

Christ Is Preached

[12]But I want you to know, brethren, that the things *which happened* to me have actually turned out for the furtherance of the gospel, [13]so that it has become evident to the whole palace guard, and to all the rest, that my chains are in Christ; [14]and most of the brethren in the Lord, having become confident by my chains, are much more bold to speak the word without fear.

[15]Some indeed preach Christ even from envy and strife, and some also from goodwill: [16]The former[a] preach Christ from selfish ambition, not sincerely, supposing to add affliction to my chains; [17]but the latter out of love, knowing that I am appointed for the defense of the gospel. [18]What then? Only *that* in every way, whether in pretense or in truth, Christ is preached; and in this I rejoice, yes, and will rejoice.

To Live Is Christ

[19]For I know that this will turn out for my deliverance through your prayer and the supply of the Spirit of Jesus Christ, [20]according to my earnest expectation and hope that in nothing I shall be ashamed, but with all boldness, as always, so now also Christ will be magnified in my body, whether by life or by death. [21]For to me, to live *is* Christ, and to die *is* gain. [22]But if *I* live on in the flesh, this *will mean* fruit from *my* labor; yet what I shall choose I cannot tell. [23]For[a] I am hard-pressed between the two, having a desire to depart and be with Christ, *which is* far better. [24]Nevertheless to remain in the flesh *is* more needful for you. [25]And being confident of this, I know that I shall remain and continue with you all for your progress and joy of faith, [26]that your rejoicing for me may be more abundant in Jesus Christ by my coming to you again.

Striving and Suffering for Christ

[27]Only let your conduct be worthy of the gospel of Christ, so that whether I come and see you or am absent, I may hear of your affairs, that you stand fast in one spirit, with one mind striving together for the faith of the gospel, [28]and not in any way terrified by your adversaries, which is to them a proof of

perdition, but to you of salvation,[a] and that from God. [29]For to you it has been granted on behalf of Christ, not only to believe in Him, but also to suffer for His sake, [30]having the same conflict which you saw in me and now hear *is* in me.

Unity Through Humility

2 Therefore if *there is* any consolation in Christ, if any comfort of love, if any fellowship of the Spirit, if any affection and mercy, [2]fulfill my joy by being like-minded, having the same love, *being* of one accord, of one mind. [3]*Let* nothing *be done* through selfish ambition or conceit, but in lowliness of mind let each esteem others better than himself. [4]Let each of you look out not only for his own interests, but also for the interests of others.

The Humbled and Exalted Christ

[5]Let this mind be in you which was also in Christ Jesus, [6]who, being in the form of

> ➤ *Let nothing be done through selfish ambition or conceit, but in lowliness of mind let each esteem others better than himself. Let each of you look out not only for his own interests, but also for the interests of others.* Phil. 2:3, 4

God, did not consider it robbery to be equal with God, [7]but made Himself of no reputation, taking the form of a bondservant, *and* coming in the likeness of men. [8]And being found in appearance as a man, He humbled Himself and became obedient to *the point of* death, even the death of the cross. [9]Therefore God also has highly exalted Him and given Him the name which is above every name, [10]that at the name of Jesus every knee should bow, of those in heaven, and of those on earth, and of those under the earth, [11]and *that* every tongue should confess that Jesus Christ *is* Lord, to the glory of God the Father.

Light Bearers

[12]Therefore, my beloved, as you have always obeyed, not as in my presence only, but now much more in my absence, work out your own salvation with fear and trembling;

↘ LEARN

● ● ● ● ● ● ● ● ● ● ● ● ● ● ● ●

2:3 • Conventional wisdom says, "If you want to succeed in life, then you need to start looking out for #1. Lie, connive, do whatever it takes to get ahead. That's how the world works!" Well, that may be how the world works, but it is *not* how the kingdom of God works. You find JOY when you put things in their right order: Jesus, Others, Yourself. Jesus Himself is our example of humility and success. He modeled perfectly what we are to do and how we are to live. Although in our era we emphasize self-esteem, Paul focused on esteeming others. *For more about* Loving Others, *see Col. 4:6.*

1:28 [a]NU-Text reads *of your salvation.*

↑ GROW (PHIL. 2:12)

● ●

To "work out your own salvation" does not mean you are to work *for* your salvation, as that is a gift of God purchased by the blood of Jesus Christ. To work out conveys the idea of carrying to the goal and fully completing. We are to work out what God has worked in, as in mining valuable ore in a mine. Why do some people succeed spiritually and others fail? Because they choose to. If you have a real desire to know God, by God's grace you will do just that. This may seem like a daunting task, but verse 13 brings clarity: "For it is God who works in you both to will and to do for His good pleasure." God will give us the strength to live the life He has called us to live. The calling of God is also the enabling of God. *For more about* How to Live Out Your Faith, *see Phil. 3:13;* God at Work, *Heb. 13:2.*

→LIVE

• • • • • • • • • • • • • • • • •

2:12 • What are you supposed to do with this great thing called salvation? Should you just put it up on a shelf and look at it and admire it? You could do that. In fact, you do need to explore it, understand it, appreciate it. But you also need to work it out. I didn't say work "for" your salvation. You can't do that; it's a gift from God. But you do need to work it out in your life. As you see what's there and explore it, bring it out into the open and let it affect your life. *For more about* How to Live Out Your Faith, *see Phil. 3:13.*

[13]for it is God who works in you both to will and to do for *His* good pleasure.

[14]Do all things without complaining and disputing, [15]that you may become blameless and harmless, children of God without fault in the midst of a crooked and perverse generation, among whom you shine as lights in the world, [16]holding fast the word of life, so that I may rejoice in the day of Christ that I have not run in vain or labored in vain.

[17]Yes, and if I am being poured out *as a drink offering* on the sacrifice and service of your faith, I am glad and rejoice with you all. [18]For the same reason you also be glad and rejoice with me.

Timothy Commended

[19]But I trust in the Lord Jesus to send Timothy to you shortly, that I also may be encouraged when I know your state. [20]For I have no one like-minded, who will sincerely care for your state. [21]For all seek their own, not the things which are of Christ Jesus. [22]But you know his proven character, that as a son with *his* father he served with me in the gospel. [23]Therefore I hope to send him at once, as soon as I see how it goes with me. [24]But I trust in the Lord that I myself shall also come shortly.

Epaphroditus Praised

[25]Yet I considered it necessary to send to you Epaphroditus, my brother, fellow worker, and fellow soldier, but your messenger and the one who ministered to my need; [26]since he was longing for you all, and was distressed because you had heard that he was sick. [27]For indeed he was sick almost unto death; but

God had mercy on him, and not only on him but on me also, lest I should have sorrow upon sorrow. [28]Therefore I sent him the more eagerly, that when you see him again you may rejoice, and I may be less sorrowful. [29]Receive him therefore in the Lord with all gladness, and hold such men in esteem; [30]because for the work of Christ he came close to death, not regarding his life, to supply what was lacking in your service toward me.

All for Christ

3 Finally, my brethren, rejoice in the Lord. For me to write the same things to you *is* not tedious, but for you *it is* safe.

[2]Beware of dogs, beware of evil workers, beware of the mutilation! [3]For we are the circumcision, who worship God in the Spirit,[a] rejoice in Christ Jesus, and have no confidence in the flesh, [4]though I also might have confidence in the flesh. If anyone else thinks he may have confidence in the flesh, I more so: [5]circumcised the eighth day, of the stock of Israel, *of* the tribe of Benjamin, a Hebrew of the Hebrews; concerning the law, a Pharisee; [6]concerning zeal, persecuting the church; concerning the righteousness which is in the law, blameless.

[7]But what things were gain to me, these I have counted loss for Christ. [8]Yet indeed I also count all things loss for the excellence of the knowledge of Christ Jesus my Lord, for whom I have suffered the loss of all things, and count them as rubbish, that I may gain Christ [9]and be found in Him, not having my own righteousness, which *is* from the law, but that which *is* through faith in Christ, the righteousness which is from God by faith; [10]that I may know Him and the power of His resurrection, and the fellowship of His sufferings, being conformed to His death, [11]if, by any means, I may attain to the resurrection from the dead.

Pressing Toward the Goal

[12]Not that I have already attained, or am already perfected; but I press on, that I may lay hold of that for which Christ Jesus has also laid hold of me. [13]Brethren, I do not count myself to have apprehended; but one thing I *do*, forgetting those things which are behind and reaching forward to those things which are ahead, [14]I press toward the goal for

3:3 [a]NU-Text and M-Text read *who worship in the Spirit of God.*

↘ LEARN

3:13 • Paul had a clear aim and focus; he wanted to know and follow Jesus. He channeled his energies into this "one thing" instead of dabbling in a thousand things. Do you have this singular aim? Or do you have double vision? Too often we permit urgent things to crowd out the important. The main thing is to keep the main thing the main thing! If you want a strong purpose and direction for your life, then maintain a single-minded ambition to serve God. "Forget the things" that are behind, including sins that have been forgiven and forgotten by God (Ps.103:12), as well as victories and accomplishments. *For more about* How to Live Out Your Faith, *see Col. 3:2.*

→ LIVE

3:18 • Some people claim to be followers of Jesus, and yet live as though they are not saved. They want to know they are going to heaven, but they want to live like hell. In essence, they want to live in two worlds and see how much they can get away with and technically still be a Christian. That's a dangerous game! The Bible makes it clear that if you have been saved, your life should change dramatically (Acts 26:18). You should seek to live as a follower of Jesus Christ because it is possible for anyone to shipwreck their faith (Heb. 3:12). *For more about* Becoming a Christian, *see Heb. 2:15;* New Life in Christ, *1 Tim. 1:15.*

the prize of the upward call of God in Christ Jesus.

[15]Therefore let us, as many as are mature, have this mind; and if in anything you think otherwise, God will reveal even this to you. [16]Nevertheless, to *the degree* that we have already attained, let us walk by the same rule,[a] let us be of the same mind.

Our Citizenship in Heaven

[17]Brethren, join in following my example, and note those who so walk, as you have us for a pattern. [18]For many walk, of whom I have told you often, and now tell you even weeping, *that they are* the enemies of the cross of Christ: [19]whose end *is* destruction, whose god *is their* belly, and *whose* glory *is* in their shame—who set their mind on earthly things. [20]For our citizenship is in heaven, from which we also eagerly wait for the Savior, the Lord

Jesus Christ, [21]who will transform our lowly body that it may be conformed to His glorious body, according to the working by which He is able even to subdue all things to Himself.

4 Therefore, my beloved and longed-for brethren, my joy and crown, so stand fast in the Lord, beloved.

Be United, Joyful, and in Prayer

[2]I implore Euodia and I implore Syntyche to be of the same mind in the Lord. [3]And[a] I urge you also, true companion, help these women who labored with me in the gospel, with Clement also, and the rest of my fellow workers, whose names *are* in the Book of Life.

[4]Rejoice in the Lord always. Again I will say, rejoice!

[5]Let your gentleness be known to all men. The Lord *is* at hand.

3:16 [a]NU-Text omits *rule* and the rest of the verse.   4:3 [a]NU-Text and M-Text read *Yes.*

↑ GROW (PHIL. 4:6)

Life is full of troubles. We have concerns about our future, our health, our family, our finances—the list goes on. Scary things happen. Prayer is the means by which God helps us overcome our anxiety. It has been said, "If your knees are shaking, kneel on them." So instead of worrying, why not pray? Maybe God will take your problem away. But even if He doesn't, you will gain perspective. You see God for who He is and your problem for what it is. If you have a big God, then you have a relatively small problem. But if you have a big problem, then maybe you have a small god. I know I *need* to pray. I need God's help—and He gives it to me. God promises His personal peace will "guard us," or literally, "mount a garrison." You are safe and saved in Jesus Christ. *For more about* Adversity, *see Phil. 4:11, 12;* Prayer, *Col. 1:9.*

➤ *Be anxious for nothing, but in everything by prayer and supplication, with thanksgiving, let your requests be made known to God; and the peace of God, which surpasses all understanding, will guard your hearts and minds through Christ Jesus.* Phil. 4:6, 7

[6]Be anxious for nothing, but in everything by prayer and supplication, with thanksgiving, let your requests be made known to God; [7]and the peace of God, which surpasses all understanding, will guard your hearts and minds through Christ Jesus.

Meditate on These Things

[8]Finally, brethren, whatever things are true, whatever things *are* noble, whatever things *are* just, whatever things *are* pure, whatever things *are* lovely, whatever things *are* of good report, if *there is* any virtue and if *there is* anything praiseworthy—meditate on these things. [9]The things which you learned and received and heard and saw in me, these do, and the God of peace will be with you.

Philippian Generosity

[10]But I rejoiced in the Lord greatly that now at last your care for me has flourished again; though you surely did care, but you lacked opportunity. [11]Not that I speak in regard to need, for I have learned in whatever state I am, to be content: [12]I know how to be abased, and I know how to abound. Everywhere and in all things I have learned both to

➤ **LEARN**
• • • • • • • • • • • • • • • •

4:11, 12 • In Philippi, Paul and Silas had been arrested, beaten, thrown in jail, and their feet placed in stocks. Their physical condition could not have been much worse. And yet in the middle of the night, this pair prayed and sang hymns to God (Acts 16:25). They had learned to be independent from both the bad *and* the good. Both abounding and suffering have their unique problems. Contentment does not come from what we have, but who we know. Hebrews 13:5 reminds us, "Be content with such things as you have. For He Himself has said, 'I will never leave you nor forsake you.'" *For more about* Adversity, *see 1 Thess. 3:3;* Worship, *Col. 3:16.*

be full and to be hungry, both to abound and to suffer need. [13]I can do all things through Christ[a] who strengthens me.

[14]Nevertheless you have done well that you shared in my distress. [15]Now you Philippians know also that in the beginning of the gospel, when I departed from Macedonia, no church shared with me concerning giving and receiving but you only. [16]For even in Thessalonica you sent *aid* once and again for my necessities. [17]Not that I seek the gift, but I seek the fruit that abounds to your account. [18]Indeed I have all and abound. I am full, having received from Epaphroditus the things *sent* from you, a sweet-smelling aroma, an acceptable sacrifice, well pleasing to God. [19]And my God shall supply all your need according to His riches in glory by Christ Jesus. [20]Now to our God and Father *be* glory forever and ever. Amen.

➤ *I can do all things through Christ who strengthens me.* Phil. 4:13

Greeting and Blessing

[21]Greet every saint in Christ Jesus. The brethren who are with me greet you. [22]All the saints greet you, but especially those who are of Caesar's household.

[23]The grace of our Lord Jesus Christ be with you all.[a] Amen.

4:13 [a]NU-Text reads *Him who.*   **4:23** [a]NU-Text reads *your spirit.*

COLOSSIANS

INTRODUCTION//

How easily we get caught up in the inflated importance of traditions! And how often we let false philosophies infiltrate and infect our faith. We also tend to worry about what other people think about us. Our vain and fickle nature predisposes us to all three traps. But in this short letter, Paul gives us reason not to worry because Christians have struggled with these things since the beginning of the church. In fact, the church at Colosse dealt with these very issues.

The apostle hoped to correct many false teachings and to encourage them in the true faith. Therefore the supremacy of Christ runs strong throughout Colossians. Jesus is "the firstborn over all creation" (1:15). "All things were created through Him and for Him. And He is before all things, and in Him all things consist" (1:16b, 17). Because of Christ's supremacy, merely human regulations have no more hold on us. The body of the sins of the flesh has been put off (2:11), and we have been forgiven.

Paul then provides basic instructions for godly living. He begins by reminding us that we were "raised with Christ" and that therefore we should "seek those things which are above, where Christ is, sitting at the right hand of God" (3:1). He reminds us to live without lust, anger, deceit, and greed, but rather to fill our lives with compassion, kindness, humility, and forgiveness. He insists that all believers have an equal standing in the eyes of God, regardless of their race, heritage, background, or sex. He provides a brief set of instructions on how a Christian household is to function (see also Ephesians 5:21—6:9), including guidance for husbands, wives, children, and servants. His key piece of advice is this: "And whatever you do, do it heartily, as to the Lord and not to men" (3:23).

Greeting

1 Paul, an apostle of Jesus Christ by the will of God, and Timothy our brother,

[2]To the saints and faithful brethren in Christ *who are* in Colosse:

Grace to you and peace from God our Father and the Lord Jesus Christ.[a]

Their Faith in Christ

[3]We give thanks to the God and Father of our Lord Jesus Christ, praying always for you, [4]since we heard of your faith in Christ Jesus and of your love for all the saints; [5]because of the hope which is laid up for you in heaven, of which you heard before in the word of the truth of the gospel, [6]which has come to you, as *it has* also in all the world, and is bringing forth fruit,[a] as *it is* also among you since the day you heard and knew the grace of God in truth; [7]as you also learned from Epaphras, our dear fellow servant, who is a faithful minister of Christ on your behalf, [8]who also declared to us your love in the Spirit.

Preeminence of Christ

[9]For this reason we also, since the day we heard it, do not cease to pray for you, and to ask that you may be filled with the knowledge of His will in all wisdom and spiritual understanding; [10]that you may walk worthy of the Lord, fully pleasing *Him*, being fruitful in every good work and increasing in the knowledge of God; [11]strengthened with all

might, according to His glorious power, for all patience and longsuffering with joy; [12]giving thanks to the Father who has qualified us to be partakers of the inheritance of the saints in the light. [13]He has delivered us from the power of darkness and conveyed *us* into the kingdom of the Son of His love, [14]in whom we have redemption through His blood,[a] the forgiveness of sins.

[15]He is the image of the invisible God, the firstborn over all creation. [16]For by Him all things were created that are in heaven and that are on earth, visible and invisible, whether thrones or dominions or principalities or powers. All things were created through Him and for Him. [17]And He is before all things, and in Him all things consist. [18]And He is the head of the body, the church, who is the beginning, the firstborn from the dead, that in all things He may have the preeminence.

↘ LEARN

1:9 • Do you have someone who regularly prays for you and your growth in Christ? Do you consistently pray that others you know will mature in their faith? We all need prayer partners who will ask the Lord to help us become increasingly like Jesus, and we all need to be praying for others that they might daily know and serve God more fully. Read through Paul's letters sometime and see how often he prays for the spiritual maturity of his friends. It's good to pray for someone's physical health, but it's even more crucial to pray for their spiritual maturity. *For more about* Prayer, *see 1 Thess. 5:17;* Fellowship, *Col. 3:16;* Growing in Christ, *1 Thess. 3:3.*

1:2 [a]NU-Text omits *and the Lord Jesus Christ.*   1:6 [a]NU-Text and M-Text add *and growing.*
1:14 [a]NU-Text and M-Text omit *through His blood.*

↓ KNOW (COL. 1:15)

Some people protest when we speak of the Trinity. "You can't find that word anywhere in the Bible," they say, and they're right. Nevertheless, you do find the teaching of the Trinity from Genesis to Revelation. "But how could that be?" they ask. "Doesn't the Bible say in Deuteronomy 6:4 that the Lord our God is one God?" Yes, our Lord is one God. We worship a single God, not multiple gods. Christians are not polytheists, but monotheists. We worship just one God. Even so, the Bible teaches that God is a Trinity, with three divine Persons who are all active simultaneously. In other words, the Father is not the same Person as the Son, and the Son is not the same Person as the Holy Spirit. There is one true God who exists in three coequal, coeternal Persons. The three Persons are of one substance, living in perfect harmony. *For more about the* Attributes of God, *see Col. 2:7; the* Holy Spirit, *1 Thess. 5:19.*

Reconciled in Christ

[19]For it pleased *the Father that* in Him all the fullness should dwell, [20]and by Him to reconcile all things to Himself, by Him, whether things on earth or things in heaven, having made peace through the blood of His cross.

[21]And you, who once were alienated and enemies in your mind by wicked works, yet now He has reconciled [22]in the body of His flesh through death, to present you holy, and blameless, and above reproach in His sight— [23]if indeed you continue in the faith, grounded and steadfast, and are not moved away from the hope of the gospel which you heard, which was preached to every creature under heaven, of which I, Paul, became a minister.

Sacrificial Service for Christ

[24]I now rejoice in my sufferings for you, and fill up in my flesh what is lacking in the afflictions of Christ, for the sake of His body, which is the church, [25]of which I became a minister according to the stewardship from God which was given to me for you, to fulfill the word of God, [26]the mystery which has been hidden from ages and from generations, but now has been revealed to His saints. [27]To them God willed to make known what are the riches of the glory of this mystery among the Gentiles: which[a] is Christ in you, the hope of glory. [28]Him we preach, warning every man and teaching every man in all wisdom, that we may present every man perfect in Christ Jesus. [29]To this *end* I also labor, striving according to His working which works in me mightily.

Not Philosophy but Christ

2 For I want you to know what a great conflict I have for you and those in Laodicea, and *for* as many as have not seen my face in the flesh, [2]that their hearts may be encouraged, being knit together in love, and *attaining* to all riches of the full assurance of understanding, to the knowledge of the mystery of God, both of the Father and[a] of Christ, [3]in whom are hidden all the treasures of wisdom and knowledge.

[4]Now this I say lest anyone should deceive you with persuasive words. [5]For though I am absent in the flesh, yet I am with you in spirit, rejoicing to see your *good* order and the steadfastness of your faith in Christ.

[6]As you therefore have received Christ Jesus the Lord, so walk in Him, [7]rooted and built up in Him and established in the faith, as you have been taught, abounding in it[a] with thanksgiving.

↘ LEARN

* * * * * * * * * * * * * * * * *

2:7 • A thankful heart is a growing heart. The Bible does not say, "Give thanks unto the Lord when you feel good," but rather, "Give thanks unto the Lord, for He is good" (Ps. 106). When we are really "rooted and built up in Him and established in the faith," we will express that to God through our thanksgiving. The more we know of God, the greater our cause for thanksgiving. Thanksgiving connects us to God's heart as almost nothing else can. It helps us to see our need and shows us God's willingness to meet that need. And it gets our eyes off of ourselves and instead focuses them on God and His infinite resources. *For more about the* Attributes of God, *see Col. 3:16;* Spiritual Disciplines, *Col. 3:16.*

[8]Beware lest anyone cheat you through philosophy and empty deceit, according to the tradition of men, according to the basic principles of the world, and not according to Christ. [9]For in Him dwells all the fullness of the Godhead bodily; [10]and you are complete in Him, who is the head of all principality and power.

Not Legalism but Christ

[11]In Him you were also circumcised with the circumcision made without hands, by putting off the body of the sins[a] of the flesh, by the circumcision of Christ, [12]buried with Him in baptism, in which you also were raised with *Him* through faith in the working of God, who raised Him from the dead. [13]And you, being dead in your trespasses and the uncircumcision of your flesh, He has made alive together with Him, having forgiven you all trespasses, [14]having wiped out the handwriting of requirements that was against us, which was contrary to us. And He has taken it out of the way, having nailed it to the cross. [15]Having disarmed principalities and powers, He made a public spectacle of them, triumphing over them in it.

1:27 [a]M-Text reads *who.*   2:2 [a]NU-Text omits *both of the Father and.*   2:7 [a]NU-Text omits *in it.*   2:11 [a]NU-Text omits *of the sins.*

→LIVE

• • • • • • • • • • • • • • •

2:13 • As soon you trust in Jesus, the devil will attack. He will whisper, "Do you *really* believe God has forgiven a sinner like you? Do you *really* believe you are going to go to heaven when you die? You're not worthy! You don't deserve it! You're not good enough!" None of us, of course, in our own righteousness is worthy or good enough. We must base our salvation not on our feelings, but on the fact of what the Word of God says. Salvation covers your past. You are saved and going to heaven. You have God's Word on it (John 3:16). *For more about* Satan, *see 1 Pet. 1:7;* Assurance of Salvation, *2 Tim. 2:19.*

Not Carnality but Christ

3 If then you were raised with Christ, seek those things which are above, where Christ is, sitting at the right hand of God. [2]Set your mind on things above, not on things on the earth. [3]For you died, and your life is hidden with Christ in God. [4]When Christ *who is* our life appears, then you also will appear with Him in glory.

> ➤ *When Christ who is our life appears, then you also will appear with Him in glory.* Col. 3:4

[16]So let no one judge you in food or in drink, or regarding a festival or a new moon or sabbaths, [17]which are a shadow of things to come, but the substance is of Christ. [18]Let no one cheat you of your reward, taking delight in *false* humility and worship of angels, intruding into those things which he has not[a] seen, vainly puffed up by his fleshly mind, [19]and not holding fast to the Head, from whom all the body, nourished and knit together by joints and ligaments, grows with the increase *that is* from God.

[20]Therefore,[a] if you died with Christ from the basic principles of the world, why, as *though* living in the world, do you subject yourselves to regulations— [21]"Do not touch, do not taste, do not handle," [22]which all concern things which perish with the using—according to the commandments and doctrines of men? [23]These things indeed have an appearance of wisdom in self-imposed religion, *false* humility, and neglect of the body, *but are* of no value against the indulgence of the flesh.

[5]Therefore put to death your members which are on the earth: fornication, uncleanness, passion, evil desire, and covetousness, which is idolatry. [6]Because of these things the wrath of God is coming upon the sons of disobedience, [7]in which you yourselves once walked when you lived in them.

[8]But now you yourselves are to put off all these: anger, wrath, malice, blasphemy, filthy language out of your mouth. [9]Do not lie to one another, since you have put off the old man with his deeds, [10]and have put on the new *man* who is renewed in knowledge according to the image of Him who created him, [11]where there is neither Greek nor Jew, circumcised nor uncircumcised, barbarian, Scythian, slave *nor* free, but Christ *is* all and in all.

2:18 [a]NU-Text omits *not.*   **2:20** [a]NU-Text and M-Text omit *Therefore.*

↑ GROW (COL. 3:2)

• •

What do you think about most of the time? Where do your thoughts wander when you're not focused on something that demands your whole attention? According to the apostle Paul, all of us should be thinking aggressively about heaven. And his counsel isn't only for those with loved ones already living there, or for someone who's getting on in years and ought to be planning a permanent move. "Set your mind" speaks of a diligent, active, single-minded investigation—as when you have lost something and are urgently searching for it. It is a focused, diligent exploration. Another way to translate this verse is, "Think heaven." The verb here appears in the present tense, which could be translated, "Keep seeking heaven." When we put it all together, Paul is telling us, "Constantly keep seeking and thinking about heaven. Your feet must be on earth, but your mind must be in heaven." *For more about* How to Live Out Your Faith, *see Col. 4:6;* Heaven, *2 Thess. 1:7.*

Character of the New Man

¹²Therefore, as *the* elect of God, holy and beloved, put on tender mercies, kindness, humility, meekness, longsuffering; ¹³bearing with one another, and forgiving one another, if anyone has a complaint against another; even as Christ forgave you, so you also *must do.* ¹⁴But above all these things put on love, which is the bond of perfection. ¹⁵And let the peace of God rule in your hearts, to which also you were called in one body; and be thankful. ¹⁶Let the word of Christ dwell in you richly in all wisdom, teaching and admonishing one another in psalms and hymns and spiritual songs, singing with grace in your hearts to the Lord. ¹⁷And whatever you do in word or deed, *do* all in the name of the Lord Jesus, giving thanks to God the Father through Him.

↘ LEARN

3:16 • God has designed us to be more like conduits than reservoirs. The Lord gives us insights into His Word and an understanding of His ways, not merely so we can amass an ocean of knowledge about Him, but rather so we can share those insights and understanding with others, both believers and unbelievers. We are to teach one another and admonish one another through things like songs and the spoken word. We go to church, not just to be fed, but also to help others. You are blessed to be a blessing. You have received so that you can give. But first, His Word must "dwell in you richly." *For more about* Worship, *see Heb. 13:15;* Fellowship, *2 Tim. 2:14;* Spiritual Disciplines, *1 Thess. 5:17;* God's Word, *1 Tim. 4:16.*

The Christian Home

¹⁸Wives, submit to your own husbands, as is fitting in the Lord.

¹⁹Husbands, love your wives and do not be bitter toward them.

²⁰Children, obey your parents in all things, for this is well pleasing to the Lord.

²¹Fathers, do not provoke your children, lest they become discouraged.

²²Bondservants, obey in all things your masters according to the flesh, not with eye-service, as men-pleasers, but in sincerity of heart, fearing God. ²³And whatever you do, do it heartily, as to the Lord and not to men, ²⁴knowing that from the Lord you will receive the reward of the inheritance; for[a] you serve the Lord Christ. ²⁵But he who does wrong will be repaid for what he has done, and there is no partiality.

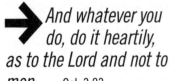

And whatever you do, do it heartily, as to the Lord and not to men . . . Col. 3:23

4 Masters, give your bondservants what is just and fair, knowing that you also have a Master in heaven.

Christian Graces

²Continue earnestly in prayer, being vigilant in it with thanksgiving; ³meanwhile praying also for us, that God would open to us a door for the word, to speak the mystery

3:24 [a]NU-Text omits *for.*

↑ GROW (COL. 3:16)

We should worship God because He is good. If you worship the Lord only when you feel like it, then you are not going to worship very often. When you go to church and the worship team or choir break into song, do you ever think, *I'm not really in a* Worship*ing mood today?* You might say, "I haven't had breakfast. I just can't worship without some breakfast in my stomach." Or, "I have a cold." Or maybe it's something worse than those things. Maybe a tragedy looms over your head. Whatever your situation, you should praise the Lord regardless of how you feel. The Bible does not say, "Give thanks unto the Lord when you feel good." No, it says, "Give thanks to the LORD, for He is good! For His mercy endures forever" (Ps. 106:1). Worship God because He is worthy of your worship! And you can do that regardless of your circumstances. *For more about* Worship, *see Heb. 13:15;* Spiritual Disciplines, *1 Thess. 5:17; the* Attributes of God, *1 Tim. 2:7.*

of Christ, for which I am also in chains, [4]that I may make it manifest, as I ought to speak.

[5]Walk in wisdom toward those *who are* outside, redeeming the time. [6]*Let* your speech always *be* with grace, seasoned with salt, that you may know how you ought to answer each one.

↘ LEARN
● ● ● ● ● ● ● ● ● ● ● ● ● ● ● ● ●

4:6 • Do you have a graceful tongue? When you speak to others, do you season your words with salt to make them palatable and healthy? Are you learning how to effectively answer those who ask about your faith? Are you growing in your ability as an effective mouthpiece for God? Paul became "all things to all men," so that he might "by all means save some" (1 Cor. 9:22). That should also be our goal. Consider the acronym THINK when speaking to others: T–Is it true? H–Is it helpful? I–Is it inspiring? N–Is it necessary? K–Is it kind? Quite frankly, if we really apply this, it would stop a great deal of what we say in its tracks. *For more about* Loving Others, *see 2 Tim. 2:14;* How to Live Out Your Faith, *2 Thess. 1:10–12.*

Final Greetings

[7]Tychicus, a beloved brother, faithful minister, and fellow servant in the Lord, will tell you all the news about me. [8]I am sending him to you for this very purpose, that he[a] may know your circumstances and comfort your hearts, [9]with Onesimus, a faithful and beloved brother, who is *one* of you. They will make known to you all things which *are happening* here.

[10]Aristarchus my fellow prisoner greets you, with Mark the cousin of Barnabas (about whom you received instructions: if he comes to you, welcome him), [11]and Jesus who is called Justus. These *are my* only fellow workers for the kingdom of God who are of the circumcision; they have proved to be a comfort to me.

[12]Epaphras, who is *one* of you, a bondservant of Christ, greets you, always laboring fervently for you in prayers, that you may stand perfect and complete[a] in all the will of God. [13]For I bear him witness that he has a great zeal[a] for you, and those who are in Laodicea, and those in Hierapolis. [14]Luke the beloved physician and Demas greet you. [15]Greet the brethren who are in Laodicea, and Nymphas and the church that *is* in his[a] house.

Closing Exhortations and Blessing

[16]Now when this epistle is read among you, see that it is read also in the church of the Laodiceans, and that you likewise read the *epistle* from Laodicea. [17]And say to Archippus, "Take heed to the ministry which you have received in the Lord, that you may fulfill it."

[18]This salutation by my own hand—Paul. Remember my chains. Grace *be* with you. Amen.

4:8 [a]NU-Text reads *you may know our circumstances and he may.* **4:12** [a]NU-Text reads *fully assured.* **4:13** [a]NU-Text reads *concern.* **4:15** [a]NU-Text reads *Nympha . . . her house.*

1 THESSALONIANS

INTRODUCTION//

Paul wrote to the church in Thessalonica to reaffirm its faithfulness to the work of Jesus Christ and to urge the people to continue living godly and holy lives as they await the return of Jesus. He recounts his last visit to the church and comments on the good report he received from Timothy about them, and so he commends them for being so willing to hold true to "the word of God, which also effectively works in you who believe" (2:13). Paul compliments the Thessalonians not only for believing, but also for standing firm in their faith as they face persecution from their countrymen. Persecution is never easy to handle for anyone—and these Thessalonians were young believers.

Paul also instructs believers about how to live in a holy way as they wait for the Lord's return. He speaks of "sanctification: that you should abstain from sexual immorality" (4:3), which was as big a problem in their culture as it is now. He urges them to continue in their spirit of brotherly love and that they "increase more and more" (4:10). As a part of this brotherly love, he provides them with ways to encourage one another, such as respecting leaders, helping the weak, praying continually, and "in everything give thanks; for this is the will of God in Christ Jesus for you" (5:18). In speaking of the Lord's return—which he mentions at the end of each chapter—he asks them to "not sleep, as others do, but let us watch and be sober . . . putting on the breastplate of faith and love" (5:6, 8). We have a living hope in Christ's return that others do not. Some might despair at the thought of death, but because of Jesus' death and resurrection, "we shall always be with the Lord" (4:17).

Greeting

1

Paul, Silvanus, and Timothy,

To the church of the Thessalonians in God the Father and the Lord Jesus Christ:

Grace to you and peace from God our Father and the Lord Jesus Christ.[a]

Their Good Example

[2]We give thanks to God always for you all, making mention of you in our prayers, [3]remembering without ceasing your work of faith, labor of love, and patience of hope in our Lord Jesus Christ in the sight of our God and Father, [4]knowing, beloved brethren, your election by God. [5]For our gospel did not come to you in word only, but also in power, and in the Holy Spirit and in much assurance, as you know what kind of men we were among you for your sake.

[6]And you became followers of us and of the Lord, having received the word in much affliction, with joy of the Holy Spirit, [7]so that you became examples to all in Macedonia and Achaia who believe. [8]For from you the word of the Lord has sounded forth, not only in Macedonia and Achaia, but also in every place. Your faith toward God has gone out, so that we do not need to say anything. [9]For they themselves declare concerning us what manner of entry we had to you, and how you turned to God from idols to serve the living and true God, [10]and to wait for His Son from heaven, whom He raised from the dead, *even* Jesus who delivers us from the wrath to come.

Paul's Conduct

2

For you yourselves know, brethren, that our coming to you was not in vain. [2]But even[a] after we had suffered before and were spitefully treated at Philippi, as you know, we were bold in our God to speak to you the gospel of God in much conflict. [3]For our exhortation *did* not *come* from error or uncleanness, nor *was it* in deceit.

[4]But as we have been approved by God to be entrusted with the gospel, even so we speak, not as pleasing men, but God who tests our hearts. [5]For neither at any time did we use flattering words, as you know, nor a cloak for covetousness—God *is* witness. [6]Nor did we seek glory from men, either from you or from others, when we might have made demands as apostles of Christ. [7]But we were gentle among you, just as a nursing *mother* cherishes her own children. [8]So, affectionately longing for you, we were well pleased to impart to you not only the gospel of God, but also our own lives, because you had become dear to us. [9]For you remember, brethren, our labor and toil; for laboring night and day, that we might not be a burden to any of you, we preached to you the gospel of God.

[10]You *are* witnesses, and God *also*, how devoutly and justly and blamelessly we behaved ourselves among you who believe; [11]as you know how we exhorted, and comforted, and charged[a] every one of you, as a father *does* his own children, [12]that you would walk worthy of God who calls you into His own kingdom and glory.

Their Conversion

[13]For this reason we also thank God without ceasing, because when you received the word of God which you heard from us, you welcomed *it* not *as* the word of men, but as it is in truth, the word of God, which also effectively works in you who believe. [14]For you, brethren, became imitators of the churches of God which are in Judea in Christ Jesus. For you also suffered the same things from your own countrymen, just as they *did* from the Judeans, [15]who killed both the Lord Jesus and their own prophets, and have persecuted us; and they do not please God and are contrary to all men, [16]forbidding us to speak to the Gentiles that they may be saved, so as always to fill up *the measure of* their sins; but wrath has come upon them to the uttermost.

Longing to See Them

[17]But we, brethren, having been taken away from you for a short time in presence, not in heart, endeavored more eagerly to see your face with great desire. [18]Therefore we wanted to come to you—even I, Paul, time and again—but Satan hindered us. [19]For what *is* our hope, or joy, or crown of rejoicing? *Is it* not even you in the presence of our Lord Jesus Christ at His coming? [20]For you are our glory and joy.

1:1 [a]NU-Text omits *from God our Father and the Lord Jesus Christ.*   2:2 [a]NU-Text and M-Text omit *even.*
2:11 [a]NU-Text and M-Text read *implored.*

Concern for Their Faith

3 Therefore, when we could no longer endure it, we thought it good to be left in Athens alone, [2]and sent Timothy, our brother and minister of God, and our fellow laborer in the gospel of Christ, to establish you and encourage you concerning your faith, [3]that no one should be shaken by these afflictions; for you yourselves know that we are appointed to this. [4]For, in fact, we told you before when we were with you that we would suffer tribulation, just as it happened, and you know. [5]For this reason, when I could no longer endure it, I sent to know your faith, lest by some means the tempter had tempted you, and our labor might be in vain.

> ### ↘ LEARN
> . . . .
> **3:3** • Jesus said, "In the world you will have tribulation" (John 16:33). Part of spiritual growth is preparing for hard times. Trials, difficulties, and even persecution make up a significant portion of the Christian life. When these painful times arrive, and they will, God wants us to be ready and to use them as platforms for growth. Instead of asking, "Why me? Why now? Why this?" the Lord encourages us to use suffering to grow closer to Him and to remember that He is fashioning us into the likeness of Christ—and Jesus suffered more than any of us ever will. The truth is, it is an honor to be persecuted for our faith (Matt. 5:11, 12). *For more about* Growing in Christ, *see 1 Thess. 4:11;* Adversity, *1 Tim. 4:16.*

Encouraged by Timothy

[6]But now that Timothy has come to us from you, and brought us good news of your faith and love, and that you always have good remembrance of us, greatly desiring to see us, as we also *to see* you— [7]therefore, brethren, in all our affliction and distress we were comforted concerning you by your faith. [8]For now we live, if you stand fast in the Lord.

[9]For what thanks can we render to God for you, for all the joy with which we rejoice for your sake before our God, [10]night and day praying exceedingly that we may see your face and perfect what is lacking in your faith?

Prayer for the Church

[11]Now may our God and Father Himself, and our Lord Jesus Christ, direct our way to you. [12]And may the Lord make you increase and abound in love to one another and to all, just as we *do* to you, [13]so that He may establish your hearts blameless in holiness before our God and Father at the coming of our Lord Jesus Christ with all His saints.

Plea for Purity

4 Finally then, brethren, we urge and exhort in the Lord Jesus that you should abound more and more, just as you received from us how you ought to walk and to please God; [2]for you know what commandments we gave you through the Lord Jesus.

[3]For this is the will of God, your sanctification: that you should abstain from sexual immorality; [4]that each of you should know how to possess his own vessel in sanctification and honor, [5]not in passion of lust, like the Gentiles who do not know God; [6]that no one should take advantage of and defraud his brother in this matter, because the Lord *is* the avenger of all such, as we also forewarned you and testified. [7]For God did not call us to

↑ GROW (1 THESS. 4:3)
. . . .
The will of God is not always easy to discern, and anyone who says he always knows God's will probably isn't being honest. At least, I don't always know God's will. Most of my life as a Christian is one of faith, not an unending series of visions and angels and pillars of fire and audible voices. Most of the time God says to us, "I have an opportunity for you right now if you will just pay attention." He *will* lead you, both supernaturally and naturally. But for the most part, finding God's will involves studying His Word, praying for direction, applying His principles, and then going out and doing the right thing. You often find God's will in the middle of the mundane. What did the Lord show you to do most recently? Start there. The will of God becomes plain when we start walking in it. *For more about* God's Will, *see 1 John 5:14, 15;* Faith, *2 Thess. 2:15.*

→LIVE
• • • • • • • • • • • • • • • •

4:3 • Christians want to know the will of God for their lives. So why does God sometimes delay in revealing it? Perhaps He is waiting for you to act on what He has already revealed in Scripture! For instance, the Bible tells us that it is God's will to be filled with the Holy Spirit (Eph. 5:15), to have an attitude of gratitude (1 Thess. 5:18), and to live a pure life (v. 3). To abstain from sexual immorality speaks to single people to remain sexually pure until marriage and faithful to one's spouse afterwards. This is clearly God's will. There are no exceptions. *For more about* God's Will, *see 1 John 5:14, 15;* Submitting to God, *1 Tim. 6:6.*

↘LEARN
• • • • • • • • • • • • • • • •

4:11 • When Paul instructs us to pursue a quiet life, to mind our own business, and to work with our own hands, he's showing us what a real Christian looks like in day-to-day living. Busybodies who leech off of others are *not* growing deeper in the Lord. Sometimes, growth best expresses itself in picking up a shovel instead of the latest devotional. Christians should be the hardest workers of all. Remember, it's not how high you jump, but how straight you walk when you hit the ground. *For more about* Growing in Christ, *2 Thess. 1:7.*

uncleanness, but in holiness. [8]Therefore he who rejects *this* does not reject man, but God, who has also given[a] us His Holy Spirit.

A Brotherly and Orderly Life

[9]But concerning brotherly love you have no need that I should write to you, for you yourselves are taught by God to love one another; [10]and indeed you do so toward all the brethren who are in all Macedonia. But we urge you, brethren, that you increase more and more; [11]that you also aspire to lead a quiet life, to mind your own business, and to work with your own hands, as we commanded you, [12]that you may walk properly toward those who are outside, and *that* you may lack nothing.

The Comfort of Christ's Coming

[13]But I do not want you to be ignorant, brethren, concerning those who have fallen asleep, lest you sorrow as others who have no hope. [14]For if we believe that Jesus died and rose again, even so God will bring with Him those who sleep in Jesus.[a]

[15]For this we say to you by the word of the Lord, that we who are alive *and* remain until the coming of the Lord will by no means precede those who are asleep. [16]For the Lord Himself will descend from heaven with a shout, with the voice of an archangel, and with the trumpet of God. And the dead in Christ will rise first. [17]Then we who are alive *and* remain shall be caught up together with them in the clouds to meet the Lord in the air. And thus we shall always be with the Lord. [18]Therefore comfort one another with these words.

The Day of the Lord

5 But concerning the times and the seasons, brethren, you have no need that I should write to you. [2]For you yourselves know perfectly that the day of the Lord

4:8 [a]NU-Text reads *who also gives.*   4:14 [a]Or *those who through Jesus sleep*

↑ GROW (1 THESS. 5:17)
• •

At its simplest, prayer is hearing from and communicating with God. All successful Christians have an active prayer life. You can pray publicly or privately. You can pray verbally or silently. Any physical position is acceptable for prayer; you can pray kneeling, standing, sitting, lying down, and even driving. You can pray with your eyes closed (*not* while driving), with your eyes opened, on your back, on your stomach, sitting down, standing up, or running. Whatever position you choose, you can pray anytime, anywhere. Sometimes we think God will hear our prayers more quickly if we offer them in a place of worship. Not necessarily true. God hears our prayers wherever we offer them. The key is to pray frequently. Pray in the morning when you get up. Pray in the afternoon when you eat or work out. Pray in the evening as you wind down for the day. Just pray! *For more about* Prayer, *see Heb. 4:16;* Spiritual Disciplines, *2 Tim. 2:15.*

so comes as a thief in the night. ³For when they say, "Peace and safety!" then sudden destruction comes upon them, as labor pains upon a pregnant woman. And they shall not escape. ⁴But you, brethren, are not in darkness, so that this Day should overtake you as a thief. ⁵You are all sons of light and sons of the day. We are not of the night nor of darkness. ⁶Therefore let us not sleep, as others *do*, but let us watch and be sober. ⁷For those who sleep, sleep at night, and those who get drunk are drunk at night. ⁸But let us who are of the day be sober, putting on the breastplate of faith and love, and *as* a helmet the hope of salvation. ⁹For God did not appoint us to wrath, but to obtain salvation through our Lord Jesus Christ, ¹⁰who died for us, that whether we wake or sleep, we should live together with Him.

¹¹Therefore comfort each other and edify one another, just as you also are doing.

Various Exhortations

¹²And we urge you, brethren, to recognize those who labor among you, and are over you in the Lord and admonish you, ¹³and to esteem them very highly in love for their work's sake. Be at peace among yourselves.

¹⁴Now we exhort you, brethren, warn those who are unruly, comfort the fainthearted, uphold the weak, be patient with all. ¹⁵See that no one renders evil for evil to anyone, but always pursue what is good both for yourselves and for all.

5:27 ᵃNU-Text omits *holy*.

¹⁶Rejoice always, ¹⁷pray without ceasing, ¹⁸in everything give thanks; for this is the will of God in Christ Jesus for you.

¹⁹Do not quench the Spirit. ²⁰Do not despise prophecies. ²¹Test all things; hold fast what is good. ²²Abstain from every form of evil.

> **Rejoice always, pray without ceasing, in everything give thanks; for this is the will of God in Christ Jesus for you.** 1 Thess. 5:16–18

Blessing and Admonition

²³Now may the God of peace Himself sanctify you completely; and may your whole spirit, soul, and body be preserved blameless at the coming of our Lord Jesus Christ. ²⁴He who calls you *is* faithful, who also will do *it*.

²⁵Brethren, pray for us.

²⁶Greet all the brethren with a holy kiss.

²⁷I charge you by the Lord that this epistle be read to all the holyᵃ brethren.

²⁸The grace of our Lord Jesus Christ *be* with you. Amen.

↓ **KNOW** (1 THESS. 5:19)

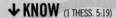

The Bible warns us against committing the sin of quenching the Holy Spirit. The word *quench* conveys the idea of extinguishing something, like pouring water on a fire. We quench the Spirit every time He leads us to do something, and either we ignore Him or refuse to do it. Perhaps the Holy Spirit is saying to you, "Do you see this thing in your life? Repent of it. Stop rationalizing and get rid of it." Too many of us say, by our actions if not by our words, "No, I am not going to quit. I am going to keep right on doing it." Such a rebellious, disobedient spirit quenches the Spirit. We quench the Holy Spirit every time we refuse to respond to His leading, urging, and nudging, as when we are led to share the gospel with someone. Don't quench the Spirit but instead yield to Him. *For more about the* Holy Spirit, *see 2 Tim. 2:19;* Sin, *1 Tim. 2:7.*

2 THESSALONIANS

INTRODUCTION//

Paul's second letter to the church at Thessalonica reiterates many of his words of encouragement given in his first letter and also provides some explanation regarding a few misinterpretations of what he had said in his initial correspondence. He begins by telling the Thessalonians that he and colleagues "boast of you among the churches of God for your patience and faith in all your persecutions and tribulations" (1:4). He claims that their positive response to persecution provides evidence of their strong faith, so that when the Lord comes again, their persecutors "shall be punished with everlasting destruction from the presence of the Lord and from the glory of His power" (1:9). Paul had perhaps only six weeks with the Thessalonians before he was forced to flee the city, so he found it necessary to correct some misunderstandings regarding "the day of the Lord." Many believers had become convinced that Christ already had returned, but Paul points out several signs that had to occur before the Second Coming.

Because of these misconceptions about Jesus' return, many believers had stopped working and were just sitting around, waiting. Paul admonishes these people for not living according to his teaching and his example. He warns them to stay away from anyone who unnecessarily burdens his fellow Christians, like those who would take hospitality and food without working or paying for it. Furthermore, he warns of idle people becoming busybodies and gossips. In light of Christ's return, he asks that his friends live in an upright way, free from such vices, and warn their brothers who had fallen into such practices. They should all pray "that the word of the Lord may run swiftly and be glorified" (3:1). And he reminds them that "the Lord is faithful, who will establish you and guard you from the evil one" (3:3).

Greeting

1

Paul, Silvanus, and Timothy,

To the church of the Thessalonians in God our Father and the Lord Jesus Christ:

[2]Grace to you and peace from God our Father and the Lord Jesus Christ.

God's Final Judgment and Glory

[3]We are bound to thank God always for you, brethren, as it is fitting, because your faith grows exceedingly, and the love of every one of you all abounds toward each other, [4]so that we ourselves boast of you among the churches of God for your patience and faith in all your persecutions and tribulations that you endure, [5]*which is* manifest evidence of the righteous judgment of God, that you may be counted worthy of the kingdom of God, for which you also suffer; [6]since *it is* a righteous thing with God to repay with tribulation those who trouble you, [7]and to *give* you who are troubled rest with us when the Lord Jesus is revealed from heaven with His mighty angels, [8]in flaming fire taking vengeance on those who do not know God, and on those who do not obey the gospel of our Lord Jesus Christ. [9]These shall be punished with everlasting destruction from the presence of the Lord and from the glory of His power, [10]when He comes, in that Day, to be glorified in His saints and to be admired among all those who believe,[a] because our testimony among you was believed. [11]Therefore we also pray always for you

> ### ↘ LEARN
> • • • • • • • • • • • • • • • •
>
> 1:7 • If we want to keep moving ahead in the present, sometimes it helps to remember what's coming in the future. That's one reason the apostle Paul spoke so much to the Thessalonian church—a congregation full of young believers—about the Second Coming of Christ and what would happen to both believers and unbelievers. God knows the hardships we may be suffering, but He also wants us to look forward to the amazing blessings He has in store for us. We all need to be heavenly-minded people (Col. 3). We can keep moving forward today by remembering what's coming tomorrow. *For more about* Growing in Christ, *see 2 Thess. 2:15;* Jesus' Return, *2 Thess. 1:10–12;* Heaven, *Rev. 7:9.*

that our God would count you worthy of *this* calling, and fulfill all the good pleasure of *His* goodness and the work of faith with power, [12]that the name of our Lord Jesus Christ may be glorified in you, and you in Him, according to the grace of our God and the Lord Jesus Christ.

The Great Apostasy

2

Now, brethren, concerning the coming of our Lord Jesus Christ and our gathering together to Him, we ask you, [2]not to be soon shaken in mind or troubled, either by spirit or by word or by letter, as if from us, as though the day of Christ[a] had come. [3]Let no one deceive you by any means; for *that Day will not come* unless the falling away comes first, and the man of sin[a] is revealed, the son of perdition, [4]who opposes and exalts himself above all that is called God or that is wor-

1:10 [a]NU-Text and M-Text read *have believed.*   2:2 [a]NU-Text reads *the Lord.*   2:3 [a]NU-Text reads *lawlessness.*

↑ GROW (2 THESS. 1:10–12)
• •

How should we behave and conduct ourselves, given the knowledge that Christ could return at any moment? Paul gives us at least one clear instruction: wake up! A lot of people in the church are fast asleep, spiritually as well as physically. They hear the Word of God, take it in, and quickly become spiritually lethargic. These earth-shaking truths should move them spiritually, but somehow they don't. Wake up, Paul says! The signs of the times are all around you. Jesus Christ is coming back! Therefore make up your mind to live in a holy, God-pleasing way. If you don't already, start looking forward to the return of Jesus, waiting for it with eager, joyful anticipation. The thought of His Second Coming should give birth to a barely-contained excitement, not a miserable, gloomy attitude. The Lord could come at any time. We need to wake up! *For more about* Jesus' Return, *see 2 Thess. 2:7;* How to Live Out Your Faith, *1 Tim. 6:6.*

shiped, so that he sits as God[a] in the temple of God, showing himself that he is God.

[5]Do you not remember that when I was still with you I told you these things? [6]And now you know what is restraining, that he may be revealed in his own time. [7]For the mystery of lawlessness is already at work; only He[a] who now restrains *will do so* until He[b] is taken out of the way. [8]And then the lawless one will be revealed, whom the Lord will consume with the breath of His mouth and destroy with the brightness of His coming. [9]The coming of the *lawless one* is according to the working of Satan, with all power, signs, and lying wonders, [10]and with all unrighteous deception among those who perish, because they did not receive the love of the truth, that they might be saved. [11]And for this reason God will send them strong delusion, that they should believe the lie, [12]that they all may be condemned who did not believe the truth but had pleasure in unrighteousness.

Stand Fast

[13]But we are bound to give thanks to God always for you, brethren beloved by the Lord, because God from the beginning chose you for salvation through sanctification by the Spirit and belief in the truth, [14]to which He called you by our gospel, for the obtaining of the glory of our Lord Jesus Christ. [15]Therefore, brethren, stand fast and hold the traditions which you were taught, whether by word or our epistle.

[16]Now may our Lord Jesus Christ Himself, and our God and Father, who has loved us and given *us* everlasting consolation and

↘ LEARN

2:15 • How does an oak tree grow from a small, insignificant acorn into a massive and sturdy plant? It doesn't do so by flitting from spot to spot, continually seeking ideal conditions for growth. Acorns become mighty oaks by staying put. In a similar way, we grow in faith when we hold firm to the teachings of the Bible and refuse to be moved from the unchanging truth of the gospel. In an unstable and rapidly changing culture, "Stand fast" may be the best advice we'll ever get. Jesus told us to "abide in Him," which means to stay in a given place (John 15). *For more about* Growing in Christ, *see 2 Tim. 2:15;* Faith, *Titus 2:14.*

good hope by grace, [17]comfort your hearts and establish you in every good word and work.

Pray for Us

3 Finally, brethren, pray for us, that the word of the Lord may run *swiftly* and be glorified, just as *it is* with you, [2]and that we may be delivered from unreasonable and wicked men; for not all have faith.

[3]But the Lord is faithful, who will establish you and guard *you* from the evil one. [4]And we have confidence in the Lord concerning

➜ But the Lord is faithful, who will establish you and guard you from the evil one. 2 Thess. 3:3

2:4 [a]NU-Text omits *as God.*   2:7 [a]Or *he* [b]Or *he*

you, both that you do and will do the things we command you.

[5]Now may the Lord direct your hearts into the love of God and into the patience of Christ.

> **→LIVE**
> . . . .
> **3:5** • If you count Jesus Christ as your Lord and Savior, you have God's unconditional love and approval because of what He's done for you. You have His love and approval when you are spiritually flourishing, as well as when you are floundering. To get this straight in your mind could mean the revolutionizing of your Christian walk. You should desire to live in a way that pleases God, *not* to gain His approval, but rather because you recognize you already have it! Nothing can separate you from God's love (Rom. 8:38, 39). Deepen your understanding of how much God really loves you. *For more about* God's Love, *see Titus 2:11.*

Warning Against Idleness

[6]But we command you, brethren, in the name of our Lord Jesus Christ, that you withdraw from every brother who walks disorderly and not according to the tradition which he[a] received from us. [7]For you yourselves know how you ought to follow us, for we were not disorderly among you; [8]nor did we eat anyone's bread free of charge, but worked with labor and toil night and day, that we might not be a burden to any of you, [9]not because we do not have authority, but

3:6 [a]NU-Text and M-Text read *they.*

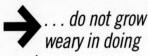

... do not grow weary in doing good. 2 Thess. 3:13

to make ourselves an example of how you should follow us.

[10]For even when we were with you, we commanded you this: If anyone will not work, neither shall he eat. [11]For we hear that there are some who walk among you in a disorderly manner, not working at all, but are busybodies. [12]Now those who are such we command and exhort through our Lord Jesus Christ that they work in quietness and eat their own bread.

[13]But *as for* you, brethren, do not grow weary *in* doing good. [14]And if anyone does not obey our word in this epistle, note that person and do not keep company with him, that he may be ashamed. [15]Yet do not count *him* as an enemy, but admonish *him* as a brother.

Benediction

[16]Now may the Lord of peace Himself give you peace always in every way. The Lord *be* with you all.

[17]The salutation of Paul with my own hand, which is a sign in every epistle; so I write.

[18]The grace of our Lord Jesus Christ *be* with you all. Amen.

1 TIMOTHY ↙

INTRODUCTION//

P aul wrote this letter to his protégé, Timothy, a half-Greek and half-Hebrew believer in Christ, to lay out the proper conduct of the church and its leaders. Paul points out that false teachers, bad practices, and unqualified leaders can harm the church. He does not mean to encourage cynicism and the distrust of church authorities, but he does want us to defer to Scripture over the authority of men. Scripture sets the standard that we are to use to provide a good example for the church.

Paul's first instructions concern worship and prayer. He asks women to dress and conduct themselves with modesty in the church. In one of the more controversial passages in Paul's letters—at least, in modern times—He also forbids women to teach or to have authority over men. These verses must be read very carefully and in the context of Paul's other writings. Whatever one's interpretation, the passage clearly does *not* mean that women cannot participate in ministry, as in other letters he refers to certain women as "fellow workers" and a "servant of the church" (or "deaconness," see Rom. 16:1, 3). Paul then gives instructions and qualifications for those working in the church. He says a church authority should be "blameless, the husband of one wife, temperate, sober-minded, of good behavior, hospitable, able to teach; not given to wine, not violent, not greedy for money, but gentle, not quarrelsome, not covetous" (3:2, 3). He tells Timothy, "Let no one despise your youth, but be an example to the believers in word, in conduct, in love, in spirit, in faith, in purity" (4:12). And he ends his letter with a double warning about the power of money to spiritually sidetrack any believer (6:5–19), and a last warning about straying from the faith through "profane and idle babblings" (6:20).

Greeting

1 Paul, an apostle of Jesus Christ, by the commandment of God our Savior and the Lord Jesus Christ, our hope,

[2]To Timothy, a true son in the faith:

Grace, mercy, *and* peace from God our Father and Jesus Christ our Lord.

No Other Doctrine

[3]As I urged you when I went into Macedonia—remain in Ephesus that you may charge some that they teach no other doctrine, [4]nor give heed to fables and endless genealogies, which cause disputes rather than godly edification which is in faith. [5]Now the purpose of the commandment is love from a pure heart, *from* a good conscience, and *from* sincere faith, [6]from which some, having strayed, have turned aside to idle talk, [7]desiring to be teachers of the law, understanding neither what they say nor the things which they affirm.

[8]But we know that the law *is* good if one uses it lawfully, [9]knowing this: that the law is not made for a righteous person, but for *the* lawless and insubordinate, for *the* ungodly and for sinners, for *the* unholy and profane, for murderers of fathers and murderers of mothers, for manslayers, [10]for fornicators, for sodomites, for kidnappers, for liars, for perjurers, and if there is any other thing that is contrary to sound doctrine, [11]according to the glorious gospel of the blessed God which was committed to my trust.

Glory to God for His Grace

[12]And I thank Christ Jesus our Lord who has enabled me, because He counted me faithful, putting *me* into the ministry, [13]although I was formerly a blasphemer, a persecutor, and an insolent man; but I obtained mercy because I did *it* ignorantly in unbelief. [14]And the grace of our Lord was exceedingly abundant, with faith and love which are in Christ Jesus. [15]This *is* a faithful saying and worthy of all acceptance, that Christ Jesus came into the world to save sinners, of whom I am chief. [16]However, for this reason I obtained mercy, that in me first Jesus Christ

> **→LIVE**
>
> **1:15 •** Justification speaks not only of what God has taken away, but also of what He has put in its place. Justification is more than forgiveness and the removal of guilt and condemnation; that denotes the negative part of what He has taken away. Justification has a positive side, as well, which includes what He has done and given to us. Justification is a legal act of God declaring the guilty guiltless before God. It is the complete acquittal of the guilty sinner. When God justifies a person, He does so by placing to his credit all the righteousness of Christ. *For more about* Forgiveness, *see Heb. 10:22;* New Life in Christ, *Titus 2:11.*

might show all longsuffering, as a pattern to those who are going to believe on Him for everlasting life. [17]Now to the King eternal, immortal, invisible, to God who alone is wise,[a] *be* honor and glory forever and ever. Amen.

Fight the Good Fight

[18]This charge I commit to you, son Timothy, according to the prophecies previously made concerning you, that by them you may wage the good warfare, [19]having faith and a good conscience, which some having rejected, concerning the faith have suffered shipwreck, [20]of whom are Hymenaeus and Alexander, whom I delivered to Satan that they may learn not to blaspheme.

Pray for All Men

2 Therefore I exhort first of all that supplications, prayers, intercessions, *and* giving of thanks be made for all men, [2]for kings and all who are in authority, that we may lead a quiet and peaceable life in all godliness and reverence. [3]For this *is* good and acceptable in the sight of God our Savior, [4]who desires all men to be saved and to come to the knowledge of the truth. [5]For *there is* one God and one Mediator between God and men, *the* Man Christ Jesus, [6]who gave Himself a ransom for all, to be testified in due time, [7]for which I was appointed a preacher and an apostle—I am speaking the truth in Christ[a] *and* not lying—a teacher of the Gentiles in faith and truth.

1:17 [a]NU-Text reads *to the only God.*   2:7 [a]NU-Text omits *in Christ.*

> **For there is one God and one Mediator between God and men, the Man Christ Jesus, who gave Himself a ransom for all** . . . 1 Tim. 2:5, 6

Men and Women in the Church

[8]I desire therefore that the men pray everywhere, lifting up holy hands, without wrath and doubting; [9]in like manner also, that the women adorn themselves in modest apparel, with propriety and moderation, not with braided hair or gold or pearls or costly clothing, [10]but, which is proper for women professing godliness, with good works. [11]Let a woman learn in silence with all submission. [12]And I do not permit a woman to teach or to have authority over a man, but to be in silence. [13]For Adam was formed first, then Eve. [14]And Adam was not deceived, but the woman being deceived, fell into transgression. [15]Nevertheless she will be saved in childbearing if they continue in faith, love, and holiness, with self-control.

Qualifications of Overseers

3 This *is* a faithful saying: If a man desires the position of a bishop,[a] he desires a good work. [2]A bishop then must be blameless, the husband of one wife, temperate, sober-minded, of good behavior, hospi-

table, able to teach; [3]not given to wine, not violent, not greedy for money,[a] but gentle, not quarrelsome, not covetous; [4]one who rules his own house well, having *his* children in submission with all reverence [5](for if a man does not know how to rule his own house, how will he take care of the church of God?); [6]not a novice, lest being puffed up with pride he fall into the *same* condemnation as the devil. [7]Moreover he must have a good testimony among those who are outside, lest he fall into reproach and the snare of the devil.

Qualifications of Deacons

[8]Likewise deacons *must be* reverent, not double-tongued, not given to much wine, not greedy for money, [9]holding the mystery of the faith with a pure conscience. [10]But let these also first be tested; then let them serve as deacons, being *found* blameless. [11]Likewise, *their* wives *must be* reverent, not slanderers, temperate, faithful in all things. [12]Let deacons be the husbands of one wife, ruling *their* children and their own houses well. [13]For those who have served well as deacons obtain for themselves a good standing and great boldness in the faith which is in Christ Jesus.

The Great Mystery

[14]These things I write to you, though I hope to come to you shortly; [15]but if I am delayed, *I write* so that you may know how you ought to conduct yourself in the house of God, which is the church of the living God, the pillar and ground of the truth. [16]And without controversy great is the mystery of godliness:

3:1 [a]Literally *overseer*   **3:3** [a]NU-Text omits *not greedy for money.*

↑ GROW (1 TIM. 2:7)

. . . .

Because God is truth, we need to be truthful. It seems like a no-brainer, doesn't it? And yet a lot of believers apparently missed the memo. Scripture tells us that lying lips are an abomination to the Lord. In fact, in a list of seven things that God hates, two items deal with lying and falsehood (Prov. 6:16–19). Tell the truth! Besides, there's another simple reason why you should tell the truth: it's just too much work to tell lies. It is hard to remember which lie you told to whom and how you told it. You end up having to tell one lie to cover up the first thing you did wrong, and then tell another lie to back up that lie, and a third lie to cover the first two lies. After a while, you get confused. It's a lot simpler to just be truthful. Walk in truth! *For more about the* Attributes of God, *see 1 Tim. 6:16;* Sin, *Heb. 3:14.*

God[a] was manifested in the flesh,
Justified in the Spirit,
Seen by angels,
Preached among the Gentiles,
Believed on in the world,
Received up in glory.

The Great Apostasy

4 Now the Spirit expressly says that in latter times some will depart from the faith, giving heed to deceiving spirits and doctrines of demons, [2]speaking lies in hypocrisy, having their own conscience seared with a hot iron, [3]forbidding to marry, *and commanding* to abstain from foods which God created to be received with thanksgiving by those who believe and know the truth. [4]For every creature of God *is* good, and nothing is to be refused if it is received with thanksgiving; [5]for it is sanctified by the word of God and prayer.

A Good Servant of Jesus Christ

[6]If you instruct the brethren in these things, you will be a good minister of Jesus Christ, nourished in the words of faith and of the good doctrine which you have carefully followed. [7]But reject profane and old wives' fables, and exercise yourself toward godliness. [8]For bodily exercise profits a little, but godliness is profitable for all things, having promise of the life that now is and of that which is to come. [9]This *is* a faithful saying and worthy of all acceptance. [10]For to this *end* we both labor and suffer reproach,[a] because we trust in the living God, who is *the* Savior of all men,

especially of those who believe. [11]These things command and teach.

Take Heed to Your Ministry

[12]Let no one despise your youth, but be an example to the believers in word, in conduct, in love, in spirit,[a] in faith, in purity. [13]Till I come, give attention to reading, to exhortation, to doctrine. [14]Do not neglect the gift that is in you, which was given to you by prophecy with the laying on of the hands of the eldership. [15]Meditate on these things; give yourself entirely to them, that your progress

> **Let no one despise your youth, but be an example to the believers in word, in conduct, in love, in spirit, in faith, in purity.** 1 Tim. 4:12

may be evident to all. [16]Take heed to yourself and to the doctrine. Continue in them, for in doing this you will save both yourself and those who hear you.

Treatment of Church Members

5 Do not rebuke an older man, but exhort *him* as a father, younger men as brothers, [2]older women as mothers, younger women as sisters, with all purity.

3:16 [a]NU-Text reads *Who.*   4:10 [a]NU-Text reads *we labor and strive.*   4:12 [a]NU-Text omits *in spirit.*

↑ GROW (1 TIM. 4:16)

When a time of crisis hits, where will you turn? When a tragedy strikes, what will you do? You will need something to give you both strength and direction—and you can find both in the Word of God. In my own times of anguish I have trusted in the Bible's message and it has sustained me and given me direction, hope, and comfort. When the ground shakes and gale-force winds blow in, little platitudes and clever sayings don't cut it. But the Word of God does. I urge you to get a good foundation in God's book, because it is only a matter of time until hardship strikes you. It happens in every life; there are no exceptions. But if you have a foundation in God's Word, you will be ready when it comes. Don't wait to try to catch up later. Build your foundation *now.* Know what the Bible teaches. *For more about* God's Word, *see 2 Tim. 2:15;* Adversity, *James 1:12.*

Honor True Widows

[3]Honor widows who are really widows. [4]But if any widow has children or grandchildren, let them first learn to show piety at home and to repay their parents; for this is good and[a] acceptable before God. [5]Now she who is really a widow, and left alone, trusts in God and continues in supplications and prayers night and day. [6]But she who lives in pleasure is dead while she lives. [7]And these things command, that they may be blameless. [8]But if anyone does not provide for his own, and especially for those of his household, he has denied the faith and is worse than an unbeliever.

[9]Do not let a widow under sixty years old be taken into the number, *and not unless* she has been the wife of one man, [10]well reported for good works: if she has brought up children, if she has lodged strangers, if she has washed the saints' feet, if she has relieved the afflicted, if she has diligently followed every good work.

[11]But refuse *the* younger widows; for when they have begun to grow wanton against Christ, they desire to marry, [12]having condemnation because they have cast off their first faith. [13]And besides they learn *to be* idle, wandering about from house to house, and not only idle but also gossips and busybodies, saying things which they ought not. [14]Therefore I desire that *the* younger *widows* marry, bear children, manage the house, give no opportunity to the adversary to speak reproachfully. [15]For some have already turned aside after Satan. [16]If any believing man or[a] woman has widows, let them relieve them, and do not let the church be burdened, that it may relieve those who are really widows.

Honor the Elders

[17]Let the elders who rule well be counted worthy of double honor, especially those who labor in the word and doctrine. [18]For the Scripture says, *"You shall not muzzle an ox while it treads out the grain,"*[a] and, *"The laborer is worthy of his wages."*[b] [19]Do not receive an accusation against an elder except from two or three witnesses. [20]Those who are sinning rebuke in the presence of all, that the rest also may fear.

[21]I charge *you* before God and the Lord Jesus Christ and the elect angels that you observe these things without prejudice, doing nothing with partiality. [22]Do not lay hands on anyone hastily, nor share in other people's sins; keep yourself pure.

[23]No longer drink only water, but use a little wine for your stomach's sake and your frequent infirmities.

[24]Some men's sins are clearly evident, preceding *them* to judgment, but those of some *men* follow later. [25]Likewise, the good works *of some* are clearly evident, and those that are otherwise cannot be hidden.

Honor Masters

6 Let as many bondservants as are under the yoke count their own masters worthy of all honor, so that the name of God and *His* doctrine may not be blasphemed. [2]And those who have believing masters, let them not despise *them* because they are brethren, but rather serve *them* because those who are benefited are believers and beloved. Teach and exhort these things.

Error and Greed

[3]If anyone teaches otherwise and does not consent to wholesome words, *even* the words of our Lord Jesus Christ, and to the doctrine which accords with godliness, [4]he is proud, knowing nothing, but is obsessed with disputes and arguments over words, from which come envy, strife, reviling, evil suspicions, [5]useless wranglings[a] of men of corrupt minds and destitute of the truth, who suppose that godliness is a *means of* gain. From such withdraw yourself.[b]

↘ LEARN

• • • • • • • • • • • • • • • •

6:6 • David said, "The LORD is my shepherd, I shall not want" (Ps 23:1). So if we are always wanting, wanting, wanting, can we truly say the Lord is *our* shepherd? So how do we deal with this dissatisfaction in our lives? Paul answers with two words: *godly contentment.* That's why the writer of Hebrews advises us, "Be content with such things as you have. For He Himself has said, 'I will never leave you nor forsake you'" (13:5). Our contentment does not come from what we have, but who we know. *For more about* How to Live Out Your Faith, *see* Titus 1:16; Submitting to God, *James 4:1, 2.*

5:4 [a]NU-Text and M-Text omit *good and.*   **5:16** [a]NU-Text omits *man or.*   **5:18** [a]Deuteronomy 25:4   [b]Luke 10:7   **6:5** [a]NU-Text and M-Text read *constant friction.*   [b]NU-Text omits this sentence.

⁶Now godliness with contentment is great gain. ⁷For we brought nothing into *this* world, *and it is* certain[a] we can carry nothing out. ⁸And having food and clothing, with these we shall be content. ⁹But those who desire to be rich fall into temptation and a snare, and *into* many foolish and harmful lusts which drown men in destruction and perdition. ¹⁰For the love of money is a root of all *kinds of* evil, for which some have strayed from the faith in their greediness, and pierced themselves through with many sorrows.

The Good Confession

¹¹But you, O man of God, flee these things and pursue righteousness, godliness, faith, love, patience, gentleness. ¹²Fight the good fight of faith, lay hold on eternal life, to which you were also called and have confessed the good confession in the presence of many witnesses. ¹³I urge you in the sight of God who gives life to all things, and *before* Christ Jesus who witnessed the good confession before Pontius Pilate, ¹⁴that you keep *this* commandment without spot, blameless until our Lord Jesus Christ's appearing, ¹⁵which He will manifest in His own time, *He who is* the blessed and only Potentate, the King of kings and Lord of lords, ¹⁶who alone has immortality, dwelling in unapproachable light, whom no man has seen or can see, to whom *be* honor and everlasting power. Amen.

Instructions to the Rich

¹⁷Command those who are rich in this present age not to be haughty, nor to trust in uncertain riches but in the living God, who gives us richly all things to enjoy. ¹⁸*Let them* do good, that they be rich in good works, ready to give, willing to share, ¹⁹storing up for themselves a good foundation for the time to come, that they may lay hold on eternal life.

Guard the Faith

²⁰O Timothy! Guard what was committed to your trust, avoiding the profane *and* idle babblings and contradictions of what is falsely called knowledge— ²¹by professing it some have strayed concerning the faith.

Grace *be* with you. Amen.

6:7 ªNU-Text omits *and it is certain.*

↓ KNOW (1 TIM. 6:16)

Sooner or later, everyone gets around to asking, "Where did God come from?" In fact, God always has existed. He did not come from something. He was not invented or created. God has no beginning nor does He have an end. Genesis 1:1 says, "In the beginning God." It is as simple as that. But who is this God who has always existed? This is much harder, because it calls for trying to wrap our finite minds around the infinite. We try to make God fit our logic; sometimes He does, but often He does not. This is no cop-out. It is a simple acknowledgement that I will never be able to fully comprehend God this side of heaven. Nevertheless, we *can* know God, which is the essence of being a Christian. Remember, if God were small enough for our minds, He would not be big enough for our needs. *For more about the* Attributes of God, *see 2 Tim. 4:8.*

2 TIMOTHY

INTRODUCTION//

I n this final letter before his death in A.D. 66–67, Paul wrote again to Timothy to encourage him to remain faithful to Christ. It is more intimate than his first letter, with more personal references and advice. Paul urges Timothy to continue to preach the gospel and maintain sound doctrine, despite any trials. He speaks of his own suffering and how through his persecution the Lord stood by him and strengthened him—even though men had abandoned him. He tells Timothy, "Do not be ashamed of the testimony of our Lord, nor of me His prisoner, but share with me in the sufferings for the gospel according to the power of God" (1:8). Paul warns Timothy not to "strive about words to no profit" and to "shun profane and idle babblings" because it results in "the ruin of the hearers" (2:14, 16).

Paul also briefly describes the last days: "Men will be lovers of themselves, lovers of money . . . unloving, unforgiving . . . lovers of pleasure rather than lovers of God, having a form of godliness but denying its power" (3:2–5). He warns Timothy that people will gather around themselves teachers willing to say whatever suits their audiences' desires. Paul therefore gives Timothy this charge: "Preach the word! Be ready in season and out of season. Convince, rebuke, exhort, with all longsuffering and teaching" (4:2). Paul wrote this letter from a dank Roman prison, and he knew that his execution, approved by the Emperor Nero, was approaching: "I am already being poured out as a drink offering, and the time of my departure is at hand" (4:6). Still, he expressed the confidence that "the Lord will deliver me from every evil work and preserve me for His heavenly kingdom" (4:18). Even as the hour of our own death approaches, we can have the same hope.

Greeting

1 Paul, an apostle of Jesus Christ[a] by the will of God, according to the promise of life which is in Christ Jesus,

[2]To Timothy, a beloved son:

Grace, mercy, *and* peace from God the Father and Christ Jesus our Lord.

Timothy's Faith and Heritage

[3]I thank God, whom I serve with a pure conscience, as *my* forefathers *did,* as without ceasing I remember you in my prayers night and day, [4]greatly desiring to see you, being mindful of your tears, that I may be filled with joy, [5]when I call to remembrance the genuine faith that is in you, which dwelt first in your grandmother Lois and your mother Eunice, and I am persuaded is in you also. [6]Therefore I remind you to stir up the gift of God which is in you through the laying on of my hands. [7]For God has not given us a spirit of fear, but of power and of love and of a sound mind.

> ➤ *For God has not given us a spirit of fear, but of power and of love and of a sound mind.* 2 Tim. 1:7

Not Ashamed of the Gospel

[8]Therefore do not be ashamed of the testimony of our Lord, nor of me His prisoner, but share with me in the sufferings for the gospel according to the power of God, [9]who has saved us and called *us* with a holy calling, not according to our works, but according to His own purpose and grace which was given to us in Christ Jesus before time began, [10]but has now been revealed by the appearing of our Savior Jesus Christ, *who* has abolished death and brought life and immortality to light through the gospel, [11]to which I was appointed a preacher, an apostle, and a teacher of the Gentiles.[a] [12]For this reason I also suffer these things; nevertheless I am not ashamed, for I know whom I have believed and am

↘ LEARN

1:8 • New believers usually can't wait to tell everyone they meet about Jesus and the salvation He freely offers. A strong desire to speak about Christ wells up naturally in their hearts. But in time, unfortunately, the enthusiasm often ebbs and many followers of Christ begin to feel a bit complacent about sharing their testimony. Paul says to us, "Don't be ashamed. Don't shrink from identifying with Jesus or with His people. Even if it costs you something to witness about the Lord, do it. Don't let fear keep you from introducing others to Jesus. Remember, you have the power of God!" *For more about* Sharing Your Faith, *see Titus 1:16.*

persuaded that He is able to keep what I have committed to Him until that Day.

Be Loyal to the Faith

[13]Hold fast the pattern of sound words which you have heard from me, in faith and love which are in Christ Jesus. [14]That good thing which was committed to you, keep by the Holy Spirit who dwells in us.

[15]This you know, that all those in Asia have turned away from me, among whom are Phygellus and Hermogenes. [16]The Lord grant mercy to the household of Onesiphorus, for he often refreshed me, and was not ashamed of my chain; [17]but when he arrived in Rome, he sought me out very zealously and found *me.* [18]The Lord grant to him that he may find mercy from the Lord in that Day—and you know very well how many ways he ministered *to me*[a] at Ephesus.

Be Strong in Grace

2 You therefore, my son, be strong in the grace that is in Christ Jesus. [2]And the things that you have heard from me among many witnesses, commit these to faithful men who will be able to teach others also. [3]You therefore must endure[a] hardship as a good soldier of Jesus Christ. [4]No one engaged in warfare entangles himself with the affairs of *this* life, that he may please him who enlisted him as a soldier. [5]And also if anyone competes in athletics, he is not crowned unless he competes according to the rules. [6]The hardworking farmer must be first to partake of the

---

1:1 [a]NU-Text and M-Text read *Christ Jesus.*   1:11 [a]NU-Text omits *of the Gentiles.*   1:18 [a]*To me* is from the Vulgate and a few Greek manuscripts.   2:3 [a]NU-Text reads *You must share.*

crops. [7]Consider what I say, and may[a] the Lord give you understanding in all things.

[8]Remember that Jesus Christ, of the seed of David, was raised from the dead according to my gospel, [9]for which I suffer trouble as an evildoer, *even* to the point of chains; but the word of God is not chained. [10]Therefore I endure all things for the sake of the elect, that they also may obtain the salvation which is in Christ Jesus with eternal glory.

[11]*This is* a faithful saying:

For if we died with *Him,*
We shall also live with *Him.*
[12]If we endure,
We shall also reign with *Him.*
If we deny *Him,*
He also will deny us.
[13]If we are faithless,
He remains faithful;
He cannot deny Himself.

Approved and Disapproved Workers

[14]Remind *them* of these things, charging *them* before the Lord not to strive about words to no profit, to the ruin of the hearers. [15]Be diligent to present yourself approved to God, a worker who does not need to be ashamed, rightly dividing the word of truth. [16]But shun profane *and* idle babblings, for

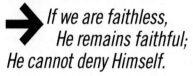

If we are faithless,
  He remains faithful;
He cannot deny Himself.

2 Tim. 2:13

2:7 [a]NU-Text reads *the Lord will give you.*

they will increase to more ungodliness. [17]And their message will spread like cancer. Hymenaeus and Philetus are of this sort, [18]who have strayed concerning the truth, saying that the resurrection is already past; and they overthrow the faith of some. [19]Nevertheless the solid foundation of God stands, having this seal: "The Lord knows those who are His," and, "Let everyone who names the name of Christ[a] depart from iniquity."

[20]But in a great house there are not only vessels of gold and silver, but also of wood and clay, some for honor and some for dishonor. [21]Therefore if anyone cleanses himself from the latter, he will be a vessel for honor, sanctified and useful for the Master, prepared for every good work. [22]Flee also youthful lusts; but pursue righteousness, faith, love, peace with those who call on the Lord out of a pure heart. [23]But avoid foolish and ignorant disputes, knowing that they generate strife. [24]And a servant of the Lord must not quarrel but be gentle to all, able to teach, patient, [25]in humility correcting those who are in opposition, if God perhaps will grant them repentance, so that they may know the truth, [26]and *that* they may come to their senses *and escape* the snare of the devil, having been taken captive by him to *do* his will.

Perilous Times and Perilous Men

3 But know this, that in the last days perilous times will come: [2]For men will be lovers of themselves, lovers of money, boasters, proud, blasphemers, disobedient to parents, unthankful, unholy, [3]unloving, unforgiving, slanderers, without self-control, brutal, despisers of good, [4]traitors, headstrong, haughty, lovers of pleasure rather than lovers of God, [5]having a form of godliness but denying its power. And from such people turn away! [6]For of this sort are those who creep into households and make captives of gullible women loaded down with sins, led away by

↘ LEARN

3:7 • There's a big difference between accumulating mounds of facts about Christian topics and actually coming to a genuine "knowledge of the truth." Nobody can grow in faith without increasing their biblical knowledge, but the mere collection of scriptural facts doesn't guarantee spiritual growth. So how can you make sure that your personal study is leading to a genuine "knowledge of the truth"? Much depends on what your study produces. If your knowledge leads to a godly life, a divine purpose, a strong faith, and love, perseverance, and a longsuffering nature, then probably you're on the right track (see v. 10). We are not to be hearers of the Word, but also doers (James 1:22). *For more about* Growing in Christ, *see Heb. 2:1.*

various lusts, [7]always learning and never able to come to the knowledge of the truth. [8]Now as Jannes and Jambres resisted Moses, so do these also resist the truth: men of corrupt minds, disapproved concerning the faith; [9]but they will progress no further, for their folly will be manifest to all, as theirs also was.

The Man of God and the Word of God

[10]But you have carefully followed my doctrine, manner of life, purpose, faith, longsuffering, love, perseverance, [11]persecutions, afflictions, which happened to me at Antioch, at Iconium, at Lystra—what persecutions I endured. And out of *them* all the Lord delivered me. [12]Yes, and all who desire to live godly in Christ Jesus will suffer persecution. [13]But evil men and impostors will grow worse and worse, deceiving and being deceived. [14]But you

2:19 [a]NU-Text and M-Text read *the Lord.*

↑ GROW (2 TIM. 4:3)

Sometimes people ask me, "What should I do if I come to a verse in the Bible that I don't agree with?" Here's my short answer: change your opinion, because you are wrong. It is that simple. Of course, you need to make sure that you understand the verse contextually. Taking verses out of context leads to all kinds of problems. Second, make sure you understand what the verse says in its original language. Third, take care that you're using an accurate translation. (This one, the New King James Version, is excellent.) Fourth, be sure that you understand the intent of the verse. But if you do all of that, and still you find your opinion differs from the Bible, then you need to change your opinion. The objective is to conform your thinking to what the Bible teaches, not try to conform the Bible to your way of thinking. *For more about* God's Word, *see Heb. 5:12–14.*

➤ *All Scripture is given by inspiration of God, and is profitable for doctrine, for reproof, for correction, for instruction in righteousness, that the man of God may be complete, thoroughly equipped for every good work.* 2 Tim. 3:16, 17

must continue in the things which you have learned and been assured of, knowing from whom you have learned *them*, [15]and that from childhood you have known the Holy Scriptures, which are able to make you wise for salvation through faith which is in Christ Jesus. [16]All Scripture *is* given by inspiration of God, and *is* profitable for doctrine, for reproof, for correction, for instruction in righteousness, [17]that the man of God may be complete, thoroughly equipped for every good work.

Preach the Word

4 I charge *you* therefore before God and the Lord Jesus Christ, who will judge the living and the dead at[a] His appearing and His kingdom: [2]Preach the word! Be ready in season *and* out of season. Convince, rebuke, exhort, with all longsuffering and teaching. [3]For the time will come when they will not endure sound doctrine, but according to their own desires, *because* they have itching ears, they will heap up for themselves teachers; [4]and they will turn *their* ears away from the truth, and be turned aside to fables. [5]But you be watchful in all things, endure afflictions, do the work of an evangelist, fulfill your ministry.

Paul's Valedictory

[6]For I am already being poured out as a drink offering, and the time of my departure is at hand. [7]I have fought the good fight, I have finished the race, I have kept the faith. [8]Finally, there is laid up for me the crown of righteousness, which the Lord, the righteous Judge, will give to me on that Day, and not to me only but also to all who have loved His appearing.

The Abandoned Apostle

[9]Be diligent to come to me quickly; [10]for Demas has forsaken me, having loved this present world, and has departed for Thessalonica—Crescens for Galatia, Titus for Dalmatia. [11]Only Luke is with me. Get Mark and

➤ *I have fought the good fight, I have finished the race, I have kept the faith. Finally, there is laid up for me the crown of righteousness . . .* 2 Tim. 4:7, 8

4:1 [a]NU-Text omits *therefore* and reads *and by* for *at*.

↓ KNOW (2 TIM. 4:8)

It's important to see how God's many attributes complement one another. Many Bible texts declare that God is all-powerful. But many more call our attention to God's infinite righteousness. The two attributes complement one another perfectly. If He were a God of perfect righteousness, yet without the power to carry out His righteousness, then we could never be sure that justice would prevail. On the other hand, if He were a God of unlimited power, yet without a righteous character, imagine how horrible and terrifying this universe would be! But since our God has revealed Himself as both all-powerful and infinitely righteous, we can feel confident that He will never misuse His power. Abraham knew the truth: "Shall not the Judge of all the earth do right"? (Gen. 18:25). Yes, He will. Always. And He will give a crown of righteousness to those who love His appearing, as well. *For more about the* Attributes of God, *see Heb. 1:8.*

bring him with you, for he is useful to me for ministry. [12]And Tychicus I have sent to Ephesus. [13]Bring the cloak that I left with Carpus at Troas when you come—and the books, especially the parchments.

[14]Alexander the coppersmith did me much harm. May the Lord repay him according to his works. [15]You also must beware of him, for he has greatly resisted our words.

[16]At my first defense no one stood with me, but all forsook me. May it not be charged against them.

The Lord Is Faithful

[17]But the Lord stood with me and strengthened me, so that the message might be preached fully through me, and *that* all the Gentiles might hear. Also I was delivered out of the mouth of the lion. [18]And the Lord will deliver me from every evil work and preserve *me* for His heavenly kingdom. To Him *be* glory forever and ever. Amen!

Come Before Winter

[19]Greet Prisca and Aquila, and the household of Onesiphorus. [20]Erastus stayed in Corinth, but Trophimus I have left in Miletus sick.

[21]Do your utmost to come before winter.

Eubulus greets you, as well as Pudens, Linus, Claudia, and all the brethren.

Farewell

[22]The Lord Jesus Christ[a] be with your spirit. Grace be with you. Amen.

4:22 [a]NU-Text omits *Jesus Christ.*

TITUS ↙

INTRODUCTION//

I n many respects, Paul's letter to Titus—his student and a leader of the church on the island of Crete—echoes the themes found in his first letter to Timothy. The apostle addresses many tough challenges facing Titus as an overseer of the Cretan churches. He lists criteria for qualifications of leadership, describes sound teaching, and encourages good works. The listed qualifications for leadership are virtually the same as those 1 Timothy 3:1–7, including monogamy, patience, honesty, and love of others (1:6–9). Paul then warns of false teachers, both the ignorant and the malicious. These people present a danger to the church, especially for new believers and young churches, because they corrupt faith and eventually discredit the church.

Paul then instructs Titus on the proper way to teach various groups within the church. He calls for older men to provide strong examples to the young, being "sober, reverent, temperate, sound in faith, in love, in patience" (2:2). Likewise, the older women are to set examples for the younger women, especially in refraining from gossip and indulgence and teaching good family morals. The young men are to exercise self-control and integrity, so that no one will look down upon them. Paul finally provides a reminder on how Christians should conduct themselves with obedience, goodness, peace, and humility. Those who claim to believe in Jesus, but do not show it by their godly actions, are in fact "abominable, disobedient, and disqualified for every good work" (1:16). Instead, we are to remember that "the grace of God that brings salvation has appeared to all men, teaching us that, denying ungodliness and worldly lusts, we should live soberly, righteously, and godly in the present age" (2:11, 12). To underscore the message, he says again, "those who have believed in God should be careful to maintain good works" (3:8).

Greeting

1 Paul, a bondservant of God and an apostle of Jesus Christ, according to the faith of God's elect and the acknowledgment of the truth which accords with godliness, [2]in hope of eternal life which God, who cannot lie, promised before time began, [3]but has in due time manifested His word through preaching, which was committed to me according to the commandment of God our Savior;

[4]To Titus, a true son in *our* common faith:

Grace, mercy, *and* peace from God the Father and the Lord Jesus Christ[a] our Savior.

Qualified Elders

[5]For this reason I left you in Crete, that you should set in order the things that are lacking, and appoint elders in every city as I commanded you— [6]if a man is blameless, the husband of one wife, having faithful children not accused of dissipation or insubordination. [7]For a bishop[a] must be blameless, as a steward of God, not self-willed, not quick-tempered, not given to wine, not violent, not greedy for money, [8]but hospitable, a lover of what is good, sober-minded, just, holy, self-controlled, [9]holding fast the faithful word as he has been taught, that he may be able, by sound doctrine, both to exhort and convict those who contradict.

The Elders' Task

[10]For there are many insubordinate, both idle talkers and deceivers, especially those

> ## ↘ LEARN
> . . . .
>
> **1:16** • Perhaps it's time to change the old saying "Practice what you preach," into something a little less job-descriptive, such as "Practice what you profess." You may not be a preacher by profession, but if you are a Christian, then certainly you profess to follow Christ. Sadly, a lot of folks these days "profess to know God, but in works they deny Him." They *don't* practice what they profess. Paul gave his cure for this spiritual disease in Acts 26:20, when he called for men and women to "repent, turn to God, and do works befitting repentance." It's still good counsel. *For more about* How to Live Out Your Faith, *see Titus 2:14;* Sharing Your Faith, *Matt. 28:18–20.*

of the circumcision, [11]whose mouths must be stopped, who subvert whole households, teaching things which they ought not, for the sake of dishonest gain. [12]One of them, a prophet of their own, said, "Cretans *are* always liars, evil beasts, lazy gluttons." [13]This testimony is true. Therefore rebuke them sharply, that they may be sound in the faith, [14]not giving heed to Jewish fables and commandments of men who turn from the truth. [15]To the pure all things are pure, but to those who are defiled and unbelieving nothing is pure; but even their mind and conscience are defiled. [16]They profess to know God, but in works they deny *Him,* being abominable, disobedient, and disqualified for every good work.

Qualities of a Sound Church

2 But as for you, speak the things which are proper for sound doctrine: [2]that the older men be sober, reverent, temper-

1:4 [a]NU-Text reads *and Christ Jesus.*   1:7 [a]Literally *overseer*

↓ KNOW (TITUS 2:13)
. . . .

Sometimes we confuse the Second Coming with the Rapture, but these are two distinct and separate events. Consider just a few of the major differences between the two events. The Rapture will be a stealth event, while the Second Coming will be a very public one. In the Rapture, we meet the Lord in the air; in the Second Coming, Jesus returns to the earth. In the Rapture, Jesus comes *for* His church; in the Second Coming He returns *with* His church. In the Rapture, He comes *before* judgment; in the Second Coming He comes *with* judgment. After the Rapture, the Tribulation begins; after the Second Coming, the Millennium begins (Rev. 20:1–7). With all these differences in mind, are you ready for the Rapture, to be caught up with the Lord in the air? It could happen at any time. Your job is to be ready and waiting, whenever He returns. *For more about* Jesus' Return, *see James 5:7.*

ate, sound in faith, in love, in patience; [3]the older women likewise, that they be reverent in behavior, not slanderers, not given to much wine, teachers of good things— [4]that they admonish the young women to love their husbands, to love their children, [5]to be discreet, chaste, homemakers, good, obedient to their own husbands, that the word of God may not be blasphemed.

[6]Likewise, exhort the young men to be sober-minded, [7]in all things showing yourself to be a pattern of good works; in doctrine showing integrity, reverence, incorruptibility,[a] [8]sound speech that cannot be condemned, that one who is an opponent may be ashamed, having nothing evil to say of you.[a]

[9]Exhort bondservants to be obedient to their own masters, to be well pleasing in all things, not answering back, [10]not pilfering, but showing all good fidelity, that they may adorn the doctrine of God our Savior in all things.

Trained by Saving Grace

[11]For the grace of God that brings salvation has appeared to all men, [12]teaching us that, denying ungodliness and worldly lusts, we should live soberly, righteously, and godly in the present age, [13]looking for the blessed hope and glorious appearing of our great God and Savior Jesus Christ, [14]who gave Himself for us, that He might redeem us from every lawless deed and purify for Himself His own special people, zealous for good works.

[15]Speak these things, exhort, and rebuke with all authority. Let no one despise you.

2:7 [a]NU-Text omits incorruptibility.   2:8 [a]NU-Text and M-Text read us.

→LIVE

• • • • • • • • • • • • • • • •

2:11 • Grace is God's unmerited favor, meaning that you can't earn it. Sometimes we think, If I do this, I will earn God's approval. If I fail, then God will not love me. No! God has extended His grace to you, which gives you access to His presence. And because He has made you accepted in the Beloved (Eph. 1:6), He smiles on you. Of course, you can displease God by your actions. I am not suggesting that God is always smiling! God does indeed get angry. But He loves you and lavishes His grace on you because that is His very nature. For more about God's Love, see Heb. 4:15; New Life in Christ, Titus 2:14.

Graces of the Heirs of Grace

3 Remind them to be subject to rulers and authorities, to obey, to be ready for every good work, [2]to speak evil of no one, to be peaceable, gentle, showing all humility to all men. [3]For we ourselves were also once foolish, disobedient, deceived, serving various lusts and pleasures, living in malice and envy, hateful and hating one another. [4]But when the kindness and the love of God our Savior toward man appeared, [5]not by works of righteousness which we have done, but according to His mercy He saved us, through the washing of regeneration and renewing of the Holy Spirit, [6]whom He poured out on us abundantly through Jesus Christ our Savior, [7]that having been justified by His grace we should become heirs according to the hope of eternal life.

[8]This is a faithful saying, and these things I want you to affirm constantly, that those who have believed in God should be careful to maintain good works. These things are good and profitable to men.

↑ GROW (TITUS 2:14)

• •

Just as running a full marathon gives birth to real sweat, so real faith gives birth to God-honoring works. If you have genuinely met Christ and He has really come into your life, then real and positive changes should occur in your life. God intends that good works should follow genuine faith. Works can't save you, but they do provide good evidence that you are saved. The hallmark of each follower of Jesus is that he or she is totally committed to doing what is right. That doesn't mean he or she is a perfect person. On this side of heaven, there are no such creatures! But men and women who have placed their faith in Christ make every effort, by the grace of God, to change into people who increasingly look and act more like Jesus Christ every day of their lives. For more about Faith, see Heb. 2:1; How to Live Out Your Faith, Titus 3:8; New Life in Christ, Philem. 5.

➤ *. . . having been justified by His grace we should become heirs according to the hope of eternal life.* Titus 3:7

Avoid Dissension

[9]But avoid foolish disputes, genealogies, contentions, and strivings about the law; for they are unprofitable and useless. [10]Reject a divisive man after the first and second admonition, [11]knowing that such a person is warped and sinning, being self-condemned.

Final Messages

[12]When I send Artemas to you, or Tychicus, be diligent to come to me at Nicopolis, for I have decided to spend the winter there. [13]Send Zenas the lawyer and Apollos on their

➘ **LEARN**
• • • • • • • • • • • • • •

3:8 • Just because doing good works can't earn our salvation or win you spiritual favor, doesn't mean we should forget about doing good works altogether. Have you "believed in God"? If so, then you must "be careful to maintain good works." Good works don't save a man, but they provide good evidence he is saved. The Spirit of God wants to work in your life to help you produce good, wholesome "fruit," which serves as a good advertisement for God. Good trees bear good fruit, Jesus said, and bad trees bear bad fruit (Matt. 7:17, 18). What kind of fruit are you bearing? *For more about* How to Live Out Your Faith, *see Heb. 9:27; the* Holy Spirit, *Heb. 10:29.*

journey with haste, that they may lack nothing. [14]And let our *people* also learn to maintain good works, to *meet* urgent needs, that they may not be unfruitful.

Farewell

[15]All who *are* with me greet you. Greet those who love us in the faith.

Grace *be* with you all. Amen.

PHILEMON

INTRODUCTION//

This short but profound letter teaches a wonderful lesson about the importance of forgiveness among Christian brothers. Paul wrote to a close friend, Philemon, with whom he worked in Colosse, to persuade him to forgive and accept his runaway slave, Onesimus. It is not clear why Onesimus ran away, though some have inferred that he stole from his master; but regardless of his actions, Paul convinced him to repent, place his faith in Christ, and return to his master. Onesimus anxiously carries the apostle's letter back to Colosse and Philemon.

Paul asks Philemon to forgive Onesimus and accept him back not only as a slave, but as a brother in Christ. This is a beautiful plea for forgiveness between Christians because Paul does not command obedience from a position of apostolic authority but out of love for both the slave and the master. He tells Philemon, "Though I might be very bold in Christ to command you what is fitting, yet for love's sake I rather appeal to you" (vv. 8, 9). He writes of Onesimus as his "own heart" (v. 12), wishing that he could keep him in Rome as a friend and aide. As much as he loves Onesimus, however, he loves Philemon as much and does not want to take any action that might offend him. Instead, Paul shows one of the greatest acts of love and asks that any debt incurred or sin committed by Onesimus against Philemon be transferred to Paul's account. This is the very core of what it means to live a Christ-like love, for on the Cross Christ took all of our debts and sins against God upon Himself. So it is fitting that the apostle closes his letter with the words, "The grace of our Lord Jesus Christ be with your spirit. Amen" (v. 25).

Greeting

Paul, a prisoner of Christ Jesus, and Timothy *our* brother,

To Philemon our beloved *friend* and fellow laborer, [2]to the beloved[a] Apphia, Archippus our fellow soldier, and to the church in your house:

[3]Grace to you and peace from God our Father and the Lord Jesus Christ.

Philemon's Love and Faith

[4]I thank my God, making mention of you always in my prayers, [5]hearing of your love and faith which you have toward the Lord Jesus and toward all the saints, [6]that the sharing of your faith may become effective by the acknowledgment of every good thing which is in you[a] in Christ Jesus. [7]For we have[a] great

> **→LIVE**
> • • • • • • • • • • • • • • •
>
> v. 5 • Paul often addressed his remarks to "the saints" in his epistles (Phil. 1:1; Col. 1:2; Philem. 5). So what exactly is a saint? A saint is any person who has put his or her faith in Jesus Christ. *Saint* means "true believer," someone who has been set apart through faith by God's grace for membership in God's family. You do not have to be canonized or perform a miracle or be perfect to be a saint. You simply need to believe in and follow Jesus Christ, and then you can rightly regard yourself as a genuine, living saint. *For more about* New Life in Christ, *see Heb. 9:13;* Following Christ, *Luke 14:26.*

joy[b] and consolation in your love, because the hearts of the saints have been refreshed by you, brother.

The Plea for Onesimus

[8]Therefore, though I might be very bold in Christ to command you what is fitting, [9]*yet* for love's sake I rather appeal *to you*—being such a one as Paul, the aged, and now also a prisoner of Jesus Christ— [10]I appeal to you for my son Onesimus, whom I have begotten *while* in my chains, [11]who once was unprofitable to you, but now is profitable to you and to me.

[12]I am sending him back.[a] You therefore receive him, that is, my own heart, [13]whom I wished to keep with me, that on your behalf he might minister to me in my chains for the gospel. [14]But without your consent I wanted to do nothing, that your good deed might not be by compulsion, as it were, but voluntary.

[15]For perhaps he departed for a while for this *purpose*, that you might receive him forever, [16]no longer as a slave but more than a slave—a beloved brother, especially to me but how much more to you, both in the flesh and in the Lord.

Philemon's Obedience Encouraged

[17]If then you count me as a partner, receive him as *you would* me. [18]But if he has wronged you or owes anything, put that on my account. [19]I, Paul, am writing with my own hand. I will repay—not to mention to you that you owe me even your own self

2 [a]NU-Text reads *to our sister Apphia.*   6 [a]NU-Text and M-Text read *us.*   7 [a]NU-Text reads *had.*   [b]M-Text reads *thanksgiving.*
12 [a]NU-Text reads *back to you in person, that is, my own heart.*

↑ GROW (PHILEM. 4–7)
• •

Do you love to spend time around Christians? If you are saved, then you will love other believers. I find that relationships deeply affect me. When I am around some people, I draw nearer to God. Hanging around certain others, however, makes the world seem a little more attractive. They might not be openly hostile to my beliefs, but something about what they say and do makes God seem a little farther away. Being in their company for an extended time makes my faith seem a little less important. That's why you ought to spend most of your time with maturing Christians. Don't isolate yourself from the world or refuse to converse with someone who doesn't know the Lord—we're called to influence others for Jesus and we want to call others to Christ—but be careful to not get dragged down, either. Ask yourself of friendships you have with others, are they a wing or are they a weight? In other words, do they speed you along in the race of life or slow you down? *For more about* Fellowship, *see Heb. 3:13;* Loving Others, *James 3:6.*

besides. [20]Yes, brother, let me have joy from you in the Lord; refresh my heart in the Lord.

[21]Having confidence in your obedience, I write to you, knowing that you will do even more than I say. [22]But, meanwhile, also prepare a guest room for me, for I trust that through your prayers I shall be granted to you.

Farewell

[23]Epaphras, my fellow prisoner in Christ Jesus, greets you, [24]*as do* Mark, Aristarchus, Demas, Luke, my fellow laborers.

[25]The grace of our Lord Jesus Christ *be* with your spirit. Amen.

HEBREWS

INTRODUCTION//

The Book of Hebrews, written for Jews who accepted Jesus as their Messiah, warns of the danger of slipping away from Christ when hardship comes because of personal association with Him. The book encourages readers to consider the superiority of Christ in all things. The unknown author writes to show that Christ is above all sources of authority, including Moses, angels, or Abraham. Christ is portrayed as both man and God (1:1—2:18). As God, He is above the angels, Moses, and Abraham. He came before them, created them, and will last beyond them. As a man, he lived without sin, something impossible for any mere human hero to do. As a man, Jesus sacrificed Himself for us, becoming the Savior of Jews and Gentiles alike. Through His sacrifice, Jesus also connected God and His people. No longer did people have to go through the high priest and make sacrifices, because Jesus was the final sacrifice. Now we can go directly to the Father through Christ. This is the new covenant, greater than the old covenant prophesied centuries before (Jer. 31:31–34).

The author then implores his readers to live by faith, citing many great examples of those who trusted God wholeheartedly. Hebrews 11 is often referred to as the "Hall of Faith," as it contains the inspiring stories of many godly men and women who remained faithful to God despite great hardship. In chapter 12, we are urged to run the spiritual race as we look to "Jesus, the author and finisher of our faith" (12:2). When we walk by faith, we grow and become stronger, reflecting more and more the glory of Christ. We must therefore "let brotherly love continue" (13:1) and trust God for the future, "since we are receiving a kingdom which cannot be shaken" (12:28).

God's Supreme Revelation

1 God, who at various times and in various ways spoke in time past to the fathers by the prophets, ²has in these last days spoken to us by *His* Son, whom He has appointed heir of all things, through whom also He made the worlds; ³who being the brightness of *His* glory and the express image of His person, and upholding all things by the word of His power, when He had by Himselfᵃ purged ourᵇ sins, sat down at the right hand of the Majesty on high, ⁴having become so much better than the angels, as He has by inheritance obtained a more excellent name than they.

The Son Exalted Above Angels

⁵For to which of the angels did He ever say:

"You are My Son,
Today I have begotten You"?ᵃ

And again:

"I will be to Him a Father,
And He shall be to Me a Son"?ᵇ

⁶But when He again brings the firstborn into the world, He says:

"Let all the angels of God worship Him."ᵃ

⁷And of the angels He says:

"Who makes His angels spirits
And His ministers a flame of fire."ᵃ

⁸But to the Son *He says:*

"Your throne, O God, is forever and
    ever;
A scepter of righteousness is the scepter
    of Your kingdom.
⁹You have loved righteousness and hated
    lawlessness;
Therefore God, Your God, has anointed
    You
With the oil of gladness more than Your
    companions."ᵃ

¹⁰And:

"You, LORD, in the beginning laid the
    foundation of the earth,
And the heavens are the work of Your
    hands.
¹¹They will perish, but You remain;
And they will all grow old like a
    garment;
¹²Like a cloak You will fold them up,
And they will be changed.
But You are the same,
And Your years will not fail."ᵃ

¹³But to which of the angels has He ever said:

"Sit at My right hand,
Till I make Your enemies Your
    footstool"?ᵃ

¹⁴Are they not all ministering spirits sent forth to minister for those who will inherit salvation?

1:3 ᵃNU-Text omits *by Himself.* ᵇNU-Text omits *our.* **1:5** ᵃPsalm 2:7 ᵇ2 Samuel 7:14 **1:6** ᵃDeuteronomy 32:43 (Septuagint, Dead Sea Scrolls); Psalm 97:7 **1:7** ᵃPsalm 104:4 **1:9** ᵃPsalm 45:6, 7 **1:12** ᵃPsalm 102:25–27 **1:13** ᵃPsalm 110:1

↓ KNOW (HEB. 1:8)
....

Jesus is God. Before the world existed, before there were planets or light or darkness or matter of any kind—in fact, before there was anything at all except the Godhead—there was Jesus Christ. From eternity He has been a member of the Trinity, coequal and coexistent with the Father and the Holy Spirit. He was *with* God and He *was* God. When Jesus came to this earth as a man, He did not become *identical* with us, but rather He became *identified* with us. He was not a man with sinful impulses, but He became identified with us in our struggle against sin. This was a total identification with humanity, without any loss of identity. He became one of us without ceasing to be Himself. He became human without ceasing to be God. Jesus did not exchange deity for humanity; He was deity in humanity. Jesus is God. *For more about* Jesus' Life, *see 2 Pet. 1:18; the* Attributes of God, *Heb. 4:15.*

Do Not Neglect Salvation

2 Therefore we must give the more earnest heed to the things we have heard, lest we drift away. [2]For if the word spoken through angels proved steadfast, and every transgression and disobedience received a just reward, [3]how shall we escape if we neglect so great a salvation, which at the first began to be spoken by the Lord, and was confirmed to us by those who heard *Him*, [4]God also bearing witness both with signs and wonders, with various miracles, and gifts of the Holy Spirit, according to His own will?

> **↘ LEARN**
> . . . .
>
> 2:1 • Most Christians who stop growing never intend for it to happen. They don't wake up one morning and say, "You know, today I think I'd like to start choking the life out of my faith." Instead, they start drifting—slowly and almost imperceptibly at first, quickly and obviously sometime later—until they wind up very far from where they ever wanted to be. The time to stop drifting is before you find yourself miles out to sea. What about you? Are you on course for solid growth? Or have the waves around you taken you farther and farther from shore? *For more about* Growing in Christ, *see Heb. 3:14;* Faith, *Heb. 11:1.*

The Son Made Lower than Angels

[5]For He has not put the world to come, of which we speak, in subjection to angels. [6]But one testified in a certain place, saying:

> "What is man that You are mindful of him,
> Or the son of man that You take care of
>   him?
> [7]You have made him a little lower than the
>   angels;
> You have crowned him with glory and
>   honor,[a]
> And set him over the works of Your
>   hands.
> [8]You have put all things in subjection
>   under his feet."[a]

For in that He put all in subjection under him, He left nothing *that is* not put under him. But now we do not yet see all things put under him. [9]But we see Jesus, who was made a little lower than the angels, for the suffering of death crowned with glory and honor, that He, by the grace of God, might taste death for everyone.

Bringing Many Sons to Glory

[10]For it was fitting for Him, for whom *are* all things and by whom *are* all things, in bringing many sons to glory, to make the captain of their salvation perfect through sufferings. [11]For both He who sanctifies and those who are being sanctified *are* all of one, for which reason He is not ashamed to call them brethren, [12]saying:

> "I will declare Your name to My brethren;
> In the midst of the assembly I will sing
>   praise to You."[a]

[13]And again:

> "I will put My trust in Him."[a]

And again:

> "Here am I and the children whom God
>   has given Me."[b]

[14]Inasmuch then as the children have partaken of flesh and blood, He Himself likewise shared in the same, that through death He might destroy him who had the power of death, that is, the devil, [15]and release those who through fear of death were all their lifetime subject to bondage. [16]For indeed He does not give aid to angels, but He does give aid to the seed of Abraham. [17]Therefore, in all things He had to be made like *His* brethren, that He might be a merciful and faithful

> **→ LIVE**
> . . . .
>
> 2:15 • We are often afraid of death and do not want to acknowledge its existence; we even avoid the very word. But one day, we all will die (Eccl. 3:2). Jesus died on the Cross to pay the price for your sin and rose again from the dead so you don't have to be afraid to die. You can know that when you die you will go straight to heaven. But if you reject God's forgiveness—if you say no to Jesus—then in that final day you will face certain judgment . . . and you will have no one to blame but yourself. *For more about* The Cross, *see Matt. 20:19;* Becoming a Christian, *1 Pet. 1:23.*

2:7 [a]NU-Text and M-Text omit the rest of verse 7.   2:8 [a]Psalm 8:4–6   2:12 [a]Psalm 22:22   2:13 [a]2 Samuel 22:3; Isaiah 8:17   [b]Isaiah 8:18

High Priest in things *pertaining* to God, to make propitiation for the sins of the people. [18]For in that He Himself has suffered, being tempted, He is able to aid those who are tempted.

> ➡ *For in that He Himself has suffered, being tempted, He is able to aid those who are tempted.* Heb. 2:18

The Son Was Faithful

3 Therefore, holy brethren, partakers of the heavenly calling, consider the Apostle and High Priest of our confession, Christ Jesus, [2]who was faithful to Him who appointed Him, as Moses also *was faithful* in all His house. [3]For this One has been counted worthy of more glory than Moses, inasmuch as He who built the house has more honor than the house. [4]For every house is built by someone, but He who built all things *is* God. [5]And Moses indeed *was* faithful in all His house as a servant, for a testimony of those things which would be spoken *afterward,* [6]but Christ as a Son over His own house, whose house we are if we hold fast the confidence and the rejoicing of the hope firm to the end.[a]

Be Faithful

[7]Therefore, as the Holy Spirit says:

> "Today, if you will hear His voice,
> [8]Do not harden your hearts as in the
>   rebellion,
> In the day of trial in the wilderness,
> [9]Where your fathers tested Me,
>   tried Me,
> And saw My works forty years.
> [10]Therefore I was angry with that
>   generation,
> And said, 'They always go astray in their
>   heart,
> And they have not known My ways.'
> [11]So I swore in My wrath,
> 'They shall not enter My rest.' "[a]

[12]Beware, brethren, lest there be in any of you an evil heart of unbelief in departing from the living God; [13]but exhort one another daily, while it is called *"Today,"* lest any of you be hardened through the deceitfulness of sin. [14]For we have become partakers of Christ if we hold the beginning of our confidence steadfast to the end, [15]while it is said:

> "Today, if you will hear His voice,
> Do not harden your hearts as in the
>   rebellion." [a]

⬎ LEARN
• • • • • • • • • • • • • • • •

3:13 • Being a part of the church is vitally important, for it is there that we "exhort one another" (among other things). The word "exhort" comes from the Greek term *parakaleo,* which literally means, "to call alongside." Some translations render it "to encourage." God consistently instructs us to exhort one another, and in this verse, He directs us to do so "daily" and "while it is called 'Today.'" This indicates He wants us to schedule regular, even urgent contact with one another. Why? Because when we avoid significant contact with other believers, it's a lot easier to slide, unnoticed, into destructive patterns of sin. *For more about* Fellowship, *see Heb. 10:24, 25.*

Failure of the Wilderness Wanderers

[16]For who, having heard, rebelled? Indeed, *was it* not all who came out of Egypt, *led* by Moses? [17]Now with whom was He angry forty years? *Was it* not with those who sinned, whose corpses fell in the wilderness? [18]And to whom did He swear that they would not

➔ LIVE
• • • • • • • • • • • • • • • •

3:14 • Christians must constantly beware of falling away or backsliding. If we are not moving forward in Christ, we are going backward. There is no standing still. In fact, the moment you cease to progress as a Christian, the process of backsliding begins. Why? Because we begin to slip back into our old, sinful ways. Although I have a natural tendency to do what is wrong, I have a supernatural tendency to do what is right. Faith and repentance must continue to be practiced after salvation. We must keep growing spiritually and depending upon Christ (Titus 2:11–14; Heb. 3:12, 13; 2 Pet. 3:17). *For more about* Growing in Christ, *see Heb. 5:12–14;* Sin, *Heb. 10:22.*

3:6 [a]NU-Text omits *firm to the end.*   **3:11** [a]Psalm 95:7–11   **3:15** [a]Psalm 95:7, 8

enter His rest, but to those who did not obey? ¹⁹So we see that they could not enter in because of unbelief.

The Promise of Rest

4 Therefore, since a promise remains of entering His rest, let us fear lest any of you seem to have come short of it. ²For indeed the gospel was preached to us as well as to them; but the word which they heard did not profit them,^a not being mixed with faith in those who heard *it*. ³For we who have believed do enter that rest, as He has said:

> *"So I swore in My wrath,*
> *'They shall not enter My rest,' "*^a

although the works were finished from the foundation of the world. ⁴For He has spoken in a certain place of the seventh *day* in this way: *"And God rested on the seventh day from all His works",*^a ⁵and again in this *place:* *"They shall not enter My rest."*^a

⁶Since therefore it remains that some *must* enter it, and those to whom it was first preached did not enter because of disobedience, ⁷again He designates a certain day, saying in David, *"Today,"* after such a long time, as it has been said:

> *"Today, if you will hear His voice,*
> *Do not harden your hearts."*^a

⁸For if Joshua had given them rest, then He would not afterward have spoken of another day. ⁹There remains therefore a rest for the people of God. ¹⁰For he who has entered His rest has himself also ceased from his works as God *did* from His.

The Word Discovers Our Condition

¹¹Let us therefore be diligent to enter that rest, lest anyone fall according to the same example of disobedience. ¹²For the word of God *is* living and powerful, and sharper than any two-edged sword, piercing even to the division of soul and spirit, and of joints and marrow, and is a discerner of the thoughts and intents of the heart. ¹³And there is no creature hidden from His sight, but all things *are* naked and open to the eyes of Him to whom we *must give* account.

Our Compassionate High Priest

¹⁴Seeing then that we have a great High Priest who has passed through the heavens, Jesus the Son of God, let us hold fast *our*

> ## ↘ LEARN
> ● ● ● ● ● ● ● ● ● ● ● ● ● ●
>
> **4:16 •** Because of your faith in Jesus, you have the right not only to appear before God's throne in prayer, but also to come into His presence "boldly." The original Greek term *parresia* means "confidently, with courage, publicly and without fear." How can you and I pray so fearlessly? We can do so because we approach God by His grace, knowing that the sinless Son of God, Jesus Christ, has paved the way for us. Times of need come to every believer, sometimes acute times of need—and because of Jesus, we may confidently approach the throne of our heavenly Father in prayer whenever we desire. *For more about* Prayer, *see James 4:2.*

4:2 ^aNU-Text and M-Text read *profit them, since they were not united by faith with those who heeded it.*   **4:3** ^aPsalm 95:11   **4:4** ^aGenesis 2:2   **4:5** ^aPsalm 95:11   **4:7** ^aPsalm 95:7, 8

↓ KNOW (HEB. 4:15)
● ●

God is not some distant, unapproachable being. He wants to draw close to us and He wants us to draw close to Him. But since God is holy—totally perfect, separate from all sin— we sinful beings had no way to have a relationship with Him. That's why Jesus had to come. As a human, but without sin, He could bridge the gap between a holy God and sinful us. Because of what Jesus did for us on the Cross, this awesome and holy God can now be our loving Father. As such, God has our best interests at heart. God is unlimited in power, ignorant of nothing, and unbound by either time or space. He is just, good, righteous, and loving. His decisions and purposes are always right and proper, always motivated by a pure goodness—and, because of Jesus—He has a deep and abiding love for us. *For more about the* Attributes of God, *see 1 Pet. 1:15, 16;* God's Love, *Heb. 12:6.*

confession. [15]For we do not have a High Priest who cannot sympathize with our weaknesses, but was in all *points* tempted as *we are,* yet without sin. [16]Let us therefore come boldly to the throne of grace, that we may obtain mercy and find grace to help in time of need.

Qualifications for High Priesthood

5 For every high priest taken from among men is appointed for men in things *pertaining* to God, that he may offer both gifts and sacrifices for sins. [2]He can have compassion on those who are ignorant and going astray, since he himself is also subject to weakness. [3]Because of this he is required as for the people, so also for himself, to offer *sacrifices* for sins. [4]And no man takes this honor to himself, but he who is called by God, just as Aaron *was.*

A Priest Forever

[5]So also Christ did not glorify Himself to become High Priest, but *it was* He who said to Him:

"You are My Son,
Today I have begotten You."[a]

[6]As *He* also says in another *place:*

"You are a priest forever
According to the order of Melchizedek";[a]

[7]who, in the days of His flesh, when He had offered up prayers and supplications, with vehement cries and tears to Him who was able to save Him from death, and was heard because of His godly fear, [8]though He was a Son, *yet* He learned obedience by the things which He suffered. [9]And having been perfected, He became the author of eternal salvation to all who obey Him, [10]called by God as High Priest *"according to the order of Melchizedek,"* [11]of whom we have much to say, and hard to explain, since you have become dull of hearing.

Spiritual Immaturity

[12]For though by this time you ought to be teachers, you need *someone* to teach you again the first principles of the oracles of God; and you have come to need milk and not solid food. [13]For everyone who partakes

only of milk *is* unskilled in the word of righteousness, for he is a babe. [14]But solid food belongs to those who are of full age, *that is,* those who by reason of use have their senses exercised to discern both good and evil.

The Peril of Not Progressing

6 Therefore, leaving the discussion of the elementary *principles* of Christ, let us go on to perfection, not laying again the foundation of repentance from dead works and of faith toward God, [2]of the doctrine of baptisms, of laying on of hands, of resurrection of the dead, and of eternal judgment. [3]And this we will[a] do if God permits.

[4]For *it is* impossible for those who were once enlightened, and have tasted the heavenly gift, and have become partakers of the Holy Spirit, [5]and have tasted the good word of God and the powers of the age to come, [6]if they fall away,[a] to renew them again to repentance, since they crucify again for themselves the Son of God, and put *Him* to an open shame.

[7]For the earth which drinks in the rain that often comes upon it, and bears herbs useful for those by whom it is cultivated, receives blessing from God; [8]but if it bears thorns and briers, *it is* rejected and near to being cursed, whose end *is* to be burned.

A Better Estimate

[9]But, beloved, we are confident of better things concerning you, yes, things that accompany salvation, though we speak in this manner. [10]For God *is* not unjust to forget your work and labor of[a] love which you have

5:5 [a]Psalm 2:7   5:6 [a]Psalm 110:4   6:3 [a]M-Text reads *let us do.*   6:6 [a]Or *and have fallen away*   6:10 [a]NU-Text omits *labor of.*

shown toward His name, *in that* you have ministered to the saints, and do minister. [11]And we desire that each one of you show the same diligence to the full assurance of hope until the end, [12]that you do not become sluggish, but imitate those who through faith and patience inherit the promises.

> ↘ **LEARN**
>
> **6:12 •** Imitation might be the sincerest form of flattery, but it's also one of the best ways for us to mature as Christians. We learn best when we have good models to follow. "I urge you, imitate me," Paul told the Corinthians; and later, "Imitate me, just as I also imitate Christ" (1 Cor. 4:16; 11:1). Think about your own life. What worthy examples do you have? Who do you know that prompts you to say, "I want to be like him (or her)"? What if the church were made of people like you? What kind of church would we have? *For more about* Growing in Christ, *see Heb. 9:13.*

God's Infallible Purpose in Christ

[13]For when God made a promise to Abraham, because He could swear by no one greater, He swore by Himself, [14]saying, *"Surely blessing I will bless you, and multiplying I will multiply you."*[a] [15]And so, after he had patiently endured, he obtained the promise. [16]For men indeed swear by the greater, and an oath for confirmation *is* for them an end of all dispute. [17]Thus God, determining to show more abundantly to the heirs of promise the immutability of His counsel, confirmed *it* by an oath, [18]that by two immutable things, in which it *is* impossible for God to lie, we might[a] have strong consolation, who have fled for refuge to lay hold of the hope set before *us.*

[19]This *hope* we have as an anchor of the soul, both sure and steadfast, and which enters the *Presence* behind the veil, [20]where the forerunner has entered for us, *even* Jesus, having become High Priest forever according to the order of Melchizedek.

The King of Righteousness

7 For this Melchizedek, king of Salem, priest of the Most High God, who met Abraham returning from the slaughter of the kings and blessed him, [2]to whom also Abraham gave a tenth part of all, first being

translated "king of righteousness," and then also king of Salem, meaning "king of peace," [3]without father, without mother, without genealogy, having neither beginning of days nor end of life, but made like the Son of God, remains a priest continually.

[4]Now consider how great this man *was,* to whom even the patriarch Abraham gave a tenth of the spoils. [5]And indeed those who are of the sons of Levi, who receive the priesthood, have a commandment to receive tithes from the people according to the law, that is, from their brethren, though they have come from the loins of Abraham; [6]but he whose genealogy is not derived from them received tithes from Abraham and blessed him who had the promises. [7]Now beyond all contradiction the lesser is blessed by the better. [8]Here mortal men receive tithes, but there he *receives them,* of whom it is witnessed that he lives. [9]Even Levi, who receives tithes, paid tithes through Abraham, so to speak, [10]for he was still in the loins of his father when Melchizedek met him.

Need for a New Priesthood

[11]Therefore, if perfection were through the Levitical priesthood (for under it the people received the law), what further need *was there* that another priest should rise according to the order of Melchizedek, and not be called according to the order of Aaron? [12]For the priesthood being changed, of necessity there is also a change of the law. [13]For He of whom these things are spoken belongs to another tribe, from which no man has officiated at the altar. [14]For *it is* evident that our Lord arose from Judah, of which tribe Moses spoke nothing concerning priesthood.[a] [15]And it is yet far more evident if, in the likeness of Melchizedek, there arises another priest [16]who has come, not according to the law of a fleshly commandment, but according to the power of an endless life. [17]For He testifies:[a]

> *"You are a priest forever*
> *According to the order of Melchizedek."*[b]

[18]For on the one hand there is an annulling of the former commandment because of its weakness and unprofitableness, [19]for the law made nothing perfect; on the other

6:14 [a]Genesis 22:17   **6:18** [a]M-Text omits *might.*   **7:14** [a]NU-Text reads *priests.*   **7:17** [a]NU-Text reads *it is testified.*   [b]Psalm 110:4

hand, *there is the* bringing in of a better hope, through which we draw near to God.

Greatness of the New Priest

[20]And inasmuch as *He was* not *made priest* without an oath [21](for they have become priests without an oath, but He with an oath by Him who said to Him:

"The Lord has sworn
And will not relent,
'You are a priest forever[a]
According to the order of
    Melchizedek' "),[b]

[22]by so much more Jesus has become a surety of a better covenant.

[23]Also there were many priests, because they were prevented by death from continuing. [24]But He, because He continues forever, has an unchangeable priesthood. [25]Therefore He is also able to save to the uttermost those who come to God through Him, since He always lives to make intercession for them.

> ➤ **Therefore He is also able to save to the uttermost those who come to God through Him, since He always lives to make intercession for them.** Heb. 7:25

[26]For such a High Priest was fitting for us, *who is* holy, harmless, undefiled, separate from sinners, and has become higher than the heavens; [27]who does not need daily, as those high priests, to offer up sacrifices, first for His own sins and then for the people's, for this He did once for all when He offered up Himself. [28]For the law appoints as high priests men who have weakness, but the word of the oath, which came after the law, *appoints* the Son who has been perfected forever.

The New Priestly Service

8 Now *this is* the main point of the things we are saying: We have such a High Priest, who is seated at the right hand of the throne of the Majesty in the heavens, [2]a Minister of the sanctuary and of the true tabernacle which the Lord erected, and not man.

[3]For every high priest is appointed to offer both gifts and sacrifices. Therefore *it is* necessary that this One also have something to offer. [4]For if He were on earth, He would not be a priest, since there are priests who offer the gifts according to the law; [5]who serve the copy and shadow of the heavenly things, as Moses was divinely instructed when he was about to make the tabernacle. For He said, *"See that you make all things according to the pattern shown you on the mountain."*[a] [6]But now He has obtained a more excellent ministry, inasmuch as He is also Mediator of a better covenant, which was established on better promises.

A New Covenant

[7]For if that first *covenant* had been faultless, then no place would have been sought for a second. [8]Because finding fault with them, He says: *"Behold, the days are coming, says the Lord, when I will make a new covenant with the house of Israel and with the house of Judah—* [9]*not according to the covenant that I made with their fathers in the day when I took them by the hand to lead them out of the land of Egypt; because they did not continue in My covenant, and I disregarded them, says the Lord.* [10]*For this is the covenant that I will make with the house of Israel after those days, says the Lord: I will put My laws in their mind and write them on their hearts; and I will be their God, and they shall be My people.* [11]*None of them shall teach his neighbor, and none his brother, saying, 'Know the Lord,' for all shall know Me, from the least of them to the greatest of them.* [12]*For I will be merciful to their unrighteousness, and their sins and their lawless deeds*[a] *I will remember no more."*[b] [13]In that He says, *"A new covenant,"* He has made the first obsolete. Now what is becoming obsolete and growing old is ready to vanish away.

The Earthly Sanctuary

9 Then indeed, even the first *covenant* had ordinances of divine service and the earthly sanctuary. [2]For a tabernacle

7:21 [a]NU-Text ends the quotation here. [b]Psalm 110:4   8:5 [a]Exodus 25:40   8:12 [a]NU-Text omits *and their lawless deeds.*
[b]Jeremiah 31:31–34

was prepared: the first *part,* in which *was* the lampstand, the table, and the showbread, which is called the sanctuary; [3]and behind the second veil, the part of the tabernacle which is called the Holiest of All, [4]which had the golden censer and the ark of the covenant overlaid on all sides with gold, in which *were* the golden pot that had the manna, Aaron's rod that budded, and the tablets of the covenant; [5]and above it were the cherubim of glory overshadowing the mercy seat. Of these things we cannot now speak in detail.

Limitations of the Earthly Service

[6]Now when these things had been thus prepared, the priests always went into the first part of the tabernacle, performing the services. [7]But into the second part the high priest *went* alone once a year, not without blood, which he offered for himself and *for* the people's sins *committed* in ignorance; [8]the Holy Spirit indicating this, that the way into the Holiest of All was not yet made manifest while the first tabernacle was still standing. [9]It *was* symbolic for the present time in which both gifts and sacrifices are offered which cannot make him who performed the service perfect in regard to the conscience— [10]*concerned* only with foods and drinks, various washings, and fleshly ordinances imposed until the time of reformation.

The Heavenly Sanctuary

[11]But Christ came *as* High Priest of the good things to come,[a] with the greater and more perfect tabernacle not made with hands, that is, not of this creation. [12]Not with the blood of goats and calves, but with His own blood He entered the Most Holy Place once for all, having obtained eternal redemption. [13]For if the blood of bulls and goats and the ashes of a heifer, sprinkling the unclean, sanctifies for the purifying of the flesh, [14]how much more shall the blood of Christ, who through the eternal Spirit offered Himself without spot to God, cleanse your conscience from dead works to serve the living God? [15]And for this reason He is the Mediator of the new covenant, by means of death, for the redemption of the transgressions under the first covenant, that those who are called may receive the promise of the eternal inheritance.

→ LIVE
• • • • • • • • • • • • • • •

9:13 • Holy living—which we simply can't manage in our natural state—will never produce salvation. But the salvation that God provides for us *will* produce holy living. To be sanctified means to be set apart to be used by God and to increasingly become more like Christ. Living a sanctified life means to work out what God has worked in. Sanctification is a part of the process of the new birth, in which God's favor toward you comes not on the basis of what you've done for Him, but on the basis of what He has done for you. *For more about* New Life in Christ, *see 1 John 4:10;* Growing in Christ, *Heb. 10:24, 25.*

The Mediator's Death Necessary

[16]For where there *is* a testament, there must also of necessity be the death of the testator. [17]For a testament *is* in force after men are dead, since it has no power at all while the testator lives. [18]Therefore not even the first *covenant* was dedicated without blood. [19]For when Moses had spoken every precept to all the people according to the law, he took the blood of calves and goats, with water, scarlet wool, and hyssop, and sprinkled both the book itself and all the people, [20]saying, *"This is the blood of the covenant which God has commanded you."*[a] [21]Then likewise he sprinkled with blood both the tabernacle and all the vessels of the ministry. [22]And according to the law almost all things are purified with blood, and without shedding of blood there is no remission.

Greatness of Christ's Sacrifice

[23]Therefore *it was* necessary that the copies of the things in the heavens should be purified with these, but the heavenly things themselves with better sacrifices than these. [24]For Christ has not entered the holy places made with hands, *which are* copies of the true, but into heaven itself, now to appear in the presence of God for us; [25]not that He should offer Himself often, as the high priest enters the Most Holy Place every year with blood of another— [26]He then would have had to suffer often since the foundation of the world; but now, once at the end of the ages, He has appeared to put away sin by the sacrifice of Himself. [27]And as it is appointed

9:11 [a]NU-Text reads *that have come.*   9:20 [a]Exodus 24:8

↘ LEARN

9:27 • As many have noted, the statistics on death are impressive: one out of every one person will die. We all have an appointment with destiny, and God, not us, has appointed both the day of our birth and death (Eccl. 3:2). When we leave this world, we will live forever either in the presence of God in heaven, or separated from Him in hell. While we remain in this world, we need to live in such a way that we are ready to meet God at any time. Only those who are prepared to die are really ready to live. *For more about* How to Live Out Your Faith, *see James 2:14.*

for men to die once, but after this the judgment, ²⁸so Christ was offered once to bear the sins of many. To those who eagerly wait for Him He will appear a second time, apart from sin, for salvation.

Animal Sacrifices Insufficient

10 For the law, having a shadow of the good things to come, *and* not the very image of the things, can never with these same sacrifices, which they offer continually year by year, make those who approach perfect. ²For then would they not have ceased to be offered? For the worshipers, once purified, would have had no more consciousness of sins. ³But in those *sacrifices there is* a reminder of sins every year. ⁴For *it is* not possible that the blood of bulls and goats could take away sins.

Christ's Death Fulfills God's Will

⁵Therefore, when He came into the world, He said:

"Sacrifice and offering You did not desire,
But a body You have prepared for Me.
⁶In burnt offerings and sacrifices for sin
You had no pleasure.
⁷Then I said, 'Behold, I have come—
In the volume of the book it is written of
Me—
To do Your will, O God.' "ᵃ

⁸Previously saying, *"Sacrifice and offering, burnt offerings, and offerings for sin You did not desire, nor had pleasure in them"* (which are offered according to the law), ⁹then He

said, *"Behold, I have come to do Your will, O God."*ᵃ He takes away the first that He may establish the second. ¹⁰By that will we have been sanctified through the offering of the body of Jesus Christ once *for all.*

Christ's Death Perfects the Sanctified

¹¹And every priest stands ministering daily and offering repeatedly the same sacrifices, which can never take away sins. ¹²But this Man, after He had offered one sacrifice for sins forever, sat down at the right hand of God, ¹³from that time waiting till His enemies are made His footstool. ¹⁴For by one offering He has perfected forever those who are being sanctified.

¹⁵But the Holy Spirit also witnesses to us; for after He had said before,

¹⁶ *"This is the covenant that I will make with them after those days, says the LORD: I will put My laws into their hearts, and in their minds I will write them,"*ᵃ ¹⁷then He adds, *"Their sins and their lawless deeds I will remember no more."*ᵃ ¹⁸Now where there is remission of these, *there is* no longer an offering for sin.

Hold Fast Your Confession

¹⁹Therefore, brethren, having boldness to enter the Holiest by the blood of Jesus, ²⁰by a new and living way which He consecrated for us, through the veil, that is, His flesh, ²¹and *having* a High Priest over the house of God, ²²let us draw near with a true heart in full assurance of faith, having our hearts sprinkled from an evil conscience and our bodies washed with pure water. ²³Let us hold fast the

→ LIVE

10:22 • When you sin, you feel guilt, which is a very *good* thing. The presence of guilt means your conscience is working as it should (Rom. 3:19). The time to get worried is when you can sin against God repeatedly and yet feel no sense of wrongdoing. Many people consider guilt a horrible thing, but it isn't, really. While there is such a thing as false guilt—driving ourselves to it unnecessarily and failing to take hold of the forgiveness of God (1 John 3:20, 21)—the horrible thing is not admitting your true guilt and allowing God to remove it. *For more about* Sin, *see Heb. 10:29;* Forgiveness, *1 John 4:10.*

10:7 ᵃPsalm 40:6–8   **10:9** ᵃNU-Text and M-Text omit *O God.*   **10:16** ᵃJeremiah 31:33   **10:17** ᵃJeremiah 31:34

↘ LEARN
• • • • • • • • • • • • • • • •

10:24, 25 • There's something about regularly assembling as a church that spurs spiritual growth. As we interact with one another, God moves among us to bring us to maturity in Christ. And yet, from the very beginning, some believers have figured they don't need to gather as members of the body of Christ. Don't count yourself among them! Every Christian needs to be an active part of a local church. We also need a group of close Christian friends. As the time of Christ's return grows nearer, we need to increasingly "stir up" one another to acts of love and good works. *For more about* Fellowship, *see Matt. 5:21–24;* Growing in Christ, *Heb. 11:6.*

➤ *And let us consider one another in order to stir up love and good works, not forsaking the assembling of ourselves together, as is the manner of some, but exhorting one another, and so much the more as you see the Day approaching.* Heb. 10:24, 25

confession of *our* hope without wavering, for He who promised is faithful. [24]And let us consider one another in order to stir up love and good works, [25]not forsaking the assembling of ourselves together, as is the manner of some, but exhorting *one another,* and so much the more as you see the Day approaching.

The Just Live by Faith

[26]For if we sin willfully after we have received the knowledge of the truth, there no longer remains a sacrifice for sins, [27]but a certain fearful expectation of judgment, and fiery indignation which will devour the adversaries. [28]Anyone who has rejected Moses' law dies without mercy on *the testimony of* two or three witnesses. [29]Of how much worse punishment, do you suppose, will he be thought worthy who has trampled the Son of God underfoot, counted the blood of the covenant by which he was sanctified a common thing, and insulted the Spirit of grace? [30]For we know Him who said, *"Vengeance is Mine, I will repay,"*[a] says the Lord.[b] And again, *"The LORD will judge His people."*[c] [31]It is a fearful thing to fall into the hands of the living God.

[32]But recall the former days in which, after you were illuminated, you endured a great struggle with sufferings: [33]partly while you were made a spectacle both by reproaches and tribulations, and partly while you became companions of those who were so treated; [34]for you had compassion on me[a] in my chains, and joyfully accepted the plundering of your goods, knowing that you have a better and an enduring possession for yourselves in heaven.[b] [35]Therefore do not cast away your confidence, which has great reward. [36]For you have need of endurance, so that after you

10:30 [a]Deuteronomy 32:35 [b]NU-Text omits *says the Lord.* [c]Deuteronomy 32:36
10:34 [a]NU-Text reads *the prisoners* instead of *me in my chains.* [b]NU-Text omits *in heaven.*

↓ KNOW (HEB. 10:29)
• •

How does someone insult the Holy Spirit of God? It happens when we tell people about Jesus and how He shed His blood for them, and they just outright reject it. "Who cares? I don't believe in any of that stuff. I don't believe the blood of Jesus means anything. The death of Jesus has nothing to do with me." Whenever *that* happens, the person is insulting the Holy Spirit. Careful! Such a person is skating on extremely thin ice. What is the worst sin a person can commit? Murder? Adultery? Rape? People can be forgiven of any of those sins, and of sins much worse, if only they will repent of their sin and put their faith in Christ. But someone who rejects Jesus Christ as Savior and Lord insults the Holy Spirit. Take care! "How shall we escape if we neglect so great a salvation?" (Heb. 2:3). *For more about the* Holy Spirit, *see Matt. 5:20;* Sin, *James 3:6.*

have done the will of God, you may receive the promise:

37 "For yet a little while,
And He[a] who is coming will come and
    will not tarry.
38 Now the[a] just shall live by faith;
But if anyone draws back,
My soul has no pleasure in him."[b]

39But we are not of those who draw back to perdition, but of those who believe to the saving of the soul.

By Faith We Understand

11 Now faith is the substance of things hoped for, the evidence of things not seen. 2For by it the elders obtained a *good* testimony.

➤ *Now faith is the substance of things hoped for, the evidence of things not seen.* Heb. 11:1

3By faith we understand that the worlds were framed by the word of God, so that the things which are seen were not made of things which are visible.

Faith at the Dawn of History

4By faith Abel offered to God a more excellent sacrifice than Cain, through which he obtained witness that he was righteous, God

⬎ LEARN
• • • • • • • • • • • • • • • • • •

11:6 • Every growing believer wants to please the Lord by the way he or she lives. If you have no desire to please God, then you're not growing. So how can you best please God? In fact, there's only one way: by believing His promises and relying on them for everything. You can't see God, and Jesus has gone to heaven. To please God, therefore, you need to step out in faith, trusting in an unseen God to fulfill every promise He has made. You receive this faith needed to please God by carefully studying and believing in His Word (Rom.10:17). *For more about* Faith, *see James 1:12;* Growing in Christ, *1 Pet. 2:2.*

testifying of his gifts; and through it he being dead still speaks.

5By faith Enoch was taken away so that he did not see death, *"and was not found, because God had taken him"*;[a] for before he was taken he had this testimony, that he pleased God. 6But without faith *it is* impossible to please *Him,* for he who comes to God must

➤ *But without faith it is impossible to please Him, for he who comes to God must believe that He is, and that He is a rewarder of those who diligently seek Him.* Heb. 11:6

10:37 aOr *that which*   10:38 aNU-Text reads *My just one.*   bHabakkuk 2:3, 4   11:5 aGenesis 5:24

↑ GROW (HEB. 11:1)
• •

Faith is belief plus action. You applied it when you first came to Christ by acting on what you accepted as true. The very existence of faith despite your circumstances is proof of God. It is a title deed from God, a confident assurance. Not everyone has this, of course, but the believer does. Some people say, "I can't have faith. I am a practical person and I need to know something is true before I can believe it." Nonsense. You apply faith every day. You apply faith when you go to the pharmacist and he fills your prescription, or when you have surgery and they put you under anesthesia and the surgeons operate on you. Faith is the means by which the infirmity of man takes hold of the affinity of God. Faith is how we connect to God. We put our trust and our faith in the Lord. *For more about* Faith, *see Heb. 11:6.*

believe that He is, and *that* He is a rewarder of those who diligently seek Him.

[7]By faith Noah, being divinely warned of things not yet seen, moved with godly fear, prepared an ark for the saving of his household, by which he condemned the world and became heir of the righteousness which is according to faith.

Faithful Abraham

[8]By faith Abraham obeyed when he was called to go out to the place which he would receive as an inheritance. And he went out, not knowing where he was going. [9]By faith he dwelt in the land of promise as *in* a foreign country, dwelling in tents with Isaac and Jacob, the heirs with him of the same promise; [10]for he waited for the city which has foundations, whose builder and maker *is* God.

[11]By faith Sarah herself also received strength to conceive seed, and she bore a child[a] when she was past the age, because she judged Him faithful who had promised. [12]Therefore from one man, and him as good as dead, were born *as many* as the stars of the sky in multitude—innumerable as the sand which is by the seashore.

The Heavenly Hope

[13]These all died in faith, not having received the promises, but having seen them afar off were assured of them,[a] embraced *them* and confessed that they were strangers and pilgrims on the earth. [14]For those who say such things declare plainly that they seek a homeland. [15]And truly if they had called to mind that *country* from which they had come out, they would have had opportunity to return. [16]But now they desire a better, that is, a heavenly *country*. Therefore God is not ashamed to be called their God, for He has prepared a city for them.

The Faith of the Patriarchs

[17]By faith Abraham, when he was tested, offered up Isaac, and he who had received the promises offered up his only begotten *son,* [18]of whom it was said, *"In Isaac your seed shall be called,"*[a] [19]concluding that God *was* able to raise *him* up, even from the dead,

from which he also received him in a figurative sense.

[20]By faith Isaac blessed Jacob and Esau concerning things to come.

[21]By faith Jacob, when he was dying, blessed each of the sons of Joseph, and worshiped, *leaning* on the top of his staff.

[22]By faith Joseph, when he was dying, made mention of the departure of the children of Israel, and gave instructions concerning his bones.

The Faith of Moses

[23]By faith Moses, when he was born, was hidden three months by his parents, because they saw *he was* a beautiful child; and they were not afraid of the king's command.

[24]By faith Moses, when he became of age, refused to be called the son of Pharaoh's daughter, [25]choosing rather to suffer affliction with the people of God than to enjoy the passing pleasures of sin, [26]esteeming the reproach of Christ greater riches than the treasures in[a] Egypt; for he looked to the reward.

[27]By faith he forsook Egypt, not fearing the wrath of the king; for he endured as seeing Him who is invisible. [28]By faith he kept the Passover and the sprinkling of blood, lest he who destroyed the firstborn should touch them.

[29]By faith they passed through the Red Sea as by dry *land, whereas* the Egyptians, attempting to do so, were drowned.

By Faith They Overcame

[30]By faith the walls of Jericho fell down after they were encircled for seven days. [31]By faith the harlot Rahab did not perish with those who did not believe, when she had received the spies with peace.

[32]And what more shall I say? For the time would fail me to tell of Gideon and Barak and Samson and Jephthah, also *of* David and Samuel and the prophets: [33]who through faith subdued kingdoms, worked righteousness, obtained promises, stopped the mouths of lions, [34]quenched the violence of fire, escaped the edge of the sword, out of weakness were made strong, became valiant in battle, turned to flight the armies of the aliens. [35]Women received their dead raised to life again.

11:11 [a]NU-Text omits *she bore a child.*   11:13 [a]NU-Text and M-Text omit *were assured of them.*   11:18 [a]Genesis 21:12
11:26 [a]NU-Text and M-Text read *of.*

Others were tortured, not accepting deliverance, that they might obtain a better resurrection. [36]Still others had trial of mockings and scourgings, yes, and of chains and imprisonment. [37]They were stoned, they were sawn in two, were tempted,[a] were slain with the sword. They wandered about in sheepskins and goatskins, being destitute, afflicted, tormented— [38]of whom the world was not worthy. They wandered in deserts and mountains, *in* dens and caves of the earth.

[39]And all these, having obtained a good testimony through faith, did not receive the promise, [40]God having provided something better for us, that they should not be made perfect apart from us.

The Race of Faith

12 Therefore we also, since we are surrounded by so great a cloud of witnesses, let us lay aside every weight, and the sin which so easily ensnares *us,* and let us run with endurance the race that is set before us, [2]looking unto Jesus, the author and finisher of *our* faith, who for the joy that was set before Him endured the cross, despising the shame, and has sat down at the right hand of the throne of God.

→ *Therefore we also, since we are surrounded by so great a cloud of witnesses, let us lay aside every weight, and the sin which so easily ensnares us, and let us run with endurance the race that is set before us, looking unto Jesus, the author and finisher of our faith . . .* Heb. 12:1, 2

The Discipline of God

[3]For consider Him who endured such hostility from sinners against Himself, lest you become weary and discouraged in your souls. [4]You have not yet resisted to bloodshed, striving against sin. [5]And you have forgotten the exhortation which speaks to you as to sons:

> "My son, do not despise the chastening of
> the Lord,
> Nor be discouraged when you are
> rebuked by Him;
> [6]For whom the Lord loves He chastens,
> And scourges every son whom He
> receives."[a]

→LIVE

12:6 • God demonstrates His unconditional love toward us in at least one unexpected way. He shows how deeply He loves us whenever He disciplines us. He reserves this kind of treatment for those who are truly His (v. 7), so the next time you cross the line spiritually and the Holy Spirit convicts you of your transgression and you feel guilt, rejoice! Take it as a heavenly reminder that you are indeed a child of God. No one enjoys the process of being disciplined by the Lord, but the ultimate outcome of such discipline will always be very good (v. 11). *For more about* God's Love, *see Heb. 12:11.*

[7]If[a] you endure chastening, God deals with you as with sons; for what son is there whom a father does not chasten? [8]But if you are without chastening, of which all have become partakers, then you are illegitimate and not sons. [9]Furthermore, we have had human fathers who corrected *us,* and we paid *them* respect. Shall we not much more readily be in subjection to the Father of spirits and live? [10]For they indeed for a few days chastened *us* as seemed *best* to them, but He for *our* profit, that *we* may be partakers of His holiness. [11]Now no chastening seems to be joyful for the present, but painful; nevertheless, afterward it yields the peaceable fruit of righteousness to those who have been trained by it.

Renew Your Spiritual Vitality

[12]Therefore strengthen the hands which hang down, and the feeble knees, [13]and make

11:37 [a]NU-Text omits *were tempted.*   12:6 [a]Proverbs 3:11, 12   12:7 [a]NU-Text and M-Text read *It is for discipline that you endure; God . . . .*

↘ LEARN

● ● ● ● ● ● ● ● ● ● ● ● ● ● ● ●

12:11 • It never feels good when God disciplines us. It hurts. We want it to stop. Often, we don't understand what He's up to. We wonder how a loving God could allow so much pain into our lives. But this verse teaches us not to ask why but what. That is, "What do I need to learn in this situation, Lord? How do you want to use it to make me more like Jesus?" Such questions of faith God will reward with "the peaceable fruit of righteousness." Discipline is actually a sign that you are indeed a child of God (Heb. 12:8). *For more about* God's Love, *see Jude 21.*

straight paths for your feet, so that what is lame may not be dislocated, but rather be healed.

¹⁴Pursue peace with all *people,* and holiness, without which no one will see the Lord: ¹⁵looking carefully lest anyone fall short of the grace of God; lest any root of bitterness springing up cause trouble, and by this many become defiled; ¹⁶lest there *be* any fornicator or profane person like Esau, who for one morsel of food sold his birthright. ¹⁷For you know that afterward, when he wanted to inherit the blessing, he was rejected, for he found no place for repentance, though he sought it diligently with tears.

The Glorious Company

¹⁸For you have not come to the mountain that[a] may be touched and that burned with fire, and to blackness and darkness[b] and tempest, ¹⁹and the sound of a trumpet and the voice of words, so that those who heard *it* begged that the word should not be spoken to them anymore. ²⁰(For they could not endure what was commanded: *"And if so much as a beast touches the mountain, it shall be stoned*[a] *or shot with an arrow."*[b] ²¹And so terrifying was the sight *that* Moses said, *"I am exceedingly afraid and trembling."*[a])

²²But you have come to Mount Zion and to the city of the living God, the heavenly Jerusalem, to an innumerable company of angels, ²³to the general assembly and church of the firstborn *who are* registered in heaven, to God the Judge of all, to the spirits of just men made perfect, ²⁴to Jesus the Mediator of the new covenant, and to the blood of

sprinkling that speaks better things than *that of* Abel.

Hear the Heavenly Voice

²⁵See that you do not refuse Him who speaks. For if they did not escape who refused Him who spoke on earth, much more *shall we not escape* if we turn away from Him who *speaks* from heaven, ²⁶whose voice then shook the earth; but now He has promised, saying, *"Yet once more I shake*[a] *not only the earth, but also heaven."*[b] ²⁷Now this, *"Yet once more,"* indicates the removal of those things that are being shaken, as of things that are made, that the things which cannot be shaken may remain.

²⁸Therefore, since we are receiving a kingdom which cannot be shaken, let us have grace, by which we may[a] serve God acceptably with reverence and godly fear. ²⁹For our God *is* a consuming fire.

Concluding Moral Directions

13 Let brotherly love continue. ²Do not forget to entertain strangers, for by so *doing* some have unwittingly entertained angels. ³Remember the prisoners as if chained with them—those who are mistreated—since you yourselves are in the body also.

⁴Marriage *is* honorable among all, and the bed undefiled; but fornicators and adulterers God will judge.

⁵*Let your* conduct *be* without covetousness; *be* content with such things as you have. For He Himself has said, *"I will never leave*

↘ LEARN

● ● ● ● ● ● ● ● ● ● ● ● ● ● ● ●

13:2 • Angels are highly involved in the lives of every believer. In fact, they are constantly at work behind the scenes, doing God's will. Sometimes they deliver us from harm (Ps. 34:7; Acts 12). We may even have met one without knowing it! Not everyone to whom we offer hospitality will be an angel, of course, but some could be. And even human guests may have something crucial to impart to us—but we'll never find out unless we open our arms, door, cupboards, refrigerator, and our hearts to those in need. Who knows? They might be angels in disguise! *For more about* God at Work, *see 1 Pet. 1:7.*

12:18 [a]NU-Text reads *to that which.* [b]NU-Text reads *gloom.* **12:20** [a]NU-Text and M-Text omit the rest of this verse.
[b]Exodus 19:12, 13   **12:21** [a]Deuteronomy 9:19   **12:26** [a]NU-Text reads *will shake.* [b]Haggai 2:6   **12:28** [a]M-Text omits *may.*

you nor forsake you."ᵃ ⁶So we may boldly say:

> "*The LORD is my helper;*
> *I will not fear.*
> *What can man do to me?*"ᵃ

Concluding Religious Directions

⁷Remember those who rule over you, who have spoken the word of God to you, whose faith follow, considering the outcome of *their* conduct. ⁸Jesus Christ *is* the same yesterday, today, and forever. ⁹Do not be carried aboutᵃ with various and strange doctrines. For *it is* good that the heart be established by grace, not with foods which have not profited those who have been occupied with them.

➤ *Jesus Christ is the same yesterday, today, and forever.* Heb. 13:8

¹⁰We have an altar from which those who serve the tabernacle have no right to eat. ¹¹For the bodies of those animals, whose blood is brought into the sanctuary by the high priest for sin, are burned outside the camp. ¹²Therefore Jesus also, that He might sanctify the people with His own blood, suffered outside the gate. ¹³Therefore let us go forth to Him, outside the camp, bearing His reproach. ¹⁴For here we have no continuing city, but we seek the one to come. ¹⁵Therefore by Him let us continually offer the sacrifice of praise to God, that is, the fruit of *our* lips, giving thanks to His name. ¹⁶But do not forget to do good and to share, for with such sacrifices God is well pleased.

¹⁷Obey those who rule over you, and be submissive, for they watch out for your souls, as those who must give account. Let them do so with joy and not with grief, for that would be unprofitable for you.

Prayer Requested

¹⁸Pray for us; for we are confident that we have a good conscience, in all things desiring to live honorably. ¹⁹But I especially urge *you* to do this, that I may be restored to you the sooner.

Benediction, Final Exhortation, Farewell

²⁰Now may the God of peace who brought up our Lord Jesus from the dead, that great Shepherd of the sheep, through the blood of the everlasting covenant, ²¹make you complete in every good work to do His will, working in youᵃ what is well pleasing in His sight, through Jesus Christ, to whom *be* glory forever and ever. Amen.

²²And I appeal to you, brethren, bear with the word of exhortation, for I have written to you in few words. ²³Know that *our* brother Timothy has been set free, with whom I shall see you if he comes shortly.

²⁴Greet all those who rule over you, and all the saints. Those from Italy greet you.

²⁵Grace *be* with you all. Amen.

13:5 ᵃDeuteronomy 31:6, 8; Joshua 1:5 **13:6** ᵃPsalm 118:6 **13:9** ᵃNU-Text and M-Text read *away.* **13:21** ᵃNU-Text and M-Text read *us.*

↑ GROW (HEB. 13:15)

Sometimes we become critics of worship rather than participants in it. "I didn't like those worship songs as much as the ones last week. I felt it was a little too loud (or wasn't loud enough). I don't like that instrument (or I like this other instrument)." But worship is not something we should critique; it is something we should do. And that is why the Bible talks about the sacrifice of praise. Sometimes, praise is a sacrifice. I don't want to offer it, but I offer it anyway, because I know God is in control. I know God loves me and that He's completely worthy of my praise. So I offer it up. Remember, worship is not about *you*. It is all about *Him*. And if we can get this firmly in mind when we sing our praises to God, it can make all the difference in the world. *For more about* Worship, *see Acts 2:42.*

JAMES

INTRODUCTION//

The Epistle of James is a handbook on practical Christian living, described as the "Proverbs of the New Testament." James, the author, was the oldest half-brother of Jesus, although he never mentions the fact.

James writes to Jewish believers scattered around the Mediterranean, issuing warnings and offering instructions on how to live. He asks his readers to "count it all joy when you fall into various trials, knowing that the testing of your faith produces patience" (1:2, 3). None of us should blame God for the temptations we face, for He does not "tempt anyone. But each one is tempted when he is drawn away by his own desires and enticed" (1:13, 14). James calls special attention to the tongue, calling it "an unruly evil, full of deadly poison" (3:8). We must be careful about our words, especially as many of us struggle to refrain from judging fellow believers. James tells us that when we judge each other, we judge the law, and by doing so we subject ourselves to harsh judgment. He tells us "there is one Lawgiver, who is able to save and to destroy. Who are you to judge another?" (4:12).

And in what is perhaps his major point, James clarifies the meaning of genuine faith. He inextricably connects faith to practical works and results. He insists on a concrete, seven-days-a-week, working faith that produces positive results. Without good works, James says, faith is dead, useless, a nonentity (2:17, 20). The kind of faith that does not produce righteousness is little different from the kind of faith the devil possesses, because even demons believe in God (2:19). Genuine faith takes hold of the promises of God and does something with them; it is active, not passive. And so Elijah's faith caused him to take a risk and stand up for God (5:17, 18).

Greeting to the Twelve Tribes

1 James, a bondservant of God and of the Lord Jesus Christ,

To the twelve tribes which are scattered abroad:

Greetings.

Profiting from Trials

²My brethren, count it all joy when you fall into various trials, ³knowing that the testing of your faith produces patience. ⁴But let patience have *its* perfect work, that you may be perfect and complete, lacking nothing. ⁵If any of you lacks wisdom, let him ask of God, who gives to all liberally and without reproach, and it will be given to him. ⁶But let him ask in faith, with no doubting, for he who doubts is like a wave of the sea driven and tossed by the wind. ⁷For let not that man suppose that he will receive anything from the Lord; ⁸*he is* a double-minded man, unstable in all his ways.

The Perspective of Rich and Poor

⁹Let the lowly brother glory in his exaltation, ¹⁰but the rich in his humiliation, because as a flower of the field he will pass away. ¹¹For no sooner has the sun risen with a burning heat than it withers the grass; its flower falls, and its beautiful appearance perishes. So the rich man also will fade away in his pursuits.

Loving God Under Trials

¹²Blessed *is* the man who endures temptation; for when he has been approved, he will

> ➤ *Blessed is the man who endures temptation; for when he has been approved, he will receive the crown of life which the Lord has promised to those who love Him.* James 1:12

receive the crown of life which the Lord has promised to those who love Him. ¹³Let no one say when he is tempted, "I am tempted by God"; for God cannot be tempted by evil, nor does He Himself tempt anyone. ¹⁴But each one is tempted when he is drawn away by his own desires and enticed. ¹⁵Then, when desire has conceived, it gives birth to sin; and sin, when it is full-grown, brings forth death.

¹⁶Do not be deceived, my beloved brethren. ¹⁷Every good gift and every perfect gift is from above, and comes down from the Father of lights, with whom there is no variation or shadow of turning. ¹⁸Of His own will He brought us forth by the word of truth, that we might be a kind of firstfruits of His creatures.

Qualities Needed in Trials

¹⁹So then,ᵃ my beloved brethren, let every man be swift to hear, slow to speak, slow to wrath; ²⁰for the wrath of man does not produce the righteousness of God.

1:19 ᵃNU-Text reads *Know this* or *This you know.*

↓ KNOW (JAMES 1:12)

Would it surprise you to learn that testing and temptation can have a positive effect? That's the surprising claim James makes. No sooner has he begun his very practical letter than he tells us three important things about temptation:
- We can endure it.
- We get a reward for enduring it.
- We will be very happy when we resist its demonic pull.

Martin Luther once said, "One Christian who has been tempted is worth a thousand who haven't." You never know how real your faith is until it's been severely tested. And so someone else has well said, "Christians are a lot like teabags. You don't know what they're made of until you put them in hot water." *For more about* Faith, *see* James 2:14; Adversity, 1 Pet. 1:7.

Doers—Not Hearers Only

[21]Therefore lay aside all filthiness and overflow of wickedness, and receive with meekness the implanted word, which is able to save your souls.

[22]But be doers of the word, and not hearers only, deceiving yourselves. [23]For if anyone is a hearer of the word and not a doer, he is like a man observing his natural face in a mirror; [24]for he observes himself, goes away, and immediately forgets what kind of man he was. [25]But he who looks into the perfect law of liberty and continues *in it,* and is not a forgetful hearer but a doer of the work, this one will be blessed in what he does.

> ↘ **LEARN**
> . . . .
> 1:23, 24 • Imagine a Christian reading his Bible. At some point God's Spirit brings home a certain text to his heart. He thinks, *I really need to do something about this.* But he never does. This is the kind of person James has in mind here. He wants us to see that unless the Word has made a change in our lives, it has not really entered our lives. God's Word can become a millstone if we do not make it a milestone. Truth acted on brings more truth, but failure to respond to truth will ultimately result in loss of truth. *For more about* God's Word, *see James 2:9, 10.*

[26]If anyone among you[a] thinks he is religious, and does not bridle his tongue but deceives his own heart, this one's religion *is* useless. [27]Pure and undefiled religion before God and the Father is this: to visit orphans and widows in their trouble, *and* to keep oneself unspotted from the world.

Beware of Personal Favoritism

2 My brethren, do not hold the faith of our Lord Jesus Christ, *the Lord* of glory, with partiality. [2]For if there should come into your assembly a man with gold rings, in fine apparel, and there should also come in a poor man in filthy clothes, [3]and you pay attention to the one wearing the fine clothes and say to him, "You sit here in a good place," and say to the poor man, "You stand there," or, "Sit here at my footstool," [4]have you not shown partiality among yourselves, and become judges with evil thoughts?

[5]Listen, my beloved brethren: Has God not chosen the poor of this world *to be* rich in faith and heirs of the kingdom which He promised to those who love Him? [6]But you have dishonored the poor man. Do not the rich oppress you and drag you into the courts? [7]Do they not blaspheme that noble name by which you are called?

[8]If you really fulfill *the* royal law according to the Scripture, *"You shall love your neighbor as yourself,"*[a] you do well; [9]but if you show partiality, you commit sin, and are convicted by the law as transgressors. [10]For whoever shall keep the whole law, and yet stumble in one *point,* he is guilty of all. [11]For He who said, *"Do not commit adultery,"*[a] also said, *"Do not murder."*[b] Now if you do not commit adultery, but you do murder, you have become a transgressor of the law. [12]So speak and so do as those who will be judged by the law of liberty. [13]For judgment is without mercy to the one who has shown no mercy. Mercy triumphs over judgment.

> → **LIVE**
> . . . .
> 2:9, 10 • Some people say, "I live by the Ten Commandments and that's all the religion I need!" The irony is that most of these people cannot even name the Ten Commandments, much less actually keep them. The commandments were not given to make us holy, but rather to show us our unholiness. The law opens our eyes and shuts our mouths (Rom. 3:19, 20). If you offend in one point of the law, you are guilty of all (v. 10). The law was given to drive us into the open arms of Jesus, who alone can change the human heart (Gal. 3:24). *For more about* God's Word, *see 1 Pet. 2:2.*

Faith Without Works Is Dead

[14]What *does it* profit, my brethren, if someone says he has faith but does not have works? Can faith save him? [15]If a brother or sister is naked and destitute of daily food, [16]and one of you says to them, "Depart in peace, be warmed and filled," but you do not give them the things which are needed for the body, what *does it* profit? [17]Thus also faith by itself, if it does not have works, is dead.

[18]But someone will say, "You have faith, and I have works." Show me your faith without your[a] works, and I will show you my faith by my[b] works. [19]You believe that there

1:26[a]NU-Text omits *among you.*   **2:8**[a]Leviticus 19:18   **2:11**[a]Exodus 20:14; Deuteronomy 5:18 [b]Exodus 20:13; Deuteronomy 5:17
2:18[a]NU-Text omits *your.*   [b]NU-Text omits *my.*

↘ LEARN

• • • • • • • • • • • • • • •

2:14 • Any declaration of faith that fails to result in a changed life is a false declaration. Faith alone justifies, but faith that justifies can never remain alone. C. H. Spurgeon asked, "Of what value is the grace I profess to receive if it does not dramatically change the way that I live? If it doesn't change the way that I live, it will never change my eternal destiny." True belief in Jesus Christ results in a radical change in your attitudes and lifestyle. Works do not save a person, but they are good evidence that he or she is saved. *For more about* Faith *and* How to Live Out Your Faith, *see James 2:18.*

is one God. You do well. Even the demons believe—and tremble! [20]But do you want to know, O foolish man, that faith without works is dead?[a] [21]Was not Abraham our father justified by works when he offered Isaac his son on the altar? [22]Do you see that faith was working together with his works, and by works faith was made perfect? [23]And the Scripture was fulfilled which says, *"Abraham believed God, and it was accounted to him for righteousness."*[a] And he was called the friend of God. [24]You see then that a man is justified by works, and not by faith only.

[25]Likewise, was not Rahab the harlot also justified by works when she received the messengers and sent *them* out another way?

[26]For as the body without the spirit is dead, so faith without works is dead also.

The Untamable Tongue

3 My brethren, let not many of you become teachers, knowing that we shall receive a stricter judgment. [2]For we all stumble in many things. If anyone does not stumble in word, he *is* a perfect man, able also to bridle the whole body. [3]Indeed,[a] we put bits in horses' mouths that they may obey us, and we turn their whole body. [4]Look also at ships: although they are so large and are driven by fierce winds, they are turned by a very small rudder wherever the pilot desires. [5]Even so the tongue is a little member and boasts great things.

See how great a forest a little fire kindles! [6]And the tongue *is* a fire, a world of iniquity. The tongue is so set among our members that it defiles the whole body, and sets on fire the course of nature; and it is set on fire by hell. [7]For every kind of beast and bird, of reptile and creature of the sea, is tamed and has been tamed by mankind. [8]But no man can tame the tongue. *It is* an unruly evil, full of deadly poison. [9]With it we bless our God and Father, and with it we curse men, who have been made in the similitude of God. [10]Out of

↘ LEARN

• • • • • • • • • • • • • • •

3:6 • Why do we get so careless with our tongues? While we would never consider assassinating even our worst enemies, often we casually assassinate another's character over Sunday brunch. When we gossip, we are doing the work of the enemy. The very word gossip hisses. What we say *matters*. Our words carry great weight, to either build up or tear others down. Unkind and untrue things said about another can destroy. Bad news and falsehood often travels faster than good news and truth. It's been said, "A lie is halfway around the world while truth is still putting its shoes on." *For more about* Loving Others, *see 1 John 3:11;* Sin, *1 John 1:9.*

2:20 [a]NU-Text reads *useless.*   2:23 [a]Genesis 15:6   3:3 [a]NU-Text reads *Now if.*

↑ GROW (JAMES 2:18)

• •

We develop our faith through regular use. Hearing the Word of God creates and bolsters my faith, but *using* my faith strengthens it. Some of us treat faith as if it were a fragile little egg. "Oh, careful with my faith! Don't drop it. *Easy.* Put it here." No, that is not what faith is. Faith is tough, resilient, and gets stronger through use. Faith is like a muscle. You build your muscle by repeatedly tearing it down and rebuilding it. And the same is true of faith. Faith always carries the idea of action. It involves movement toward its object. Faith is a restless, living thing. It cannot remain inoperative. Faith *moves*. Faith *acts*. Faith *does*. It doesn't just sit. It has to move. Faith is the refusal to panic. Faith has no back door. *For more about* Faith, *see 1 Pet. 1:7;* How to Live Out Your Faith, *1 Pet. 1:15, 16.*

the same mouth proceed blessing and cursing. My brethren, these things ought not to be so. [11]Does a spring send forth fresh *water* and bitter from the same opening? [12]Can a fig tree, my brethren, bear olives, or a grapevine bear figs? Thus no spring yields both salt water and fresh.[a]

Heavenly Versus Demonic Wisdom

[13]Who *is* wise and understanding among you? Let him show by good conduct *that his* works *are done* in the meekness of wisdom. [14]But if you have bitter envy and self-seeking in your hearts, do not boast and lie against the truth. [15]This wisdom does not descend from above, but *is* earthly, sensual, demonic. [16]For where envy and self-seeking *exist*, confusion and every evil thing *are* there. [17]But the wisdom that is from above is first pure, then peaceable, gentle, willing to yield, full of mercy and good fruits, without partiality and without hypocrisy. [18]Now the fruit of righteousness is sown in peace by those who make peace.

Pride Promotes Strife

4 Where do wars and fights *come* from among you? Do *they* not *come* from your *desires for* pleasure that war in your members? [2]You lust and do not have. You murder and covet and cannot obtain. You fight and war. Yet[a] you do not have because you do not ask. [3]You ask and do not receive, because you ask amiss, that you may spend *it* on your pleasures. [4]Adulterers and[a] adulteresses! Do you not know that friendship

> ### ↘ LEARN
> • • • • • • • • • • • • • • • •
> 4:1, 2 • James put his finger on the real source of our problems: self. Jesus said that if we want to find ourselves, we must lose ourselves. If we want to find life, we must lose it in following Jesus. This is God's trade-in program. The things so many people chase after in life—pleasure, happiness, fulfillment, meaning—come not so much from seeking them but rather as the beautiful after-effect of knowing and walking with God. To put it briefly, James insists that the Christ-centered life must take the place of a self-centered life. God and others must come before me. *For more about* Submitting to God, *see 1 Pet. 5:7.*

with the world is enmity with God? Whoever therefore wants to be a friend of the world makes himself an enemy of God. [5]Or do you think that the Scripture says in vain, "The Spirit who dwells in us yearns jealously"?

[6]But He gives more grace. Therefore He says:

> "God resists the proud,
> But gives grace to the humble."[a]

Humility Cures Worldliness

[7]Therefore submit to God. Resist the devil and he will flee from you. [8]Draw near to God and He will draw near to you. Cleanse *your* hands, *you* sinners; and purify *your* hearts, *you* double-minded. [9]Lament and mourn and weep! Let your laughter be turned to mourning and *your* joy to gloom. [10]Humble yourselves in the sight of the Lord, and He will lift you up.

3:12 [a]NU-Text reads *Neither can a salty spring produce fresh water.*   4:2 [a]NU-Text and M-Text omit *Yet.*   4:4 [a]NU-Text omits *Adulterers and.*   4:6 [a]Proverbs 3:34

↑ GROW (JAMES 4:2)
• •
Prayer is God's appointed way of obtaining things. That's one reason why we should pray, although it's not the only reason. Still, prayer is God's way of giving you the things you need. God may want to give you many good things and do many wonderful things for you, but you have yet to receive them *because you have not asked.* God will not always give you everything that you ask for, of course. He doesn't heal every person who asks for a divine touch, but He will heal some. If you want God to do something for you, but He hasn't yet done it, perhaps He's waiting for you to pray about it. What have you got to lose? Sure, the Lord could say no. But what if He says yes? James says, "You do not have because you do not ask." Take your requests to God. *For more about* Prayer, *see 1 John 5:14, 15;* Spiritual Disciplines, *2 John 6.*

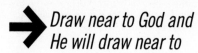

Draw near to God and He will draw near to you. . . . James 4:8

Do Not Judge a Brother

[11]Do not speak evil of one another, brethren. He who speaks evil of a brother and judges his brother, speaks evil of the law and judges the law. But if you judge the law, you are not a doer of the law but a judge. [12]There is one Lawgiver,[a] who is able to save and to destroy. Who[b] are you to judge another?[c]

Do Not Boast About Tomorrow

[13]Come now, you who say, "Today or tomorrow we will[a] go to such and such a city, spend a year there, buy and sell, and make a profit"; [14]whereas you do not know what *will happen* tomorrow. For what *is* your life? It is even a vapor that appears for a little time and then vanishes away. [15]Instead you *ought* to say, "If the Lord wills, we shall live and do this or that." [16]But now you boast in your arrogance. All such boasting is evil. [17]Therefore, to him who knows to do good and does not do *it*, to him it is sin.

Rich Oppressors Will Be Judged

5 Come now, *you* rich, weep and howl for your miseries that are coming upon *you!* [2]Your riches are corrupted, and your garments are moth-eaten. [3]Your gold and silver are corroded, and their corrosion will be a witness against you and will eat your flesh like fire. You have heaped up treasure in the last days. [4]Indeed the wages of the laborers who mowed your fields, which you kept back by fraud, cry out; and the cries of the reapers have reached the ears of the Lord of Sabaoth.[a] [5]You have lived on the earth in pleasure and luxury; you have fattened your hearts as[a] in a day of slaughter. [6]You have condemned, you have murdered the just; he does not resist you.

Be Patient and Persevering

[7]Therefore be patient, brethren, until the coming of the Lord. See *how* the farmer waits for the precious fruit of the earth, waiting patiently for it until it receives the early and latter rain. [8]You also be patient. Establish your hearts, for the coming of the Lord is at hand.

[9]Do not grumble against one another, brethren, lest you be condemned.[a] Behold, the Judge is standing at the door! [10]My brethren, take the prophets, who spoke in the name of the Lord, as an example of suffering and patience. [11]Indeed we count them blessed who endure. You have heard of the perseverance of Job and seen the end *intended by* the Lord—that the Lord is very compassionate and merciful.

[12]But above all, my brethren, do not swear, either by heaven or by earth or with any other oath. But let your "Yes" be "Yes," and *your* "No," "No," lest you fall into judgment.[a]

◥ LEARN

5:7 • Never study Bible prophecy merely to tantalize or entertain yourself. Rather, use Jesus' Second Coming to motivate yourself to personal godliness and bold evangelism. Pondering the return of Christ should have a purifying effect. So when James tells you to be patient, he is not promoting passive resignation, but rather a patient, expectant waiting on the Lord. The apostle John tells us, "Everyone who has this hope in Him [the hope of Christ's imminent return] purifies himself, just as He is pure" (1 John 3:3). So nurture an excited, expectant readiness, like a kid on Christmas Eve who's watching and waiting. *For more about* Jesus' Return, *see 1 Pet. 1:13.*

Meeting Specific Needs

[13]Is anyone among you suffering? Let him pray. Is anyone cheerful? Let him sing psalms. [14]Is anyone among you sick? Let him call for the elders of the church, and let them pray over him, anointing him with oil in the name of the Lord. [15]And the prayer of faith will save the sick, and the Lord will raise him up. And if he has committed sins, he will be forgiven. [16]Confess *your* trespasses[a] to one another, and pray for one another, that you may be healed. The effective, fervent prayer of a righteous man avails much. [17]Elijah was a man with a nature like ours, and he prayed earnestly that

→ *. . . The effective, fervent prayer of a righteous man avails much.* James 5:16

it would not rain; and it did not rain on the land for three years and six months. [18]And he prayed again, and the heaven gave rain, and the earth produced its fruit.

Bring Back the Erring One

[19]Brethren, if anyone among you wanders from the truth, and someone turns him back, [20]let him know that he who turns a sinner from the error of his way will save a soul[a] from death and cover a multitude of sins.

5:20 [a]NU-Text reads *his soul.*

1 PETER

INTRODUCTION//

Peter, one of the first apostles called by Christ, is a very important figure in church history. Jesus occasionally took Peter with Him on special occasions, such as His transfiguration (Matt.17:1), and to witness his agony in Gethsemene (Mark 14:33). As Jesus predicted, Peter denied the Lord (Mark 14:71, 72), but later was recommissioned by Christ Himself (John 21). The first section of the Book of Acts deals with Peter's life and ministry.

In his first letter, Peter focuses on suffering, bringing words of comfort to the Christian victims of vicious persecution. Peter writes that their faith will be proved genuine and "may be found to praise, honor, and glory at the revelation of Jesus Christ" (1:7). Because of this, we are to "be holy in all" our conduct (1:15). We are to love each other and rid ourselves of "all malice, all deceit, hypocrisy, envy, and all evil speaking" (2:1). He reminds us that "it is better, if it is the will of God, to suffer for doing good than for doing evil" (3:17).

Peter instructs his readers to "Honor all people. Love the brotherhood. Fear God. Honor the king" (2:17). They were to do so because "by doing good you may put to silence the ignorance of foolish men" (2:15). Likewise, he instructs elders to care for the younger believers. He calls everyone to "have fervent love for one another" (4:8) and to live every aspect of their lives for God. If we do not conduct ourselves in this way, our suffering is deserved, and no glory comes either to God or to us. But when we suffer according to God's will, "rejoice to the extent that you partake of Christ's sufferings, that when His glory is revealed, you may also be glad with exceeding joy" (4:13).

Greeting to the Elect Pilgrims

1 Peter, an apostle of Jesus Christ,

To the pilgrims of the Dispersion in Pontus, Galatia, Cappadocia, Asia, and Bithynia, ²elect according to the foreknowledge of God the Father, in sanctification of the Spirit, for obedience and sprinkling of the blood of Jesus Christ:

Grace to you and peace be multiplied.

A Heavenly Inheritance

³Blessed *be* the God and Father of our Lord Jesus Christ, who according to His abundant mercy has begotten us again to a living hope through the resurrection of Jesus Christ from the dead, ⁴to an inheritance incorruptible and undefiled and that does not fade away, reserved in heaven for you, ⁵who are kept by the power of God through faith for salvation ready to be revealed in the last time.

⁶In this you greatly rejoice, though now for a little while, if need be, you have been grieved by various trials, ⁷that the genuineness of your faith, *being* much more precious than gold that perishes, though it is tested by fire, may be found to praise, honor, and glory at the revelation of Jesus Christ, ⁸whom having not seen[a] you love. Though now you do not see *Him,* yet believing, you rejoice with joy inexpressible and full of glory, ⁹receiving the end of your faith—the salvation of *your* souls.

¹⁰Of this salvation the prophets have inquired and searched carefully, who prophesied of the grace *that would come* to you,

¹¹searching what, or what manner of time, the Spirit of Christ who was in them was indicating when He testified beforehand the sufferings of Christ and the glories that would follow. ¹²To them it was revealed that, not to themselves, but to us[a] they were ministering the things which now have been reported to you through those who have preached the gospel to you by the Holy Spirit sent from heaven—things which angels desire to look into.

Living Before God Our Father

¹³Therefore gird up the loins of your mind, be sober, and rest *your* hope fully upon the grace that is to be brought to you at the revelation of Jesus Christ; ¹⁴as obedient children, not conforming yourselves to the former lusts, *as* in your ignorance; ¹⁵but as He who called you *is* holy, you also be holy in all *your* conduct, ¹⁶because it is written, *"Be holy, for I am holy."*[a]

1:8 [a]M-Text reads *known.*   1:12 [a]NU-Text and M-Text read *you.*   1:16 [a]Leviticus 11:44, 45; 19:2; 20:7

> **↘ LEARN**
>
> 1:13 • Meditating on the Second Coming of Christ is no mere idle speculation. This is so important that *at this very moment* we are to rest our hope fully in it. To "gird up the loins of your mind" means to think clearly about this and exercise self-control, in expectation of His glorious return. It is a good thing while on earth to think of heavenly things. Because life here is so fleeting and short, but eternity is forever. Heaven is a prepared place for prepared people. If Jesus Christ were to return today, would you be ready? *For more about* Jesus' Return, *see 2 Pet. 3:11.*

↑ GROW (1 PET. 1:7)

God is in total control of every circumstance of your life. The devil can do *nothing* in your life without the expressed permission of God. But why would God give Satan such permission? He does so because Satan's attacks will demonstrate what you're made of. When the devil attacks, his assault will reveal whether you are a genuine believer. Some people will say, "This tragedy shattered my faith. How can I believe in God anymore?" When I hear something like that, I always wonder, *Did you have real faith to begin with?* Randy Alcorn said, "A faith that cannot be shaken is a faith that has been shaken." And if your faith is real, it will get you through even a catastrophe because character is not *made* in crisis, but *revealed* in crisis. Trials, temptations, and crises separate the wheat from the chaff, the true from the false, the real from the unreal. *For more about* Faith, *see Matt. 14:28–31;* Satan, *Rev. 12:10;* God at Work, *1 Pet. 3:21;* Adversity, *1 Pet. 4:1, 2.*

[17]And if you call on the Father, who without partiality judges according to each one's work, conduct yourselves throughout the time of your stay *here* in fear; [18]knowing that you were not redeemed with corruptible things, *like* silver or gold, from your aimless conduct *received* by tradition from your fathers, [19]but with the precious blood of Christ, as of a lamb without blemish and without spot. [20]He indeed was foreordained before the foundation of the world, but was manifest in these last times for you [21]who through Him believe in God, who raised Him from the dead and gave Him glory, so that your faith and hope are in God.

→LIVE

● ● ● ● ● ● ● ● ● ● ● ● ● ● ● ●

1:23 • Being born into God's family has nothing to do with *descent*. You cannot be born a Christian. Nor does new birth have anything to do with *desire*. You cannot simply make yourself a Christian by exercising your will. Finally, new birth has nothing to do with *determination* (John 1:13). You cannot be reborn through a ceremony, by reciting a creed, or by kneeling at a bench. To become a Christian you must come humbly before God, admit your sinfulness, turn from it, and believe in and receive His Son, Jesus Christ. Jesus said, "You must be born again" (John 3). *For more about* Becoming a Christian, *see Matt. 10:32.*

The Enduring Word

[22]Since you have purified your souls in obeying the truth through the Spirit[a] in sincere love of the brethren, love one another fervently with a pure heart, [23]having been born again, not of corruptible seed but incorruptible, through the word of God which lives and abides forever,[a] [24]because

"*All flesh is as grass,*
And all the glory of man[a] as the flower of the grass.
The grass withers,
And its flower falls away,
[25]*But the word of the LORD endures forever.*"[a]

Now this is the word which by the gospel was preached to you.

2 Therefore, laying aside all malice, all deceit, hypocrisy, envy, and all evil speaking, [2]as newborn babes, desire the pure milk of the word, that you may grow thereby,[a] [3]if indeed you have tasted that the Lord *is* gracious.

↘LEARN

● ● ● ● ● ● ● ● ● ● ● ● ● ● ● ●

2:2 • "How's your appetite?" asks the doctor when you feel ill. He knows healthy people have good appetites. Hungry people are healthy people. In the same way, healthy babies crave their mothers' milk. They want it, demand it, cry for it. Peter says that young believers should desire the nourishment of God's Word with the milk-loving fervor of infants. God's Word is pure, just as the old life was full of deceit (v. 1), and that is why the Bible enables believers to grow in the Christian life. As we learn about Jesus and His Father—the heart of the Bible's message—we become both productive and joyful. *For more about* God's Word, *see 2 Pet. 2:1;* Growing in Christ, *2 Pet. 1:12.*

1:22 [a]NU-Text omits *through the Spirit.*   1:23 [a]NU-Text omits *forever.*   1:24 [a]NU-Text reads *all its glory.*   1:25 [a]Isaiah 40:6–8
2:2 [a]NU-Text adds *up to salvation.*

↑ GROW (1 PET. 1:15, 16)

● ●

Because God is holy, we should be holy. Unfortunately, most people have a negative impression of holiness. "You are so holier than thou!" But in fact we should indeed desire to be holy people. In fact, the Bible *commands* you to be holy. By "holy" I don't mean arrogance or having a false piety; some people call themselves holy, but it's nothing more than pride. They look down their noses at everybody and act in a very condescending way. That is *not* holiness; that's just being arrogant. In fact, the holiest people in the world are also the humblest people. When you begin *really* living a holy life, you will become increasingly aware of how far you have to go. Perhaps if we spelled holiness differently it might help us to understand it better. Be wholly committed to the Lord and you will live a holy life (Josh. 14:8). *For more about the* Attributes of God, *see 1 John 3:11;* How to Live Out Your Faith, *2 John 6.*

The Chosen Stone and His Chosen People

[4]Coming to Him *as to* a living stone, rejected indeed by men, but chosen by God *and* precious, [5]you also, as living stones, are being built up a spiritual house, a holy priesthood, to offer up spiritual sacrifices acceptable to God through Jesus Christ. [6]Therefore it is also contained in the Scripture,

> "Behold, I lay in Zion
> A chief cornerstone, elect, precious,
> And he who believes on Him will by no
>   means be put to shame."[a]

[7]Therefore, to you who believe, *He is* precious; but to those who are disobedient,[a]

> "The stone which the builders rejected
> Has become the chief cornerstone,"[b]

[8]and

> "A stone of stumbling
> And a rock of offense."[a]

They stumble, being disobedient to the word, to which they also were appointed.
[9]But you *are* a chosen generation, a royal priesthood, a holy nation, His own special people, that you may proclaim the praises of Him who called you out of darkness into His marvelous light; [10]who once *were* not a people but *are* now the people of God, who had not obtained mercy but now have obtained mercy.

Living Before the World

[11]Beloved, I beg *you* as sojourners and pilgrims, abstain from fleshly lusts which war against the soul, [12]having your conduct honorable among the Gentiles, that when they speak against you as evildoers, they may, by *your* good works which they observe, glorify God in the day of visitation.

Submission to Government

[13]Therefore submit yourselves to every ordinance of man for the Lord's sake, whether to the king as supreme, [14]or to governors, as to those who are sent by him for the punishment of evildoers and *for the* praise of those who do good. [15]For this is the will of God, that by doing good you may put to silence the ignorance of foolish men— [16]as free, yet not using liberty as a cloak for vice, but as bondservants of God. [17]Honor all *people.* Love the brotherhood. Fear God. Honor the king.

Submission to Masters

[18]Servants, *be* submissive to *your* masters with all fear, not only to the good and gentle, but also to the harsh. [19]For this *is* commendable, if because of conscience toward God one endures grief, suffering wrongfully. [20]For what credit *is it* if, when you are beaten for your faults, you take it patiently? But when you do good and suffer, if you take it patiently, this *is* commendable before God. [21]For to this you were called, because Christ also suffered for us,[a] leaving us[b] an example, that you should follow His steps:

> [22] "Who committed no sin,
>   Nor was deceit found in His mouth";[a]

[23]who, when He was reviled, did not revile in return; when He suffered, He did not threaten, but committed *Himself* to Him who judges righteously; [24]who Himself bore our sins in His own body on the tree, that we, having died to sins, might live for righteousness—by whose stripes you were healed. [25]For you were like sheep going astray, but have now returned to the Shepherd and Overseer[a] of your souls.

Submission to Husbands

3 Wives, likewise, *be* submissive to your own husbands, that even if some do not obey the word, they, without a word, may be won by the conduct of their wives, [2]when they observe your chaste conduct *accompanied* by fear. [3]Do not let your adornment be *merely* outward—arranging the hair, wearing gold, or putting on *fine* apparel— [4]rather *let it be* the hidden person of the heart, with the incorruptible *beauty* of a gentle and quiet spirit, which is very precious in the sight of God. [5]For in this manner, in former times, the holy women who trusted in God also adorned themselves, being submissive to their own husbands, [6]as Sarah obeyed Abraham, calling him lord, whose daughters

2:6 [a]Isaiah 28:16   2:7 [a]NU-Text reads *to those who disbelieve.*   [b]Psalm 118:22   2:8 [a]Isaiah 8:14
2:21 [a]NU-Text reads *you.*   [b]NU-Text and M-Text read *you.*   2:22 [a]Isaiah 53:9   2:25 [a]Greek *Episkopos*

you are if you do good and are not afraid with any terror.

A Word to Husbands

[7]Husbands, likewise, dwell with *them* with understanding, giving honor to the wife, as to the weaker vessel, and as *being* heirs together of the grace of life, that your prayers may not be hindered.

Called to Blessing

[8]Finally, all *of you be* of one mind, having compassion for one another; love as brothers, *be* tenderhearted, *be* courteous;[a] [9]not returning evil for evil or reviling for reviling, but on the contrary blessing, knowing that you were called to this, that you may inherit a blessing. [10]For

"He who would love life
And see good days,
Let him refrain his tongue from evil,
And his lips from speaking deceit.
[11]Let him turn away from evil and do good;
Let him seek peace and pursue it.
[12]For the eyes of the LORD are on the righteous,
And His ears are open to their prayers;
But the face of the LORD is against those who do evil."[a]

Suffering for Right and Wrong

[13]And who *is* he who will harm you if you become followers of what is good? [14]But even if you should suffer for righteousness' sake, *you are* blessed. *"And do not be afraid of their threats, nor be troubled."*[a] [15]But sanctify the Lord God[a] in your hearts, and always *be* ready to *give* a defense to everyone who asks you a reason for the hope that is in you, with meekness and fear; [16]having a good conscience, that when they defame you as evildoers, those who revile your good conduct in Christ may be ashamed. [17]For *it is* better, if it is the will of God, to suffer for doing good than for doing evil.

Christ's Suffering and Ours

[18]For Christ also suffered once for sins, the just for the unjust, that He might bring

---

→ LIVE

3:21 • Salvation is past, present, and future. If you have placed your faith in Jesus, God already has saved you. It's a done deal (Eph. 2:8). Second, God is saving you right now. He is saving you every day from the power and control of sin (2 Cor. 1:10). And if that were not enough, He will also save you in the future. He'll save you from the coming judgment awaiting those who have failed to put their trust in Jesus Christ (Rom. 5:9). God has saved you. God is saving you. And God will yet save you in the future. *For more about* Assurance of Salvation, *see 1 John 2:19;* God at Work, *2 Pet. 3:8, 9.*

---

us[a] to God, being put to death in the flesh but made alive by the Spirit, [19]by whom also He went and preached to the spirits in prison, [20]who formerly were disobedient, when once the Divine longsuffering waited[a] in the days of Noah, while *the* ark was being prepared, in which a few, that is, eight souls, were saved through water. [21]There is also an antitype which now saves us—baptism (not the removal of the filth of the flesh, but the answer of a good conscience toward God), through the resurrection of Jesus Christ, [22]who has gone into heaven and is at the right hand of God, angels and authorities and powers having been made subject to Him.

4 Therefore, since Christ suffered for us[a] in the flesh, arm yourselves also with the same mind, for he who has suffered in the flesh has ceased from sin, [2]that he no longer should live the rest of *his* time in the flesh for the lusts of men, but for the will of God. [3]For we *have spent* enough of

---

↘ LEARN

4:1, 2 • Suffering for Christ is no accident. When hardship or difficulty hits us because of our connection to Jesus, Scripture encourages us to use the painful experience to grow deeper in Him, to curb our appetite for sin, and to follow the example of Jesus, who desired more than anything else to please His heavenly Father. If we allow suffering to shape us as God intends, we will emerge on the other side of the pain with a stronger, more resilient, and far richer relationship with Christ than we have ever known. Suffering will either make us bitter or better. *For more about* Adversity, *see 1 Pet. 4:12, 13.*

3:8 [a]NU-Text reads *humble.*   **3:12** [a]Psalm 34:12–16   **3:14** [a]Isaiah 8:12   **3:15** [a]NU-Text reads *Christ as Lord.*   **3:18** [a]NU-Text and M-Text read *you.*   **3:20** [a]NU-Text and M-Text read *when the longsuffering of God waited patiently.*   **4:1** [a]NU-Text omits *for us.*

our past lifetime[a] in doing the will of the Gentiles—when we walked in lewdness, lusts, drunkenness, revelries, drinking parties, and abominable idolatries. [4]In regard to these, they think it strange that you do not run with *them* in the same flood of dissipation, speaking evil of *you.* [5]They will give an account to Him who is ready to judge the living and the dead. [6]For this reason the gospel was preached also to those who are dead, that they might be judged according to men in the flesh, but live according to God in the spirit.

Serving for God's Glory

[7]But the end of all things is at hand; therefore be serious and watchful in your prayers. [8]And above all things have fervent love for one another, for *"love will cover a multitude of sins."*[a] [9]*Be* hospitable to one another without grumbling. [10]As each one has received a gift, minister it to one another, as good stewards of the manifold grace of God. [11]If anyone speaks, *let him speak* as the oracles of God. If anyone ministers, *let him do it* as with the ability which God supplies, that in all things God may be glorified through Jesus Christ, to whom belong the glory and the dominion forever and ever. Amen.

Suffering for God's Glory

[12]Beloved, do not think it strange concerning the fiery trial which is to try you, as though some strange thing happened to you; [13]but rejoice to the extent that you partake of Christ's sufferings, that when His glory is revealed, you may also be glad with exceeding joy. [14]If you are reproached for the name of Christ, blessed *are you,* for the Spirit of glory and of God rests upon you.[a] On their part He is blasphemed, but on your part He is glorified. [15]But let none of you suffer as a murderer, a thief, an evildoer, or as a busybody in other people's matters. [16]Yet if *anyone suffers* as a Christian, let him not be ashamed, but let him glorify God in this matter.[a]

[17]For the time *has come* for judgment to begin at the house of God; and if *it begins* with us first, what will *be* the end of those who do not obey the gospel of God? [18]Now

> *"If the righteous one is scarcely saved,*
> *Where will the ungodly and the sinner*
> *appear?"*[a]

[19]Therefore let those who suffer according to the will of God commit their souls *to Him* in doing good, as to a faithful Creator.

Shepherd the Flock

5 The elders who are among you I exhort, I who am a fellow elder and a witness of the sufferings of Christ, and also a partaker of the glory that will be revealed: [2]Shepherd the flock of God which is among you, serving as overseers, not by compulsion but willingly,[a] not for dishonest gain but eagerly; [3]nor as being lords over those entrusted to you, but being examples to the flock; [4]and when the Chief Shepherd appears, you will receive the crown of glory that does not fade away.

4:3 [a]NU-Text reads *time.*　　**4:8** [a]Proverbs 10:12　　**4:14** [a]NU-Text omits the rest of this verse.　　**4:16** [a]NU-Text reads *name.*
4:18 [a]Proverbs 11:31　　**5:2** [a]NU-Text adds *according to God.*

↓ KNOW (1 PET. 4:12, 13)

Why does God allow bad things to happen to good people? And to take it a step further, why does God allow bad things to happen to *godly* people? One thing is for sure: being a Christian does *not* exempt you from suffering. Christians get cancer, have heart attacks, and die. Christians get killed in automobile accidents. Tragedy comes into our lives without invitation. So why do bad things happen to godly people? Here's my answer: *I don't know.* That is not to say no answers exist, but simply that I don't know them. Still, I know God is good and that He is in control. And I know He works all things together for good. That will have to be enough, for now. When we have suffered and survived, however, we have a platform to help others who can see no light at the end of the tunnel (2 Cor.1:3–7). *For more about* Adversity, *see 2 Pet. 3:8, 9.*

> **→LIVE**
> • • • • • • • • • • • • • • • • •
> 5:7 • Because God has adopted you into His family, He has promised to take care of you. Your Father knows you need many things, so do not worry about that. Instead, focus on seeking first His kingdom and His righteousness, and all of these other things—what you will eat, drink, wear, and live in—will be added to you (Matt. 6:33). So cast your worries, concerns and anxieties on the Lord. God *will* take care of you, for you are His child. Your Father loves to bless you! Jesus told us to come to him with our burdens (Matt.11:28). *For more about* Submitting to God, *see Rev. 1:4.*

Submit to God, Resist the Devil

⁵Likewise you younger people, submit yourselves to *your* elders. Yes, all of *you* be submissive to one another, and be clothed with humility, for

> "God resists the proud,
>   But gives grace to the humble."^a

⁶Therefore humble yourselves under the mighty hand of God, that He may exalt you in due time, ⁷casting all your care upon Him, for He cares for you.

⁸Be sober, be vigilant; because^a your

> **→** *Therefore humble yourselves under the mighty hand of God, that He may exalt you in due time, casting all your care upon Him, for He cares for you.* 1 Pet. 5:6, 7

> **→** *Be sober, be vigilant; because your adversary the devil walks about like a roaring lion, seeking whom he may devour. Resist him, steadfast in the faith, knowing that the same sufferings are experienced by your brotherhood in the world.* 1 Pet. 5:8, 9

adversary the devil walks about like a roaring lion, seeking whom he may devour. ⁹Resist him, steadfast in the faith, knowing that the same sufferings are experienced by your brotherhood in the world. ¹⁰But may^a the God of all grace, who called us^b to His eternal glory by Christ Jesus, after you have suffered a while, perfect, establish, strengthen, and settle *you.* ¹¹To Him *be* the glory and the dominion forever and ever. Amen.

Farewell and Peace

¹²By Silvanus, our faithful brother as I consider him, I have written to you briefly, exhorting and testifying that this is the true grace of God in which you stand.

¹³She who is in Babylon, elect together with *you,* greets you; and *so does* Mark my son. ¹⁴Greet one another with a kiss of love.

Peace to you all who are in Christ Jesus. Amen.

5:5 ^aProverbs 3:34   5:8 ^aNU-Text and M-Text omit *because.*   5:10 ^aNU-Text reads *But the God of all grace . . . will perfect, establish, strengthen, and settle you.* ^bNU-Text and M-Text read *you.*

⬂ 2 PETER

INTRODUCTION//

By the time Peter wrote his second letter, many heresies and errors in belief had infiltrated the church. In order to keep the church strong, Peter clarifies a few core beliefs and reminds his readers of what they had been taught. He insists that God has provided everything we need for life and righteousness (1:3). He reminds us what righteousness looks like, from faith to self-control to godliness to love (1:5–7). Peter tells believers that they need to remember all of this, as it can be easily forgotten (1:13). Peter also reminds his readers that everything he taught them was based on his eyewitness experience; it is no fable. And beyond that, everything that happened to Jesus was foretold in the Prophets.

Peter then warns of false teachers who would spread heresy and slander against the Lord and His work. God knows who is blameless and who is lawless, and He will protect godly men and "reserve the unjust under punishment for the day of judgment" (2:9). While false teachers promise liberty to their followers, in fact they themselves are captives to sin and have nothing to offer. Finally, Peter speaks of the hope of the Lord's coming. Some Christians were growing impatient as they waited for Jesus to return because they expected His arrival within a generation of His advent. Therefore some scoffers denied that He ever would come. Peter therefore writes, "The Lord is not slack concerning His promise, as some count slackness, but is longsuffering toward us, not willing that any should perish but that all should come to repentance" (3:9). Though God is patient—and we should be grateful He is!—when Christ returns, He will arrive suddenly. Because of this, Peter counsels us to live blamelessly while we look for Jesus' Second Coming.

Greeting the Faithful

1 Simon Peter, a bondservant and apostle of Jesus Christ,

To those who have obtained like precious faith with us by the righteousness of our God and Savior Jesus Christ:

²Grace and peace be multiplied to you in the knowledge of God and of Jesus our Lord, ³as His divine power has given to us all things that *pertain* to life and godliness, through the knowledge of Him who called us by glory and virtue, ⁴by which have been given to us exceedingly great and precious promises, that through these you may be partakers of the divine nature, having escaped the corruption *that is* in the world through lust.

Fruitful Growth in the Faith

⁵But also for this very reason, giving all diligence, add to your faith virtue, to virtue knowledge, ⁶to knowledge self-control, to self-control perseverance, to perseverance godliness, ⁷to godliness brotherly kindness, and to brotherly kindness love. ⁸For if these things are yours and abound, *you* will be neither barren nor unfruitful in the knowledge of our Lord Jesus Christ. ⁹For he who lacks these things is shortsighted, even to blindness, and has forgotten that he was cleansed from his old sins.

¹⁰Therefore, brethren, be even more diligent to make your call and election sure, for if you do these things you will never stumble; ¹¹for so an entrance will be supplied to you abundantly into the everlasting kingdom of our Lord and Savior Jesus Christ.

Peter's Approaching Death

¹²For this reason I will not be negligent to remind you always of these things, though you know and are established in the present truth. ¹³Yes, I think it is right, as long as I am in this tent, to stir you up by reminding *you,* ¹⁴knowing that shortly I *must* put off my tent, just as our Lord Jesus Christ showed me. ¹⁵Moreover I will be careful to ensure that you always have a reminder of these things after my decease.

The Trustworthy Prophetic Word

¹⁶For we did not follow cunningly devised fables when we made known to you the power and coming of our Lord Jesus Christ, but were eyewitnesses of His majesty. ¹⁷For He received from God the Father honor and glory when such a voice came to Him from the Excellent Glory: "This is My beloved Son, in whom I am well pleased." ¹⁸And we heard

↘ LEARN

1:12 • Healthy, growing Christians not only cultivate a strong desire to learn more about their faith, their salvation, and their God; they also make it their habit to periodically review and rehearse what they have learned. We forget so easily! We remember what we ought to forget and forget what we ought to remember. Lessons we thought we had mastered once and for all tend to slip away if we do not consciously recall them. That is why the Bible urges us to remember key lessons and important doctrines. By reminding ourselves of what we already know, we pave the way for future growth. *For more about* Growing in Christ, *see 2 Pet. 3:18.*

↓ KNOW (2 PET. 1:18)

The apostle Peter described that amazing moment when Jesus was transfigured. The true miracle was not that for a few amazing moments He shined like the sun, but rather that He did not do it all of the time! Jesus veiled His deity, but He never violated it. Wherever He walked, you could point to Him and say, "There's God among us." Imagine if you had been one of the apostles, able to lay your eyes on Jesus. You could feel his flesh as the two of you shook hands. You'd look at Him in the eyes and say, "So *that* is God in human form." It really is astonishing: The apostles realized, *God is there. That is God speaking to us. That is God we just reached out and touched—God, in human form.* The Son of God became a man that men might become sons of God. *For more about* Jesus' Life, *see Matt. 1:23.*

this voice which came from heaven when we were with Him on the holy mountain.

[19]And so we have the prophetic word confirmed,[a] which you do well to heed as a light that shines in a dark place, until the day dawns and the morning star rises in your hearts; [20]knowing this first, that no prophecy of Scripture is of any private interpretation,[a] [21]for prophecy never came by the will of man, but holy men of God[a] spoke *as they were moved* by the Holy Spirit.

Destructive Doctrines

2 But there were also false prophets among the people, even as there will be false teachers among you, who will secretly bring in destructive heresies, even denying the Lord who bought them, *and* bring on themselves swift destruction. [2]And many will follow their destructive ways, because of whom the way of truth will be blasphemed. [3]By covetousness they will exploit you with deceptive words; for a long time their judgment has not been idle, and their destruction does[a] not slumber.

↘ LEARN

• • • • • • • • • • • • • •

2:1 • False prophets never advertise themselves as wolves in sheep's clothing. They do not march into your community or slide into your church with loudspeakers blaring, "I have come to turn you away from the true faith!" They don't immediately stick their hands in your wallet or demand total control of your life. No, they "secretly" bring in "destructive heresies." Very often, their false teachings center around some badly warped views about Jesus, especially concerning His divinity or His mission. They'll tell you that Jesus never claimed to be God, or that He was a great moral teacher but nothing else. Beware! *For more about* God's Word, *see 1 John 4:1, 2.*

Doom of False Teachers

[4]For if God did not spare the angels who sinned, but cast *them* down to hell and delivered *them* into chains of darkness, to be reserved for judgment; [5]and did not spare the ancient world, but saved Noah, *one of* eight *people,* a preacher of righteousness, bringing in the flood on the world of the ungodly; [6]and turning the cities of Sodom and Gomorrah

into ashes, condemned *them* to destruction, making *them* an example to those who afterward would live ungodly; [7]and delivered righteous Lot, *who was* oppressed by the filthy conduct of the wicked [8](for that righteous man, dwelling among them, tormented *his* righteous soul from day to day by seeing and hearing *their* lawless deeds)— [9]*then* the Lord knows how to deliver the godly out of temptations and to reserve the unjust under punishment for the day of judgment, [10]and especially those who walk according to the flesh in the lust of uncleanness and despise authority. *They are* presumptuous, self-willed. They are not afraid to speak evil of dignitaries, [11]whereas angels, who are greater in power and might, do not bring a reviling accusation against them before the Lord.

Depravity of False Teachers

[12]But these, like natural brute beasts made to be caught and destroyed, speak evil of the things they do not understand, and will utterly perish in their own corruption, [13]*and* will receive the wages of unrighteousness, *as* those who count it pleasure to carouse in the daytime. *They are* spots and blemishes, carousing in their own deceptions while they feast with you, [14]having eyes full of adultery and that cannot cease from sin, enticing unstable souls. They have a heart trained in covetous practices, *and are* accursed children. [15]They have forsaken the right way and gone astray, following the way of Balaam the *son of* Beor, who loved the wages of unrighteousness; [16]but he was rebuked for his iniquity: a dumb donkey speaking with a man's voice restrained the madness of the prophet.

[17]These are wells without water, clouds[a] carried by a tempest, for whom is reserved the blackness of darkness forever.[b]

Deceptions of False Teachers

[18]For when they speak great swelling *words* of emptiness, they allure through the lusts of the flesh, through lewdness, the ones who have actually escaped[a] from those who live in error. [19]While they promise them liberty, they themselves are slaves of corruption; for by whom a person is overcome, by him also he is brought into bondage. [20]For if, after

1:19 [a]Or *We also have the more sure prophetic word.*   1:20 [a]Or origin   1:21 [a]NU-Text reads *but men spoke from God.*
2:3 [a]M-Text reads *will not.*   2:17 [a]NU-Text reads *and mists.*   [b]NU-Text omits *forever.*   2:18 [a]NU-Text reads *are barely escaping.*

they have escaped the pollutions of the world through the knowledge of the Lord and Savior Jesus Christ, they are again entangled in them and overcome, the latter end is worse for them than the beginning. [21]For it would have been better for them not to have known the way of righteousness, than having known *it*, to turn from the holy commandment delivered to them. [22]But it has happened to them according to the true proverb: *"A dog returns to his own vomit,"*[a] and, "a sow, having washed, to her wallowing in the mire."

God's Promise Is Not Slack

3 Beloved, I now write to you this second epistle (in *both of* which I stir up your pure minds by way of reminder), [2]that you may be mindful of the words which were spoken before by the holy prophets, and of the commandment of us,[a] the apostles of the Lord and Savior, [3]knowing this first: that scoffers will come in the last days, walking according to their own lusts, [4]and saying, "Where is the promise of His coming? For since the fathers fell asleep, all things continue as *they were* from the beginning of creation." [5]For this they willfully forget: that by the word of God the heavens were of old, and the earth standing out of water and in the water, [6]by which the world *that* then existed perished, being flooded with water. [7]But the heavens and the earth *which* are now preserved by the same word, are reserved for fire until the day of judgment and perdition of ungodly men.

[8]But, beloved, do not forget this one thing, that with the Lord one day *is* as a thousand years, and a thousand years as one day. [9]The Lord is not slack concerning *His* promise, as

> **The Lord is not slack concerning His promise, as some count slackness, but is longsuffering toward us, not willing that any should perish but that all should come to repentance.** 2 Pet. 3:9

some count slackness, but is longsuffering toward us,[a] not willing that any should perish but that all should come to repentance.

The Day of the Lord

[10]But the day of the Lord will come as a thief in the night, in which the heavens will

↘ LEARN

3:8, 9 • There are two primary sides to God's timing, and often we don't appreciate them equally. We like the part that emphasizes His patience. If God judged us the moment we sinned, we'd all be in trouble! It's the second part—the way He often delays taking action, from our point of view—that troubles us. We wonder, *Where is He? Why doesn't He help me? How long will I have to suffer like this?* But God is never late. He's always on time—*His* time. The Lord is waiting for more people to come into His kingdom before He returns. *For more about* Adversity, *see 1 John 2:5;* God at Work, *1 John 5:14, 15.*

2:22 [a]Proverbs 26:11   3:2 [a]NU-Text and M-Text read *commandment of the apostles of your Lord and Savior* or *commandment of your apostles of the Lord and Savior.*   3:9 [a]NU-Text reads *you.*

↑ GROW (2 PET. 3:18)

Choice is everything in spiritual growth. It's not the luck of the draw or some random event. It happens when you make the choice to do the right thing. It comes down to this: You will either go forward as a Christian or you will go backward. You will either progress or regress. You will either gain ground or lose ground. Nobody stands still. Make the commitment to grow spiritually every day, to learn, to advance in your faith. Don't make it your goal merely to hold your own or to maintain your position. Decide to gain ground daily in your relationship with Jesus Christ, and you will grow spiritually. Commit yourself to it. Choose to grow! Paul understood this and explains it to us in Philippians 3:12–15. Don't rest on your spiritual laurels or live in the past. Keep moving forward as a follower of Jesus! *For more about* Growing in Christ, *see 1 John 4:1, 2.*

→LIVE
● ● ● ● ● ● ● ● ● ● ● ● ● ● ● ●

3:11 • Knowing of the Lord's imminent return should have a spiritual impact on us. First, it should purify us spiritually (1 John 3:2, 3). A real litmus test of your spiritual condition is how you react to Jesus coming back at any moment. If you think you can live in an ungodly way in light of this, then something is not right (Matt. 24:48, 49). But if you live in eager expectation and look forward to His return, that indicates your life is indeed right with God. When Jesus says He is coming back, we should respond, "Even so, come, Lord Jesus!" (Rev. 22:20). *For more about* Jesus' Return, *see Rev. 3:11.*

according to His promise, look for new heavens and a new earth in which righteousness dwells.

Be Steadfast

¹⁴Therefore, beloved, looking forward to these things, be diligent to be found by Him in peace, without spot and blameless; ¹⁵and consider *that* the longsuffering of our Lord *is* salvation—as also our beloved brother Paul, according to the wisdom given to him, has written to you, ¹⁶as also in all his epistles, speaking in them of these things, in which are some things hard to understand, which untaught and unstable *people* twist to their own destruction, as *they do* also the rest of the Scriptures.

¹⁷You therefore, beloved, since you know *this* beforehand, beware lest you also fall from your own steadfastness, being led away with the error of the wicked; ¹⁸but grow in the grace and knowledge of our Lord and Savior Jesus Christ.

To Him *be* the glory both now and forever. Amen.

pass away with a great noise, and the elements will melt with fervent heat; both the earth and the works that are in it will be burned up.ᵃ ¹¹Therefore, since all these things will be dissolved, what manner *of persons* ought you to be in holy conduct and godliness, ¹²looking for and hastening the coming of the day of God, because of which the heavens will be dissolved, being on fire, and the elements will melt with fervent heat? ¹³Nevertheless we,

3:10 ᵃNU-Text reads *laid bare* (literally *found*).

1 JOHN

INTRODUCTION//

John, along with Peter and James, was one of three apostles who spent extensive time with Jesus. Inspired by the Holy Spirit, John pulls few punches in this short letter, written sometime between A.D. 85–95. He points out that a person either is or is not a child of God; there is no middle ground. One's behavior must provide the evidence. In almost proverbial fashion he lays down the foundations for right living. He does so to answer questions raised by antichrists, or those who denied Jesus as Lord. Virtually everything John says either reinforces the truth of the gospel, or provides tests for someone's true spiritual allegiance.

John, known as the "love apostle," referred to himself in his Gospel as "the disciple whom Jesus loved" (John 21:20). It is not surprising, therefore, that we see a strong emphasis on the need to love. Children of God love others as God has loved them; if they don't, then they deny God and are not saved. Either you walk in the light or in darkness (1:5–10). If you claim not to sin or if you continue to consciously live in sin, then you are denying the truth of salvation (3:9, 10). And the only way to overcome sin is to have faith in Jesus Christ. John writes, "Who is he who overcomes the world, but he who believes that Jesus is the Son of God?" (5:5). John does not intend his message to instill doubt about salvation—in fact, he writes, "These things I have written to you who believe in the name of the Son of God, that you may know that you have eternal life" (5:13). He declares that by committing our lives to Jesus, we can overcome sin and live lives full of divine love.

What Was Heard, Seen, and Touched

1 That which was from the beginning, which we have heard, which we have seen with our eyes, which we have looked upon, and our hands have handled, concerning the Word of life— [2]the life was manifested, and we have seen, and bear witness, and declare to you that eternal life which was with the Father and was manifested to us— [3]that which we have seen and heard we declare to you, that you also may have fellowship with us; and truly our fellowship *is* with the Father and with His Son Jesus Christ. [4]And these things we write to you that your[a] joy may be full.

Fellowship with Him and One Another

[5]This is the message which we have heard from Him and declare to you, that God is light and in Him is no darkness at all. [6]If we say that we have fellowship with Him, and walk in darkness, we lie and do not practice the truth. [7]But if we walk in the light as He is in the light, we have fellowship with one another, and the blood of Jesus Christ His Son cleanses us from all sin.

[8]If we say that we have no sin, we deceive ourselves, and the truth is not in us. [9]If we

> ➡️ *If we confess our sins, He is faithful and just to forgive us our sins and to cleanse us from all unrighteousness.* 1 John 1:9

1:4 [a]NU-Text and M-Text read *our.*   **2:7** [a]NU-Text reads *Beloved.*

confess our sins, He is faithful and just to forgive us *our* sins and to cleanse us from all unrighteousness. [10]If we say that we have not sinned, we make Him a liar, and His word is not in us.

2 My little children, these things I write to you, so that you may not sin. And if anyone sins, we have an Advocate with the Father, Jesus Christ the righteous. [2]And He Himself is the propitiation for our sins, and not for ours only but also for the whole world.

The Test of Knowing Him

[3]Now by this we know that we know Him, if we keep His commandments. [4]He who says, "I know Him," and does not keep His commandments, is a liar, and the truth is not in him. [5]But whoever keeps His word, truly the love of God is perfected in him. By this we know that we are in Him. [6]He who says he abides in Him ought himself also to walk just as He walked.

[7]Brethren,[a] I write no new commandment

to you, but an old commandment which you have had from the beginning. The old commandment is the word which you heard from the beginning.[b] [8]Again, a new commandment I write to you, which thing is true in Him and in you, because the darkness is passing away, and the true light is already shining.

[9]He who says he is in the light, and hates his brother, is in darkness until now. [10]He who loves his brother abides in the light, and there is no cause for stumbling in him. [11]But he who hates his brother is in darkness and walks in darkness, and does not know where he is going, because the darkness has blinded his eyes.

Their Spiritual State

[12]I write to you, little children,
    Because your sins are forgiven you for
        His name's sake.
[13]I write to you, fathers,
    Because you have known Him *who is*
        from the beginning.
I write to you, young men,
    Because you have overcome the wicked
        one.
I write to you, little children,
    Because you have known the Father.
[14]I have written to you, fathers,
    Because you have known Him *who is*
        from the beginning.
I have written to you, young men,
    Because you are strong, and the word of
        God abides in you,
    And you have overcome the wicked one.

Do Not Love the World

[15]Do not love the world or the things in the world. If anyone loves the world, the love of the Father is not in him. [16]For all that *is* in the world—the lust of the flesh, the lust of the eyes, and the pride of life—is not of the Father but is of the world. [17]And the world is passing away, and the lust of it; but he who does the will of God abides forever.

Deceptions of the Last Hour

[18]Little children, it is the last hour; and as you have heard that the[a] Antichrist is coming, even now many antichrists have come, by which we know that it is the last hour. [19]They

➜ LIVE
● ● ● ● ● ● ● ● ● ● ● ● ● ● ● ● ●

2:19 ● Can you lose your salvation? That's a hard question, but I think I have a better one. Are you a Christian to begin with? Sometimes we see a person who claims to make a commitment to Christ, but eventually he returns to his old life and never comes back to Jesus. So did he lose his salvation? I would rather ask, *Was he saved to start with?* Because if he leaves, never to return, it seems to me he was never a Christian in the first place. When a believer goes astray, he'll always come home to the Lord. A nonbeliever won't. *For more about* Assurance of Salvation, *see Jude 21.*

went out from us, but they were not of us; for if they had been of us, they would have continued with us; but *they went out* that they might be made manifest, that none of them were of us.

[20]But you have an anointing from the Holy One, and you know all things.[a] [21]I have not written to you because you do not know the truth, but because you know it, and that no lie is of the truth. [22]Who is a liar but he who denies that Jesus is the Christ? He is antichrist who denies the Father and the Son. [23]Whoever denies the Son does not have the Father either; he who acknowledges the Son has the Father also.

Let Truth Abide in You

[24]Therefore let that abide in you which you heard from the beginning. If what you heard from the beginning abides in you, you also will abide in the Son and in the Father. [25]And this is the promise that He has promised us—eternal life.

[26]These things I have written to you concerning those who *try to* deceive you. [27]But the anointing which you have received from Him abides in you, and you do not need that anyone teach you; but as the same anointing teaches you concerning all things, and is true, and is not a lie, and just as it has taught you, you will[a] abide in Him.

The Children of God

[28]And now, little children, abide in Him, that when[a] He appears, we may have confidence and not be ashamed before Him at His

2:7 [b]NU-Text omits *from the beginning.*   2:18 [a]NU-Text omits *the.*   2:20 [a]NU-Text reads *you all know.*
2:27 [a]NU-Text reads *you abide.*   2:28 [a]NU-Text reads *if.*

coming. ²⁹If you know that He is righteous, you know that everyone who practices righteousness is born of Him.

3 Behold what manner of love the Father has bestowed on us, that we should be called children of God!ᵃ Therefore the world does not know us,ᵇ because it did not know Him. ²Beloved, now we are children of God; and it has not yet been revealed what we shall be, but we know that when He is revealed, we shall be like Him, for we shall see Him as He is. ³And everyone who has this hope in Him purifies himself, just as He is pure.

➤ *Behold what manner of love the Father has bestowed on us, that we should be called children of God!* 1 John 3:1

Sin and the Child of God

⁴Whoever commits sin also commits lawlessness, and sin is lawlessness. ⁵And you know that He was manifested to take away our sins, and in Him there is no sin. ⁶Whoever abides in Him does not sin. Whoever sins has neither seen Him nor known Him.

⁷Little children, let no one deceive you. He who practices righteousness is righteous, just as He is righteous. ⁸He who sins is of the devil, for the devil has sinned from the beginning. For this purpose the Son of God was manifested, that He might destroy the works of the devil. ⁹Whoever has been born of God does not sin, for His seed remains in him; and he cannot sin, because he has been born of God.

The Imperative of Love

¹⁰In this the children of God and the children of the devil are manifest: Whoever does not practice righteousness is not of God, nor is he who does not love his brother. ¹¹For this is the message that you heard from the beginning, that we should love one another, ¹²not as Cain who was of the wicked one and murdered his brother. And why did he murder

him? Because his works were evil and his brother's righteous.

¹³Do not marvel, my brethren, if the world hates you. ¹⁴We know that we have passed from death to life, because we love the brethren. He who does not love *his* brotherᵃ abides in death. ¹⁵Whoever hates his brother is a murderer, and you know that no murderer has eternal life abiding in him.

The Outworking of Love

¹⁶By this we know love, because He laid down His life for us. And we also ought to lay down *our* lives for the brethren. ¹⁷But whoever has this world's goods, and sees his brother in need, and shuts up his heart from him, how does the love of God abide in him?

¹⁸My little children, let us not love in word or in tongue, but in deed and in truth. ¹⁹And by this we knowᵃ that we are of the truth, and shall assure our hearts before Him. ²⁰For if our heart condemns us, God is greater than our heart, and knows all things. ²¹Beloved, if our heart does not condemn us, we have confidence toward God. ²²And whatever we ask we receive from Him, because we keep His commandments and do those things that are pleasing in His sight. ²³And this is His commandment: that we should believe on the

➤ *. . . let us not love in word or in tongue, but in deed and in truth.* 1 John 3:18

3:1 ᵃNU-Text adds *And we are.* ᵇM-Text reads *you.*   3:14 ᵃNU-Text omits *his brother.*   3:19 ᵃNU-Text reads *we shall know.*

name of His Son Jesus Christ and love one another, as He gave us[a] commandment.

The Spirit of Truth and the Spirit of Error

[24]Now he who keeps His commandments abides in Him, and He in him. And by this we know that He abides in us, by the Spirit whom He has given us.

4 Beloved, do not believe every spirit, but test the spirits, whether they are of God; because many false prophets have gone out into the world. [2]By this you know the Spirit of God: Every spirit that confesses that

↘ LEARN

• • • • • • • • • • • • • • •

4:1, 2 • How do you tell a false prophet from a true one? How do you "test the spirits, whether they are of God"? First, note that this is a duty of growing Christians. We are to weigh carefully everything our teachers say. One crucial test concerns what they say about Jesus. Those who deny He "has come in the flesh" may agree that He was a great man, perhaps even the Savior—but they reject the notion that Jesus is the eternal Word, forever one with the Father (John 1:1). We are to reject any teacher who rejects Jesus' deity. *For more about* God's Word, *see 2 John 6;* Growing in Christ, *Matt. 5:21–24.*

Jesus Christ has come in the flesh is of God, [3]and every spirit that does not confess that[a] Jesus Christ has come in the flesh is not of God. And this is the *spirit* of the Antichrist, which you have heard was coming, and is now already in the world.

[4]You are of God, little children, and have overcome them, because He who is in you is

greater than he who is in the world. [5]They are of the world. Therefore they speak *as* of the world, and the world hears them. [6]We are of God. He who knows God hears us; he who is not of God does not hear us. By this we know the spirit of truth and the spirit of error.

Knowing God Through Love

[7]Beloved, let us love one another, for love is of God; and everyone who loves is born of God and knows God. [8]He who does not love does not know God, for God is love. [9]In this the love of God was manifested toward us, that God has sent His only begotten Son into the world, that we might live through Him. [10]In this is love, not that we loved God, but that He loved us and sent His Son *to be* the propitiation for our sins. [11]Beloved, if God so loved us, we also ought to love one another.

→ LIVE

• • • • • • • • • • • • • • •

4:10 • The word *propitiation* carries the idea of appeasement or satisfaction. Why was propitiation necessary? Christians answer that God's holy wrath rests on evil. So who does the propitiating? Pagans answer that *we* do. We have offended the gods and we must now appease them. By contrast, the Bible says we cannot placate the righteous anger of God. We have no means to do so. But God in His love and mercy has done for us what we could never do for ourselves. God presented Christ as the atonement for our sins. Thus God sacrificed Himself to save us from Himself. *For more about* New Life in Christ, *see Jude 3;* Forgiveness, *Matt. 5:21–24.*

3:23 [a]M-Text omits *us.*   4:3 [a]NU-Text omits *that* and *Christ has come in the flesh.*

↓ KNOW (1 JOHN 3:20)

God is omniscient, which means He knows everything. What's more, God's knowledge is eternal. God doesn't learn new things, unlike us. He knows what will happen tomorrow, and next century. Neither does He forget what He has learned, like we often do. God remembers everything at all times. He never has a lapse in memory, never forgets someone, never has something slip His mind. But it gets much more personal than that. He knows all about *you.* So whatever you are facing right now, the Lord knows all about it. It deeply concerns Him. He doesn't just see you, He sees through you. He knows every thought you have. That is why it is so preposterous to believe that we can hide *anything* from God. And that is why you can have complete confidence in Him, because He knows everything about you—and still wants only the best for you. *For more about the* Attributes of God, *see Jude 25.*

Seeing God Through Love

[12]No one has seen God at any time. If we love one another, God abides in us, and His love has been perfected in us. [13]By this we know that we abide in Him, and He in us, because He has given us of His Spirit. [14]And we have seen and testify that the Father has sent the Son *as* Savior of the world. [15]Whoever confesses that Jesus is the Son of God, God abides in him, and he in God. [16]And we have known and believed the love that God has for us. God is love, and he who abides in love abides in God, and God in him.

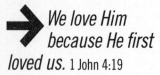

We love Him because He first loved us. 1 John 4:19

The Consummation of Love

[17]Love has been perfected among us in this: that we may have boldness in the day of judgment; because as He is, so are we in this world. [18]There is no fear in love; but perfect love casts out fear, because fear involves torment. But he who fears has not been made perfect in love. [19]We love Him[a] because He first loved us.

Obedience by Faith

[20]If someone says, "I love God," and hates his brother, he is a liar; for he who does not love his brother whom he has seen, how can[a] he love God whom he has not seen? [21]And this commandment we have from Him: that he who loves God *must* love his brother also.

5 Whoever believes that Jesus is the Christ is born of God, and everyone who loves Him who begot also loves him who is begotten of Him. [2]By this we know that we love the children of God, when we love God and keep His commandments. [3]For this is the love of God, that we keep His commandments. And His commandments are not burdensome. [4]For whatever is born of God overcomes the world. And this is the victory that has overcome the world—our[a] faith. [5]Who is he who overcomes the world, but he who believes that Jesus is the Son of God?

Who is he who overcomes the world, but he who believes that Jesus is the Son of God? 1 John 5:5

The Certainty of God's Witness

[6]This is He who came by water and blood—Jesus Christ; not only by water, but by water and blood. And it is the Spirit who bears witness, because the Spirit is truth. [7]For there are three that bear witness in heaven: the Father, the Word, and the Holy Spirit; and these three are one. [8]And there are three

4:19 [a]NU-Text omits *Him*.   4:20 [a]NU-Text reads *he cannot*.   5:4 [a]M-Text reads *your*.

↑ GROW (1 JOHN 5:14, 15)

Do you ever say, "God never answers my prayers"? If so, what do you mean? "Well, I prayed for this, and it didn't happen. God doesn't answer my prayers." But hold on! No is as much of an answer as is yes. Generally we don't like that answer, but it's still an answer. It would be more accurate to say, "I don't like God's answers to my prayers," than to say, "God doesn't answer my prayers." Consider this: If your request is wrong, then God will say "No." If the timing is wrong, then God will say "Slow." If *you* are wrong, then God will say "Grow." But if the request is right and the timing is right and you are right, then God will say "Go." So is there something you can do to hear God say go more often? Yes. Learn to pray according to the will of God. *For more about* Prayer, *see* Matt. 6:10; God at Work, Jude 25; God's Will, Matt. 6:10.

that bear witness on earth:[a] the Spirit, the water, and the blood; and these three agree as one.

[9]If we receive the witness of men, the witness of God is greater; for this is the witness of God which[a] He has testified of His Son. [10]He who believes in the Son of God has the witness in himself; he who does not believe God has made Him a liar, because he has not believed the testimony that God has given of His Son. [11]And this is the testimony: that God has given us eternal life, and this life is in His Son. [12]He who has the Son has life; he who does not have the Son of God does not have life. [13]These things I have written to you who believe in the name of the Son of God, that you may know that you have eternal life,[a] and that you may *continue to* believe in the name of the Son of God.

Confidence and Compassion in Prayer

[14]Now this is the confidence that we have in Him, that if we ask anything according to His will, He hears us. [15]And if we know that He hears us, whatever we ask, we know that we have the petitions that we have asked of Him.

[16]If anyone sees his brother sinning a sin *which does* not *lead* to death, he will ask, and He will give him life for those who commit sin not *leading* to death. There is sin *leading* to death. I do not say that he should pray about that. [17]All unrighteousness is sin, and there is sin not *leading* to death.

Knowing the True—Rejecting the False

[18]We know that whoever is born of God does not sin; but he who has been born of God keeps himself,[a] and the wicked one does not touch him.

[19]We know that we are of God, and the whole world lies *under the sway of* the wicked one.

[20]And we know that the Son of God has come and has given us an understanding, that we may know Him who is true; and we are in Him who is true, in His Son Jesus Christ. This is the true God and eternal life.

[21]Little children, keep yourselves from idols. Amen.

5:8 [a]NU-Text and M-Text omit the words from *in heaven* (verse 7) through *on earth* (verse 8). Only four or five very late manuscripts contain these words in Greek.   **5:9** [a]NU-Text reads *God, that.*   **5:13** [a]NU-Text omits the rest of this verse.   **5:18** [a]NU-Text reads *him.*

2 JOHN

INTRODUCTION//

John's brief second letter declares that true Christian love involves more than a mere emotional feeling. Rather, it is grounded in the truth. John also warns of false teachers and urges believers not to receive them. As in his first letter, John's central tenet is that we must walk with God and love one another wholeheartedly. Sometimes we find this hard to figure out. What does it mean to love one another? John lays out his clear understanding: "This is love, that we walk according to His commandments" (v. 6). Because God's central command is love (Matt. 22:36–40), John's statement emphasizes walking in obedience out of love. The practical kind of love that John endorses certainly includes feelings of affection, but it goes far beyond that.

John also writes consistently about "the truth." He mentions loving in the truth, knowing the truth, and walking in the truth (vv. 1–4). The truth he has in mind is the truth of salvation: God loves us, Jesus died for us, and through faith we are forgiven of our sins. Standing behind all this is the fact that Jesus Himself is the truth. John's Gospel records Jesus' greatest "I am" statement, "I am the way and the truth and the life" (John 14:6). This means that we should live not only in the knowledge of our salvation, but also in Jesus Himself, dedicating our entire lives and beings to Him. John concludes his short letter with a further warning about false teachers. Such warnings crop up throughout the epistles because in every age some people misinterpret or warp a small aspect of the truth, thus disfiguring the whole thing—and too often they lead the unsuspecting into spiritual oblivion. That is why we must stay vigilant in our faith and our walk in the truth.

Greeting the Elect Lady

The Elder,

To the elect lady and her children, whom I love in truth, and not only I, but also all those who have known the truth, [2]because of the truth which abides in us and will be with us forever:

[3]Grace, mercy, *and* peace will be with you[a] from God the Father and from the Lord Jesus Christ, the Son of the Father, in truth and love.

Walk in Christ's Commandments

[4]I rejoiced greatly that I have found *some* of your children walking in truth, as we received commandment from the Father. [5]And now I plead with you, lady, not as though I wrote a new commandment to you, but that which we have had from the beginning: that we love one another. [6]This is love, that we

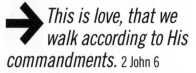

> ➤ *This is love, that we walk according to His commandments.* 2 John 6

walk according to His commandments. This is the commandment, that as you have heard from the beginning, you should walk in it.

Beware of Antichrist Deceivers

[7]For many deceivers have gone out into the world who do not confess Jesus Christ *as* coming in the flesh. This is a deceiver and an antichrist. [8]Look to yourselves, that we[a] do not lose those things we worked for, but *that* we[b] may receive a full reward.

[9]Whoever transgresses[a] and does not abide in the doctrine of Christ does not have God. He who abides in the doctrine of Christ has both the Father and the Son. [10]If anyone comes to you and does not bring this doctrine, do not receive him into your house nor greet him; [11]for he who greets him shares in his evil deeds.

John's Farewell Greeting

[12]Having many things to write to you, I did not wish *to do so* with paper and ink; but I hope to come to you and speak face to face, that our joy may be full.

[13]The children of your elect sister greet you. Amen.

3 [a]NU-Text and M-Text read *us*.   8 [a]NU-Text reads *you*.   [b]NU-Text reads *you*.   9 [a]NU-Text reads *goes ahead*.

↑ GROW (2 JOHN 6)
. . . .

Do you obey the commands of Christ? This is a big problem for many of us. We say we are Christians, but we disregard what the Bible says. We say we love Jesus, but we don't obey His commands. We call ourselves spiritual, but we do whatever we want, regardless of what God's Word might say. Something is deeply wrong with such a scenario! If you are really a Christian, then you will love and obey the Word of God. But how are you going to obey the Word if you don't read the Word? So, first you have to read the Bible to know what His commandments are; only then can you live in line with them. This is why Bible memorization is so important. When you hide the Word of God in your heart, you have something in memory to draw upon in times of temptation and trial (Ps. 119:11). *For more about* God's Word, *see Jude 3;* How to Live Out Your Faith, *3 John 11;* Spiritual Disciplines, *Rev. 2:17.*

3 JOHN

INTRODUCTION//

John wrote his third letter to commend a believer named Gaius for the hospitality he has shown to traveling teachers of the gospel. During this time, church leaders such as John, Paul, and Peter would travel around the Roman Empire visiting as many churches as possible. They would also send out their disciples and other church elders to guide and teach Christians so that everyone would get the true gospel and learn correct practices. This was important, because many people had begun to introduce false theologies and practices into the church. These faithful traveling leaders had no money or possessions, other than what they carried, so they could not stay in hotels or rent houses for their stays. They relied on the charity and hospitality of their Christian brothers. Gaius was well known for his generosity and hospitality, and John praises him for his commitment to the work of the Lord and his unbounded love for his brothers. Gaius is a shining example of how we ought to live. The core of living a Christ-like life is loving as He did, selflessly and continually. This short letter shows us the importance of loving our neighbors, even when we do not know them. Hospitality means not only being someone's friend, but also giving freely of what you have to meet someone else's need.

John also mentions the negative example of a man named Diotrephes. This man put himself before any traveling leaders and turned them away because he did not like to be second to anyone. He used the church to gain power and respect for himself. Even today many follow the way of Diotrephes; that is why we must remain vigilant, watching out so that we are not fooled and so that we can keep other people from being fooled as well.

Greeting to Gaius

The Elder,

To the beloved Gaius, whom I love in truth:

[2]Beloved, I pray that you may prosper in all things and be in health, just as your soul prospers. [3]For I rejoiced greatly when brethren came and testified of the truth *that is* in you, just as you walk in the truth. [4]I have no greater joy than to hear that my children walk in truth.[a]

Gaius Commended for Generosity

[5]Beloved, you do faithfully whatever you do for the brethren and[a] for strangers, [6]who have borne witness of your love before the church. *If* you send them forward on their journey in a manner worthy of God, you will do well, [7]because they went forth for His name's sake, taking nothing from the Gentiles. [8]We therefore ought to receive[a] such, that we may become fellow workers for the truth.

Diotrephes and Demetrius

[9]I wrote to the church, but Diotrephes, who loves to have the preeminence among them, does not receive us. [10]Therefore, if I come, I will call to mind his deeds which he does, prating against us with malicious words. And not content with that, he himself does not receive the brethren, and forbids those who wish to, putting *them* out of the church.

[11]Beloved, do not imitate what is evil, but what is good. He who does good is of God, but[a] he who does evil has not seen God. [12]Demetrius has a *good* testimony from all, and from the truth itself. And we also bear witness, and you know that our testimony is true.

Farewell Greeting

[13]I had many things to write, but I do not wish to write to you with pen and ink; [14]but I hope to see you shortly, and we shall speak face to face.

Peace to you. Our friends greet you. Greet the friends by name.

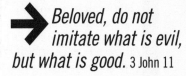

Beloved, do not imitate what is evil, but what is good. 3 John 11

4 [a]NU-Text reads *the truth*.   5 [a]NU-Text adds *especially*.   8 [a]NU-Text reads *support*.   11 [a]NU-Text and M-Text omit *but*.

JUDE

INTRODUCTION//

The Book of Jude, one of the shortest books in the New Testament, focuses on the proliferation of false teachers in Jude's time, as well as on the great apostasy—the falling away from the faith—that will occur before the return of Jesus Christ. Written around A.D. 65 by Jude, one of Jesus' half-brothers, it warns against specific heresies that were starting to develop at that time. Eventually known as the gnostics, these teachers ignored the biblical call to morality and denied that Jesus is God (v. 4). In essence, they turned grace into a justification for sin. They claimed that because of God's love, they could commit any sins they wanted to and still be forgiven—a recurring problem that has plagued the church throughout its long history. These people committed some of the worst sins imaginable: denying what Christ did for us, turning from the right, and instead willfully choosing the wrong. Jude warns of their impending doom and warns us not to follow their wicked ways. He cites the historical examples of the Exodus and Sodom of Gomorrah in order to remind us that God never treats sin lightly (vv. 5–7). Long ago the conviction and judgment of such people was prophesied, and they will get the full measure of punishment they deserve.

In order to avoid their fate, we are to build up ourselves in our "most holy faith, praying in the Holy Spirit" (v. 20). We are to keep ourselves in the love of God, which means we are to remain close to Him, following Him wholeheartedly, careful to eagerly obey His commandments. Those who struggle, we are to help; and God Himself "is able to keep you from stumbling, and to present you faultless before the presence of His glory with exceeding joy" (v. 24).

Greeting to the Called

Jude, a bondservant of Jesus Christ, and brother of James,

To those who are called, sanctified[a] by God the Father, and preserved in Jesus Christ:

[2]Mercy, peace, and love be multiplied to you.

Contend for the Faith

[3]Beloved, while I was very diligent to write to you concerning our common salvation, I found it necessary to write to you exhorting you to contend earnestly for the faith which was once for all delivered to the saints. [4]For certain men have crept in unnoticed, who long ago were marked out for this condemnation, ungodly men, who turn the grace of our God into lewdness and deny the only Lord God[a] and our Lord Jesus Christ.

1 [a]NU-Text reads *beloved.*   4 [a]NU-Text omits *God.*

Old and New Apostates

[5]But I want to remind you, though you once knew this, that the Lord, having saved the people out of the land of Egypt, afterward destroyed those who did not believe. [6]And the angels who did not keep their proper domain, but left their own abode, He has reserved in everlasting chains under darkness for the judgment of the great day; [7]as Sodom and Gomorrah, and the cities around them in a similar manner to these, having given themselves over to sexual immorality and gone after strange flesh, are set forth as an example, suffering the vengeance of eternal fire.

[8]Likewise also these dreamers defile the flesh, reject authority, and speak evil of dignitaries. [9]Yet Michael the archangel, in contending with the devil, when he disputed about the body of Moses, dared not bring against him a reviling accusation, but said, "The Lord rebuke you!" [10]But these speak evil of whatever they do not know; and whatever

they know naturally, like brute beasts, in these things they corrupt themselves. [11]Woe to them! For they have gone in the way of Cain, have run greedily in the error of Balaam for profit, and perished in the rebellion of Korah.

Apostates Depraved and Doomed

[12]These are spots in your love feasts, while they feast with you without fear, serving *only* themselves. *They are* clouds without water, carried about[a] by the winds; late autumn trees without fruit, twice dead, pulled up by the roots; [13]raging waves of the sea, foaming up their own shame; wandering stars for whom is reserved the blackness of darkness forever.

[14]Now Enoch, the seventh from Adam, prophesied about these men also, saying, "Behold, the Lord comes with ten thousands of His saints, [15]to execute judgment on all, to convict all who are ungodly among them of all their ungodly deeds which they have committed in an ungodly way, and of all the harsh things which ungodly sinners have spoken against Him."

Apostates Predicted

[16]These are grumblers, complainers, walking according to their own lusts; and they mouth great swelling *words,* flattering people to gain advantage. [17]But you, beloved, remember the words which were spoken before by the apostles of our Lord Jesus Christ: [18]how they told you that there would be mockers in the last time who would walk according to their own ungodly lusts. [19]These are sensual persons, who cause divisions, not having the Spirit.

Maintain Your Life with God

[20]But you, beloved, building yourselves up on your most holy faith, praying in the Holy Spirit, [21]keep yourselves in the love of God, looking for the mercy of our Lord Jesus Christ unto eternal life.

> ➤ *... keep yourselves in the love of God, looking for the mercy of our Lord Jesus Christ unto eternal life.* Jude 21

[22]And on some have compassion, making a distinction;[a] [23]but others save with fear, pulling *them* out of the fire,[a] hating even the garment defiled by the flesh.

Glory to God

[24]Now to Him who is able to keep you[a]
    from stumbling,
 And to present *you* faultless
 Before the presence of His glory with
    exceeding joy,
[25]To God our Savior,[a]
 Who alone is wise,[b]
 Be glory and majesty,
 Dominion and power,[c]
 Both now and forever.
 Amen.

12 [a]NU-Text and M-Text read *along.*   22 [a]NU-Text reads *who are doubting* (or *making distinctions*).   23 [a]NU-Text adds *and on some have mercy with fear* and omits *with fear* in first clause.   24 [a]M-Text reads *them.*   25 [a]NU-Text reads *To the only God our Savior.*
[b]NU-Text omits *Who . . . is wise* and adds *Through Jesus Christ our Lord.* [c]NU-Text adds *Before all time.*

↓ KNOW (JUDE 25)
....

Everything everywhere is subject to God's ultimate control. God can do what He wants, when He wants, wherever He wants. Why? Because He rules as a sovereign Lord, with the authority, power, and wisdom to act exactly as He sees fit in every situation. This means God is able to do whatever He pleases, with whomever He chooses, whenever He wishes. It is not up to a vote; His is a majority of One. God is the Master and we are the servants. He is the Potter and we are the clay. He is the Vine and we are the branches. He is the Giver and we are the recipients. Quite frankly, God can (and does!) impose His will without asking permission or explaining His reasons. Daniel says He "does according to His will," and "No one can restrain His hand or say to Him, 'What have You done?'" (Dan. 4:35). *For more about the* Attributes of God, *see* Rev. 4:8; God at Work, Matt. 7:7.

REVELATION ↙

INTRODUCTION//

The word *revelation* means, "the unveiling." The Book of Revelation is therefore the unveiling of things to come. The apostle John wrote Revelation around A.D. 95 while in exile on the Greek island of Patmos. This letter recounts an astonishing vision given to John of the events directly leading to and following the Second Coming of Jesus Christ. During His earthly ministry and after His resurrection, Christ told His followers that one day He would return for them. Since the day He ascended to heaven, Christians have looked for His return. Many early believers thought it would happen in their lifetimes, and every generation since then has thought the same thing. And so long as looking forward to His return means building up our faith and striving to live in a more Christ-like manner, rather than sitting idly while we wait, this is a good way to express our Christian convictions. Revelation is the only book of the Bible that promises a special blessing to the person who hears and keeps its truths.

Despite some odd images and frightening pictures, above all, John's book declares a message of incredible hope. Revelation reinforces in the strongest of terms the promise that Christ *will* return. The wicked and those who have turned against God will suffer everything promised in this vision, but God will save those who overcome through their faith in Jesus. When the Day of Judgment comes, our names are written in the Book of Life (20:11–15), and we will live forever with Jesus in the restored kingdom of God (21:1—22:6). Though life may be hard today, we have an amazing life to look forward to. Revelation expounds the greatest promise ever made. John gives us unique and amazing insights into the future dwelling place of believers, including heaven and the new earth.

Introduction and Benediction

1 The Revelation of Jesus Christ, which God gave Him to show His servants— things which must shortly take place. And He sent and signified *it* by His angel to His servant John, [2]who bore witness to the word of God, and to the testimony of Jesus Christ, to all things that he saw. [3]Blessed *is* he who reads and those who hear the words of this prophecy, and keep those things which are written in it; for the time *is* near.

↘ LEARN

• • • • • • • • • • • • • • • •

1:3 • The Book of Revelation is the only book in the Bible with a special blessing promised for those who read it. There are three prerequisites for receiving the promised blessing. First, you must read the book for yourself. Second, you must "hear the words of this prophecy." If you ask the Holy Spirit to open your spiritual ears to hear what God is saying, you will benefit. Third, the blessing comes to those who "keep those things which are written in it." You win when you apply these truths to your life and get ready for the return of Jesus Christ. *For more about* God's Word, *see Rev. 12:10.*

Greeting the Seven Churches

[4]John, to the seven churches which are in Asia:

Grace to you and peace from Him who is and who was and who is to come, and from

→ LIVE

• • • • • • • • • • • • • • • •

1:4 • Before you can have the peace *of* God, you must first have peace *with* God, which comes only through Jesus. We do not have peace with God through our ethical efforts or our religious righteousness. Peace is not an effort, but an effect, the effect of Christ's person and work. If a man has peace, it is because he has ended his personal war with God. In doing so he has accepted God's terms, which are unconditional surrender. And make no mistake about it, prior to our conversion we were at war with God. Neutrality toward God does not exist. *For more about* New Life in Christ, *see Rev. 2:17.*

the seven Spirits who are before His throne, [5]and from Jesus Christ, the faithful witness, the firstborn from the dead, and the ruler over the kings of the earth.

To Him who loved us and washed[a] us from our sins in His own blood, [6]and has made us kings[a] and priests to His God and Father, to Him *be* glory and dominion forever and ever. Amen.

[7]Behold, He is coming with clouds, and every eye will see Him, even they who pierced Him. And all the tribes of the earth will mourn because of Him. Even so, Amen.

[8]"I am the Alpha and the Omega, *the* Beginning and *the* End,"[a] says the Lord,[b] "who is and who was and who is to come, the Almighty."

Vision of the Son of Man

[9]I, John, both[a] your brother and companion in the tribulation and kingdom and patience of Jesus Christ, was on the island that is called Patmos for the word of God and for the testimony of Jesus Christ. [10]I was in the Spirit on the Lord's Day, and I heard behind me a loud voice, as of a trumpet, [11]saying, "I am the Alpha and the Omega, the First and the Last,"[a] and, "What you see, write in a book and send *it* to the seven churches which are in Asia:[b] to Ephesus, to Smyrna, to Pergamos, to Thyatira, to Sardis, to Philadelphia, and to Laodicea."

[12]Then I turned to see the voice that spoke with me. And having turned I saw seven golden lampstands, [13]and in the midst of the seven lampstands One like the Son of Man, clothed with a garment down to the feet and girded about the chest with a golden band. [14]His head and hair *were* white like wool, as white as snow, and His eyes like a flame of fire; [15]His feet *were* like fine brass, as if refined in a furnace, and His voice as the sound of many waters; [16]He had in His right hand seven stars, out of His mouth went a sharp two-edged sword, and His countenance *was* like the sun shining in its strength. [17]And when I saw Him, I fell at His feet as dead. But He laid His right hand on me, saying to me,[a] "Do not be afraid; I am the First and the Last. [18]I *am* He who lives, and was dead, and behold, I am alive forevermore. Amen.

1:5 [a]NU-Text reads *loves us and freed;* M-Text reads *loves us and washed.*   1:6 [a]NU-Text and M-Text read *a kingdom.*
1:8 [a]NU-Text and M-Text omit *the Beginning and the End.* [b]NU-Text and M-Text add *God.*   1:9 [a]NU-Text and M-Text omit *both.*
1:11 [a]NU-Text and M-Text omit *I am* through third *and.* [b]NU-Text and M-Text omit *which are in Asia.*
1:17 [a]NU-Text and M-Text omit *to me.*

And I have the keys of Hades and of Death. [19]Write[a] the things which you have seen, and the things which are, and the things which will take place after this. [20]The mystery of the seven stars which you saw in My right hand, and the seven golden lampstands: The seven stars are the angels of the seven churches, and the seven lampstands which you saw[a] are the seven churches.

The Loveless Church

2 "To the angel of the church of Ephesus write,

'These things says He who holds the seven stars in His right hand, who walks in the midst of the seven golden lampstands: [2]"I know your works, your labor, your patience, and that you cannot bear those who are evil. And you have tested those who say they are apostles and are not, and have found them liars; [3]and you have persevered and have patience, and have labored for My name's sake and have not become weary. [4]Nevertheless I have *this* against you, that you have left your first love. [5]Remember therefore from where you have fallen; repent and do the first works, or else I will come to you quickly and remove your lampstand from its place—unless you repent. [6]But this you have, that you hate the deeds of the Nicolaitans, which I also hate.

↘ LEARN
• • • • • • • • • • • • • •

2:4 • This verse can be rendered, "You no longer love me as you did at first." These believers were so busy maintaining their separation from the world that they neglected their adoration of Christ. They had substituted perspiration for inspiration, work for worship. But labor is no substitute for love—think of two newlyweds, just back from their honeymoon. These early believers had forgotten their passion and devotion for Christ. Gone was their excitement and open display of love with no inhibitions. It is a serious thing to leave your first love, because love is the root of either success or failure. *For more about* Loving God, *see Luke 11:34–36.*

[7]"He who has an ear, let him hear what the Spirit says to the churches. To him who overcomes I will give to eat from the tree of life, which is in the midst of the Paradise of God." '

→ LIVE
• • • • • • • • • • • • • • • •

2:5 • Let's say that after you became a Christian, you slipped a bit. Somehow you lost some ground. How do you get back to being right with God? The Bible gives us three R's: **R**emember. **R**epent. **R**epeat. First, you must *remember:* "Hey, there was a time when my commitment to Christ was stronger. I used to walk more closely with Him than I am today." Remembering is a point of reference. Second, you must *repent.* Change your current direction and stop doing what you are doing. Third, you must *repeat.* Go back to doing what you were doing before you slipped. *For more about* Sin, *see Rev. 3:15, 16.*

The Persecuted Church

[8]"And to the angel of the church in Smyrna write,

'These things says the First and the Last, who was dead, and came to life: [9]"I know your works, tribulation, and poverty (but you are rich); and *I know* the blasphemy of those who say they are Jews and are not, but *are* a synagogue of Satan. [10]Do not fear any of those things which you are about to suffer. Indeed, the devil is about to throw *some* of you into prison, that you may be tested, and you will have tribulation ten days. Be faithful until death, and I will give you the crown of life.

[11]"He who has an ear, let him hear what the Spirit says to the churches. He who overcomes shall not be hurt by the second death." '

The Compromising Church

[12]"And to the angel of the church in Pergamos write,

'These things says He who has the sharp two-edged sword: [13]"I know your works, and where you dwell, where Satan's throne *is.* And you hold fast to My name, and did not deny My faith even in the days in which Antipas *was* My faithful martyr, who was killed among you, where Satan dwells. [14]But I have a few things against you, because you have there those who hold the doctrine of Balaam, who taught Balak to put a stumbling block before the children of Israel, to eat things sacrificed to idols, and to commit sexual immorality. [15]Thus you also have those who hold the doctrine of the Nicolaitans, which thing I hate.[a] [16]Repent, or else I will come to you

---

1:19 [a]NU-Text and M-Text read *Therefore, write.*   1:20 [a]NU-Text and M-Text omit *which you saw.*
2:15 [a]NU-Text and M-Text read *likewise* for *which thing I hate.*

quickly and will fight against them with the sword of My mouth.

[17]"He who has an ear, let him hear what the Spirit says to the churches. To him who overcomes I will give some of the hidden manna to eat. And I will give him a white stone, and on the stone a new name written which no one knows except him who receives *it*." '

→LIVE

• • • • • • • • • • • • • • • •

2:17 • Theologians often use the term *identification* to describe our union with Christ. How closely do we exist with Jesus? Although the apostle Paul often spoke of his loss and giving up things when he identified with Christ, he didn't do so in order to earn God's favor. We deny ourselves and discipline ourselves, not to get spiritual brownie points, but to make room for Jesus in our lives, to fully experience His fullness. As part of His work in our salvation, Christ offers us intimate knowledge of Himself and a life saturated with that knowledge. How closely do you identify with Christ? *For more about* New Life in Christ, *see Matt. 5:20;* Spiritual Disciplines, *Mark 4:9.*

The Corrupt Church

[18]"And to the angel of the church in Thyatira write,

'These things says the Son of God, who has eyes like a flame of fire, and His feet like fine brass: [19]"I know your works, love, service, faith,[a] and your patience; and *as for* your works, the last *are* more than the first. [20]Nevertheless I have a few things against you, because you allow[a] that woman[b] Jezebel, who calls herself a prophetess, to teach and seduce[c] My servants to commit sexual immorality and eat things sacrificed to idols. [21]And I gave her time to repent of her sexual immorality, and she did not repent.[a] [22]Indeed I will cast her into a sickbed, and those who commit adultery with her into great tribulation, unless they repent of their[a] deeds. [23]I will kill her children with death, and all the churches shall know that I am He who searches the minds and hearts. And I will give to each one of you according to your works.

[24]"Now to you I say, and[a] to the rest in Thyatira, as many as do not have this doctrine, who have not known the depths of Satan, as they say, I will[b] put on you no other burden. [25]But hold fast what you have till I come. [26]And he who overcomes, and keeps My works until the end, to him I will give power over the nations—

[27] '*He shall rule them with a rod of iron;*
　　They shall be dashed to pieces like the
　　　　　potter's vessels'[a]—

as I also have received from My Father; [28]and I will give him the morning star.

[29]"He who has an ear, let him hear what the Spirit says to the churches." '

The Dead Church

3 "And to the angel of the church in Sardis write,

'These things says He who has the seven Spirits of God and the seven stars: "I know your works, that you have a name that you are alive, but you are dead. [2]Be watchful, and strengthen the things which remain, that are ready to die, for I have not found your works perfect before God.[a] [3]Remember therefore how you have received and heard; hold fast and repent. Therefore if you will not watch, I will come upon you as a thief, and you will not know what hour I will come upon you. [4]You[a] have a few names even in Sardis who have not defiled their garments; and they shall walk with Me in white, for they are worthy. [5]He who overcomes shall be clothed in white garments, and I will not blot out his name from the Book of Life; but I will confess his name before My Father and before His angels.

[6]"He who has an ear, let him hear what the Spirit says to the churches." '

The Faithful Church

[7]"And to the angel of the church in Philadelphia write,

'These things says He who is holy, He who is true, *"He who has the key of David, He who opens and no one shuts, and shuts and no one opens":*[a] [8]"I know your works. See, I have set before you an open door, and no one can shut it;[a] for you have a little strength,

---

2:19 [a]NU-Text and M-Text read *faith, service.*　2:20 [a]NU-Text and M-Text read *I have against you that you tolerate.* [b]M-Text reads *your wife Jezebel.* [c]NU-Text and M-Text read *and teaches and seduces.*　2:21 [a]NU-Text and M-Text read *time to repent, and she does not want to repent of her sexual immorality.*　2:22 [a]NU-Text and M-Text read *her.*　2:24 [a]NU-Text and M-Text omit *and.* [b]NU-Text and M-Text omit *will.*　2:27 [a]Psalm 2:9　3:2 [a]NU-Text and M-Text read *My God.*　3:4 [a]NU-Text and M-Text read *Nevertheless you have a few names in Sardis.*　3:7 [a]Isaiah 22:22　3:8 [a]NU-Text and M-Text read *which no one can shut.*

have kept My word, and have not denied My name. ⁹Indeed I will make *those* of the synagogue of Satan, who say they are Jews and are not, but lie—indeed I will make them come and worship before your feet, and to know that I have loved you. ¹⁰Because you have kept My command to persevere, I also will keep you from the hour of trial which shall come upon the whole world, to test those who dwell on the earth. ¹¹Behold,ᵃ I am coming quickly! Hold fast what you have, that no one may take your crown. ¹²He who overcomes, I will make him a pillar in the temple of My God, and he shall go out no more. I will write on him the name of My God and the name of the city of My God, the New Jerusalem, which comes down out of heaven from My God. And *I will write on him* My new name.

¹³"He who has an ear, let him hear what the Spirit says to the churches." '

The Lukewarm Church

¹⁴"And to the angel of the church of the Laodiceansᵃ write,

'These things says the Amen, the Faithful and True Witness, the Beginning of the creation of God: ¹⁵"I know your works, that you are neither cold nor hot. I could wish you were cold or hot. ¹⁶So then, because you are lukewarm, and neither cold nor hot,ᵃ I will vomit you out of My mouth. ¹⁷Because you say, 'I am rich, have become wealthy, and have need of nothing'—and do not know that you are wretched, miserable, poor, blind, and naked— ¹⁸I counsel you to buy from Me gold refined in the fire, that you may be rich; and white garments, that you may be clothed,

↘ LEARN

· · · · · · · · · · · · · · · · · ·

3:15, 16 • What's your spiritual temperature? It's important to know because it indicates your spiritual health. According to the Scripture, there are three possible answers: 1) burning hot; 2) icy cold; 3) miserably lukewarm. If you have a burning heart, then you're on fire for God. You're active, alive, making a difference for time and eternity. A cold heart describes someone who's going through the motions, but without life or passion. And a lukewarm heart—surprise!—offends Jesus most of all. In fact, He says it makes Him so sick He wants to vomit. So I ask again: what's your spiritual temperature? *For more about* Sin, *see Rev. 3:19.*

that the shame of your nakedness may not be revealed; and anoint your eyes with eye salve, that you may see. ¹⁹As many as I love, I rebuke and chasten. Therefore be zealous and repent. ²⁰Behold, I stand at the door and knock. If anyone hears My voice and opens the door, I will come in to him and dine

→ LIVE

· · · · · · · · · · · · · · · · · ·

3:19 • Sometimes we feel as though we will never overcome sin in our lives, and so we may reason, "I'm always going to sin, so I might as well make the most of it." Some believers try to exploit the grace of God. After all, won't God forgive them? Clearly, this is not the teaching of the Bible. Do not forget that even though God is faithful and righteous to forgive us our sins— when we confess them and forsake them—yet still there may be repercussions for our sinful choices. You reap what you sow. And sometimes these repercussions can be very serious. *For more about* Sin, *see Mark 1:14.*

3:11 ᵃNU-Text and M-Text omit *Behold.*   **3:14** ᵃNU-Text and M-Text read *in Laodicea.*   **3:16** ᵃNU-Text and M-Text read *hot nor cold.*

↑ GROW (REV. 3:11)

· ·

The biblical teaching about Christ's return provides a powerful litmus test of your spiritual condition. How do you tend to react when you hear that Jesus could come back at any time? If you're right with God, then the message probably motivates you and purifies you and energizes you for further energetic service to Jesus. It encourages you to continue to move ahead in developing your relationship with God. But something very different happens when you hear about Jesus' Second Coming at a time in your life when you're *not* right with God. The idea that Jesus could return at any moment alarms you, worries you, maybe even angers you. The person who is not where he or she should be spiritually often dreads the idea of Jesus' imminent return. But the person who is watching and waiting for Christ's Second Advent can hardly wait for that great Day. Come quickly, Lord Jesus! *For more about* Jesus' Return, *see Rev. 13:1.*

➡ *Behold, I stand at the door and knock. If anyone hears My voice and opens the door, I will come in to him and dine with him, and he with Me.* Rev. 3:20

with him, and he with Me. ²¹To him who overcomes I will grant to sit with Me on My throne, as I also overcame and sat down with My Father on His throne.

²²"He who has an ear, let him hear what the Spirit says to the churches." ' "

The Throne Room of Heaven

4 After these things I looked, and behold, a door *standing* open in heaven. And the first voice which I heard *was* like a trumpet speaking with me, saying, "Come up here, and I will show you things which must take place after this."

²Immediately I was in the Spirit; and behold, a throne set in heaven, and *One* sat on the throne. ³And He who sat there was[a] like a jasper and a sardius stone in appearance; and *there was* a rainbow around the throne, in appearance like an emerald. ⁴Around the throne *were* twenty-four thrones, and on the thrones I saw twenty-four elders sitting, clothed in white robes; and they had crowns[a] of gold on their heads. ⁵And from the throne proceeded lightnings, thunderings, and

voices.[a] Seven lamps of fire *were* burning before the throne, which are the[b] seven Spirits of God.

⁶Before the throne *there was*[a] a sea of glass, like crystal. And in the midst of the throne, and around the throne, *were* four living creatures full of eyes in front and in back. ⁷The first living creature *was* like a lion, the second living creature like a calf, the third living creature had a face like a man, and the fourth living creature *was* like a flying eagle. ⁸*The* four living creatures, each having six wings, were full of eyes around and within. And they do not rest day or night, saying:

"Holy, holy, holy,[a]
Lord God Almighty,
Who was and is and is to come!"

⁹Whenever the living creatures give glory and honor and thanks to Him who sits on the throne, who lives forever and ever, ¹⁰the twenty-four elders fall down before Him who sits on the throne and worship Him who lives forever and ever, and cast their crowns before the throne, saying:

¹¹"You are worthy, O Lord,[a]
To receive glory and honor and power;
For You created all things,
And by Your will they exist[b] and were created."

The Lamb Takes the Scroll

5 And I saw in the right *hand* of Him who sat on the throne a scroll written inside and on the back, sealed with seven seals.

4:3 [a]M-Text omits *And He who sat there was* (which makes the description in verse 3 modify the throne rather than God).
4:4 [a]NU-Text and M-Text read *robes, with crowns.*   **4:5** [a]NU-Text and M-Text read *voices, and thunderings.*   [b]M-Text omits *the.*
4:6 [a]NU-Text and M-Text add *something like.*   **4:8** [a]M-Text has *holy* nine times.   **4:11** [a]NU-Text and M-Text read *our Lord and God.*
[b]NU-Text and M-Text read *existed.*

↓ KNOW (REV. 4:8)
• •

God is holy. If anything comes out plainly in the Scriptures, it is this fact. And because God is holy, He hates sin. Have we lost sight of this? Have we traded reverence for relevance? A lot of churches want to grow numerically and will do whatever seems necessary to attract more people, so it becomes all about cultural connection and social relevance. Now, I am all for connecting with our culture and for being relevant. But do I have to stop being reverent? The early church had enormous reverence for God; they called it "fearing God" (Col. 3:22; see also Acts 2:43; 13:26). This fear doesn't mean cowering because you are afraid He will smack you (though we often deserve it). In the Bible, fear means a wholesome dread of displeasing Him. The Lord is so good and so holy! Let's desire to live in such a way that we bring honor to His holy name. *For more about* How to Live Out Your Faith, *see Matt. 7:21–23; the* Attributes of God, *Rev. 15:3.*

↘ LEARN
• • • • • • • • • • • • • • • •

4:11 • Why are you here on this earth? What is your purpose in life? To find happiness, pleasure, or personal fulfillment? No! You exist primarily to bring pleasure to God. Some people, of course, think the world exists to revolve around them. They end up squandering their lives because happiness consistently remains beyond their reach—always just around the next corner, in that next relationship, that next experience, that next possession, that next accomplishment. When you seek to fulfill your God-ordained purpose, however—to know, glorify, and worship God—*then* you find the happiness you have been seeking. By seeking God, you find happiness, not the other way around. *For more about* Submitting to God, *see Matt. 19:21–24.*

²Then I saw a strong angel proclaiming with a loud voice, "Who is worthy to open the scroll and to loose its seals?" ³And no one in heaven or on the earth or under the earth was able to open the scroll, or to look at it.

⁴So I wept much, because no one was found worthy to open and read[a] the scroll, or to look at it. ⁵But one of the elders said to me, "Do not weep. Behold, the Lion of the tribe of Judah, the Root of David, has prevailed to open the scroll and to loose[a] its seven seals."

⁶And I looked, and behold,[a] in the midst of the throne and of the four living creatures, and in the midst of the elders, stood a Lamb as though it had been slain, having seven horns and seven eyes, which are the seven Spirits of God sent out into all the earth. ⁷Then He came and took the scroll out of the right hand of Him who sat on the throne.

Worthy Is the Lamb

⁸Now when He had taken the scroll, the four living creatures and the twenty-four elders fell down before the Lamb, each having a harp, and golden bowls full of incense, which are the prayers of the saints. ⁹And they sang a new song, saying:

"You are worthy to take the scroll,
  And to open its seals;
  For You were slain,
  And have redeemed us to God by Your
    blood

Out of every tribe and tongue and people
    and nation,
¹⁰And have made us[a] kings[b] and priests to
    our God;
  And we[c] shall reign on the earth."

¹¹Then I looked, and I heard the voice of many angels around the throne, the living creatures, and the elders; and the number of them was ten thousand times ten thousand, and thousands of thousands, ¹²saying with a loud voice:

"Worthy is the Lamb who was slain
  To receive power and riches and wisdom,
  And strength and honor and glory and
    blessing!"

**➤ *Worthy is the Lamb
who was slain
To receive power and riches
and wisdom,
And strength and honor and
glory and blessing!***

Rev. 5:12

¹³And every creature which is in heaven and on the earth and under the earth and such as are in the sea, and all that are in them, I heard saying:

"Blessing and honor and glory and power
  Be to Him who sits on the throne,
  And to the Lamb, forever and ever!"[a]

¹⁴Then the four living creatures said, "Amen!" And the twenty-four[a] elders fell down and worshiped Him who lives forever and ever.[b]

First Seal: The Conqueror

6 Now I saw when the Lamb opened one of the seals;[a] and I heard one of the four living creatures saying with a voice like thunder, "Come and see." ²And I looked, and

---

5:4 [a]NU-Text and M-Text omit *and read.*   **5:5** [a]NU-Text and M-Text omit *to loose.*   **5:6** [a]NU-Text and M-Text read *I saw in the midst . . . a Lamb standing.*   **5:10** [a]NU-Text and M-Text read *them.* [b]NU-Text reads *a kingdom.* [c]NU-Text and M-Text read *they.* **5:13** [a]M-Text adds *Amen.*   **5:14** [a]NU-Text and M-Text omit *twenty-four.* [b]NU-Text and M-Text omit *Him who lives forever and ever.* **6:1** [a]NU-Text and M-Text read *seven seals.*

behold, a white horse. He who sat on it had a bow; and a crown was given to him, and he went out conquering and to conquer.

Second Seal: Conflict on Earth

³When He opened the second seal, I heard the second living creature saying, "Come and see."ᵃ ⁴Another horse, fiery red, went out. And it was granted to the one who sat on it to take peace from the earth, and that *people* should kill one another; and there was given to him a great sword.

Third Seal: Scarcity on Earth

⁵When He opened the third seal, I heard the third living creature say, "Come and see." So I looked, and behold, a black horse, and he who sat on it had a pair of scales in his hand. ⁶And I heard a voice in the midst of the four living creatures saying, "A quartᵃ of wheat for a denarius,ᵇ and three quarts of barley for a denarius; and do not harm the oil and the wine."

Fourth Seal: Widespread Death on Earth

⁷When He opened the fourth seal, I heard the voice of the fourth living creature saying, "Come and see." ⁸So I looked, and behold, a pale horse. And the name of him who sat on it was Death, and Hades followed with him. And power was given to them over a fourth of the earth, to kill with sword, with hunger, with death, and by the beasts of the earth.

Fifth Seal: The Cry of the Martyrs

⁹When He opened the fifth seal, I saw under the altar the souls of those who had been slain for the word of God and for the testimony which they held. ¹⁰And they cried with a loud voice, saying, "How long, O Lord, holy and true, until You judge and avenge our blood on those who dwell on the earth?" ¹¹Then a white robe was given to each of them; and it was said to them that they should rest a little while longer, until both *the number of* their fellow servants and their brethren, who would be killed as they *were,* was completed.

Sixth Seal: Cosmic Disturbances

¹²I looked when He opened the sixth seal, and behold,ᵃ there was a great earthquake; and the sun became black as sackcloth of hair, and the moonᵇ became like blood. ¹³And the stars of heaven fell to the earth, as a fig tree drops its late figs when it is shaken by a mighty wind. ¹⁴Then the sky receded as a scroll when it is rolled up, and every mountain and island was moved out of its place. ¹⁵And the kings of the earth, the great men, the rich men, the commanders,ᵃ the mighty men, every slave and every free man, hid themselves in the caves and in the rocks of the mountains, ¹⁶and said to the mountains and rocks, "Fall on us and hide us from the face of Him who sits on the throne and from the wrath of the Lamb! ¹⁷For the great day of His wrath has come, and who is able to stand?"

The Sealed of Israel

7 After these things I saw four angels standing at the four corners of the earth, holding the four winds of the earth, that the wind should not blow on the earth, on the sea, or on any tree. ²Then I saw another angel ascending from the east, having the seal of the living God. And he cried with a loud voice to the four angels to whom it was granted to harm the earth and the sea, ³saying, "Do not harm the earth, the sea, or the trees till we have sealed the servants of our God on their foreheads." ⁴And I heard the number of those who were sealed. One hundred *and* forty-four thousand of all the tribes of the children of Israel *were* sealed:

⁵of the tribe of Judah twelve thousand *were*
     sealed;ᵃ
  of the tribe of Reuben twelve thousand
     were sealed;
  of the tribe of Gad twelve thousand *were*
     sealed;
⁶of the tribe of Asher twelve thousand *were*
     sealed;
  of the tribe of Naphtali twelve thousand
     were sealed;
  of the tribe of Manasseh twelve thousand
     were sealed;

6:3 ᵃNU-Text and M-Text omit *and see.*   6:6 ᵃGreek *choinix;* that is, approximately one quart   ᵇThis was approximately one day's wage for a worker.   6:12 ᵃNU-Text and M-Text omit *behold.*   ᵇNU-Text and M-Text read *the whole moon.*   6:15 ᵃNU-Text and M-Text read *the commanders, the rich men.*   7:5 ᵃIn NU-Text and M-Text *were sealed* is stated only in verses 5a and 8c; the words are understood in the remainder of the passage.

[7]of the tribe of Simeon twelve thousand *were* sealed;
of the tribe of Levi twelve thousand *were* sealed;
of the tribe of Issachar twelve thousand *were* sealed;
[8]of the tribe of Zebulun twelve thousand *were* sealed;
of the tribe of Joseph twelve thousand *were* sealed;
of the tribe of Benjamin twelve thousand *were* sealed.

A Multitude from the Great Tribulation

[9]After these things I looked, and behold, a great multitude which no one could number, of all nations, tribes, peoples, and tongues, standing before the throne and before the Lamb, clothed with white robes, with palm branches in their hands, [10]and crying out with a loud voice, saying, "Salvation *belongs* to our God who sits on the throne, and to the Lamb!" [11]All the angels stood around the throne and the elders and the four living creatures, and fell on their faces before the throne and worshiped God, [12]saying:

"Amen! Blessing and glory and wisdom,
Thanksgiving and honor and power and might,
Be to our God forever and ever.
Amen."

[13]Then one of the elders answered, saying to me, "Who are these arrayed in white robes, and where did they come from?"
[14]And I said to him, "Sir,[a] you know."

So he said to me, "These are the ones who come out of the great tribulation, and washed their robes and made them white in the blood of the Lamb. [15]Therefore they are before the throne of God, and serve Him day and night in His temple. And He who sits on the throne will dwell among them. [16]They shall neither hunger anymore nor thirst anymore; the sun shall not strike them, nor any heat; [17]for the Lamb who is in the midst of the throne will shepherd them and lead them to living fountains of waters.[a] And God will wipe away every tear from their eyes."

Seventh Seal: Prelude to the Seven Trumpets

8 When He opened the seventh seal, there was silence in heaven for about half an hour. [2]And I saw the seven angels who stand before God, and to them were given seven trumpets. [3]Then another angel, having a golden censer, came and stood at the altar. He was given much incense, that he should offer *it* with the prayers of all the saints upon the golden altar which was before the throne. [4]And the smoke of the incense, with the prayers of the saints, ascended before God from the angel's hand. [5]Then the angel took the censer, filled it with fire from the altar, and threw *it* to the earth. And there were noises, thunderings, lightnings, and an earthquake.
[6]So the seven angels who had the seven trumpets prepared themselves to sound.

First Trumpet: Vegetation Struck

[7]The first angel sounded: And hail and fire followed, mingled with blood, and they

7:14 [a]NU-Text and M-Text read *My lord.*   7:17 [a]NU-Text and M-Text read *to fountains of the waters of life.*

↓ KNOW (REV. 7:9)
. . . .

What will we do in heaven? Don't worry that you'll find it boring; in fact, heaven will be a very active place. First, you'll be worshiping God—which is, by the way, why you were created. God made you to bring Him glory. Heaven will also be a place of great productivity; we'll rule together with Christ. We will eat in heaven and be able to sit down with the great saints of old and enjoy a five-course meal. We'll also be reunited with saved loved ones. But the main event of heaven, of course, will be Jesus. We long for heaven, but really we long for God Himself. And God will be there! You'll be able to ask Him anything, tell Him anything, and hear everything He has to say to you. After all, you'll have all the time in the world when you get to heaven. *For more about* Heaven, *see Rev. 15:3.*

were thrown to the earth.[a] And a third of the trees were burned up, and all green grass was burned up.

Second Trumpet: The Seas Struck

[8]Then the second angel sounded: And *something* like a great mountain burning with fire was thrown into the sea, and a third of the sea became blood. [9]And a third of the living creatures in the sea died, and a third of the ships were destroyed.

Third Trumpet: The Waters Struck

[10]Then the third angel sounded: And a great star fell from heaven, burning like a torch, and it fell on a third of the rivers and on the springs of water. [11]The name of the star is Wormwood. A third of the waters became wormwood, and many men died from the water, because it was made bitter.

Fourth Trumpet: The Heavens Struck

[12]Then the fourth angel sounded: And a third of the sun was struck, a third of the moon, and a third of the stars, so that a third of them were darkened. A third of the day did not shine, and likewise the night.

[13]And I looked, and I heard an angel[a] flying through the midst of heaven, saying with a loud voice, "Woe, woe, woe to the inhabitants of the earth, because of the remaining blasts of the trumpet of the three angels who are about to sound!"

Fifth Trumpet: The Locusts from the Bottomless Pit

9 Then the fifth angel sounded: And I saw a star fallen from heaven to the earth. To him was given the key to the bottomless pit. [2]And he opened the bottomless pit, and smoke arose out of the pit like the smoke of a great furnace. So the sun and the air were darkened because of the smoke of the pit. [3]Then out of the smoke locusts came upon the earth. And to them was given power, as the scorpions of the earth have power. [4]They were commanded not to harm the grass of the earth, or any green thing, or any tree, but only those men who do not have the seal of God

on their foreheads. [5]And they were not given *authority* to kill them, but to torment them *for* five months. Their torment *was* like the torment of a scorpion when it strikes a man. [6]In those days men will seek death and will not find it; they will desire to die, and death will flee from them.

[7]The shape of the locusts was like horses prepared for battle. On their heads were crowns of something like gold, and their faces *were* like the faces of men. [8]They had hair like women's hair, and their teeth were like lions' *teeth*. [9]And they had breastplates like breastplates of iron, and the sound of their wings *was* like the sound of chariots with many horses running into battle. [10]They had tails like scorpions, and there were stings in their tails. Their power *was* to hurt men five months. [11]And they had as king over them the angel of the bottomless pit, whose name in Hebrew *is* Abaddon, but in Greek he has the name Apollyon.

[12]One woe is past. Behold, still two more woes are coming after these things.

Sixth Trumpet: The Angels from the Euphrates

[13]Then the sixth angel sounded: And I heard a voice from the four horns of the golden altar which is before God, [14]saying to the sixth angel who had the trumpet, "Release the four angels who are bound at the great river Euphrates." [15]So the four angels, who had been prepared for the hour and day and month and year, were released to kill a third of mankind. [16]Now the number of the army of the horsemen *was* two hundred million; I heard the number of them. [17]And thus I saw the horses in the vision: those who sat on them had breastplates of fiery red, hyacinth blue, and sulfur yellow; and the heads of the horses *were* like the heads of lions; and out of their mouths came fire, smoke, and brimstone. [18]By these three *plagues* a third of mankind was killed—by the fire and the smoke and the brimstone which came out of their mouths. [19]For their power[a] is in their mouth and in their tails; for their tails *are* like serpents, having heads; and with them they do harm.

[20]But the rest of mankind, who were not killed by these plagues, did not repent of the works of their hands, that they should not

---

8:7 [a]NU-Text and M-Text add *and a third of the earth was burned up.*   8:13 [a]NU-Text and M-Text read *eagle.*
9:19 [a]NU-Text and M-Text read *the power of the horses.*

worship demons, and idols of gold, silver, brass, stone, and wood, which can neither see nor hear nor walk. [21]And they did not repent of their murders or their sorceries[a] or their sexual immorality or their thefts.

The Mighty Angel with the Little Book

10 I saw still another mighty angel coming down from heaven, clothed with a cloud. And a rainbow *was* on his head, his face *was* like the sun, and his feet like pillars of fire. [2]He had a little book open in his hand. And he set his right foot on the sea and *his* left *foot* on the land, [3]and cried with a loud voice, as *when* a lion roars. When he cried out, seven thunders uttered their voices. [4]Now when the seven thunders uttered their voices,[a] I was about to write; but I heard a voice from heaven saying to me,[b] "Seal up the things which the seven thunders uttered, and do not write them."

[5]The angel whom I saw standing on the sea and on the land raised up his hand[a] to heaven [6]and swore by Him who lives forever and ever, who created heaven and the things that are in it, the earth and the things that are in it, and the sea and the things that are in it, that there should be delay no longer, [7]but in the days of the sounding of the seventh angel, when he is about to sound, the mystery of God would be finished, as He declared to His servants the prophets.

John Eats the Little Book

[8]Then the voice which I heard from heaven spoke to me again and said, "Go, take the little book which is open in the hand of the angel who stands on the sea and on the earth."

[9]So I went to the angel and said to him, "Give me the little book."

And he said to me, "Take and eat it; and it will make your stomach bitter, but it will be as sweet as honey in your mouth."

[10]Then I took the little book out of the angel's hand and ate it, and it was as sweet as honey in my mouth. But when I had eaten it, my stomach became bitter. [11]And he[a] said to me, "You must prophesy again about many peoples, nations, tongues, and kings."

The Two Witnesses

11 Then I was given a reed like a measuring rod. And the angel stood,[a] saying, "Rise and measure the temple of God, the altar, and those who worship there. [2]But leave out the court which is outside the temple, and do not measure it, for it has been given to the Gentiles. And they will tread the holy city underfoot *for* forty-two months. [3]And I will give *power* to my two witnesses, and they will prophesy one thousand two hundred and sixty days, clothed in sackcloth."

[4]These are the two olive trees and the two lampstands standing before the God[a] of the earth. [5]And if anyone wants to harm them, fire proceeds from their mouth and devours their enemies. And if anyone wants to harm them, he must be killed in this manner. [6]These have power to shut heaven, so that no rain falls in the days of their prophecy; and they have power over waters to turn them to blood, and to strike the earth with all plagues, as often as they desire.

The Witnesses Killed

[7]When they finish their testimony, the beast that ascends out of the bottomless pit will make war against them, overcome them, and kill them. [8]And their dead bodies *will lie* in the street of the great city which spiritually is called Sodom and Egypt, where also our[a] Lord was crucified. [9]Then *those* from the peoples, tribes, tongues, and nations will see their dead bodies three-and-a-half days, and not allow[a] their dead bodies to be put into graves. [10]And those who dwell on the earth will rejoice over them, make merry, and send gifts to one another, because these two prophets tormented those who dwell on the earth.

The Witnesses Resurrected

[11]Now after the three-and-a-half days the breath of life from God entered them, and they stood on their feet, and great fear fell on those who saw them. [12]And they[a] heard a loud voice from heaven saying to them, "Come up here." And they ascended to heaven in a cloud, and their enemies saw them. [13]In the

---

9:21 [a]NU-Text and M-Text read *drugs.*   **10:4** [a]NU-Text and M-Text read *sounded.*   [b]NU-Text and M-Text omit *to me.*
10:5 [a]NU-Text and M-Text read *right hand.*   **10:11** [a]NU-Text and M-Text read *they.*   **11:1** [a]NU-Text and M-Text omit *And the angel stood.*
11:4 [a]NU-Text and M-Text read *Lord.*   **11:8** [a]NU-Text and M-Text read *their.*   **11:9** [a]NU-Text and M-Text read *nations see . . . and will not allow.*   **11:12** [a]M-Text reads *I.*

same hour there was a great earthquake, and a tenth of the city fell. In the earthquake seven thousand people were killed, and the rest were afraid and gave glory to the God of heaven.

[14]The second woe is past. Behold, the third woe is coming quickly.

Seventh Trumpet: The Kingdom Proclaimed

[15]Then the seventh angel sounded: And there were loud voices in heaven, saying, "The kingdoms[a] of this world have become *the kingdoms* of our Lord and of His Christ, and He shall reign forever and ever!" [16]And the twenty-four elders who sat before God on their thrones fell on their faces and worshiped God, [17]saying:

"We give You thanks, O Lord God Almighty,
The One who is and who was and who is to come,[a]
Because You have taken Your great power and reigned.
[18]The nations were angry, and Your wrath has come,
And the time of the dead, that they should be judged,
And that You should reward Your servants the prophets and the saints,
And those who fear Your name, small and great,
And should destroy those who destroy the earth."

[19]Then the temple of God was opened in heaven, and the ark of His covenant[a] was seen in His temple. And there were lightnings, noises, thunderings, an earthquake, and great hail.

The Woman, the Child, and the Dragon

12 Now a great sign appeared in heaven: a woman clothed with the sun, with the moon under her feet, and on her head a garland of twelve stars. [2]Then being with child, she cried out in labor and in pain to give birth.

[3]And another sign appeared in heaven: behold, a great, fiery red dragon having seven heads and ten horns, and seven diadems on his heads. [4]His tail drew a third of the stars of heaven and threw them to the earth. And the dragon stood before the woman who was ready to give birth, to devour her Child as soon as it was born. [5]She bore a male Child who was to rule all nations with a rod of iron. And her Child was caught up to God and His throne. [6]Then the woman fled into the wilderness, where she has a place prepared by God, that they should feed her there one thousand two hundred and sixty days.

Satan Thrown Out of Heaven

[7]And war broke out in heaven: Michael and his angels fought with the dragon; and the dragon and his angels fought, [8]but they did not prevail, nor was a place found for them[a] in heaven any longer. [9]So the great dragon was cast out, that serpent of old, called the Devil and Satan, who deceives the whole world; he was cast to the earth, and his angels were cast out with him.

[10]Then I heard a loud voice saying in heaven, "Now salvation, and strength, and the kingdom of our God, and the power of His Christ have come, for the accuser of our brethren, who accused them before our God day and night, has been cast down. [11]And they overcame him by the blood of the Lamb and by the word of their testimony, and they did not love their lives to the death. [12]Therefore rejoice, O heavens, and you who dwell in them! Woe to the inhabitants of the earth and the sea! For the devil has come down to you, having great wrath, because he knows that he has a short time."

↘ LEARN

. . . .

12:10 • You must learn to distinguish between Satan's accusations—Scripture calls the devil "the accuser of the brethren"—and the Spirit's conviction. A feeling of guilt and shame is not necessarily bad! When the Spirit of God convicts you, He lovingly uses the Word of God to bring you back into fellowship with your heavenly Father. When Satan accuses you, however, he uses your own sins in a hateful way to make you feel helpless and hopeless. Judas listened to the devil and hanged himself. Peter wept bitterly when he looked at Jesus' face, but later came back into fellowship with Christ. *For more about* God's Word, *see Rev. 22:7*; Satan, *Rev. 20:10.*

11:15 [a]NU-Text and M-Text read *kingdom . . . has become.*   11:17 [a]NU-Text and M-Text omit *and who is to come.*   11:19 [a]M-Text reads *the covenant of the Lord.*   12:8 [a]M-Text reads *him.*

The Woman Persecuted

[13]Now when the dragon saw that he had been cast to the earth, he persecuted the woman who gave birth to the male *Child.* [14]But the woman was given two wings of a great eagle, that she might fly into the wilderness to her place, where she is nourished for a time and times and half a time, from the presence of the serpent. [15]So the serpent spewed water out of his mouth like a flood after the woman, that he might cause her to be carried away by the flood. [16]But the earth helped the woman, and the earth opened its mouth and swallowed up the flood which the dragon had spewed out of his mouth. [17]And the dragon was enraged with the woman, and he went to make war with the rest of her offspring, who keep the commandments of God and have the testimony of Jesus Christ.[a]

The Beast from the Sea

13 Then I[a] stood on the sand of the sea. And I saw a beast rising up out of the sea, having seven heads and ten horns,[b] and on his horns ten crowns, and on his heads a blasphemous name. [2]Now the beast which I saw was like a leopard, his feet were like *the feet of* a bear, and his mouth like the mouth of a lion. The dragon gave him his power, his throne, and great authority. [3]And I saw one of his heads as if it had been mortally wounded, and his deadly wound was healed. And all the world marveled and followed the beast. [4]So they worshiped the dragon who gave authority to the beast; and they worshiped the beast, saying, "Who *is* like the beast? Who is able to make war with him?"

[5]And he was given a mouth speaking great things and blasphemies, and he was given authority to continue[a] for forty-two months. [6]Then he opened his mouth in blasphemy against God, to blaspheme His name, His tabernacle, and those who dwell in heaven. [7]It was granted to him to make war with the saints and to overcome them. And authority was given him over every tribe,[a] tongue, and nation. [8]All who dwell on the earth will worship him, whose names have not been written in the Book of Life of the Lamb slain from the foundation of the world.

[9]If anyone has an ear, let him hear. [10]He who leads into captivity shall go into captivity; he who kills with the sword must be killed with the sword. Here is the patience and the faith of the saints.

The Beast from the Earth

[11]Then I saw another beast coming up out of the earth, and he had two horns like a lamb and spoke like a dragon. [12]And he exercises all the authority of the first beast in his presence, and causes the earth and those who dwell in it to worship the first beast, whose deadly wound was healed. [13]He performs great signs, so that he even makes fire come down from heaven on the earth in the sight of men. [14]And he deceives those[a] who dwell on the earth by those signs which he was granted to do in the sight of the beast, telling those who dwell on the earth to make an image to the beast who was wounded by the sword and lived. [15]He was granted *power* to give breath to the image of the beast, that the image of the beast should both speak and

12:17 [a]NU-Text and M-Text omit *Christ.*   13:1 [a]NU-Text reads *he.*   [b]NU-Text and M-Text read *ten horns and seven heads.*
13:5 [a]M-Text reads *make war.*   13:7 [a]NU-Text and M-Text add *and people.*   13:14 [a]M-Text reads *my own people.*

↑ GROW (REV. 13:1)

I believe we are living in the last days. The Bible tells us that the Antichrist, the Beast, plays a significant role in those end times. Yet the Bible does not tell you to look for the Antichrist; it instructs you to look for Jesus Christ. You need to place your focus and attention on the Savior, not on the serpent's henchman. This doesn't mean, of course, that you should stand on a street corner and stare into the sky like a raving idiot. When the Bible tells you to "look up," it wants you to live with a sense of anticipation and in a state of readiness (Luke 21:28). Be ready to go at any time! And consider this, if the Antichrist is close to being revealed—and I believe he is—then the coming of Jesus Christ is even closer. *For more about* Jesus' Return, *see Rev. 22:7.*

cause as many as would not worship the image of the beast to be killed. [16]He causes all, both small and great, rich and poor, free and slave, to receive a mark on their right hand or on their foreheads, [17]and that no one may buy or sell except one who has the mark or[a] the name of the beast, or the number of his name.

[18]Here is wisdom. Let him who has understanding calculate the number of the beast, for it is the number of a man: His number is 666.

The Lamb and the 144,000

14 Then I looked, and behold, a[a] Lamb standing on Mount Zion, and with Him one hundred and forty-four thousand, having[b] His Father's name written on their foreheads. [2]And I heard a voice from heaven, like the voice of many waters, and like the voice of loud thunder. And I heard the sound of harpists playing their harps. [3]They sang as it were a new song before the throne, before the four living creatures, and the elders; and no one could learn that song except the hundred and forty-four thousand who were redeemed from the earth. [4]These are the ones who were not defiled with women, for they are virgins. These are the ones who follow the Lamb wherever He goes. These were redeemed[a] from among men, being firstfruits to God and to the Lamb. [5]And in their mouth was found no deceit,[a] for they are without fault before the throne of God.[b]

The Proclamations of Three Angels

[6]Then I saw another angel flying in the midst of heaven, having the everlasting gospel to preach to those who dwell on the earth— to every nation, tribe, tongue, and people— [7]saying with a loud voice, "Fear God and give glory to Him, for the hour of His judgment has come; and worship Him who made heaven and earth, the sea and springs of water."

[8]And another angel followed, saying, "Babylon[a] is fallen, is fallen, that great city, because she has made all nations drink of the wine of the wrath of her fornication."

[9]Then a third angel followed them, saying with a loud voice, "If anyone worships the beast and his image, and receives his mark on his forehead or on his hand, [10]he himself shall also drink of the wine of the wrath of God, which is poured out full strength into the cup of His indignation. He shall be tormented with fire and brimstone in the presence of the holy angels and in the presence of the Lamb. [11]And the smoke of their torment ascends forever and ever; and they have no rest day or night, who worship the beast and his image, and whoever receives the mark of his name."

[12]Here is the patience of the saints; here are those[a] who keep the commandments of God and the faith of Jesus.

[13]Then I heard a voice from heaven saying to me,[a] "Write: 'Blessed are the dead who die in the Lord from now on.' "

"Yes," says the Spirit, "that they may rest from their labors, and their works follow them."

Reaping the Earth's Harvest

[14]Then I looked, and behold, a white cloud, and on the cloud sat One like the Son of Man, having on His head a golden crown, and in His hand a sharp sickle. [15]And another angel came out of the temple, crying with a loud voice to Him who sat on the cloud, "Thrust in Your sickle and reap, for the time has come for You[a] to reap, for the harvest of the earth is ripe." [16]So He who sat on the cloud thrust in His sickle on the earth, and the earth was reaped.

Reaping the Grapes of Wrath

[17]Then another angel came out of the temple which is in heaven, he also having a sharp sickle.

[18]And another angel came out from the altar, who had power over fire, and he cried with a loud cry to him who had the sharp sickle, saying, "Thrust in your sharp sickle and gather the clusters of the vine of the earth, for her grapes are fully ripe." [19]So the angel thrust his sickle into the earth and gathered the vine of the earth, and threw it into the great winepress of the wrath of God. [20]And the winepress was trampled outside the city, and blood came out of the winepress, up

---

13:17 [a]NU-Text and M-Text omit or.   14:1 [a]NU-Text and M-Text read the. [b]NU-Text and M-Text add His name and.
14:4 [a]M-Text adds by Jesus.   14:5 [a]NU-Text and M-Text read falsehood. [b]NU-Text and M-Text omit before the throne of God.
14:8 [a]NU-Text reads Babylon the great is fallen, is fallen, which has made; M-Text reads Babylon the great is fallen. She has made.
14:12 [a]NU-Text and M-Text omit here are those.   14:13 [a]NU-Text and M-Text omit to me.   14:15 [a]NU-Text and M-Text omit for You.

to the horses' bridles, for one thousand six hundred furlongs.

Prelude to the Bowl Judgments

15 Then I saw another sign in heaven, great and marvelous: seven angels having the seven last plagues, for in them the wrath of God is complete.

[2]And I saw *something* like a sea of glass mingled with fire, and those who have the victory over the beast, over his image and over his mark[a] *and* over the number of his name, standing on the sea of glass, having harps of God. [3]They sing the song of Moses, the servant of God, and the song of the Lamb, saying:

"Great and marvelous *are* Your works,
  Lord God Almighty!
Just and true *are* Your ways,
  O King of the saints![a]
[4]Who shall not fear You, O Lord, and
    glorify Your name?
For *You* alone *are* holy.
For all nations shall come and worship
    before You,
For Your judgments have been
    manifested."

[5]After these things I looked, and behold,[a] the temple of the tabernacle of the testimony in heaven was opened. [6]And out of the temple came the seven angels having the seven plagues, clothed in pure bright linen, and having their chests girded with golden bands. [7]Then one of the four living creatures gave to the seven angels seven golden bowls full of the wrath of God who lives forever and ever. [8]The temple was filled with smoke from the glory of God and from His power, and no one was able to enter the temple till the seven plagues of the seven angels were completed.

16 Then I heard a loud voice from the temple saying to the seven angels, "Go and pour out the bowls[a] of the wrath of God on the earth."

First Bowl: Loathsome Sores

[2]So the first went and poured out his bowl upon the earth, and a foul and loathsome sore came upon the men who had the mark of the beast and those who worshiped his image.

Second Bowl: The Sea Turns to Blood

[3]Then the second angel poured out his bowl on the sea, and it became blood as of a dead *man;* and every living creature in the sea died.

Third Bowl: The Waters Turn to Blood

[4]Then the third angel poured out his bowl on the rivers and springs of water, and they became blood. [5]And I heard the angel of the waters saying:

"You are righteous, O Lord,[a]
The One who is and who was and who is
    to be,[b]
Because You have judged these things.
[6]For they have shed the blood of saints and
    prophets,

15:2 [a]NU-Text and M-Text omit *over his mark.*   **15:3** [a]NU-Text and M-Text read *nations.*   **15:5** [a]NU-Text and M-Text omit *behold.*
16:1 [a]NU-Text and M-Text read *seven bowls.*   **16:5** [a]NU-Text and M-Text omit *O Lord.*   [b]NU-Text and M-Text read *who was, the Holy One.*

↓ KNOW (REV. 15:3)

Because God is holy and righteous, He is also just. And because He is just, a severe penalty waits for all lawbreakers. Some of us say that we don't like justice . . . until someone rips us off. *Then* we want the full weight of justice to come down on our side. Well, guess what? God is perfectly and infinitely just. That means that if you have broken His commandments and so far seem to be getting away with it, one day you will appear in a heavenly court where full and final justice will be administered. I don't care who your defense attorney is, you are *not* getting out of this one. Unless you have Jesus Christ to defend you, there is only one verdict for you: guilty. Because God is perfectly just, He will judge sin perfectly. Heaven has no appeals court, nor does it need one. *For more about* Heaven, *see Rev. 21:2; the* Attributes of God, *Mark 10:18.*

And You have given them blood to drink. For[a] it is their just due."

[7]And I heard another from[a] the altar saying, "Even so, Lord God Almighty, true and righteous *are* Your judgments."

Fourth Bowl: Men Are Scorched

[8]Then the fourth angel poured out his bowl on the sun, and power was given to him to scorch men with fire. [9]And men were scorched with great heat, and they blasphemed the name of God who has power over these plagues; and they did not repent and give Him glory.

Fifth Bowl: Darkness and Pain

[10]Then the fifth angel poured out his bowl on the throne of the beast, and his kingdom became full of darkness; and they gnawed their tongues because of the pain. [11]They blasphemed the God of heaven because of their pains and their sores, and did not repent of their deeds.

Sixth Bowl: Euphrates Dried Up

[12]Then the sixth angel poured out his bowl on the great river Euphrates, and its water was dried up, so that the way of the kings from the east might be prepared. [13]And I saw three unclean spirits like frogs *coming* out of the mouth of the dragon, out of the mouth of the beast, and out of the mouth of the false prophet. [14]For they are spirits of demons, performing signs, *which* go out to the kings of the earth and[a] of the whole world, to gather them to the battle of that great day of God Almighty.

[15]"Behold, I am coming as a thief. Blessed *is* he who watches, and keeps his garments, lest he walk naked and they see his shame."

[16]And they gathered them together to the place called in Hebrew, Armageddon.[a]

Seventh Bowl: The Earth Utterly Shaken

[17]Then the seventh angel poured out his bowl into the air, and a loud voice came out of the temple of heaven, from the throne, saying, "It is done!" [18]And there were noises and thunderings and lightnings; and there was a great earthquake, such a mighty and great earthquake as had not occurred since men were on the earth. [19]Now the great city was divided into three parts, and the cities of the nations fell. And great Babylon was remembered before God, to give her the cup of the wine of the fierceness of His wrath. [20]Then every island fled away, and the mountains were not found. [21]And great hail from heaven fell upon men, *each hailstone* about the weight of a talent. Men blasphemed God because of the plague of the hail, since that plague was exceedingly great.

The Scarlet Woman and the Scarlet Beast

17 Then one of the seven angels who had the seven bowls came and talked with me, saying to me,[a] "Come, I will show you the judgment of the great harlot who sits on many waters, [2]with whom the kings of the earth committed fornication, and the inhabitants of the earth were made drunk with the wine of her fornication."

[3]So he carried me away in the Spirit into the wilderness. And I saw a woman sitting on a scarlet beast *which was* full of names of blasphemy, having seven heads and ten horns. [4]The woman was arrayed in purple and scarlet, and adorned with gold and precious stones and pearls, having in her hand a golden cup full of abominations and the filthiness of her fornication.[a] [5]And on her forehead a name *was* written:

MYSTERY, BABYLON THE GREAT,
THE MOTHER OF HARLOTS AND
OF THE ABOMINATIONS
OF THE EARTH.

[6]I saw the woman, drunk with the blood of the saints and with the blood of the martyrs of Jesus. And when I saw her, I marveled with great amazement.

The Meaning of the Woman and the Beast

[7]But the angel said to me, "Why did you marvel? I will tell you the mystery of the

16:6 [a]NU-Text and M-Text omit *For.*   **16:7** [a]NU-Text and M-Text omit *another from.*   **16:14** [a]NU-Text and M-Text omit *of the earth and.*   **16:16** [a]M-Text reads *Megiddo.*   **17:1** [a]NU-Text and M-Text omit *to me.*   **17:4** [a]M-Text reads *the filthiness of the fornication of the earth.*

woman and of the beast that carries her, which has the seven heads and the ten horns. [8]The beast that you saw was, and is not, and will ascend out of the bottomless pit and go to perdition. And those who dwell on the earth will marvel, whose names are not written in the Book of Life from the foundation of the world, when they see the beast that was, and is not, and yet is.[a]

[9]"Here *is* the mind which has wisdom: The seven heads are seven mountains on which the woman sits. [10]There are also seven kings. Five have fallen, one is, *and* the other has not yet come. And when he comes, he must continue a short time. [11]The beast that was, and is not, is himself also the eighth, and is of the seven, and is going to perdition.

[12]"The ten horns which you saw are ten kings who have received no kingdom as yet, but they receive authority for one hour as kings with the beast. [13]These are of one mind, and they will give their power and authority to the beast. [14]These will make war with the Lamb, and the Lamb will overcome them, for He is Lord of lords and King of kings; and those *who are* with Him *are* called, chosen, and faithful."

[15]Then he said to me, "The waters which you saw, where the harlot sits, are peoples, multitudes, nations, and tongues. [16]And the ten horns which you saw on[a] the beast, these will hate the harlot, make her desolate and naked, eat her flesh and burn her with fire. [17]For God has put it into their hearts to fulfill His purpose, to be of one mind, and to give their kingdom to the beast, until the words of God are fulfilled. [18]And the woman whom you saw is that great city which reigns over the kings of the earth."

The Fall of Babylon the Great

18 After these things I saw another angel coming down from heaven, having great authority, and the earth was illuminated with his glory. [2]And he cried mightily[a] with a loud voice, saying, "Babylon the great is fallen, is fallen, and has become a dwelling place of demons, a prison for every foul spirit, and a cage for every unclean and hated bird! [3]For all the nations have drunk of the wine of the wrath of her fornication, the kings of the earth have committed fornication with her, and the merchants of the earth have become rich through the abundance of her luxury."

[4]And I heard another voice from heaven saying, "Come out of her, my people, lest you share in her sins, and lest you receive of her plagues. [5]For her sins have reached[a] to heaven, and God has remembered her iniquities. [6]Render to her just as she rendered to you,[a] and repay her double according to her works; in the cup which she has mixed, mix double for her. [7]In the measure that she glorified herself and lived luxuriously, in the same measure give her torment and sorrow; for she says in her heart, 'I sit *as* queen, and am no widow, and will not see sorrow.' [8]Therefore her plagues will come in one day—death and mourning and famine. And she will be utterly burned with fire, for strong *is* the Lord God who judges[a] her.

The World Mourns Babylon's Fall

[9]"The kings of the earth who committed fornication and lived luxuriously with her will weep and lament for her, when they see the smoke of her burning, [10]standing at a distance for fear of her torment, saying, 'Alas, alas, that great city Babylon, that mighty city! For in one hour your judgment has come.'

[11]"And the merchants of the earth will weep and mourn over her, for no one buys their merchandise anymore: [12]merchandise of gold and silver, precious stones and pearls, fine linen and purple, silk and scarlet, every kind of citron wood, every kind of object of ivory, every kind of object of most precious wood, bronze, iron, and marble; [13]and cinnamon and incense, fragrant oil and frankincense, wine and oil, fine flour and wheat, cattle and sheep, horses and chariots, and bodies and souls of men. [14]The fruit that your soul longed for has gone from you, and all the things which are rich and splendid have gone from you,[a] and you shall find them no more at all. [15]The merchants of these things, who became rich by her, will stand at a distance for fear of her torment, weeping and wailing, [16]and saying, 'Alas, alas, that great city that was clothed in fine linen, purple, and scarlet, and adorned with gold and precious stones

---

17:8 [a]NU-Text and M-Text read *and shall be present.*   **17:16** [a]NU-Text and M-Text read *saw, and the beast.*
18:2 [a]NU-Text and M-Text omit *mightily.*   **18:5** [a]NU-Text and M-Text read *have been heaped up.*
18:6 [a]NU-Text and M-Text omit *to you.*   **18:8** [a]NU-Text and M-Text read *has judged.*   **18:14** [a]NU-Text and M-Text read *been lost to you.*

and pearls! [17]For in one hour such great riches came to nothing.' Every shipmaster, all who travel by ship, sailors, and as many as trade on the sea, stood at a distance [18]and cried out when they saw the smoke of her burning, saying, 'What *is* like this great city?'

[19]"They threw dust on their heads and cried out, weeping and wailing, and saying, 'Alas, alas, that great city, in which all who had ships on the sea became rich by her wealth! For in one hour she is made desolate.'

[20]"Rejoice over her, O heaven, and *you* holy apostles[a] and prophets, for God has avenged you on her!"

Finality of Babylon's Fall

[21]Then a mighty angel took up a stone like a great millstone and threw *it* into the sea, saying, "Thus with violence the great city Babylon shall be thrown down, and shall not be found anymore. [22]The sound of harpists, musicians, flutists, and trumpeters shall not be heard in you anymore. No craftsman of any craft shall be found in you anymore, and the sound of a millstone shall not be heard in you anymore. [23]The light of a lamp shall not shine in you anymore, and the voice of bridegroom and bride shall not be heard in you anymore. For your merchants were the great men of the earth, for by your sorcery all the nations were deceived. [24]And in her was found the blood of prophets and saints, and of all who were slain on the earth."

Heaven Exults over Babylon

19 After these things I heard[a] a loud voice of a great multitude in heaven, saying, "Alleluia! Salvation and glory and honor and power *belong* to the Lord[b] our God! [2]For true and righteous *are* His judgments, because He has judged the great harlot who corrupted the earth with her fornication; and He has avenged on her the blood of His servants *shed* by her." [3]Again they said, "Alleluia! Her smoke rises up forever and ever!" [4]And the twenty-four elders and the four living creatures fell down and worshiped God who sat on the throne, saying, "Amen! Alleluia!" [5]Then a voice came from the throne, saying, "Praise our God, all

➤ *. . . Praise our God, all you His servants and those who fear Him, both small and great!* Rev. 19:5

you His servants and those who fear Him, both[a] small and great!"

[6]And I heard, as it were, the voice of a great multitude, as the sound of many waters and as the sound of mighty thunderings, saying, "Alleluia! For the[a] Lord God Omnipotent reigns! [7]Let us be glad and rejoice and give Him glory, for the marriage of the Lamb has come, and His wife has made herself ready." [8]And to her it was granted to be arrayed in fine linen, clean and bright, for the fine linen is the righteous acts of the saints.

[9]Then he said to me, "Write: 'Blessed *are* those who are called to the marriage supper of the Lamb!' " And he said to me, "These are the true sayings of God." [10]And I fell at his feet to worship him. But he said to me, "See *that you do* not *do that!* I am your fellow servant, and of your brethren who have the testimony of Jesus. Worship God! For the testimony of Jesus is the spirit of prophecy."

Christ on a White Horse

[11]Now I saw heaven opened, and behold, a white horse. And He who sat on him *was* called Faithful and True, and in righteousness He judges and makes war. [12]His eyes *were* like a flame of fire, and on His head *were* many crowns. He had[a] a name written that no one knew except Himself. [13]He *was* clothed with a robe dipped in blood, and His name is called The Word of God. [14]And the armies in heaven, clothed in fine linen, white and clean,[a] followed Him on white horses. [15]Now out of His mouth goes a sharp[a] sword, that with it He should strike the nations. And He Himself will rule them with a rod of iron. He Himself treads the winepress of the fierceness and wrath of Almighty God. [16]And He has on *His* robe and on His thigh a name written:

KING OF KINGS AND
LORD OF LORDS.

18:20 [a]NU-Text and M-Text read *saints and apostles.*   **19:1** [a]NU-Text and M-Text add *something like.*
[b]NU-Text and M-Text omit *the Lord.*   **19:5** [a]NU-Text and M-Text omit *both.*   **19:6** [a]NU-Text and M-Text read *our.*
19:12 [a]M-Text adds *names written, and.*   **19:14** [a]NU-Text and M-Text read *pure white linen.*   **19:15** [a]M-Text adds *two-edged.*

The Beast and His Armies Defeated

[17]Then I saw an angel standing in the sun; and he cried with a loud voice, saying to all the birds that fly in the midst of heaven, "Come and gather together for the supper of the great God,[a] [18]that you may eat the flesh of kings, the flesh of captains, the flesh of mighty men, the flesh of horses and of those who sit on them, and the flesh of all *people,* free[a] and slave, both small and great."

[19]And I saw the beast, the kings of the earth, and their armies, gathered together to make war against Him who sat on the horse and against His army. [20]Then the beast was captured, and with him the false prophet who worked signs in his presence, by which he deceived those who received the mark of the beast and those who worshiped his image. These two were cast alive into the lake of fire burning with brimstone. [21]And the rest were killed with the sword which proceeded from the mouth of Him who sat on the horse. And all the birds were filled with their flesh.

Satan Bound 1000 Years

20 Then I saw an angel coming down from heaven, having the key to the bottomless pit and a great chain in his hand. [2]He laid hold of the dragon, that serpent of old, who is *the* Devil and Satan, and bound him for a thousand years; [3]and he cast him into the bottomless pit, and shut him up, and set a seal on him, so that he should deceive the nations no more till the thousand years were finished. But after

these things he must be released for a little while.

The Saints Reign with Christ 1000 Years

[4]And I saw thrones, and they sat on them, and judgment was committed to them. Then *I saw* the souls of those who had been beheaded for their witness to Jesus and for the word of God, who had not worshiped the beast or his image, and had not received *his* mark on their foreheads or on their hands. And they lived and reigned with Christ for a[a] thousand years. [5]But the rest of the dead did not live again until the thousand years were finished. This *is* the first resurrection. [6]Blessed and holy *is* he who has part in the first resurrection. Over such the second death has no power, but they shall be priests of God and of Christ, and shall reign with Him a thousand years.

Satanic Rebellion Crushed

[7]Now when the thousand years have expired, Satan will be released from his prison [8]and will go out to deceive the nations which are in the four corners of the earth, Gog and Magog, to gather them together to battle, whose number *is* as the sand of the sea. [9]They went up on the breadth of the earth and surrounded the camp of the saints and the beloved city. And fire came down from God out of heaven and devoured them. [10]The devil, who deceived them, was cast into the lake of fire and brimstone where[a] the beast and the false prophet *are.* And they will be tormented day and night forever and ever.

19:17 [a]NU-Text and M-Text read *the great supper of God.*   **19:18** [a]NU-Text and M-Text read *both free.*   **20:4** [a]M-Text reads *the.*
20:10 [a]NU-Text and M-Text add *also.*

↓ KNOW (REV. 20:10)

The Bible calls the devil "the god of this age" who has spiritually "blinded" those "who do not believe, lest the light of the gospel of the glory of Christ, who is the image of God, should shine on them" (2 Cor. 4:4). Jesus came to destroy both the devil and his works (Heb. 2:14; 1 John 3:8). The battle has raged ever since Adam and Eve believed Satan's lie in the Garden of Eden. After the devil deceived Adam and Eve and brought about their spiritual ruin, God told him that he would crawl on his belly all the days of his life and eat dust. And then the Lord gave us the very first messianic passage in the Bible. He told Satan that although he would "bruise" Eve's "Seed," that Seed—the Messiah—would one day bruise Satan's head (Gen. 3:15). Both prophecies were fulfilled at the Cross. *For more about* Satan, *see Luke 4:1.*

The Great White Throne Judgment

[11]Then I saw a great white throne and Him who sat on it, from whose face the earth and the heaven fled away. And there was found no place for them. [12]And I saw the dead, small and great, standing before God,[a] and books were opened. And another book was opened, which is *the Book* of Life. And the dead were judged according to their works, by the things which were written in the books. [13]The sea gave up the dead who were in it, and Death and Hades delivered up the dead who were in them. And they were judged, each one according to his works. [14]Then Death and Hades were cast into the lake of fire. This is the second death.[a] [15]And anyone not found written in the Book of Life was cast into the lake of fire.

All Things Made New

21 Now I saw a new heaven and a new earth, for the first heaven and the first earth had passed away. Also there was no more sea. [2]Then I, John,[a] saw the holy city, New Jerusalem, coming down out of heaven from God, prepared as a bride adorned for her husband. [3]And I heard a loud voice from heaven saying, "Behold, the tabernacle of God *is* with men, and He will dwell with them, and they shall be His people. God Himself will be with them *and be* their God. [4]And God will wipe away every tear from their eyes; there shall be no more death, nor sorrow, nor crying. There shall be no more pain, for the former things have passed away."

[5]Then He who sat on the throne said, "Behold, I make all things new." And He said to me,[a] "Write, for these words are true and faithful."

[6]And He said to me, "It is done![a] I am the Alpha and the Omega, the Beginning and the End. I will give of the fountain of the water of life freely to him who thirsts. [7]He who overcomes shall inherit all things,[a] and I will be his God and he shall be My son. [8]But the cowardly, unbelieving,[a] abominable, murderers, sexually immoral, sorcerers, idolaters, and all liars shall have their part in the lake which burns with fire and brimstone, which is the second death."

The New Jerusalem

[9]Then one of the seven angels who had the seven bowls filled with the seven last plagues came to me[a] and talked with me, saying, "Come, I will show you the bride, the Lamb's wife."[b] [10]And he carried me away in the Spirit to a great and high mountain, and showed me the great city, the holy[a] Jerusalem, descending out of heaven from God, [11]having the glory of God. Her light *was* like a most precious stone, like a jasper stone, clear as crystal. [12]Also she had a great and high wall with twelve gates, and twelve angels at the gates, and names written on them, which are *the names* of the twelve tribes of the children of Israel: [13]three gates on the east, three gates

20:12 [a]NU-Text and M-Text read *the throne*.   **20:14** [a]NU-Text and M-Text add *the lake of fire*.   **21:2** [a]NU-Text and M-Text omit *John*.
21:5 [a]NU-Text and M-Text omit *to me*.   **21:6** [a]M-Text omits *It is done*.   **21:7** [a]M-Text reads *overcomes, I shall give him these things*.
21:8 [a]M-Text adds *and sinners*.   **21:9** [a]NU-Text and M-Text omit *to me*.   [b]M-Text reads *I will show you the woman, the Lamb's bride*.
21:10 [a]NU-Text and M-Text omit *the great* and read *the holy city, Jerusalem*.

↓ KNOW (REV. 21:2)

The Bible describes heaven as a city. Many of us have a hard time imagining this, because when we think of cities, we tend to picture noisy, crowded places with urban blight, neighborhoods overrun with graffiti, vacant lots filled with trash, and violent crime around every corner. But try to think of cities in a different way. Try to think of a perfect city, without crime or decay, or debauchery. Everyone there loves everyone else. This city has a wonderful and rich culture with a wild variety of art, music, goods, services, events, and restaurants readily available. Restaurants? In heaven? Well, why not? We know feasting will take place there (Luke 22:18). Just as earthly cities have their own unique qualities, so the New Jerusalem, the heavenly city, will have many of its own utterly distinctive qualities. Imagine the sights just waiting to be explored! *For more about* Heaven, *see Rev. 21:10–21.*

↘ LEARN

21:10–21 • Much is made about heaven, and rightly so. Here, heaven comes to earth as the New Jerusalem. Abraham waited for this city "which has foundations, whose builder and maker is God" (Heb. 11:10). It will have no crime, no corruption, no division. Here we will enter a new spiritual dimension incomprehensible to us now. The city has streets of translucent gold and walls of jasper (similar to diamonds). While men today live to accumulate gold, God paves the streets with it! And the city is transparent because nobody has anything to hide—and no one wants to be out of sight of Jesus. *For more about* Heaven, *see John 14:2.*

on the north, three gates on the south, and three gates on the west.

¹⁴Now the wall of the city had twelve foundations, and on them were the names[a] of the twelve apostles of the Lamb. ¹⁵And he who talked with me had a gold reed to measure the city, its gates, and its wall. ¹⁶The city is laid out as a square; its length is as great as its breadth. And he measured the city with the reed: twelve thousand furlongs. Its length, breadth, and height are equal. ¹⁷Then he measured its wall: one hundred *and* forty-four cubits, *according* to the measure of a man, that is, of an angel. ¹⁸The construction of its wall was *of* jasper; and the city *was* pure gold, like clear glass. ¹⁹The foundations of the wall of the city *were* adorned with all kinds of precious stones: the first foundation *was* jasper, the second sapphire, the third chalcedony, the fourth emerald, ²⁰the

fifth sardonyx, the sixth sardius, the seventh chrysolite, the eighth beryl, the ninth topaz, the tenth chrysoprase, the eleventh jacinth, and the twelfth amethyst. ²¹The twelve gates *were* twelve pearls: each individual gate was of one pearl. And the street of the city *was* pure gold, like transparent glass.

The Glory of the New Jerusalem

²²But I saw no temple in it, for the Lord God Almighty and the Lamb are its temple. ²³The city had no need of the sun or of the moon to shine in it,[a] for the glory[b] of God illuminated it. The Lamb *is* its light. ²⁴And the nations of those who are saved[a] shall walk in its light, and the kings of the earth bring their glory and honor into it.[b] ²⁵Its gates shall not be shut at all by day (there shall be no night there). ²⁶And they shall bring the glory and the honor of the nations into it.[a] ²⁷But there shall by no means enter it anything that defiles, or causes[a] an abomination or a lie, but only those who are written in the Lamb's Book of Life.

The River of Life

22 And he showed me a pure[a] river of water of life, clear as crystal, proceeding from the throne of God and of the Lamb. ²In the middle of its street, and on either side of the river, *was* the tree of life, which bore twelve fruits, each *tree* yielding its fruit every month. The leaves of the tree *were* for the healing of the nations. ³And there shall

---

21:14 [a]NU-Text and M-Text read *twelve names.*   **21:23** [a]NU-Text and M-Text omit *in it.*   [b]M-Text reads *the very glory.*   **21:24** [a]NU-Text and M-Text omit *of those who are saved.*   [b]M-Text reads *the glory and honor of the nations to Him.*   **21:26** [a]M-Text adds *that they may enter in.*   **21:27** [a]NU-Text and M-Text read *anything profane, nor one who causes.*   **22:1** [a]NU-Text and M-Text omit *pure.*

↑ GROW (REV. 22:7)

Sometimes I hear people say, "I can't understand all that Bible prophecy stuff. Antichrist this, Millennium that, Rapture over here. I don't know what it means. I can't sort it out. I'll just let someone else figure it all out." Now, wait a second. You don't want to ignore biblical prophecy, because the Bible has a lot to say about it. In fact, the Book of Revelation promises a special blessing to those who hear and keep the words of this prophecy. God must have wanted us to learn Bible prophecy, because 30 percent of the Scripture is dedicated to this topic. And God wants us to know that He keeps His Word! Just as surely as He kept His Word with prophecies that foretold the birth of the Messiah, so He wants us to know He will keep His Word about the prophecies pertaining to the return of the Messiah. *For more about* God's Word, *see Luke 1:1–4;* Jesus' Return, *Matt. 24:42–44.*

be no more curse, but the throne of God and of the Lamb shall be in it, and His servants shall serve Him. [4]They shall see His face, and His name *shall be* on their foreheads. [5]There shall be no night there: They need no lamp nor light of the sun, for the Lord God gives them light. And they shall reign forever and ever.

The Time Is Near

[6]Then he said to me, "These words *are* faithful and true." And the Lord God of the holy[a] prophets sent His angel to show His servants the things which must shortly take place.

[7]"Behold, I am coming quickly! Blessed *is* he who keeps the words of the prophecy of this book."

[8]Now I, John, saw and heard[a] these things. And when I heard and saw, I fell down to worship before the feet of the angel who showed me these things.

[9]Then he said to me, "See *that you do* not *do that.* For[a] I am your fellow servant, and of your brethren the prophets, and of those who keep the words of this book. Worship God." [10]And he said to me, "Do not seal the words of the prophecy of this book, for the time is at hand. [11]He who is unjust, let him be unjust still; he who is filthy, let him be filthy still; he who is righteous, let him be righteous[a] still; he who is holy, let him be holy still."

Jesus Testifies to the Churches

[12]"And behold, I am coming quickly, and My reward *is* with Me, to give to every one according to his work. [13]I am the Alpha and the Omega, *the* Beginning and *the* End, the First and the Last."[a]

[14]Blessed *are* those who do His com-

mandments,[a] that they may have the right to the tree of life, and may enter through the gates into the city. [15]But[a] outside *are* dogs and sorcerers and sexually immoral and murderers and idolaters, and whoever loves and practices a lie.

[16]"I, Jesus, have sent My angel to testify to you these things in the churches. I am the Root and the Offspring of David, the Bright and Morning Star."

[17]And the Spirit and the bride say, "Come!" And let him who hears say, "Come!" And let him who thirsts come. Whoever desires, let him take the water of life freely.

A Warning

[18]For[a] I testify to everyone who hears the words of the prophecy of this book: If anyone adds to these things, God will add[b] to him the plagues that are written in this book; [19]and if anyone takes away from the words of the book of this prophecy, God shall take away[a] his part from the Book[b] of Life, from the holy city, and *from* the things which are written in this book.

. . . Surely I am coming quickly. Rev. 22:20

I Am Coming Quickly

[20]He who testifies to these things says, "Surely I am coming quickly."

Amen. Even so, come, Lord Jesus!

[21]The grace of our Lord Jesus Christ *be* with you all.[a] Amen.

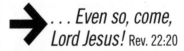

. . . Even so, come, Lord Jesus! Rev. 22:20

22:6 [a]NU-Text and M-Text read *spirits of the prophets.*   **22:8** [a]NU-Text and M-Text read *am the one who heard and saw.*
22:9 [a]NU-Text and M-Text omit *For.*   **22:11** [a]NU-Text and M-Text read *do right.*   **22:13** [a]NU-Text and M-Text read *the First and the Last, the Beginning and the End.*   **22:14** [a]NU-Text reads *wash their robes.*   **22:15** [a]NU-Text and M-Text omit *But.*
22:18 [a]NU-Text and M-Text omit *For.*   [b]M-Text reads *may God add.*   **22:19** [a]M-Text reads *may God take away.*
[b]NU-Text and M-Text read *tree of life.*   **22:21** [a]NU-Text reads *with all;* M-Text reads *with all the saints.*

ESSENTIALS//
WHAT EVERY CHRISTIAN NEEDS TO KNOW ABOUT GOD AND JESUS

WHO IS GOD?

Let's start with some basic yet essential foundational truths that every Christian needs to know about God and life.

1. God exists and is the Creator of the universe and humankind.

It is worth noting that the Bible never tries to prove the existence of God. It just says, "In the beginning God created the heavens and the earth" (Gen. 1:1). You can't go back any further than that! Now, certain people would like to eliminate the major player here. They'd rather the verse read, "In the beginning, the heavens and the earth. . . ." But if I eliminate God, then I have a big problem. In the beginning . . . what?

Some would say, "In the beginning, a mass of gases were floating in space." But that's not the beginning. Where did the mass of gases come from? Where did the space come from? The Bible simply says, "In the beginning God."

Eventually, every child gets around to asking the question, "Where did God

come from?" And there is no easy answer for that, except to say, God has *always* existed. He is self-existent. He has existed from the beginning. God has no beginning, nor does He have an end.

"In the beginning God. . . ." The Bible doesn't tell us when the beginning was, it just says God was there to begin it all.

2. God is omnipresent.

God is present everywhere, at all times. There is no place where God is not. Psalm 139:7–12 tells us quite a bit about what we call the attributes of God:

> Where can I go from Your Spirit? Or where can I flee from Your presence? If I ascend into heaven, You are there; If I make my bed in hell, behold, You are there. If I take the wings of the morning, and dwell in the uttermost parts of the sea, even there Your hand shall lead me, and Your right hand shall hold me. If I say, "Surely the darkness shall fall on me," even the

night shall be light about me; indeed, the darkness shall not hide from You, but the night shines as the day; the darkness and the light are both alike to You. (vv. 7–12)

Depending on what side of the fence you are on spiritually, these words can be either comforting or frightening. When you trust in Jesus Christ as your Lord and Savior, you have the promise that He will never leave you or forsake you (Heb. 13:5). If you are alone or frightened, God's omnipresence is of great comfort. The Bible tells us, "When you pass through the waters, I will be with you; and through the rivers, they shall not overflow you. When you walk through the fire, you shall not be burned, nor shall the flame scorch you" (Is. 43:2).

We are never alone, for God is with us wherever we go. Jesus said, "Lo, I am with you always, even to the end of the age" (Matt. 28:20).

3. God is omnipotent.

God has unlimited power. His strength and might have no limits.

All of us have heard the question, "Can God do absolutely *anything* He wants? And if He can do anything, can He do something 'un-Godlike'?"

The short answer to these questions is no. To say God is all-powerful is not to say He can do anything, including something sinful, for that would be against His holy nature. For instance, the Bible says God "cannot deny Himself" (2 Tim. 2:13). God cannot do anything inconsistent with His perfect, divine nature. God can neither die nor lie. So what is impossible for God? Not that which is too difficult for His power, but that which is contrary to His nature.

Omnipotence means God is an infinite power who can never be depleted, drained, or exhausted. He is infinitely perfect, in that He is limitless, eternal, and self-existent. God does not need to draw on any outside source of power for anything. Job said to God, "I know that You can do everything, and that no purpose of Yours can be withheld from You" (Job 42:2). God Himself asked, "Is anything too hard for the LORD?" (Gen. 18:14). And Jeremiah answered the question, "There is nothing too hard for You" (Jer. 32:17).

4. God is sovereign.

God is able to do what He pleases, with whomever He chooses, whenever He wishes. God has His plans and purposes that He will unfold at the time and in the manner of His choosing. Even the pagan King Nebuchadnezzar said, "All inhabitants of the earth are reputed as nothing; He does according to His will in the army of heaven and among the inhabitants of the earth. No one can restrain His hand or say to Him, 'What have You done?' " (Dan. 4:35).

He is the Master; we are the servants.

He is the Potter; we are the clay.

He is the Vine; we are the branches.

He is the Giver; we are the recipients.

Frankly, God can do all of this without asking permission or explaining His reasons. The psalmist said, "For I know that the LORD is great, and our Lord is above all gods. Whatever the LORD pleases He does" (Ps. 135:5, 6). And, "But our God is in heaven; He does whatever He pleases" (Ps. 115:3). Chuck Swindoll defined God's sovereignty this way:

"To say that God is sovereign is to say that He is supreme. He is in full control of all things. All. He is Almighty. He is the possessor of all power both on earth, above earth, below earth, in all matters pertaining to all existence. Over all nature. Over all events. Over all blessings. All disasters and calamities. All humanity. All life in the realm of the seen and the unseen. Good and evil. No one can defeat His purposes or thwart His plans. He is never surprised. He never learns. He is never frustrated. Nothing is ever an afterthought."

5. God is truth.

God's knowledge is perfect and flawless, and He is the final standard of truth. This means that He, and He alone, is the true God and that His knowledge and words are true and are the final standard of truth. There are, of course, many false gods out there: "But the LORD is the true God; He is the living God and the everlasting King" (Jer. 10:10). Jesus said, "And this is eternal life, that they may know You, the only true God, and Jesus Christ whom You have sent" (John 17:3).

The final court of arbitration is God Himself. There simply is no higher authority.

Clearly, we humans are not the source of truth, for we are deeply flawed in our ability to know what is true and false, right and wrong. So the apostle Paul writes, "But indeed, O man, who are you to reply to God? Will the thing formed say to him who formed it, 'Why have you made me like this?' " (Rom. 9:20).

Jesus used this key word to describe His own character: "I am . . . the truth" (John 14:6).

Scripture tells us, "It is impossible for God to lie" (Heb. 6:18). In dramatic contrast, Satan is "a liar and the father of it" (John 8:44). When we lie, we behave more like children of the devil than children of God.

6. God is holy.

If there is one thing we see repeatedly in Scripture, it is the fact of God's holiness. God is so pure and unblemished (Hab. 1:13) that He cannot look at evil (Is. 59:1, 2). When Isaiah had a glimpse of His holiness, note what he saw: "I saw the Lord sitting on a throne . . . Above it stood seraphim . . . And one cried to another and said: 'Holy, holy, holy' " (Is. 6:1–3). The psalmist asked, "Who may ascend to the hill of the LORD? Or who may stand in His holy place? He who has clean hands and a pure heart, who has not lifted up his soul to an idol, nor sworn deceitfully" (Ps. 24:3, 4).

Because God is holy, He hates sin. This is why the death of Jesus Christ was necessary. As all the sin of the world was poured upon God's holy, sinless, and beloved Son, God had to look away. This is why Jesus cried out on the Cross,

"My God, My God, why have You forsaken Me?" (Matt. 27:46).

7. God is righteous.

Holiness describes God's character, while righteousness and justice describe His actions in dealing with humankind. "For the LORD is righteous, He loves righteousness; His countenance beholds the upright" (Ps. 11:7). In the Book of Exodus we read the account of a plague of hail sent on Egypt, and then the following words from Pharaoh: "I have sinned this time. The LORD is righteous, and my people and I are wicked" (9:27). Pharaoh acknowledged the perfect justice of God in punishing him for his sin.

It is important to understand how these attributes of God complement one another. We have seen that God is omnipotent; now we see He is also righteous. Consider this: If He were a God of perfect righteousness without the power to carry out that righteousness, we could never be sure that justice would ultimately prevail. On the other hand, if He were a God of unlimited power, yet without righteousness in His character, how unthinkably horrible this universe would be! Unrighteousness would stand at the center of all existence—and nothing we could do would change it.

We ought to thank God that "all His ways are justice, a God of truth and without injustice; righteous and upright is He" (Deut. 32:4).

8. God is good.

The word *good* applied to God can be understood to mean that God is the final standard of good, and all that God is and does is worthy of approval. Does this mean that God's goodness is contingent on my approval for it to be true? No, it means that God is good, whether I believe it or not.

Again, He is the final court of arbitration.

Jesus said, "No one is good but One, that is, God" (Luke 18:19). The Psalms frequently point to the fact that God is good: "Oh, give thanks to the LORD, for He is good!" (Ps.106:1; 107:1). David said, "Taste and see that the LORD is good" (Ps. 34:8). But if God is good and therefore the ultimate standard of good, then we have a definition of the meaning of *good* that will greatly help us in the study of ethics and morality. In other words, it will give us a worldview and life-view.

For instance, when I don't know why something has happened, I fall back on what I know is true. I don't trade what I do know for what I don't know. A crisis may hit and we wonder, *Why did this happen?* The short answer is, I don't know. But what *do* I know?

I know that God is good.

"But what is *good*?" you might ask. Answer: *Good* is what God approves.

We may ask, "Why is what God approves good?" Answer: Because He approves it!

You might protest, "But that's circular reasoning!" No, actually that is biblical reasoning.

Remember, there is no higher standard of goodness than God's own perfect character and His approval of whatever is consistent with that character.

9. God is loving.

Scripture tells us simply, "God is love" (1 John 4:8). It says not merely that He *has* love or even that He is *loving*, but that He Himself is *love!*

Today we have a shallow, Hollywood version of love that is closer to lust than to anything else. Lust is jumping in bed with someone. By contrast, love is marrying that person, consistently doing what is best for him or her, and staying faithful for the rest of your life.

God's love for us is unchanging, consistent, inexhaustible. God says, "Yes, I have loved you with an everlasting love; therefore with lovingkindness I have drawn you" (Jer. 31:3). It's one thing to *say* you love someone; it's quite another to show it. The apostle Paul writes, "God demonstrates His own love toward us, in that while we were still sinners, Christ died for us" (Rom. 5:8).

Perhaps all of God's moral attributes are included in the two attributes of holiness and love.

In His holiness, He is unapproachable.

In His love, He approaches us.

SO WHAT?

We have seen that God is truth, holy, righteous, good and loving. He is omniscient, omnipresent, omnipotent, and sovereign. Someone might say, "So what? What does this all mean to us?"

Actually, it means a lot. For theology without doxology means very little.

1. God is truth, therefore we His children must be truthful.

The Scripture tells us that "Lying lips are an abomination to the LORD" (Prov. 12:22; see also Is. 59:3, 4). It is significant to note that in a list of "seven things God hates" in Proverbs 6, two of them have to do with lying:

"These six things the LORD hates, yes, seven are an abomination to Him: a proud look, a lying tongue, hands that shed innocent blood, a heart that devises wicked plans, feet that are swift in running to evil, a false witness who speaks lies, and one who sows discord among brethren" (vv. 16–19).

Besides, it's a lot of work to live in a lie. You lie, and then you have to tell a lie to cover your lie, and then another lie to cover that one. It gets so confusing and exhausting! Here is a better idea: just speak and live in truth! The apostle John writes, "For I rejoiced greatly when brethren came and testified of the truth that is in you, just as you walk in the truth. I have no greater joy than to hear that my children walk in truth" (3 John 3, 4).

2. God is holy, therefore we should seek to be holy.

The apostle Peter writes, "But as He who called you is holy, you also be holy in all your conduct, because it is written, 'Be holy, for I am holy.' And if you call on the Father, who without partiality judges according to each one's work, conduct yourselves throughout the time of your stay here in fear" (1 Pet. 1:15–17).

We tend to think of holiness in a negative light. People will critically say of another whom they think is looking down on them, "You're holier than thou!"—as if living a godly and holy life is putting yourself above others. Or you may see someone living in sin and you quote a Bible verse, and they shoot back, "You're so holier than thou."

"Oh, sorry. I'll be unholier than thou, then," we might sheepishly respond.

Understand this: to be holy does not mean you are arrogant. In fact, the godliest people I know are the most humble. The first step in seeking to be holy is to realize you are unholy! As soon as Isaiah saw the holy God, He realized he was an unholy man. Prior to chapter 6, Isaiah had a lot of "woes" for other people. But when he personally encountered God, he said, "Woe is *me*!" (Is. 6:5, italics mine). Don't let anyone ever discourage you from seeking to live a holy life. To live holy is to live *wholly* committed to Him.

The Bible tells the story of a man named Caleb who lived a godly and holy life. His secret was that he "wholly followed the Lord God" (Josh. 14:14). To be holy is to live wholly. It also means to learn to hate sin.

WHO IS JESUS CHRIST?

The question is sometimes asked, "What is God like?" If you want to know what God is like, then look at Jesus Christ, for He was not a mere representative of God, but God Himself among us. He was not a glorified man, but God in human form. Jesus Christ was God with skin on!

Jesus embodied all the attributes of God that we just looked at, such as omnipotence and omniscience, yet He was a man who walked our planet, breathed our air, and felt our pain.

He was so wise He could predict future world events.

He was so humble He got on His knees and washed His friends' dirty feet.

He was so powerful He could calm the wind and waves with a word.

He was so approachable that children climbed into His arms.

Jesus was God, spelling Himself out in language we could all understand. There has never been a figure like Him, striding across the human stage. He stands apart from all others. We literally divide human time by His birth. His very name ripples with power!

Consider several essential things you need to know about Jesus Christ.

1. Jesus is God.

Before there was a world, before there were planets, before there was light or darkness, before there was matter, before there was anything but the Godhead—there was Jesus.

John's Gospel tells us, "In the beginning was the Word, and the Word was with God, and the Word was God. He was in the beginning with God" (John 1:1, 2). Jesus Christ is co-equal, co-eternal, co-existent with the Father and Holy Spirit. He was "with God." He was God and is God. Jesus was deity in diapers.

Yet, Jesus did not stay in the safety of heaven. He entered our world. He walked in our shoes . . . and then some. He lived our life, and then He died our death.

Jesus did not become identical to us, but He did become identified with us. In fact, He could not have identified with us any more closely than He did. It was total identification, without any loss of identity, for He became one of us without ceasing to be Himself. He became human without ceasing to be God.

The Bible clearly points out that Jesus Christ was and is God Himself. Even before the Creation of the universe, Jesus was always there, as God, without beginning or end. Jesus said of Himself, "I am the Alpha and the Omega, the Beginning and the End, the First and the Last" (Rev. 22:12).

There never was a time when Christ did not exist. The word translated "was," in the original Greek text, appears as an imperfect tense, which means, "was continuing." So a better translation of John 1:1 might be, "In the beginning was continuing the Word, and the Word was continuing with God and the Word was continually God." When John says, "The Word was with God" (v. 1), it literally means, "The Word was continually toward God." In other words, the Father and Son were continually face to face. The preposition "with" bears the idea of nearness, along with a sense of movement toward God. That is to say, there has always existed the deepest equality and intimacy in the Trinity. In

His prayer recorded in John 17, Jesus said to His Father, "And now, O Father, glorify Me together with Yourself, with the glory which I had with You before the world was" (v. 5).

2. Jesus, who was God, became a man.

When we think of what happened on the first Christmas, we think of the birth of Jesus.

And of course that's right. But the nativity was just as much about a departure from heaven as it was about an arrival on earth. Isaiah says, "For unto us a Child is born, unto us a Son is given; and the government will be upon His shoulder. And His name will be called Wonderful, Counselor, Mighty God, Everlasting Father, Prince of Peace" (9:6). From our perspective on earth, "unto us a child is born." But from heaven's perspective, "unto us a Son is given." Notice that Jesus is "the Mighty God, the Everlasting Father." As the Bible says, "The virgin shall conceive . . . and shall call His name Immanuel" (Is. 7:14). *Immanuel* means "God is with us."

The Bible teaches that Jesus was born of a virgin named Mary. He was supernaturally conceived in her womb by the Holy Spirit (Luke 1:35). Christ was God, not because He was virgin born; He was virgin born because He was God. Dietrich Bonhoeffer asked, "If Jesus Christ is not true God, how could He help us? If not true man, how could He help us?"

It is important for us to know that Jesus never became God. He was God before He was born and He remained God after He became man. His deity was pre-human, pre-earthly, pre-Bethlehem, pre-Mary. He always was God, even in His mother's womb.

Some ask, "In the Incarnation, did Jesus lay aside His deity as He came to this world?" The answer is NO. The apostle Paul wrote in Philippians 2:7, "But made Himself of no reputation, taking the form of a bondservant"—literally, "He *emptied* Himself." This was a self-renunciation, not an emptying Himself of deity, nor an exchange of deity for humanity. Jesus did not cease being God or divest Himself of divine attributes in order to become man. Rather, He took on a human nature (an addition, not a subtraction) and submitted the use of His divine attributes to the will of the Father.

At times, He displayed His omniscience. He knew all about the woman at the well (John 4) and the future details contained in the Olivet Discourse (Matt. 24). He predicted His own death and resurrection and He knew who would betray Him. At other times, in accordance with His Father's will, some knowledge was veiled by His humanity. As the Christmas carol says, "Veiled in flesh, the Godhead see, hail incarnate deity."

3. Jesus veiled His deity; He never voided it.

The apostle Paul wrote, "Who [Jesus], being in the form of God, did not consider it robbery to be equal with God, but made Himself of no reputation, taking the form of a bondservant, and coming in the likeness of men. And being found in appearance as a man, He humbled Himself and became obedient to the point of death, even the death of the cross" (Phil. 2:6–8).

Let's consider some facets of the very real humanity of Jesus.

A. Jesus became tired, like we do (John 4:6).

When He met the woman at the well, we are told He was weary. He did not float from place to place; He walked, just like every other man.

B. He knew physical hunger (Matt. 4:2).

After He fasted for forty days in the wilderness, we read that "He was hungry." He never did a miracle for His own benefit. During His temptation in the wilderness, for instance, Satan told Him to turn a stone to bread, but Jesus refused (Luke 4:3, 4).

C. He got thirsty (John 19:28).

When on the Cross, no doubt extremely dehydrated, He said, "I thirst!" Ironically, this from the very One who created water. He could have spoken but a word, and a fountain would have gushed forth. But He didn't.

D. He grew weak physically.

On His way to Calvary, bearing His cross, He fell beneath the tree's great weight. A man named Simon, from Cyrene, had the great privilege of carrying it for Jesus for a short distance. Jesus died like a man in the sense that His body ceased to function, just as ours does when we die.

E. Jesus knew anger.

He didn't get angry as we do when we fly off the handle (can you imagine God having a temper-tantrum?). Jesus never got angry with sinners, *per se*, but primarily with those who misrepresented God to the people. Jesus, with righteous indignation, drove the moneychangers out of the temple because they were preying on the people instead of praying for them. They were keeping people from approaching God (Matt. 21:12, 13).

F. Jesus felt sadness.

When He stood at the tomb of Lazarus, He wept—probably in sympathy with those who had lost one they loved, but also perhaps a sadness for Lazarus himself, who would be called back from the glories of heaven to earth (John 11:35). He also wept over the city of Jerusalem, knowing the devastation that would befall her because of her sinfulness. The Greek word used is strong, signifying bitter anguish, as though one mourned the dead. It was audible (Luke 19:41)! The Bible says, "We do not have a High Priest who cannot sympathize with our weaknesses, but was in all points tempted as we are, yet without sin" (Heb. 4:15).

G. Jesus was tempted.

Here's another one that may surprise you: Jesus was tempted! "But doesn't the Bible teach that God was perfect?" someone asks. "If so, how could Jesus be tempted? Doesn't the Bible say, 'God cannot be tempted by evil?'" (James 1:13).

So then, was Jesus, who was God, tempted or not?

Answer: He was tempted, but He did not have the ability to give in. Luke 4 tells He was driven to the wilderness to be tempted by Satan. Jesus felt the presence and pressure of temptation like we do. But remember, Jesus did not have that sinful nature that you and I have, so there was not that necessary element present for temptation to succeed. Jesus was tempted, but He was not vulnerable to it like you and I are.

But why was He tempted?

The Bible answers, "Therefore, in all things He had to be made like His brethren, that He might be a merciful and faithful High Priest in things pertaining to God, to make propitiation for the sins of the people. For in that He Himself has suffered, being tempted, He is able to aid those who are tempted" (Heb. 2:17, 18).

Jesus knows what it is like to walk in your shoes! So never say, "No one knows what I am going through!" Jesus is there to help you when you are being tempted. Remember, He will never give you more then you can handle (1 Cor. 10:13).

Jesus had to die on the Cross for our sins. He came specifically to die on the Cross for the sin of the world. This brings us to why Jesus came to this earth in the first place.

To give us the ultimate teachings ever? To some degree that is true, for His teachings were that and more—but that is not all of it.

To set the perfect example of how a man should be? Again, yes, Jesus is the ultimate example, but that is not the primary reason He came.

To do miracles and heal people? He did that and far more, but that is not primarily why He came.

Jesus came to reclaim that which was lost in the Garden of Eden. He came to show us what God is like. But the primary reason Jesus came was to die on the Cross for our sins. In other words, Jesus Christ, the very Son of God, came to this earth to die on a cross. The Bible says He came to "taste death for everyone" (Heb. 2:9). Jesus said, "The Son of Man did not come to be served, but to serve, and to give His life a ransom for many" (Mark 10:45). To ransom is to deliver a person by the paying of a price. We were in a slave market and He paid the price for us. In other words, Jesus Christ, the very Son of God, came to this earth to die on a cross.

"For you know the grace of our Lord Jesus Christ, that though He was rich, yet for your sakes He became poor, that you through His poverty might become rich" (2 Cor. 8:9). He was born to die, that we might live. The Incarnation was for the purpose of the atonement. The birth of Jesus was so there would be the death of Jesus. The Cross was Jesus' goal and destination from the very beginning.

But why did Jesus have to suffer and die like this?

1. Jesus died on the Cross to show His love for us.

Jesus said, "For God so loved the world that He gave His only begotten Son" (John 3:16). Paul wrote, "Christ also loved the church and gave Himself for her" (Eph. 5:25). He also said of Jesus, "The Son of God . . . loved me, and gave Himself for me" (Gal. 2:20). If you are ever tempted to doubt God's love for you, just look at the Cross.

2. Jesus died on the Cross to absorb the wrath of God.

If God were not just, there would be no demand for His Son to suffer and die. And if God were not loving, there would be no willingness for His Son to suffer and die. But God is both just and loving. At the Cross, His love was willing to meet the demands of justice. God says in His Word, "The soul who sins shall die" (Ezek. 18:4). Paul writes, "All have sinned and fall short of the glory of God" (Rom. 3:23). So, sin is not small, because it is not against a small god. The seriousness of an insult rises with the dignity of the one insulted. We sinned against and offended God. So, that just and loving God sent Jesus as the substitute for us. God's wrath, that should have fallen on you, was placed on Him instead!

3. Jesus died on the Cross in order to neutralize Satan and cancel legal demands against us.

Jesus declared, " 'Now is the judgment of this world; now the ruler of this world will be cast out. And I, if I am lifted up from the earth, will draw all peoples to Myself.' This He said, signifying by what death He would die" (John 12:31–33). Paul wrote, "Having wiped out the handwriting of requirements that was against us, which was contrary to us. And He has taken it out of the way, having nailed it to the cross. Having disarmed principalities and powers,

He made a public spectacle of them, triumphing over them in it" (Col. 2:14, 15). Sin's power no longer need stand as a barrier between God and man.

If we are saved from the consequences of our bad deeds, it will not be because they weighed less than our good deeds. There is no salvation by balancing records. There is salvation only by cancelling records! This is why Jesus suffered and died for us. Paul wrote, "And you, being dead in your trespasses and the uncircumcision of your flesh, He has made alive together with Him, having forgiven you all trespasses, having wiped out the handwriting of requirements that was against us, which was contrary to us. And He has taken it out of the way, having nailed it to the cross" (Col. 2:13, 14).

4. Jesus suffered and died to provide our forgiveness and justification.

The Bible says we have been justified by His blood (Rom. 5:9). To be justified means you are forgiven of the wrong you have done. But it also is a legal term that means, "Just as if it never happened." He forgave you of your debt and then put the riches of Christ in your account!

5. Jesus Christ rose bodily from the grave three days after His death on the Cross.

To be a true Christian you must believe that Jesus Christ was supernaturally conceived in the womb of Mary, that He died on the Cross, and bodily rose again from the dead. Paul reminded us, "For I delivered to you first of all that which I also received: that Christ died for our sins according to the Scriptures,

and that He was buried, and that He rose again the third day according to the Scriptures, and that He was seen by [Peter], then by the twelve" (1 Cor. 15:3–5). This is foundational teaching for every believer. This is why the devil tried to discredit the resurrection of Jesus two thousand years ago and persists to this present day. That is because the death and resurrection of Jesus spells his defeat. Satan knows that if you believe this great truth, it will change your life.

Paul dealt with this denial and addressed it in 1 Corinthians 15:13–15, "But if there is no resurrection of the dead, then Christ is not risen. And if Christ is not risen, then our preaching is empty and your faith is also empty. Yes, and we are found false witnesses of God, because we have testified of God that He raised up Christ, whom He did not raise up—if in fact the dead do not rise."

What does the resurrection of Jesus mean to us today? For the believer, it means at least five crucial things:

1. The resurrection of Jesus assures me that I am accepted by God.

Paul wrote of Jesus, "Who was delivered up because of our offenses, and was raised because of our justification" (Rom. 4:25). If Jesus had never risen, I could have no assurance that I am right with God. But now, I do.

2. The resurrection of Jesus assures me that Jesus is now interceding in heaven for me!

Paul wrote, "Who is he that condemns? Christ Jesus, who died—more than that, who was raised to life—is at the right hand of God and is also interceding for us" (Rom. 8:34). One of Satan's most effective strategies is to accuse you before God after he has pulled you down through temptation. On more than one occasion he is referred to as an accuser: "The accuser of our brethren . . . who accused them before our God day and night, has been cast down" (Rev. 12:10).

Before we sin, while he is tempting us, he whispers, "You can Get away with this. . . ." After we sin he shouts. "You will *never* get away with that! God doesn't love you anymore, after what you did! In fact, you have lost your salvation!"

As though God's love and forgiveness was *ever* based on our worthiness!

Our defense against the accusations of the devil is the interceding Son of God. The apostle John wrote, "My little children, these things I write to you, so that you may not sin. And if anyone sins, we have an Advocate with the Father, Jesus Christ the righteous" (1 John 2:1). Because of the Resurrection, I know Jesus is interceding for me.

3. The resurrection of Jesus assures me that I have all the power I need to live the Christian life.

The history of humankind has been the story of discovering and using power. First it was man power. Then steam power. Now nuclear power. But we seem to lack will-power. Humankind is able to harness the powers of the universe, but cannot control itself.

But because of the resurrection of Jesus, I have all the power I need to live. Paul wrote, "But if the Spirit of Him who raised Jesus from the dead dwells in you, He who raised Christ from the dead will also give life to your mortal bodies through His Spirit who dwells in you. Therefore, brethren, we are debtors—not to the flesh, to live according to the flesh" (Rom. 8:11, 12).

4. The resurrection of Jesus assures me that I, too, will live forever!

Paul wrote, "But now Christ is risen from the dead, and has become the firstfruits of those who have fallen asleep. For since by man came death, by Man also came the resurrection of the dead. For as in Adam all die, even so in Christ all shall be made alive" (1 Cor. 15:20–22). And Jesus Himself said, "Because I live, you will live also" (John 14:19).

5. Jesus Christ, born of a virgin, died on a cross and rose again from the dead. He is alive, and now wants admittance into the human heart.

Becoming a Christian is more than simply believing a creed and going to church (though that should be a part of it). Being a Christian is having Jesus Christ Himself come and take up residence in your heart and life as your Savior and Lord. John wrote, "But as many as received Him, to them He gave the right to become children of God, to those who believe in His name" (John 1:12). And Jesus said, "Behold, I stand at the door and knock. If anyone hears My voice and opens the door, I will come in to him and dine with him, and he with Me" (Rev. 3:20).

Jesus will not force His way into any life. He gave to us free will and it is up to us to decide whether we want to accept or reject Him. There is no neutrality when it comes to Christ. We are either for or against Him (Matt. 12:30). To not say yes to Him is, by default, to say no.

If you would like to make a commitment to follow Jesus Christ, go to the front of this Bible, to the section called "The Plan of Salvation" on page xxx.

TOPICAL INDEX//
SCRIPTURES AND FEATURES